MAGILL'S LITERARY ANNUAL 2022

Essay-Reviews of 150 Outstanding Books Published in the United States During 2021

With an Annotated List of Titles

Volume II
M-Z
Indexes

Edited by
Jennifer Sawtelle

SALEM PRESS
A Division of EBSCO Information Services, Inc.
Ipswich, Massachusetts

GREY HOUSE PUBLISHING

Cover photo: Neilson Barnard/Getty Images

Copyright © 2022, by Salem Press, a Division of EBSCO Information Services, Inc. All rights in this book are reserved. No part of this work may be used or reproduced in any manner whatsoever or transmitted in any form or by any means, electronic or mechanical, including photocopy, recording, or any information storage and retrieval system, without written permission from the copyright owner. For permissions requests, contact permissions@ebscohost.com.

Magill's Literary Annual, 2022, published by Grey House Publishing, Inc., Amenia, NY, under exclusive license from EBSCO Information Services, Inc.

For information contact Grey House Publishing/Salem Press, 4919 Route 22, PO Box 56, Amenia, NY 12501.

∞ The paper used in these volumes conforms to the American National Standard for Permanence of Paper for Printed Library Materials, Z39.48-1992 (R2009).

Publisher's Cataloging-In-Publication Data
(Prepared by The Donohue Group, Inc.)

Names: Magill, Frank N. (Frank Northen), 1907-1997, editor. | Wilson, John D., editor. | Kellman, Steven G., 1947- editor. | Goodhue, Emily, editor. | Poranski, Colin D., editor. | Akre, Matthew, editor. | Spires, Kendal, editor. | Toth, Gabriela, editor. | Sawtelle, Jennifer, editor.
Title: Magill's literary annual.
Description: <1977->: [Pasadena, Calif.] : Salem Press | <2015->: Ipswich, Massachusetts : Salem Press, a division of EBSCO Information Services, Inc. ; Amenia, NY : Grey House Publishing | Essay-reviews of ... outstanding books published in the United States during the previous year. | "With an annotated list of titles." | Editor: 1977- , F.N. Magill; <2010-2014>, John D. Wilson and Steven G. Kellman; <2015>, Emily Goodhue and Colin D. Poranski; <2016>, Matthew Akre, Kendal Spires, and Gabriela Toth; <2017->, Jennifer Sawtelle. | Includes bibliographical references and index.
Identifiers: ISSN: 0163-3058
Subjects: LCSH: Books--Reviews--Periodicals. | United States--Imprints--Book reviews--Periodicals. | Literature, Modern--21st century--History and criticism--Periodicals. | Literature, Modern--20th century--History and criticism--Periodicals.
Classification: LCC PN44 .M333 | DDC 028.1--dc23

FIRST PRINTING
PRINTED IN THE UNITED STATES OF AMERICA

CONTENTS

Complete Annotated List of Contents. vii

The Madness of Crowds—*Louise Penny* 349
Major Labels—*Kelefa Sanneh* 354
Malibu Rising—*Taylor Jenkins Reid* 358
A Marvellous Light—*Freya Marske* 363
Mary Jane—*Jessica Anya Blau* 367
Matrix—*Lauren Groff*. 372
Me (Moth)—*Amber McBride*. 377
The Memoirs of Stockholm Sven—*Nathaniel Ian Miller* 381
Milk Blood Heat—*Dantiel W. Moniz* 386
The Mirror Season—*Anna-Marie McLemore*. 391
A Most Remarkable Creature—*Jonathan Meiburg*. 396
My Broken Language—*Quiara Alegría Hudes*. 401
My Heart Is a Chainsaw—*Stephen Graham Jones* 406
My Monticello—*Jocelyn Nicole Johnson* 411

The Night Always Comes—*Willy Vlautin* 416
No Gods, No Monsters—*Cadwell Turnbull* 421
No One Is Talking about This—*Patricia Lockwood* 426
Noor—*Nnedi Okorafor* 431

Oh William!—*Elizabeth Strout* 435
On Juneteenth—*Annette Gordon-Reed* 439
Once There Were Wolves—*Charlotte McConaghy* 444
The Other Black Girl—*Zakiya Dalila Harris* 449
The (Other) You—*Joyce Carol Oates* 454
The Outlier—*Kai Bird* 459

A Passage North—*Anuk Arudpragasam* 464
People We Meet on Vacation—*Emily Henry* 469
Playlist for the Apocalypse—*Rita Dove* 474
Poet Warrior—*Joy Harjo* 478
Project Hail Mary—*Andy Weir* 482
The Promise—*Damon Galgut* 487
The Prophets—*Robert Jones Jr.* 492
A Psalm for the Wild-Built—*Becky Chambers* 497
Punch Me Up to the Gods—*Brian Broome* 502

The Queen of the Cicadas—*V. Castro* 507

Razorblade Tears—*S. A. Cosby* 511
The Reading List—*Sara Nisha Adams* 516
Remote Control—*Nnedi Okorafor* 520
The Removed—*Brandon Hobson*. 525
Rescuing the Planet—*Tony Hiss* 530
Revolution in Our Time—*Kekla Magoon*. 535
Run: Book One—*John Lewis and Andrew Aydin*. 540

The Second—*Carol Anderson* 545
Second Place—*Rachel Cusk* 550
Seek You—*Kristen Radtke* 555
The Sentence—*Louise Erdrich* 560
She Who Became the Sun—*Shelley Parker-Chan* 565
A Sitting in St. James—*Rita Williams-Garcia* 569
Skinship—*Yoon Choi* 573
Smile—*Sarah Ruhl* 578
A Snake Falls to Earth—*Darcie Little Badger* 582
Somebody's Daughter—*Ashley C. Ford* 587
The Souvenir Museum—*Elizabeth McCracken* 591
Squirrel Hill—*Mark Oppenheimer* 596
The Storyteller—*Dave Grohl* 601
The Sum of Us—*Heather McGhee* 606
The Sunflower Cast a Spell to Save Us from the Void—*Jackie Wang* 611
The Sweetness of Water—*Nathan Harris* 615
A Swim in a Pond in the Rain—*George Saunders* 620

The Tangleroot Palace—*Marjorie Liu* 625
Tastes Like War—*Grace M. Cho* 629
These Precious Days—*Ann Patchett* 634
Three Girls from Bronzeville—*Dawn Turner* 639
The Twilight Zone—*Nona Fernández* 644

Unbound—*Tarana Burke* 649
Under a White Sky—*Elizabeth Kolbert*. 654

Velvet Was the Night—*Silvia Moreno-Garcia* 658

Wake—*Rebecca Hall* 663
We Begin at the End—*Chris Whitaker* 668
When the Stars Go Dark—*Paula McLain* 673
When We Cease to Understand the World—*Benjamín Labatut* 678
Whereabouts—*Jhumpa Lahiri* 683
White Smoke—*Tiffany D. Jackson* 688

CONTENTS

The Wild Fox of Yemen—*Threa Almontaser* 692
Winter in Sokcho—*Elisa Shua Dusapin* 697
Winter Recipes from the Collective—*Louise Glück* 702
The Woman They Could Not Silence—*Kate Moore* 707
A World on the Wing—*Scott Weidensaul* 712
The Wrong End of the Telescope—*Rabih Alameddine* 717

You Don't Have to Be Everything—*Diana Whitney* 721

Category Index 727
Title Index 733

COMPLETE ANNOTATED LIST OF CONTENTS

VOLUME I

1000 Years of Joys and Sorrows 1
    1000 Years of Joys and Sorrows *is both a memoir by the internationally renowned artist Ai Weiwei and an intimate biography of the artist's father, Ai Qing. Through the life stories of these two creative minds, the volume offers a complex and troubling history of China from within, encompassing the years from the rise of Mao Zedong to the present.*

Afterparties 6
    Afterparties *is a collection of nine short stories featuring Cambodian American characters, including immigrants and those descended of refugees who fled the communist Khmer Rouge genocide in Cambodia in the late 1970s and established new lives in the United States.*

All In 11
    In All In: An Autobiography, *tennis champion Billie Jean King and cowriters Johnette Howard and Maryanne Vollers chronicle King's dual careers in tennis and activism over more than half a century.*

All That She Carried: The Journey of Ashley's Sack, a Black Family Keepsake . . 16
    In her seventh book, American author and historian Tiya Miles explores the history behind a nineteenth-century matrilineal heirloom, and in turn elucidates what life was like for generations of African American women who lived through the era of slavery, Reconstruction, and legalized racial segregation.

American Baby: A Mother, a Child, and the Shadow History of Adoption. 21
    The nonfiction work American Baby *explores adoption in the United States, especially in the post–World War II era, by focusing on one particular case in which a young, unwed mother was coerced into giving her baby up for adoption.*

American Melancholy. 26
    In her twelfth collection of poetry, Joyce Carol Oates reflects on America's particular brand of melancholy, with poems ranging from unethical psychological experiments conducted in the twentieth century, to incidents of racism, to the loss of her husband.

American Republics: A Continental History of the United States, 1783–1850. . . 31
    A comprehensive history of the fragility and instability of the United States in the decades following the American Revolution.

And Now I Spill the Family Secrets 36
    Margaret Kimball's illustrated memoir And Now I Spill the Family Secrets *explores the author's family's struggles with mental illness. The diligence with which information was guarded about her mother's attempted suicide when Kimball was young drives her to look deeper into her family history and its dysfunctionality in an effort to better understand her mother and to piece together a coherent narrative of the past.*

The Anthropocene Reviewed 41
    In forty-four short essays, novelist and blogger John Green examines aspects of everyday life in the twenty-first century to help readers grasp the wonders and travails of life in the Anthropocene, the current geological age in which humans have exerted significant influence on the planet.

Aristotle and Dante Dive into the Waters of the World 46
    Written by award-winning author Benjamin Alire Sáenz, Aristotle and Dante Dive into the Waters of the World *follows the relationship between two gay Mexican American teenagers as they try to maintain their love for one another in the dangerously homophobic world of 1980s Texas.*

Arsenic and Adobo 50
    Arsenic and Adobo *is the first in the* Tita Rosie's Kitchen Mystery *series, following pastry chef Lila Macapagal as she investigates the murder of her ex-boyfriend, who died in front of her at her family's restaurant.*

Beasts of a Little Land 54
    Juhea Kim's debut novel, Beasts of a Little Land, *is an epic family drama set against the tumultuous backdrop of the fight for Korean independence.*

Beautiful Country 59
    Qian Julie Wang's memoir Beautiful Country *(2021) tells the story of her family's immigration to the United States from China. Drawing on her childhood experiences, Wang recounts the first five years she and her family lived as undocumented immigrants in New York City.*

Beautiful World, Where Are You 64
    Beautiful World, Where Are You, *best-selling Irish novelist Sally Rooney's third novel, follows two friends in their late twenties: Alice, a famous novelist, and Eileen, an underpaid editor at a literary magazine, as they grapple with the challenges of modern romance.*

COMPLETE ANNOTATED LIST OF CONTENTS

Between Two Kingdoms: A Memoir of a Life Interrupted 69
    In her book Between Two Kingdoms: A Memoir of a Life Interrupted, *American writer Suleika Jaouad chronicles her battle with leukemia and the long road to remission.*

Bewilderment 74
    In Bewilderment, *Richard Powers's thirteenth novel, the author continues his concern with the health of our planet and its human inhabitants, this time by focusing on a father-son relationship.*

Billy Summers 79
    Stephen King's sixty-third novel, Billy Summers, *follows a hitman, a former US Marine Corps sniper, on his last job.*

Black Birds in the Sky: The Story and Legacy of the 1921 Tulsa Race Massacre . . 84
    Young-adult author Brandy Colbert offers a compelling, accessible history of the 1921 Tulsa Race Massacre and the societal context and the lead-up to it in Black Birds in the Sky, *published a century later. This straightforward account incorporates firsthand reports as well as the work of other historians, provoking further consideration around why information about the massacre was so long suppressed.*

The Black Church: This Is Our Story, This Is Our Song 89
    From the transatlantic slave trade to the civil rights movement to the Black Lives Matter movement of today, renowned scholar Henry Louis Gates Jr. lays out the role of the Black Church in American society. He shows how religion has often been the epicenter of life for Black people in the United States, serving as one of the oldest and most valuable resources in the fight for liberation and equality as well as a profound influence on artistic expression. But he also explores negative aspects such as insularity and intolerance, ultimately painting a vivid, multidimensional portrait of a complex institution that remains a powerful force.

Blackout 94
    Blackout *is a collection of six interwoven love stories about Black teens whose plans to attend a Brooklyn block party are disrupted by a historic blackout.*

The Book of Form and Emptiness 100
    Ruth Ozeki's novel The Book of Form and Emptiness *is a Zen parable about the mercurial nature of reality and the navigation of grief following an unexpected loss. Ozeki, a Zen Buddhist priest, offers an unruly, compelling, and impeccably written narrative that begs the question: What is real?*

Broken (In the Best Possible Way). 104
    Broken (In the Best Possible Way) *is a collection of thirty-seven essays by humorist Jenny Lawson. The essays cover a variety of issues, including serious topics like mental health and medical insurance, as well as entertaining subjects like her father's fascination with stray animals and a list of ideas that could be presented on the television series Shark Tank.*

Call Us What We Carry. 109
    Call Us What We Carry *is a best-selling poetry collection by Amanda Gorman, who won legions of fans after she recited her poem "The Hill We Climb" at the inauguration of President Joe Biden in 2021. The book recalls the upheaval of the coronavirus disease 2019 (COVID-19) pandemic with an eye toward the violence in America's past.*

Chatter: The Voice in Our Head, Why It Matters, and How to Harness It 114
    Chatter *is a guide to using the brain's capacity for self-talk to replace negative thoughts with empowering ones. It is the debut book by American psychologist Ethan Kross.*

The Chosen and the Beautiful. 119
    In The Chosen and the Beautiful, *a reimagining of F. Scott Fitzgerald's* The Great Gatsby, *socialite Jordan Baker navigates the tumultuous summer of 1922 in a world filled with magic and demonic influence.*

Cloud Cuckoo Land. 124
    In this ambitious novel, Anthony Doerr explores the lives of characters living in far-flung times and places, all of whom are connected by their relationship to an ancient Greek book titled Cloud Cuckoo Land.

The Code Breaker: Jennifer Doudna, Gene Editing, and the
    Future of the Human Race. 129
    In The Code Breaker: Jennifer Doudna, Gene Editing, and the Future of the Human Race, *Walter Isaacson explores the life and career of Nobel Prize-winning scientist Jennifer Doudna and chronicles her work, alongside fellow researchers from around the world, to develop gene-editing tools based on the DNA sequences known as CRISPR.*

The Committed 134
    In his novel The Committed, *Viet Thanh Nguyen provides a sequel to his Pulitzer Prize–winning* The Sympathizer *(2015). The perpetually ambivalent former North Vietnamese spy joins the exodus of people from his country and ends up in Paris, where he falls in with a gang of drug dealers. His presence in the land of the colonial oppressors of his homeland, as well as the birthplace of existential philosophy, leads to a protracted exploration of his conflicted sense of identity.*

COMPLETE ANNOTATED LIST OF CONTENTS

Concrete Rose 139
    In Concrete Rose, *Maverick Carter, a Black teenager approaching his senior year in high school, struggles to face the consequences of his own behavior while drawing strength from the extended family and caring community around him.*

Crossroads 143
    Jonathan Franzen's sixth novel, Crossroads, *is a multigenerational work following a brief period in the 1970s within the Hildebrandt family. The novel, reported to be the first in a trilogy, explores the many sides of familial responsibility, Christian faith, adolescence, and the complications of adult relationships through chapters rotating among the points of view of its main characters.*

Crying in H Mart 148
    This memoir centers around the death of the author's mother after a grueling battle with cancer, confronting horrific suffering and death in honest terms before probing the author's journey of grief in the months that follow. Throughout, the memoir explores Michelle Zauner's biracial and bicultural upbringing between the United States and South Korea.

Damnation Spring 153
    People have worked over the course of generations bringing down the ancient redwoods of Northern California for profit, but by the late 1970s, as the groves dwindle and environmentalists lobby to preserve what remains, the small logging town and one of its families at the heart of Damnation Spring *face a profound moment of reckoning. Part domestic saga, part environmental thriller, Ash Davidson's meticulously researched debut novel chronicles the seasons spanning from 1977 to 1978.*

The Dangers of Smoking in Bed 157
    The Dangers of Smoking in Bed *is a collection of horror stories by best-selling Argentine author Mariana Enríquez that explores the dark side of human nature and the way in which historical atrocities continue to haunt the places where they occurred.*

The Doctors Blackwell: How Two Pioneering Sisters Brought
    Medicine to Women—and Women to Medicine 162
    Janice P. Nimura offers a fascinating overview of the lives of two impressive nineteenth-century women, Elizabeth and Emily Blackwell, who became, respectively, the first and third female medical doctors in the United States. The Blackwell sisters changed the face (and gender) of medicine both in America and throughout the world.

Empire of Pain: The Secret History of the Sackler Dynasty 167
    Patrick Radden Keefe's Empire of Pain *details how, over the course of three generations, the pioneering Sackler family became one of the richest in the United States, in large part through the development and aggressive sales of a highly addictive drug called OxyContin. Through his study, Keefe explores the significant issues of ambition, ethics, accountability, and greed in the context of big business and powerful wealth.*

Everybody: A Book about Freedom. 172
    Author Olivia Laing's book Everybody *is an exploration of the concept of freedom that specifically focuses on varying degrees of human bodily freedom across different aspects of life.*

The Failed Promise: Reconstruction, Frederick Douglass,
    and the Impeachment of Andrew Johnson. 177
    The Failed Promise *provides piercing insight into the tumultuous Reconstruction era, focusing on the perspective of Frederick Douglass amid the conflict between President Andrew Johnson and the Radical Republicans. It shows how Douglass and other Black leaders contributed to Johnson's impeachment and how Johnson's acquittal contributed to the failure to secure civil rights for Black Americans in the wake of the US Civil War.*

Falling. 183
    T. J. Newman's first novel, Falling *(2021), is a thriller that unfolds at 35,000 feet, as a commercial airline pilot must solve an ethical dilemma posed by a terrorist threat directed against both his passengers and his own family.*

Finding the Mother Tree: Discovering the Wisdom of the Forest 188
    Part science and part memoir, Finding the Mother Tree *is the weaving together of author Suzanne Simard's personal life story, the history of her research into the mysteries of forest ecology, and her ideas about how to address society's needs for forest products while supporting the natural regeneration of the forest.*

Firekeeper's Daughter. 193
    In Firekeeper's Daughter, *a young woman recovering from recent tragedies works with undercover law enforcement to investigate a methamphetamine ring responsible for the deaths of several members of her community.*

First Person Singular 198
    First Person Singular *is a collection of eight short stories by the international bestselling author Haruki Murakami.*

COMPLETE ANNOTATED LIST OF CONTENTS

The Five Wounds 203
    In American author Kirstin Valdez Quade's debut novel, a Mexican American family struggles to overcome the enduring effects of intergenerational trauma, loss, and hardship.

Floaters 208
    In Martin Espada's Floaters, *the poet connects the public and political to the personal through cycles of poems with subjects taken from the national news, Espada's personal life, and his relationships, both familial and not.*

Four Hundred Souls: A Community History of African America, 1619–2019 . . . 212
    Four Hundred Souls is a collection of eighty essays and ten poems edited by award-winning historians Ibram X. Kendi and Keisha Blain. This community chronicle of African America begins with the twenty or so Africans held aboard the White Lion that docked at Jamestown, Virginia, in 1619. It spans four hundred years to 2019 with a reassertion that Black lives matter and concludes with a call for a future where ancestors' dreams can be fully realized.

The Free World: Art and Thought in the Cold War 217
    In The Free World: Art and Thought in the Cold War, *Louis Menand provides an expansive exploration of the period after World War II through a cultural, ideological lens on the United States and its European influences.*

From a Whisper to a Rallying Cry: The Killing of Vincent Chin and
    the Trial that Galvanized the Asian American Movement. 222
    Paula Yoo's From a Whisper to a Rallying Cry *tells the story of the murder of Vincent Chin, a hate crime that took place in the city of Detroit, Michigan, in 1982 and helped to inspire what some historians recognize as the Asian American movement.*

Fuzz: When Nature Breaks the Law 227
    In Fuzz: When Nature Breaks the Law, *Mary Roach explores the numerous ways in which humans and wildlife come into conflict and the varied efforts to resolve those conflicts.*

Garbo 232
    In Garbo, *the distinguished veteran editor and biographer Robert Gottlieb presents a thought-provoking study of the legendary screen icon Greta Garbo. In addition to offering some clues as to Garbo's enigmatic personality, Gottlieb provides a beautifully illustrated introduction to her glamorous career in film, which spanned the transition from silent films to talkies.*

Girlhood 237
    Melissa Febos's essay collection Girlhood *explores the ways in which women experience abuse, harassment, and exploitation from a young age and how these experiences shape who they become. Writing from the perspective of her own life and the lives of the many women she interviewed while researching her book, Febos creates a vivid tapestry of experiences that spans generations and continents, culminating in a unified, engrossing portrait of what it means to be a woman.*

Great Circle 242
    Maggie Shipstead's third novel, Great Circle, *is a globe-trotting epic in which a pioneering female aviator and a modern Hollywood actor navigate emotional isolation and gender politics in separate stories that converge in a surprising twist.*

The Ground Breaking: The Tulsa Race Massacre and an
    American City's Search for Justice 247
    The Ground Breaking *presents a detailed history of the 1921 Tulsa Race Massacre, building on the author's decades of research into the event. It gives special focus to the aftermath of the event, including official efforts to suppress information about it and eventual efforts to reckon with Tulsa's history of racial terror.*

Halfway Home: Race, Punishment, and the Afterlife of Mass Incarceration. . . . 252
    Halfway Home *is an award-winning narrative nonfiction study of the lives of incarcerated and formerly incarcerated Black men and women, based on an ethnographic study that began in 2008 as well as the lived experiences of the author, Reuben Jonathan Miller.*

Harlem Shuffle 257
    Harlem Shuffle *is best-selling author Colson Whitehead's eighth novel, a crime thriller that explores Black life in 1960s New York City.*

Heaven 262
    In Mieko Kawakami's novel Heaven, *a bullied fourteen-year-old boy is befriended by a girl who is herself an outcast and helps him to understand the nature of suffering, friendship, and forgiveness.*

Hell of a Book 267
    This inventive work takes an absurdist approach to examining the traumatic impact of race on American society, following a successful Black author on a book tour who begins to question reality.

COMPLETE ANNOTATED LIST OF CONTENTS

Home Is Not a Country 272
    Home Is Not a Country, *a verse novel from award-winning poet Safia Elhillo, tells the story of Nima, a fourteen-year-old Muslim immigrant growing up in an American suburb after the 9/11 terrorist attacks.*

The Hospital: Life, Death, and Dollars in a Small American Town 276
    Writer Brian Alexander examines the operations of a small, private nonprofit hospital in Bryan, Ohio, including the stories of the people who work there and some of their patients as well as the hospital's vital struggle to maintain its independent status.

How the Word Is Passed: A Reckoning with the History of
    Slavery across America 281
    How the Word Is Passed, *a history and memoir by* The Atlantic *staff writer and poet Clint Smith, chronicles how the United States' collective history and memory are framed regarding transatlantic enslavement. He visits eight public historic sites and monuments in the United States and Gorée Island off the coast of Senegal.*

Intimacies 286
    A short, electrifying novel, Intimacies *details the personal and professional life of a woman who has moved to The Hague to serve as an interpreter in an international court dedicated to prosecuting crimes associated with war, human rights, and genocide.*

Invisible Child: Poverty, Survival and Hope in an American City 291
    Invisible Child *details the life of Dasani Coates, a girl growing up in New York City, as a way of understanding the larger issues of poverty, homelessness, and inequity in American life.*

Islands of Abandonment: Nature Rebounding in the Post-Human Landscape . . 296
    In Islands of Abandonment, *journalist and author Cal Flyn offers an examination of areas across the world where human habitation has largely disappeared, and how nature reclaims these environments over time.*

King of the Blues: The Rise and Reign of B. B. King 301
    In King of the Blues: The Rise and Reign of B. B. King, *Daniel de Visé chronicles the life and career of the titular acclaimed blues singer and guitarist, whom he presents as one of the most influential American musicians of the twentieth century.*

Klara and the Sun 306
    In Klara and the Sun, *the Nobel Prize–winning novelist Kazuo Ishiguro presents readers with a penetrating meditation on love, mortality, and faith, set against the backdrop of a dystopian near future.*

Last Night at the Telegraph Club 311
    Winner of the 2021 National Book Award for Young People's Literature, Last Night at the Telegraph Club *is an exploration of queerness and identity in McCarthy-era Chinatown, San Francisco.*

The Letters of Shirley Jackson 315
    Edited by Laurence Jackson Hyman and Bernice M. Murphy, The Letters of Shirley Jackson *collects nearly three hundred letters that trace the life and career of acclaimed writer Shirley Jackson.*

Libertie 320
    Told through the perspective of the eponymous main character, Libertie *is the diaspora tale of one Black woman growing into herself and reckoning with what freedom truly means.*

The Life I'm In 324
    The Life I'm In *is the long-awaited sequel to* The Skin I'm In *(1998) and explores the life of the previous book's antagonist, Char. Fleeing a troubled home life, Char ends up involved in sex trafficking.*

Light Perpetual 328
    Francis Spufford's second novel, Light Perpetual, *imagines what might have become of five young British children had their lives not been cut short in a German bombing during World War II.*

The Lincoln Highway 333
    Amor Towles's third novel, The Lincoln Highway, *follows four boys during a ten-day trip from Morgen, Kansas, to New York City to retrieve a family fortune.*

A Little Devil in America: Notes in Praise of Black Performance 338
    Award-winning cultural critic, poet, and essayist Hanif Abdurraqib offers a cultural and historical consideration of Black performance—a term broadly and fruitfully interpreted—in the United States in A Little Devil in America: Notes in Praise of Black Performance. *In addition to providing discussions of the work of various Black artists, the book parses modes of performance ranging from the artistic, like dance and music, to the seemingly mundane; fighting is a form of performance, as is the intimacy of a haircut or a hug.*

The Love Songs of W. E. B. Du Bois 343
    Honorée Fanonne Jeffers's debut novel tells the story of the complex Black, American Indian, and White family of Ailey Pearl Garfield in Georgia, over the course of multiple generations.

COMPLETE ANNOTATED LIST OF CONTENTS
VOLUME II

The Madness of Crowds 349
    A murder mystery set during the COVID-19 pandemic, The Madness of Crowds *is the seventeenth book in Canadian author Louise Penny's best-selling Chief Inspector Gamache series.*

Major Labels: A History of Popular Music in Seven Genres 354
    Written by journalist and music critic Kelefa Sanneh, Major Labels *explores the evolution of rock, R&B, country, punk, hip-hop, dance, and pop music between the mid-1900s and the early 2020s.*

Malibu Rising. 358
    In Malibu Rising, *family secrets come to light, conflicts come to a head, and four siblings come into their own amid a wild 1983 party.*

A Marvellous Light 363
    A Marvellous Light, *the first book in a planned trilogy, introduces Robin Blyth and Edwin Courcey, civil service employees whose jobs are to curtail rumors and incidents of magical disruptions. In this first book, they are drawn into a conspiracy over the Last Contract and a trio of magical objects which, if combined, could spell the doom of the world.*

Mary Jane. 367
    In the novel Mary Jane, *Jessica Anya Blau tells the story of Mary Jane Dillard, whose carefree experiences with sex, drugs, and rock and roll during the summer of 1975 cause her to question everything she has thought to be accurate in her world.*

Matrix 372
    A luminous novel set in twelfth-century England, Matrix *chronicles Marie de France's struggle to build a meaningful life for herself after she is sent to live in an abbey of nuns.*

Me (Moth). 377
    Me (Moth) *tells the story of two teens who struggle to find their own identities as well as love after personal tragedy. Moth's parents and brother have been killed in a car accident while Sani's parents have failed to protect him from an abusive stepfather. The two learn to live again while taking a summer road trip across the country.*

The Memoirs of Stockholm Sven............................. 381
  In his impressive debut novel, The Memoirs of Stockholm Sven, *Nathaniel Ian Miller presents a gripping account of survival and friendship in the harsh world of the Arctic. In 1916, Sven Ormson, a Swedish worker dissatisfied with life in Stockholm, heads north to the frozen world of Spitsbergen, hoping for a challenging and interesting life of adventure.*

Milk Blood Heat 386
  In her debut book of short stories, Dantiel Moniz delves into the lives of women, from adolescence through adulthood, to explore the connections between them and the boundaries they accept or challenge, and ultimately to illuminate the human condition.

The Mirror Season 391
  This gripping young adult novel blends magical realism and fairy tale themes with contemporary drama as two young people drawn together by a cruel sexual assault help each other heal.

A Most Remarkable Creature: The Hidden Life and Epic Journey of the
  World's Smartest Birds of Prey 396
  In A Most Remarkable Creature, *musician and naturalist Jonathan Meiburg presents an engaging look at a group of falcons called caracaras. Unusually omnivorous and intelligent for raptors, caracaras have fascinated observers for centuries, and Meiburg's quest to discover more about the bird leads him on explorations spanning the continent of South America.*

My Broken Language.. 401
  In this memoir, renowned playwright Quiara Alegría Hudes probes the intersection of her childhood years in rural Pennsylvania, the urban Puerto Rican culture of her mother's extended family in Philadelphia, and her father's life in White suburbia after her parents split up. Through personal stories about navigating between homes, languages, and cultures, she finds her own authentic voice and calls for greater inclusivity in publishing.

My Heart Is a Chainsaw.................................... 406
  Written by bestselling horror novelist Stephen Graham Jones, My Heart Is a Chainsaw *is a coming-of-age story about an Indigenous teenager who finds her life becoming increasingly more like the slasher films that she loves.*

My Monticello 411
  Jocelyn Nicole Johnson's debut collection, My Monticello, *contains five short stories and a novella, the latter of which presents a dystopian vision of the future. Each of the texts explores race, racism, and the Black American experience in the United States.*

COMPLETE ANNOTATED LIST OF CONTENTS

The Night Always Comes. 416
    Willy Vlautin's sixth novel, The Night Always Comes, *focuses on a young, hardworking woman in Portland, Oregon, who is desperately trying to attain the security of home ownership in a rapidly changing, increasingly hostile urban environment.*

No Gods, No Monsters 421
    No God, No Monsters sets the stage for Cadwell Turnbull's rich and sprawling Convergence Saga, in which so-called "monsters"—werewolves, witches and other supernatural beings—reveal themselves to humans in the aftermath of a fatal police shooting.

No One Is Talking about This. 426
    Patricia Lockwood's debut novel, No One Is Talking about This, *details the experiences of a young influencer and public speaker. Using an experimental, abstract style, Lockwood juxtaposes the narrator's experience on social media with the divergent, subsequent experience of caring for a niece born with a serious medical condition.*

Noor. 431
    In Noor, *by Nnedi Okorafor, an Igbo auto mechanic with cybernetic limbs is on the run in near-future Nigeria after being attacked by a group of men. She flees with a Fulani herdsman who has been accused of terrorism and attempts to hide in a secret city located at the center of a sandstorm called the Red Eye.*

Oh William! 435
    Oh William!, the third book in Elizabeth Strout's Lucy Barton series, explores successful writer Lucy Barton's relationship with her ex-husband William as they each navigate late middle age and come to terms with the lives they have lived.

On Juneteenth. 439
    In On Juneteenth, *Pulitzer Prize–winning author and historian Annette Gordon-Reed examines the holiday known as Juneteenth, which commemorates the day of the official 1865 order that those who had been enslaved in Texas were now free. Gordon-Reed, whose family has lived in Texas for generations, considers Juneteenth in the specific context of a state typically considered synonymous with White men, dispelling popular myths about Texas and exploring its complex and diverse origins while adding her own experiences growing up in the twilight days of Jim Crow.*

Once There Were Wolves. 444
    Once There Were Wolves follows biologist Inti Flynn as she leads a team of scientists reintroducing wolves to the wilds of Scotland. As the wolves begin to flourish in their new environment, Inti struggles to overcome her own personal demons.

The Other Black Girl 449
    The Other Black Girl *tells the story of Nella Rogers, a young African American woman working in the predominantly White publishing business. When another African American woman joins the staff, Nella is thrilled. However, when strange threats start appearing on her desk, Nella begins to question her job, her friends, and herself.*

The (Other) You 454
    The (Other) You *is a collection of short stories that follow characters who are challenged by the idea of a life that is full of regrets, that is not what appears to be, or that could have been completely different.*

The Outlier: The Unfinished Presidency of Jimmy Carter 459
    In The Outlier, *the Pulitzer Prize–winning biographer Kai Bird presents a revisionist account of the presidency of Jimmy Carter, arguing that this political outsider's one term in office was enormously consequential and far from a failure. Bird explores Carter's attempts to pursue intelligent and humane policies at a time when the United States was buffeted by dramatic social and economic change.*

A Passage North. 464
    A Passage North *(2021), Anuk Arudpragasam's second novel, revisits the long, bloody Sri Lankan Civil War, this time focusing on the aftereffects of violence on innocent civilians.*

People We Meet on Vacation 469
    People We Meet on Vacation *is the story of two best friends with a tradition of traveling together every summer who have one last trip to determine if there is something more to their relationship.*

Playlist for the Apocalypse 474
    Playlist for the Apocalypse *is a collection of poetry by Pulitzer Prize–winning American poet Rita Dove, with its diverse works bringing together themes of history, contemporary society, and change.*

Poet Warrior. 478
    A memoir describing the author's journey toward becoming a poet, and the influences that her family, her mentors, the Muskogee culture, and the natural world had on her thinking and her art

Project Hail Mary 482
    In Andy Weir's science-fiction drama Project Hail Mary, *a science teacher and a lost alien try to save both of their worlds from a microorganism that eats solar energy.*

COMPLETE ANNOTATED LIST OF CONTENTS

The Promise. 487
    Damon Galgut's ninth novel, The Promise, *examines the dysfunctional White South African Swart family against the backdrop of sweeping social changes occurring in the nation over the course of thirty troubled years.*

The Prophets 492
    Set on an antebellum plantation in Mississippi, Robert Jones Jr.'s debut novel, The Prophets, *is a love story about two enslaved boys whose relationship demonstrates that some bonds can never be broken.*

A Psalm for the Wild-Built 497
    In A Psalm for the Wild-Built, *a monk takes on a new vocation, provides comfort to the people of Panga, and encounters a robot that will challenge their understanding of life.*

Punch Me Up to the Gods. 502
    Debut memoirist Brian Broome covers the story of his upbringing in Ohio and coming to embrace and accept his identity as both a Black man and a gay man.

The Queen of the Cicadas. 507
    While staying at a historical Texas farmhouse that has been converted into a guesthouse, a woman learns the true details behind an urban legend of a gruesome murder and a vengeful ghost. She becomes obsessed with the story, which then begins to intersect with her life in ways that are strange and terrifying—but ultimately transformative.

Razorblade Tears 511
    In the fast-paced thriller Razorblade Tears, *two fathers team up to avenge the murder of their gay sons.*

The Reading List 516
    In The Reading List, *an isolated widower meets a seventeen-year-old high school student who works as a librarian at his local library. When a chance occurrence takes place—the discovery of an anonymous reading list—the threads of their lives begin to tangle.*

Remote Control 520
    In Remote Control, *a young girl with a frightening yet awe-inspiring power comes of age in near-future Ghana.*

The Removed 525
In Brandon Hobson's fourth novel, The Removed *(2021), a Cherokee family in Oklahoma celebrates its heritage as descendants of survivors from the brutal nineteenth-century Trail of Tears and commemorates the life of a family member lost to modern violence.*

Rescuing the Planet: Protecting Half the Land to Heal the Earth. 530
Tony Hiss's Rescuing the Planet: Protecting Half the Land to Heal the Earth *focuses on efforts underway across North America to conserve plant and animal habitats to slow climate change, reduce extinctions, preserve biodiversity, and protect 50 percent of US land and water by 2050.*

Revolution in Our Time: The Black Panther Party's Promise to the People 535
Kekla Magoon offers an exhilarating and deeply informative history of the radical Black Panther Party, countering their image as mainly a violent group with a thoughtful focus on their social work. She invites readers to think critically about the Panthers' legacy and see in themselves the capacity for political action and change.

Run: Book One 540
Run: Book One *is the first book in a sequel to the congressman John Lewis's award-winning graphic trilogy,* March. *The* March *books told the story of Lewis's childhood as the son of Georgia sharecroppers and his rise as a prominent figure in the civil rights movement.* Run: Book One *lays the groundwork for Lewis's run for public office, as he grapples with national unrest following the passage of the Voting Rights Act of 1965.*

The Second: Race and Guns in a Fatally Unequal America 545
Academic Carol Anderson's well-researched and meticulously sourced nonfiction work The Second: Race and Guns in a Fatally Unequal America *posits a compelling argument that the Second Amendment to the US Constitution was based on strong anti-Black bias that has continued to this day.*

Second Place 550
Second Place *is a novel written in the form of a long letter from a woman known as "M" to her correspondent "Jeffers." The novel centers around the relationship between M and a painter, "L"—or, rather, how M's relationship with L's paintings fatefully intertwined the lives of M and L over the months with which the novel is concerned.*

COMPLETE ANNOTATED LIST OF CONTENTS

Seek You: A Journey through American Loneliness 555
Graphic artist and writer Kristen Radtke's second book, Seek You: A Journey through American Loneliness, *dissects America's growing epidemic of loneliness and social isolation. Radtke first conceived of the book in 2016, four years before a global pandemic made such suffering painfully acute, and it casts a wide net among disparate concepts while also drawing on experiences and observations from Radtke's own life with the hope that in shared affliction people might reach out to one another to save themselves.*

The Sentence 560
In The Sentence, *Louise Erdrich's eighteenth novel, the employees of a Native American–owned bookstore in Minneapolis try to survive a pandemic, police brutality, and unfriendly visits from the ghost of a former customer.*

She Who Became the Sun 565
She Who Became the Sun *is the debut novel of Australian Shelley Parker-Chan, a former diplomat in Southeast Asia. This fantasy novel centers on a girl who assumes her brother's identity to fulfill her destiny in Mongol-ruled fourteenth century China, as it ponders the nature of fate, queer identity, and desire.*

A Sitting in St. James 569
A Sitting in St. James *is a sweeping work of historical fiction by young adult author Rita Williams-Garcia. Set on a sugar plantation in St. James Parish, Louisiana, the novel is an unflinching portrait of slavery in the pre–Civil War South that focuses on the members of a White enslaving family.*

Skinship 573
Yoon Choi's debut fiction collection, Skinship, *features eight stories about the varied experiences of Koreans, Korean immigrants, and Korean Americans.*

Smile: The Story of a Face 578
In this memoir recounting a decade living with a serious case of Bell's palsy, a condition that causes facial paralysis, noted playwright Sarah Ruhl meditates on many different topics relevant to her sudden inability to smile.

A Snake Falls to Earth 582
A Snake Falls to Earth *is an Indigenous futurist young adult novel based in Apache tradition, telling the intersecting coming-of-age stories of a young human girl and a snake boy from the spirit world.*

Somebody's Daughter. 587
    In this riveting memoir, writer Ashley C. Ford recalls growing up with an incarcerated father and a volatile, temperamental mother. The book reveals how these relationships permeated every aspect of Ford's early life, from the challenges of poverty to her very sense of identity.

The Souvenir Museum 591
    The Souvenir Museum is a collection of tragicomic short stories about oddball characters dealing with love, grief, fear, and heartbreak as they explore the many variations of family relationships.

Squirrel Hill: The Tree of Life Synagogue Shooting and the
    Soul of a Neighborhood 596
    Squirrel Hill is the account of how a Jewish community in Pittsburgh fared after an anti-Semitic attack took the lives of eleven worshippers at the Tree of Life synagogue in the deadliest attack on Jewish people in American history.

The Storyteller: Tales of Life and Music 601
    The Storyteller is a memoir by one of the most prominent American rock musicians of the late twentieth and early twenty-first centuries, Dave Grohl, the onetime drummer for Nirvana and the founder and lead vocalist of the Foo Fighters.

The Sum of Us: What Racism Costs Everyone and
    How We Can Prosper Together 606
    Focusing on the intersection of economics, politics, and race, Heather McGhee argues that America has a long history of enacting policies that are designed to target people of color, but that also have a profoundly damaging impact on White people.

The Sunflower Cast a Spell to Save Us from the Void 611
    In her debut full-length poetry collection, The Sunflower Cast a Spell to Save Us from the Void, *Jackie Wang uses dream-like imagery and language to touch on a variety of topics, from identity and interpersonal connection to memory and loss.*

The Sweetness of Water. 615
    The Sweetness of Water presents a look at life in rural Georgia in the confusing weeks and months following the American Civil War. White landowner George Walker, his wife Isabelle, their veteran son Caleb, and the formerly enslaved brothers Prentiss and Landry all find their lives intertwined in unexpected ways.

COMPLETE ANNOTATED LIST OF CONTENTS

A Swim in a Pond in the Rain: In Which Four Russians Give a
  Master Class on Writing, Reading, and Life 620
  In A Swim in a Pond in the Rain: In Which Four Russians Give a Master Class on Writing, Reading, and Life, author and professor George Saunders gathers seven Russian short stories that he has used in his creative writing classes, commenting on what each one can teach the aspiring writer about the craft of fiction.

The Tangleroot Palace 625
  The Tangleroot Palace collects seven of Marjorie Liu's previously published stories exploring powerful magic, hostile landscapes, and complex women.

Tastes Like War 629
  In her memoir Tastes Like War, Grace M. Cho looks back on her relationship with her mother, a Korean immigrant who struggled with schizophrenia.

These Precious Days 634
  This collection of essays by acclaimed novelist Ann Patchett explores varied subjects such as friendship, death, memory, and the life of a writer and bookstore owner.

Three Girls from Bronzeville: A Uniquely American Memoir of Race,
  Fate, and Sisterhood 639
  In this memoir, novelist Dawn Turner shares her lived experiences from childhood to the present day shaped by community, love, loss, and self-reflection. From Chicago's South Side to college a few hours away to putting down roots in a rural community, Turner shows the impacts of urban planning, inequitable education, and how a couple of poor decisions can have lifelong implications at the intersection of race and gender.

The Twilight Zone 644
  The second novel of Nona Fernández to be translated from Spanish to English, The Twilight Zone continues the author's unique blend of fact and fiction in its examination of the violence of the Pinochet dictatorship in Chile.

Unbound: My Story of Liberation and the Birth of the Me Too Movement 649
  Unbound is a memoir by activist Tarana Burke covering major events in her life, from the sexual assault she endured in childhood to her founding of the "Me Too" movement, one of the most influential social movements in contemporary American history.

Under a White Sky: The Nature of the Future 654
    Under a White Sky: The Nature of the Future *is the follow-up to Elizabeth Kolbert's Pulitzer Prize–winning book* The Sixth Extinction, *in which she wrote that human beings are living through a mass extinction event. In* Under a White Sky, *she assesses the damage humans have wrought and offers a grim prescription.*

Velvet Was the Night 658
    Velvet Was the Night, *a tense neo-noir set in 1970s Mexico City during a period of violent political turbulence, follows an unhappy secretary and a low-level government enforcer as they stumble across dangerous secrets while searching for a missing woman.*

Wake: The Hidden History of Women-Led Slave Revolts 663
    Wake: The Hidden History of Women-Led Slave Revolts *gives life to historian Rebecca Hall's extensive, thorough research about resistance in the era of chattel slavery, exploring the experiences of enslaved women in eighteenth-century New York and African women who revolted on transatlantic slaving ships. Unusually,* Wake *also depicts Hall's efforts to uncover these stories, digging, often fruitlessly, through archives in New York City, London, and Liverpool.*

We Begin at the End. 668
    We Begin at the End *takes place in a small town devastated by the tragic death of seven-year-old Sissy Radley. Thirty years later, the boy held responsible for her death is released from prison, setting off a new chain of violent events.*

When the Stars Go Dark 673
    When the Stars Go Dark *is a thriller by best-selling author Paula McLain that follows the kidnapping of three different girls through the eyes of a detective who is grappling with her own traumatic past.*

When We Cease to Understand the World 678
    Benjamín Labatut's When We Cease to Understand the World *is a series of increasingly fictional accounts of major scientific breakthroughs of the twentieth century, the modes of destruction each one offers, and the price of progress.*

Whereabouts 683
    Whereabouts, *Jhumpa Lahiri's fourth book of fiction and her first novel originally written in Italian, explores a woman's solitary life in spare and haunting prose.*

COMPLETE ANNOTATED LIST OF CONTENTS

White Smoke 688
 New York Times *best-selling young adult author Tiffany D. Jackson's novel* White Smoke *is a gothic horror set in a small Midwestern town where Mari's mother has won a three-year writing residency that offers a rent-free home. Struggling with profound anxiety, a very particular phobia, and addiction, Mari is unmoored when strange things start happening around the family's newly renovated old house.*

The Wild Fox of Yemen. 692
 The Wild Fox of Yemen, *the debut poetry volume of Yemeni American writer Threa Almontaser, is a powerful collection of poems that explore themes of identity, history, and survival.*

Winter in Sokcho 697
 Elisa Shua Dusapin's debut novel, Winter in Sokcho, *originally published in French in 2016 and translated into English in 2021, tells the story of a young biracial woman grappling with her identity and relationships in a desolate Korean resort town.*

Winter Recipes from the Collective. 702
 Winter Recipes from the Collective *is a haunting collection of poems that meditate on the nature of life, death, and memory.*

The Woman They Could Not Silence: One Woman, Her Incredible Fight for
 Freedom, and the Men Who Tried to Make Her Disappear 707
 The Woman They Could Not Silence *follows the story of Elizabeth Packard, a woman who was involuntarily admitted without trial in the nineteenth century to an institution for people with mental illness by her husband. Packard's intelligence and will are explored through her journey to legally prove her sanity as well as inspire change for women and people with mental illness.*

A World on the Wing: The Global Odyssey of Migratory Birds 712
 In A World on the Wing: The Global Odyssey of Migratory Birds, *nature writer and birder Scott Weidensaul explores the lengthy and often-dangerous migrations undertaken by numerous bird species and the efforts to track, study, and ultimately protect migratory birds and their habitats.*

The Wrong End of the Telescope 717
 Mina Simpson, a doctor who emigrated from Lebanon to the United States, agrees to volunteer at a refugee camp in Greece at the request of a friend. As the novel unfolds, she shares the stories of the refugees she meets, reflects on her own life, and criticizes the author telling her story.

You Don't Have to Be Everything: Poems for Girls Becoming Themselves. . . . 721
   In You Don't Have to Be Everything, *Diana Whitney has compiled an empowering anthology of poems that foster self-understanding and explore the complexity of adolescent girls and their wide range of emotions, from longing to rage and everything in between.*

The Madness of Crowds

Author: Louise Penny (b. 1958)
Publisher: Minotaur Books (New York). pp 436.
Type of work: Novel
Time: 2021
Locale: Three Pines, Québec

A murder mystery set during the COVID-19 pandemic, The Madness of Crowds *is the seventeenth book in Canadian author Louise Penny's best-selling Chief Inspector Gamache series.*

Principal characters

ARMAND GAMACHE, the chief inspector of homicide for the provincial police force of Québec
ABIGAIL ROBINSON, a genius statistician with an incendiary solution for "improving" the world
JEAN-GUY BEAUVOIR, Gamache's son-in-law, a police officer
HANIYA DAOUD, a Sudanese-born political activist and Nobel Peace Prize nominee
DEBBIE SCHNEIDER, Robinson's assistant
IDOLA, Gamache's infant granddaughter, who has Down syndrome

While writing her first draft of *The Madness of Crowds* (2021), Louise Penny did not mention the coronavirus disease 2019 (COVID-19) pandemic until two-thirds of the way through the story. "I thought it would be the last thing people would want to hear about after living through so much sadness," she explained in an interview with *Literary Hub*. However, it soon became apparent that the book would be more resonant if its characters were grappling with vestiges of the pandemic in the same way that its readers were. Consequently, in the next draft, Penny decided to bring up the virus on the first page.

Despite this decision, *The Madness of Crowds* does not feel like a "pandemic novel," but more like a compelling installment in the Chief Inspector Gamache murder mystery series that just so happens to examine the moral issues surrounding the pandemic. This blend of mystery storytelling and social commentary is typical of Penny's Chief Inspector Gamache series. Ostensibly, the Inspector Gamache books are best categorized as "cozy mysteries"—a gentle subcategory of the crime-writing genre typically set in idyllic small towns that does not explicitly depict violence or sex, instead allowing it to happen "offstage." Some aspects of the series fit neatly within this genre; Penny sets much of the action in a quaint fictional town in Québec called Three Pines and often steers away from gruesome and salacious storytelling. However, the series is also unlike most cozy mysteries in that it is rife with social commentary and often weaves real events into its plotlines. In the series' earlier books, Penny used Inspector Gamache's homicide cases to discuss everything from police corruption to systemic racism. Specifically, in the series' fourteenth book, *Kingdom of the Blind* (2018), Penny weaves the story of a deadly wave of drug addiction into Gamache's investigation, drawing inspiration from contemporary headlines about the opioid epidemic.

Louise Penny

A large part of what makes *The Madness of Crowds* such an engaging read is that its plot feels both terrifying and plausible at the same time. When the book begins, distribution of COVID-19 vaccines has begun and the world is starting to reopen again. One wintery day, Inspector Gamache is asked to organize the security for an event at a local university where a statistician named Professor Abigail Robinson is scheduled to give a lecture. Known as a controversial genius, Robinson claims to have a solution to the myriad problems that the pandemic has caused on the economy and healthcare system: euthanize members of society who are sick, old, or disabled; amid the chaos of the pandemic, Robinson's ideas have grown in popularity. Despite abhorring her work, Gamache dutifully agrees to oversee the event and ends up saving Robinson when an attempt is made on her life. However, later that week Robinson's assistant, Debbie Schneider, is murdered in what appears to be an act of violence that may have been intended for Robinson. As Gamache investigates the case, he quickly discovers that the situation is far more complicated than it initially appeared and that many of the crime's suspects are hiding their own dark secrets. As is typical of the mystery genre in general and Penny's writing in particular, *The Madness of Crowds* takes many unexpected twists and turns before ending in an entirely unexpected place.

In addition to its dynamic plot loaded with social commentary, the novel also draws strength from Penny's exceptionally crafted characters. This includes the series' recurring cast of Three Pines' townspeople, Gamache's family, and the officers of the local police force. These recurring characters provide a warm feeling of familiarity as well as much of the novel's humor and lighter moments, but by setting up new conflicts between them, Penny also ensures that these characters never feel stagnant. One of the best examples of a new conflict occurs between Gamache and his son-in-law Jean-Guy, who already have a complicated relationship because they also work together on the police force. Jean-Guy wants to ban Robinson from speaking because his infant daughter, Idola, has Down syndrome and thus is the kind of person for whom Robinson advocates euthanasia. Gamache despises Robinson for the same reason but feels bound by the duties of his job to oversee the event and ensure that no one is hurt. The moral dilemma that stems from conflict between Jean-Guy and Gamache's personal beliefs and professional duties builds throughout the novel, adding tension and testing their relationship in a way that feels authentic.

As enjoyable as it is to watch the dynamics of complex ongoing relationships play out, the new characters introduced in *The Madness of Crowds* often prove even more engaging than the recurring ones. Penny ensures these newcomers feel fresh and interesting by setting them up as foils to Gamache, his family, and colleagues. The character of Abigail Robinson is particularly fascinating; while her eugenicist proposal is undeniably evil, she also comes across as intelligent, funny, and magnetic. When she speaks, other characters struggle to not succumb to her charm, even if they hate her and everything she stands for. This both makes it believable that Robinson has fans and influence, despite the disturbing nature of her proposal, and sets her apart as a female antagonist depicted as highly charismatic.

Another great addition to the cast is Haniya Daoud, a young Sudanese political activist and Nobel Peace Prize nominee who fights for women and children's rights in countries affected by war and oppressive regimes. She herself was enslaved and sexually abused as a child and still carries the physical and emotional scars from this experience. Penny goes beyond this traumatic backstory to give Daoud greater depth and make her a fully rounded character; what makes her particularly interesting is that she is a deeply moral person who is not particularly "nice." Despite being a Nobel Peace Prize nominee, she has a combative personality and is unconcerned with how others see her. This becomes clear in her first encounter with Gamache. After the two are introduced, Daoud immediately calls Gamache "feeble" and a hypocrite for calling himself a good man while protecting Robinson, who is proposing mass murder. Although readers may agree with Daoud's arguments, some may find her caustic attitude toward the protagonist difficult to stomach. Her aggressive behavior toward Gamache and others nevertheless provides an interesting contrast with her peaceful political intentions. It also sets up an interesting parallel with Robinson, who behaves in a charming, polite manner yet preaches a violent ideology centered on mass euthanasia.

Penny has always used the Chief Inspector Gamache series as a vehicle for exploring morality, and this inclination has never been better utilized than it is in *The Madness of Crowds*. The novel focuses on several moral issues, but at its core is the question of whether all lives have equal value. Robinson's argument is that they do not—the weak should be sacrificed for the good of everyone else. Daoud believes that the weak must be protected at all costs, which sometimes requires one to kill one's oppressors. Gamache, on the other hand, believes in the sanctity of human life and subsequently feels that all lives are worth saving, no matter the quality of the person; his opposition to any form of killing places him in conflict with both Robinson and Daoud. Gamache's true commitment to his principles is illustrated in the dramatic scene early in the novel when he saves Robinson from a shooter, despite believing that she is dangerous and evil.

Although the moral questions about equality and the value of human lives at the center of *The Madness of Crowds* are in many ways timeless, Penny presents them in a context very specific to the year when the book was published. Indeed, the COVID-19 pandemic drives much of the plot, particularly the first act; in a move unusual for the mystery genre, the novel's inciting murder does not take place until the second act. The pandemic also helps frame the novel's main ideological debate. Robinson's argument that sometimes it is necessary to sacrifice members of society for the good of everyone else echoes a sentiment some people shared at the beginning of the pandemic. These individuals believed that measures such as mandatory lockdowns, mask-wearing requirements, and physical distancing for the sake of protecting older adults and immunocompromised people from COVID-19 was not worth the hardship, inconvenience, and economic impact. While these people generally did not go as far as Robinson or speak in such explicit terms, Penny suggests that this implied willingness to sacrifice certain groups of people to preserve the greater good places them in the same ideological camp. Penny does not highlight these parallels ham-handedly, but rather lets readers discover them on own their own. Penny's own beliefs about these issues are embodied by Gamache himself, a character she has presented as consistently upholding the values of hope, kindness, and justice throughout the series' seventeen books.

Upon its 2021 release, *The Madness of Crowds* received acclaim from both readers and critics alike. Most reviews highlighted the timeliness of the book and the deft way in which Penny weaves sharp, intelligent commentary about the present into what could have easily been a run-of-the-mill murder mystery. In her review for *New York Journal of Books*, Carolyn Haley praised Penny's ability to "humanize this difficult concept." She felt the novel succeeded as a new entry in the mystery series, but more importantly worked as a meditation on the moral issues surrounding the pandemic, due to Penny's creation of a complex world with "no oversimplified, easy-way-out viewpoints."

In his review for the *Free Lance Star*, Jay Strafford also praised the novel's moral ambiguity, considering it a thoughtful examination of the "duality of human nature." Although he was impressed with the novel's deeper themes, Strafford also felt that it succeeded on its own terms as a work of fiction, calling it "rich with inspired storytelling and thoughtful prose" and considered it a fitting addition to a mystery series already "renowned for its intelligent storylines and thoughtful examination of moral issues."

While Penny has showcased corruption and evil in her earlier works, *The Madness of Crowds* has a sharper edge to it as a result of its subject matter and reflection on the pandemic. Consequently, *The Madness of Crowds* may not provide readers the same level of comfort and escapism as earlier Inspector Gamache novels, something a few critics commented on. Carol Memmott, writing for the *Washington Post*, felt that *The Madness of Crowds* was indeed one of Penny's "darkest works" but could still provide some comfort due to the "natural beauty of Three Pines and the quirky residents we would love to have as our neighbors."

Ultimately, *The Madness of Crowds* is a satisfying blend of a classic mystery story line with rich, relevant social commentary. It manages to deliver the expected twists and turns of any Chief Inspector Gamache plot yet breaks exciting new ground for the series' cast of characters. However, what makes this work particularly relevant for the year of its release is Penny's willingness to tackle heavy ethical questions about equality and the value of human life; in these critical debates, Penny and her steadfast hero Gamache are not afraid to take a firm stance.

Author Biography
Louise Penny's long-running, best-selling Chief Inspector Gamache mystery series has won many awards, including the 2006 Gold Dagger from the Crime Writers' Association and multiple Agatha Awards. In 2017 she was awarded the Order of Canada for her contributions to Canadian culture.

Emily E. Turner

Review Sources
Haley, Carolyn. Review of *The Madness of Crowds*, by Louise Penny. *NY Journal of Books*, 24 Aug. 2021, www.nyjournalofbooks.com/book-review/madness-crowds-novel. Accessed 14 Dec. 2021.
Review of *The Madness of Crowds*, by Louise Penny. *Kirkus Reviews*, 2 Nov. 2021, www.kirkusreviews.com/book-reviews/louise-penny/the-madness-of-crowds/. Accessed 14 Dec. 2021.
Memmott, Carol. "Louise Penny's Latest Novel Imagines a Post-Covid World. Things Are Still Pretty Complicated." Review of *The Madness of Crowds*, by Louise Penny. *The Washington Post*, 21 Aug. 2021, www.washingtonpost.com/entertainment/books/louise-pennys-latest-mystery-imagines-a-post-covid-world-things-are-still-pretty-complicated/2021/08/21/8fb152a8-f6d5-11eb-9738-8395ec2a44e7_story.html. Accessed 14 Dec. 2021.
Stafford, Jay. "Book Review: Louise Penny Examines Human Duality in *The Madness of Crowds*." *The Free Lance Star*, 4 Sept. 2021, fredericksburg.com/entertainment/arts/books/book-review-louise-penny-examines-human-duality-in-the-madness-of-crowds/article_fb085ee1-5d3b-5273-80db-201ef8fdb2f7.html. Accessed 17 Dec. 2021.

Major Labels
A History of Popular Music in Seven Genres

Author: Kelefa Sanneh (b. 1976)
Publisher: Penguin Press (New York).
496 pp.
Type of work: Music, history
Time: Twentieth and twenty-first centuries
Locale: The United States

Written by journalist and music critic Kelefa Sanneh, Major Labels *explores the evolution of rock, R&B, country, punk, hip-hop, dance, and pop music between the mid-1900s and the early 2020s.*

Early in his fascinating book *Major Labels* (2021), longtime music critic and journalist Kelefa Sanneh states that if has learned anything firsthand about musicians, it is that they hate labels. "I don't know why it can't just be 'good music,'" they bemoan, resentful of the fact that their work is being judged exclusively within the context of whatever genre they have been contained to. For these musicians, being assigned a genre means that they cannot experiment outside its boundaries without some kind of backlash. The events surrounding "Old Town Road," he emphasizes, illustrate this phenomenon well; in 2019, the smash hit was removed from the Billboard country music chart because the publication ruled that it did not "embrace enough elements of today's country music," despite the fact that rapper-singer Little Nas X had written it to have a country influence. Sanneh states that this level of genre obsessiveness can be problematic—especially because it is often led by record executives who are more interested in selling the music to specific demographics than anything else.

While *Major Labels* acknowledges that the strict adherence to genres can pose serious challenges like these, at its core the book is a defense of them and their important role in the period of popular music spanning from the mid-1990s into the early 2020s. According to Sanneh, genres have not only provided certain groups of listeners with a sense of community but have also shaped the way that music is made. This argument may seem controversial to anyone who operates on the belief that truly great songs "transcend genres" and cannot be put into little boxes. However, such controversy is on brand for Sanneh, who built his career on incendiary hypotheses while writing about music for such publications as the *New York Times* and the *New Yorker.*

In *Major Labels,* Sanneh continues his quest to spark heated conversations. Each of the book's chapters focuses on the evolution of a different genre of mainstream music, centering primarily between the post-Beatles late 1960s and 2021. In addition

Kelefa Sanneh

to documenting the different stages of seven genres' development, the chapters also pose provocative ideas about them that often go against mainstream thought. In the chapter "Pop," for example, Sanneh claims that radio hits by Britney Spears are just as authentic and important as classic rock songs by artists like Bruce Springsteen. In "Hip Hop," he argues that rap music does not have to be socially conscious to be good and that demanding the genre only produce songs about the struggles of Black people would hurt the creativity of what he believes to be the greatest cultural movement that America has ever produced. It is through these kinds of ideas, which populate each of the chapters, that Sanneh repeatedly proves that he has fresh takes on age-old debates.

In the hands of a lesser writer, it is easy to imagine that *Major Labels* could be dull considering the sheer amount of intricate history that it imparts to its readers. Fortunately, Sanneh's warm and engaging writing style combined with his willingness to share personal stories from his own life as a music lover prevent it from ever feeling like a textbook. He begins all of the chapters, which are written in an essayist style, with an anecdote about the genre that gently lures his readers into some of the bigger ideas that he intends to explore in the subsequent pages. The first few pages of "Rock," for example, relay the story of Pamela Des Barres, who is the author of *I'm with the Band: Confessions of a Groupie* (1987). Her autobiography chronicles her adventures in rock 'n' roll when it was at its peak in the late 1960s and throughout the 1970s. According to Sanneh, Des Barres's depiction of this time perfectly captures the enormous impact that rock 'n' roll had on American culture and how subsequently rock stars were treated like gods. He then provides a detailed account of how the genre evolved over the next five decades by exploring the many different forms it took, including glitter rock, heavy metal, and alternative. His conclusion that rock 'n' roll has become repertory music is like so many of the other insightful points he makes throughout the book in that it feels both revelatory and true at the same time.

It is important to note that while Sanneh makes divisive arguments throughout *Major Labels*, they never come across as dismissive or condescending. The author has love for all seven of the book's genres and is not some record store snob trying to demonstrate his superiority by writing about his musical taste. Instead, Sanneh has a populist perspective when it comes to music. Genres, he argues, help people differentiate themselves from others. They provide them with an identity and sense of belonging to a specific community. This phenomenon is illustrated well with country music, which, Sanneh points out, reflects the feelings and experiences of its predominantly White audiences. As a man with a Black father and a White mother who is also a country music fan, however, he notes that he has never found the Whiteness of country music to be off-putting but simply an intrinsic aspect of the genre.

The theme of race is omnipresent throughout *Major Labels* and becomes especially evident in the chapter "R&B." Through a highly engaging and educational essay, Sanneh argues that more than any other genre, R&B has reflected the nation's musical segregation throughout history. He reveals that the term "rhythm and blues" (R&B) first emerged in the 1940s with a new style of Black music. When that music was appropriated and repackaged as "rock 'n' roll" by White artists, R&B had to reinvent itself. As the years went on, any time an R&B singer like Stevie Wonder, Michael Jackson, Prince, or Beyoncé had a mainstream hit it was relabeled as "pop music." Conversely, Black music that did not appeal to White audiences was called R&B. Just as it is in American history, race proves to be an incredibly complex subject when it comes to American music. Fortunately, Sanneh is a deft guide.

Arguably the most interesting chapter in *Major Labels* is "Punk." It would be easy to dismiss the genre's loud, angry songs as "unmusical," so some readers might be surprised that Sanneh has actually devoted a whole chapter to it. However, he convincingly demonstrates that punk does have historical significance, especially to generations of young Americans, by exploring what it meant to him growing up. For example, he illustrates that the genre was often about defiance and political idealism by describing how he used to attend underground punk vegetarian potlucks where members would discuss their various causes and organize activities. The chapter also relays the genre's history by diving into punk's many seemingly disparate subgenres, from grunge to the feminist riot grrrl. As Sanneh details the genre's history, his passion spills onto the pages and it makes for a particularly fun masterclass.

Reception of *Major Labels* has been mostly positive, with many critics extolling the book for the quality of Sanneh's writing. In his review for the *New York Times*, Dwight Garner stated that Sanneh "has a subtle and flexible style, and great powers of distillation. He's a reliable guide to music's foothills, as well as its mountains." Other critics have focused more on Sanneh's talents as a historian—specifically his thoroughness and talent for conveying large amounts of information in an accessible, digestible way. Writing for the *New York Journal of Books*, Jonah Raskin stated, "Over the past 50 years, the music scene in the US and in England has become so complex and complicated that *Major Labels* is absolutely essential reading as a road map. . . . Sanneh gets the contradictions, never loses sight of them, and nails them incisively."

Although the majority of critics have had nothing but praise in their reviews for *Major Labels*, some have been quicker to point out its flaws. One of the more common complaints about the book has been that it does not feel relevant to the year of its publication. In his review for *The Observer*, Sean O'Hagan wrote, "Given that pop's present fluidity is making genre traditionalism seem suddenly, hopelessly outdated, *Major Labels* may yet become an elegy for a time when it mattered above all else. Why it mattered so much, though it is often lost in the telling, is the essential question that propels this book. Why it no longer matters so much is perhaps the more pressing one." There is something to be said about O'Hagan's critique. Although Sanneh quite convincingly begins the book by saying that genres are important and should be defended, there are several times when it feels like he has disproven his own point. This is especially true in certain chapters, like "Rock," when he talks about how the genre he is discussing has faded in relevance. Sanneh's discussion of how genres' boundaries are more permeable than ever and subsequently more hybrid music is being produced also makes the book, as a whole, seem outdated. Because of this, *Major Labels* might be better classified as a history book than a cutting-edge examination of pop culture. While this is likely not what Sanneh wanted to accomplish when he sat down to write it, it does not mean the book is therefore uninteresting or less important.

At its core, *Major Labels* feels like an overdue addition to the canon of music literature. As a music critic with Black heritage, Sanneh brings much-needed insight to the role that race has played throughout the history of popular music—something that many White critics would overlook. His decision to include a memoir element throughout the book also makes it feel more personal, as if it were written by a friend. Combined with the fact that Sanneh is a superbly fun and engaging writer, *Major Labels* can be enjoyed by a wide variety of people—everyone from vinyl record collectors to readers who want to feel nostalgic about old bands to Gen Z kids who know little to nothing about the past fifty years of music. As the anonymous reviewer for *Kirkus* aptly concluded, *Major Labels* is, at the end of the day, "a pleasure—and an education—for any music fan."

Author Biography

Kelefa Sanneh is a music critic who has written for many different publications, including *The Source*, the *New York Times*, and *Rolling Stone*. He began writing as a staff member for the *New Yorker* in 2008. *Major Labels* (2021) is his first book.

Emily E. Turner

Review Sources

Garner, Dwight. "*Major Labels* Wraps Popular Music—All of It—in a Warm Embrace." Review of *Major Labels: A History of Popular Music in Seven Genres*, by Kelefa Sanneh. *The New York Times*, 4 Oct. 2021, www.nytimes.com/2021/10/04/books/review-major-labels-kelefa-sanneh.html. Accessed 5 Jan. 2022.

Review of *Major Labels: A History of Popular Music in Seven Genres*, by Kelefa Sanneh. *Kirkus*, 14 July 2021, www.kirkusreviews.com/book-reviews/kelefa-sanneh/major-labels/. Accessed 7 Jan. 2022.

O'Hagan, Sean. "*Major Labels*, by Kelefa Sanneh Review—An Unapologetic Defense of Music's Defining Categories." *The Observer*, Guardian News and Media, 10 Oct. 2021, www.theguardian.com/books/2021/oct/10/major-labels-by-kelefa-sanneh-review-an-unapologetic-defence-of-musics-defining-categories. Accessed 5 Jan. 2022.

Raskin, Jonah. Review of *Major Labels: A History of Popular Music in Seven Genres*, by Kelefa Sanneh. *New York Journal of Books*, www.nyjournalofbooks.com/book-review/major-labels-history. Accessed 7 Jan. 2022.

Malibu Rising

Author: Taylor Jenkins Reid (b. 1983)
Publisher: Ballantine Books (New York).
  384 pp.
Type of work: Novel
Time: 1956–83
Locale: Malibu, California

In Malibu Rising, *family secrets come to light, conflicts come to a head, and four siblings come into their own amid a wild 1983 party.*

Principal characters

NINA RIVA, the oldest of the Riva siblings, a twenty-five-year-old surfer and model
JEREMY MICHAEL "JAY" RIVA, her twenty-four-year-old brother, a championship-winning surfer
HUDSON "HUD" RIVA, her twenty-three-year-old brother, a photographer
KATHERINE ELIZABETH "KIT" RIVA, her twenty-year-old sister, a surfer
JUNE COSTAS, a.k.a. June Riva, the biological mother of Nina, Jay, and Kit and the adoptive mother of Hud
MICHAEL DOMINIC "MICK" RIVA, the Riva siblings' father, a popular singer
BRANDON RANDALL, a professional tennis player and Nina's estranged husband
ASHLEY, Hud's girlfriend and Jay's ex-girlfriend
LARA VORHEES, a bartender with whom Jay has fallen in love
CASEY GREENS, a young woman with ties to the Riva family

The city of Malibu, California, is highly susceptible to fire. As the prologue to the 2021 novel *Malibu Rising* makes clear, a number of factors play a role in Malibu's particular flammability, including the region's dry climate and spark-carrying Santa Ana winds. But the especially burnable nature of Malibu is also indicative of that region's and its residents' capacity for transformation, in which the new can emerge only out of the destruction of the old. The fire itself is inevitable; the only questions are when it will begin, who will spark the first flame, and how both landscape and people will be reshaped. Written by bestselling author Taylor Jenkins Reid and set within the same universe as her earlier novels *The Seven Husbands of Evelyn Hugo* (2017) and *Daisy Jones & the Six* (2019), *Malibu Rising* chronicles the events leading up to the Malibu fire of 1983, the result of a wild party held by the Riva siblings. In revealing that the party will end with a fire, the prologue creates not only dramatic irony but also a sense of anticipation and a mystery of sorts. The reader, unlike the characters themselves, knows that the Riva house will, at some point in the course of the party,

Taylor Jenkins Reid

go up in flames. However, the prologue does not explain how or why, and the novel's slow reveal of the circumstances surrounding the fire and its ultimate consequences proves both entertaining and satisfying.

The present-day events of *Malibu Rising* take place on August 27, 1983, and center on the four Riva siblings, lifelong residents of Malibu who have become celebrities over the previous several years. The oldest of the siblings, Nina, is a twenty-five-year-old surfer who reluctantly began modeling some years prior as a means of supporting her family. While Nina's modeling brought her both fame and professional success, she is unhappy with her life, particularly because her husband, professional tennis player Brandon Randall, has recently left her for another woman. The second-oldest Riva sibling, Jay, is a championship-winning surfer who has gained widespread notice due in part to the efforts of twenty-three-year-old brother Hud, an accomplished photographer whose photographs of Jay surfing have graced multiple magazine covers. Hud is in fact half-brother to his three siblings, born out of one of their father Mick Riva's many extramarital affairs. Hud's biological mother chose not to raise him and instead brought him to the Riva household, where he was raised alongside his siblings by adoptive mother June Riva and grew particularly close to Jay, who is only about a month older. As of August 1983, however, Hud worries that his close relationship with Jay may be in danger because he is now in a relationship with Jay's ex-girlfriend Ashley—a relationship that actually began as an affair while Ashley and Jay were still together. Jay himself has fallen in love with a bartender named Lara and has begun to pursue her more seriously while avoiding thinking about an upsetting medical diagnosis that could harm his career. Meanwhile, the youngest Riva sibling, twenty-year-old Kit, grapples with a not-fully-acknowledged truth about herself while also seeking greater recognition as a talented surfer in her own right, not only as a Riva.

As *Malibu Rising* begins, the four Riva siblings are preparing to host their annual end-of-summer party, Malibu's most notorious celebration of the year, at the house Nina once shared with Brandon. The first half of the novel is broken up into chapters chronicling each hour between 7:00 a.m. and 7:00 p.m., the period leading up to the party, as well as flashback chapters that offer insight into the family history of the Rivas and the events that have brought them to this specific point. The flashback narrative begins in 1956, when June Costas, the daughter of local Malibu restaurant owners, falls in love with aspiring singer Mick Riva. Readers familiar with Reid's earlier work may recognize Mick, who is a minor character in *Daisy Jones & the Six* and the third husband of the title character in *The Seven Husbands of Evelyn Hugo*. Following a courtship that results in Nina's conception, June and Mick marry, and Mick begins what will become a highly successful singing career while June raises their children at their seaside home in Malibu. While the relationship starts off strong, June eventually divorces Mick because of his serial infidelities and spends the next several years raising the children on her own. The couple reunites, during which they remarry and Kit is born, but Mick ultimately abandons the family amid a new affair with a backup singer.

While their childhood has some bright spots, including the four siblings' discovery and mastery of surfing, life is difficult for the Riva siblings following Mick's second departure. Nina, as the oldest, is forced to take on more and more responsibility in the household as June descends into alcoholism. Following June's sudden death, the seventeen-year-old Nina is thrust into the role of head of household. Nina accepts that role out of necessity and sacrifices her own childhood for the sake of her siblings, dropping out of high school, taking over the family restaurant, and eventually accepting an offer to model despite her discomfort with the attention now being paid to her physical appearance. Though key to the Riva family's wellbeing, Nina's focus on her duty to her family is often to her own detriment, and her pattern of repressing her own wants and needs in favor of those of the people around her—which continues into her marriage—proves harmful to her psyche.

The Riva siblings' tumultuous shared history has shaped the strong bonds between them, but those bonds are tested over the latter half of *Malibu Rising*, which spans the period between 7:00 p.m. on August 27, 1983, and 7:00 a.m. the following morning. What begins with a slow trickle of guests soon grows out of hand, with attendees swinging from chandeliers, shooting guns in the house, stealing Nina's possessions, and consuming copious amounts of cocaine. More pressing for the Rivas is the arrival of several unexpected guests, including Brandon, who attempts to convince Nina to take him back. As the party grows increasingly wild, a number of secrets come to light, and the inevitable fire is kindled at last.

An entertaining and lively novel, *Malibu Rising* is a strong period piece that is deeply immersed in its Southern California setting, which Reid has previously featured to great effect in her earlier novels set in the same universe. It also skillfully evokes the early 1980s era in which the present-day portions of the novel are set. Reid's omniscient narration proves to be an effective means of telling the story, delving at times into the perspectives of various side characters, in addition to those of the Rivas, in order to convey necessary information or simply to flesh out the world around the central characters. The novel is perhaps most effective in its depiction of the four Riva siblings, whose bonds, conflicts, and character arcs remain the focal point of the work even amid the 1980s Hollywood debauchery of the climactic party. Of particular note are the ways in which the siblings break free from their previous patterns of behavior or the patterns set out for them by their family members, thus counteracting Nina's revelation midway through the novel that "family histories repeat." Jay and Hud embrace a new level of honesty with one another, while Kit becomes more honest with herself and rejects the norms that society seeks to force upon her. Nina herself comes alarmingly close to making the same mistake as her mother in taking her unfaithful husband back, briefly agreeing to resume her relationship with Brandon after his arrival at the party. While the personal journeys of the Riva siblings are all important from a narrative perspective, Nina's personal growth and success in breaking the cycle of dysfunction represent a particularly satisfying victory that many of the novel's readers will likely appreciate.

Reviews of *Malibu Rising* were largely positive, with critics praising Reid's characters and narrative as well as the novel's overall tone and feel. The anonymous reviewer for *Publishers Weekly* described the novel as "fast-paced and addictive," and the critic for *Kirkus* characterized it as "compulsively readable." The *Kirkus* reviewer also praised Reid's depiction of the relationships between the Riva siblings, whose history, flaws, and love for one another were highlights of the novel for many reviewers. Writing for the *Evening Standard*, Madeleine Feeny particularly commended Reid's depiction of Nina and her story arc, as well as the novel's "sensitive depictions of betrayal, alcoholism and the distorting drug of fame." *Malibu Rising*'s evocation of its setting and the surf culture in which the Riva siblings are immersed also caught the attention of critics. In a review for the *New York Times*, for example, Elinor Lipman noted that the "descriptions and lingo" of surfing and surf culture "sound to this non-surfing reader authentic, insider-ish, without straining."

A few reviewers did critique some aspects of the novel, however, including elements of its plot and language. The reviewer for *Publishers Weekly*, for instance, wrote that "the novel's climactic scenes verge on melodramatic," while Feeny asserted that Reid "doesn't shy away from cliché" in her prose. Yet even when making such points, critics generally approved of the work as a whole. Tellingly, Feeny noted that the novel's clichés actually help make it a quick, easy read—which will likely appeal to many readers—and do not obscure the fact that the narrative's "emotional depth is real."

Author Biography

Taylor Jenkins Reid is the author of seven novels, including *The Seven Husbands of Evelyn Hugo* (2017) and *Daisy Jones & the Six* (2019).

Joy Crelin

Review Sources

Feeny, Madeleine. "*Malibu Rising* by Taylor Jenkins Reid Review: A Great Beach Read." *Evening Standard*, 17 May 2021, www.standard.co.uk/culture/books/malibu-rising-taylor-jenkins-reid-book-review-b935613.html. Accessed 16 Feb. 2022.

Lipman, Elinor. "Welcome to the Party of the Century. Leave Your Scruples at the Door." Review of *Malibu Rising*, by Taylor Jenkins Reid. *The New York Times*, 1 June 2021, www.nytimes.com/2021/05/29/books/review/malibu-rising-taylor-jenkins-reid.html. Accessed 16 Feb. 2022.

Review of *Malibu Rising*, by Taylor Jenkins Reid. *Kirkus*, 17 Mar. 2021, www.kirkusreviews.com/book-reviews/taylor-jenkins-reid/malibu-rising/. Accessed 16 Feb. 2022.

Review of *Malibu Rising*, by Taylor Jenkins Reid. *Publishers Weekly*, 10 Feb. 2021, www.publishersweekly.com/978-1-5247-9865-9. Accessed 16 Feb. 2022.

Merry, Stephanie. "Taylor Jenkins Reid's *Malibu Rising* Is a Fiery Mix of Celebrity Culture and Family Drama." *The Washington Post*, 31 May 2021, www.washingtonpost.com/entertainment/books/malibu-rising-book-review/2021/05/27/4d047ed4-bd56-11eb-b26e-53663e6be6ff_story.html. Accessed 16 Feb. 2022.

Rancilio, Alicia. "Review: Taylor Jenkins Reid Soars with *Malibu Rising*." *ABC News*, 1 June 2021, abcnews.go.com/Entertainment/wireStory/review-taylor-jenkins-reid-soars-malibu-rising-78024118. Accessed 16 Feb. 2022.

A Marvellous Light

Author: Freya Marske
Publisher: Tordotcom (New York). 384 pp.
Type of work: Novel
Time: 1908
Locale: London

A Marvellous Light, the first book in a planned trilogy, introduces Robin Blyth and Edwin Courcey, civil service employees whose jobs are to curtail rumors and incidents of magical disruptions. In this first book, they are drawn into a conspiracy over the Last Contract and a trio of magical objects which, if combined, could spell the doom of the world.

Principal characters

REGINALD "REGGIE" GATLING, Assistant in the Office of Special Domestic Affairs and Complaints
SIR ROBERT "ROBIN" BLYTH, Reggie's replacement as Assistant in the Office of Special Domestic Affairs and Complaints
EDWIN COURCEY, magical liaison to the Chief Minister of the Magical Assembly
ADELAIDE MORRISSEY, Robin's secretary
MAUD BLYTH, Robin's younger sister
WALT COURCEY, Edwin's oldest brother, powerful magician

In *A Marvellous Light* (2021), Freya Marske's debut novel, the author takes science-fiction/fantasy fans on a trip back to Edwardian England where two men from very different worlds are introduced as a result of a mistake. Their unlikely meeting forces the two men together to pursue a mystery that leads to a conspiracy to rule the world, falling in love along the way.

The story begins with the torture of Reginald "Reggie" Gatling, the Assistant in the Office of Special Domestic Affairs and Complaints. Reggie reveals that an object his captors desire has been hidden in his office. Though it is suggested Reggie has been killed, his family and coworkers believe he has disappeared or transferred positions, respectively. The story jumps ahead several weeks to find Reggie's replacement, Sir Robert "Robin" Blyth in his new office. Robin has no idea what his new job entails or even why he has been assigned to it. On the verge of complete frustration, Robin is shocked when his secretary, Miss Adelaide Morrissey, leaves him in the hands of Mr. Edwin Courcey, a stony-faced young man who has been introduced as a "special liaison." Thrust into a position for which he has no aptitude, Edwin takes it upon himself

Freya Marske

to test Robin's ability to handle the truth and reveals the existence of magic. Robin is further tested when he is accosted by a mysterious figure who places a curse on his arm in an attempt to manipulate him into helping his attackers find something called the Last Contract.

Thus begins the quest that Robin and Edwin must undertake: to discover a way to remove the curse, find out what happened to Reggie, and search for the mysterious Last Contract. The story follows the two men as they travel to Edwin's family's estate where a magical library might hold the key. In between researching potential cures, Robin is treated to a variety of activities bordering on amusing and cruel at the hands of Edwin's sister and a group of her friends. His own headstrong sister, Maud, takes it upon herself to follow him to the country, placing both Edwin and Robin in a precarious position with the others when Edwin refuses to allow either Robin's or Maud's memory of magic to be erased. In the meantime, Edwin and Robin begin to acknowledge a budding attraction to each other. The story continues to trace their romantic relationship as the two men work through the puzzle that has been placed in front of them.

One thematic element explored in the novel is that of opposites. The most obvious example of this is the dichotomy of the non-magical world of Robin Blyth and the magical world of Edwin Courcey. Robin has led a life free of magic until his first day of the new job. Edwin, however, has lived with magic his whole life. Within the magical world there is another binary: those whose magic is strong versus those whose magic is weak or non-existent. Surprisingly to Edwin, Robin readily adapts to the magical world, offering only questions about this new experience. The answers to Robin's questions smoothly world-build, so readers learn alongside him. However, Edwin's magical world is often less friendly or exciting than Robin might anticipate. Since Edwin is the youngest son and is less magical than the rest of his family, he has been a life-long victim of bullying. Not only did his schoolmates sneer at him, but his older brother and father mercilessly treat him as less-than. Even his more friendly sister and her group of friends taunt his abilities. Through their budding friendship and Robin's growing attraction, Edwin begins to accept himself and to see his own strengths.

Family is another thematic concern where Marske presents opposites. After the death of Robin's self-centered parents, he is left in charge of a bankrupt estate as well as Maud, who is eighteen. While keeping his sister home would be less stressful for Robin, she insists that sending her to college—a comparatively uncommon choice for women of the time—would be more fulfilling. Robin clearly loves his sister, and readers learn that the two have been taking care of each other's emotional needs since their glory-seeking parents only saw them as unimportant extensions of themselves. Edwin's family is vastly different. While Robin's parents primarily ignored him, Edwin's father and older brother openly criticized him for what they declared as his lack of magical ability. His sister, her husband, and their friends do not dislike Edwin as openly as the older patriarchs do; however, they often callously provoke him. Only Edwin's mother genuinely cares for him, but she has an ongoing illness and is often too withdrawn from the family to offer temperance.

Partially as a result of their upbringing, Robin and Edwin are further disconnected. While Robin found fulfillment in social pursuits, Edwin became an introvert. Physically, Robin is athletic and well-built. He prefers physical action and can be found boxing or doing other energetic activities to work out his aggressions. He is intelligent, but he is not as brilliant as Edwin, who, even as a child, chose books as a refuge. This preference for indoor activities contributes to Edwin's slimmer stature and pale coloring. Edwin's studious nature also provides a strong contrast to Robin's physical abilities as the two learn to complement each other's strengths to solve the puzzle of the last contract and the missing item that Reggie had hidden.

Marske herself points out that land ownership is additionally a significant theme of the novel. In the acknowledgements section, she calls *A Marvellous Light* "a book about the responsibility we owe to the places we live." Robin has to learn to accept accountability for the land he has been left in his parents' will. In an effort to make a positive change for himself and Maud, as well as those who depend on him, he takes a stand by firing his parents' incompetent land manager and rehiring the previous person who could be honest about what needed to be improved. Edwin's relationship with land is more complicated. Magical landowning families imbue their land with their blood, creating a bond between the land and their families. Edwin has always found his presence on the family estate to give him a prickly feeling, but after he unwittingly becomes the master of another estate, he begins to understand that it was his attitude toward his home that had been the problem. He was not being rejected by the estate as he had thought; he was, instead, rejecting it. His new position as the owner of Sutton Cottage, one of the oldest magical estates in the country, teaches him the value of making a place into a home.

The romantic relationship between the two protagonists provides another theme throughout the novel. Marske introduces the fact that both Robin and Edwin are gay men very early in the story, and their attraction to each other grows fairly quickly considering the short time frame of the plot. Their thoughts about each other are often erotic, and there are several graphic, and somewhat lengthy, sex scenes. The author also provides commentary on the difficulties of being gay men during the Edwardian period in England as she offers allusion to the trial and imprisonment of Oscar Wilde for sodomy.

The critical reception of the novel glows with compliments. Several reviewers noted similarities between Marske's debut and works by other authors, such as C. L. Polk, Everina Maxwell, Robinette Kowal, and Casey McQuiston. Outside of these comparisons, the romance between Edwin and Robin is highly touted. A *Publishers*

Weekly review claimed the "sensual erotic scenes" as one reason readers will return for the sequels, while Caitlyn Paxson for *NPR* argued that the romantic relationship is responsible for "stealing the show from the mystery plot." Jenna Jay, in a review of the novel for *Booklist*, concurred, stating that it "is sure to capture the hearts of romance and fantasy readers alike." Plot, setting, characterization, dialogue, the magic itself and the temptation of two more books are additional areas of comment. In a review for *Library Journal*, Kristi Chadwick announced, "Marske's debut is a delightful blend of Edwardian fantasy and romance, with enough twists and questions to have readers clamoring for the next in the planned series." In addition, Paxson claimed she "would happily return to Marske's magic-infused England for more adventures with Robin, Edwin and their friends and relations."

Author Biography

Freya Marske has been recognized with the 2020 Australian National SF (Ditmar) Award for Best New Talent for her writing and was nominated for the Hugo Award for coauthoring the *Be The Serpent* podcast. She has published short stories in a number of sources. *A Marvellous Light* is her first novel.

Theresa L. Stowell, PhD

Review Sources

Chadwick, Kristi. Review of *A Marvellous Light*, by Freya Marske. *Library Journal*, Sept. 2021, p. 55. *Literary Reference Center Plus*, search.ebscohost.com/login.asp x?direct=true&db=lkh&AN=151944193&site=lrc-plus. Accessed 18 Jan. 2022.

El-Mohtar, Amal. "Memory, That Unreliable Narrator: New Science Fiction and Fantasy." Review of *Elder Race*, by Adrian Tchaikovsky; *You Feel it Just Below the Rips*, by Jeffrey Cranor and Kanina Matthewson; *A Marvellous Light*, by Freya Marske; *Far from the Light of Heaven*, by Tade Thompson; *AI 2041*, by Kai-Fu Lee; and *The Perishing*, by Natashia Deón. *The New York Times*, 3 Dec. 2021, www.nytimes.com/2021/12/03/books/review/new-science-fiction-fantasy.html. Accessed 18 Jan. 2022.

Jay, Jenna. Review of *A Marvellous Light*, by Freya Marske. *Booklist*, 15 Sept. 2021, p. 28. *Literary Reference Center Plus*, search.ebscohost.com/login.aspx?direct=tr ue&db=lkh&AN=152387365&site=lrc-plus. Accessed 18 Jan. 2022.

Review of *A Marvellous Light*, by Freya Marske." *Publishers Weekly*, 16 Aug. 2021, p. 66. *Literary Reference Center Plus*, search.ebscohost.com/login.aspx?direct=tr ue&db=lkh&AN=151926687&site=lrc-plus. Accessed 18 Jan. 2022.

Paxson, Caitlyn. "*A Marvellous Light* Infuses Magic and Adventures into 19th Century England." *NPR*, 22 Dec. 2021, www.npr.org/2021/12/22/1065740632/a-marvellous-light-infuses-magic-and-adventures-into-19th-century-england. Accessed 18 Jan. 2022.

Mary Jane

Author: Jessica Anya Blau
Publisher: Custom House (New York). 320 pp.
Type of work: Novel
Time: 1975
Locale: Baltimore, Maryland

In the novel Mary Jane, *Jessica Anya Blau tells the story of Mary Jane Dillard, whose carefree experiences with sex, drugs, and rock and roll during the summer of 1975 cause her to question everything she has thought to be accurate in her world.*

Principal characters

MARY JANE DILLARD, a fourteen-year-old nanny
BETSY DILLARD, her mother
GERALD DILLARD, her father
IZZY CONE, the five-year-old girl Mary Jane will nanny
BONNIE CONE, Izzy's mother
DR. RICHARD CONE, Izzy's father, a psychiatrist
JIMMY BENDINGER, a rock star recovering from a heroin addiction
SHEBA, an actor and former child TV star who is married to Jimmy

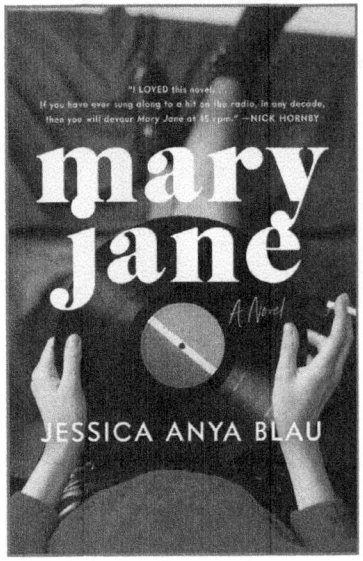

Author Jessica Anya Blau has long written about characters who grow up in unique families. She typically sets her novels in California, and occasionally during the 1970s. For example, *The Summer of Naked Swim Parties* (2008) tells the story of two sisters in 1970s California who must deal with the turbulence of growing up in the home of their eccentric parents. *Mary Jane* (2021), Blau's fifth novel, is told from the first-person point of view, and incorporates many of the same elements as Blau's earlier coming-of-age tales. Set in 1975, the descriptive language transports the reader back in time through clothing, pop culture references, and most importantly, the era's social norms. While the turmoil of the 1960s in the United States is over, the battle between the mainstream culture and counterculture continues, with different characters in the novel representing different aspects of this conflict.

Fourteen-year-old Mary Jane Dillard's life is reminiscent of the stereotypical American idyll, with her mother Betsy being a strict and structured homemaker while her father Gerald works. The Dillard household, representing a "typical" suburban White family, is always clean and organized. The family follows a schedule that does not afford them any flexibility, however. All activities are routine and predictable, including nightly family dinners, visits to the country club, and Sundays at church.

Jessica Anya Blau

The story begins with Mary Jane at the residence of the Cone family, where she is interviewing for a summer nannying job caring for Dr. Richard and Bonnie Cone's five-year-old daughter, Izzy. While Mary Jane likes Mrs. Cone, she is confused as to how she spends her time and wonders why the family needs a summer nanny. Mary Jane is also distracted by the messiness and disorder in the Cones's household and knows that her mother would harshly judge the family's living situation. Despite these reservations, Mary Jane accepts the job.

Shortly after Mary Jane begins her nanny duties, Dr. Cone informs her that a celebrity couple will be living with them for the summer as one of them receives treatment for heroin addiction, and makes it clear to Mary Jane that no one must know about their summer guests. Amid this secrecy, Mary Jane cannot wait to see who the celebrities are and is interested to better understand addiction. As Dr. Cone explains little about the exact nature of the issue, Mary Jane becomes convinced that she herself is a sex addict. While she has never even kissed anyone, she is concerned she is addicted to sex simply because she thinks about it so often.

When the celebrity houseguests arrive, Mary Jane is speechless. The wife, Sheba, a former child star, is one of Mary Jane's favorite actors. Sheba is married to Jimmy, a famous rock musician struggling with heroin addiction; he has come to the Cones's house for a summer of treatment and rehabilitation, and Sheba is along for the ride to offer her husband moral support. Mary Jane does not take long to get comfortable around the celebrities and the Cones, and they all welcome her with open arms. While Mary Jane is fascinated with everyone, Izzy easily becomes her favorite member of the house. The two of them have a lot of fun together, and Mary Jane finds creative ways to engage Izzy while cleaning and organizing the house. Mary Jane may be bothered by her own mother's strict and stoic nature, but the lessons she has learned regarding household management come in handy in her role as a nanny, which evolves to include housekeeping.

Mary Jane works diligently to keep her mother in the dark about the daily goings-on at the Cone household, because she knows her summer employment would end abruptly if her mother learned of the reality of life there. Mary Jane's mother would be horrified by the recreational drug use Sheba and Jimmy engage in, Jimmy's attempts to work on his sobriety, and the adult conversations Mary Jane has been participating in around the dinner table. Her mother would also disapprove of more trivial things, such as Mrs. Cone not wearing a bra. Initially, it is difficult for Mary Jane to lie to her mother, but in time it gets easier as she commits to making it through the summer in her position. While Mary Jane is enjoying this change of scenery, she also wants to be sure Izzy is properly taken care of while the adults are busy. As a result, she finds herself living two lives. Throughout the week, she enjoys a carefree existence with freedom, good music, and meals she has prepped for herself and the Cone household. On the weekends, when she is home with her parents, it is back to business as usual.

Later in the novel, the Cones, their houseguests, and Mary Jane spend a week on a secluded beach in the middle of summer. During this week, the dynamics of the group shift drastically. Jimmy has remained sober after an early slip-up, but he breaks his promise to Sheba not to act on their open marriage. Making matters worse, Izzy and Mary Jane catch Jimmy in the act with a neighbor from Roland Park. Mary Jane convinces Izzy that Jimmy and the neighbor were wrestling, and they decide to keep it a secret to prevent Sheba from becoming upset. After Izzy goes to bed, Mary Jane and the adults have a group therapy session to unpack the day's events. At this time, Mary Jane gains a deeper understanding of addiction, realizing she is not a sex addict. Sheba admits to missing the spotlight while hiding out in Maryland, Jimmy announces his desire to avoid the spotlight, and Mrs. Cone shares how unhappy she is in her marriage. When the group returns home, they fall back into their routine, with these newly revealed truths hanging over them.

After returning to the city, Jimmy, Sheba, Izzy, and Mary Jane travel to a part of Baltimore that Mary Jane's mother disapproves of to purchase some albums. During their visit to the record store, the owners recognize Jimmy and Sheba; as the group prepares to leave, the store owners ask to take a photo. Little do they know this photo will ultimately disrupt their rhythm for the remainder of summer. The picture makes its way to the front page of the local newspaper, and Mary Jane's parents see it. Mary Jane's father orders her to immediately cut ties with the Cones and their houseguests, and punishes her by sentencing her to stay in her bedroom until school begins. She constantly worries about Izzy and misses the affectionate interactions she has become accustomed to over the prior months. As summer nears its end, uncertainty grows as to whether Mary Jane will be able to exist within the confines of her home after experiencing such an emotional awakening. Blau builds anticipation and heightens uncertainty as she brings the novel to an unexpected yet satisfying ending.

Overall, *Mary Jane* is a classic coming-of-age story. One of the strengths of this novel is how it makes Mary Jane's innocence evident without making it a barrier to her growth. She is allowed to slowly begin to explore a world she has not been privy to, and manages to be open rather than judgmental in the way her parents have been. This journey of discovery presents her with many opportunities for fun and excitement. However, it also forces her to confront things that her parents were able to shield her from, such as drug addiction. Mary Jane's balancing act between the positive and negative aspects of engaging with the wider world, and how she makes peace with both ends of the spectrum, helps motivate her efforts to break free of her strict family. While she is not as openly rebellious or troubled as some protagonists in coming-of-age tales, such as the iconic Holden Caulfield of *Catcher in the Rye* (1951), Mary Jane's willingness to live life on her own terms makes her a rebel regardless.

Mary Jane received starred reviews upon its publication in 2021. Rebecca Munro, writing for *Book Reporter*, praised the novel's messages about family, which Blau is able to depict through Mary Jane's willingness to confront an unfamiliar world very different from her sheltered upbringing. Writing about Mary Jane's discovery of the contrast between her own "intensely compartmentalized family" and the Cones, who lacked such boundaries and restrictions, Munro argued that Mary Jane's discovery of this alternate way of living drives home the book's message that what people learn from their parents is not always correct. Mary Jane's "joyful" engagement with the world on her own terms, in addition to being "hilarious," also touches on some more challenging lessons. In particular, Munro felt the novel's examination of Jimmy's addiction helps teach Mary Jane the valuable lesson that, to quote the novel, "people you loved could do things you didn't love. And, still, you could keep loving them." Munro noted how this helps Mary Jane realize her family's view of love operates like a "meritocracy," whereas unconditional love "can arise naturally, organically and unstoppably."

Many other reviews similarly commented on *Mary Jane*'s examination of family, including one's ability to choose their own family other than the one they were born into. Calling the novel a "breezy coming-of-age tale" in her *New York Journal of Books* review, critic Fran Hawthorne described the novel as something of a love story between Mary Jane and the entire Cone family; while Blau vividly depicts the Cones's perpetually messy home as a place "like a college dorm after a drunken party," the experience of living in a house where "everyone is always hugging and kissing" allows Mary Jane to learn valuable lessons about love and family. She experiences many tender moments with the Cones; for example, when she tells Izzy that she loves her, Mary Jane realizes that she had "never said that before, not to anyone." While Hawthorne enjoyed the novel's humor and moments of "genuine love," she did take issue with some perceived plot holes, particularly Mary Jane's strict mother not knowing more about her daughter's employers.

Some reviews commented on the novel's engaging storytelling and vivid setting, feeling that it would be well-suited to a film or TV adaptation. In her *New York Times* review, Allegra Goodman wrote that *Mary Jane* has the "bouncy rhythm of classic television," adding, "Blau's story is so clear and bright that you can watch the movie in your mind." However, Goodman did echo Hawthorne's concerns about the plot's credulity, and considered some elements of the plot to be "far-fetched," such as the feasibility of Jimmy staying at the Cones's home for an entire summer of treatment. Additionally, Goodman felt that some of the secondary characters required further development and felt somewhat one-dimensional. Still, despite these reservations, Goodman considered the novel a success, in part due to Blau's "deft hand with comic juxtaposition and fantasy."

Author Biography
Jessica Anya Blau is a writer whose previous novels include *The Summer of Naked Swim Parties* (2008), *Drinking Closer to Home* (2011), and *The Trouble with Lexie* (2016). Her work has appeared in several outlets and she has taught writing at Johns Hopkins University and the Fashion Institute of Technology.

LaShawnda Fields

Review Sources
Goodman, Allegra. "The Babysitter Knows All." Review of *Mary Jane*, by Jessica Anya Blau. *The New York Times*, 11 May 2021, www.nytimes.com/2021/05/11/books/review/mary-jane-jessica-anya-blau.html. Accessed 22 Jan. 2022.
Hawthorne, Fran. Review of *Mary Jane*, by Jessica Anya Blau. *New York Journal of Books*, www.nyjournalofbooks.com/book-review/mary-jane-novel. Accessed 22 Jan 2022.
Munro, Rebecca. Review of *Mary Jane*, by Jessica Anya Blau. *Book Reporter*, 14 May 2021, www.bookreporter.com/reviews/mary-jane. Accessed 22 Jan. 2022.

Matrix

Author: Lauren Groff (b. 1978)
Publisher: Riverhead Books (New York). 272 pp.
Type of work: Novel
Time: The twelfth century
Locale: England

A luminous novel set in twelfth-century England, Matrix *chronicles Marie de France's struggle to build a meaningful life for herself after she is sent to live in an abbey of nuns.*

Principal characters

MARIE, the novel's protagonist, a fictionalized version of Marie de France
CECILY, her childhood servant, friend, and lover
ELEANOR OF AQUITAINE, queen of England and France and her unrequited love
ABBESS EMME, the elderly nun who leads the abbey when she first arrives there
WEVUA, the nun responsible for the novices, who inducts her into the abbey
GODA, her rival in the abbey
RUTH, a longtime friend and ally in the abbey
NEST, a healer who reawakens her sexuality
WULFHILD, a child she takes into the abbey and who later manages the abbey's finances
AVICE, a headstrong young nun
TILDE, a fellow novice and lifelong friend

Matrix (2021), the critically acclaimed writer Lauren Groff's sixth book of fiction, is a brilliant portrait of a medieval woman's struggle to construct a meaningful life for herself in a harsh and unfair world. At the novel's opening, seventeen-year-old Marie has been exiled from the court of Westminster and is to become prioress of a poor abbey in rural England. The daughter of a prince who raped her mother, Marie is an unacknowledged half-sister to Queen Eleanor of Aquitaine. Marie adores Eleanor and the royal court and is crushed by the queen's decision to send her away. Marie has little religious faith and no interest in becoming a nun, and she believes that her talents for languages, warfare, and managing an estate will be wasted at the abbey. Moreover, her servant, friend, and lover, Cecily, will not be allowed to travel with her. Despite her formidable intelligence and will, Marie's life is shaped by factors outside of her control: her parentage, her illegitimacy, and her tall, gaunt frame and unlovely visage. Eleanor dismisses Marie with a particularly cruel joke, saying that "anyone with eyes

Lauren Groff

could see she had always been meant for holy virginity." For Marie, her banishment to the abbey is a form of "living death."

Although Marie has been appointed prioress of the abbey, she is also a young novice who must be initiated into abbey life, and her early days are marked by discipline and suffering. The officious Sister Wevua is put in charge of Marie and her fellow novices. Marie is rousted from her bed every few hours to pray with the other nuns according to the strictures of their Rule, and like those other women she is constantly cold and hungry. After the wealth and comfort of the court at Westminster, the poverty of the abbey comes as a shock. The kindly but scattered Abbess Emme is incapable of managing the institution's affairs or of providing for the sisters' basic needs. This new life is poor not just in material terms, but in its lack of culture, art, literature, music, and conversation.

Marie rebels against the strictures that have been laid upon her, making one attempt after another to regain some measure of the freedom that she enjoyed in her courtly life. She rides out on her horse one day, skipping all of her prescribed duties, but is beaten upon her return. Taking a different tact, she wakes night after night to compose a series of poems meant to impress Eleanor. Although she dedicates the volume to Eleanor's husband and sends it off to the court, she receives no reply. This snub is worse than any beating at the hands of her superior: it means that there will be no reversal of Marie's sentence, and that her future truly lies with this abbey.

At this low point in her life, Marie undergoes a sudden and remarkable transformation. She experiences the first of many visions that will appear to her, seeing all at once the role she could play in transforming the life of the abbey. She sets to work reviewing the abbey's financial accounts and finds that the place is being appallingly mismanaged. Turning her forceful personality squarely on this new project, she collects outstanding tithes that local tributaries have failed to pay, removes renters who are enriching themselves at the abbey's expense, and weeds out graft and abuse throughout the institution. She finds a new source of income by creating a scriptorium and having her nuns adopt a practice that was normally reserved for monks. Later in the novel, she will abrogate to herself priestly duties like saying Mass and hearing confession. Riding about the countryside on the abbey's business, Marie makes herself a fearsome presence and gradually transforms her abbey into a prosperous and respected institution. Groff jumps quickly from year to year, so that some fifty pages into the novel Marie is middle-aged and has firmly established herself as abbess.

Marie is a remarkable character, a woman of vast ambition and determination living in a time in which these qualities were thought fit only for men. Interestingly, the abbey is not her first experience living in a society of women. As a girl, Marie was raised by her mother and her fierce aunts, who took her with them on the failed Second Crusade. Though they never reached their goal of Jerusalem, this army of women saw combat and carved out for themselves a rare measure of autonomy. Eleanor's court, too, was created and ruled by a powerful woman. In managing the abbey, Marie creates yet another model for how women can form a society and wield power. Spurred on both by her visions and by her own sense of pride, Marie sets her nuns to ever more ambitious projects, such as building a vast labyrinth around the abbey to protect it from intruders. One of the questions running through the book is whether Marie's visions are truly inspired by God or are rather the impulses of her own boundless drive to create a legacy for herself. Reflecting on the difference between herself and her fellow nuns late in her life, Marie will realize that "greatness was not the same as goodness." While everything she has done benefits her order, Marie is driven by an ambition and a desire for greatness that sets her apart from her contemplative sisters.

Groff based Marie on the historical figure Marie de France, author of a series of poems devoted to courtly love and the earliest known French female poet. Little is known of the real Marie, which gives Groff an opportunity to imagine a rich life for her fictionalized version of the poet, interweaving her story with the historical events and personages of her time. Historical fiction can sometimes fall into the trap of overemphasizing setting, such that a story becomes waterlogged with details, references, and asides meant to evoke a particular period. Groff, however, is remarkably deft at depicting the culture and history surrounding Marie in a way that emphasizes rather than distracts from her story. Eleanor of Aquitaine, for example, emerges as a fully formed and vital character, rather than a piece of historical window dressing.

By the same token, Groff refers to power struggles within Eleanor's family without presenting the reader with an unnecessary roster of historical names and personages. Readers may remember on their own that Eleanor's sons are the well-regarded King Richard the Lionhearted and the ignoble King John. These kings figure in many stories, from Shakespeare's *King John* to the legends of Robin Hood. The more readers remember or learn about the novel's historical setting, the more parallels and resonances will they find with Marie's story. Marie and her nuns, for example, are contemporaries of Robin Hood and his merry men, another band of disenfranchised people who carve out a new society for themselves in the wilderness. Likewise, King John's struggles with the church hierarchy and the English nobles, which eventually led to John's being forced to sign the Magna Carta, are a fascinating parallel to Marie's own power struggles. Ultimately, though, Groff's triumph in this novel lies in conveying historical setting not through facts, references, and asides, but through the power of her language. She invokes the Middle Ages on the level of the word and the line, telling Marie's story in a voice that captures the cadences of a different time and place.

While *Matrix* is set in the twelfth century, it is deeply concerned with issues and problems of our own time. Many reviewers have praised the novel for its relevance. As Ron Charles wrote in his *Washington Post* review, "It seems clear that Groff is using this ancient story as a way of reflecting on how women might survive and thrive in a culture increasingly violent and irrational." Like Margaret Atwood's classic *The Handmaid's Tale* (1985), *Matrix* portrays an imagined and seemingly distant society that nevertheless stands as a warning about how women's rights are being threatened in the present day. The novel addresses many other contemporary issues as well. From a pandemic to climate change to political upheaval and violence, we live in unsettled times. The Middle Ages may speak to contemporary American readers in a way it might not have a generation ago. The sense of dread that pervades Groff's novel—and Marie's recurring desire to better protect the people she loves from manifold threats—has become a familiar one. One subtle but powerful thread that runs through *Matrix* is a concern for the environment and the future of the planet. Although Marie is oblivious to the harm that her various projects cause to the local ecosystem, the narrator takes note of how her labyrinth destroys bird habitats and her dam floods ancient trees and displaces native salamanders. Marie and her nuns will be succeeded by "even more ravenous people," who "will heat the world imperceptibly until after centuries it will be too hot to bear humanity." Yet by the same token, Marie and her community may have offered future generations "a different path for the next millennium;" the abbey represents a more harmonious and responsible way to live with each other and with the earth. At its core, Marie's story is therefore one of stewardship: the choices one must make about people, resources, and the earth that sustains all of humanity. If historical fiction can sometimes offer an escape from the present, Groff's novel holds up a mirror to it.

Matrix was nominated for the National Book Award and received overwhelmingly positive reviews. In the *New York Times*, Kathryn Harrison asserted that "the greatest pleasure of this novel is also its most subtle." While Groff's "deft pyrotechnics" allow her to depict Marie's mystical visions and other dramatic set pieces of the novel, Harrison prized the book for its "dogged progress of a grand life." Praising Groff as "one of the most beloved and critically acclaimed fiction writers in the country," Charles noted that after enduring "almost two years of quarantine and social distancing, her new novel about a 12th-century nunnery feels downright timely." Writing for *NPR*, Keishel Williams called the book "inspiring," and commended Groff's literary prowess, writing that "with masterful wordplay and pacing, Groff builds what could have been a mundane storyline into something quite impossible to put down." Because Groff's previous book, *Fates and Furies* (2015), was a beloved best seller, expectations were high for her new novel. With *Matrix*, Groff has exceeded those expectations, staking out bold new territory and further establishing herself as one of the finest novelists of the twenty-first century.

Author Biography

Lauren Groff's previous novels included *The Monsters of Templeton* (2003), *Arcadia* (2012), and *Fates and Furies* (2015), as well as the short story collections *Delicate Edible Birds* (2009) and *Florida* (2018). A three-time National Book Award finalist, she has been published in venues including the *Atlantic* and the *New Yorker*.

Matthew J. Bolton

Review Sources

Berry, Lorraine. "Review: Lauren Groff's Perfectly Timely Feminist Medieval Utopia." Review of *Matrix*, by Lauren Groff. *The Los Angeles Times*, 7 Sept. 2021, www.latimes.com/entertainment-arts/books/story/2021-09-07/lauren-groffs-feminist-medieval-utopia-novel-is-exactly-what-we-need-right-now. Accessed 31 Dec. 2021.

Charles, Ron. "In Lauren Groff's Hands, the Tale of a Medieval Nunnery Is Must-Read Fiction." Review of *Matrix*, by Lauren Groff. *The Washington Post*, 31 Aug. 2021, www.washingtonpost.com/entertainment/books/lauren-groff-matrix-book-review/2021/08/30/ecb4a0d4-0915-11ec-aea1-42a8138f132a_story.html. Accessed 15 Dec. 2021.

Harrison, Kathryn. "In Lauren Groff's New Novel, Nothing—and Everything—Is Sacred." Review of *Matrix*, by Lauren Groff. *The New York Times*, 31 Aug. 2021, www.nytimes.com/2021/08/31/books/review/matrix-lauren-groff.html. Accessed 15 Dec. 2021.

Review of *Matrix*, by Lauren Groff. *Kirkus*, 16 June 2021, www.kirkusreviews.com/book-reviews/lauren-groff/matrix/. Accessed 31 Dec. 2021.

Williams, Keishel. "A Poet-Nun Inspired This Tale of Medieval Ambition, Pleasure and Aspiration." Review of *Matrix*, by Lauren Groff. *National Public Radio*, 6 Sept. 2021, www.npr.org/2021/09/06/1031907772/matrix-lauren-groff-book-review. Accessed 15 Dec. 2021.

Me (Moth)

Author: Amber McBride
Publisher: Feiwel and Friends (New York). 256 pp.
Type of work: Verse novel
Time: Present day
Locales: New York, Virginia, New Mexico

Me (Moth) tells the story of two teens who struggle to find their own identities as well as love after personal tragedy. Moth's parents and brother have been killed in a car accident while Sani's parents have failed to protect him from an abusive stepfather. The two learn to live again while taking a summer road trip across the country.

Principal characters

MOTH, a Black high school junior who is struggling with grief
SANI, her friend, a Navajo and White high school junior
AUNT JACK, her aunt
GRAY-BEARDED GRANDFATHER, her grandfather, a Hoodoo rootworker
JIM, MARCIA, and ZACHARY, her parents and brother

Amber McBride's debut young-adult novel-in-verse *Me (Moth)* (2021) has been widely recognized. Listed as a finalist for the 2021 National Book Award for Young People's Literature, the book has also garnered a 2022 William C. Morris Award Finalist, a BookPage Best Book of 2021, a Shelf Awareness Best Book of 2021, an NPR Best Book of the Year 2021, a School Library Journal Best Book of 2021, a Time Magazine Best Children's Book of 2021, and one of *People* magazine's Best Children's Books of 2021.

McBride takes a unique approach by presenting the story as a series of "mellifluous" free verse poems, which the National Book Award judges also cited for their "haunting lyricism" and characterized as "equal parts ancestor veneration and land acknowledgment that honors the spiritual traditions of African and Native people." In her note at the end of the book, McBride thanks her aunt, who is a member of the Navajo Nation, and discusses Hoodoo, a Black Southern "magic system created out of misfortune" during slavery from a blend of West African spiritual traditions and Christianity.

The book starts with an epigraph featuring Jericho Brown's poem "Crossing." This poem sets the tone of the novel, establishing the purpose of the characters. The epigraph is followed by over 150 free verse poems that act as chapters in presenting the story of Moth, a teenager who is the only survivor of a car accident that killed her parents and brother. Intertwined into Moth's story is the story of Sani, another outcast teen who shows up in her class one day.

The story itself is set two years after the deaths of Moth's family when their car fell apart on a highway. Moth, the only survivor, lives with her Aunt Jack and attending a school where she feels like an outsider, one of only a few Black students, "who don't talk to me." She feels so invisible in school that she declares "I don't mind being nothing." Moth is isolated until a new student, Sani, starts at school, just days before the end of her junior year. When he sits next to her on the bus, she finally finds someone who will talk to her; they both avoid becoming involved with their classmates. As summer

Amber McBride

starts, Aunt Jack leaves Moth home alone and her friendship with Sani grows. Soon after, Sani's stepfather attacks him, so the teens leave on a road trip across the country. On their way, they visit historical sites, learn to love, and regain their desire to grasp their music: for Sani, this means composing, singing, and playing guitar; for Moth, it means she begins to dance again. Intertwined throughout the physical journey that drives the story are Moth's memories of her grandfather and his practice of Hoodoo as well as Sani's retellings of Navajo creation stories.

In addition to the use of poetry to tell the story, there are a number of other noteworthy literary elements throughout the novel. For instance, one of the most important themes for teens is that of mental health, and McBride explores this issue through both teens. Moth, not surprisingly, deals with depression, grief, and survivor's guilt after the death of her family. She watches her aunt fall into an overuse of alcohol as a way to cope, a method that fails miserably, leaving both Jack and Moth even more miserable. Moth also struggles with loneliness and low self-esteem, feeling that she is unworthy of notice until Sani enters and actually sees Moth, even when she tries to hide from herself. Sani deals with mental health issues as well. At several points in the novel, Sani takes medication, which is meant to settle his mind, but like the alcohol that fails to soothe Jack's heart, the pills Sani takes fail to help him. At moments, his life is so overwhelming that he even considers suicide, behavior that causes Moth even more grief, but as the two begin to connect more strongly, they help each other find a way to embrace their artistic expression, which brings each a sense of peace, again. Through the gift of music, Moth's ability to dance and Sani's desire to sing return, helping both of them learn to live again.

A second literary direction McBride introduces can be found in the combination of foreshadowing and irony. As the teens travel across the country, Moth shares stories of her deceased grandfather, a Hoodoo practitioner, with Sani, while he shares aspects of his Navajo upbringing with her through a series of creation stories that become symbolic of the friends' own re-creation. One particularly ironic connection involving Moth's grandfather is her memory of him telling her his "best friend was Navajo" like Sani. Moth also remembers Gray-Bearded Grandfather telling her that the Hoodoo he practiced shared magic with Native American magic, further connecting the teens in ways neither could have predicted. During their road trip, the two stop at a cemetery in Nashville where Moth and her grandfather had visited years earlier. While there, Moth discovers a buried picture of herself and her grandfather as well as an envelope with a Juilliard application, items that represent each teen. Much later, as the story draws close to the end, Moth dreams of her grandfather and Sani together when Sani was a child. Sprinkled throughout these memories and dreams of Gray-Bearded Grandfather are fragments of the Hoodoo practice he had taught his granddaughter. These instances involving her grandfather also foreshadow the surprising end of the novel, offering clues that readers will recognize as having led to the finale.

Sani's creation stories begin to appear in a poem titled "Creation According to Sani." In this poem, Sani shares the tale of the Four Worlds. The first three worlds are places that need to be escaped, but in the fourth world the first man and woman "find balance. They live & live until it is time to die peacefully," something Moth and Sani long to be able to do as well. The creation stories continue as Moth comes to a point when she believes she and Sani "could stay in this Fifth World we created with stories & song lyrics & dance."

In addition to Hoodoo traditions and Navajo creation stories, McBride incorporates references to violence perpetuated by White Americans against African Americans and Native Americans at several points throughout the book as Moth and Sani travel across the country, visiting historical sites. A poem titled "Places We Decide to Stop" provides a list of eleven locations they plan to see on their way to New Mexico. Among these stops are Thomas Jefferson's Monticello Plantation, where Moth notes "He didn't own their souls, though" and leaves pieces of pancake she took from their breakfast to as an offering "for the ancestors." The Crossroads of the Trail of Tears at Fort Smith National Historical Site in Arkansas is a place where McBride focuses on the devastation Native Americans faced, as Sani says, "Father taught me that there are five hundred sixty-eight Native American tribes but only three hundred twenty-six reservations. There are many forts with plaques thanking settlers for pushing west, for goldrushing & eating the land."

McBride also weaves in poems about Moth's namesake insect. Several poems relate stages of the moth's life cycle or talk about different kinds of moths. This extended metaphor opens the story as the first poem, titled "Moth (egg):" presents Moth's background and introduces Sani. A poem titled "Moths" shares the four life stages of the insect and suggests that Moth herself is ready to move out of the cocoon in which she has been imprisoned. The poem "Black Witch Moth" ends with the image of a migration just as Moth and Sani prepare to travel. The comparison continues with an additional eight poems providing yet another link to Moth's magic.

Though the story could easily drag readers into melancholy, McBride skillfully intertwines light moments that provide a sense of hope. Moth's ability to make Sani feel loved and his ability to make her feel seen save both of them. Though Moth has not danced since her family's deaths, she learns to enjoy moving again, and Sani begins to sing and compose after having hidden his talents under his stepfather's tyranny. Their budding romance also brings a positive note to what could otherwise be seen as only a sad tale.

The critical reviews of the work were largely positive. In her review for *The Horn Book Magazine* Nicholl Denice Montgomery noted that McBride "beautifully handles themes of death, grief, first love, and abuse" while calling the book "engaging" and "vivid." *School Library Journal's* reviewer says it is a "searing debut" and points out that each poem is "tightly composed, leading into the next for a poignant and richly layered narrative." *Booklist*'s review lauds the author's ability to "artfully [weave] Black Southern hoodoo traditions with those of the Navajo/Dine people, creating a beautiful and cross-cultural reverence for the earth, its inhabitants, and our ancestors." This review also praises the hidden messages, the romance, and the presentation of change as the characters grow and develop. *Publishers Weekly* adds to the rave reviews by arguing that McBride "skillfully renders" the love story of these two teens "while covering serious topics such as grief and mental health, including suicidal ideation." Macmillan Publishers was so confident in this novel that they contracted McBride for a second work.

Author Biography

Amber McBride teaches in the English department at the University of Virginia. Her work has appeared in *The Cincinnati Review, Ploughshares, Provincetown Arts, The Rumpus* and elsewhere. Her debut novel-in-verse, *Moth (Me)*, was a finalist for the 2021 National Book Award for Young People's Literature among other honors.

Theresa L. Stowell, PhD

Review Sources

Marshall, Melanie. Review of *Me (Moth)*, by Amber McBride. *Booklist*, 28 June 2021, p. 73. *Literary Reference Center Plus*, search.ebscohost.com/login.aspx?direct=true&db=lkh&AN=151464513&site=lrc-plus. Accessed 20 Jan. 2022.

Review of *Me (Moth)*, by Amber McBride. *Publishers Weekly*, 28 June 2021, p. 79, *Literary Reference Center Plus*, search.ebscohost.com/login.aspx?direct=true&db=lkh&AN=151118769&site=lrc-plus. Accessed 20 Jan. 2022.

Montgomery, Nicholl Denice. Review of *Me (Moth)*, by Amber McBride. *The Horn Book Magazine*, 1 Jan. 2022, p.115. *Literary Reference Center Plus*, search.ebscohost.com/login.aspx?direct=true&db=lkh&AN=154206494&site=lrc-plus. Accessed 20 Jan. 2022.

Ruscio, Erica. Review of *Me (Moth)*, by Amber McBride. *School Library Journal*, 1 Aug. 2021, p. 90, *Literary Reference Center Plus*, search.ebscohost.com/login.aspx?direct=true&db=lkh&AN=151483369&site=lrc-plus. Accessed 20 Jan. 2022.

Stevenson, Deborah. Review of *Me (Moth)*, by Amber McBride. *Bulletin of the Center for Children's Books*, vol. 74, no. 11, 2021, p. 480, doi:10.1353/bcc.2021.0398. Accessed 20 Jan. 2022.

The Memoirs of Stockholm Sven

Author: Nathaniel Ian Miller
Publisher: Little, Brown (New York). 336 pp.
Type of work: Novel
Time: Largely 1916–46
Locale: Spitsbergen (Svalbard)

In his impressive debut novel, The Memoirs of Stockholm Sven, *Nathaniel Ian Miller presents a gripping account of survival and friendship in the harsh world of the Arctic. In 1916, Sven Ormson, a Swedish worker dissatisfied with life in Stockholm, heads north to the frozen world of Spitsbergen, hoping for a challenging and interesting life of adventure.*

Principal characters

SVEN ORMSON, a Stockholm industry worker dissatisfied with his life who seeks a new life in the Arctic archipelago region of Spitsbergen, or Svalbard
OLGA, his younger sister, who encourages him to pursue his dream
CHARLES MACINTYRE, a geologist who befriends him
MATTHEW HARE, the manager of the British mining operation at Camp Morton
SAMUEL GIBBLET, a steward at Camp Morton
TAPIO, a Finnish socialist trapper who becomes a mentor to Sven
HELGA, Olga's daughter who comes to live with Sven
SKULD, Helga's daughter who grows up with Sven
ILLYA, a Jewish Ukrainian of anarchist leanings who befriends Sven
LUDMILLA, a married Russian woman who has an affair with Sven

Nathaniel Ian Miller's *The Memoirs of Stockholm Sven* (2021) is an ambitious and engrossing first novel. It is a tale, narrated from the first-person point of view, of a Swedish man who seeks adventure, and then isolation, in the terrain of Spitsbergen, an Arctic island archipelago, during the period of World War I. The premise of the book evokes the classic literary archetype of a hero on a quest, which can be traced back to *The Epic of Gilgamesh* (ca. 2100 BCE) and Homer's *The Odyssey* (ca. 750 BCE). It also echoes the classic accounts of European explorers, who tested themselves and found beauty and meaning in extreme environments, such as Charles Montagu Doughty's *Travels in Arabia Deserta* (1888) and the writings of Fridtjof Nansen about his Arctic expeditions. Indeed, in Miller's novel Nansen's books are among those that fire the imagination of his protagonist and feed his dream of engaging in his own travels in the Arctic.

Given the setting, a reader might reasonably expect a stark and grueling tale of one man's lonely struggle with the forces of nature, confronting cold, snow, and ice, and the many dangers of a harsh and forbidding environment. Along the way would come a good deal of natural history, including details of the lifecycles of polar bears, seals, and other wildlife encountered in the region, as well as careful descriptions of icebergs, glaciers, and the physical geography of the Arctic Circle. However, an exhaustive anatomy of the wildlife and physical characteristics of Spitsbergen in the first half of the twentieth century is not what the reader gets in *The Memoirs of Stockholm Sven*; this novel bears little resemblance to a *National Geographic* travelogue. While there are some impressive sketches of icy landscapes, background description in Miller's book is kept to a minimum. In its pages, the titular protagonist spends as much, or more, time dealing with other humans than struggling against nature. Ironically, this book about a man seeking solitude becomes a story about people and relationships. Sven's quest transforms into a developmentally delayed bildungsroman. The existential struggle for survival gives way to a broader, more social examination of meaning.

Nathaniel Ian Miller

As someone who was a resident in the Arctic Circle expeditionary program, Miller brings solid expertise to a novel set in the far North. While his prose renditions of icebergs, glaciers, and barren tundra convey authority, he has also mastered his history. The central character of Sven Ormson is based on what is thought to be known about a real man, a hunter also named Sven who lived a solitary existence in the remote region near Raudfjorden for many years. Like the fictional Sven, he had worked as a miner and his embrace of the wilderness may have been encouraged by damage to his face suffered in an avalanche. The main source for what little is known of the historical Sven is Christiane Ritter's *Eine Frau erlebt die Polarnacht* (*A Woman in the Polar Night*, 1938), a memoir of her sojourn with her husband in Spitsbergen in the early 1930s. But even her knowledge of Sven was secondhand, as she never met the man. In a literary tit for tat, Miller has his Sven hear of but never meet Christiane Ritter. Out of these bare bones of historical gossip and legend, Miller weaves the tapestry of his Sven's memoir.

Though the Sven of the novel lives at the furthest fringe of civilization, he is not unaffected by events elsewhere. His career in the North is bracketed by world wars. He travels to Spitsbergen in 1916, at the height of World War I. While Spitsbergen was controlled by Norway, a neutral state, it could not help but be affected by the wars because of the foreign mining concessions in the territory. Among the powers competing for Spitsbergen's resources are the British and, following the Russian Revolution, the Soviets. Miller does a fine job of recreating the cosmopolitan atmosphere of a frontier land valued only for the resources that could be extracted from it. Throughout the book, Sven experiences reverberations from the epochal events ravaging European history in the early twentieth century. His growing list of acquaintances often bear the scars, physical and psychic, of these traumatic developments. Eventually, history will catch up with Sven himself. He is forced to leave his home by the imminent arrival of German troops after their invasion of Norway in the early years of World War II.

At the beginning of the book, Sven Ormson is a working-class man in Stockholm who is thoroughly dissatisfied with his life. His alienation is complete; not only does he despise his dead-end industry jobs but he finds no meaning in his life. He can find no solace in religion, regarding God as a fairy tale to comfort the weak-minded, and he cannot work up any enthusiasm over secular efforts to create an earthly paradise. Because he, himself, is his only measure of things, the thought of death appalls him. A world without him in it is emotionally if not intellectually incomprehensible. Sven's existential malaise haunts him, but his solipsism is his real problem, with his only release from his lonely misery being the occasional prostitute and reading about Arctic exploration. From an early age he had been fascinated by the adventures of explorers like Fridtjof Nansen and Roald Amundsen. Lingering outside Stockholm's Polar Institute, he attempts to catch glimpses of explorers, hoping to see something in their eyes that made them different from the ordinary run of men.

Yet for years Sven takes no concrete action to realize his dreams. He remains wedded to his rut, his most positive act being a decision to help his sister Olga with her children when she falls into a postpartum depression. It is Olga who changes the course of Sven's life when, recognizing his spiritual sickness, she takes the crucial steps to make him aware of and encourage him to take a position with a Norwegian mining company in Spitsbergen. This sets a pattern that will persist throughout the novel; Sven's life will be shaped more by the decisions of others than by his own. He is a somewhat passive protagonist, more an observer and chronicler than a person who actively takes charge of events. His story can be boiled down to a series of crises precipitated or resolved by the people in his life. His triumph is that he eventually resolves his existential issues and makes something meaningful out of the unpredictable flow of time.

At first Spitsbergen is a disappointment for Sven. He finds the mining town of Longyear City more squalid and boring than the slums of Stockholm. His work in the dark, dangerous coalpits leave him depressed and in despair. The only bright spot in his life is an encounter with Charles MacIntyre, a British geologist. MacIntyre notices Sven's love of books and seeks him out as a source of conversation and companionship, laying the foundation for a lifelong friendship. When Sven is severely injured in an avalanche at the mine that mangles his face and destroys his right eye, MacIntyre helps sustain him.

Horrified at his injuries, Sven wants to avoid contact with other people as much as possible. His geologist friend gets him a job as a steward at a British mining camp. Here, he meets Lieutenant Matthew Hare, a shell-shocked veteran. Hare introduces Sven to the antiwar poems of Siegfried Sassoon and other British warrior poets. At the British camp Sven also meets a trio of hunters and trappers. Their leader is Tapio, a Finnish socialist very much worried about the civil war between Reds and Whites dividing his country as the Russian Empire collapses and the Bolsheviks preach world revolution. Tapio takes Sven under his wing. Born a city dweller whose only knowledge of the North comes from books, Sven has much to learn, and that knowledge does not come easily. Gradually, he develops the skills to survive in the wild. After more tragedy, it is Tapio who sets him up at Raudfjorden in the far north Haakon Land.

This is where the legend of Stockholm Sven really begins, as he learns to live by himself, though he does have the company of his devoted dog, Eberhard, and Tapio occasionally makes extended visits. Then the life of this lone trapper gets very crowded indeed. His sister's daughter, Helga, arrives with her own infant daughter, Skuld, suddenly making Sven a family man. More interpersonal complications ensue with visits to a Soviet mining concession, where he finds romance with a Russian woman named Ludmilla and friendship with a Jewish Ukrainian anarchist named Illya. By the second half of the book, the story of Sven is fully centered on his relationships, with the Arctic landscape a chilly backdrop to the interpersonal drama. The ice and rock become a metaphor, with Spitsbergen as bleak as Sven's dark view of life. When he finds meaning in human connection, he leaves it behind.

Nathaniel Ian Miller creates a memorable voice in Sven's fictional memoir. It is terse and muscular, believably the prose of a thoughtful man who came of age in the early twentieth century. The story, like its Arctic environment, is hard and often unforgiving. Death comes frequently, and murders are described briefly but graphically. The existential atmosphere is perhaps inevitable in a tale filled with brooding Scandinavians. The power of the book lies in the way that Miller's Sven, deemed by Alice Cary in a review for *BookPage* as "an unforgettable narrator who asks essential questions of human connection," transcends all this. The anonymous reviewer for *Kirkus*, like other critics, praised the power of Sven's account of his life, writing that "readers will love the beauty and depth of his story." With *The Memoirs of Stockholm Sven*, Miller demonstrates that he can balance believable characters with vivid action, and ideas with moral insight. The novel was well-received by critics overall, including starred reviews from both *Kirkus* and *Publishers Weekly*, and several reviewers agreed that the book is the auspicious debut of a serious novelist.

Author Biography
Nathaniel Ian Miller has had his award-winning writings published in outlets such as the *Virginia Quarterly Review* and various local newspapers. *The Memoirs of Stockholm Sven* is his first novel.

Daniel P. Murphy

Review Sources
Cary, Alice. Review of *The Memoirs of Stockholm Sven*, by Nathaniel Ian Miller. *BookPage*, Nov. 2021, www.bookpage.com/reviews/the-memoirs-of-stockholm-sven/. Accessed 25 Jan. 2022.

McGuire, Ian. "A Debut Novel of a Life in the Arctic, Beyond History's Reach." Review of *The Memoirs of Stockholm Sven*, by Nathaniel Ian Miller. *The New York Times*, 26 Oct. 2021, www.nytimes.com/2021/10/26/books/review/nathaniel-ian-miller-memoirs-stockholm-sven.html. Accessed 21 Jan. 2022.

Review of *The Memoirs of Stockholm Sven*, by Nathaniel Ian Miller. *Kirkus*, 28 July 2021, www.kirkusreviews.com/book-reviews/nathaniel-ian-miller/the-memoirs-of-stockholm-sven/. Accessed 21 Jan. 2022.

Review of *The Memoirs of Stockholm Sven*, by Nathaniel Ian Miller. *Publishers Weekly*, 4 Aug. 2021, www.publishersweekly.com/978-0-316-59255-0. Accessed 25 Jan. 2022.

Milk Blood Heat

Author: Dantiel W. Moniz
Publisher: Grove Press (New York).
  208 pp.
Type of work: Short fiction
Time: Present day
Locales: Jacksonville, Florida; northern Florida

In her debut book of short stories, Dantiel Moniz delves into the lives of women, from adolescence through adulthood, to explore the connections between them and the boundaries they accept or challenge, and ultimately to illuminate the human condition.

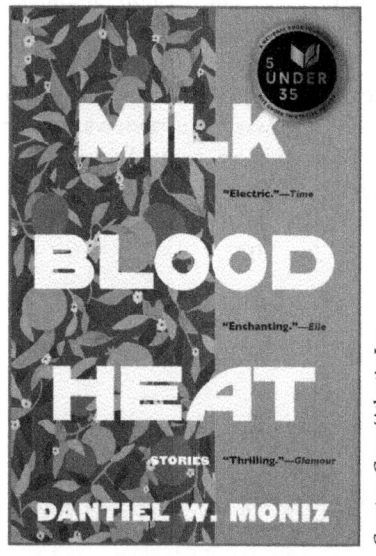

Dantiel Moniz's *Milk Blood Heat* (2021) is, as numerous reviewers noted, a stunning debut. Set in present day northern Florida, the eleven stories included in the collection range widely in topic but connect through their focus on the lives of women on the brink of change. Whether Moniz depicts the friendship between adolescent girls, young women struggling with issues such as miscarriage or unintended pregnancy, or a late middle-aged man grappling with his wife's impending death from cancer, all her characters strive to find ways forward. She reveals many strengths as a writer, including highly realistic characterization and dialogue, dexterity in linking deeply personal details and universal themes, and a knack for open-ended, thought-provoking endings. The result is a strong, memorable collection that establishes Moniz as an important voice in American literature.

While several themes emerge from this collection of stories, the two most prominent are women connecting across generations and characters examining their place in the world and the boundaries that exist or are created between themselves and others. The theme of connectivity is especially evident in "An Almanac of Bones," where Moniz focuses on the relationship between three generations of women in one family. Sylvie, the narrator, is eleven and has lived with her grandmother since the age of two. Sylvie's mother, Helen, left Sylvie in her own mother's care while she traveled the world and had adventures. Helen makes unannounced, sporadic visits, and the latest coincides with one of her grandmother's moon festivals, where local women gather in celebration of the full moon. At various points in the beginning of the story, Sylvie wonders why her mother gave birth to her if she was not going to stay to raise her, and when her mother does arrive, she does not act like a traditional mother. An exchange between Sylvie and Helen begins to showcase the complex layers of emotion between the two:

"What does your friend's mother do?" she asked, like she already knew the answer and it was laughable.

"Stays," I said. Maybe I imagined it, but I thought I heard her inhale, a small sound, like a flinch. She asked, "Is that what makes a good mother?"

She was the one with all the answers, woman of the world. I clutched the glass tight in my hands, bracing myself. "How would I know anything about mothers?"

Sylvie's resentment of her mother's absence is palpable. Traditional mothers stay with their children and care for them, but hers does not, and though Helen often brings small gifts, it is not until years later that Sylvie realizes these offerings—as well as her mother's blunt honesty—were Helen's way of asking for acceptance and understanding. Helen tells Sylvie, "You learn to be who you are, or you die as someone else." Helen understood herself and realized she would not make a good mother. Sylvie's grandmother, who loves and accepts her daughter as she is, also accepts her role in raising Sylvie. She understands that her daughter, Helen, must be true to herself, and that does not include the daily care of a child. Meanwhile, Moniz emphasizes an even broader form of female interconnectivity through the moon festival. From a young age, Sylvie has been a part of the circle of women that participate in this tradition, and she begins to see herself as part of something bigger, "an unbroken chain," she calls it, both in the wider world and within her own family.

Many of the characters in Moniz's stories also struggle with boundaries and finding their place in the world. For example, in the title story, "Milk Blood Heat," Ava, the protagonist, is thirteen and going through all the turmoil of that age. Her new and intense friendship with a girl named Kiera is driven by what Ava feels is a shared sense of deep sadness, although she also notes the sharp differences between them. Kiera is White and from a two-parent family, while Ava has brown skin and is raised by her mother. Kiera's parents encourage her to express herself, which Ava's mother, who has a more traditional approach to parenting, frowns upon. The girls make a blood pact to seal their friendship, and they spend much of their time discussing death.

Ava believes her mother does not understand her. Her mother has criticized the amount of time Ava and Kiera spend together and the lack of supervision the two seem to have at Kiera's house. Ava often comes home dirty and unkempt because they have been playing outside, causing further tension with her mother. Ava feels criticized rather than loved. When tragedy strikes later in the story, however, and Ava has

Dantiel W. Moniz

difficulty sharing her feelings about it, her mother shows, through her actions of braiding Ava's hair and quietly and patiently waiting for Ava to share her feelings, that she does understand. She is trying to support her daughter in the best way she can. Thus, Ava and her mother begin to heal the rift between them and, as Ava crosses into womanhood with the onset of her period, she also begins to better understand the boundaries between mother and daughter as well as life and death.

While themes of connectivity and boundaries are vividly depicted in the stories centering on early adolescence, they apply equally well to the adult women narrators in other pieces. In "Feast," Rayna miscarried a much-desired child, and despite everyone's sympathy and understanding, she cannot move past her grief and depression, which worsen to the point of hallucinations. Rayna sees the disembodied hands of a small child moving up and down the curtains. These images actually comfort her somewhat, since they keep her baby alive in a sense, but they also plague her as a reminder of her loss. These images signal that she is not yet willing to separate herself from that pregnancy and potential child, and it causes her to disconnect from her husband and his young daughter from an earlier marriage.

Family concerns are also at the forefront in "Necessary Bodies," and here they are linked to the many other issues and worries of contemporary society. The protagonist, Billie, experiences an unexpected pregnancy, and other than her husband and her best friend, she keeps that news to herself. She is not sure she wants to be a mother, and she is purposely withholding the information from her own mother because she knows her mother desperately wants to be a grandmother. Billie allows herself some time to wallow in this dilemma, and she creates a mental list that not only includes the pros and cons of having the baby, but wider-ranging concerns, such as climate change, that add to her anxiety. "She was thinking a million things, some of which had plagued her even before she'd found out: What if the state floods; we reelect that terrible man; if I'm bad at it; I do it and decide I don't want to do it; if I don't do it and miss it . . . if none of this can be sustained, not our love or our planet?" Billie worries about how having the baby will affect her life, her aspirations, and her marriage, and she questions how to integrate motherhood into an already complicated life. Should she cross the threshold into motherhood and allow all the changes that will ensue or continue living the life with which she is comfortable? Billie and Rayna struggle in different ways, but both contemplate how having a child or losing one changes their life and their relationships.

Reviews of *Milk Blood Heat* were overwhelmingly positive, and most critics raved about Moniz's deft writing skills and vivid characters. Colette Bancroft, in a review for the *Tampa Bay Times*, particularly noted how powerfully Moniz writes about adolescent girls, capturing their complexity, vulnerability, and energy. She also commended the way in which the stories mostly spotlight Black characters and often acknowledge how race plays into relationships, yet only as one element in a complex web of factors. Both Michele Filgate, in the *Washington Post*, and Aram Mrjoian, in the *Chicago Review of Books*, remarked on the skill Moniz demonstrates in crafting the endings to her stories, which are neither pat nor predictable. "Moniz always lands on an image or mood that you can feel in your own chest," Filgate wrote, while Mrjoian commented that "It's refreshing to read a collection that never seems to capitulate on length or development." Moniz's attention to structure results in thoughtful, often open-ended conclusions, suggesting that there are no easy answers for her characters or their struggles.

A few reviewers did offer some critiques. Notably, in a piece for the *New York Times*, Chelsea Leu suggested that "some stories become one-note in their effort to make a point." Specifically, she felt "Tongues" is too obvious in posing religious patriarchy as an antagonist, and that Moniz's one story focusing on a male character, "The Loss of Heaven," veers into stereotype. Yet Leu concluded that the "well-honed righteousness" of Moniz's writing otherwise works to powerful effect and applauded that "it's women and girls who really hold sway in this book, their cares and secrets and self-delusions." Overall, these stories are nuanced and memorable, making *Milk Blood Heat* read more like a triumphant collection of a mid-career writer than a debut. The book earned Moniz recognition on the National Book Foundation's 5 Under 35 list of up-and-coming young writers in 2021 and was featured on numerous recommended lists by various publications, including *Time*'s 100 Must-Read Books of 2021.

Author Biography
Dantiel W. Moniz has published short stories in numerous literary journals and magazines, winning the Alice Hoffman Prize for Fiction, a Pushcart Prize, and a MacDowell Fellowship. She teaches fiction at the University of Wisconsin-Madison. *Milk Blood Heat* is her debut collection.

Marybeth Rua-Larsen

Review Sources
Bancroft, Colette. "Dantiel Moniz's '*Milk Blood Heat*' Tells Moving Stories of Human Need." Review of *Milk Blood Heat*, by Dantiel Moniz. *Tampa Bay Times*, 11 Feb. 2021, www.tampabay.com/life-culture/arts/books/2021/02/12/dantiel-monizs-milk-blood-heat-tells-moving-stories-of-human-need/. Accessed 9 Dec. 2021.

Filgate, Michele. "Review: Dantiel W. Moniz's '*Milk Blood Heat*' Thrums with Life While Considering Death." Review of *Milk Blood Heat*, by Dantiel Moniz. *The Washington Post*, 1 Feb. 2021, www.washingtonpost.com/entertainment/books/milk-blood-heat-book-review/2021/02/01/3771573a-617c-11eb-9061-07abc-c1f9229_story.html. Accessed 8 Dec. 2021.

LeBlanc, Lauren. "Survivor Stories in '*Milk Blood Heat*.'" Review of *Milk Blood Heat*, by Dantiel Moniz. *The Boston Globe*, 4 Feb. 2021, www.bostonglobe.com/2021/02/04/arts/survivor-stories-milk-blood-heat/. Accessed 8 Dec. 2021.

Leu, Chelsea. "In Three New Collections, Characters on the Edge." Review of *Milk Blood Heat*, by Dantiel Moniz; *The Dangers of Smoking in Bed*, by Mariana Enriquez; and *Wild Swims*, by Dorthe Nors. *The New York Times*, 2 Feb. 2021, www.nytimes.com/2021/02/02/books/review/the-dangers-of-smoking-in-bed-mariana-enriquez-milk-blood-heat-dantiel-moniz-wild-swims-dorthe-nors.html. Accessed 8 Dec. 2021.

Mitchell, Emily. Review of *Milk Blood Heat*, by Dantiel Moniz. *Washington Independent Review of Books*, 8 Feb. 2021, www.washingtonindependentreviewofbooks.com/index.php/bookreview/milk-blood-heat-stories. Accessed 8 Dec. 2021.

Mrjoian, Aram. "Dantiel W. Moniz's '*Milk Blood Heat*' Is a Debut to Remember." Review of *Milk Blood Heat*, by Dantiel Moniz. *Chicago Review of Books*, 4 Feb. 2021, chireviewofbooks.com/2021/02/04/dantiel-w-monizs-milk-blood-heat-is-a-debut-to-remember/. Accessed 8 Dec. 2021.

The Mirror Season

Author: Anna-Marie McLemore
Publisher: Feiwel and Friends (New York). 320 pp.
Type of work: Novel
Time: Present day
Locale: San Juan Capistrano, California

This gripping young adult novel blends magical realism and fairy tale themes with contemporary drama as two young people drawn together by a cruel sexual assault help each other heal.

Principal characters

GRACIELA 'CIELA' CRISTALES, a high school student who works at her family's pastelería and is known as "La Bruja de los Pasteles" (the Pastry Witch) for her ability to sense customers' needs
LOCK THOMAS, a new student at Ciela's school who is targeted by bullies
JESSAMYN 'JESS' BEVERLY, Ciela's best friend and former girlfriend, who is a year ahead in school and about to graduate
PJ, a popular boy who bullies Lock and Ciela
CHRIS, another popular student and bully
VICTORIA, a popular girl who bullies Lock and Ciela
BRIGID, another popular student and bully

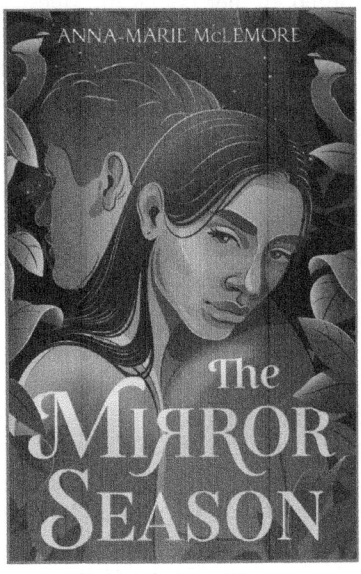

The Mirror Season (2021), Anna-Marie McLemore's seventh young adult novel, was inspired by both the author's own experience and the Hans Christian Andersen fairy tale "The Snow Queen" (1844). In Andersen's original story, a magic mirror shatters and fragments of it enter people's eyes, causing them to see only evil and ugliness, or pierce their chests, turning their hearts to ice. In *The Mirror Season*, high school student Ciela survives a sexual assault and begins to find roses that turn into shards of mirrored glass. One shard enters her eye, distorting her perceptions and blocking the gift she inherited from her *bisabuela* (great-grandmother), the ability to sense which pastry is right for each customer in her family's bakery. She continues to find pieces of mirrored glass, which she tries to hide to protect her family and friends, but she is too late to save Lock, a boy who was drugged and sexually assaulted at the same party where Ciela was attacked. When Ciela meets Lock again at school, she notices a glint of silver in his eye and blames herself for allowing the mirrored glass to escape. These tinges of magical realism help McLemore craft a highly engaging novel that takes on difficult, weighty issues in a nuanced and spirited fashion.

Ciela, who provides first-person narration, is proud of her Mexican American heritage and comfortable in her queer identity. Still, she sometimes faces discrimination from the richer, White students at Astin, the prestigious private school she attends on scholarship. For example, in the aftermath of the sexual assault many of her classmates assume that she consented to sex, especially because her attackers are from the popular crowd. Ciela is well aware of her marginalized status, and this has made her wary and untrusting. As the book opens she tells herself there is no point in reporting the assault. It is once she resolves to keep quiet that she sees the first mirrored rose and feels the impact of the magical shard.

Anna-Marie McLemore

Complicating Ciela's silence is her new connection to Lock. He appeared at the party as a stranger from out of town, surrounded by rumors and teasing that he claimed to be waiting until marriage to have sex. The novel begins with Ciela dropping him off nearly unconscious at the hospital after he is drugged, not expecting to ever see him again. Yet he then shows up as a new student at Astin, also on a scholarship as he is from a poor, rural background. There he is further targeted for harassment as an outsider with unusual interests like crocheting. The rich and popular boys Chris and PJ—Ciela's attackers—and their equally cruel girlfriends Victoria and Brigid try to humiliate Lock with sexually-themed pranks, such as sticking condoms to his locker. Despite her wariness, Ciela begins to stick up for Lock, and the two form a tentative alliance.

Initially thrown together in the most traumatic way possible, Ciela and Lock find themselves unexpectedly bonding. As Ciela helps Lock to heal from his trauma, she finds her magical pastry gift returning. She introduces him to the world of *pan dulce* (Mexican pastry) and tacos, and he takes her to the secret forest where he has been replanting neighborhood trees tagged for removal by the town. They meet each other's families and talk about their shared experience as survivors of sexual assault, though not in great detail. Ciela does not want to push Lock to tell more than he is ready to, and she has secrets of her own she is not yet ready to reveal.

On one level, *The Mirror Season* is a love story. Ciela and Lock, both survivors, become allies, then friends, then find themselves moving into attraction and a deeper love. Chris and PJ make crude jokes about Ciela being a lesbian and not liking guys, but her sexuality is more complicated. She is pansexual, as she explains to Lock: she is attracted to people for who they are, regardless of their gender identity or sexual orientation. Thus, while she was previously in a relationship with Jess, a woman, she does not date women exclusively. The deepening of Lock and Ciela's relationship allows McLemore to explore the issue of consent. Both characters have been hurt by things done to them without permission, but with each other they reclaim choice and desire and become more than victims.

Throughout the novel, however, Ciela has been withholding one key fact about the assault from Lock and from the reader. Lock knows Ciela was there at the party and that she was the one who took him to the hospital, but because he was drugged he does not remember the details. When he finally learns the truth about what happened that night, his shock makes him back away from Ciela and threatens their new relationship. The novel's climax comes during La Fiesta de las Golondrinas, a yearly festival celebrating the return of the swallows to San Juan Capistrano in March. Ciela works at the festival, selling pastries with her aunt, and Lock attends with his family. Chris, PJ, Victoria, and Brigid show up, angry because Ciela has threatened to expose their part in the attacks to the authorities, and force a final confrontation. In the end, Ciela must make the wrenching choice of whether it is worth it to tell difficult truths.

The Mirror Season continues McLemore's penchant for using the lens of magical realism to explore issues of family, community, inequality, and identity, particularly in the lives of characters who are seldom represented in traditional fairy tales. In her reimagined takes on classic stories, formerly marginalized characters—especially people of color and LGBTQ characters—are centered. For example, her novel *Blanca & Roja* (2018) is a Latinx retelling of "Snow-White and Rose-Red," while *Dark and Deepest Red* (2020) draws inspiration from another Hans Christian Andersen fairy tale, "The Red Shoes." Even McLemore's novels that are not based upon one specific tale, like 2016's *When the Moon Was Ours*, incorporate elements of magical realism and Latinx folklore. *The Mirror Season* further showcases her talent for incorporating traditional stories into unique young adult works for modern readers. In addition to fairy tales, McLemore cited Mexican writer Laura Esquivel's magical realist novel *Like Water for Chocolate* (1989) as an important early influence, and echoes of its blending of supernatural elements with traditional Mexican recipes can also be seen in *The Mirror Season*. Like many writers in the magical realist tradition, McLemore uses language that is lush and lyrical, with vivid images that are sometimes surreal.

The Mirror Season, which was longlisted for the National Book Award for Young People's Literature, received an overwhelmingly positive response from critics. Most reviews focused on McLemore's lyrical prose, clever integration of fairy tale themes with a contemporary story, and—perhaps most importantly—sensitive handling of the difficult topic of sexual assault. For example, Colleen Mondor acknowledged in a review for *Locus* that it "is not an easy book to read," given the brutality of its core subject, but praised McLemore as a "fearless writer" and an "exceptional talent" whose work is not to be missed. The trauma of sexual assault and the healing journey of survivors has been addressed before in young adult literature, notably in Laurie Halse Anderson's *Speak* (1999), but the experiences of male survivors are seldom explored, making Lock's story all the more important. Ciela, too, highlights the diversity of such traumatizing experience. In a review for the *Horn Book Magazine*, Gabi Huesca remarked how the book provides important "insight into the often-overlooked experiences of women of color, boys, and queer and trans survivors of sexual assault." Lock and Ciela's story may make it easier for survivors of all identities to understand that they are not alone. In an afterword to *The Mirror Season*, McLemore explains that the novel draws upon her own experience and that of a male survivor, and encourages survivors to seek help through trusted friends, counselors, or the organization Rape, Abuse & Incest National Network (RAINN).

A starred review in *Booklist* called *The Mirror Season* an "empowering" and "transformative" story about "healing and finding the way back to your own magic." *Publishers Weekly* and *Kirkus* also provided starred reviews, with the latter especially praising McLemore's "poetic and vulnerable prose." Notably, McLemore incorporates Spanish phrases into Ciela's narration, a device which feels natural given the character's Mexican American heritage. The names of traditional pastries, poetic and fanciful in themselves, are woven throughout the narrative: *las conchas de sirenas* (mermaid shells), *pan de yema* (egg yolk bread), *pajaritos* (little birds). Ciela also uses Spanish terms for family members—such as *tía* for aunt—for concepts, and for emotions. For the most part, the terms are easily understood in context, and sometimes an English equivalent is used later. Writing for *School Library Journal*, Ruth Quiroa felt that McLemore's "rich, symbolic descriptions" are strengthened by her use of "equally symbolic Spanish translanguaging."

Quiroa also aptly compared *The Mirror Season*'s structure to that of a "puzzle being slowly pieced together." Because the reader sees the story from Ciela's point of view, we know what she knows—and what other characters, including Lock and Ciela's parents, do not know—but we still do not know everything. Although we understand that both Lock and Ciela were sexually assaulted on the night of the party, and we know that Chris, PJ, Victoria, and Brigid were involved, the narrative does not describe the incident in full detail until close to the end of the story. This structure is typical of the trauma narrative, in which snippets of memory are teased out before being fully revealed. While this could be seen as leading to a twist ending, it is handled with skill and sensitivity and never feels cheap or manipulative.

Ultimately, *The Mirror Season* received near-unanimous critical praise as a difficult but necessary work. A compelling and beautifully written young adult novel, it gives a voice to characters often overlooked in mainstream culture. Though it is a story of deep and painful trauma that acknowledges darkness, it offers hope of resilience and healing that will likely resonate with many readers.

Author Biography
Anna-Marie McLemore is the author of several acclaimed young adult novels, including *The Weight of Feathers* (2015), *When the Moon Was Ours* (2016), Wild Beauty (2017), and *Blanca & Roja* (2018). They received a Lambda Literary Emerging Writer Fellowship, the James Tiptree Jr. Award, and a Stonewall Honor Award, among other honors.

Kathryn Kulpa

Review Sources

Huesca, Gabi K. Review of *The Mirror Season*, by Anna-Marie McLemore. *The Horn Book Inc.*, May-June 2021, www.hbook.com/story/review-of-the-mirror-season . Accessed 20 Jan. 2022.

Leary, Alaina. Review of *The Mirror Season*, by Anna-Marie McLemore. *Booklist*, 15 Apr. 2021, www.booklistonline.com/The-Mirror-Season/pid=9745349. Accessed 20 Jan. 2022.

Review of *The Mirror Season*, by Anna-Marie McLemore. *Kirkus*, 25 Dec. 2020, www.kirkusreviews.com/book-reviews/anna-marie-mclemore/the-mirror-season/. Accessed 20 Jan. 2022.

Review of *The Mirror Season*, by Anna-Marie McLemore. *Publishers Weekly*, 21 Jan. 2021, www.publishersweekly.com/978-1-250-62412-3. Accessed 20 Jan. 2022.

Mondor, Colleen. Review of *The Mirror Season*, by Anna-Marie McLemore. *Locus*, 16 Apr. 2021, locusmag.com/2021/04/colleen-mondor-reviews-the-mirror-season-by-anna-marie-mclemore. Accessed 20 Jan. 2022.

Quiroa, Ruth. Review of *The Mirror Season*, by Anna-Marie McLemore. *School Library Journal,* vol. 67, no. 5, May 2021. *MasterFILE Complete*, search.ebscohost.com/login.aspx?direct=true&db=f6h&AN=149976854&site=eds-live. Accessed 20 Jan. 2021.

A Most Remarkable Creature
The Hidden Life and Epic Journey of the World's Smartest Birds of Prey

Author: Jonathan Meiburg (b. 1976)
Publisher: Alfred A. Knopf (New York). 384 pp.
Type of work: Natural history, nature, travel
Time: Prehistory to the present day
Locales: South America, the Falkland Islands, and Great Britain

In A Most Remarkable Creature, *musician and naturalist Jonathan Meiburg presents an engaging look at a group of falcons called caracaras. Unusually omnivorous and intelligent for raptors, caracaras have fascinated observers for centuries, and Meiburg's quest to discover more about the bird leads him on explorations spanning the continent of South America.*

Principal personages

JONATHAN MEIBURG, the author, an American journalist, musician, and naturalist
ROBIN WOODS, a British ornithologist who is an expert on the wildlife of the Falkland Islands
CHARLES DARWIN, an English naturalist best known for his theory of evolution
CHARLES BARNARD, an American ship captain who was marooned on the Falkland Islands in the early nineteenth century
WILLIAM HENRY HUDSON, a naturalist and writer born in Argentina and most famous for his novel Green Mansions: A Romance of the Tropical Forest (1904)
LEN HILL, a.k.a. "the Penguin King," a British businessman who created a wildlife park called Birdland
GEOFF PEARSON, a British falconer
JULIA CLARKE, an American paleontologist whose work has offered clues to the origins of caracaras
SEAN MCCANN, a Canadian biologist who accompanied the author on an expedition into the forests of Guyana
CARLA DOVE, a curator of birds at the Smithsonian National Museum of Natural History

With *A Most Remarkable Creature: The Hidden Life and Epic Journey of the World's Smartest Birds of Prey* (2021), Jonathan Meiburg, best known as the lead singer of the band Shearwater, makes an auspicious debut as an author. He has chosen to write about an unusual topic: caracaras, a species of bird little known to his English-speaking readership, and one that has attracted scant interest even amongst the scientific community. Caracaras belong to the falcon family, but they are a far cry from the streamlined raptors that have been treasured by aristocratic hunters around the world, served as mascots for military academies, and inspired classic detective stories. Meiburg describes the various branches of the caracara family as being built like "a crow on a falcon chassis, with results falling somewhere between elegant, menacing, and whimsical." Unlike better-known breeds of falcons, caracaras are omnivorous, eating everything from other birds, insects, and animal feces to organic bits of human trash. Such is their taste for carrion that some caracaras are often seen in company with vultures. Also, unlike other falcons, caracaras are notable for their sociability, intelligence, curiosity, and willingness to interact with humans. In this they are more akin to crows and parrots. Caracaras have been observed being playful and solving rudimentary problems, and their survival has been assured so far by brains rather than brawn.

Meiburg celebrates the adaptability and resilience of caracaras wherever he finds them, whether it is in the wild, on the fringe of human settlement, or in captivity in a thoroughly domesticated environment like modern England. He does this through an engaging narrative style that effectively balances erudition with anecdote, and analysis with vivid storytelling. In addition to introducing his readers to fascinating animals and their intriguing behaviors, he also brilliantly describes the colorful people who study and interact with them. This makes for a fast-moving and enthralling reading experience. Meiburg's *A Most Remarkable Creature* is itself a remarkable debut book and an example of popular nature writing at its best.

Meiburg first encountered caracaras in 1997, when a fellowship to study isolated communities led him to the Falkland Islands, a remote group of islands in the South Atlantic Ocean. There, he took advantage of an opportunity to visit a large penguin breeding ground. While wandering over the rocky ground, congested with colonies of penguins and other birds, he was approached by a pair of striated caracaras—brown, raven-sized raptors with chestnut legs and yellow feet. Of the thousands of birds in the area, these were the only two that seemed interested in him. They came close and looked directly at him, one cocking its head in an almost human fashion. Meiburg wanted to give these creatures something, but he had no food to offer. Instead, he took a pen from his pocket and laid it down before them. The birds looked at the pen for a moment, sizing it up. Then one of them advanced and grasped it with one of its talons. The other quickly lunged after the unfamiliar object, and jostling over their new toy, the birds and pen disappeared over a cliff.

This unexpected meeting spurred a lifelong fascination with caracaras that resulted in this book. Meiburg learned that the striated caracaras were known locally as "Johnny rooks," and had long been regarded as "cheeky" pests because of their ingenious and seemingly mischievous willingness to make off with human food and tools. During the War of 1812, Charles Barnard, an American sealer marooned on the Falklands by British sailors, was plagued by Johnny rooks that ransacked his caches of penguin eggs and even carried off the club that he used to hunt. When famed naturalist Charles Darwin and the HMS *Beagle* arrived in 1834, Johnny rooks stole men's hats and even a compass. Almost two centuries later, Meiburg's own hat was not safe from the attentions of the acquisitive caracaras. Meiburg became astonished at the fearlessness, cleverness, and playfulness of these birds. He wondered how they found their way to the Falkland Islands, where they face the evolutionary perils of any species living on islands shared with humans. In 1908, the Falkland authorities put a price on Johnny rook beaks, and the birds were nearly wiped out before the bounty was lifted. By the 1990s, the Johnny rook population had risen to just a few thousand. Yet these birds that had been hunted to the brink of extinction did not act like an endangered species. Despite the twentieth century slaughter, the descendants of caracaras that pilfered so freely from Barnard and the crew of the *Beagle* still felt no compunction about approaching Meiburg. Instead of retreating from humans, caracaras continued to satisfy their curiosity about humans whenever given the opportunity. For Meiburg, they are indeed "a most remarkable creature." He believes Johnny rooks and other species of caracaras offer fascinating insights into evolution and survival in a rapidly changing world.

Meiburg ranges widely in his exploration of caracaras, even into prehistory. Readers get a brief but lively disquisition on the disastrous effects of an asteroid strike near what is now the Yucatan Peninsula some sixty-six million years ago. The enormous impact of this collision caused massive tidal waves and threw so much debris into the air that the earth fell into a global winter. The environmental effects of this catastrophe killed off much of the world's plant and animal life. This put an end to the age of the great dinosaurs. However, not all dinosaurs perished. Some smaller, feathered dinosaurs—the ancestors of modern birds—survived. They lived in places like Antarctica, less directly affected by the cataclysm unleashed by the asteroid. Antarctica in this period was a lush, tropical environment that sheltered many creatures whose descendants would spread into other areas as the slow workings of plate tectonics brought continents together and falling and rising seas alternately exposed and then submerged land bridges between distant territories.

The precursors of modern caracaras were able to move into South America before Antarctica became an ice-covered wasteland. Meiburg spends some time with a team of paleontologists in southern Chile, exploring the fossil record of feathered dinosaurs who made this journey across a now-lost pathway between the continents. Over time, proto caracaras spread throughout the continent and onto adjacent islands like the

Falklands, eventually differentiating into ten species. Along the way, caracaras took a different evolutionary path than that of their relatives in the falcon family. They became generalists rather than specialists as they confronted their environment. Instead of a concentration on speed, sight, and hunting prowess, caracaras proved more adaptable, emphasizing sociability and intelligence as they scavenged a living. They now exist in a wide range of habitats, from the Andes Mountains to the Argentine pampas. However, one place where they do not live is North America. Meiburg argues that this is because South and North America only connected five to six million years ago, rather recently in geological terms. As a result, the animal life in the two halves of the Americas remains very different.

Much of the book traces Meiburg's journeys in pursuit of different varieties of caracaras. He travels to Britain to visit caracaras in captivity. Most of these are Johnny rooks, whose forebears were imported by Len Hill, also known as the "Penguin King," an eccentric businessperson who ran a theme park called Birdland in Britain. For a time, he owned two islands in the Falklands that he mined for birds to stock his park or trade for other species. Most of the descendants of Hill's Johnny rooks live in falconry centers, where they stand out in demonstrations of game-playing and problem-solving unthinkable for other breeds of falcons. Meiburg also stops by the Smithsonian Institution in Washington, DC, to examine a mounted specimen of the Guadalupe caracara, a rare island-bound bird that did not survive the interest of human collectors. Back in the caracaras' homeland of South America, Meiburg visits the Altiplano, a soaring plateau high in the Andes. This is the homeland of the mountain caracara, whose feathers figured prominently in the headdresses of Incan emperors. The longest section in the book recounts an expedition Meiburg takes into the deep forests of Guyana with a Canadian biologist and three Amerindian guides. This trip was inspired in part by his admiration for the writings of William Henry Hudson, a British writer born in Argentina. A great lover of nature, Hudson appreciated and wrote about the unusual qualities of caracaras. Hudson's most famous novel, *Green Mansions* (1904), was set in Guyana. In addition to honoring the memory of a favorite author, Meiburg looks for the red-throated caracara, an endangered species with a taste for wasp nests.

By the time Meiburg finishes retelling his last adventure, and *A Most Remarkable Creature* comes to an end, most readers will wish the book would go on longer. Meiburg's graceful writing wears well, and he proves his case about the fascinating qualities of caracaras. Reviewers have largely agreed with such accolades. Writing for the *Wall Street Journal*, Christoph Irmscher heaped praise on Meiburg as a "lavishly talented nature writer" who "weaves a seamless narrative from the most diverse observations." Likewise, the anonymous reviewer for *Kirkus* noted that "the narrative rarely lags," despite the book being devoted to just one obscure bird, and the starred review in *Publishers Weekly* proclaimed that readers "will be thrilled by his lyrical account, and eager to see where Meiburg goes next."

Author Biography
Jonathan Meiburg is a musician best known as the leader of the rock band Shearwater. After receiving a Thomas J. Watson Fellowship in 1997 that enabled him to travel to several remote regions of the world, he began publishing articles and interviews. *A Most Remarkable Creature* is his first book.

Daniel P. Murphy

Review Sources
Eagan, Robert. Review of *A Most Remarkable Creature: The Hidden Life and Epic Journey of the World's Smartest Birds of Prey*, by Jonathan Meiburg. *Library Journal*, 1 Mar. 2021, www.libraryjournal.com/?reviewDetail=a-most-remarkable-creature-the-hidden-life-and-epic-journey-of-the-worlds-smartest-birds-of-prey-2108070. Accessed 27 Sept. 2021.

Irmscher, Christoph. "'A Most Remarkable Creature' Review: The Curious Caracara." Review of *A Most Remarkable Creature: The Hidden Life and Epic Journey of the World's Smartest Birds of Prey*, by Jonathan Meiburg. *The Wall Street Journal*, 2 Apr. 2021, www.wsj.com/articles/a-most-remarkable-creature-review-the-curious-caracara-11617375314. Accessed 13 Sept. 2021.

Review of *A Most Remarkable Creature: The Hidden Life and Epic Journey of the World's Smartest Birds of Prey*, by Jonathan Meiburg. *Kirkus*, 15 Dec. 2020, www.kirkusreviews.com/book-reviews/jonathan-meiburg/a-most-remarkable-creature/. Accessed 13 Sept. 2021.

Review of *A Most Remarkable Creature: The Hidden Life and Epic Journey of the World's Smartest Birds of Prey*, by Jonathan Meiburg. *Publishers Weekly*, 8 Jan. 2021, www.publishersweekly.com/978-1-101875-70-4. Accessed 27 Sept. 2021.

Sandstrom, Karen. "A Particular Fascination with a Peculiar Bird." Review of *A Most Remarkable Creature: The Hidden Life and Epic Journey of the World's Smartest Birds of Prey*, by Jonathan Meiburg. *The Washington Post*, 6 May 2021, www.washingtonpost.com/outlook/a-particular-fascination-with-a-peculiar-bird/2021/05/06/9dd82f00-7de0-11eb-85cd-9b7fa90c8873_story.html. Accessed 13 Sept. 2021.

My Broken Language

Author: Quiara Alegría Hudes (b. 1977)
Publisher: One World (New York). 336 pp.
Type of work: Memoir
Time: Largely 1980s through the present
Locales: Philadelphia, Pennsylvania; New Haven, Connecticut; Providence, Rhode Island

In this memoir, renowned playwright Quiara Alegría Hudes probes the intersection of her childhood years in rural Pennsylvania, the urban Puerto Rican culture of her mother's extended family in Philadelphia, and her father's life in White suburbia after her parents split up. Through personal stories about navigating between homes, languages, and cultures, she finds her own authentic voice and calls for greater inclusivity in publishing.

Principal personages
QUIARA ALEGRÍA HUDES, the author
OBDULIA PEREZ, her grandmother
VIRGINIA, her mother
GIL SCOTT-HERON, a musician and spoken-word poet
PAULA VOGEL, a playwright and graduate mentor of Hudes

My Broken Language (2021) begins with a relocation, as five-year-old Quiara Alegría Hudes and her parents leave the West Philadelphia neighborhood that is home to her mother's large Puerto Rican family and relocate to a rural property in Malvern, Pennsylvania. Although Malvern was only an hour from Philadelphia, young Hudes's migration was absolute. With her mother's exhausting daily commute into the city for work, her parents never found the opportunity to return on days off to see the extended family. Approximately two years later, Hudes's parents had separated, and she found herself thrust back into life in West Philly, though commuting regularly between her parents' homes. Her White, English-speaking father settled into life in suburbia, which Hudes began to see as "manicured Americana." Meanwhile, her commutes in and out of Philadelphia made her uncomfortably aware that her mother's urban and Spanish-speaking family experienced the disparity of "derelict squalor." English initially represented the language of her father and her schooling. Later, it would also become the language of her profession. Spanish, the mother tongue of her family members who had relocated from Puerto Rico, was the vibrant and essential yet hidden language of her personal life.

In many ways, this memoir represents Hudes's search for cultural and linguistic authenticity, as she struggled with the challenges of living in between worlds—whether linguistically or in terms of race and ethnicity. But it is also more. Her book is a journey of deepening research, literacy, and fluency that brings realities of Latina experience, as seen through the stories of her female family members, into the spotlight of theater, literature, and the public intellectual eye. Calling out the silence through which her family members have endured the damages of systematic racism, Hudes urges positive action: "We must be our own librarians because we alone are literate in our bodies. By naming our pain and voicing our imperfections, we declare our tremendous survival."

Quiara Alegría Hudes

Hudes organizes her memoir into four parts. The first, titled "I Am the Gulf between English and Spanish," tells the story of her young childhood, including her early memories of both parents, and lays the foundations for the rift that develops between her paternal and maternal worlds. Titled "All the Languages of My Perez Women, and Yet All This Silence . . .," the second part follows Hudes from her parents' separation through her teenage years. Notably, these chapters introduce her education in music (she describes music as her one "chosen" language) as well as her increasing confrontation with her mother's Santería faith and the Puerto Rican cultural roots of her ancestry. The third part of the book, "How Qui Qui Be?," encompasses the conclusion of Hudes's high school years, her undergraduate experiences at Yale University, and her post-college years of working as a professional musician. These years encompassed several watershed experiences. This section of the book begins with a chapter dedicated to a fateful evening with her father and stepmother during which they revealed their deep-seated racism, expecting her to be complicit in their comments due to her own fair skin tone. It concludes with a chapter that is shaped around the performer Gil Scott-Heron asking Hudes about who she is authentically—to which she had no ready answer. Her subsequent realization that "if you ask for an audience, you best have something to say" eventually led her to apply to graduate school and launch her career as a playwright. The book's fourth part, "Break Break Break My Mother Tongue" deals with Hudes's years in graduate school, which she also presents as years in which she learned to be true to her "broken Spanish" and, through this, how to speak through, with, and for her "Philly Rican" family.

In addition to its effective writing style and its poignancy, *My Broken Language* has gained critical attention for the "feel-good narratives of cross-cultural exchange," as stated by Alicia Ramírez in a review for the *Christian Science Monitor*. As the child of a White man of Jewish ancestry and a Spanish-speaking Brown woman born and raised in Puerto Rico, Hudes was raised in between and across two realms and at times felt like an observing other. Among her maternal relatives, she sat quietly and watched while they danced. She was uncomfortable with her mother's mysticism, which was a secret, yet dominant, theme of her young teenage years. While she was integrated unquestioningly within her mother's extended family, her father's suburban household kept her at a distance. One fateful evening after she was accepted into Yale, her father and stepmother engaged Hudes in a thinly veiled conversation about "the inner-city problem," revealing the depth of their racism and its application to the Perez family. Hudes discusses with affecting candor how, in retrospect, she had comprehended that her fair skin tone "provided familiarity . . . it gained me access to a conversation that blistered my heart." She describes this pivotal conversation as being "as much of a birth as I can claim in life," forcing the decision to stop remaining nonconfrontationally silent and to identify definitively as Puerto Rican rather than White, while also clarifying the racism that cleaved her family in two.

This highly personal experience of racism is, significantly, explored alongside the systemic racism under which Hudes's Perez relatives suffered. Hudes presents an intimate, affectionate view of her family, through which their personal struggles are often tied to racial injustice. From a young age, Hudes watched her cousins die tragically young. Eventually, she found patterns in the deaths and connected the family tragedies to the HIV/AIDS and drug epidemics. She chafed against the family silences and shame, which hid the cause of suffering and death. But she also learned that her family was not unique in its suffering, as public health announcements, medical clinics, and other social support systems were not available for the inner-city Black and Brown population. And when Hudes's mother made a real impact by developing a support program for the neighborhood, Hudes got a front-row seat to witness the lack of administrative support and funding for the initiative, which was shuttered shortly thereafter.

Although the inner-city area where Hudes's grandmother lived was a cherished enclave of family, Hudes also reveals it to be an environment in which her relatives were trapped. While attending a magnet high school, she listened to classmates express disdain for "welfare queens" and other urban stereotypes and realized that these racialized slurs could be used against members of her family. In response, Hudes introduces the story of her elder cousin Nuchi, a loving but struggling mother. One afternoon, Hudes was helping Nuchi to dye her hair when she learned Nuchi could not read a simple instruction on the bottle of dye, revealing that she was fully illiterate despite having a high school diploma. Nuchi explained that she was able to pass from one grade to the next in her urban public school simply by keeping herself invisible by standing in the back. Hudes, already a passionate reader of sophisticated literature, was immediately stunned by the disparity and injustice of her cousin's illiteracy. She thought of heading to the Free Library of Philadelphia to seek answers and solace in its shelves but paused as she understood that "now, praying in the temple of my literary saints was revealed as its own sick privilege." Later, she carried the weight of this inequity with her to Yale and into her career as a writer.

My Broken Language is also principally a compelling celebration of Hudes's Puerto Rican ancestry. Always observing and curious, Hudes gradually probed deeper through oral history, reading, travel, and, eventually, her own craft as a writer and intellectual. In one powerful chapter titled "Unwritten Recipes," she recounts learning to cook *arroz blanco* (white rice) with her grandmother Obdulia Perez. Through an engaging structure, in nine approximate steps, she lays out a recipe of sorts, interspersed with a recounting of her grandmother's rich life story. Over the course of many migrations while raising children and then grandchildren, Perez's story is one of a resilience centered around the family table. In one life story, Perez heard a threatening knock on her door and wound up inviting Philadelphia police into her home, correcting them that the plants growing on her windowsill were cooking herbs, not marijuana, through the magic of a meal. Later, when forced to move by gentrification, she found herself even deeper in the concrete jungle. With nowhere to grow food and more mouths to feed, Perez realized it was time to become an activist.

Other passages dig deeply into her mother's faith practices. From a young age, her mother had felt the powerful tug of religion, through spiritual visions that would wrack her mind and body. After her mother separated from her atheist father, this religious tendency became a prominent, if secretive, element of Hudes's childhood. Hudes explores her own curiosity, and sometimes her revulsion, to her mother's faith. Eventually, she came to understand the deep Indigenous roots of her mother's faith practice and the ties that it brought to their ancestry and homeland, and her mother later asked her adult daughter to use her skills at writing to begin to share the deep stories of her ancestry. Finally, Hudes had found her professional calling, the passionate voice that could motivate her to push through the struggles of generations of silence and racism and "into the light" of public scrutiny.

My Broken Language is the story of the author's journey to find her true sense of self and professional calling. Through literary analysis, then music, and eventually writing (whether for the stage or otherwise), Hudes honed her intellectual and creative skills. Importantly, she shares her struggle to find a defining creative mission—which, in the end, is linked inseparably to her racial and cultural identity. In pursuit of this professional calling, Hudes was the first in her family to go to college. She struggled against imposter syndrome and worked long hours to afford her elite college studies. Yet, during these many achievements, she also combated her keen awareness of the "sick privilege" that her own academic gifts afforded her. She was driven forward by the twinned goals of celebrating her family and her heritage while also combating structural injustice. Her creative voice found itself through the haunting and personal quandary, *"Why do I get Sterling Library and Nuchi doesn't?"*.

Author Biography
Quiara Alegría Hudes is an acclaimed playwright, screenwriter, and essayist known for her Pulitzer Prize–winning drama *Water by the Spoonful* and the award-winning musical *In the Heights*.

Julia A. Sienkewicz, PhD

Review Sources

Bowen, Kirsten. Review of *My Broken Language*, by Quiara Alegría Hudes. *Broad Street Review*, 5 Apr. 2021, www.broadstreetreview.com/reviews/my-broken-language-by-quiara-alegria-hudes. Accessed 31 Oct. 2021.

Delgado, Anjanette. Review of *My Broken Language*, by Quiara Alegría Hudes. *New York Journal of Books*, www.nyjournalofbooks.com/book-review/my-broken-language-memoir. Accessed 31 Oct. 2021.

Review of *My Broken Language*, by Quiara Alegría Hudes. *Kirkus*, 19 Jan. 2021, www.kirkusreviews.com/book-reviews/quiara-alegria-hudes/my-broken-language/. Accessed 9 Dec. 2021.

Padilla Peralta, Dan-El. "Three New Memoirs Reveal the 'Vertigo' of Life in the Diaspora." Review of *My Broken Language*, by Quiara Alegría Hudes, et al. *The New York Times*, 1 June 2021, www.nytimes.com/2021/06/01/books/review/crying-in-h-mart-michelle-zauner-my-broken-language-quiara-alegria-hudes-nuestra-america-claudio-lomnitz.html. Accessed 31 Oct. 2021.

Ramírez, Alicia. "'A Migrant in My Own Life': A Playwright Looks Deep Within." Review of *My Broken Language*, by Quiara Alegría Hudes. *The Christian Science Monitor*, 30 Apr. 2021, www.csmonitor.com/Books/Book-Reviews/2021/0430/A-migrant-in-my-own-life-A-playwright-looks-deep-within. Accessed 31 Oct. 2021.

My Heart Is a Chainsaw

Author: Stephen Graham Jones (b. 1972)
Publisher: First Saga Press (New York). 416 pp.
Type of work: Novel
Time: Present day
Locale: Proofrock, Idaho

Written by bestselling horror novelist Stephen Graham Jones, My Heart Is a Chainsaw *is a coming-of-age story about an Indigenous teenager who finds her life becoming increasingly more like the slasher films that she loves.*

Principal characters

JADE DANIELS, a seventeen-year-old outcast obsessed with slasher films
LETHA MONDRAGON, a pretty, popular girl in her school
MR. HOLMES, Jade's history teacher
SHERIFF HARDY, the town's chief law enforcement officer
THEO MONDRAGON, Letha's wealthy father
TAB, Jade's alcoholic and abusive father
REXALL, an obnoxious friend of Jade's father

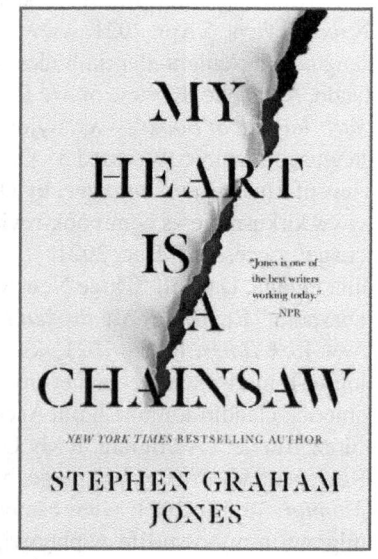

The slasher film, which typically involves a lone killer hunting down defenseless victims, has long been a part of American cinema. Firmly established as their own genre by the late 1970s, these typically low budget productions often relied on unknown actors and gruesome violence to bring terrifying stories to the big screen. As the genre continued to gain momentum throughout the 1980s, audiences were introduced to characters like Michael Myers, Freddy Krueger, and Jason Voorhees—all deranged killers known for their mercilessness. The genre's frequent low production value, inane plots, and excessive violence helped many slasher films go on to become cult classics among horror fans and win over new audiences long after their original releases.

Stephen Graham Jones is one such fan. Throughout his prolific career, the Blackfeet author has written numerous horror stories, many of which include werewolves, zombies, monsters, and evil spirits. With a talent for blending realism with the supernatural, Jones has been praised by critics for his ability to use the horror genre to discuss issues that affect Native Americans, including poverty, colonialism, and the preservation of Native identity. For example, his 2020 novel *The Only Good Indians* is ostensibly a horror story about a group of men who leave the Blackfeet Reservation after a disturbing event in their youth, and are later haunted by a deadly elk-shaped

Stephen Graham Jones

demon. Yet at its core, the novel centers on the identity crisis that many Indigenous people endure when they try to adapt to a culture that has historically tried to destroy their own.

My Heart Is a Chainsaw (2021) is not only Jones's latest work of horror fiction, but also a love letter to the slasher film genre. Jones is an outspoken fan of slasher films, and has cited director Wes Craven as a major influence, particularly due to his ability to create strong female characters. Craven also happens to be one of the heroes of Jade Daniels, the protagonist of *My Heart Is a Chainsaw*.

A social outcast, Jade is a half Native American seventeen-year-old with an encyclopedic knowledge of slasher films, which she loves due to their themes of revenge. Slasher films are the lens through which she views the world, so when people begin turning up brutally murdered in her small, fictional hometown of Proofrock, Idaho, she uses the films as a guide to anticipate what will happen next. Along the way, she befriends Letha Mondragon, a purehearted classmate who Jade determines is "the Final Girl," the only slasher character who can stand up to the murderer and survive. As Jade prepares Letha to take on this role and tries to understand the chaos unfolding, her obsession with the murderer intensifies, all the way up to the novel's violent, dramatic conclusion.

One of *My Heart Is a Chainsaw*'s most distinguishing features is the way that Jones strikes a balance between explaining slasher film tropes and bringing them to life. This becomes evident in the novel's first few pages, which depict two young lovers going out on a lake in the middle of the night, unaware that something sinister is lurking nearby. This scene is familiar for anyone who watches horror films, as it includes young, sexually active adults alone in a dark, isolated wooded area. The novel also includes several other delightfully clichéd characters and story beats that Jade often points out in a meta fashion. For example, the character of Sheriff Hardy tries to function as a paternal figure to Jade. However, when she tells him there is an evil murderer in town, he does not believe her, representative of how most adults in horror films do not believe children.

Another way that Jones cleverly weaves slasher films into the novel is by including papers that Jade has written on the subject for her history teacher, Mr. Holmes. In each of Jade's papers, which make up the book's alternating chapters, she describes the types of killers that populate the slasher genre and how its narratives typically unfold. In addition to being extremely analytical, Jade provides examples of real films to illustrate her points. Through Jade, Jones manages to fill any knowledge gaps that readers might have on the topic, enhancing their enjoyment of his play on classic slasher themes.

Features such as Jade's papers allow *My Heart Is a Chainsaw* to succeed as both an homage to classic slasher films, as well as an original work of horror fiction that tackles larger issues. Set in an isolated lakeside town, the novel examines the socioeconomic divide that exists between working class and wealthy people. Jones uses the changes taking place in Proofrock as a way to discuss gentrification, represented by the contrast between Jade's impoverished home and the new property development where Letha and her father, Theo, live.

The novel's characters also feel fresh and original, and Jones has a knack for depicting unsavory characters. For example, Rexall, Jade's father's alcoholic friend who constantly makes sexually suggestive jokes to Jade, manages to come across as authentically sleazy rather than as an over-the-top caricature. There is also a twisted darkness that Jones captures about Jade's parents; her abusive father rarely speaks, and her mother only exists in the glaringness of her absence.

One of the most compelling characters of *My Heart Is a Chainsaw* is the character of Jade herself, the novel's unconventional heroine. Strong but extremely damaged, she wields her obsession with slasher films as a buffer towards anyone who tries to get too close to her. Isolated from her peers and constantly avoiding her father at home, Jade exists on the fringes of her own narrative. She cannot imagine herself ever being worthy of the "Final Girl" designation or confronting the villain herself, and gives the responsibility to her friend Letha instead.

Through Jade, Jones provides a heart-wrenching depiction of the struggles that many Native American teenagers endure in the United States today. It is implied throughout the chapters that Jade suffers from mental health issues rooted in trauma and hardship that she endured as a young child. Grappling with a sense of self-loathing, she often feels like she has nowhere to go or any options for a better life, and as a result has attempted suicide. Her struggles eventually become a way to emphasize the novel's message of the importance of communities taking care of their children. Not only have Jade's parents failed her, but so has the entire town of Proofrock. Although Sheriff Hardy, Mr. Holmes, and Letha all try to help Jade at some point, their efforts often feel punitive or alienating to her. Early on it becomes clear that Jade has always needed, but sadly lacked, a support system to protect her, care for her, and enable her to thrive.

Overall, *My Heart Is a Chainsaw* is a refreshing addition to the horror genre that in many ways feels comparable to the work of Stephen King. Specifically, Jones shares King's talent for exciting worldbuilding within the confines of small, fictional towns, as well as his ability to develop myths about supernatural forces that have the same gravity as older fables and myths. The novel also belongs to the trend of Indigenous creators who came to prominence in the 2010s and 2020s by using their art to bring stories about contemporary Native life to larger audiences, and in turn challenge longstanding negative stereotypes about Native American peoples. Jones's literary success has placed him at the forefront of this movement, which also includes Indigenous authors like Tommy Orange, Darcie Little Badger, and Kelli Jo Ford, as well as filmmaker Sterlin Harjo, whose 2021 television show *Reservation Dogs* told the story of four Native American teenagers and became a critical and commercial success.

Reception of *My Heart Is a Chainsaw* has been largely positive, with most critics lauding its deft storytelling and compelling characters. In its glowing review, *Publishers Weekly* concluded, "Horror fans won't need to have seen all of the films referenced to be blown away by this audacious extravaganza," confirming that Jones succeeds in making his homage to slashers accessible to readers of all tastes and backgrounds. Ellen Morton also comments on this fact in her review for the *Washington Post*, noting that the novel is so entertaining that it made her, someone who does not like gore, want to begin watching horror films. She praised the novel's plot in particular, writing, "Everything promised in the first act is gleefully delivered in the third with comedy, pathos, and a machete clutched in the hands of an unforgettable character."

Another common point of praise among critics was how *My Heart Is a Chainsaw* uses horror as a tool to make necessary social commentary. In his review for National Public Radio, Gabino Iglesias remarks how the novel is similar to Jones's previous works, such as *The Only Good Indian* (2020) and *Attack of the 50 Foot Indian* (2020), in that it "lures" readers in with its promise of horror and, then provides them with "smart, soulful goodness" by forcing them to "rethink revenge and triumph in the shadow of trauma."

My Heart Is a Chainsaw is not perfect, however. At times, Jones's prose can be so dense that it requires rereading, particularly during the third act's action sequences. Furthermore, some critics commented that Jones packs so many elements into the story that some of the points he tries to get across do not resonate as strongly as they should. In her review for the *New York Times*, Danielle Trussoni praised the scope of the work, stating, "Jones is a heady writer; gentrification, class and race all come into play here." However, she also felt the "unfocused" plot moved too quickly.

Despite these minor shortcomings, *My Heart Is a Chainsaw* succeeds as an exciting new entry into the horror canon, and its main character Jade as a worthy new heroine in the slasher genre. Jones is not afraid to depict her in all her complexity, and some readers may become frustrated with her refusal to assimilate, be quiet, and follow the rules. However, it is this defiance, along with her twisted, slasher-obsessed worldview, that makes her so compelling. As readers learn more about Jade, they may start to feel defiant, too—perhaps even moved to make their community a better place for its most vulnerable members.

Author Biography
Stephen Graham Jones is a *New York Times* best-selling author of nearly thirty novels, novellas, and short story collections. He is the recipient of, among many other awards, the Texas Institute of Letters Jesse Jones Award for Fiction, the LA Times Ray Bradbury Prize, and the Bram Stoker Award.

Emily E. Turner

Review Sources

Iglesias, Gabino. "Slasher Films Provide the Lens That Frames This Horror Story." Review of *My Heart Is a Chainsaw*, by Stephen Graham Jones. *National Public Radio*, 1 Sept. 2021, www.npr.org/2021/09/01/1031875240/my-heart-is-a-chainsaw-stephen-graham-jones-review. Accessed 10 Nov. 2021.

Mandelo, Lee. "Slasher 101: *My Heart Is a Chainsaw*, by Stephen Graham Jones." *Tor.com*, 31 Aug. 2021, www.tor.com/2021/08/31/book-reviews-my-heart-is-a-chainsaw-by-stephen-graham-jones/. Accessed 8 Dec. 2021.

Morton, Ellen. "*My Heart Is a Chainsaw* Will Delight Horror Fans." Review of *My Heart Is a Chainsaw*, by Stephen Graham Jones. *The Washington Post*, 30 Aug. 2021, www.washingtonpost.com/entertainment/books/stephen-graham-jones-heart-is-a-chainsaw-review/2021/08/30/54ee2214-09a3-11ec-9781-07796ffb56fe_story.html. Accessed 10 Nov. 2021.

Review of *My Heart Is a Chainsaw*, by Stephen Graham Jones. *Publishers Weekly*, 1 Mar. 2021, www.publishersweekly.com/978-1-982137-63-2. Accessed 10 Nov. 2021.

Trussoni, Danielle. "Read It and Scream." Review of *My Heart Is a Chainsaw*, by Stephen Graham Jones. *The New York Times*, 25 Oct. 2021, www.nytimes.com/2021/10/25/books/new-horror-books.html. Accessed 10 Nov. 2021.

My Monticello

Author: Jocelyn Nicole Johnson (b. 1971)
Publisher: Henry Holt (New York). 240 pp.
Type of work: Novella, short fiction
Locale: Virginia

Jocelyn Nicole Johnson's debut collection, My Monticello, contains five short stories and a novella, the latter of which presents a dystopian vision of the future. Each of the texts explores race, racism, and the Black American experience in the United States.

Principal characters
PROFESSOR ADAMS, narrator of the short story "Control Negro"
VIRGINIA, subject of "Virginia Is Not Your Home"
RICHARD LORDLY, African immigrant and student in "Something Sweet on Our Tongues"
MR. ATTAH, Nigerian immigrant and protagonist of "The King of Xandria"
UNNAMED NARRATOR, a would-be homeowner in "Buying a House ahead of the Apocalypse"
DA'NAISHA LOVE, the narrator of the novella "My Monticello"
MAVIOLET, Da'Naisha's grandmother
KNOX, Da'Naisha's White boyfriend

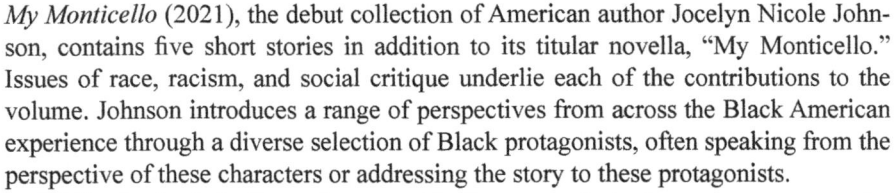

My Monticello (2021), the debut collection of American author Jocelyn Nicole Johnson, contains five short stories in addition to its titular novella, "My Monticello." Issues of race, racism, and social critique underlie each of the contributions to the volume. Johnson introduces a range of perspectives from across the Black American experience through a diverse selection of Black protagonists, often speaking from the perspective of these characters or addressing the story to these protagonists.

While the book is focused geographically on a relatively narrow context—the southeastern United States, Virginia in particular—Johnson manages to create characters with a variety of perspectives, ranging from urban to rural, female to male, and American-born to immigrant. The book also explores two interracial relationships, both involving the relationship of a Black woman and a White man, which offer opportunities for reflection on the intimate dynamics of race within relationships.

This is not the only lens through which Johnson examines racism in the United States. Throughout the volume, Johnson offers significant material for reflection on the history, present, and future of race and racism in the US. Her fiction incorporates allusions to some real events of the 2010s and uses this context to paint a vision of the future that is somewhat pessimistic. For example, in the novella "My Monticello," Johnson's fiction offers a dire, dystopian vision of future race wars building from the real events that unfolded at the August 2017 "Unite the Right" rally in Charlottesville, Virginia, a gathering of right-wing groups during which a counterprotester was killed.

Each of the five short stories, some of which have been previously published, introduces a different cast of characters and contexts. The volume opens with the story "Control Negro," which is narrated by Professor Adams, a Black American sociologist and teacher. Adams addresses his biological son throughout the story; this son had previously been unaware of his relationship with Adams and was raised as part of a different family with a different father. In the story, Adams explains how his son's whole life has been the result of an experiment to create a "Control Negro," an individual "otherwise equivalent to those broods of average American Caucasian males" in colleges across the country. Adams hopes this "Control Negro" could help answer a pressing research question: "Given the right conditions, could America extend her promise of Life and Liberty to me too, to someone like me?" Of course, the story has little to do with a real, academic approach, but it makes use of the professor's cold, analytical construct to confront the systemic violence and discrimination against Black men in the United States.

Jocelyn Nicole Johnson

Two stories—"Something Sweet on Our Tongues" and "The King of Xandria"—engage with the environment of public schools, thus building on Johnson's expertise from many years in the classroom as a teacher. "Something Sweet on Our Tongues" is focused on schoolchildren living in a low-income urban community. Told from the perspective of one of the children, the story examines issues central to the experience of many working-class communities, including food insecurity, violence in schools, and unstable homes. Instigated by Melvin Moses Green, a child who is abused at home and bullies his classmates, the students violently attack classmate Richard Lordly, an African immigrant who is also the highest-performing student in the class. The story presents public education in working-class communities as a space devoid of hope or effective support for children and their families.

"The King of Xandria" touches on similar issues. It follows Mr. Attah, a recent immigrant from Nigeria, as he struggles against an inhospitable environment in Alexandria, Virginia. He has lost his job and overstayed his visa, but what pushes Attah to the point of breakdown is the school district's assertion that his son, Alex, requires special education. The story touches on the sociopolitical crises of Nigeria, as Attah was driven to come to the United States with his children after his wife was randomly killed in the family's home country. If the family returns to Nigeria, Attah and his children feel they have nothing to go back to. However, in Virginia, Attah must struggle with differing notions of self-worth and manliness, for both himself and his son. Meanwhile, the story also demonstrates the bureaucracy of the public education system, confronting, controlling, and locking ranks against a Black father who attempts to advocate for his son. The school's persistence on this issue raises the question as to whether school administrators have made any attempt to work individually with Alex, or if they quickly decided to force him into remedial classes.

The two remaining short stories, "Virginia Is Not Your Home" and "Buying a House ahead of the Apocalypse," are both written from the perspective of a Black American woman. In "Virginia Is Not Your Home," a rural Virginian woman repudiates her name, "Virginia" (and nickname "Ginny"), as well as her birthplace. She aspires to a cosmopolitan lifestyle—she nearly graduates from college, but after meeting a French artist in Europe, she drops out and marries him without finishing her degree. Over the years, Ginny's high-flying lifestyle disintegrates. First, the couple return to the US at her French husband's wish, with Virginia serving as his ticket to American legitimacy. Then, after their finances crumble, they return to Virginia to live with her parents, the beginning of a long downslide that crushes Ginny's dreams. While loosely concerned with race, this story more prominently considers the question of home and the ties that sometimes bind stronger than dreams.

"Buying a House ahead of the Apocalypse," which is written as a bulleted list, reflects the anxieties of a would-be homeowner in the face of a discriminatory housing market and a tense sociopolitical moment. The woman imagines which qualities might make a secure concept of home, even as she laments her youthful failure to make a safe and happy home for her now-grown daughter, and confronts a social and political context that presages an "apocalypse."

This fixation with societal collapse recurs in the title novella, "My Monticello," the part of the volume on which most critical attention has focused. The novella is told from the perspective of Da'Naisha Love, a Black woman and Charlottesville, Virginia, native who is studying education at the University of Virginia (UVA). At UVA, Da'Naisha has begun dating a White man named Knox.

As the story opens, Da'Naisha flees her childhood home, which belongs to her grandmother, MaViolet, as an armed mob of White supremacists attacks the neighborhood. Da'Naisha, Knox, MaViolet, and a handful of neighbors jump into a small camper and manage to escape. With no plan, little gas, and only a few supplies, they drive to Monticello, the historic home of former US president Thomas Jefferson located in the hills outside of Charlottesville. Da'Naisha is familiar with the site since she worked there during a summer job; fortunately, one of the guards remaining on the property recognizes her and lets the group stay. The group of neighbors are, essentially, refugees, made homeless by the race-based violence that has broken out in the region and only worsened over the years.

As the story unfolds, it is clear that by this time, US society has begun to unravel. The electrical grid is down due to the unpredictable climate, gasoline is in short supply, and the streets are controlled by armed vigilantes; uncertain threats are everywhere. While some pockets of suburban idyll still exist, residents never know when a neighbor might suddenly display a hate group's flag. While critics have written about Da'Naisha's group as a collection of Black and minority resisters, a strict Black and White dichotomy is not exactly what Johnson presents. Neighbors Carol and Ira are White and working class; Knox is also White, though he is from a wealthy background. Meanwhile, a Latino family joins the group only later on, after hiding at Monticello for several days. While the story is clearly about the race-based nature of the threat against Da'Naisha and her diverse companions, exact definitions of who is "White," "Black," or something else is often somewhat deliberately blurred. Through much of the narrative, Da'Naisha struggles with whether Knox truly belongs among them. The name and affiliation of the hate group that forced Da'Naisha and the others to flee Charlottesville are not specified, but the threat is clearly real and terrifying, with plenty of allusions to Nazi Germany.

The central symbolism of "My Monticello" is the historical place and person with which Monticello is associated: Thomas Jefferson. As the story unfolds, the reader learns that MaViolet and, thus, Da'Naisha, are descendants of Jefferson, through the lineage of Sally Hemings, an enslaved woman with whom Jefferson fathered children. MaViolet has even attended multiple events at the historic site. But, even before the family's relationship to Jefferson was publicly acknowledged, MaViolet had made sure that her daughter and granddaughter knew of their connection to him. Da'Naisha's own feelings about Monticello are conflicted, naturally associating the place with the dark, intertwined legacies of slavery and sexual violence connected to this ancestry. Knox wants to talk with Da'Naisha about the fascinating truth that Monticello is "partly [hers]," but Da'Naisha recoils from discussing the Hemings-Jefferson relationship with her White boyfriend. When he ponders whether Hemings and Jefferson loved one another "at some level," she corrects him, saying that no love can exist with such a power differential. Da'Naisha then wonders if loving Knox means hating herself.

When the group first arrives at Monticello, they live in the environs of the visitors' center. After a few days, though, and spurred by MaViolet's worsening asthma, they move into the historic mansion house, where Da'Naisha settles MaViolet into Jefferson's own bed. By contrast, and in a symbolic reversal of the home's original race dynamics, Carol and Ira choose to live in the reconstructed quarters of the home's enslaved residents. When Da'Naisha leads the small group of refugees in writing their own constitution, they agree on the sharing of property and labor, and they vow to protect one another. As Da'Naisha and the other refugees begin forming a new society on their mountain citadel, outside forces begin to threaten them once again, and the refugees prepare to fight for their lives.

My Monticello earned widespread critical praise upon its publication in 2021. Bridgett M. Davis, writing for the *New York Times*, called the collection a "startling and powerful debut" and complimented Johnson's ability to weave contemporary events into her fiction. She drew parallels between Johnson's stories and the work of Black American author Toni Morrison; both writers, she argued, successfully used fiction in a "quest to access the interior lives of [their] ancestors." Maureen Corrigan, writing for National Public Radio, echoed Davis's praise of the collection's inspirational foundations in contemporary events such as the Unite the Right rally and also lauded Johnson's "precise, pictorial writing style." This writing style, along with Johnson's ability to present a range of emotions in characters faced with challenging circumstances, also earned praise from Carr Harkrader of the *Washington Independent Review of Books*. Calling the collection a "mesmerizing antidote" for historical nostalgia, Harkrader complimented Johnson's ability to examine racism and other pressing issues without succumbing to cliché.

Author Biography
Jocelyn Nicole Johnson is a teacher and writer who has received fellowships from Hedgebrook and Tin House. Her writing has appeared in the *Guardian*, *Guernica*, and other publications, and her first book, *My Monticello*, was published in 2021.

Julia A. Sienkewicz, PhD

Review Sources
Corrigan, Maureen. "*My Monticello* Grapples with the Past, Present and Future of American Racism." Review of *My Monticello*, by Jocelyn Nicole Johnson. *NPR*, 2 Nov. 2021, www.npr.org/2021/11/02/1045277325/my-monticello-review-jocelyn-nicole-johnson. Accessed 4 Jan. 2022.

Davis, Bridgett M. "Jocelyn Nicole Johnson Makes Virginia's Past Present in *My Monticello*." *The New York Times*, 4 Oct. 2021, www.nytimes.com/2021/10/04/books/review/jocelyn-nicole-johnson-my-monticello.html. Accessed 4 Jan. 2022.

Grant, Colin. "*My Monticello* by Jocelyn Nicole Johnson Review—an American Tragedy." *The Guardian*, 16 Dec. 2021, www.theguardian.com/books/2021/dec/16/my-monticello-by-jocelyn-nicole-johnson-review-an-american-tragedy. Accessed 4 Jan. 2022.

Gray, Anissa. "Jocelyn Nicole Johnson's *My Monticello* Explores America's Racist Past—and Present—with Grace." *The Washington Post*, 15 Oct. 2021, www.washingtonpost.com/entertainment/books/jocelyn-nicole-johnsons-my-monticello-explores-americas-racist-past--and-present--with-grace/2021/10/14/65c872a6-2c7b-11ec-985d-3150f7e106b2_story.html. Accessed 4 Jan. 2022.

Harkrader, Carr. Review of *My Monticello*, by Jocelyn Nicole Johnson. *Washington Independent Review of Books*, 2 Nov. 2021, www.washingtonindependentreviewofbooks.com/bookreview/my-monticello-fiction. Accessed 4 Jan. 2022.

The Night Always Comes

Author: Willy Vlautin (b. 1967)
Publisher: Harper (New York). 224 pp.
Type of work: Novel
Time: Present day
Locale: Portland, Oregon, and environs

Willy Vlautin's sixth novel, The Night Always Comes, *focuses on a young, hardworking woman in Portland, Oregon, who is desperately trying to attain the security of home ownership in a rapidly changing, increasingly hostile urban environment.*

Principal characters

LYNETTE, a young woman working multiple jobs and trying to buy the house she lives in
KENNY, her older brother, who has developmental disabilities
DOREEN, her mother
GLORIA, her friend, a beautiful escort

The Night Always Comes (2021) opens at a moment of stress for a poverty-stricken family living in a run-down rented house near the freeway in North Portland, Oregon. Told from a third-person viewpoint, the book focuses on the character of Lynette, who is barely thirty but already world-weary. She works long hours: mornings at a pastry shop, evenings at the bar of a restaurant-cocktail lounge. In between she attends community college. At night, she secretly works as a high-paid escort. Her labor is complicated by the necessity of arranging constant daily care for her older brother Kenny, who has developmental disabilities and cannot speak. Their overweight, worn-out mother, Doreen, whose husband abandoned the family when Lynette was an infant, lives with her children and works at a superstore.

Lynette toils hard with a particular goal in mind: to purchase their current residence, the house she has always lived in. Though the building is in poor shape, their hands-off landlord has not raised the monthly rent in more than a decade, meaning it costs less than half what even a small apartment would cost elsewhere in the city. Now the landlord wants to sell and has offered Lynette and family a relative bargain on the house, with a price of $280,000. This is all the more attractive because Portland is undergoing extensive urban renewal—marked by a plethora of construction cranes—which is a boon for investors, but a disaster for the working class, many of whom cannot afford the trappings of upscale gentrification. Lynette's sense of urgency to buy the property is heightened by a fixed deadline to make the deal.

Willy Vlautin

Three years before, Lynette and Doreen agreed to buy the place. Lynette, who envisions all the improvements they will undertake to make the house more livable, has saved $80,000 from her various jobs (especially the clandestine one) for the down payment. Doreen, whose credit is better than her daughter's, is supposed to take out a loan for the remainder. But now, just days from signing the purchase agreement, Doreen is balking. She refuses to be tied to a dilapidated, overpriced dwelling for the rest of her life. She wants nice things that she has denied herself, and to demonstrate her changed attitude, buys a new car.

Doreen's sudden change of heart causes bitter arguments between mother and daughter. Episodes from the younger woman's past, which will be more fully revealed throughout the story, are brought up and flung in her face. Lynette as a teen ran away from home and was missing for almost a year. She attempted suicide. She later had a nice boyfriend but ruined the relationship.

Her mother's reneging on their deal sends Lynette into a forty-eight-hour frenzy of activity as she tries to collect on outstanding debts. The more money she has for the down payment, she calculates, the smaller the loan will have to be, and the greater the chance she can persuade Doreen to honor their agreement. The action-packed two-day spree reveals much about Lynette's character, especially her capacity to do whatever it takes to achieve her goals.

Lynette's first stop is at a hotel, where she regularly meets an unnamed wealthy older married man for sex. Though they have been intimate two dozen times, she has never before spoken personally with her client. This time, she tells him about her house-buying dilemma and asks for investment advice. He is uncomfortable communicating on that level, and tipping her generously, tells her they will never meet again. When he goes to shower, she takes his car key and steals his vehicle, a top-of-the line Mercedes. Afterward, she drops in unannounced at the luxurious residence of another longtime escort client, a young technology executive, whom she browbeats into coughing up what he owes for past services.

Next is a visit to the upscale apartment of fellow escort Gloria. Lynette hopes to be reimbursed for $8,000 she lent Gloria for a driving-under-the-influence (DUI) charge. Gloria claims to be broke; besides, she is about to go off on a trip with her latest sugar daddy. Gloria says Lynette can stay in her apartment while she is gone, gives her a spare key, and departs. At the apartment, Lynette finds a small but heavy safe, which she suspects contains the money she is owed. After-hours, she visits the restaurant where she works to recruit ex-con cleaner Cody Henson to help steal and open the safe. Their tenuous partnership brings Lynette into contact with a succession of shady characters after the safe is made to disgorge its contents: a bundle of cash, expensive jewelry, and a half-kilo of uncut cocaine. Some of the accomplices she encounters are willing to kill for the goods, and Lynette must be willing to fight to protect herself and retain what she feels is rightfully hers.

As a protagonist, Lynette, who is introspective enough to recognize and learn from her own flaws, has redeeming features that offset her criminal inclinations. She is, for example, conscientious and patient in caring for her brother. She scrimps on personal luxuries to achieve her goal of becoming a homeowner; the details of the small challenges she faces daily resonate as markers of working-class life. For example, the broken heater and unreliable ignition of her old car are mentioned often, reflecting the tedious grind of regularly dealing with such problems. But it is her relationship with Doreen that truly makes Lynette a complex and interesting character. Their mother-daughter connection is complicated and highly contentious, but not without familial affection. A particularly poignant moment comes when Doreen discusses the aftermath of Lynette attempting suicide as a teenager (driven by a sexual assault by one of Doreen's boyfriends): "Just seeing your pile of dirty underwear on the floor made me so happy. Because a girl who changes her underwear must want to live."

The main plot is tightly paced and engaging, drawing the reader in to Lynette's desperate mission. Despite (or perhaps in part because of) her many misfortunes, she proves to be resourceful as her plans take unexpected turns and she does not panic when threatened with violence. Fortunately for her, most of the crooks she deals with in the caper of the safe, though physically sinister, are rather inept. Though she is bruised and bloodied during her nightmare tour of the dark, shadowy, rain-slick corners of the city, she remains unbowed. Her dedication and belief in a better future gives an optimistic tinge to what could otherwise easily be a depressing story of all-too-realistic struggles in modern society.

Throughout, *The Night Always Comes* presents a fast-paced, entertaining blend of character study, noirish suspense, social commentary, and a paean to the city of Portland. Author Willy Vlautin, who moved to Portland in the 1990s, effectively captures its nuances as a unique place—as well as the social forces causing rapid change. Indeed, the setting serves as a major factor in the story. Many real-life landmarks—such as the Pearl District, Portland Community College, and the Original Hotcake House—are mentioned in passing. A longtime working musician, Vlautin also plugs actual local bands operating in the city, like Dead Moon, Calamity Jane, Crackerbash, Oblivion Seekers, and the Maroons, by noting their posters hanging on the walls of a character's home. These realistic details ultimately help underscore how Portland is an exemplar of the effects of gentrification. Most obvious here is the rise of housing insecurity and homelessness among the working poor, who find themselves effectively barred from elements of the traditional American dream such as home ownership, career advancement, and even basic stability and safety. In this way, Vlautin continues his penchant for focusing on characters living at the fringes of society, as displayed in his previous novels *The Motel Life* (2006), *Northline* (2008), *Lean on Pete* (2010), *The Free* (2014), and *Don't Skip Out on Me* (2018) as well as his songwriting. He manages to lift various examples of the downtrodden into the light, to show the good—the honesty and the honor—that lurks beneath the dusty surface.

Critics were generally very positive about *The Night Always Comes*. The anonymous reviewer for *Kirkus*, for example, stated that it "plays out like a modern noir take on a Tennessee Williams play" and hailed it as "a soulful thriller for the age of soulless gentrification." Writing for the *New York Journal of Books*, Mark Stevens noted the author's "spare, matter-of-fact prose," appropriate for shining "a light on those who are scratching out a living," and praised the "noir flavor that gives the story an extra layer of tension." In a review for the *Big Issue*, Doug Johnstone compared Vlautin's novels to "Tom Waits songs in book form, stories of hardworking people down on their luck, trying to get by and find a little happiness and kindness where they can," and called *The Night Always Comes* the author's "finest work to date."

A few reviewers did find elements to critique. Writing for the Portland-area *Willamette Week*, Christen McCurdy said, "Vlautin's prose is generally crisp and straightforward, making the book a quick read, with a slight exception: Every few chapters there's a scene of heavy dialogue between two characters who typically speak in long paragraphs, often about an emotionally fraught subject." Alanna Bennett argued a similar point in the *New York Times*, suggesting that the novel "stalls out during its many long monologues spelling out exactly what each character is thinking in clunky detail," though she noted that the book "regains its footing . . . in the moments where we get to live in Lynette's inner world." Bennett also felt that Vlautin's "etchings of the city's poor, white population are at times overwrought," and especially felt that Doreen falls flat as a character.

Despite such minor misgivings, the broad critical consensus is that with *The Night Always Comes* Vlautin has produced yet another strong work that shows his skill in depicting parts of society that often go overlooked. He illuminates the lives of worthwhile individuals among the nameless, faceless masses who toil in the shadows, working tirelessly toward objectives they may never realize. For characters like his—and the real humans they represent—the notion of moving forward regardless of long odds is part of their internal fiber, and simply giving up is never a viable option.

Author Biography
A longtime professional musician and songwriter, Willy Vlautin cofounded the bands Richmond Fontaine and the Delines. He published his first novel, *The Motel Life*, in 2006 and went on to win several literary awards for his fiction, which tends to focus on working-class themes.

Jack Ewing

Review Sources

Bennett, Alanna. "Who Can Actually Afford to Live in Portland?" Review of *The Night Always Comes*, by Willy Vlautin. *The New York Times*, 6 Apr. 2021, www.nytimes.com/2021/04/06/books/review/the-night-always-comes-willy-vlautin.html. Accessed 9 Aug. 2021.

Johnstone, Doug. "*The Night Always Comes* by Willy Vlautin: An Arrow Through the Reader's Heart." *The Big Issue*, 3 July 2021, www.bigissue.com/culture/books/the-night-always-comes-willy-vlautin-an-arrow-through-the-readers-heart/. Accessed 9 Aug. 2021.

McCurdy, Christen. "Book Review: Willy Vlautin's *The Night Always Comes* is a Harrowing Portrait of a Changing Portland." *Willamette Week*, 6 Apr. 2021, www.wweek.com/arts/books/2021/04/06/book-review-willy-vlautins-the-night-always-comes-is-a-harrowing-portrait-of-a-changing-portland/. Accessed 9 Aug. 2021.

Review of *The Night Always Comes*, by Willy Vlautin. *Kirkus*, 13 Jan. 2021, www.kirkusreviews.com/book-reviews/willy-vlautin/the-night-always-comes/. Accessed 9 Aug. 2021.

Piehl, Norah. Review of *The Night Always Comes*, by Willy Vlautin. *Bookreporter*, 30 Apr. 2021, www.bookreporter.com/reviews/the-night-always-comes. Accessed 9 Aug. 2021.

Stevens, Mark. Review of *The Night Always Comes*, by Willy Vlautin. *New York Journal of Books*, www.nyjournalofbooks.com/book-review/night-always-comes-novel. Accessed 9 Aug. 2021.

No Gods, No Monsters

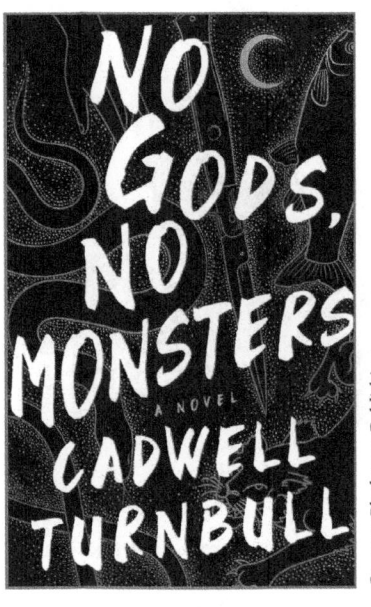

Author: Cadwell Turnbull
Publisher: Blackstone (Ashland). 387 pp.
Type of work: Novel
Time: Present day
Locales: Massachusetts; St. Thomas, US Virgin Islands; Virginia

No God, No Monsters *sets the stage for Cadwell Turnbull's rich and sprawling Convergence Saga, in which so-called "monsters"—werewolves, witches and other supernatural beings—reveal themselves to humans in the aftermath of a fatal police shooting.*

Principal characters
CALVIN, a man with the ability to travel across parallel timelines in his sleep
LAINA, a young woman seeking justice for her murdered brother
REBECCA, a young woman and werewolf
RIDLEY, Laina's husband; an asexual trans man and community organizer
SONDRA, a Virgin Islands senator and weredog
DRAGON, a child shapeshifter
HARRY, a biologist

No Gods, No Monsters (2021), Cadwell Turnbull's second novel, is the first of a projected fantasy and science fiction series called the Convergence Saga, which imagines the conflicts and chaos that would emerge if monsters and other mythical creatures actually existed. The book draws on a range of genres, including fantasy and Afrofuturism, a growing subgenre of science fiction that blends fantasy, science fiction, and history to tell stories about African Americans and other members of the global Black diaspora. Although the novel incorporates classic fantasy elements such as magic, werewolves, and other creatures, it also relies heavily on its grounding in science fiction. As a genre, science fiction has long been a conduit for political ideas from a range of perspectives, as it offers a way for writers to use fictional worlds to examine real social and political issues. For example, Octavia Butler, often considered the mother of Afrofuturism, used the lens of science fiction to examine racism and other issues African Americans faced in the twentieth-century United States. Turnbull blends this rich literary tradition with a contemporary setting to create a complex fantasy world and populates it with a diverse cast of characters prepared to tackle its challenges.

Cadwell Turnbull

Courtesy Blackstone Publishing

The story begins in the aftermath of a fatal police shooting. Laina, one of the main protagonists, is grieving the death of her brother, Lincoln, who had struggled with drug addiction and was shot and killed by a police officer. Laina wants justice for her brother, so when a disembodied voice offers her video footage of the shooting, she eagerly accepts. In addition to offering her closure, Laina hopes the footage can help rally people to join the fight against police brutality and racism.

The video of the police shooting is disturbing, but also surprising in ways Laina never anticipated. In the video, a police officer shoots a terrifying wolf creature, who only in death is revealed to be the human Lincoln. Despite her confusion, Laina leaks the video, precipitating the Fracture, the book's central event. During the Fracture, werewolves and other monsters, previously unseen by humans and existing only as the stuff of legend, reveal their existence. This revelation, along with other unseen forces, threaten to draw all of humanity into an all-out war.

The events in the immediate aftermath of the leak play out in a very realistic way. Much like the real-life videos of police killings on which it is based, footage of Lincoln's death sparks protest. At this point, when the Fracture becomes a major part of the narrative, the story delves deeper into its fantasy and science fiction themes. In one scene, a group of protesters reveal themselves to be werewolves and block a highway, causing a media frenzy. While the werewolves are the first to appear, other shapeshifters and supernatural creatures from regional legend and lore soon make themselves known as well.

These monsters, as they are called by the media, are depicted as a marginalized class, but Turnbull resists limiting his story to a simple conflict between powerful humans and oppressed monsters. There are also gods, ancient secret societies, and complex relationship dynamics that thwart any attempt to categorize *No Gods, No Monsters* as a simple allegory about racism. Its scope casts a far wider net to tell a hopeful story about how diverse and flawed people can come together to build a better world. Turnbull uses recurring images and a cast of diverse, vividly drawn characters to drive this point home. One character, Harry, is a biologist who studies honeybees. He describes how colonies function as a single unit, with thousands of bees reacting to their environment in tandem. The power of insect colonies is demonstrated again elsewhere in the book, when a mage performs magic with the aid of a colony of ants.

The value of cooperation and community-building is perhaps most demonstrated through the character of Laina's husband Ridley, who is overtly interested in the political possibilities of community. He is the cofounder of a worker-owned bookstore, and a member of an anarchist collective. Ridley's politics and reality are challenged when he is faced first with the existence of monsters, and then by the full and terrible breadth of the structure of the universe, with gods at the top, humans in the middle, and monsters at the bottom. The book's title stems from Ridley's politics, playing on the anarchist slogan, "No Gods, No Masters," which rejects the traditional authority of religion and hierarchical society in favor of a community based on equality. Ridley hears a variation of this chant—"No Gods, No Monsters"—at a monster allyship march, and interprets it as a "call against hierarchy and discrimination" and demand for equal rights between humans and monsters.

Turnbull also addresses colonialism in *No Gods, No Monsters*, particularly through the storylines set in St. Thomas in the US Virgin Islands. One character in the book, Sondra, is a senator in St. Thomas, and is also secretly a weredog—a creature similar to a werewolf, but native to the islands. Through Sondra, Turnbull lays the groundwork for a plotline that explores the Caribbean islands' relationship to the United States, which took over the territory in 1917. This is familiar ground for Turnbull, whose first novel, *The Lesson* (2019), is an allegory about colonialism in the Caribbean, framed as an alien invasion story.

Turnbull demonstrates an impressive ability to weave together the stories of various characters and give each of them unique attributes and backstories. In addition to Laina, Ridley, and Sondra, *No Gods, No Monsters* features a man named Calvin, who has the powerful but terrifying ability to travel to parallel universes in his sleep. Calvin serves as the book's omniscient narrator, bearing silent witness to the struggles of others from a place outside of time. However, Calvin also has his own problems. When the book begins, he is leaving a teaching position in North Carolina—along with a possible love interest—to return to his home in St. Thomas. Calvin is still grieving the murder of his brother Cory, who, like Laina's brother Lincoln, was shot and killed while trying to recover from addiction. Calvin reunites with Cory's daughter, who claims to speak with her dead father in her dreams. Calvin's engagement with parallel universes gives expression to his desire to change the past. He is haunted by visions of moments that could have been; in one vision, he sees a figure that looks like himself sitting on the couch, choosing to talk to his brother all night instead of leaving him alone to relapse. While Calvin's role in the story beyond his narration initially seems unclear, his deeper connection to the events following the Fracture may lie in his visit to a real historical figure named Hugh Everett, a quantum physicist who pioneered the concept of the multiverse, a model of the universe that contains a possibly infinite number of alternate timelines and realities.

No Gods, No Monsters was published to widespread acclaim in 2021. Many reviewers commented on its successful balance of complex worldbuilding, social commentary, and clear storytelling. Amal El-Mohtar, who reviewed the novel for the *New York Times*, attributed this successful outcome to Turnbull's confident clarity and "beautiful, conversational prose." She particularly praised Turnbull's ability to "inhabit" each character while seamlessly weaving together different settings and storylines; despite the constant shifts between setting and points of view, El-Mohtar said she "never felt lost or confused." In a review for *Tor*, Martin Cahill praised Turnbull's unusual decisions about who and what to place at the center of his story. Commenting on the story's warring secret societies, magicians, and monsters, Cahill felt another writer would have "shoved them into the spotlight as the highlight of the book." According to Cahill, Turnbull avoided relying too heavy on these fantasy and science fiction elements, and in fact "barely spends any time with them." Cahill observed that Turnbull spent much more time depicting the "day-to-day humans of this story, [who] are just as caught up in their own complex web of relationships and hardships and fears." This decision—a bold one, given how popular fantasy tropes are—speaks to Turnbull's rejection of traditional hierarchy, and is somewhat anarchist in its "laser focus" on the human interior of each character, not one of whom could be described as a clear, traditional protagonist. Cahill also noted that the novel's narration, which is entirely from the various points of view of its characters, is unusual in fantasy or science fiction writing, and is far more typical of realist literary fiction. Unlike many fantasy and science fiction works, which sometimes lean too heavily on exciting action and worldbuilding at the expense of character development, *No Gods, No Monsters* takes a radically different approach. Cahill felt this results in a story in which "the reader cares more for the characters caught in the middle of this whirlwind than they do for the storm itself."

While this character-driven approach impressed some reviewers, others did find issues with it. Jason Sheehan for *NPR* noted how Turnbull balances the "fantastical" and the "mundane," evident in the sharp contrasts between more tedious scenes, such as Ridley's drawn-out anarchist meetings, and moments of violence, such as a child chewing off a character's arm. While Sheehan admired this unique approach, he also wished that Turnbull provided a deeper dive into the world of *No Gods, No Monsters*. Sheehan felt that the novel only offered the "barest hints" at the scope and depth of its universe, and that Turnbull's preference for writing scenes of "workaday realism" came at the expense of fleshing out the story's rich mythology. Meanwhile, while most reviewers appreciated Turnbull's incorporation and discussion of concepts such as asexuality, polyamory, and worker-owned business models, the deep explanation of these concepts can feel overly didactic at times. Yet despite these small issues, *No Gods, No Monsters* succeeds not only as the foundation of a much larger epic narrative, but also as a timely commentary on race, equality, and building community in a time of conflict.

Author Biography
Cadwell Turnbull, a novelist and short story writer, published his first novel, *The Lesson*, in 2019. It won the Neukom Institute Literary Award in 2020.

Molly Hagan

Review Sources

Cahill, Martin. "What Makes a Monster? The Complexities of *No Gods, No Monsters* by Cadwell Turnbull." *Tor*, 17 Sept. 2021, www.tor.com/2021/09/17/book-reviews-no-gods-no-monsters-by-cadwell-turnbull/. Accessed 15 Dec. 2021.

El-Mohtar, Amal. "Beasts and Baseball: New Science Fiction and Fantasy." Review of *No Gods, No Monsters*, by Cadwell Turnbull. *The New York Times*, 21 Sept. 2021, www.nytimes.com/2021/09/21/books/review/lincoln-michel-ryka-aoki-cadwell-turnbull.html. Accessed 15 Dec. 2021.

Review of *No Gods, No Monsters*, by Cadwell Turnbull. *Kirkus Reviews*, 10 July 2021, www.kirkusreviews.com/book-reviews/cadwell-turnbull/no-gods-no-monsters/. Accessed 15 Dec. 2021.

Review of *No Gods, No Monsters*, by Cadwell Turnbull. *Publisher's Weekly*, 5 Mar. 2021, www.publishersweekly.com/978-1-982603-72-4. Accessed 15 Dec. 2021.

Sheehan, Jason. "If Monsters Were Real, This Book Knows What You'd Really Do—Nothing." Review of *No Gods, No Monsters*, by Cadwell Turnbull. *NPR*, 5 Sept. 2021, www.npr.org/2021/09/05/1031846954/no-gods-no-monsters-review-cadwell-turnbull. Accessed 15 Dec. 2021.

No One Is Talking about This

Author: Patricia Lockwood (b. ca. 1983)
Publisher: Riverhead Books (New York). 224 pp.
Type of work: Novel
Time: Present day
Locale: United States

Patricia Lockwood's debut novel, No One Is Talking about This, *details the experiences of a young influencer and public speaker. Using an experimental, abstract style, Lockwood juxtaposes the narrator's experience on social media with the divergent, subsequent experience of caring for a niece born with a serious medical condition.*

Principal characters

NARRATOR, a social media celebrity and public speaker
BABY, the narrator's niece, who was born with Proteus syndrome
SISTER, the narrator's sister and Baby's mother
HUSBAND, the narrator's husband
MOTHER, the narrator's mother
FATHER, the narrator's father, a former police officer

Prior to the publication of *No One Is Talking about This* (2021), her fiction debut, Patricia Lockwood was best known as a poet, essayist, and memoirist. She gained a loyal following from the comedy, political commentary, and poetry she posted on her Twitter account starting in the late 2000s and early 2010s, but her true breakthrough came with her poem "Rape Joke" (2013), for which she received a Pushcart Prize. The poem was praised for its dark humor and commentary on rape culture, and was republished in her acclaimed 2014 poetry collection *Motherland Fatherland Homosexuals*. Shifting away from poetry, Lockwood published a critically acclaimed memoir, *Priestdaddy* (2017), focusing primarily on her relationship with her father, a married Catholic priest who converted to Catholicism from Lutheranism.

In *No One Is Talking about This*, Lockwood revisits some of the same themes and subjects she touches on in earlier works, including family, with her signature brand of irreverent humor. She explores the phenomena of what it means to be "extremely online" as a fluid experience, simultaneously intangible and real. In doing so, she explores and dissects her own attempts to reconcile two irreconcilable things—profound tragedy and triviality. To balance these two seemingly opposite concepts, Lockwood's narrator bounces between these extremes, offering meditations on serious topics such as death in addition to discussions of more trivial matters, such as paparazzi photos of American actor Jason Momoa. Lockwood's signature blend of humor and social commentary, along with her own experience writing and publishing her work online, makes her well-suited to explore the strangeness of modern online experiences.

The story follows the trials of an unnamed narrator who lives both a real, embodied life as well as a literal "life online," which she experiences by engaging with the "portal," a device she can use to traverse the internet, call her mother, and Tweet life's most central questions. One particular tweet, "Can a dog be twins?", went viral and established her as a celebrity. In her physical existence, the narrator makes her living as an influencer and a public speaker by virtue of her pseudo-celebrity status. She feels comfort and fulfillment in her a marriage to a husband who, in moments of panic, opens the portal to show her pictures of roast chickens, her internet-era coping mechanism.

All this takes place in the context of political chaos in the United States; the country's current leader is a despot who constantly pursues the erosion of civil rights—most imminently to the narrator, reproductive rights. The narrator communicates her story in a series of sequential but otherwise disconnected vignettes. They read as the structural component of a commentary about the ways in which the narrator's inner voice has been invaded with the abbreviated, lingo-filled language of social media, the portal's most potent form of connection and influence. Only as the story unfolds does it become clear that is the novel is not a disorganized stream of consciousness, but rather a chronological narrative.

In Part One, the narrator poses the absurd, somewhat humorous question that first originated from many sleepless nights during her childhood and persists in her mind: "How did French people know what they were saying?" She later comments on the unabashed pleasure she derives from forming sentences that would prove indecipherable to the vast majority of people. Subsequently, she chronicles her horror at her mother's internet-related faux pas: a cross-generational miscommunication of the meaning attached to the eggplant emoji. Though these narrations are seemingly unrelated and may even seem trivial, they all detail the difficult balance between the need to be understood and understand oneself, and the desire to create things not meant to be shared or understood.

These meandering questions call attention to the complexity of language and communication, especially as they change over time. For example, the narrator's cat has an obscene name; the narrator knows that, were she alive one hundred years ago, she likely would have chosen a more innocent or sweet name, such as Mittens. The

Patricia Lockwood

narrator later details a man's cross-country barefoot trek, undertaken with the aim of bringing awareness to climate change. This trip ended abruptly when the man was struck and killed by a car as he walked along the roadside. The narrator describes how she furiously analyzes images of a now-dead man's foot wounds, which he fastidiously documented in the portal alongside his other experiences on the road. In these moments, the narrator tries to identify the experience of being human amid the mass consumption she encounters on social media. With such examples, the book explores the far-reaching effects of social media and the internet's influence on even the most mundane things, like the name of a pet.

Lockwood also takes moments to discuss the concept of American exceptionalism, the idea that the US is a unique nation incomparable to others; a concept that has contributed to the malignment and marginalization of many beliefs, food, words, and clothing wrongly typified as "non-American." She points out moments when the internet allows people to transcend these barriers and enjoy universal things and experiences. The narrator uses some extreme examples of cultural exchange to make this argument, for example pointing out that "Charlie Bit My Finger," a popular American viral video from 2007, was downloaded onto al-Qaeda terrorist leader Osama bin Laden's computer and discovered by the CIA, an inarguably absurd footnote in history. This observation seems to confirm that, in some respects, the ubiquity of the internet can undermine toxic nationalism and an "us-versus-them" mentality.

Part Two finds the narrator navigating wildly different circumstances after she relocates to her home state of Ohio after learning that her pregnant sister is expecting to give birth to a daughter with Proteus syndrome, a rare and often fatal genetic condition. No longer in a place of her choosing, and now feeling politically outnumbered and emotionally overwhelmed, the narrator considers who she could have become had she never moved away. She likens her own life path to the experience of men who grew up in internet chat rooms and consider themselves lucky for having moved on after they understood enough to be funny, but just before they were fully consumed by the vitriol and offensive beliefs they encountered there. Further, the narrator contrasts her own behavior, which is often humorous or juvenile, with her family's constant grappling with deeply complex moral and emotional issues. In this, she strikes at the heart of what it means to be alive and considers small moments of pleasure and ordinary existence to be the greatest source of meaning. She lists many examples: listening to the song "Africa" by Toto on a drive to visit her newborn niece in the hospital, the sound of rain on the roof, holding a seizing child while watching a Hallmark movie, and a trip to the dentist. In impossible circumstances, people still must feed, teach, and hold their children, and in contemporary society they still engage in frivolities on social media.

These realizations lead the narrator to consider a new question; what does it mean to experience a shared reality—or to not? In doing so, she comes to see both the portal and its recorded reality in a different light, choosing to engage more fully in the connections she shares with the people in her physical life. With this in mind, she also comes to understand that the relationships she has built on social media as being extensions of these connections, united by the commonality of having lived and known tragedies all their own.

No One Is Talking about This enjoyed much critical renown upon its publication, and was a finalist for the Booker Prize, among other honors. Jordan Kisner, in a review for the *Atlantic*, said that Lockwood's "genius for irony" was "matched by the radiance of her reverence." Lily Scherlis, writing for *Harvard Review Online*, argued that the narrator of *No One Is Talking about This* is positioned as navigating the internet with the audience, not before or despite them, and invites readers along for her journey. In the *Times*, Francesca Angelini called Lockwood's narrator "fabulously irreverent," and felt the book was a well-needed addition to the limited number of novels that address the subject of online life. However, some critics did take issue with aspects of the novel. In his review for the *New York Times*, for example, Merve Amre remarked that the experience of reading the book did not leave him with the feeling that he had read a good novel, but rather a text so native to the internet zeitgeist that he was not quite sure what to call it. Still, Amre praised the work's "restless narrator" and her "witty, tidy paragraphs" of mental wanderings. Indeed, despite its unusual approach to storytelling, many reviewers felt the novel succeeded in its aims. Writing for the *Guardian*, Mark O'Connell felt his emotional involvement with Lockwood's characters signified the novel's success, writing, "I was with these people, in their pain and hilarity. I was, for the first time, and in the old and funniest way, laughing out loud."

Author Biography

Patricia Lockwood is an American writer and poet whose works include the poetry collections *Balloon Pop Outlaw Black* (2012) and *Motherland Fatherland Homosexuals* (2014) and the memoir *Priestdaddy* (2017). She has also written essays for a range of publications, including the *New York Times* and the *New Yorker*.

Annie Brown

Review Sources

Angelini, Francesca, and Alexander Nurnberg. "Fiction Reviews - *No One Is Talking about This* by Patricia Lockwood; Maxwell's Demon by Steven Hall." *The Sunday Times*, 12 Feb. 2021, www.thetimes.co.uk/article/fiction-reviews-no-one-is-talking-about-this-by-patricia-lockwood-maxwells-demon-by-steven-hall-kplvdd72d. Accessed 8 Feb. 2022.

Emre, Merve. "Patricia Lockwood's First Novel Reaches for the Sublime, Online and Off." Review of *No One Is Talking about This*, by Patricia Lockwood. *The New York Times*, 16 Feb. 2021, www.nytimes.com/2021/02/16/books/review/no-one-is-talking-about-this-patricia-lockwood.html. Accessed 8 Feb. 2022.

Kisner, Jordan. "Extremely Online and Wildly Out of Control." Review of *No One Is Talking about This*, by Patricia Lockwood. *The Atlantic*, 13 Feb. 2021, www.theatlantic.com/magazine/archive/2021/03/patricia-lockwood-no-one-is-talking-about-this/617798/. Accessed 8 Feb. 2022.

McAlpin, Heller. "You Actually Will Be Talking about *No One Is Talking about This.*" *NPR*, 18 Feb. 2021, www.npr.org/2021/02/18/968718574/you-actually-will-be-talking-about-no-one-is-talking-about-this. Accessed 8 Feb. 2022.

O'Connell, Mark. "*No One Is Talking about This* by Patricia Lockwood Review – Life in the Twittersphere." *The Guardian*, 12 Feb. 2021, www.theguardian.com/books/2021/feb/12/no-one-is-talking-about-this-by-patricia-lockwood-review-life-in-the-twittersphere. Accessed 8 Feb. 2022.

Scherlis, Lily. Review of *No One Is Talking about This*, by Patricia Lockwood. *Harvard Review Online*, Harvard University, 1 Mar. 2021, harvardreview.org/book-review/no-one-is-talking-about-this/. Accessed 8 Feb. 2022.

Noor

Author: Nnedi Okorafor (b. 1974)
Publisher: DAW Books (New York).
 224 pp.
Type of work: Novel
Time: Near future
Locale: Nigeria

In Noor, *by Nnedi Okorafor, an Igbo auto mechanic with cybernetic limbs is on the run in near-future Nigeria after being attacked by a group of men. She flees with a Fulani herdsman who has been accused of terrorism and attempts to hide in a secret city located at the center of a sandstorm called the Red Eye.*

Principal characters
AO, born Anwuli Okwudili, an Igbo auto mechanic with cybernetic prosthetics
DANGOTE NUHU ADAMU, a.k.a. DNA, a Fulani herdsman accused of terrorism
BABA SOLA, a mystical soothsayer
ZAGORA, inventor of the Noor

Anwuli Okwudili, the hero of Nnedi Okorafor's 2021 novel *Noor*, prefers to be called AO—not for the initials of her birth name, but for "Autobionic Organism." Living in a near-future version of Nigeria, AO, who was born with numerous physical ailments, has undergone augmentations that make her half-human, half-machine. In addition to her synthetic organs, she has a shining, silver neural implant on her forehead, a robotic arm, and cybernetic prosthetic legs that never tire or experience heat, cold, or pain. Refreshingly, AO embraces her body and herself; it is other people who are the problem. When the book begins, AO's fiancé has just left her. Unsettled by her various nonhuman abilities, he departs with the cutting words that AO must hear again and again: "What kind of woman are you?" People like AO are persecuted, and sometimes hunted, in Okorafor's near-future Nigeria. As AO explains, "To replace an organ or two with cybernetic, 3D-printed, non-human parts was fine . . . But if you were one of those people who *seemed* to be '*more* machine than human' for whatever reason, one of those who 'refused to obey the laws of nature and die,' you were a demon." On a trip to the market to gather items for a comforting meal, AO is attacked by a group of men. They are no match for her, of course, but killing them, even in defense, means big trouble. Without stopping to consider where or how, she flees. In her escape, she encounters a Fulani herdsman named Dangote Nuhu Adamu, or DNA, who happens to be on the run himself.

Nnedi Okorafor (Courtesy Penguin Random House)

Okorafor, a prolific and award-winning science-fiction writer, was born to Nigerian immigrants and raised in Illinois and Nigeria. She has called Nigeria her "muse" and sets most of her stories there. Among her best-known works are her adult novel *Who Fears Death* (2010), which won the World Fantasy Award for Best Novel, and *Binti*, the title novella of the *Binti* trilogy, winner of the Hugo and Nebula Awards, the genre's most coveted accolades.

Okorafor refers to her aesthetic as "Africanfuturism," which she defines as a subgenre of science fiction, and "Africanjujuism," which she defined in a 2019 blog post as "a subcategory of fantasy that respectfully acknowledges the seamless blend of true existing African spiritualities and cosmologies with the imaginative." Okorafor has emphasized that her vision is distinct from the more familiar "Afrofuturism," a term scholar Mark Dery coined in 1994 to describe speculative fiction centered on African American themes and concerns. Okorafor's books are deeply rooted in African culture, history, and lore, and *Noor* is no exception as it explicitly engages with the history and culture of Nigeria; for example, making note of the profound differences between the north and south.

In *Noor*, AO flees the prosperous and marginally more progressive south for the north, a region unforgiving in its climate and its view of people like her. In Okorafor's fictional Nigeria, the country, ravaged by climate change, is exploited for its wind power. Powerful wind turbines, called Noors, harvest clean energy but have also produced an "enormous never-ending sandstorm" called the Red Eye, whose "dust will turn your eyes red within moments and kill you within minutes," Okorafor writes. The Red Eye occupies much of the northern desert. The Noors are operated by a megacorporation called Ultimate Corp, which has a stranglehold on nearly every aspect of Nigeria's economy. One can see echoes of the global superstore Amazon but also the Nigeria-based Dangote Group, one of the largest multinational conglomerates in Africa. Ultimate Corp is so ubiquitous; even its detractors cannot escape it. AO is critical of the company but notes that they designed and implanted all of her prosthetics. They are a powerful foe, operating countless surveillance drones throughout the country. To escape them, AO eventually ditches her car and continues her escape on foot. Okorafor creates a familiar, twenty-first century urgency when AO's attack is captured on film and goes viral. The footage, which shows a cybernetic woman killing five men, adds fuel to existing anti-cybernetic bigotry AO faces.

DNA has a similar problem, though he has no machine augmentations. Born to a nomadic community of Fulani herdsman, DNA wants nothing more than to continue to care for his cattle as his family has done for generations. But the Muslim Fulani people are similarly ostracized and misunderstood. A recent attack, purportedly committed by

Fulani herdsmen, has put all of Nigeria on edge. Television news anchors stoke fear, claiming, erroneously, that the attack is part of an ongoing war. "For decades, these herdsmen have terrorized peaceful farmers trying to live their lives," says one anchorwoman, whom Okorafor intriguingly describes as having braided eyebrows. DNA and his friends are accused of being terrorists and are subsequently attacked. After the attack, DNA and AO join forces and decide to make for the only place people like them might hide: a secret city of outcasts that is rumored to exist at the center of the raging Red Eye.

There is plenty of adventure in *Noor*, but a revelation about the extent of AO's machine capabilities brings together the various major strands of Okorafor's tale. In a genre where sequels and series are common, it is surprising and, frankly, disappointing, that *Noor* appears to be a stand-alone novel. Okorafor's world-building is unimpeachably good, but the climax and conclusion feel rushed with some threads—though not enough to suggest a follow-up—left dangling. Take the intriguing tale of Zagora. Early in the book, AO recites from memory a detailed story about the young woman who invented the Noor—who claimed inspiration from real-life activist Greta Thunberg—but Zagora never reenters the story in a way that satisfies.

The most intriguing aspect of *Noor* is AO, herself. After a car accident at fourteen, AO opts to obtain prosthetic legs. In the world of the novel, this is a dangerous and excruciating process in which one's nerves must slowly fuse with the new cybernetic limbs. Learning to walk again, a doctor concedes that they do not like to tell patients the essential truth of the procedure, "that in order to truly master usage [of one's limbs], you had to die another death by pain." Listening to a podcast about Zagora becomes AO's saving grace. The experience instills rage but also her fighting spirit. In AO's characteristically blunt voice, Okorafor writes, "I realized that there are times when you either save yourself or you don't." AO's experience shares similarities with Okorafor's own painful experience when, at nineteen, she underwent back surgery for scoliosis, and a rare complication left her paralyzed from the waist down. Okorafor has said that waking from surgery to discover this was the darkest moment of her life. Like AO, Okorafor found a life raft, not in a podcast, but in writing. Okorafor eventually learned to walk again but her speed and balance were never the same.

In a larger sense, *Noor* offers powerful critiques of inequity, colonialism, and capitalist exploitation. As Nigerians in the novel turn against one another, fighting over who the "real" Nigerians are, Ultimate Corp quietly assumes political and economic power. Gabrielle Sanchez, who reviewed *Noor* for the *AV Club*, noted that AO's body offers its own commentary, representing a necessary balance between nature and technology. Okorafor emphasizes the need to differentiate between good tech and bad, like the ever-present "pomegranate of eyes"—as AO describes them—of surveillance drones. As for the good tech, "the scale of life-giving technologies matches the richness offered by nature's bounties like plantains, water, and marijuana," Sanchez wrote. "All of this anchors a compelling reflection on man's principal role in climate disaster and the need to use technology to continue living in an altered world." *Noor* received starred reviews from both *Kirkus* and *Publishers Weekly*, with the latter calling it "a must-read." It also won enthusiastic reviews from the science-fiction publications *Tor* and *Locus*. While *Noor* is disappointingly brief, Gary K. Wolfe for *Locus* praised the novel's brevity, writing that it "may be Okorafor's most tightly plotted novel to date, but it still manages to explore in unsettling ways some of her most passionate themes, including sense of identity, the role of the outsider, cultural intolerance, horrific corporate malfeasance, and government indifference or complicity," he wrote. "It's such a fast-moving tale that the real punch doesn't quite hit you until it's over, but it's quite a punch."

Author Biography
Nnedi Okorafor is an award-winning Nigerian American novelist. Her young adult novel *Zahrah the Windseeker* (2005) won the Wole Soyinka Prize for Literature in Africa in 2008. Her 2015 novella, *Binti*, won a Hugo and a Nebula Award and became the title novella in her acclaimed *Binti* trilogy. Her first adult novel was *Who Fears Death* (2010).

Molly Hagan

Review Sources
Murad, Mahvesh. "A Familiar-Looking Future: *Noor* by Nnedi Okorafor." *Tor*, 16 Nov. 2021, www.tor.com/2021/11/16/book-reviews-noor-by-nnedi-okorafor/. Accessed 16 Jan. 2022.
Review of *Noor*, by Nnedi Okorafor. *Kirkus*, 29 Sept. 2021, www.kirkusreviews.com/book-reviews/nnedi-okorafor/noor/. Accessed 16 Jan. 2022.
Review of *Noor*, by Nnedi Okorafor. *Publishers Weekly*, 27 Aug. 2021, www.publishersweekly.com/978-0-7564-1609-6. Accessed 16 Jan. 2022.
Sanchez, Gabrielle. "It's Nature vs. Technology in Nnedi Okorafor's Fast-Paced Novel, *Noor*." *AV Club*, 15 Nov. 2021, www.avclub.com/it-s-nature-vs-technology-in-nnedi-okorafor-s-fast-pac-1848022178. Accessed 16 Jan. 2022.
Wolfe, Gary K. "Gary K. Wolfe Reviews *Noor* by Nnedi Okorafor." *Locus*, 27 Dec. 2021, locusmag.com/2021/12/gary-k-wolfe-reviews-noor-by-nnedi-okorafor/. Accessed 16 Jan. 2022.

Oh William!

Author: Elizabeth Strout (b. 1956)
Publisher: Random House (New York). 256 pp.
Type of work: Novel
Time: Present day
Locales: New York City; Maine

Oh William!, the third book in Elizabeth Strout's Lucy Barton series, explores successful writer Lucy Barton's relationship with her ex-husband William as they each navigate late middle age and come to terms with the lives they have lived.

Principal characters

LUCY BARTON, a successful writer now in her early sixties
WILLIAM GERHARDT, her ex-husband and father of the couple's two children
DAVID ABRAMSON, her recently deceased second husband
CHRISSIE, Lucy and William's elder daughter
BECKA, Lucy and William's younger daughter
CATHERINE COLE, William's mother, an important influence on William and Lucy
ESTELLE, William's current wife, a much younger woman in her forties
BRIDGET, Estelle and William's daughter

In 2016, Elizabeth Strout's novel *My Name is Lucy Barton* introduced the character Lucy Barton, a New York-based writer and mother who endured a childhood mired in abuse and poverty. Strout continued Lucy's story with the short-story collection *Anything is Possible* (2017), which turns its attention to the small town where Lucy was born and raised, examining many side characters who influenced Lucy's upbringing. *Oh William!* (2021) shifts its focus back to Lucy's adult life as a successful writer in her sixties living in New York City. She and her first husband, William Gerhardt, have divorced since their first appearance in *My Name is Lucy Barton*, their daughters are grown, and the family has found a new rhythm that includes William's third wife Estelle and the couple's child, Bridget. Set in the aftermath of the death of Lucy's second husband, David Abramson, and William's separation from Estelle, the novel centers on the relationship between Lucy and William, and examines how Lucy deals with loss, aging, and the trauma of her past.

Lucy's familiar voice guides the story to her present-day situation, with the anticipation of the story that follows. Told through a first-person narration that mingles a rather straightforward story with Lucy's thoughtful observations of herself and others,

Elizabeth Strout
Courtesy Penguin Random House

the novel succeeds as a satisfying new entry in the Lucy Barton series, but also stands on its own as a character-driven novel.

The novel's opening page quickly establishes the context of Lucy's present-day life and bridges the gap between *My Name is Lucy Barton* and *Oh William!*, revealing her divorce from William years earlier and the recent death of her second husband, David Abramson. Lucy also provides background on her life with William and who he is as a person. This careful move also allows Strout to address the passage of time between the first and third novels in a way that feels emotionally authentic rather than rushed. A meta element is introduced as well, fitting the novel's status as a kind of fictional memoir; as Lucy tells the reader, "Because I am a novelist, I have to write this almost like a novel, but it is true—as true as I can make it." The novel, told in fragments, next skips to a sympathetic description of William, who is now seventy-one years old. These carefully placed fragments throughout the book create a rich quilting effect, weaving backstory and character development into the story's action. For example, later in the book Lucy interjects memories of her now-deceased former mother-in-law Catherine Cole. These pairings lend an intimacy to Lucy's story, skipping through time and place as she works through her emotions and tries to understand new developments in her relationship with William.

While Strout gives plenty of space to Lucy's emotions and memories, she also manages to develop a gripping plot about a road trip Lucy and William take to Maine in order for him to investigate a family secret; this unexpected reunion between the two forms the narrative backbone of the novel. The pacing is well executed, as Strout takes her time moving Lucy through scenes such as a birthday party at William's that introduces the reader to his home life with his new wife Estelle and a lengthy scene with Lucy and her daughters at lunch while shopping. This depiction of slices of Lucy's everyday life fleshes her out as a three-dimensional character, and the effect is powerful. With a few short descriptions and a strong sense of place, Strout creates a rich world despite her often sparse prose These detailed moments in Lucy's current life also lend Lucy a helpful comparison when she contemplates the impoverished and traumatic childhood she left behind.

Strout's earlier Lucy Barton novels depict the extreme poverty and trauma Lucy overcame in her hometown, and *Oh William!* does an excellent job of bringing up that backstory for new readers without being repetitive for established fans. While she survived a childhood full of abuse and neglect, Lucy still carries the trauma of these experiences, and even as a successful, happy adult sometimes feels "invisible." She reveals this while retelling a story about being stuck in an airport in Washington, DC, during a snowstorm. She approaches a couple who are planning to head back to New York City via train, who are somewhat dismissive but allow her to accompany them. Later, when Lucy is giving a reading in the suburban Connecticut town where this couple lives, the wife shows up, overly friendly toward Lucy now that she realizes Lucy is famous. A moment like this skillfully pulls the reader into Lucy's psychology. While other people might see through the superficiality of an encounter such as that, Lucy's past results in her internalizing many small things and taking every moment personally. These insights into Lucy's psychology reveal that she is a survivor who often struggles and has to fight for her place in the world, but is also filled with joy. Throughout *Oh William!*, Lucy flashes back to more harrowing moments from her childhood, though she quickly moves on, seemingly not to inflict further pain on herself emotionally. By keeping these flashbacks brief, Strout is able to depict the impact of these past traumas on Lucy's present, without getting too bogged down in backstory.

Because of her background and her position as the story's narrator, Lucy is a wonderful medium for the voices of others; her work as a writer also makes her well-suited to this task. During remembered painful conversations with her mother, the reader understands their dynamic with only a few words, while Lucy's moments with own daughters reveals the intimacy that exists between the three of them as women and family. Her most impactful moments, however, might be those spent remembering Catherine, William's deceased mother. Lucy and William learn later in the novel that Catherine herself grew up poorer than Lucy, but always made a point of bringing up Lucy's background in order to shame her. The ambivalence that sprouts from this realization adds a new emotional depth to Lucy's memories of Catherine, as Lucy comes to recognize the parts of herself Catherine was likely fighting to keep secret as she created a new life in an upper middle class world.

Oh William! received overwhelmingly positive reception from critics, who in particular praised the power of Strout's prose, the characterization of the book's central figures, and the depth and complexity of feeling with which the author imbues the text as among the book's greatest strengths. Joan Frank, writing for the *Washington Post*, said that "so much intimate, fragile, desperate humanness infuses these pages, it's breathtaking." In her review for NPR, Heller McAlpin noted that "a memoir, fictional or otherwise, is only as interesting as its central character, and Lucy Barton could easily hold our attention through many more books." McAlpin felt that Strout demonstrated "impressive nuance and subtlety" in her depiction of William and Lucy's relationship, and was able to "pack" the relatively short novel with rich character development and complex emotions.

Critics were also impressed with the way that *O William!* continues the narrative told in *My Name is Lucy Barton* and *Anything is Possible* and how the new book interacts with its two predecessors. Jonathan Myerson, writing in the *Guardian*, compared the trilogy to a longform television series which, by "cumulative effect," becomes greater than the sum of its parts. He noted, "Elizabeth Strout seems to be generating a similarly holistic—and original—form of fiction writing," and praised how her work has a strong impact when taken all together. "Each new title," he wrote, "seems only to refine and distill the Pulitzer winner's already gorgeous skills."

Even critics who initially met some aspects of the novel with resistance soon found their objections overcome. For example, Jennifer Egan of the *New York Times* found Lucy Barton's inner voice to be fumbling, loose, and mannered, which she felt was surprising since the character is a successful writer. However, after considering the matter further, Egan realized that this intentional lack of inner fluency is in fact a savvy move on Strout's part. "The tension between Lucy's inner voice and her worldly identity turns out to be exactly what Strout wants the reader to track," Egan argued. Egan also spoke highly of *Oh William!*'s skillful exploration of relationships, particularly the "tiny offenses" that can cause marriages to deteriorate over time and the small joys that can prevent such resentment from taking root.

The success of *Oh William!* as the latest entry in the Lucy Barton series opens the possibility that Strout is finished with Lucy Barton's story. However, the text also leaves many possibilities to explore, with a notably open-ended finale. Regardless of Strout's next move, the trilogy she has published has already managed to paint a beautiful portrait of a woman who is constantly searching—and sometimes even finding—her place in the world.

Author Biography

Elizabeth Strout is the author of the Pulitzer Prize–winning novel *Olive Kitteridge* (2008). Her other books include her debut novel *Amy and Isabelle* (1998), which won the *Los Angeles Times* Art Seidenbaum Award and the *Chicago Tribune* Heartland Prize; *I Am Lucy Barton* (2016); *Anything is Possible* (2017); and *Olive, Again* (2019).

Melynda Fuller

Review Sources

Egan, Jennifer. "Elizabeth Strout Gets Meta in Her New Novel about Marriage." *The New York Times*, 18 Oct. 2021, www.nytimes.com/2021/10/18/books/review/oh-william-elizabeth-strout.html. Accessed 24 Jan. 2022.

Frank, Joan. "Elizabeth Strout's *Oh William!* Is Yet another Dazzler." *The Washington Post*, 11 Nov. 2021, www.washingtonpost.com/entertainment/books/elizabeth-strout-oh-william/2021/10/19/fff4396c-305b-11ec-93e2-dba2c2c11851_story.html. Accessed 24 Jan. 2022.

McAlpin, Heller. "Lucy Barton Returns - And Reconnects with an Old Love - In *Oh William!*" *NPR*, 19 Oct. 2021, www.npr.org/2021/10/19/1047132621/elizabeth-strout-oh-william-review. Accessed 24 Jan. 2022.

Myerson, Jonathan. "*Oh William!* by Elizabeth Strout Review – Lucy Barton's Return Brings Intense Pleasures." *The Guardian*, 24 Oct. 2021, www.theguardian.com/books/2021/oct/24/oh-william-by-elizabeth-strout-review-lucy-bartons-return-brings-intense-pleasures. Accessed 24 Jan. 2022.

Review of *Oh William!*, by Elizabeth Strout. *Kirkus*, 19 Oct. 2021, www.kirkusreviews.com/book-reviews/elizabeth-strout/oh-william/. Accessed 24 Jan. 2022.

On Juneteenth

Author: Annette Gordon-Reed (b. 1958)
Publisher: Liveright (New York). 152 pp.
Type of work: Essays
Time: Various points throughout history to the present day
Locale: Largely Texas

In On Juneteenth, *Pulitzer Prize–winning author and historian Annette Gordon-Reed examines the holiday known as Juneteenth, which commemorates the day of the official 1865 order that those who had been enslaved in Texas were now free. Gordon-Reed, whose family has lived in Texas for generations, considers Juneteenth in the specific context of a state typically considered synonymous with White men, dispelling popular myths about Texas and exploring its complex and diverse origins while adding her own experiences growing up in the twilight days of Jim Crow.*

Principal personages

ANNETTE GORDON-REED, the author, a Black historian who grew up in Texas during the mid- to late twentieth century
MAJ. GEN. GORDON GRANGER, Union general who brought the news of emancipation to those enslaved in Texas in 1865
STEPHEN F. AUSTIN, the "Father of Texas" who brought Anglo-Americans to Texas when it was still a Mexican province, for the purpose of establishing cotton plantations
ESTEBANICO, a North African man who traveled through Texas with the explorer Álvar Núñez Cabeza de Vaca in the 1500s
CYNTHIA ANN PARKER, an Anglo-American woman who was kidnapped and raised among the Comanches; her son was the famous Comanche Nation leader Quanah Parker

On June 19, 1865, approximately two months after the Confederacy surrendered at Appomattox, Virginia, and two years after the signing of the Emancipation Proclamation, Union soldiers led by Maj. Gen. Gordon Granger arrived in Galveston, Texas, bringing official news that those who were enslaved in the state were now free. Though nationwide prohibition of slavery would not come legislatively until the ratification of the Thirteenth Amendment in December of that year, the date of Granger's arrival—June 19, shortened to "Juneteenth"—came to recognize the end of chattel slavery in

Annette Gordon-Reed

the United States. It soon served as a popular holiday among descendants of the enslaved, particularly those in Texas. Commemorations by Americans of various races ultimately spread across the country over the ensuing years, and in 2021 Juneteenth was declared a federal holiday. In her book of essays *On Juneteenth*, Pulitzer Prize–winning Black historian and proud Texan Annette Gordon-Reed considers the holiday past and present. Along the way she delves into the broader history of Texas as well as her own family's Juneteenth celebrations, adding rich layers of both factual and personal detail.

Recalling indulging in red soda, eating barbeque, and setting off firecrackers, Gordon-Reed writes that she was "initially annoyed, at least mildly so," when she discovered that people outside of Texas also "claimed" the holiday. Juneteenth is a national cause for celebration, of course, but Gordon-Reed wondered if people elsewhere understood the special meaning of the holiday for Texans. "My twinge of possessiveness grew out of the habit of seeing my own state, and the people who reside there, as special," she writes. "The things that happened there couldn't have happened in other places. Non-Texans could never really understand." In these essays, Gordon-Reed does her best to provide this understanding, presenting the complex history of the state's origins in addition to its place in and impact on the country as a whole, all while interweaving recollections of her own experiences growing up in East Texas in the 1950s and 1960s. Through her authoritative factual accounts and personal narratives, she compellingly seeks to illuminate the significance of the holiday, and the nationwide persistence of racism, through an honest, nuanced Texan context.

Critics have noted that the memoir aspects of *On Juneteenth* are atypical but welcome for Gordon-Reed, though she also continues to demonstrate her excellent ability to provide a realistic, multifaceted discussion of a topic of historical significance. Gordon-Reed is best known for her scholarship on President Thomas Jefferson and his relationship with Sally Hemings, an African American woman whom he enslaved. She published her first book about Jefferson and Hemings, *Thomas Jefferson and Sally Hemings: An American Controversy*, in 1997. In it she argues that Jefferson and Hemings had children together, and that previous historians had intentionally ignored evidence of those children to protect Jefferson's reputation. The book was explosively controversial at the time; the fact that the relationship is now common knowledge is thanks, overwhelmingly, to Gordon-Reed. Her work represented an early battle in the contemporary conflict over who can claim authorship of the American story. Not only did Gordon-Reed's work offer a complicated and unflattering view of a largely beloved Founding Father, but it also emphasized that the history of Black and White Americans has always been deeply intertwined. Previous scholarship about early

American history rarely presented Black people beyond "the strict confines of the plantation," Gordon-Reed points out in *On Juneteenth*. The story of Jefferson and Hemings was seen as a vehicle for correcting the record, and her work on Juneteenth serves a similar purpose.

Throughout *On Juneteenth*, Gordon-Reed complicates dominant narratives about Texas, a place synonymous in the American imagination with cowboys that look like John Wayne and pioneers battling nameless American Indians on the lonely frontier. "Texas is a White man," she writes. She describes how even as a child she recognized this mythology, though it bore no relationship to her own experience. In a review of *On Juneteenth* for the *New York Times*, Jennifer Szalai observed this and noted, "This discrepancy—between abstractions on the one hand and lived experience on the other—is something that seems to have fueled Gordon-Reed's curiosity as a historian." Gordon-Reed grew up in a city called Conroe in East Texas, a region known for its thick pine forests. She recalls her surprise when, in college, a friend (from New England) asked her what it was like to live so close to the desert, assuming that the entire state resembles its western half. Texas is vast—"larger than Kenya, almost three times the size of the United Kingdom"—and exceptionally diverse. Gordon-Reed is especially attentive to racial and ethnic diversity throughout the region's history, for example highlighting the earliest Indigenous inhabitants and discussing a man named Estebanico, probably one of the first Africans in the area, who traveled through Texas with the explorer Álvar Núñez Cabeza de Vaca in the 1500s. Historian Daina Ramey Berry, who reviewed *On Juneteenth* for the *Washington Post*, especially appreciated Gordon-Reed's mention of Estebanico, noting that his appearance in the historical record "forces us to reconsider Black history" in America.

Texas became a Mexican province, and, later, an independent state. This lineage is often presented as an expression of Texas's inherent independence and devotion to protecting states' rights against federal overreach. Gordon-Reed, however, stresses that it had more to do with chattel slavery. In support of this observation, she provides the specific historical context around Anglo-American development of Texas and the lead-up to the separation from Mexico. When Stephen F. Austin, the man popularly known as the "Father of Texas," arrived in what is present-day Texas but was then a Mexican province, he did so with the clear intention of establishing cotton plantations, like those across the American South, on the fertile soil near the Gulf coast. By 1829 Mexico had decreed slavery illegal, and despite some exemptions granted to Texas, early White settlers successfully rebelled in 1836 to form a republic where they could continue enslaving human beings, which they viewed as necessary to their development of the land.

As she intriguingly details, Gordon-Reed's roots in East Texas run deep. Her mother's family arrived in the region in the 1820s, and her father's family as far back as the 1860s. Juneteenth, she writes, was not distant history for her family. "For my great-grandmother, my grandparents, and relatives in their generation, this was the celebration of the freedom of people they had actually known," she writes. But these celebrations were also tempered by Jim Crow and White terrorism. Gordon-Reed writes about a local Black man named Bob White, who was accused of raping a White woman in 1936. White was repeatedly and brutally beaten and forced to confess to the crime. Following his conviction, he made appeals that reached the US Supreme Court, which ruled that the beatings White suffered violated his right to due process under the Fourteenth Amendment. White's case went back to court in Conroe in 1941. During the retrial, the husband of the woman who had accused White walked to the front of the courtroom and shot White in the head, killing him. The husband turned himself in, but after a swift trial he was acquitted. This story offers an affectingly stark illustration of what "justice under the law" looked like for Black people in Conroe, and the racial legacy of slavery in Texas as a whole.

Gordon-Reed was born in 1958, and at six years old she unwittingly became the vanguard of a new era in Conroe, being the first Black student to attend the town's White elementary school. Her family received death threats, but Gordon-Reed only came to know of them later. She parses her experience with the same rigor she applies to other histories. Because she is respectfully wary of making definitive statements about the past, even when it comes to herself, her writing can seem meandering at times, however. As Gordon-Reed got older, court rulings forced the full integration of Conroe's schools, and she contemplates the myriad effects on the Black community. She notes that integration, while indisputably a good thing overall, deprived Black students of the Black teachers, like her mother, who had known them and been so deeply invested in their success. "The children were to be integrated, not the teaching staff," she recalls. "Putting Black teachers at the head of classrooms of mainly White students was never the school district's priority."

Attending a predominantly White school certainly influenced Gordon-Reed's first understanding of Texas history. Slavery, particularly its importance in the development of Texas, she writes, was hardly mentioned, while events like the standoff at the Alamo were given undue attention. She also cites the popular story of Cynthia Ann Parker, a White woman who was kidnapped by Comanche warriors when she was a child and grew to become a respected member of the tribe. Her son, Quanah Parker, became an influential Comanche Nation leader. Gordon-Reed interrogates the sensational tale from all angles and resists the urge to draw a single conclusion from it. "It seemed to me that so many wrong things were packed into this one narrative," she writes. Such myths about Texas, Gordon-Reed argues, obscure more than they reveal. People often ask her how she can love Texas based on her knowledge of past and contemporary occurrences as well as culture. Her history is Texas history, she tells them, and she acknowledges the importance of taking a critical stance regardless of affection. "We can't be of real service to the hopes we have for places—and people, ourselves included—without a clear-eyed assessment of their (and our) strengths and weaknesses," she writes.

On Juneteenth was largely well-received by critics, many of whom noted its timely and refreshingly open-minded approach. Szalai praised Gordon-Reed for being exemplary by "revisiting her own experiences, questioning her own assumptions—and showing that historical understanding is a process, not an end point." Summarizing the overall merits of the book in a starred review for *BookPage*, Deborah Mason wrote that the author's essays "seamlessly merge history and memoir into a complex portrait of her beloved, turbulent Texas, revealing new truths about a state that, more than any other, embodies all the virtues and faults of America."

Author Biography
Annette Gordon-Reed, an award-winning author and historian, is the Carl M. Loeb University Professor at Harvard University. Her works include *The Hemingses of Monticello: An American Family* (2008), which won both the National Book Award for Nonfiction and the Pulitzer Prize in History. In 2010 President Barack Obama awarded her a National Humanities Medal.

Molly Hagan

Review Sources
Brands, H. W. "Annette Gordon-Reed's Surprising Recollections of Texas." Review of *On Juneteenth*, by Annette Gordon-Reed. *The New York Times*, 7 May 2021, www.nytimes.com/2021/05/07/books/review/on-juneteenth-annette-gordon-reed.html. Accessed 28 Jan. 2022.

Mason, Deborah. Review of *On Juneteenth*, by Annette Gordon-Reed. *BookPage*, May 2021, www.bookpage.com/reviews/26211-annette-gordon-reed-juneteenth-history/. Accessed 17 Feb. 2022.

Review of *On Juneteenth*, by Annette Gordon-Reed. *Kirkus*, 24 Feb. 2021, www.kirkusreviews.com/book-reviews/annette-gordon-reed/on-juneteenth/. Accessed 28 Jan. 2022.

Review of *On Juneteenth*, by Annette Gordon-Reed. *Publishers Weekly*, 12 Feb. 2021, www.publishersweekly.com/978-1-63149-883-1. Accessed 28 Jan. 2022.

Ramey Berry, Daina. "Annette Gordon-Reed's *On Juneteenth* Complicates Notions of Black History." *The Washington Post*, 14 May 2021, www.washingtonpost.com/outlook/annette-gordon-reeds-on-juneteenth-complicates-notions-of-black-history/2021/05/13/f153ff16-a6b6-11eb-bca5-048b2759a489_story.html. Accessed 28 Jan. 2022.

Szalai, Jennifer. "The Historian Annette Gordon-Reed Gets Personal in *On Juneteenth*." *The New York Times*, 21 Apr. 2021, www.nytimes.com/2021/04/21/books/review-on-juneteenth-annette-gordon-reed.html. Accessed 28 Jan. 2022.

Once There Were Wolves

Author: Charlotte McConaghy
  (b. ca. 1989)
Publisher: Flatiron Books (New York).
  272 pp.
Type of work: Novel
Time: Present day
Locale: Scotland

Once There Were Wolves follows biologist Inti Flynn as she leads a team of scientists reintroducing wolves to the wilds of Scotland. As the wolves begin to flourish in their new environment, Inti struggles to overcome her own personal demons.

Principal characters
INTI FLYNN, an Australian biologist and the team's lead scientist
AGGIE FLYNN, her traumatized twin sister
DUNCAN MACTAVISH, the local police chief and Inti's romantic interest
GUS HOLLOWAY, Aggie's husband, a doctor
STUART BURNS, a sheep farmer and domestic abuser
RED MCRAE, a local farmer opposed to the wolves

Writer Charlotte McConaghy found significant acclaim with her mainstream debut novel, *Migrations* (2020). That book tells the story of a flawed woman who travels to the North Pole in an effort to study Arctic terns, a species of birds that migrate between the poles. McConaghy builds on that success with *Once There Were Wolves* (2021), another novel about a woman haunted by her past who tries to avoid emotional entanglements while working with animals that could soon be on the endangered species list.

Like its predecessor, *Once There Were Wolves* falls firmly in the growing genre of ecofiction, a subgenre of fiction focused on nature and environmental issues. The genre rose in prominence during the 1970s as people became more concerned about environmental pollution and grew in the first decades of the 2000s as awareness of climate change became more prevalent. Authors such as Kim Stanley Robinson and Carl Hiaasen achieved notable success writing ecofiction or incorporating elements of the genre into their work. McConaghy's first two novels carry on this tradition.

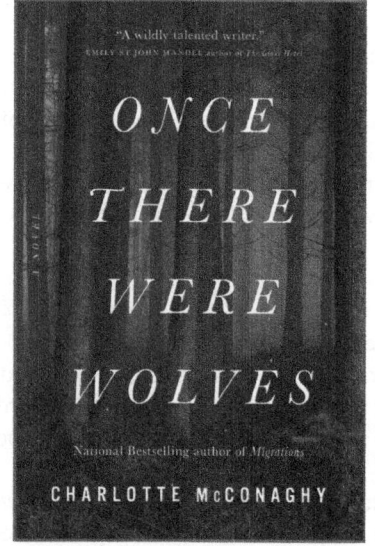

In *Once There Were Wolves*, main character Inti Flynn's life's work has centered on studying wolves. At the beginning of the novel, Inti and her team of biologists arrive in the Scottish Highlands to reintroduce wolves to the area, an effort known as the Cairngorms Wolf Project. Accompanying Inti is her sister Aggie, who is nearly catatonic due to a traumatic experience and requires constant care. As Inti's team strives to revitalize the land by bringing back a predatory species as part of a strategy to combat climate change, they also work to convince the local townspeople of the necessity of this mission. Evan, one of Inti's colleagues, explains the importance of apex predators, pointing out the positive "ripple down" effect they have on an area's food chain and ecosystem, leading to greater biodiversity, animal and plant populations, and more captured carbon emissions.

Of course, there is opposition to the Cairngorms Wolf Project. One local farmer, Red McRae, finds the reintroduction of wolves unacceptable, fearing it could "destroy the Highlander way of life." This fear, along with concerns that the wolves could kill people or the farmers' animals, leads to conflict between the locals and the scientists. Inti tries to teach Red and the other locals about the wolves in an effort to change their attitudes, but the situation worsens when a local sheep farmer, Stuart Burns, turns up dead, with slash marks all over his body. This leads to rampant speculation as to who, or what, could have killed him. Amid this atmosphere of distrust and violence, Inti tries to find a balance between her ongoing scientific work and a budding romance with Duncan MacTavish, the local police chief—who may have been involved in Burns's death.

Charlotte McConaghy

The novel uses Inti's work with wolves to examine the parallels between animals and humans. Though the wolf reintroduction project requires objectivity, Inti and her partners become emotionally attached to the animals. Inti's attachment grows so deep, she must close her eyes whenever she shoots the wolves with tranquilizer darts. Her scientific objectivity is further tested when Red kills the male of a mated pair, leaving the female pregnant and alone. Since wolves mate for life and require a pack to help care for their young, Inti begins to watch this female more closely. As she studies the wolf, she is further struck by the similarities between humans and wolves.

However, these parallels between humans and wolves go beyond family structure and caring for the young. The world of *Once There Were Wolves* is saturated with violence on many levels, and McConaghy suggests that humans are the most dangerous predators of all. Some of the novel's most visible "human predators" can be found in the townspeople who hunt the wolves, fearing that the wolves will slaughter their sheep, cattle, or children. While Inti criticizes their fear of wolves and claims that humans are the real "monsters," the locals' very real concerns about the safety of their children and farm animals demonstrates how fear and a desire to protect loved ones can inspire acts of terrible violence. The idea of human predators is also at the center of the mystery of Stuart's death, as his wounds look like slashes from a wolf but could be from a human killer. As controversy swirls in the town as to who could have been capable of such violence and many people begin to blame the wolves, Inti worries that Duncan may have been capable of committing the crime. In turn, Duncan wonders if Inti could be somehow involved. This uncertainty helps generate a sense of paranoia and deepen the novel's tension as it speeds with thriller-like efficiency towards its conclusion.

McConaghy also examines the theme of humans as predators through the lens of domestic abuse. This connection begins with Inti's flashbacks to childhood in her mother's study, which she calls "a place of bruises and blood and death," due to her mother's work as a police officer specializing in domestic violence cases. Her mother warns Inti that "people harm each other," and tries to teach her daughter that people are mostly "irredeemable." When Inti learns that her mother grew up in an abusive home, the intergenerational trauma of domestic violence becomes clearer. Domestic violence has touched the lives of other characters as well. Aggie's traumatized state stems from her abusive marriage, and Duncan is also a domestic violence survivor. The backstory of Stuart, who before his violent death was abusive towards his wife, brings domestic violence into the story's present-day narrative, and forces the characters to confront earlier traumas.

Amid this atmosphere of fear and violence, Inti's protective nature shines through. She feels deep empathy toward both the wolves and other people, in part due a neurological condition known as mirror-touch synesthesia, a real condition that causes Inti's brain to "recreate the sensory experiences of living creatures, of all people" if she can see them. It is the reason that, when Inti was a child, her mother felt the need to "toughen" Inti's spirit as a buffer against the intense feelings she has for others. While Inti admits that her mother's lessons made her feel "embarrassed" about her ability and become less forgiving than she was as a child, she retains her ability to form these deep, empathic bonds with both humans and animals.

Inti's protective instincts are particularly strong towards her sister Aggie, for whom Inti acts as something of a caretaker. While Aggie is Inti's twin, they have very different personalities. When they were young, Aggie was a reckless partier who looked out for her sister, whereas Inti was quiet and studious. However, by the start of the novel, the sisters' personalities and roles have switched; Inti is now angry and headstrong, but Aggie, traumatized by her abusive marriage, is a shell of her former self. For most of the novel, she rarely speaks and is entirely dependent on Inti, placing added pressure on Inti as she attempts to carry out her wolf rewilding mission.

This desire to protect others steers many of Inti's decisions, but also hinders her ability to protect herself. The strength of Inti's emotional connection to the wolves, bolstered by the effects of her synesthesia, leads her to take reckless action to protect them from the townspeople. Additionally, her relationship with Duncan, already emotionally fraught due to the past traumas both have suffered and their current involvement with Stuart's death, enters even more difficult territory as Inti allows him deeper into her life. The way Inti's empathy for the wolves and other people propels her toward dangerous and sometimes self-destructive behavior provides much of the novel's emotional weight.

Upon the novel's publication in August 2021, it became an instant commercial and critical success. In her review for the *Los Angeles Times*, Lorraine Berry called the book "stunning," and praised McConaghy's ability to tackle big questions about climate change and how humans ought to address it. Berry argued that the novel could "engender empathy and, subsequently, action" in people who are concerned about climate change but feel helpless to stop it. Berry also commented on the complexity of Inti as a character and felt that McConaghy was able to adequately examine trauma, hatred, and other complex emotions. Writing for the *Washington Review of Books*, Chris Rutledge also praised *Once There Were Wolves*, calling it a "thoughtful and enjoyable" story that revealed its complex, multilayered plot through a "deliberate unfolding of mysteries." Rutledge felt the book's environmental themes were its strongest element, in particular "Inti's sensual connection to nature." Despite McConaghy's examination of the dark side of humanity, Rutledge felt that the book's message was ultimately a hopeful one, that "invites us to consider the role trust plays in our lives . . . and [accept] help from unlikely places."

However, other reviews were more mixed. Harriet Lane of the *New York Times* considered a few aspects of the plot to be unrealistic, including the novel's "strange and unconvincing" Scottish setting. Lane also took issue with aspects of the plot, including Duncan leading the investigation of Stuart's death despite being a suspect himself, and felt that much of the novel's story and character building served only as a "vehicle for environmental messaging." Despite these issues, Lane described the novel as "heartfelt and earnest," if not entirely satisfying.

Overall, *Once There Were Wolves* captures attention through its combination of complex characters, a twisting plot, and strong messages about climate change and other issues in today's world. McConaghy keeps tension strong by intertwining Inti's memories of her childhood and professional years with her emotionally fraught present to offer insight into multiple aspects of her life. Readers interested in climate change, animal protection, and the ability of humans to prevail in the hardest of circumstances will likely find themselves entranced by this novel.

Author Biography

Charlotte McConaghy is an Australian author with degrees in screenwriting and screen arts who began her career with many published works of science fiction and fantasy. Her 2020 novel *Migrations* was her adult literary fiction debut and became an international best seller.

Theresa L. Stowell, PhD

Review Sources

Berry, Lorraine. "As Species Vanish, a New Novel Asks: Can 'Re-Wilding' Help Civilize Humans?" Review of *Once There Were Wolves*, by Charlotte McConaghy. *The Los Angeles Times*, 6 Aug. 2021, www.latimes.com/entertainment-arts/books/story/2021-08-06/as-species-vanish-a-new-novel-asks-can-re-wilding-help-civilize-humans. Accessed 16 Dec. 2021.

Brady, Amy. Review of *Once There Were Wolves*, by Charlotte McConaghy. *Scientific American*, vol. 325, no. 2, Aug. 2021, p. 80. *EBSCOhost*, search.ebscohost.com/login.aspx?direct=true&db=buh&AN=151340485. Accessed 30 Nov. 2021.

Lane, Harriet. "Hungry Beasts: Human and Animal Predators in the Scottish Highlands." Review of *Once There Were Wolves*, by Charlotte McConaghy. *The New York Times*, 3 Aug. 2021, www.nytimes.com/2021/08/03/books/review/once-there-were-wolves-charlotte-mcconaghy.html. Accessed 30 Nov. 2021.

Review of *Once There Were Wolves*, by Charlotte McConaghy. *Kirkus*, 19 May 2021, www.kirkusreviews.com/book-reviews/charlotte-mcconaghy/once-there-were-wolves/. Accessed 30 Nov. 2021.

Review of *Once There Were Wolves*, by Charlotte McConaghy. *Publishers Weekly*, 9 June 2021, www.publishersweekly.com/9781250244147. Accessed 30 Nov. 2021.

Seaman, Donna. Review of *Once There Were Wolves*, by Charlotte McConaghy. *Booklist*, July 2021, www.booklistonline.com/Once-There-Were-Wolves-/pid=9747772. Accessed 30 Nov. 2021.

The Other Black Girl

Author: Zakiya Dalila Harris
Publisher: Atria Books (New York).
 368 pp.
Type of work: Novel
Time: 1983–2018
Locale: New York, New York

The Other Black Girl tells the story of Nella Rogers, a young African American woman working in the predominantly White publishing business. When another African American woman joins the staff, Nella is thrilled. However, when strange threats start appearing on her desk, Nella begins to question her job, her friends, and herself.

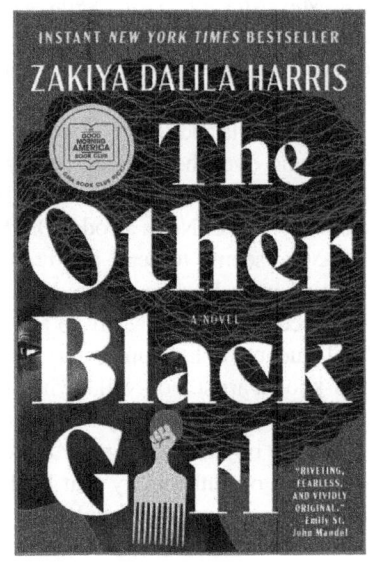

Principal characters

NELLA ROGERS, an assistant editor at Wagner Books, one of the firm's few Black employees
HAZEL-MAY MCCALL, a new employee at Wagner, the "other Black girl"
DIANA GORDON, bestselling author who got her start at Wagner
KENDRA RAE PHILLIPS, Diana Gordon's editor and Nella's role model
RICHARD WAGNER, Nella's boss, the editor-in-chief at Wagner Books
SHANI, a waitress and former reporter forced out of the publishing industry

In her debut novel, *The Other Black Girl* (2021), Zakiya Dalila Harris explores the complications of surviving as an African American in the predominantly White New York City publishing world. Though the novel focuses mainly on Nella Rogers, a young Black editorial assistant, Harris varies the point of view throughout by formatting the story with a prologue followed by four parts divided into chapters. Part I focuses primarily on Nella Rogers; however, Parts II, III and IV include chapters focused on three supporting characters: Kendra Rae Phillips, Shani, and Diana Gordon.

The main storyline follows Nella Rogers, an editorial assistant for Wagner Books, a New York City publishing house. In the early 1980s, Wagner became famous for printing a landmark book written and edited by two African American women, author Diana Gordon and editor Kendra Rae Phillips. This work was the basis of Nella's college research and became an inspiration to her, even though Kendra disappeared shortly after the book was published. Nella is initially excited to work for the same publisher as these groundbreaking women, and she has plans to further promote racial justice in both their books and their company. As Wagner's only Black employee in a white-collar position, Nella aims to increase the number of minority employees in the professional departments where she works as an editorial assistant. She is thrilled when Wagner finally hires another "Black girl," Hazel-May McCall. Now, Nella feels she has someone who will understand the challenges she faces and can help her survive as a fellow outsider.

Though Nella and Hazel-May become friendly and bond over their shared interests, experiences, and hair care routines, something about Hazel-May strikes Nella as odd. On the surface, Hazel-May seems to lead an interesting life. She grew up in Harlem, created and promoted a well-recognized writing group for Black high school students in her community, and is dating a well-known artist. For Nella, who grew up in a primarily White community in Connecticut and has a White boyfriend, Hazel-May represents a certain type of authenticity that Nella feels she herself lacks. However, Hazel-May also seems too friendly, too ambitious, and too willing to compromise her values, leading Nella to question her new colleague's motives and feelings.

Zakiya Dalila Harris

Courtesy Nicole Mondestin

Nella's hesitation over Hazel devolves into a deeper distrust as she watches her ingratiate herself with their White coworkers. A particularly disturbing turn in their relationship occurs after Hazel-May undermines Nella to her boss and other colleagues after Nella shares an honest appraisal of an author's racist portrayal of an African American character. When Nella starts getting threatening notes telling her to leave Wagner, she wonders if Hazel-May could be behind them.

As the turmoil in Nella's professional life escalates, there are hints of a different source of these notes, an even larger threat that has been lurking in the background for decades and possibly began at Wagner. In chapters that stand apart from Nella's storyline, set in both the 1980s and the present day, Harris provides deeper insight into the lives of Nella's literary role models, editor Kendra Rae Phillips and author Diana Gordon, during their innovative work advancing African American women's literature in the 1980s. Harris also tells the present-day story of a young woman named Shani, a waitress and former reporter. When the story opens, Kendra is preparing to flee New York after calling out racism in the publishing industry; she is also suffering from a mysterious burning and itching in her scalp. Kendra's former colleague and childhood friend, bestselling author Diana Gordon, falls out with Kendra over the latter's activism, and chooses to preserve her good relationship with Wagner Books and the rest of the publishing industry. Shani is a former reporter who wrote about African American issues until she was chased out of her position by another Black woman, and now works as a waitress in New York City. The backstories of Kendra, Diana, and Shani initially seem disparate, but eventually tie into the conflict between Nella and Hazel-May, propelling it towards a conclusion with implications that reach far beyond the Wagner office.

The novel touches on many contemporary issues affecting African Americans. Nella's activism inside and outside of her workplace helps provides her with a sense of a larger purpose; for example, she is involved in protests over the killing of a Black man by police. However, this activist stance also lands her in hot water at work; her White colleagues are not particularly sensitive to racial justice issues, and Hazel-May endears herself to Wagner's mostly White workforce by also being dismissive of Nella's feelings and opinions.

The novel's focus on the hair of its Black characters is also a major theme. This is first introduced in the prologue; as Kendra feels a burning in her scalp, she thinks back to her teenage years, and remembers her and her friends doing each other's hair. Nella's initial realization that another African American girl has been hired at Wagner is based on the scent of Hazel-May's hair product, as well as Hazel-May's connection to a popular Harlem salon. While this examination of the role of hair in African American culture may be educational for some readers and adds a strong sense of cultural authenticity, it also serves as a narrative device, through the inclusion of a mysterious hair product that ties into the workplace struggles of both Kendra and Nella.

The publishing world, which Harris herself had been a part of, is central to the story. The lack of publication of books by Black authors is addressed, alongside the lack of people of color in professional positions within the publishing industry. Nella's attempt to publish a Black author's work lands on deaf ears; she is told by a White colleague, "From a financial standpoint, this book just doesn't seem worth the gamble. I just didn't connect with the characters." After hearing these kinds of rejections many times, Nella stops fighting to get these books published, and "slowly but surely, in the hopes of making the ride a bit smoother—in the hopes of getting a promotion . . . accepted every excuse." Nella's acceptance of this demonstrates the reality that many employees of color are forced to give up some of their personal values and identities to advance their careers.

This connects to the most significant issue Harris brings up with the novel: the question whether to preserve or sacrifice racial identity. This conflict is first demonstrated in the relationship between Kendra and Diana. Kendra recognizes that her professional experience is different than Diana's, even though they grew up in the same neighborhood and had been friends. Ironically, Diana's education and subsequent teaching career at Howard University, a historically Black university, had given her "the blessed gift of tunnel vision. She'd been blessed with the ability to forget White people existed, if only for a little while." However, Kendra's experience attending a predominantly White university led to her feeling "smothered by them." As a result, Diana had been allowed to live more freely and experience true acceptance, whereas Kendra never had the opportunity to work in an environment that was so supporting of Black people and learned that acceptance could not be assumed. Nella, who like Kendra was forced to learn how to navigate living and working in a mostly White world, begins the novel with this awareness, and retains it as the realities of her workplace remind her of it again and again.

Throughout the novel, Harris weaves in many references to African American literature. The most obvious allusion is the main character's name, Nella. It is no coincidence that Harris examines the issues of assimilating into White society with a main character named after Nella Larsen, the Harlem Renaissance author of *Passing* (1929), the story of a young Black woman who pretends to be White to live a better life. As with the protagonist of *Passing*, Nella feels she must hide aspects of her identity to survive and thrive as an outsider in a world not always welcoming to Black people. Harris mentions other African American literary icons, including Toni Morrison, whose experience as a Black woman in the publishing industry provides some solace to Nella as she tries to justify to herself that the microaggressions she has experienced at work do not mean as much as she imagines they do.

The Other Black Girl debuted to positive reviews upon its publication in 2021. In a review for National Public Radio, Bethanne Patrick praised Harris for taking what could have been a standard "office novel" and injecting it with enough thrills, horror, and cultural commentary to create a work of "sad and wholly earned brilliance." She also complimented the novel's thoughtful examination of the tradeoff between "success" and "authenticity" that many Black women are forced to make in their professional lives.

However, while most reviewers enjoyed the book, some felt the narrative lacked cohesion. Regina Porter of the *Guardian* praised the novel's scope, humor, and satire of office life and cultural issues, but felt it came across as "two novels woven together as one." She also argued that it failed to give enough depth to some of its supporting characters. Naomi Jackson of the *Washington Post* echoed these complaints with the narrative, calling the shifts between the past and present "awkward" and a major plot point "underdeveloped." Yet even with these critiques in mind, Jackson praised the novel's examination of the publishing industry's "long legacy of anti-Blackness," and considered it a worthy addition to "an exciting wave of recent fiction by Black millennial writers."

Author Biography
Zakiya Dalila Harris is a former editorial assistant. *The Other Black Girl* is her debut novel.

Theresa L. Stowell, PhD

Review Sources
DeZelar-Tiedman, Christine. Review of *The Other Black Girl*, by Zakiya Dalila Harris. *Library Journal*, vol. 146, no. 6, June 2021, pp. 102–104. EBSCOhost, search.ebscohost.com/login.aspx?direct=true&db=buh&AN=150506478. Accessed 3 Nov. 2021.

Gill, Stacey. Review of *The Other Black Girl*, by Zakiya Dalila Harris. *Publishers Weekly*, vol. 268, no. 16, Apr. 2021, p. 26. EBSCOhost, search.ebscohost.com/login.aspx?direct=true&db=lfh&AN=149873667. Accessed 3 Nov. 2021.

Hashimoto, Sarah. Review of *The Other Black Girl*, by Zakiya Dalila Harris. *Library Journal*, vol. 146, no. 9, Sept. 2021, p. 39. EBSCOhost, search.ebscohost.com/login.aspx?direct=true&db=ehh&AN=151944148. Accessed 3 Nov. 2021.

Jackson, Naomi. "'The Other Black Girl' Should be at the Top of Your Summer Reading List." Review of *The Other Black Girl*, by Zakiya Dalila Harris. *The Washington Post*, 9 June 2021, www.washingtonpost.com/entertainment/books/other-black-girl-zakiya-dalila-harris-book-review/2021/06/09/bb7919f0-c923-11eb-a11b-6c6191ccd599_story.html. Accessed 21 Dec. 2021.

Review of *The Other Black Girl*, by Zakiya Dalila Harris. *New York Times Book Review*, July 2021, p. 19. EBSCOhost, search.ebscohost.com/login.aspx?direct=true&db=f5h&AN=151580380. Accessed 3 Nov. 2021.

Review of *The Other Black Girl*, by Zakiya Dalila Harris. *New Yorker*, vol. 97, no. 21, July 2021, p. 71. EBSCOhost, search.ebscohost.com/login.aspx?direct=true&db=lfh&AN=151444054. Accessed 3 Nov. 2021.

Review of *The Other Black Girl*, by Zakiya Dalila Harris. *Publishers Weekly*, vol. 268, no. 10, Mar. 2021, p. 29. EBSCOhost, search.ebscohost.com/login.aspx?direct=true&db=lfh&AN=149140911. Accessed 3 Nov. 2021.

Porter, Regina. "'The Other Black Girl' by Zakiya Dalila Harris Review: An Audacious Debut." *The Guardian*, 16 June 2021, www.theguardian.com/books/2021/jun/16/the-other-black-girl-by-zakiya-dalila-harris-review-an-audacious-debut. Accessed 21 Dec. 2021.

The (Other) You

Author: Joyce Carol Oates (b. 1938)
Publisher: Ecco (New York). 304 pp.
Type of work: Short fiction
Time: Present day
Locales: Yewville, New York; Hazelton-on-Hudson, New York; Mairead, Italy

The (Other) You is a collection of short stories that follow characters who are challenged by the idea of a life that is full of regrets, that is not what appears to be, or that could have been completely different.

Joyce Carol Oates published her first short story collection, *By the North Gate*, in 1963, and *The (Other) You* (2021) is her forty-third collection. This collection is broken into two parts. The first section contains eight stories, and the second section contains seven; the stories range from three to forty-three pages in length. Most of the stories focuses on the idea of what might have changed in a person's life if a different choices had been made, either by the characters themselves or by someone else; like many of Oates's earlier stories, this collection depicts a bleak, gloomy world with plenty of violence and few happy endings.

Oates develops this encompassing theme through the treatment of smaller themes and connections that recur across the collection's different stories, framed by the use of recurring locations. For example, Yewville, New York, is a small town where the unnamed character of the first story, "The (Other) You," runs a bookstore in her later years. It also appears in the final story, "The Unexpected," as the hometown of a famous writer who returns to visit over three decades after she left. This setting is not new for Oates, as it has appeared in many of her earlier works, including the novel *Wonderland* (1971), the short story collection *Heat and Other Stories* (1991), and her short story "Bad Girls," from the young adult collection *Small Avalanches and Other Stories* (2003). A second location that will be familiar to Oates' fans is Hazelton-on-Hudson, New York, a town featured in "Sinners in the Hands of an Angry God" as well as other earlier publications, including the novel *American Appetites* (1989). Another location Oates repeats in this collection is a restaurant called the Purple Onion Café; it appears in "The Women Friends," "Waiting for Kizer," and "Final Interview." This restaurant was the setting of a terrorist attack that may or may not have happened, and Oates explores this event, and the uncertainty surrounding it, in all three stories.

One of the secondary themes Oates includes is the loss of mental acuity due to age. This is first introduced in "The Women Friends," the second story in the collection. In

Joyce Carol Oates

this story, two lifelong friends plan a lunch date at the Purple Onion Café. While Francine waits for Sylvie, she dwells on a surgery she has recently undergone; unfortunately, one of the side effects of the surgery is "a curious mild dislocation regarding time" that confuses her about her friend's late arrival. Though Sylvie eventually arrives, readers are left to wonder if Francine's interaction with her old friend is real or an illusion. There are two main hints that something is not quite right with this supposed reality; the café had been the site of a suicide bombing that killed three people the previous year, and Francine's own fear regarding Sylvie's behavior raises the possibility that Francine's perception of this event is inaccurate. As Francine ponders how her close friend Sylvie could abandon her, she thinks of a possible explanation: "Because you are not alive." True to Oates's style, she leaves the question unanswered, and the true nature of the story's reality uncertain.

Later in the first section, the story "Blue Guide" follows a retired professor and his wife as they travel to Italy to revisit the town where he did his graduate work. While he remembers it fondly, glorifying its place and people, the reality of thirty years has ravaged all of his favorite places. As he tries to navigate the town using the Blue Guide, a tourist book that provides maps and descriptions, he is befuddled by the changes; his wife is frightened by his confusion. The professor's secret desire to see a young woman he had developed an obsession with while he was a student leads him and his wife on a rambling journey around the city that his wife cannot understand. The stories "Where Are You?" and "Assassin" also include stories with characters experiencing mental confusion.

Most of the stories also deal with trauma and loss in some way. "Sinners in the Hands of an Angry God" tells the story of Luce and Andrew, an aging couple whose home in Hazelton-on-Hudson survived a wildfire that had destroyed most of their neighborhood. Luce's survivor's guilt over this, combined with the fact that she and her husband have outlived many of their friends, leads Andrew to accuse her of "catastrophizing." In "Hospice/Honeymoon," a wife hopes to rekindle her marriage as her husband lies dying, waiting to enter hospice. In "The Crack," one of the few stories to feature younger characters, a ten-year-old girl arrives home from school, hoping for solace from her mother after injuring her ankle, only to find a wake taking place in her apartment. She hears her parents judging their daughter rather than grieving. In "Nightgrief," parents of a teen who had committed suicide try to survive in the home where he died. This connection to death recurs throughout the collection. In addition to the stories mentioned above, the three pieces set in the Purple Onion Café all reference the suicide bombing that killed a socially isolated teen and his three victims, and in "The (Other) You" and "Subaqueous," women deal with the loss of their husbands.

The touted theme of the collection is its surreal explanation of what would happen if its characters or the people around them had made different choices. This is particularly clear in the first story, "The (Other) You," where the widowed main character wonders how her life would have changed if she had received a full-ride scholarship and pursued higher education. The final story, "The Unexpected," confronts a successful writer with the image of the woman that she might have become had she stayed in her hometown instead of venturing out to pursue her dreams. Several other stories mention how life may have been different if its female character had decided to have children. However, the story that explores this theme in the greatest depth is "Waiting for Kizer." In this story, a man named Matt Smith waits at the Purple Onion Café for Nate Kizer, a childhood friend. While there, he meets Matthew Smith, another man who is also waiting for Kizer. As the two get to know each other, Matt Smith realizes that he and Matthew Smith are the same man whose life was changed as the result of a childhood accident involving Kizer. Matt Smith and Matthew Smith ponder the differences in their lives and reflect on whether they had saved Kizer from drowning, or whether he had saved them. When a third man, Maynard Smith, appears, the question becomes even more complicated.

Connected to this theme is the question of narrator reliability. For instance, in the stories where the characters seem to be grasping at reality, Oates often retells the events using a different sequence, heightening the sense of uncertainty. This is evident in "Waiting for Kizer," due to its three varying depictions of the same man, and even more so in "The Blue Guide." The vast changes in the city of Mairead, Italy, clash with the professor's idealized memories; his recollections of the young girl he fell in love with when he was a student are perhaps even more unreliable. In "The Final Interview," the story of a cantankerous writer waiting for a harsh interviewer, the writer experiences his arrival at the Purple Onion multiple times. Meanwhile, the suicide bomber's story is told through short chapters that relay the bomber's own experience, the writer's memory of reading of the situation, and the interviewer's thoughtless questions about the tragedy.

Many of Oates's titles and themes function as callbacks to some of her earlier works. For example, the title of "Where Are You" is reminiscent of two of Oates's earlier stories, "Where Are You Going, Where Have You Been?" (1966) and "Where is Here" (1990). Additionally, the title of the story "Assassin" is very similar to that of her novel *The Assassins* (1975). Beyond these references to her own works, Oates also incorporates allusions to classic American literature. "Sinners in the Hands of an Angry God" is perhaps where this is most obvious. Other than the title, which references a 1741 sermon by American preacher Jonathan Edwards of the same name, there is a more subtle allusion to the so-called "rest cure" described in Charlotte Perkins Gilman's 1892 short story, "The Yellow Wallpaper." The rest cure, as its name implies, recommended long periods of rest and low activity as a cure for depression, anxiety, and other mental health conditions. Luce, the main character in "Sinners in the Hands of an Angry God," discusses this approach: "Sufferers of depression are recommended gardening, music. Not so much reading, certainly not writing, for such exercises of the brain activate *thinking*. Not a good idea."

The collection met with mixed critical reception upon its publication in 2021. Several critics commented on the somber mood of the stories. For instance, Helen Schulman, in her *New York Times* review, called the works "mournful," "trenchant," and "moody," and praised Oates's "steely and prescient gaze." For Schulman, what stood out most was Oates's commentary on the "vanishing possibilities of life." In a more mixed review, Alicia Lutes of *USA Today* concluded, "The (Other) You" is an expertly crafted collection of stories made to bum you out." While Lutes praised Oates's willingness to experiment with style and technique, she felt the collection was, at times, "predictable," due to its pervasive brutality and pessimism. In his review for the *New York Journal of Books*, Townsend Walker also criticized the collection. Arguing that it was "not easy to approach," he felt that some stories relied on "trick endings" that detracted from the messages they were trying to impart. On a more positive note, a reviewer for *Publishers Weekly* described Oates's writing as "fierce and formidable," as well as "unsettling;" the reviewer identified the main themes as "obsession, remorse, and violence." Other critical commentary centered around the themes of the collection and the methods Oates uses to achieve those ideas. A reviewer for *Kirkus* pointed out that the stories are "crackling with pent-up emotion and deadly devices," and identified Oates's "trademark theme" as "people talking past and against each other instead of getting a clue."

Author Biography

Joyce Carol Oates is a novelist, playwright, short story writer, poet, and essayist noted for her prolific output. Her 1969 novel, *them*, won the National Book Award. Oates has also served as a professor at numerous colleges and universities in both the United States and Canada. She has additionally published under the pseudonyms Rosamond Smith and Lauren Kelly.

Theresa L. Stowell, PhD

Review Sources

Lutes, Alicia. "*The (Other) You* Review: Joyce Carol Oates' Latest Bleak Collection Will Bum You Out." *USA Today*, 9 Feb. 2021, www.usatoday.com/story/entertainment/books/2021/02/09/other-you-review-joyce-carol-oates-latest-bleak-bummer/4444459001/. Accessed 11 Feb. 2022.

Review of *The (Other) You*, by Joyce Carol Oates. *Kirkus Reviews*, vol. 88, no. 23, Dec. 2020, www.kirkusreviews.com/book-reviews/joyce-carol-oates/the-other-you/. Accessed 11 Feb. 2022.

Review of *The (Other) You*, by Joyce Carol Oates. *Publishers Weekly*, vol. 267, no. 42, Oct. 2020, p. 41, www.publishersweekly.com/978-0-06-303520-1. Accessed 11 Feb. 2022.

Schulman, Helen. "Joyce Carol Oates's New Stories Consider the Roads Not Taken." Review of *The (Other) You*, by Joyce Carol Oates. *The New York Times*, Feb. 2021, p.18, www.nytimes.com/2021/02/09/books/review/joyce-carol-oates-other-you.html. Accessed 11 Feb. 2022.

Strauss, Leah. Review of *The (Other) You*, by Joyce Carol Oates. *Booklist*, vol. 117, no. 7, Dec. 2020, pp. 24-25. *EBSCOhost*, search.ebscohost.com/login.aspx?direct=true&db=lfh&AN=147230278&site=eds-live. Accessed 11 Feb. 2022.

Walker, Townsend. Review of *The (Other) You*, by Joyce Carol Oates. *New York Journal of Books*, www.nyjournalofbooks.com/book-review/other-you-stories. Accessed 16 Feb. 2022.

The Outlier
The Unfinished Presidency of Jimmy Carter

Author: Kai Bird (b. 1951)
Publisher: Crown (New York). 784 pp.
Type of work: Biography, history
Time: 1924–81
Locale: The United States

In The Outlier, *the Pulitzer Prize–winning biographer Kai Bird presents a revisionist account of the presidency of Jimmy Carter, arguing that this political outsider's one term in office was enormously consequential and far from a failure. Bird explores Carter's attempts to pursue intelligent and humane policies at a time when the United States was buffeted by dramatic social and economic change.*

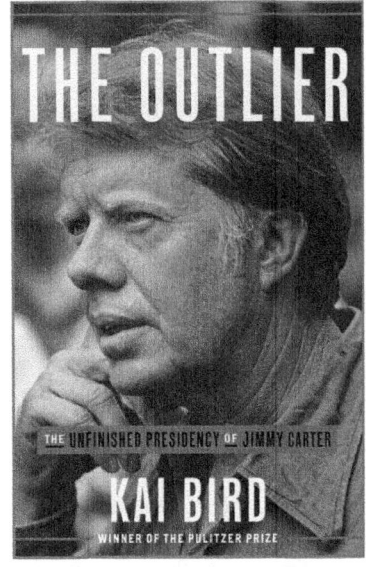

Principal personages
JIMMY CARTER, the thirty-ninth president of the United States
ROSALYNN CARTER, his wife and confidante
LILLIAN CARTER, his mother
BILLY CARTER, his brother, whose business connections to Libya embarrassed the president
WALTER MONDALE, vice president of the United States, 1977–81
EDWARD "TED" KENNEDY, his political rival, senator from Massachusetts
CYRUS VANCE, US secretary of state, 1977–80
ZBIGNIEW BRZEZINSKI, national security advisor, 1977–81
CHARLES KIRBO, Carter's trusted advisor, a lawyer
HAMILTON JORDAN, political strategist and White House chief of staff, 1979–80
JODY POWELL, White House press secretary, 1977–81

As Jimmy Carter nears his one-hundredth year, his tumultuous presidency is being reassessed. He has been the subject of several recent biographies, including Carter administration veteran Stuart Eizenstat's *President Carter: The White House Years* (2018) and Jonathan Alter's *His Very Best: Jimmy Carter, A Life* (2020). Kai Bird's *The Outlier: The Unfinished Presidency of Jimmy Carter* (2021) is an ambitious effort to rehabilitate Carter's once-tattered presidential reputation. For many Americans, Carter's name is inextricably associated with the humiliation of the Iran hostage crisis and the economic miseries of 1970s stagflation, and Carter is remembered for presiding over a period of malaise. Bird acknowledges the many challenges that Carter faced

Kai Bird (Courtesy Penguin Random House)

but argues that he compiled a remarkable record in a brief but consequential presidency.

Bird believes that Carter's upbringing in the deep South is essential to understanding his approach to politics and governance, and he explores his childhood in depth in part 1 of the book, titled "The Pre-Presidency." As a Southerner, Carter came from a part of the United States that had experienced the bitterness of defeat. His South was also still scarred by the injustices of Jim Crow's enforced segregation. It was also notable that Black people outnumbered White people in Carter's corner of Georgia. Though most of Carter's playmates were Black, he could not help but notice the difference between his prospects and theirs. Nor could he avoid the benevolent but implacable paternalism with which his father treated the workers in his peanut business. Only the eccentrically egalitarian attitude of his mother, Lillian, kept him from internalizing the racism of his region. In later years, Carter would make many references to the writings of William Faulkner; he shared the Nobel Prize–winning author's conviction that the peculiar history of the South, overshadowed by the legacy of slavery and war, fostered a tragic vision of life distinct from the triumphalist narrative dominant in the rest of the country. This perspective made Carter skeptical about claims of American exceptionalism and left him intensely conscious of the limits to human aspiration and action. As president, he would urge his fellow citizens to recognize restraints on American power and the need to husband declining resources.

In the section of *The Outlier* on Carter's upbringing, Bird explains how Carter was indelibly shaped by his fervently Christian upbringing. A lifelong member of his local Baptist church, he was always open about his Christian commitment. No Fundamentalist, Carter embraced a liberal strain of Protestantism. Although always interested in doctrine, Carter's Christianity found its best expression in active service to humanity. His was a religion of deeds rather than declarations. As such, it smoothly reinforced his political ambitions; office-seeking became a secularized form of ministry enabling him to pursue tangible improvements in the world. In the White House, Carter's speeches would occasionally devolve into sermons to a national congregation that was often disinclined to hearken to his admonitions.

Carter's mother encouraged her children to read, even at the dinner table, starting a habit that would endure a lifetime. This intellectual regimen nurtured an already high innate intelligence. His brainpower and his father's political connections gained him admission to the United States Naval Academy. Upon graduation, Carter joined the nuclear submarine program. However, the budding nuclear engineer's career was cut short by the death of his father, which prompted him to resign his commission so he could return to Georgia and manage the family business. But Carter never completely lost the aura of a bookish engineer. Even in the White House he immersed himself in the technical details of projects and legislation, often reading 250 or more pages of position papers a day. He was conscious of his impressive intellect and was unabashed at showing it. He privately confessed that there were many times when he saw himself as the smartest man in the room. Carter's intelligence was an obvious advantage as he grappled with complicated problems during his presidency. It proved a liability, though, when this made him impatient in his dealings with Capitol Hill legislators fixated on their political interests. The backslapping and socializing intrinsic to campaigning and legislating repelled Carter. Ironically, he was a politician who loathed politics. Carter believed that rectitude and brains should be enough in a president; sadly, he was wrong, and his fellow Americans would demand something else.

A key event that Bird focuses on in discussing Carter's rise to the presidency is the civil rights movement. Carter grew his family business during years when Georgia was roiled by the civil rights movement. Though sympathetic to the struggle for Black American equality, Carter kept a low profile on the issue. This discretion became more of a challenge when he decided to run for the state senate in 1962. When the polls closed in the Democratic primary, Carter's opponent was ahead by 139 votes. Carter realized that this was the result of fraud in one county, and with the help of an Atlanta lawyer named Charles Kirbo, succeeded in getting the election overturned. From this point on, Kirbo would be a close and valued friend and political counselor. After two terms in the state senate, where, by Georgia standards, he was a moderate on racial issues, Carter ran for governor in 1966 but lost to the segregationist Lester Maddox. Determined to win the governorship on a second try in 1970, Carter ran as a populist outsider who would take on the vested interests in Atlanta. He met with civil rights leaders but also appealed to segregationists by praising George Wallace, an Alabama governor who fought against racial integration. Carter later acknowledged shame over this element of his victorious 1970 campaign, but it also revealed a ruthlessly competitive streak in his character.

Once in office, Carter shocked many by declaring "the time for racial discrimination is over." He compiled an admirable record in office, reorganizing the state bureaucracy, supporting equal opportunity in education, and increasing the role of Black politicians in state government, even intentionally angering segregationists by hanging a portrait of Dr. Martin Luther King Jr. in the statehouse. Limited by state law to one term, Carter began to contemplate a campaign for the presidency. By this time, he had gathered around him a group of brilliant young political operatives that included political strategist Hamilton Jordan and press spokesman Jody Powell. Carter and his team realized that the Vietnam War and the Watergate scandal had left many Americans disillusioned with the Washington establishment. As Carter left the governorship, he built a campaign centered on running against Washington. Carter promised the American people, "I'll never lie to you." This proved to be a winning strategy in 1976, sweeping Carter to victory in the Democratic primaries, and a narrow triumph in the general election. The narrowness of Carter's victory margin was a harbinger of things to come.

Bird does not only focus on the positives of Carter's life; he likewise brings attention to some of Carter's mistakes and flaws. For instance, he tells of how during the campaign, Carter unwisely agreed to an interview in *Playboy* where he admitted to sometimes having lust in his heart for other women. The press blew up this "story" into a major embarrassment for Carter, hurting his electoral momentum. The dominant media outlets did not know what to make of a born-again Christian who seemingly emerged out of nowhere. The same went for the power brokers in Washington, who were unimpressed with a man who had run against them. The "Georgia Gang" that Carter brought with him to the White House were looked down upon as unassimilable outsiders and subjected to unflattering and usually false press reports.

Despite this, Carter managed to accomplish a great deal, and Bird highlights these accomplishments in part 2 of the book, which focuses on Carter's presidency. During his administration, Carter championed consumer safety protections while beginning the economic deregulation of various industries that led to everything from cheaper airfares to the proliferation of craft beers. Carter responded to the rapid rise in oil prices of the 1970s by calling for energy conservation and the development of more environmentally friendly renewable energy sources. He ended a chapter in American imperialism by negotiating a phased turnover of the Panama Canal to Panamanian sovereignty. He rejected the cold realpolitik of his predecessors by making human rights the centerpiece of his foreign policy, heartening lovers of freedom around the world. Yet he could still deal with great powers, normalizing relations with China and negotiating an arms agreement with the Soviet Union. When the Soviets invaded Afghanistan, he began a military buildup later amplified by President Ronald Reagan. Only Carter's personal diplomacy brought about a peace agreement between Israel and Egypt.

However, Carter failed to consolidate his political position. The American public paid less attention to his hard work and achievements than to the rising misery index that added inflation and unemployment rates. Carter paid a heavy price for his determination to do the right thing, as when he criticized Israeli policy on the West Bank, costing him Jewish votes. Carter's pragmatism led to differences with liberal Democrats hoping to reignite the Great Society. This eventually led to Senator Ted Kennedy unsuccessfully challenging him in the 1980 Democratic primaries, a devastating blow to Carter's effort to unite the party before facing a strong challenge from Ronald Reagan. Bird is unabashedly liberal, and treads lightly with the Massachusetts senator who did almost as much as Ronald Reagan to end Carter's presidency. On the other hand, Bird harshly criticizes National Security Advisor Zbigniew Brzezinski, an ardent Cold Warrior and no favorite of liberals, whom he believes played a crucial role in persuading Carter to offer shelter to the former Iranian Shah, precipitating the disastrous hostage crisis.

In *The Outlier*, Kai Bird makes a compelling case that Jimmy Carter's presidency deserves a positive reassessment. He balances sympathy for an enigmatic chief executive with incisive analysis and presents it from an unbiased viewpoint. A gift for storytelling along with clear and clean prose make a long book seem short. Many reviewers agreed with this assessment. In his review for the *Christian Science Monitor*, Steve

Donoghue praised Bird's "enormous amount of research" and "refreshing lack of partisanship." Likewise, the *Kirkus* reviewer called the book "the best study to date of the Carter era and a substantial contribution to the history of the 1970s." While the *New York Times* reviewer Timothy Naftali's overall evaluation of *The Outlier* was positive, he did find some faults, such as Bird's exploration of Carter's foreign policy. Calling the book "much less insightful on Carter's Cold War positions" and "too detailed for the general reader" in places, Naftali did concede that "the narrative is more nuanced when the focus is on the Middle East." Overall, *The Outlier* offers the general reader and specialist alike a rewarding account of a tumultuous period in modern American history.

Author Biography

Kai Bird is the executive director of the Leon Levy Center for Biography at the City University of New York. Among his many books are *American Prometheus: The Triumph and Tragedy of J. Robert Oppenheimer* (2005), which won the Pulitzer Prize in Biography, and *The Good Spy: The Life and Death of Robert Ames* (2014).

Daniel P. Murphy

Review Sources

Donoghue, Steve. "'The Outlier' Paints a Complex Portrait of Jimmy Carter." Review of *The Outlier: The Unfinished Presidency of Jimmy Carter*, by Kai Bird. *The Christian Science Monitor*, 19 Aug. 2021, www.csmonitor.com/Books/Book-Reviews/2021/0819/The-Outlier-paints-a-complex-portrait-of-Jimmy-Carter. Accessed 30 Nov. 2021.

Naftali, Timothy. "The Many Successes of Jimmy Carter—and His Ultimate Failure." Review of *The Outlier: The Unfinished Presidency of Jimmy Carter*, by Kai Bird. *The New York Times*, 16 June 2021, www.nytimes.com/2021/06/15/books/review/kai-bird-the-outlier-jimmy-carter.html. Accessed 2 Feb. 2022.

Review of *The Outlier: The Unfinished Presidency of Jimmy Carter*, by Kai Bird. *Kirkus*, 13 Mar. 2021, www.kirkusreviews.com/book-reviews/kai-bird/the-outlier/. Accessed 30 Nov. 2021.

Review of *The Outlier: The Unfinished Presidency of Jimmy Carter*, by Kai Bird. *Publishers Weekly*, 12 Jan. 2021, www.publishersweekly.com/978-0-451-49523-5. Accessed 2 Feb. 2022.

Sargent, Daniel. "Postmodern America Didn't Deserve Jimmy Carter." Review of *The Outlier: The Unfinished Presidency of Jimmy Carter*, by Kai Bird. *Foreign Policy*, 24 July 2021, foreignpolicy.com/2021/07/24/postmodern-america-didnt-deserve-jimmy-carter/. Accessed 30 Nov. 2021.

Suri, Jeremi. "Jimmy Carter's Missing Ingredient: Presidential Charisma." Review of *The Outlier: The Unfinished Presidency of Jimmy Carter*, by Kai Bird. *The Washington Post*, 18 June 2021, www.washingtonpost.com/outlook/jimmy-carters-missing-ingredient-presidential-charisma/2021/06/17/9a12f806-c583-11eb-93f5-ee9558eecf4b_story.html. Accessed 30 Nov. 2021.

A Passage North

Author: Anuk Arudpragasam (b. 1988)
Publisher: Hogarth Books (New York). 290 pp.
Type of work: Novel
Time: Present day
Locale: Sri Lanka

A Passage North (2021), Anuk Arudpragasam's second novel, revisits the long, bloody Sri Lankan Civil War, this time focusing on the aftereffects of violence on innocent civilians.

Principal characters

KRISHAN, the narrator, a young Tamil employee for a nongovernmental organization
APPAMMA, his octogenarian grandmother, another Tamil
RANI, his grandmother's caretaker, who lost two sons in the civil war
ANJUM, his former lover, an Indian activist

In his first novel, *The Story of a Brief Marriage* (2016), Anuk Arudpragasam examines the history and legacy of the Sri Lankan Civil War (1983–2009) through the eyes of contemporary characters. In his second novel, *A Passage North* (2021), Arudpragasam tackles many of the same issues, with his trademark philosophical touch. Though it has much to recommend it, *A Passage North* may be a challenging read, for two major reasons.

A major obstacle to understanding is the author's style, which seems to have more in common with nineteenth-century literature than contemporary styles. Those familiar with conventions in many contemporary works—convoluted plots, brisk language, blocks of dialogue that break the text into digestible bits, short chapters with cliffhangers that encourage page-turning—may find Arudpragasam's writing style overly complicated and hard to follow. His complex sentences, though well-constructed and grammatically correct, often run to hundreds of words at a time and follow one after another in long, unbroken streams. The story is told from the viewpoint of its third-person narrator, Krishan, who free associates in a stream of consciousness among many far-flung topics, ranging from ancient Sanskrit poems to the interpretation of eye contact between strangers on public transport, from philosophical musings about the meaning of life to extended reminiscences about past events from history and his own life. Krishan is described as "permanently suspended in the blissful but always vanishing space between desire and satisfaction." Paragraphs can run as long as several

Anuk Arudpragasam

pages, and dialogue is often summarized, rather than written out as an exchange between characters. Divisions are long, solid, and dense: the novel, separated into three parts, consists of just ten chapters.

A second barrier is the background, the complex history of Sri Lanka, which may be unfamiliar subject matter for many readers. *A Passage North* concerns and frequently comments on the troubled history of Sri Lanka, a large island off the southeast coast of India that was known as Ceylon until it gained independence from Great Britain in 1948. Much of Sri Lanka's history involves conflict between two ethnic groups with their own languages, religions, and cultures. These two groups are the Tamils, a minority who make up about 11 percent of the population, live primarily in the northeast of the island, and are mostly Hindu. The nation's ethnic majority, who are politically and culturally dominant outside the island's northeast, are the Sinhalese, who make up nearly three-quarters of the country's population and are mainly Buddhist. During their colonial rule of the island, the British favored the Tamils and placed them in important positions of power. Once the British left, the Sinhalese, on the strength of their numbers, gradually assumed control of the government and passed laws that were considered discriminatory against Tamils. One such law, the Sinhala Only Act of 1956, declared Sinhala the official language of Sri Lanka, in what many Tamils perceived as a direct attack on their culture. The increasing tension between the Tamils and the Sinhalese escalated into frequent outbreaks of violence in which the outnumbered Tamils experienced massive casualties at the hands of government-sanctioned Sinhalese mobs. This violence helped spur an effort to establish a Tamil state in the north, under the direction of the Liberation Tigers of Tamil Eelam (LTTE), a leading separatist organization often referred to as the Tamil Tigers. The Sri Lankan government began a vicious civil war, which lasted more than twenty-five years (1983–2009) and claimed roughly 150,000 lives, most of them civilians, before the government declared total victory in 2009.

A Passage North opens years after the end of this war, though its effects are still being felt and the trauma it caused still hangs heavily over Sri Lankan society. The main characters are representative: Krishan lives with his widowed mother and his paternal grandmother, Appamma, and all three have endured the loss of Krishan's father. His father was killed—along with at least fifty other people—in the 1996 LTTE suicide bombing of the Central Bank in Colombo, the capital. As with the many other real events Arudpragasam weaves into the text, the bombing helps ground the novel firmly in the context of Sri Lanka's history and ongoing challenges.

The story begins with Krishan's receipt of two messages that simultaneously advance the slim plot and allow Arudpragasam to slow the pace of the novel through extensive flashbacks. These flashbacks reveal many details of Krishan's earlier life, including his time as a PhD student in India, his social work, and his severe survivor's guilt and obsession with the violence enacted by both sides during the civil war. Also recalled is Appamma's proud and vibrant past, when she used to regularly visit her younger half-brother, a separatist exile in London, England, before her health began to deteriorate as she grew older. Appamma's condition necessitated the hiring of a caretaker named Rani, who has depression and post-traumatic stress disorder (PTSD) following the deaths of two sons in the civil war. The arrangement worked surprisingly well, and Rani lived amicably beside Appamma for two years before returning to her home in the north to commemorate the fifth anniversary of her younger son's sudden death but does not return as scheduled from her trip.

The reason for Rani's failure to return sets the plot in motion. The first message Krishan receives is a phone call from Rani's daughter informing Krishan that her mother died after falling into a village well and breaking her neck. The incident creates slight suspense and raises many possibilities. Rani could have been murdered, a victim of lingering sectarian violence. Her death could have been an accident, an aftereffect of the unsteadiness Rani experienced following many electroshock therapy sessions and the multiple strong medications she took for depression, anxiety, and several physical conditions. Perhaps Rani, still despondent from the deaths of her two sons in the civil war, died by suicide. These questions hang over Krishan as he decides to attend Rani's funeral to represent his family, as his mother works full time and Appamma is too frail to travel. The funeral will be held in northern Sri Lanka at a village near Kilinochchi, "ground zero" for the recent war. He will bring twenty thousand rupees, donated by Appamma, to help Rani's family pay for funeral expenses.

A second message complicates Krishan's mental state even further. This one is from Anjum, his former lover. While Krishan has not seen her for years for several years, Anjum writes to him about her life and wants to know how he is doing.

Both messages serve as fodder for Krishan's thoughts during his train ride north, which consumes the whole of "Journey," part 2 of the novel. The trip reminds him of a train ride from Delhi, India, to Bombay (that is, Mumbai) that he took four years earlier with Anjum, when their intense relationship began to fall apart. This in turn leads Krishan to reminisce about how he first encountered Anjum at a "panel in Delhi on the modern Indian state and queerness." Already obsessed with Anjum, who is bisexual, Krishan attended other LGBTQ+ events hoping to meet her; while he successfully won her over, he eventually lost her when their relationship ended. Wondering how to answer Anjum's recent email, Krishan philosophizes about how people no longer in one's life continue to evolve even after the end of a relationship: "There was a tendency . . . to believe that they'd remained the same while you yourself had evolved, as if other people and places ceased moving once you'd left them behind, as if their time remained still while only yours continued to advance."

When not thinking of his former girlfriend or wondering what he will discover at Rani's funeral, Krishan's restless mind flits from subject to subject, allowing the author to examine recent events in Sri Lankan history, along with many influential works of ancient culture. Krishan contemplates the Sanskrit poem of yearning, *The Cloud Messenger*. He considers Ashvaghosha's *The Life of Buddha* and compares Siddhartha Gautama's disillusionment about old age, sickness, and death with Rani's situation. He dwells at length upon the *Sivapuranam*, an ancient Tamil song about reincarnation, one of the novel's many references to Buddhism.

The final section of *A Passage North*, "Burning," is the richest, in language, imagery, and emotion, as it details the elaborate ceremonies surrounding Rani's funeral and cremation. Krishan ponders Rani's fate and the "line between accidental and planned death." He claims, "All it took sometimes was a silent half-wish . . . for death to become something the deceased would, eventually, be pushed toward."

Critical reception of *A Passage North* was largely positive, but many critics had certain reservations. For example, Tara K. Menon of the *New York Times* commended the novel both for its "condemnation of the many atrocities committed by the Sri Lankan government on its Tamil civilians" and for being "a searching work of philosophy." Menon noted that the novel is "full of melancholy" but "avoids despair," though she critiqued how Arudpragasam's "sentences strain" under the heavy burden of making "sweeping statements about the human condition." The *Guardian* reviewer Marcel Theroux agreed that Arudpragasam is "a patient and meticulous observer" but complained that "the book's rhetorical flourishes . . . [mask] an insubstantial story and unclear motivation." He concluded that the novel "gives us glimpses of extraordinary characters" but spends too much time dwelling on the "sophomoric musings of its hero," whom he deemed a "frustratingly passive protagonist."

Peter Gordon, writing for the *Asian Review of Books*, criticized the book's plot, arguing that "very little happens, nothing is resolved." However, he praised *A Passage North*'s prose and deep themes, "with its long, thoughtful sentences and deliberate construction, [and] its emphasis on sentiment and philosophy over plot." He also complimented Arudpragasam's "delicate and detailed characterizations." While most reviewers echoed Gordon's praise of the writing itself, some felt it detracted from the plot and action. Blake Morrison, critic for the *London Review of Books*, lauded "the expansiveness of the prose, which is slow, fluid and . . . quietly contemplative" while also noting that there are passages where the prose tends to "zone out." Morrison suggested the author could benefit from a more critical editor.

A Passage North presents a challenge, but the effort is worth it. There are numerous well-rendered, striking passages, starting with the opening line: "The present, we assume, is eternally before us, one of the few things in life from which we cannot be parted." The novel goes on to impart many clear-eyed reflections and thought-provoking ideas that, while related specifically to recent Sri Lankan history, could easily be applied to human suffering anywhere on earth.

Author Biography
Anuk Arudpragasam's first novel, *The Story of a Brief Marriage* (2016), won the DSC Prize for South Asian Literature and was shortlisted for the Dylan Thomas Prize. *A Passage North* (2021) was shortlisted for the Booker Prize.

Jack Ewing

Review Sources
Deboo, Khorshed. "Requiem for a Remembrance. A Review of *A Passage North* by Anuk Arudpragasam." *Himal Southasian*, 26 Oct. 2021, www.himalmag.com/requiem-for-a-remembrance-a-passage-north-anuk-arudpragasam-review-2021. Accessed 26 Dec. 2021.
Gordon, Peter. Review of *A Passage North*, by Anuk Arudpragasam. *Asian Review of Books*, 21 July 2021, asianreviewofbooks.com/content/a-passage-north-by-anuk-arudpragasam. Accessed 26 Dec. 2021.
Gunawardana, Dilan. "Memory Shrines: Anuk Arudpragasam's Elegant Political Novel amid Sri Lanka's Civil War." Review of *A Passage North*, by Anuk Arudpragasam. *Australian Book Review*, no. 438, Dec. 2021, www.australianbookreview.com.au/abr-online/current-issue/972-december-2021-no-438/8636-dilan-gunawardana-reviews-a-passage-north-by-anuk-arudpragasam. Accessed 26 Dec. 2021.
Menon, Tara K. "The Bombs May Have Stopped, but War's Scars Still Run Deep." Review of *A Passage North*, by Anuk Arudpragasam. *The New York Times*, 13 July 2021, www.nytimes.com/2021/07/13/books/review/anuk-arudpragasam-passage-north.html. Accessed 26 Dec. 2021.
Morrison, Blake. "Always Somewhere Else." Review of *A Passage North*, by Anuk Arudpragasam. *London Review of Books*, vol. 43, no. 21, 4 Nov. 2021, www.lrb.co.uk/the-paper/v43/n21/blake-morrison/always-somewhere-else. Accessed 26 Dec. 2021.
Theroux, Marcel. "*A Passage North* by Anjuk Arudpragasam Review—A Journey into the Trauma of War." *The Guardian,* 15 July 2021, www.theguardian.com/books/2021/jul/15/a-passage-north-by-anuk-arudpragasam-review-a-journey-into-the-trauma-of-war. Accessed 26 Dec. 2021.

People We Meet on Vacation

Author: Emily Henry
Publisher: Berkley (New York). 400 pp.
Type of work: Novel
Time: Unknown
Locales: Largely New York, Ohio, and California

People We Meet on Vacation *is the story of two best friends with a tradition of traveling together every summer who have one last trip to determine if there is something more to their relationship.*

Principal characters
POPPY, a free-spirited travel writer
ALEX, her best friend from college, a teacher
RACHEL, her best friend in New York
SARAH, Alex's on-again, off-again girlfriend

Most people are familiar with the romantic comedy genre of film and literature, which can trace its roots back to sixteenth-century plays of William Shakespeare. Stories that fall within this canon are commonly lighthearted in tone and focus on characters who have feelings for one another but are kept apart because of their own shortcomings or other circumstances that are ironically within their control. People love romantic comedies for many reasons but, more often than not, it is for their happy endings; just as Shakespeare's comedic plays typically ended in betrothal, contemporary stories within the genre also have the central couple overcoming their differences to profess their love for one another.

Initially writing for young adults, author Emily Henry has built her career on writing about love. This fact becomes immediately clear in the title of her first young adult novel, *The Love That Split the World* (2016), which blends drama with magical realism. Although her debut was positively received, it was not until her fifth book, the New York Times Best Seller *Beach Read* (2020), her first written for adults, that critics deemed Henry one of the most exciting new voices in romance. *Beach Read* both embraces the romantic comedy's well-worn tropes while simultaneously challenging them—resulting in a story that many critics and readers were quick to celebrate as "fresh." *People We Meet on Vacation* (2021) is the follow-up to the smash success of *Beach Read*, and although it is not as subversive as its predecessor, it is still a well-wrought story about love-challenged characters.

The narrative setup of many romance novels can often feel underdeveloped when compared to the relationship between the central couple. Fortunately, this is not the case in *People We Meet on Vacation*, which is anchored by a very clever and detailed plot. It follows Poppy, a thirty-something-year-old woman who works as a travel writer in New York City and does not want to be tied down. The only steady presence in her life is her best friend from college, Alex. Every year, Poppy and Alex take a week-long vacation together in a different location around the world. After several years of this tradition, however, they travel to Croatia, where something happens that causes them to stop speaking to one another. When the novel begins, it has been two years since the Croatia trip. Upon realizing how depressed she has become without Alex, Poppy becomes determined to win his friendship back and sets up a plan to spend time with him on a trip to Palm Springs, where she must face her feelings for him once and for all. Ultimately, this proves to be a fun, fresh premise.

Emily Henry

In *People We Meet on Vacation*, Henry demonstrates once again that she excels at rendering real-world settings. Through Poppy and Alex's adventures, she successfully transports readers everywhere from Europe to tropical islands, California, New Orleans, New York City, and Ohio without ever creating a sense of whiplash. This is a testament to her ability to capture the sensory details of places without being overwhelming. It is important to note that the book's many different settings feel authentic rather than romanticized, which in turn infuses the tone with a kind of realism that is unusual for the genre.

People We Meet on Vacation also showcases Henry's talent for creating multidimensional characters. Poppy, for example, has a good job and sense of humor but does not like making herself vulnerable in relationships because she was bullied badly in high school. Meanwhile, Alex has characteristics that make him the prototypical leading man in that he is attractive, smart, and caring. However, he is also an introverted worrier whose standoffish personality results from the fact that he lost his mother at a young age and had to take care of his father and brothers. Henry's decision to utilize such flawed protagonists proves to be successful—both Poppy and Alex are compelling because they feel real and subsequently relatable.

A large part of what makes *People We Meet on Vacation* an enjoyable read is the way in which Henry winks at popular romantic comedy tropes. Using the complicated history of Poppy and Alex's relationship, the novel explores whether heterosexual men and women can be friends. This is the same question at the heart of Nora Ephron's classic film *When Harry Met Sally...* (1989). It is not surprising, then, that several critics have made comparisons to the film, and to learn that Henry has been inspired by it, including its dialogue—a fact that she has revealed in interviews. Another familiar romantic comedy trope that Henry includes in the book is the idea that opposites attract.

While Poppy is a self-proclaimed "wild child" who values her freedom above all else, Alex is a khaki-wearing high school teacher with no plans to move out of small-town Ohio. Their divergent personalities and perspectives infuse the story with conflict, which in turn creates the kindling necessary for romantic sparks.

Despite combining many familiar romantic comedy ingredients in *People We Meet on Vacation*, Henry succeeds in preventing the book from ever feeling stale. One of the primary ways she accomplishes this is through its structure, which consists of chapters that toggle back and forth between two timelines. The primary story line takes place in the present and follows Poppy as she joins Alex on a one-week vacation in Palm Springs, ostensibly for her job but really to try to save their friendship. The second story line follows Poppy and Alex through the history of their friendship—from the time they met at college at the University of Chicago chronologically through their annual summer trips, which later culminate in the fateful Croatia trip. The mystery surrounding what happened in Croatia acts as a propulsive force in this second story line, generating a feeling of suspense that is highly engaging. Meanwhile, Henry keeps her readers on the edge of their seats in the present-day story line through the "will they, won't they" tension between Poppy and Alex as they find themselves increasingly unable to ignore the emotional truth behind the chemistry that has drawn them together since the first day they met.

There is a certain timeliness to *People We Meet on Vacation* that makes it feel especially relevant to the year that it was published. The characters of Poppy and Alex are thirty-something
representatives of their generation consumed by "millennial ennui" who are unsure of what makes them happy. Furthermore, Poppy started her career as a social media "influencer" and does not know if she wants children or to get married. While other authors might poke fun at these millennial stereotypes, Henry respects her characters and ensures that their emotions always come across as valid. In turn, she provides readers with a snapshot of the times and the fears that many people struggle with in modern society.

Another facet of *People We Meet on Vacation* that makes it feel especially enjoyable in 2021 is that it focuses so much on travel. At the time the novel was released, most of the world had been in lockdown for over a year because of the coronavirus disease 2019 (COVID-19) pandemic. Having begun writing the book before the onset of the pandemic, Henry's decision to still exclude the existence of the pandemic altogether and have Poppy and Alex spend most of their time moving freely to different exciting locations elevates the book's sense of fantasy. Somehow the carefree, joyful way they are able to travel makes their relationship feel even more romantic.

While, like its predecessor, Henry's 2021 effort claimed a place on the New York Times Best Sellers list, when compared to the reception of *Beach Read*, reviews of *People We Meet on Vacation* have been somewhat mixed. A handful of critics claimed that its pacing lags and that the obstacles keeping Poppy and Alex apart are formulaic. *Publishers Weekly* commented on this fact in its otherwise positive review, stating, "Watching them dance around the inevitable grows tiresome as things drag on, but Henry's skills with sensory detail and lovable characters shine through." It is true that some readers might find Poppy and Alex's efforts to stay friends rather than succumb to their romantic feelings to be tedious. Henry goes to great lengths to keep the characters apart and there are moments when the plot or characters' logic feels contrived. However, these flaws are nothing in comparison to the novel's strengths.

There are many reasons why readers will enjoy *People We Meet on Vacation*. Perhaps first and foremost is the chemistry between Poppy and Alex, which Henry elevates through their dialogue. The way the two characters converse is a blend of how friends speak to one another in real life and the flirty, barbed style that Elizabeth Bennet and Mr. Darcy use in Jane Austen's *Pride and Prejudice* (1813). Alicia Rancilio discusses this fact in her review for Associated Press, stating, "What Henry is especially skilled at is writing dialogue. The banter between Poppy and Alex is so natural, quick and witty that it would make Shonda Rhimes do a slow clap. It also reminds the reader why these two come alive with each other in a way that they do not with anyone else." Angela Haupt made a similar observation in a review for the *Washington Post* when she wrote, "If the friends-to-lovers trope is ever in danger of feeling tired, Henry saves it with sassy wordplay. Plus, the connection between Poppy and Alex feels genuine, like the romance next door."

Ultimately, *People We Meet on Vacation* provides readers with a pleasurable escape—a fact commented on by Amy Pugsley in her review for *Flair* magazine, in which she recommended "taking a virtual vacation" by "diving into this contemporary romance." *People We Meet on Vacation* has a lot to offer readers who love the romantic comedy genre, whether it is the opportunity to imagine traveling freely during a pandemic or simply watching a romance develop between relatable characters. As *Kirkus* concluded in its review, the book is, in its purest essence, an updated version of *When Harry Met Sally* that "hits all the perfect notes."

Author Biography

The author of six novels, Emily Henry's 2020 book *Beach Read* was also a New York Times Best Seller.

Emily E. Turner

Review Sources

Haupt, Angela. "Emily Henry's *People We Meet on Vacation* is a Pitch-Perfect Beach Read." *The Washington Post*, 12 May 2021, www.washingtonpost.com/entertainment/books/people-we-meet-on-vacation/2021/05/11/0773422a-b274-11eb-ab43-bebddc5a0f65_story.html. Accessed 1 Dec. 2021.

Review of *People We Meet on Vacation*, by Emily Henry. *Kirkus*, 3 Mar. 2021, www.kirkusreviews.com/book-reviews/emily-henry/people-we-meet-on-vacation-henry/. Accessed 30 Nov. 2021.

Review of *People We Meet on Vacation*, by Emily Henry. *Publishers Weekly*, 26 Jan. 2021, www.publishersweekly.com/978-1-984806-75-8. Accessed 20 Nov. 2021.

Pugsley, Amy. Review of *People We Meet on Vacation*, by Emily Henry. *Flair*, 6 July 2021, flair-magazine.com/botm-people-we-meet-on-vacation-by-emily-henry/. Accessed 30 Nov. 2021.

Rancilio, Alicia. "Witty Friends Bond in *People We Meet on Vacation*." Associated Press, 10 May 2021, apnews.com/article/reviews-entertainment-arts-and-entertainment-3b7aa0265f9dffee5d4525eb3d1c4381. Accessed 8 Dec. 2021.

Playlist for the Apocalypse

Author: Rita Dove (b. 1952)
Publisher: W. W. Norton (New York). 128 pp.
Type of work: Poetry

Playlist for the Apocalypse is a collection of poetry by Pulitzer Prize–winning American poet Rita Dove, with its diverse works bringing together themes of history, contemporary society, and change.

In popular culture, poets are often portrayed as solitary individuals—outsiders who spend their time quietly putting their most intimate thoughts and feelings on the page. This archetype seems based on some of the genre's most famous historic figures, the agoraphobic Emily Dickinson, for example, or lonely New England woods resident, Henry David Thoreau. Yet Rita Dove is perhaps one of the best examples shattering this myopic perception of poets. Throughout her dynamic, highly acclaimed career, Dove has been everything from a Fulbright Scholar to a Pulitzer Prize winner to the first African American to be named the US Poet Laureate. More than that, however, she proved that the societal role of poets does not have to be confined to that of a passive observer—poets can also be activists who use their voice to inspire change. In her tenure as US Poet Laureate from 1993 to 1995, for instance, she spearheaded numerous events to not only generate interest in poetry but also generate a deeper understanding of the nation's cultural diversity.

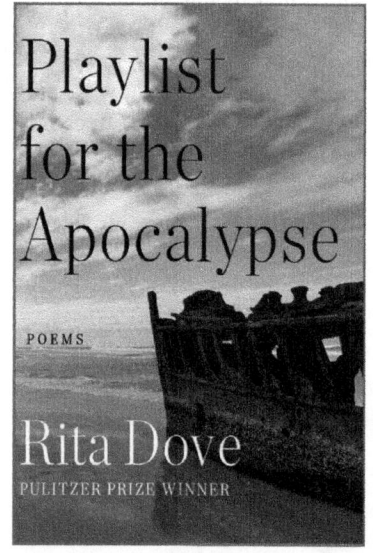

Playlist for the Apocalypse (2021) is Dove's eleventh collection of poetry and in many ways the most reflective of the multifaceted elements that make her one of the United States' greatest poets. Many critics have long found it difficult to categorize her work because she is the kind of writer who refuses to be pigeonholed and the myriad subjects her collections focus on are always unpredictable. The Pulitzer Prize–winning *Thomas and Beulah* (1986), for example, relays a semi-fictional account of her maternal grandparents' lives through a series of poems. *American Smooth* (2004) comprises poems about her experiences as a competitive ballroom dancer. Meanwhile, the poems of *Sonata Mulattica* (2009) focus on the friendship between the biracial violinist George Polgreen Bridgetower and Ludwig van Beethoven. While *Playlist for the Apocalypse* is not as singularly focused, it still feels connected to these previous works in the way that it boasts beautifully crafted verse and is anchored in the human experience.

Playlist for the Apocalypse is Dove's first collection of new poems in twelve years and proves to be a stunning return. The book is divided up into six seemingly unrelated sections that each have a unique focus—from the history of the word "ghetto" to a section told from the perspective of a springtime cricket to a series of "angry odes." In an interview with *Guernica*, Dove noted that she assembled the collection by printing out various poems she had written dating back as far as 1989, spreading them out on the floor, and walking around to try and find ones that fit together. After groups of thematically connected pieces were organized into what would become the book's sections, she began writing new pieces to fill in the gaps. When read chronologically together, these sections give way to an undeniably fraternal feeling—they may have disparate qualities but thanks to their shared creator and worldview, they undoubtedly belong together. In turn, the title word "playlist" seems especially appropriate considering that most of the poems were written separately but, through Dove's thoughtful curation, generate a complementary tone.

Rita Dove

Arguably the most prevalent theme in *Playlist for the Apocalypse* is American society and culture. This is largely due to the fact that US history and racial politics are reoccurring threads. In the section entitled "A Standing Witness," for example, Dove writes a series of "testimonies" from an unnamed woman who uses each poem to recount one significant event from the past fifty years of American history. These poems move through time chronologically beginning in 1968 with the aftermath of Martin Luther King Jr.'s and Robert Kennedy's assassinations. Another poem describes musician Jimi Hendrix playing the national anthem at Woodstock in 1969 while those that follow span subjects such as the Watergate scandal, *Roe v. Wade*, the AIDS epidemic, the advent of the internet, and the Obama and Trump presidencies. While the book's other sections do not focus so directly on US history, they still have poems that revolve around the nation's complex past. For example, the section "Spring Cricket" has two poems that explore the Negritude literary movement of the 1930s. One of the most powerful poems in the section "After Egypt" is about the 2012 killing of Black teen Trayvon Martin. Ultimately, *Playlist for the Apocalypse* may be about many different things, but its depiction of difficult moments in history, and especially racially motivated tragedies, demonstrates that the past is still shaping people's lives today and should not be ignored.

As effective as Dove is at writing poems about big sociopolitical issues, she is equally talented at crafting verse that captures small, personal moments. In the section "Time's Arrow," for example, she has a poem entitled "Scarf" that describes how beautiful she finds the sensation of silk on her neck to be. In "Family Reunion," she highlights the transcendence of her extended family's accents, genes, and food. Just as powerfully, the section "Eight Angry Odes" comprises a cathartic series of poems about the different things that anger and upset her. Such emotional instigators include everything from a group of giggling teenage girls who take too long to cross the street to an achy right knee to the experience of buying an anniversary gift for her husband. One poem in this section, "Insomnia Etiquette," describes what a typical night of not sleeping is like for her, writing "it's just me and you, / Brother Night—moonless, / plunked down behind enemy lines / with no maps, no matches." What is so compelling about these more personal poems is that they provide a more intimate look at the author as an individual while also touching on things that are so relatable that many readers will feel an enjoyable sense of comradery.

Of all the more personal poems found in *Playlist for the Apocalypse*, arguably the most powerful can be found in the final section, "Little Book of Woe." It is here that Dove publicly reveals publicly for the first time that she has been struggling with relapsing-remitting multiple sclerosis (MS) for the past twenty years. In this section's first poem, "Soup," she recalls how in the moment that her doctor officially diagnosed her with MS she found herself wanting to think about nothing else other than soup. As she processes a future with a debilitating disease, she describes memories from her youth that she associates with soup, as well as her desire to make soup later that night and all of the ingredients she plans on using. It is a profoundly human and heartbreaking poem about how when people are faced with devastating news, they often want nothing more than comfort and the opportunity to focus on something they can control. Throughout the other poems of "Little Book of Woe," Dove uses her literary prowess to capture the many different types of physical pain she struggles with and the way that MS has changed the way she views her own mortality. It is a beautiful and unflinching depiction of what living with a chronic debilitating disease is like, which many readers will feel grateful for.

At many points while reading *Playlist for the Apocalypse* it is easy to be in awe of Dove's brilliant literary talent. So many of her poems appear to be simple on the page and yet they have profound things to say about life and humanity. Equally impressive is the way that she moves with ease between different poetic styles and forms. Some of her poems are elegant and stoic while others are highly playful. In her depiction of the 1990s in "World Wide Web," for example, she begins with the stanza, "Hubba Bubba Bubble tape, / chicken pita wrap to go, / Pop Rocks, Push Pops, Dipping Dots, / Oreos!" Yet although Dove's poems cannot be contained to a singular style, there are some qualities that most of them share. Perhaps more than anything, there is a lyrical quality to so many of her poems, such that they feel as though they could easily be transformed into songs. This is likely a reflection of Dove's own passions, which include singing, dancing, and playing the cello. Regardless of where the musicality of her poems come from, it makes for a transformative reading experience—and makes the collection's title all the more apt.

It is difficult to find any significant flaws in *Playlist for the Apocalypse*, which comes across as the work of a well-established master of craft. Many readers may find their only complaint to be that the collection reads quickly and consequently is over too fast; fortunately, rereading the poems proves a rewarding way to stay emerged in Dove's luminous writing, as previously unnoticed nuances and interpretations can emerge. Unsurprisingly, critical reception of the book was overwhelmingly positive. It was a finalist for the 2021 NAACP Image Award, and reviewers consistently praised Dove's eminently readable style. Writing for *The Chicago Review of Books*, for example, Meredith Boe noted, "As always, her words are raw, poignant, and accessible." Indeed, readers from all backgrounds will be able to enjoy the book's poems and get something valuable from them. Dove has a way of effortlessly nudging her readers' minds into territories that might be new for them but completely necessary.

Many critics were also quick to extol the implications of what Dove's poems have to say. In his review for the *New York Times*, Dwight Garner suggested that the collection ranks among Dove's best, concluding, "You sense the books of many poets of Dove's generation slipping to the back of the bookcase. Not hers." Similarly, *Publishers Weekly* stated that, "Dove brilliantly breathes new life into the present age, revealing it as a time for urgent change." Indeed, one of the most resonant qualities of *Playlist for the Apocalypse* is how timely and necessary it feels. Although many of the poems look back to the past, they do so in a way to provide context for the present moment—a moment that in the wake of a global pandemic and growing political tension seems akin to the "apocalypse" that Dove refers to in the book's title. However, despite pointing out the apocalyptic qualities of the world today, she never leaves her readers feeling hopeless. Instead, *Playlist for the Apocalypse* proves to be a collection of galvanizing work that presents being alive and human in such a beautiful way that it will make people want to fight for a better tomorrow.

Author Biography

Rita Dove has served as poet laureate of the United States (1993–95), Virginia's poet laureate from (2004–6), and chancellor of the Academy of American Poets (2005–11). Her awards include the 1987 Pulitzer Prize for Poetry, a 1996 National Humanities Medal, a 2011 National Medal of Arts, and the 2021 American Academy of Arts and Letters Gold Medal for Poetry.

Emily E. Turner

Review Sources

Boe, Meredith. "Reflections on Democracy and Individuality in *Playlist for the Apocalypse*." Review of *Playlist for the Apocalypse*, by Rita Dove. *The Chicago Review of Books*, 4 Aug. 2021, chireviewofbooks.com/2021/08/04/playlist-for-the-apocalypse/. Accessed 12 Feb. 2022.

Garner, Dwight. "In *Playlist for the Apocalypse*, the Weight of American History and of Mortality." Review of *Playlist for the Apocalypse*, by Rita Dove. *The New York Times*, 9 Aug. 2021, www.nytimes.com/2021/08/09/books/review-playlist-for-apocalypse-rita-dove.html. Accessed 12 Feb. 2022.

Review of *Playlist for the Apocalypse*, by Rita Dove. *Publishers Weekly*, 14 Aug. 2021, www.publishersweekly.com/978-0-393-86777-0. Accessed 12 Feb. 2022.

Poet Warrior

Author: Joy Harjo (b. 1951)
Publisher: W. W. Norton (New York).
 Illustrated. 240 pp.
Type of work: Memoir, poetry
Time: 1950s to present day
Locale: The United States

A memoir describing the author's journey toward becoming a poet, and the influences that her family, her mentors, the Muskogee culture, and the natural world had on her thinking and her art

Principal personages
JOY HARJO, the author
WYNEMA BAKER FOSTER, her mother, who figures prominently but is not named in the book
ALLEN W. FOSTER JR., her father
LOIS HARJO, her aunt, an artist and teacher of art
THE MONSTER, her stepfather, whose name is never given
DONA JO HARJO-WEBB, her cousin
THE OLD ONES, Mvskoke elders
MERIDEL LE SUEUR, her mentor

Joy Harjo is now in her third term as the Poet Laureate of the United States but one reading this powerful memoir might conclude that Harjo, if asked to describe herself, would not even mention that high honor. Her identity seems to center more closely on being Mvskoke, a member of the Muscogee (Creek) Nation, and a member of a large extended family, both living and dead. This book, her second memoir, describes how she came to be a poet and how that journey has affected her life. The theme of journey recurs throughout the book. The Mvskoke people are one of the nations from the southeastern United States who in the 1830s were forced to give up their ancestral homelands and move to the Indian Territory in what is now Oklahoma. This uprooting had tremendous, mostly negative impacts on the people and their culture, yet a vibrant Mvskoke community abides in eastern Oklahoma and continues to pass on its traditions and folk-learning, including the brutal lessons of that journey. In *Poet Warrior* (2021), Harjo relates these lessons as well as those she has learned on her own long road to personal and creative maturity.

As a child, Harjo would hide under the kitchen table to listen to the elders in her family talk. She loved the stories, and long before she envisioned any vocation as a poet, she fell in love with words. "I loved words," she writes. "How they felt in my mouth. I would taste them. Sing them." Like many children, she also learned the hard lesson that not all words used by adults are to be repeated by children. Through a difficult childhood, which included abuse as well as the typical adolescent angst, she came to find reading, poetry, and rock-and-roll music a refuge from the fearful aspects of her life. Harjo is clearly proud of her Mvskoke heritage and sees her poetry as a tool that can used to promote recognition of her culture. Early on, she determined that the goal of her writing would be to make others see Indigenous people as humans. She sees herself as a warrior for her people, for Indigenous people generally, and for women of all races. In autobiographical poems throughout the book, early on she refers to herself as Girl-Warrior but later as Poet Warrior. She believes this role was designated for her by the Old Ones, a collective representation of traditional Mvskoke elders, who often appear to her in dreams. In one poem, she writes:

Joy Harjo

>Poet Warrior reached for a gun.
>She was given a paintbrush,
>A saxophone, a pen.
>These will be your instruments of power
>The Old Ones said.

Although this poem appears around halfway through the book, it might be taken as kind of an outline of Harjo's quest to find herself and her voice. Earlier, she notes, "As much as I loved poetry, I often felt alone in my love. Being a poet is nothing anyone could aspire to be." Even when she had become established as a noted, working poet, she admits to being uncertain what kind of life that was supposed to be. She began her higher education at the University of New Mexico as a pre-med student but soon turned to art. She worked hard to develop her skill as a poet but mentions little about her formal education except noting that she graduated from the prestigious Iowa Writer's Workshop. She attended the Institute of American Indian Art in Albuquerque and later taught there. When she began teaching in the public university system, however, she eventually concluded she was losing her way and quit because she did not want to conform to the type of teacher and writer the system seemed to demand.

Throughout the book, she cites an eclectic mix of poets who inspired her and features their poetry. Some are poets whom most well-read Americans would recognize, such as Emily Dickinson, Walt Whitman, and Langston Hughes. Others are prominent Native Nations (a descriptor she prefers over "Native American") poets, such as N. Scott Momaday and Leslie Marmon Silko. Some are Indigenous poets from around the world, such as the Ugandan poet Okot p'Bitek. Harjo also writes about her first mentor, the Iowa-born socialist activist Meridel Le Sueur, who was influenced by the radical farm protest movements of the Upper Midwest in the early 1900s and by stories told to her by Native women. Harjo met Le Sueur in the 1970s at an event at the University of New Mexico, where they began a friendship that lasted until Le Sueur died in 1996.

Poet Warrior is a hybrid memoir that combines prose and poetry and often blurs the distinctions between them. Some of Harjo's poems are listed with a title, others just flow along as part of the story, although their titles and publication history are given in credits at the end of the book. All the poems, whether titled or not, are integral to the memoir's narrative. Even in the prose sections, Harjo's writing is often lyrical. Describing a time in her early adult life, when she was raising two children and attending school, she writes, "My children were slick otters of joy in these rough waters of living."

While Harjo often writes of "big" themes and existential struggles, she also deals with the more mundane aspects of life, such as cooking and eating, themes that recur throughout the book. Harjo concludes that the world begins at a kitchen table because everyone must eat. She also includes a poem entitled "Genealogy of Cooks and Cooking." When her husband tells her that Mvskoke men traditionally treated women with respect, Harjo laughs and asks, "Then why aren't you cooking my dinner?"

Since the theme of journeying is prominent in this book, it follows that memory is also important. Harjo recalls discussing with a cousin how history "lives within us" even they did not know it. She also knows that memories can be painful, noting, "I don't want to forget, though sometimes memory appears to be an enemy bringing only pain." But painful memories often teach powerful lessons, and Harjo is aware that no valuable lessons come without pain. She stayed close to her father even though he had been unfaithful and abusive to her mother and eventually abandoned the family. With empathetic understanding she eventually came to see that the roots of his anger, which exploded in violence toward her mother and herself, actually lay in the past long before he had met her mother. Her stepfather abused her, and though she calls him "the monster" whenever she writes of him, she concludes that he was one of her greatest teachers, because his abuse forced her to turn to spiritual realties to learn to cope with life.

Since memory and family are prominent themes in this book, it is notable that Harjo writes about some family members without any reference to their names. It is not hard to see why she would not want to use the name of her abusive stepfather. She mentions her father and brother by name but does not name her mother, even though she is Harjo's first teacher and figures prominently throughout the memoir. Harjo dedicates a poem to her first granddaughter, who is named, and there is a photo with the names of her two older grandchildren in the caption.

Reviewers have noted that the book does not follow a linear progression through Harjo's life. This appears to be intentional. Early in the book, Harjo notes, "Life never goes in a straight line in our Native communities. Time moves slower." While the book begins with part 1, "Ancestral Roots" and her youth and ends with her life as a grandmother at the time the book was written, other things are in a kind of jumbled order, and some important milestones do not appear at all. For example, part 5, "Teachers," in which she writes about those who influenced her writing, does not come until late the book. Perhaps Harjo pays little attention to the framework of time because she believes we continue to interact with those who have died. She believes the Old Ones have directed her through dreams or visions throughout her life and that friends and relatives from her own past continue to visit and counsel her. The natural world also speaks to her—owls have brought her messages about the imminent passing of a loved one, and a snake once gave her a message to pass on to Leslie Marmon Silko.

Reviewers have generally praised *Poet Warrior*, using words such as "beautiful" (NPR), "gorgeous, compassionate" (*Kirkus*), and "mesmerizing" (*Publishers Weekly*) in describing it, and this praise is well deserved. Several have noted that this is not a book to be read hurriedly; one might be tempted to skim over the poetry to get on with the story, but the poetry advances the narrative and such skimming would result in missing some of the deepest and most meaningful messages in the book. One should read this book somewhat like Harjo experienced the words she collected as a young woman—tasting them, singing them, and seeing how they feel in your mouth.

Author Biography

Award-winning poet Joy Harjo has published nine poetry collections and a previous memoir, *Crazy Brave* (2012). In 2019 she became the twenty-third poet laureate of the United States. She is the first Native American poet laureate appointed to the post and the second poet laureate to serve three terms.

Mark S. Joy, PhD

Review Sources

Iglesias, Gabino. "*Poet Warrior* Centers on the Role of the Poetry, Art and Music in Joy Harjo's Life." Review of *Poet Warrior: A Memoir*, by Joy Harjo *NPR*, 8 Sept. 2021, www.npr.org/2021/09/08/1035033419/poet-warrior-centers-on-the-role-of-poetry-art-and-music-in-joy-harjo-s-life. Accessed 2 Dec. 2021.

Review of *Poet Warrior: A Memoir*, by Joy Harjo. *Kirkus Reviews*, 7 Sept. 2021, www.kirkusreviews.com/book-reviews/joy-harjo/poet-warrior/. Accessed 2 Dec. 2021.

Review of *Poet Warrior: A Memoir*, by Joy Harjo. *Publishers Weekly*, 25 June 2021, www.publishersweekly.com/978-0-393-24852-4. Accessed 2 Dec. 2021.

Winik, Marion. "Review: *Poet Warrior*, by Joy Harjo." *Star Tribune*, 3 Sept. 2021, www.startribune.com/review-poet-warrior-by-joy-harjo/600093597/. Accessed 2 Dec. 2021.

Project Hail Mary

Author: Andy Weir (b. 1972)
Publisher: Ballantine Books (New York). 496 pp.
Type of work: Novel
Time: Near future
Locales: Earth, outer space, 40 Eridani

In Andy Weir's science-fiction drama Project Hail Mary, *a science teacher and a lost alien try to save both of their worlds from a microorganism that eats solar energy.*

Principal characters

RYLAND GRACE, a junior high school science teacher recruited by the United Nations to investigate the Astrophage crisis
ROCKY, an alien from the Eridani star system also trying to solve the Astrophage crisis
EVA STRATT, Dutch scientist in charge of the Hail Mary space program back on earth
OLESYA ILYUKHINA, engineer aboard the Hail Mary spacecraft
YÁO LI-JIE, commander of the Hail Mary spacecraft

Andy Weir, a former computer scientist, skyrocketed to fame as a novelist when his first science-fiction novel, *The Martian*, became a surprise national best seller after he began self-publishing it in 2011. Weir, a lifelong science aficionado interested in space, demonstrated a knack for both storytelling and research in his debut, which tells the story of a lone astronaut marooned on Mars who must utilize his scientific knowledge to survive until he can be rescued. Many of the scientific principles and ideas discussed in *The Martian* reflected cutting-edge space science, and the book received praise not only from readers and literary critics but also from the scientific community for its accuracy. The success of *The Martian* was, in part, due to Weir's decision to tell much of the story through the point of view of its main character, Mark Watney, an astronaut and botanist who translates difficult scientific concepts for readers in an approachable and humorous way.

Weir attempted to replicate this success with his sophomore novel, *Artemis* (2017), which leaned more heavily into the fantasy side of the science-fiction genre and was set in the fictional city of Artemis, located on an inhabited version of Earth's moon. Set in the future, *Artemis* tells the story of a minor smuggler named Jasmine "Jazz" Bashara who is drawn into a corporate heist with political implications. In *Artemis*, Weir returned to the themes that drove his success with *The Martian*, incorporating scientific theories and ideas about near-future technology into the book. However, without the use of a science-trained narrator like his protagonist in *The Martian*, some critics found that many of Weir's more scientific digressions pulled focus away from the plot and led to moments of awkward contrast between complex scientific ideas and the novel's adventure-driven plot.

With his third novel, *Project Hail Mary* (2021), Weir returns to some of the techniques that made *The Martian* a success. Like his debut, *Project Hail Mary* features a protagonist with a background in science. However, unlike *The Martian*'s Mark Watney, who was a professional botanist and astronaut, the protagonist of *Project Hail Mary*, middle school science teacher Ryland Grace, is even more closely aligned with the perspective of an ordinary person. Although Grace knows a lot about science, he is also a civilian, which allows him to act as a surrogate for the reader, guiding them through both the science and the technicalities of space science as an administrative and governmental effort. By portraying Grace as both an insider and an outsider to the events of the book, Weir is able to indulge freely in his excitement about plausible scientific futures without glossing over explanations or getting lost in technical jargon.

Andy Weir

While Grace is a return to the Watney-style scientist hero that Weir cultivated in his first novel, *Project Hail Mary* is far more speculative and far more of a "science fantasy" book than *The Martian*, which was very much a "near future" book grounded in both current technology and contemporary human culture. *Project Hail Mary*'s incorporation of elements such as advanced space travel technology and aliens places it in a genre distinct from Weir's earlier works, though the author tries to keep even the most fantasy-driven elements grounded in modern science. For example, the new species of alien life introduced in the novel is based on real-life speculation about the kinds of organisms that might exist in the universe; as a result, this book also features Weir's first attempt to incorporate "astrobiology," the scientific study of extraterrestrial life. The inclusion of astrobiology compliments Weir's continued use of astronomy and astrophysics, which he drew on in his two earlier novels.

Weir also employs another narrative technique that allows him to lay out the backstory and world-building by utilizing a main character who, at least initially, suffers from severe amnesia. At the start of the novel, Grace awakens on a floating starship accompanied by the bodies of his two deceased crewmates, with no memory of his own identity or how he ended up on the ship. While the recent events of Grace's life are a mystery, he is fortunate to remember much of what he knows about science and technology and is gradually able to piece together what happened to him. The use of amnesia as a narrative device is not new but serves Weir's goal of inviting readers to "discover" the plot alongside Grace as he pieces together his lost memories.

As Grace's memories return, aspects of his past, along with the novel's backstory, are revealed through flashbacks. Readers learn that the sun has been dimming, forcing Earth's inhabitants to confront a particularly grave crisis. Probes allow the international space agencies to figure out that the sun is infected by a single-celled organism known as an "Astrophage," literally meaning "star eater," that feeds off of solar energy, reproduces uncontrollably, and will eventually dim the sun to such a level that the earth will pass into a devastating and potentially apocalyptic new Ice Age. Scientists also discover that the Astrophage infection has spread to many different stars visible from Earth or from satellite monitoring stations. Grace, a molecular biologist, becomes the scientific advisor for a United Nations effort to address the problem and helps them plan an expedition to the Tau Ceti star system, which has somehow resisted an Astrophage infection.

The United Nations outfits a ship called the *Hail Mary*, which will travel to Tau Ceti to discover why the star has not been infected. If the mission succeeds, the crew is supposed to send automated probes, known as "beetles," back to Earth with information on how to combat the problem; however, the crew of the *Hail Mary* will not have fuel to return and so will remain stranded in space and eventually die there. Grace eventually remembers that he was not supposed to be on the mission and was only originally hired to train one of the crew's scientists on how to take certain measurements. However, after an accident on Earth killed the ship's crew, Grace ended up on the mission to space. By the time Grace awakens from an induced coma years after the start of the voyage, an accident has led to the death of his two crewmates.

As he tries to recall how he ended up on the *Hail Mary*, Grace is also forced to deal with other challenges in the present day. He eventually realizes that his ship managed to reach Tau Ceti and is in stable orbit, but he also discovers another ship orbiting the star. This ship, it turns out, contains the sole survivor of an extraterrestrial crew sent from the star 40 Eridani, which is also suffering from Astrophage infection. The alien, a member of the Eridian species, is a spider-like creature covered in stone, adapted to its home planet's atmosphere of extreme pressure and density and filled with ammonia at concentrations lethal to humans.

The sole survivor on the alien ship, whom Grace nicknames "Rocky," is an engineer but lacks the biological knowledge to complete its mission, forcing Grace and Rocky to share their skills and try to work together to save themselves and their home planets. When exploring how Grace and Rocky learn to communicate and collaborate, Weir speculates about some interesting topics in the field of astrobiology, such as how humans could communicate with an alien speaking an entirely different kind of language. Grace solves this problem by using a computer program that records and translates the tonal language of the Eridian aliens. Once the pair figure out how to communicate, Rocky and Grace begin working together to figure out a way to kill the Astrophage, offering them a chance to not only save their home planets but possibly even make it home alive.

Weir's *Project Hail Mary* earned many positive reviews, but some aspects of the novel were criticized. Many of the critics enjoyed the story line, action, and Weir's witty portrayals of Grace and other characters but found flaws in the narrative's predictable elements and reliance on overused science-fiction tropes. Writing for the *Washington Post*, reviewer Mary Kowal singled out Weir's use of an amnesiac hero as the most glaring example of this reliance on old tropes. Kowal also noted that Weir, though well versed in space science, seemed to have forgotten the common administrative process of utilizing detailed checklists to ensure that small mistakes do not become major meltdowns. She argued that the lack of "checklists" is exactly what allows the accidents that provide narrative tension but found it convenient and unrealistic that such a mission would have been undertaken without a certain level of administrative redundancy designed to prevent such disasters. Kowal also pointed out some other plot holes, including questioning how the Eridians were able to possess robotics without having computers.

Other reviewers also found fault with Weir's decision to stray from the scientific realism for which his works are known. They noted the presence of advanced "technologies" that go far beyond the limits of current scientific knowledge, and felt these technologies provide overly simplistic solutions to the novel's problems. Lawrence De Maria, reviewing the book for the *Washington Independent Review of Books*, felt that, compared to the scientific veracity of *The Martian*, Weir took far greater liberties with scientific fact in *Project Hail Mary*, joking that "apparently, poetic license increases exponentially the further one gets from Earth." Writing for *USA Today*, reviewer Brian Truitt took less issue with Weir's scientific ideas but noted that the shifting back and forth between flashbacks and Grace's present-day adventures on the ship sometimes detracts from what is otherwise an engrossing read; still, he felt it succeeded as both a sci-fi thriller and "hard science buddy comedy."

Indeed, despite some perceived faults, critics and audiences generally considered *Project Hail Mary* a satisfying return to some of the elements that made *The Martian* such a tremendous success. Reviewer Alec Nevala-Lee called the book a "course correction" in his *New York Times* review, noting that Weir had essentially revived the "scientist hero" trope that first emerged during World War II and that he had used so successfully in *The Martian*. Nevala-Lee considered the work an "engaging space odyssey" and a worthy addition to Weir's canon.

Author Biography

Andy Weir is a science-fiction novelist and former computer programmer whose three published novels have all become best sellers. The success of his 2011 self-published debut *The Martian* helped him to secure subsequent book deals from mainstream publishers. In 2016, he won the John W. Campbell Award for Best New Writer for *The Martian*.

Micah Issitt

Review Sources

De Maria, Lawrence. Review of *Project Hail Mary*, by Andy Weir. *Washington Independent Review of Books*, 18 June 2021, www.washingtonindependentreviewofbooks.com/index.php/bookreview/project-hail-mary. Accessed 15 Dec. 2021.

Kowal, Mary Robinette. "Andy Weir's *Project Hail Mary* Is a Bestseller. It also Has Some Problems." *The Washington Post*, 23 May 2021, www.washingtonpost.com/entertainment/books/andy-weirs-project-hail-mary-is-a-bestseller-it-also-has-some-problems/2021/05/22/7ccd3578-b8bc-11eb-a5fe-bb49dc89a248_story.html. Accessed 15 Dec. 2021.

Nevala-Lee, Alec. "Alone on a Spaceship, Trying to Save the World." Review of *Project Hail Mary*, by Andy Weir. *The New York Times*, 4 May 2021, www.nytimes.com/2021/05/04/books/review/andy-weir-project-hail-mary.html. Accessed 15 Dec. 2021.

Review of *Project Hail Mary*, by Andy Weir. *Kirkus*, 4 May 2021, www.kirkusreviews.com/book-reviews/andy-weir/project-hail-mary/. Accessed 15 Dec. 2021.

Truitt, Brian. "Review: Andy Weir's *Project Hail Mary* Is an Out-of-This-World Tale of Science and Friendship." *USA Today*, 4 May 2021, www.usatoday.com/story/entertainment/books/2021/05/04/project-hail-mary-review-andy-weir-book-intergalactic-excellence/4915934001/. Accessed 15 Dec. 2021.

The Promise

Author: Damon Galgut (b. 1963)
Publisher: Europa Editions (New York).
   256 pp.
Type of work: Novel
Time: 1986–2018
Locale: South Africa

Damon Galgut's ninth novel, The Promise, *examines the dysfunctional White South African Swart family against the backdrop of sweeping social changes occurring in the nation over the course of thirty troubled years.*

Principal characters
HERMAN "MANIE" SWART, a.k.a. Pa, the family patriarch, operator of a reptile park
RACHEL SWART, a.k.a. Ma, his wife and mother of their three children
ANTON SWART, his son and oldest child
ASTRID SWART, his older daughter
AMOR SWART, his younger daughter
SALOME, the Swart family's longtime Black servant
LUKAS, Salome's son, the same age as Amor
MARINA LAUBSCHER, his sister, the Swart children's aunt
OCKIE LAUBSCHER, Marina's husband, the Swart children's uncle

In Damon Galgut's novel *The Promise* (2021), the first—and most important—character readers encounter is Amor Swart, who is thirteen years old in 1986. Amor is considered peculiar by other members of her family, primarily because she cares more for the welfare of others than for herself. Her oddity is excused by the fact she was struck by a bolt of lightning seven years earlier, which blew off her little toe, left scars on her feet, and may have given her the power of telekinesis. Amor is driven by her aunt and uncle, Marina and Ockie Laubscher, from the school she is attending to her home near Pretoria, South Africa. Home is a sprawling house with "twenty-four doors on the outside that have to be locked at night," surrounded by acres of farmland on the veld (a vast, rural grassland in South Africa). The property was purchased long before by her grandfather, a descendent of the Voortrekkers, Afrikaans-speaking Dutch pioneers in the region. The occasion of Amor's return is the death from cancer at age forty of her mother, Rachel. Before Rachel died, she had rejected the Dutch Reformed Church, to which she had converted upon marriage, and returned to her former religion of Judaism. This was in retaliation for her husband, Manie's refusal to keep his pledge to give up gambling and frequenting prostitutes. Much to Manie's chagrin, a rabbi will

Damon Galgut
Courtesy Marthinius Basson

perform the burial services at Rachel's funeral because of her return to the Jewish faith; furthermore, her husband will not be allowed to be buried beside his wife in the Jewish cemetery.

Amidst these tensions, the whole immediate family has gathered for the funeral. In addition to her father, Herman "Manie" Swart, operator of a popular reptile park called Scaly City, plus other friends, relatives, and a shady evangelical minister, Amor's older siblings are also present. Her nineteen-year-old brother, Anton, a rifleman in military service who killed a woman during a demonstration in the waning days of apartheid, has been granted a week-long pass. Her sister, Astrid, an anorexic, paranoid teenager afraid of everything—"dark, poverty, thunderstorms, getting fat, earthquakes, tidal waves, crocodiles, the blacks, the future, the orderly structure of society coming undone"—has recently lost her virginity to a young man who will become her first husband. In the background, unable to attend the funeral because of her race, is Salome, a Black servant who was acquired with the land. Salome has long lived nearby on farm property with her son, Lukas, in a tumbledown three-room shack.

It is this humble dwelling that serves as a major point of conflict in Galgut's novel. Weeks before, Amor witnessed her mother on her deathbed extracting a promise from Manie to give the house to Salome. After the funeral, Amor reminds her father of his promise. She also tells Anton of what she overheard, but he informs his sister that under the laws of apartheid, Salome could not own the property anyway. Amor returns to school. Anton returns to military camp but decides to desert instead, discarding his rifle and uniform before fleeing to hide in the wilderness of the Republic of Transkei, a breakaway state that existed between 1976 and 1994 in the southeastern part of South Africa.

In the novel's second of four parts, it is 1995, and apartheid has ended. Nelson Mandela, a Black man, is now head of the South African government, having ascended "from a cell to a throne." The economy is booming, and South Africa has become a nation that "defies gravity." Once again, the Swart clan has collected at the farm. This time, it is Manie ("Pa") who is of concern. While attempting to break a world record for staying in a glass cage among venomous reptiles, he was bitten by a cobra and lies comatose in a hospital intensive care unit. Family members are older, if not wiser. Because conscription ended, Anton survived without repercussion his desertion to Transkei—"holding on, holding out, an old South African tradition"—and now lives in Johannesburg on the generosity of an older woman. Astrid, now married to the man who deflowered her, is mother of twins born in 1988. Amor, living in London, has to be laboriously tracked down and informed of her father's dire condition, so she can fly home. Pa dies in the middle of June, making his children orphans. Amor arrives in time for the funeral; Salome's son, Lukas, helps dig Herman's grave at the family cemetery. The burial ceremony takes a bizarre turn when Marina, the children's aunt, who read an article about "a dodgy funeral home," demands that the coffin be opened to ensure that her brother is alone inside. The funeral director complies, and when the coffin lid is lifted to reveal Herman's grotesquely swollen body, Astrid's children are traumatized.

The following day, the family lawyer reads Manie's will to the assembled siblings. Most of the Swart estate is put into a trust, of which family members are equal beneficiaries to a fund that provides a monthly income. The farm and surrounding property are not included in the trust but are available for the use of surviving family members. When Amor asks about the promise made to give Salome her house, she is told there is nothing in the will about such a bequest. Anton decides to remain on the farm to take advantage of the terms of the trust. Amor heads for Durban to try nursing and winds up working in the HIV ward of a hospital. In the final two sections of the novel, Amor returns twice more to the farm: once in 2004 and again in 2017. Both times she is attending a funeral, and the passage of time reveals the huge political and cultural changes taking place in South Africa. Much will happen to Amor and her siblings over this time period, but Amor will never forget the promise made to Salome.

By any measure, *The Promise* is a remarkable achievement. The carefully composed, multilayered novel (inspired, according to interviews with the author, on true events) is simultaneously a sharply focused family drama, a playful soap opera, a biting satire, a well-observed social commentary on recent South African history, and a fond homage to the rugged beauty of the author's native land. Besides the main plot points—namely, who in the Swart family will survive, and whether the promise made at the beginning of the story will ever be honored—there is a strong undercurrent of religious thought that encompasses fundamental Christianity, evangelism, Judaism, native spirituality, and Eastern philosophy. Crisp dialogue (even following the modern trend of eschewing quotation marks) rings true and is often marked by dark humor. There are a multitude of marvelous, well-phrased passages containing kernels of truth that readers may want to repeat aloud, such as "time is a river that washes the world away," and "refusal only works on other people, on fate it has no effect." The third-person, present-tense narration is stylishly inventive, showing the varied perspectives not only of all major and many minor characters, but also glancing viewpoints from walk-ons, like a homeless man, mortuary attendants, a carjacker, police detectives, and even a jackal prowling for carrion.

Critical reception of *The Promise* was almost universally positive. Rave reviews by the dozens employed words and phrases like "bleakly funny," "gleeful," "bravura," and "stunning." Rand Richards Cooper of the *New York Times* (15 Apr. 2021) especially enjoyed the novel's "protean tone, now menacing, now darkly mirthful," which "offers all the virtues of realist fiction, plus some extras." Cooper further praised the novel's "cinematic present tense and kaleidoscopic point of view [which] create a mosaic of what everyone in the room is thinking at a given moment." Similarly, Paul Perry of *Independent Ireland* (25 July 2021) called *The Promise* "a masterpiece of guile and empathy." He pointed out that "the plot is just the vehicle for a story that reveals the dark heart of South Africa's recent and turbulent history." Moreover, Perry considered the novel "significant and exciting . . . meditative, lyrical, and self-conscious." William Skidelsky of the *Financial Times* (15 June 2021) built upon such comments, calling *The Promise* "Galgut's fullest exploration yet of the poisonous legacy of apartheid." The reviewer focused on the author's choice of using characters "unconnected to the story" and noted that "the intriguing effect of this technique—a kind of hyperomniscience—is to create an almost physical sense of immediacy," which helps readers feel they are present with the characters. The *New Yorker*'s James Woods (12 Apr. 2021) in his long analysis agreed, praising the author's "appreciation of modernist techniques and emphases." He compared Galgut's work to that of Virginia Woolf and William Faulkner, particularly their use of a "free-floating narrator." Woods further called attention to the author's storytelling strengths, noting how he "uses his narrator playfully, assisted by nicely wayward run-on sentences" and his "free indirect style," which brings life to the book in combination with "the steady beat of humor."

Galgut, after two near misses in 2003 and 2010, won the Booker Prize with *The Promise* in 2021. Now at the height of his creative powers, readers will surely anticipate his next novel, for which the author must be reckoned a favorite to be awarded additional honors.

Author Biography

Damon Galgut published his first novel, *A Sinless Season*, in 1984. His novel *The Quarry* (1995) was adapted into feature films in 1998 and 2020. Both *The Good Doctor* (2003) and *In a Strange Room* (2010) were shortlisted for the Man Booker Prize, before *The Promise* won the award in 2021.

Jack Ewing

Review Sources

Bain, Keith. "On White Lies and Hope for Salvation: 'The Promise' by Damon Galgut." Review of *The Promise*, by Damon Galgut. *Daily Maverick*, 6 July 2021, www.dailymaverick.co.za/article/2021-07-06-on-white-lies-and-hope-for-salvation-the-promise-by-damon-galgut/. Accessed 6 Jan. 2022.

Cooper, Rand Richards. "A Family, and a Nation Under Apartheid, Tears at the Seams." Review of *The Promise*, by Damon Galgut. *The New York Times*, 15 Apr. 2021, www.nytimes.com/2021/04/15/books/review/damon-galgut-promise.html. Accessed 6 Jan. 2022.

Mierowsky, Marc. "Four Funerals and a Farm." Review of *The Promise*, by Damon Galgut. *Australian Book Review*, Oct. 2021, www.australianbookreview.com.au/abr-online/current-issue/968-october-2021-no-436/8330-marc-mierowsky-reviews-the-promise-by-damon-galgut. Accessed 6 Jan. 2022.

Perry, Paul. "Damon Galgut's The Promise Is a Masterpiece of Guile and Empathy." Review of *The Promise*, by Damon Galgut. *Independent Ireland*, 25 July 2021, www.independent.ie/entertainment/books/book-reviews/damon-galgutsthe-promise-is-a-masterpiece-of-guile-and-empathy-40683256.html. Accessed 6 Jan. 2022.

Skidelsky, William. "The Promise by Damon Galgut—a Poisonous Legacy." Review of *The Promise*, by Damon Galgut. *The Financial Times*, 15 June 2021, www.ft.com/content/43cf6632-858a-4419-a573-2d487405aee5. Accessed 6 Jan. 2022.

Wood, James. "A Family at Odds Reveals a Nation in the Throes." Review of *The Promise*, by Damon Galgut. *The New Yorker*, 12 Apr. 2021, www.newyorker.com/magazine/2021/04/19/a-family-at-odds-reveals-a-nation-in-the-throes. Accessed 6 Jan. 2022.

The Prophets

Author: Robert Jones Jr. (b. 1971)
Publisher: G. P. Putnam's Sons (New York). 388 pp.
Type of work: Novel
Time: Antebellum period
Locale: Halifax Plantation, Mississippi

Set on an antebellum plantation in Mississippi, Robert Jones Jr.'s debut novel, The Prophets, *is a love story about two enslaved boys whose relationship demonstrates that some bonds can never be broken.*

Principal characters

ISAIAH, an enslaved youth with a gentle and impressionable personality
SAMUEL, his lover, an enslaved youth with a cold, hard personality
MAGGIE, an enslaved woman with rare psychic gifts
PAUL, an enslaver, the owner of the Halifax plantation
RUTH, Paul's wife
ESSIE, an enslaved woman and Isaiah's close friend
AMOS, Essie's husband and a budding preacher

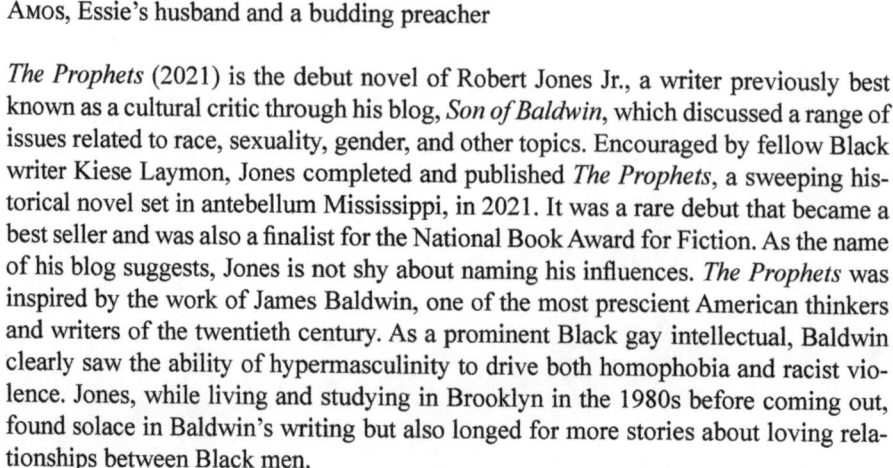

The Prophets (2021) is the debut novel of Robert Jones Jr., a writer previously best known as a cultural critic through his blog, *Son of Baldwin*, which discussed a range of issues related to race, sexuality, gender, and other topics. Encouraged by fellow Black writer Kiese Laymon, Jones completed and published *The Prophets*, a sweeping historical novel set in antebellum Mississippi, in 2021. It was a rare debut that became a best seller and was also a finalist for the National Book Award for Fiction. As the name of his blog suggests, Jones is not shy about naming his influences. *The Prophets* was inspired by the work of James Baldwin, one of the most prescient American thinkers and writers of the twentieth century. As a prominent Black gay intellectual, Baldwin clearly saw the ability of hypermasculinity to drive both homophobia and racist violence. Jones, while living and studying in Brooklyn in the 1980s before coming out, found solace in Baldwin's writing but also longed for more stories about loving relationships between Black men.

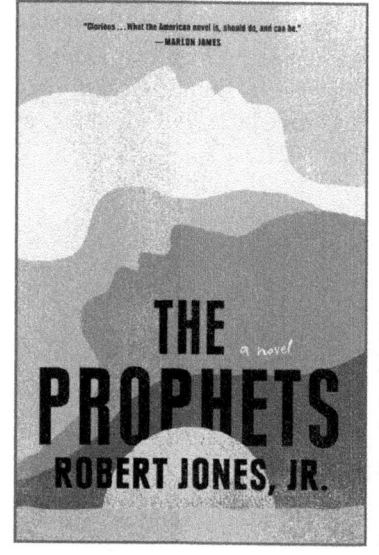

    The Prophets provides such a story and more. Through his work on *Son of Baldwin*, Jones encountered stories about gender fluidity in West African tradition. This discovery lies at the heart of *The Prophets*, which highlights the ways in which the profound violence of chattel slavery was both gendered and enforced through rape, including forced unions between unwilling partners. As a result of this narrative focus, the novel is rife with sexual violence. Beyond showing the violence of plantation slavery, Jones also recalls the forgotten African ancestors of these enslaved African Americans who embraced more generous views of sexuality, suggesting this loss of a more accepting culture as another enduring scar of enslavement.

The Prophets is narrated in the third person but through the eyes of many characters. At the center of the story are Isaiah and Samuel, two enslaved youths suggested to be in their late teens. Isaiah is thoughtful but also, at least in Samuel's eyes, too impressionable. His first survival instinct is to obey, whereas Samuel's is to fight. The two meet when Isaiah first arrives at the cotton plantation, situated deep in the Mississippi wilderness. It is called the Halifax plantation, but evocatively known to the enslaved people there as the Empty. Isaiah, a child, arrives chained to some twenty other people. Samuel is the first to approach him, carrying a ladle of water. The gesture seems both holy and sexual—Jones is movingly adept at painting the two as the same. Samuel, Jones writes, "moved the ladle toward Isaiah's face. Isaiah parted his lips and closed his eyes. He gulped as warm, sweet water leaked from the corners of his mouth." When Isaiah looks up, Samuel moves in such a way that his body blocks the sun and his outline seems to glow, imagery that paints an almost Christlike figure.

Robert Jones Jr.

This is not the only moment when *The Prophets* incorporates aspects of the Christian Bible, but it also paints Christianity as a tool of oppression used by White enslavers. This relationship between Christianity and oppression is intriguing but ultimately a little confusing. *The Prophets* reads like an allegory, but its meaning is not always entirely clear. Like the Samuel and Isaiah of the Bible, the Samuel and Isaiah of the Empty are prophets, even if they would not describe themselves as such. Memories and visions appear to them out of thin air. Other characters have biblical names, but the correlation is fuzzier, or perhaps, requires a deep familiarity with the Bible to understand the exact connection. Amos, an enslaved man, is also named for a prophet, but his role in the book is more accurately described as that of a betrayer.

As the story's conflicted villain, Amos is one of the more compelling characters in the book. He arrives at the Empty with Isaiah and in fact, carries the knowledge of Isaiah's true name. But in a misguided attempt to protect his wife, Essie, he concludes that he must turn the plantation against Samuel and Isaiah's relationship. With the encouragement of Paul, the plantation's cruel, God-fearing owner, Amos becomes a preacher. He sermonizes against Isaiah and Samuel's union, in hopes of having them split up and sold to other enslavers. By pursuing his disastrous aims with righteous zeal, Amos becomes a tragic figure in the classical sense.

Another central figure is Maggie, an older enslaved woman who serves as the plantation's cook. Like another character, Sarah, she retains the knowledge of her West African ancestors and has the rare ability to communicate with them and draw upon their powers. Like Isaiah and Samuel, she receives visions, but her mystical abilities go beyond those of a mere seer, as she can also conjure spells. In one compelling scene, she calls upon several other enslaved women to gather roots and herbs for a ritual healing circle. Maggie has a soft spot for Isaiah and Samuel but has an understandable disgust for nearly everyone else, given the atrocities she has endured. She seeks revenge when and where she can, adding snake venom to the sweet tea or ground glass to the hominy grits.

Years earlier, Maggie was forced to breastfeed the children of Ruth, who is Paul's wife and the plantation's confounding mistress. Maggie considers this task to be the most degrading of all. The reason springs from her argument for why she does not add urine or excrement to her enslavers' food. "She wouldn't allow them the pleasure, the privilege of having any part of her freely given," Jones writes. Maggie watches as other enslaved women are forced to act as wet nurses for White children and fears the day she will be forced "to act as a cow" for an enslaver's child. When Ruth approaches her with a chillingly casual command—"I'll help you unfasten your dress"—the idea for a brutal act of vengeance occurs to her. She rubs poisonous nightshade petals on her nipples, killing Ruth's first child to be born alive. Maggie harbors disdain for all children, Black and *toubab*, a West African word for White people, or colonizers. For her, enslaved children are "foolish, helpless, and unlovable," but this resentment is "mitigated by what she knew they would one day endure." This kernel of sympathy for enslaved children allows her to demonstrate kindness toward Isaiah and Samuel.

Maggie's link with her African heritage connects to the book's other thread, a story set among the Kosongo people, a West African ethnic group ruled by a female king. There, Jones introduces the characters of Kosii and Elewa. Clear forebears of Samuel and Isaiah, they are two of the king's male subjects who are marrying each other. The most striking aspect of this precolonial kingdom, though, is not its freer understanding of gender and sexuality, but its generosity and care toward all people. Children enjoy a high place in society, and strangers, even unsettling ones, are welcomed with open arms. Such effortless and selfless love does not exist on the Empty, save for the love between Samuel and Isaiah. A society built on violence, Jones seems to suggest, can only destroy itself and offers hope to neither oppressed nor oppressor. Elewa predicts this; before dying, he curses the White colonizers who have begun enslaving his people, declaring, "May you writhe in ever-pain. May you never find satisfaction. May your children eat themselves alive."

The Prophets received effusive reviews from critics who compared Jones to Baldwin as well as another African American literary legend, Toni Morrison. "It is not hyperbole to say that *The Prophets* . . . evokes the best of Toni Morrison, while being its own distinct and virtuosic work," the Zimbabwean author Novuyo Rosa Tshuma wrote in her review for the *Guardian*. Writer Lauren Michele Jackson for the *New Yorker* disagreed on this point, however, and suggested that Jones's echoes of Morrison's style and symbolism obscure his own voice and, at times, the humanity of his characters. Jackson noted the author's tendency to describe natural surroundings using metaphors for the violence of slavery—the soil is soaked in blood, the trees at the property's edges are sentinels that speak only of the deaths they have seen, and the birds, without mercy for human plight, "fly over in judgement." Jackson assumed that these "brutal observations" are included to both awe the reader and "bestow gravitas on the enslaved condition, perhaps as a means of repair, of compensating for the elisions of historical records." Unfortunately, she added, "These tones of transcendence and glory have a way of obstructing interiority, the lifeblood of the novel." In particular, she felt Jackson's tone constrains his character development, "[leaving] little gap between who someone is and what has been made of them."

However, Jackson's issues with the novel were not echoed in many other reviews. *The Prophets* received a starred review from *Publishers Weekly*, and a reviewer for *Kirkus* described it as an "ambitious, imaginative, and important tale of Black queerness through history." Poet Danez Smith, who reviewed the book for the *New York Times*, wrote that they had reservations about entering the world of the novel, since "Black historical fiction can salt real wounds both fresh and inherited." Despite this uncertainty going in, they were ultimately deeply moved by the novel. To their delight and surprise, Smith found "an often lyrical and rebellious love story embedded within a tender call-out to Black readers." In particular, Smith was drawn to Jones's precolonial vision of a West African society and the "long queer Black history" it paints, "a history of rising against, of ever making one's way back to freedom." Tshuma expressed a similar view and found the book's "tremendous generosity of spirit" inspiring. She acknowledged the novel has small flaws but urged a gentle approach to them, writing, "where it falters, it does so in the way of ambitious novels—in a bid to innovate."

Author Biography

Robert Jones Jr. is a cultural critic and author of the popular blog *Son of Baldwin*. His first novel, *The Prophets* (2021), was a finalist for the National Book Award and was a *New York Times* Best Seller.

Molly Hagan

Review Sources

Jackson, Lauren Michele. "*The Prophets*, a Novel of Queer Love during Slavery, Burdened by History." *The New Yorker*, 3 Feb. 2021, www.newyorker.com/books/under-review/the-prophets-a-novel-of-queer-love-during-slavery-burdened-by-history. Accessed 29 Dec. 2021.

Review of *The Prophets*, by Robert Jones Jr. *Kirkus Reviews*, 4 Aug. 2020, www.kirkusreviews.com/book-reviews/robert-jones-jr/the-prophets-jones/. Accessed 29 Dec. 2021.

Smith, Danez. "*The Prophets* Explores Black Love and Memory in a Time of Trauma." *The New York Times*, 6 Jan. 2021, www.nytimes.com/2021/01/06/books/review/the-prophets-robert-jones-jr.html. Accessed 29 Dec. 2021.

Tshuma, Novuyo Rosa. "*The Prophets* by Robert Jones, Jr. Review—a Virtuosic Debut." *The Guardian*, 9 Jan. 2021, www.theguardian.com/books/2021/jan/09/the-prophets-by-robert-jones-jr-review-a-virtuosic-debut. Accessed 29 Dec. 2021.

White, Edmund. Review of *The Prophets*, by Robert Jones Jr. *Publishers Weekly*, 27 Aug. 2020, www.publishersweekly.com/978-0-593-08568-4. Accessed 29 Dec. 2021.

A Psalm for the Wild-Built

Author: Becky Chambers (b. 1985)
Publisher: Tordotcom (New York). 160 pp.
Type of work: Novella
Time: Unknown
Locale: Panga

In A Psalm for the Wild-Built, *a monk takes on a new vocation, provides comfort to the people of Panga, and encounters a robot that will challenge their understanding of life.*

Principal characters
SIBLING DEX, a monk devoted to the god Allalae and a traveling provider of tea service
SPLENDID SPECKLED MOSSCAP, a wild-built robot tasked with initiating contact with humankind

Becky Chambers is the author of critically acclaimed works of science fiction such as the Wayfarers series, which began with *The Long Way to a Small, Angry Planet* (2014) and won the 2019 Hugo Award for Best Series. She followed those works with the publication of *A Psalm for the Wild-Built* (2021), a novella, or a short novel, set in a new and intriguing universe, in 2021. The narrative takes place on Panga, a moon that features a single continent occupied by humans, animals, and robots. While Panga was once an industrialized moon filled with roads, factories, and petroleum-based technologies similar to those on contemporary Earth, the people of that moon turned away from the industrialized way of life many years before the start of the novel, trading ecologically destructive building practices and lifestyles for ecologically friendly ones and relinquishing their claim on half of the moon's continent, allowing the settlements once located there to be overtaken by nature. One particularly pivotal aspect of that post–Factory Age period, known as the Transition, concerned the moon's robots. Originally built to labor in Panga's factories, the robots abruptly gained consciousness, left the factories, and declined to join human society, instead choosing to disappear into the wilderness. The terms of the so-called Parting Promise between humans and robots guaranteed that the robots would be granted the same rights and freedoms accorded to Panga's human population if they chose to return to human society; however, robots would ultimately have the right to decide whether to reinitiate contact with humanity.

As *A Psalm for the Wild-Built* begins, human monk Sibling Dex has grown dissatisfied with their life at Meadow Den Monastery, where they tend the monastery's gardens as part of their service to the god Allalae, one of the six gods of the Pangan pantheon. Though the monastery, located within Panga's sole City, has been home

Becky Chambers

to twenty-nine-year-old Dex for nearly a decade, Dex feels called both to pursue a new vocation and to leave the City in the hope of hearing the sound of crickets, which no longer live in the area. Dex changes their vocation to that of tea monk, a devotee of Allalae who provides tea service to those in need of it. Beyond serving members of the public cups of tea that meet their specific needs, providing tea service also entails serving as a therapist of sorts and, in some cases, simply allowing busy people to take a short break from their lives and responsibilities. While the self-taught Dex's first attempt to provide tea service goes poorly, they remain steadfast in their pursuit of their new vocation. Over the next two years, Dex develops into a skilled tea monk known for their tasty tea blends as well as for the helpful service they provide, becomes a welcome figure in the human settlements throughout rural Panga, and develops pleasant relationships with the people they meet along the way.

After those two years, however, Dex begins to realize that something is wrong; they struggle to get a good night's sleep, once again long to hear the sound of crickets, which they have not yet encountered in human-occupied areas; and no longer feel fulfilled in their work. Dex struggles particularly with their dissatisfaction with their vocation, grappling with feelings of guilt over being unhappy when their life is, in most respects, a good and comfortable one. A turning point for Dex comes when they listen to some pre-Transition recordings of cricket sounds and, on a whim, review the information about where each one was recorded. One particular recording had been recorded at Hart's Brow Hermitage, a pre-Transition monastery located in one of the regions of Panga that had been abandoned by humans and given back to the wilderness. Intrigued by the possibility that crickets might still exist there, Dex begins to consider traveling to the hermitage despite the potential dangers of such a journey, which would take them far from the roads and villages with which they had become deeply familiar in the course of their work as a tea monk. Despite the risks, Dex soon sets out for the hermitage, taking their ox-bike and wagon from the familiar roads of human-occupied Panga to the eroding asphalt roads paved by humans of the distant past.

Not long into the journey, Dex encounters an unexpected being: the robot Splendid Speckled Mosscap. The first robot Dex has ever seen, Mosscap is in fact the first robot to have made contact with a human in many years, and it confirms to Dex that the majority of robots still want to live apart from humans. However, the robots had grown concerned about how humankind had fared after the robots' departure. At a meeting of robots they determined that one of their number should venture out into human civilization, check on humankind's well-being, and determine what, if anything, human beings now need. Mosscap reveals that it volunteered for that mission and wants

Dex to take it with them when they return to the human-occupied portion of Panga, where it hopes to learn what it needs to know. Dex, however, is reluctant to help Mosscap, as they believe their own inability to determine what they personally need makes them unfit to help a robot learn what humankind needs as a whole. Nevertheless, Dex accepts Mosscap's offer to lead them to the Hart's Brow Hermitage, as Mosscap is knowledgeable about the terrain and the many hazards of the wilderness.

As Dex and Mosscap travel together, the book takes a turn toward the philosophical, with human and robot sharing their unique perspectives, gaining a greater understanding of each other, and debating whether an individual must have a purpose. Their conversations likewise shed further light on the world of the narrative and the beings within it. For instance, while Dex initially believes that Mosscap and its fellow robots are the same robots that left the factories many years before, Mosscap reveals that it and many of its fellow are wild-built, or assembled from the components of multiple earlier robots that had broken down and thus experienced a sort of death. As a robot who has spent its entire conscious existence in the wilderness, Mosscap is an effective foil for Dex, capable of challenging many of their preconceptions and prompting Dex to consider a new perspective on the personal and professional dissatisfaction they have been experiencing. Indeed, Dex's quandary and search for fulfilment are deeply relatable and will likely resonate with any readers who have experienced similar dissatisfaction in their own lives. The book leaves the narrative open ended and the two characters' ultimate fates unknown, as *A Psalm for the Wild-Built* is not a stand-alone novel but the first installment in Chambers's Monk and Robot series.

In addition to offering compelling characters and raising thought-provoking questions, *A Psalm for the Wild-Built* is particularly intriguing due to Chambers's optimistic vision of a society that has reshaped itself to survive major environmental and societal upheaval. After industrialization proved untenable and the emergence of robot consciousness forced humankind to reassess its relationship with its robotic workforce, the residents of Panga collectively made changes to their society—shifting from fossil fuels to solar power and from traditional building materials to recycled or biodegradable ones, for instance—and to their ways of life that have apparently made them happier and more fulfilled in the long run. While the Factory Age and the Transition era are long past and are thus not central to the narrative, the lessons of those eras remain in evidence and are deeply relevant to readers concerned about Earth's own environment. At one point, Dex muses about the limited efficacy of individual efforts to make change, noting that while environmentally friendly buildings were being constructed on an individual basis prior to the Transition, Panga's human population was not able to make headway in managing their approaching ecological crisis until they collectively made large-scale, systemic changes. Though touching on such serious issues, the book as a whole is optimistic and light rather than grim and heavy, and Chambers shies away from the cynicism or defeatism that some writers might express in the face of Earth's own environmental challenges. The dedication to the work—"for anybody who could use a break"—proves especially apt in that context. Just as Dex offers a much-needed break to those seeking tea service and receives their own respite thanks to Mosscap, *A Psalm for the Wild-Built* offers comfort to the reader and a break from the pressures of life on twenty-first-century Earth.

A Psalm for the Wild-Built has received largely positive reviews leading up to and following its publication. Critics focused extensively on the work's tone and feel, which the anonymous reviewer for *Publishers Weekly* described as "cozy" and "wholesome," as well as the experience of reading the book, which *NewScientist* reviewer Jacob Aron characterized as "joyful." The *Publishers Weekly* critic further identified *A Psalm for the Wild-Built* as a strong addition to Chambers's body of work, noting that it was consistent with the author's "characteristic nuance and careful thought." Writing for NPR, Amal El-Mohtar commented approvingly on the book's intriguing central narrative and underlying questions, including its exploration of "what might drive someone to seek discomfort in a world where everyone's basic needs are met." The interactions between Dex and Mosscap were likewise of particular interest to several reviewers: Aron praised the relationship between the two characters in the review for *NewScientist*. While reviews of the book were largely positive, some reviewers critiqued elements of the work. *Strange Horizons* critic Gautam Bhatia, for instance, wrote that the book at times "strays into the realm of the didactic" when dealing with topics such as environmentalism and further argued that some aspects of the world-building were not explored sufficiently. However, Bhatia appreciated the work as a whole, noting that *A Psalm for the Wild-Built* is particularly noteworthy for "the questions it raises, how it articulates them, and in the paths that it illumines."

Author Biography

Becky Chambers is the author of the award-winning Wayfarers science-fiction series (2014–21) as well as the 2019 novella *To Be Taught If Fortunate*.

Joy Crelin

Review Sources

Aron, Jacob. "*A Psalm for the Wild-Built* by Becky Chambers Is Joyful Sci-Fi Reading." Review of *A Psalm for the Wild-Built*, by Becky Chambers. *NewScientist*, 30 June 2021, www.newscientist.com/article/mg25033410-800-a-psalm-for-the-wild-built-by-becky-chambers-is-joyful-sci-fi-reading/. Accessed 4 Oct. 2021.

Bhatia, Gautam. Review of *A Psalm for the Wild-Built*, by Becky Chambers. *Strange Horizons*, 23 Aug. 2021, strangehorizons.com/non-fiction/a-psalm-for-the-wild-built-by-becky-chambers/. Accessed 4 Oct. 2021.

El-Mohtar, Amal. "A Monk and a Robot Meet in a Forest . . . and Talk Philosophy in This New Novel." Review of *A Psalm for the Wild-Built*, by Becky Chambers. *NPR*, 18 July 2021, www.npr.org/2021/07/18/1017119290/a-monk-and-a-robot-meet-in-a-forest-and-talk-philosophy-in-this-new-novel. Accessed 4 Oct. 2021.

M., Daryl. Review of *A Psalm for the Wild-Built*, by Becky Chambers. *Los Angeles Public Library*, 26 July 2021, www.lapl.org/books-emedia/lapl-reads/review/psalm-wild-built. Accessed 4 Oct. 2021.

Review of *A Psalm for the Wild-Built*, by Becky Chambers. *Publishers Weekly*, 8 Feb. 2021. *Literary Reference Center Plus*, search.ebscohost.com/login.aspx?direct=true&db=lkh&AN=148534689&site=lrc-plus. Accessed 4 Oct. 2021.

Punch Me Up to the Gods

Author: Brian Broome (b. ca. 1970)
Publisher: Houghton Mifflin Harcourt (Boston). 250 pp.
Type of work: Memoir
Time: 1970s to the present
Locales: Ohio; Pittsburgh, Pennsylvania

Debut memoirist Brian Broome covers the story of his upbringing in Ohio and coming to embrace and accept his identity as both a Black man and a gay man.

Principal personages
BRIAN BROOME, the author
TUAN, a young boy whom he witnesses being criticized and admonished by his father for crying while waiting at a bus stop

Writer Brian Broome's book-length debut, *Punch Me Up to the Gods* (2021), a memoir focusing largely on his early life, has received widespread critical acclaim. Some reviewers have justifiably claimed that Broome's debut deserves to be seen as an apt and important contribution to the growing genre of literature, memoirs, and nonfiction focusing on the unique experiences of Black LGBTQ people living in America.

The structure of Broome's *Punch Me Up to the Gods* is not straightforward. Rather than organizing his thoughts in chronological order, he chooses to create a thematic memoir in which various milestones and important moments are grouped together through shared themes and ideas. Two interesting structural devices serve to frame the story while also adding layers of depth and emotional resonance. The first structural device fashions each section after a line from Gwendolyn Brooks's famous poem "We Real Cool." This results in eight sections with the titles "We Real Cool," "We Left School," "We Lurk Late," "We Strike Straight," "We Sing Sin," "We Thin Gin," "We Jazz June," and "We Die Soon." The poem is often taken as a reflection on misspent youth, with the subjects perceptively wasting their lives and risking death with their self-destructive activities. Some scholars have argued that the poem can be seen as a poignant reflection of Black American rebellion against authority and power. Both interpretations are reflected in Broome's honest and heavy, but also at the same time often engagingly humorous, memoir, in which the artist describes various adventures in his own "misspent" youth while also providing deep reflections on the risk of rebellion, the stultifying effect of the pressure to conform, and the youthful terror of feeling that one does not fit in to constructed societal or cultural norms.

Punch Me Up to the Gods / BROOME

While Brooks's poem provides a thematic structure, Broome also unifies all of the chapters by relating his own experiences to a story he begins telling, early in the book, about something he witnessed while waiting for a public bus. Broome relates how he saw a young Black boy named Tuan hurt himself after falling. The boy cried in pain and his father chastised him for crying and told him to "be a man." This event resonated deeply with Broome, who recalls, in looking at the moments of his own childhood, when he was also pressured to "be a man" in ways that felt inauthentic and unnatural to him. Broome returns to the story of Tuan to make an affecting point about the way that masculinity is conceptualized, and the way that young Black men are pressured to embrace societal expectations about gender. The book is therefore a record of how Broome learned to overcome the pressure to conform in his own life and learned to risk social ostracism and other cultural penalties to express himself in a more genuine manner.

Brian Broome

Anyone who has felt compelled to adopt representations or signifiers of masculinity that felt inauthentic might be able to identify with much of what Broome describes in his memoir, but Broome's focus is also on the particular pressures and expectations associated with masculinity in Black American culture. Through excerpts from his life in Ohio and later in Pittsburgh, Broome looks at various situations that, for him, are indicative of the prejudicial ideas about the masculine/feminine dynamic that he sees as common to Black culture in America, and he seeks to speak to other Black individuals struggling with their own sense of autonomy and identity within this culture.

One of the stories Broome tells is from when he was ten years old and some of his friends, including a boy named Corey, had been teasing him because he did not behave in ways seen as appropriate for his race and gender; instead, he notes, he was not interested in or good at sports, was bookish, and played with girls. Corey arranged for him to have the opportunity to prove that he was not gay or a "sissy" by having sex with a random girl in a barn. Describing this intensely uncomfortable moment, Broome explains the tremendous pressure that he felt to embody the masculine ideal that his friends expected while also noting that the young woman had likewise been nonchalantly reduced to a sexual object for Broome's use, which is something he reflected on more deeply in the years after the event. As he discusses the toxicity of being forced to mime an exploitative version of masculinity in front of his friends, he also explores how the embodiment of gender roles, in the context of Black masculinity, carries an expectation of misogyny and the exploitation of women.

As Broome's sense of his same-sex sexual orientation and gender expression developed, his family, friends, and acquaintances at times helped and at other times hindered his identification process. This provides an important lesson on the ways in which others can amplify the expectations of conformity, but also how love and friendship can be important to expressing and accepting one's genuine identity. With each opportunity to accept and share his identity as a gay man, he has taken a risk. This has included the risk of losing friends or the respect/love of family members but also a very real, visceral threat to his well-being. In the Black American culture that he inhabits, as he was growing up it was not uncommon for those who failed to conform to become targets of bigoted violence, whether by peers or parents. The title of the book refers to the idea that, as he says in the first chapter, "Any Black boy who did not signify how manly he was at all times deserved to be punched back up to God to be remade, reshaped."

Broome explains that, for men who are Black and gay, there is a sense of not belonging in any community. Black men already feel disconnected from mainstream American society because of racism, and those who are also gay face prejudice from within the Black community. The threat of intolerance was not theoretical or distant for young Broome but was direct and ever-present in his life due to his father's belief that he could correct his son's "feminine" behavior with violence. He endured his father's ill-conceived attempts to batter him into conformity, as well as the violence of other bullies, and these stories provide a personal, authentic view of the victimization experienced by young men who are Black and gay.

In college, Broome's roommates attempted to force him to acknowledge that he was gay, an action that robbed him of agency and turned his coming out into an attack from which he needed to recover. This assault sent him on a soul-searching journey back home that ultimately led him to Pittsburgh, a city with just enough diversity and cosmopolitan culture that it provided opportunities for public LGBTQ expression. This came with some difficulty for Broome, but he credits the LGBTQ community already established in the city with helping him to reach a more genuine expression of himself. In one section of the book, Broome discusses attending his first Pride parade in the 1990s and feeling like an outsider, looking in, and not wanting to be identified as part of the crowd by onlookers; however, he gradually began to adopt a different attitude and credits seeing people in bars, clubs, and at events embracing their LGBTQ identity with helping him to gradually envision being able to self-identify as gay publicly.

Sections of the book move from Broome's early youth through his teenage years and into adulthood, but the next section might take readers right back to his youth again. The unusual structure, which carries the reader through stages in Broome's life in a cyclical pattern, has an artistic purpose, allowing him to revisit the past from new perspectives, but the book also increases in depth and emotional poignance. Early chapters contain far more humor, while Broome saves some of the more harrowing and tragic events of his life for later chapters. Especially impactful are Broome's efforts to cope with his depression and feelings of loneliness by turning to drugs. His struggle with drug addiction is explored in several chapters, and he effectively demonstrates how his inability to find comfort and acceptance in his identity was inextricably tied to his feelings of self-worth; his eventual victory over substance abuse coincides with his growing sense of himself. Other sections of the book, weaving from childhood to adulthood and back again, are more lighthearted and even humorous. His description of trying to play basketball to impress a White lover who believed he should be able to play the game because of his race is written to highlight the slapstick results of this ill-fated experiment. Other sections relate humorous but also heartbreaking moments in his gradual exploration of the aesthetic of his sexuality. A number of sections, for instance, find Broome questioning and exploring gender norms in clothing, which fall into different periods in his life, from an early fascination with clothing considered feminine to later shopping trips where he would sneak into the girls' section in the department store, hiding from his mother while exploring the possibilities in the form of different colors and fabrics not typically available to him.

Toward the end of the book, Broome details a trip he took to France, which he compares and contrasts to the writings of James Baldwin, the Black, gay icon of the civil rights era who lived in Paris and wrote a great deal about the experience of being Black and gay in this era. Reflecting on his own path and trying to approach some degree of the self-awareness that Baldwin demonstrated in his writing, Broome hopes that, although he may never match the mastery of Baldwin, he will be able to contribute something meaningful to this important discussion of Blackness and identity. He ends the book with a letter written to Tuan. He hopes that someday, Tuan might read the book, and he expresses his wish that, if that day ever comes, Tuan is already living in a reality free from the bonds of forced gender and racial roles like those that Broome was made to endure in his own tortured youth.

Punch Me Up to the Gods has drawn positive reviews from a number of critics. *Publishers Weekly* called it a "magnificent and harrowing memoir that digs into the traumas of growing up Black and gay in Ohio in the late 1970s and early '80s." *Kirkus* called the book "beautifully written," and a "must-read." In a review for the *New York Times*, critic and writer Darnell L. Moore described the book as "a gift" to all disenfranchised Black and LGBTQ boys. Though Broome writes that he will never have the heft and skill of Baldwin, one of his self-professed heroes and an inspiration to him in his life as a writer and poet, his deeply personal and yet engrossingly entertaining memoir reveals a unique and special talent that makes it stand out from much of what is published in the genre. With both a poetic sensibility to his prose and the exposition of his emotional vulnerability, Broome has created an inspiring example of just how moving and resonant the best memoir writing can be.

Author Biography

Writer Brian Broome, who has been involved in the University of Pittsburgh's writing program as a fellow and teacher, has had his work published in various outlets. *Punch Me Up to the Gods* is his first book.

Micah Issitt

Review Sources

Dunham, Dana. "The Powers of Kinesthetic Communication in 'Punch Me Up to the Gods.'" Review of *Punch Me Up to the Gods*, by Brian Broome. *Chicago Review of Books*, 24 May 2021, chireviewofbooks.com/2021/05/24/the-powers-of-kinesthetic-communication-in-punch-me-up-to-the-gods/. Accessed 19 Oct. 2021.

Moore, Darnell L. "In a New Memoir, the Miracle of Black Queer Self-Creation." Review of *Punch Me Up to the Gods*, by Brian Broome. *The New York Times*, 18 May 2021, www.nytimes.com/2021/05/18/books/review/punch-me-up-to-the-gods-brian-broome.html. Accessed 19 Oct. 2021.

Review of *Punch Me Up to the Gods*, by Brian Broome. *Kirkus*, 20 Mar. 2021, www.kirkusreviews.com/book-reviews/brian-broome/punch-me-up-to-the-gods/. Accessed 19 Oct. 2021.

Review of *Punch Me Up to the Gods*, by Brian Broome. *Publishers Weekly*, 10 Feb. 2021, www.publishersweekly.com/978-0-358-43910-3. Accessed 19 Oct. 2021.

The Queen of the Cicadas

Author: V. Castro
Publisher: Flame Tree Press (New York). 224 pp.
Type of work: Novel
Time: 1950s; 2019
Locales: Texas, Mexico

While staying at a historical Texas farmhouse that has been converted into a guesthouse, a woman learns the true details behind an urban legend of a gruesome murder and a vengeful ghost. She becomes obsessed with the story, which then begins to intersect with her life in ways that are strange and terrifying—but ultimately transformative.

Principal characters
BELINDA MONTOYA, a modern woman burnt out from work as a lawyer seeking a purpose in life
JACOB, her son
MILAGROS SANTOS, a Mexican migrant farm worker in Texas in the 1950s who is murdered
HECTOR, the owner of the guesthouse that was once the farm where Milagros worked
MICTECACÍHUATL, the Aztec Queen of the Dead

The Queen of the Cicadas (2021) opens with its protagonist, Belinda, on her way to a longtime friend's wedding, returning to her native Texas after some years of living in Philadelphia. Belinda—twice divorced, recently laid off from her job as a lawyer, and mother to a teenage son with whom she struggles to communicate—has been drifting aimlessly through her life. She is tired, jaded, unhappy, and approaching middle age; she drinks to excess to cope with her dissatisfaction with where she has found herself. She does not, initially, expect much of this trip—it will be a brief break in the monotony of her daily life, to which she assumes she will then return.

The wedding is held on what used to be a farm; the main house has now been converted into a guesthouse. From the guesthouse's charismatic owner, Hector, Belinda learns that the place has a surprising connection to the urban legend of the Queen of the Cicadas, which she learned as a girl growing up nearby. The Queen of the Cicadas is said to be a vengeful, murderous ghost who can be invoked through a Bloody Mary–like ritual: saying her name and then *chicharra*, the Spanish word for "cicada," three times while standing before a mirror.

V. Castro

The legend, Hector says, is based on the true story of a farm worker, Milagros, who worked at this very farm in the 1950s. Taken into the United States by a family friend working there through the Bracero Program, which brought millions of Mexicans to the United States on short-term contracts between 1942 and 1964, Milagros dreamed only of making enough money to travel to California and join up with the labor movement led by Cesar Chavez. However, she caught the attention of the nephew of the farm's owner who oversaw the work in the fields, a White man named Billy, and he repeatedly made unwanted sexual advances toward her. She attempted to dissuade him, but these efforts had no effect whatsoever. These attentions led Billy's jealous wife, Tanya, and a group of her friends to murder Milagros in retaliation for her supposed "seduction." Local police were not interested in making the effort or stirring up trouble for farmers dependent upon migrant Mexican workers to find the killer, or killers, of a victim they viewed as unimportant due to her race and gender. Milagros's ghost, it is said, thus returned to take her revenge on the women involved in her death, and still appears when summoned to wreak further havoc.

Belinda becomes fascinated by the story, and when the wedding is over, she stays behind at the guesthouse to track down the facts behind it. Hector joins her in this search. He too, it becomes clear, has been adrift in life, struggling to keep the guesthouse afloat and nursing a recent breakup with the man he thought he would settle down and start a family with. The search for Milagros's true history provides direction and purpose to both of them, and a strong friendship—almost a familial bond—forms between them as they work to piece together the story.

The novel then alternates between the past and the present, placing Milagros's story alongside Belinda's research and attempts to track down survivors (at one point even traveling to Mexico in search of Milagros's remaining family). After a harrowing, detailed description of Milagros's slow and brutal death, it is revealed that at the moment of her death, she called upon Mictecacíhuatl, the Aztec Queen of the Dead. She prayed to this deity as a child growing up in San Luis Potosí, Mexico, and in the last moments of her life, she falls back on this old belief—and the deity answers. It is the deity, the reader learns, rather than Milagros herself, who is behind the deaths of Milagros's killers. Mictecacíhuatl has taken Milagros's spirit into herself, and now kills to gain life energy to bring about Milagros's rebirth as her daughter, a deity in her own right.

Initially, Mictecacíhuatl's visitations in the mortal world are classic scenes of otherworldly horror, with plenty of disturbing descriptions of the gory fates of those who have harmed Milagros or otherwise angered the deity. (This is usually those who have harmed Mexican Americans, such as ICE officers in search of undocumented immigrants to arrest.) But when Mictecacíhuatl is captured in a video that is disseminated around the world, the story takes a more unusual turn, as Belinda becomes a sort of vessel chosen to usher in the dawn of a renewed version of the Aztec religion. The people around her are drawn into these mystical happenings as well: her son begins receiving prophetic visions, and Hector is encouraged to explore his heritage as the child of a family of *curanderos*, or folk healers with shamanistic qualities. Through Jacob's visions and Hector's latent psychic abilities, even more hidden stories of the past are revealed, tracing Milagros's ancestors back to the era of the Spanish conquistadors' colonization of Mexico.

In addition to chronicling the unfolding of this new, or reconstituted, religion, the latter half of the book also covers developments in the personal lives of Belinda and Hector. Having found meaning in their involvement with Mictecacíhuatl's plans, the two of them have grown enough to right some of the wrongs in their relationships. While this may seem like a shockingly positive swerve for what begins as a horror novel, this section of the book is still tinged with darkness. To bring about the world Mictecacíhuatl envisions, some sacrifices must be made.

The book proves even more engaging in that it ultimately stands as less a straight, conventional horror story than a fantasy in which justice is served for the long history of brutality suffered by Mexican immigrants in the United States, and their descendants gain access to a new form of power that comes along with a renaissance of aspects of their culture almost lost to colonialism. It is also important to note that in this new order, women hold much of the power, as deities and vessels for those deities' will in the mortal world. *The Queen of the Cicadas* is very much concerned with making women's voices heard—in addition to the points of view of Belinda and Milagros, even Mictecacíhuatl herself narrates a chapter. Meanwhile, even the most sympathetic male characters, Hector and Jacob, never serve as viewpoint characters in their own right, but rather as conduits through which stories of women from the past are shared.

Marketed as a horror novel, despite its less-than-straightforward relationship to the genre, *The Queen of the Cicadas* received more attention from horror sites and blogs than from mainstream literary review outlets. However, what critical attention it did receive was largely positive, including starred reviews from *Kirkus*, *Publishers Weekly*, *Booklist*, and *Library Journal*. Only one review, for the speculative fiction magazine *Locus*, was notably negative, with reviewer Paula Guran criticizing the novel's plotting as weak.

Most reviews praised the book for taking a familiar premise in an unusual direction. "Readers seeking originality and a fresh take on well-worn horror tropes should pick up this novel by a dynamic and innovative voice in horror," A. E. Siraki wrote for *Booklist*. The anonymous critic for *Kirkus* stated that *The Queen of the Cicadas* "shifts seamlessly from deliciously gory horror narrative to family saga to a tale of righteous vengeance," handling all of its disparate genre components equally well. Similarly, the anonymous reviewer for *Publishers Weekly* wrote that the novel "merges brutal realism and supernatural terror to create a fierce, memorable tale."

Critics also lauded the novel's frank examination of ugly aspects of the United States' past and present and its handling of themes of racial justice and women's stories. Siraki wrote that *The Queen of the Cicadas* "serves as a painful chronicle of racial violence against Latinx people," while the *Kirkus* reviewer praised "its unflinching condemnation of colonialism on both sides of the Mexican-American border." Becky Spratford, meanwhile, writing for *Library Journal*, said that the novel "belatedly but firmly delivers justice to forgotten women from all over the world."

Finally, many reviewers noted that the book's horror aspects are well-executed and memorable examples of their genre. The reviewer for *Publishers Weekly* called the novel "visceral and disturbing in the best of ways," and Siraki wrote that it "does not pull any punches" in its depiction of horrific happenings, whether supernatural or tragically realistic. Spratford called *The Queen of the Cicadas* "engrossing, violent, and exultant," and recommended it to "fans of gruesome, vengeance-themed horror."

The Queen of the Cicadas is a dense book, packing a surprising number of plot threads into its relatively small page count and zigzagging between genres at a breakneck pace, especially in the later parts of the novel. It provides a kaleidoscopic view of Mexican women in several times and places; these women are often downtrodden and forgotten, but each has her own power and agency. Readers hoping for a more traditional horror narrative may be disappointed by the turn the novel takes toward the end, but it stands out as a unique, affecting, and inventive fantasy that focuses on giving power to those who have historically been powerless, and voices to those who have been voiceless.

Author Biography

V. Castro is the author of the novellas *Hairspray and Switchblades* (2020) and *Goddess of Filth* (2021), as well as several short stories that have appeared in horror anthologies. *The Queen of the Cicadas* is her first novel.

Emma Joyce

Review Sources

Guran, Paula. Review of *The Queen of the Cicadas*, by V. Castro. *Locus*, 19 Aug. 2021, locusmag.com/2021/08/paula-guran-reviews-the-queen-of-the-cicadas-by-v-castro. Accessed 3 Jan. 2022.

Review of *The Queen of the Cicadas*, by V. Castro. *Kirkus*, 31 Mar. 2021, www.kirkusreviews.com/book-reviews/v-castro/queen-cicadas. Accessed 3 Jan. 2022.

Review of *The Queen of the Cicadas*, by V. Castro. *Publishers Weekly*, 26 Feb. 2021, www.publishersweekly.com/978-1-78758-603-1. Accessed 3 Jan. 2022.

Siraki, A. E. Review of *The Queen of the Cicadas*, by V. Castro. *Booklist*, 1 June 2021, www.booklistonline.com/ProductInfo.aspx?pid=9747912. Accessed 3 Jan. 2022.

Spratford, Becky. Review of *The Queen of the Cicadas*, by V. Castro. *Library Journal*, 1 June 2021, www.libraryjournal.com/review/the-queen-of-the-cicadas-2110064. Accessed 3 Jan. 2022.

Razorblade Tears

Author: S. A. Cosby (b. ca. 1973)
Publisher: Flatiron Books (New York). 336 pp.
Type of work: Novel
Time: Present day
Locale: Virginia

In the fast-paced thriller Razorblade Tears, *two fathers team up to avenge the murder of their gay sons.*

Principal characters
IKE RANDOLPH, a former gang member and ex-convict who has created a new life for himself
BUDDY LEE JENKINS, a hard-drinking ex-convict
ISIAH RANDOLPH, Ike's son, a reporter who is murdered on the night of his wedding anniversary
DEREK JENKINS, Buddy Lee's son and Isiah's husband, who is also murdered
MYA, Ike's wife, a nurse
ARIANNA, Isiah and Derek's three-year-old daughter

Razorblade Tears (2021) is a propulsive thriller that will keep readers on the edge of their seats while also calling on them to consider contemporary issues of race, class, gender, and sexual identity. The story begins with Ike Randolph, a Black ex-convict, feeling familiar tensions as two police officers arrive at his door. However, it turns out they are not there about his past, which he has left behind, but rather to inform him that his son, Isiah, has been killed. The narrative then skips to the funeral of Isiah and his husband Derek, who were murdered on the night of their wedding anniversary outside of a restaurant in Richmond, Virginia. Ike struggles to contain his grief and his deep regret; for many years, he had let his own homophobia drive a wedge between himself and his son. A former gang member, Ike has built a landscaping company and a new life for himself and his family. Yet faced with the sudden loss of his son, he finds his old anger and capacity for violence welling up inside of himself. At home, he and his wife Mya struggle to relate to each other and to raise their granddaughter, Arianna. Ike cannot help but think that he is somehow to blame for his son's death and his wife's grief.

Some months after the funeral, Ike is approached by Derek's father, Buddy Lee Jenkins. Because the police have made no progress in the case, Buddy Lee proposes that he and Ike begin investigating it themselves. Buddy Lee is White and Ike is Black, and the two come from very different cultures and backgrounds. While Ike has made a new life for himself out of sheer force of will, Buddy Lee seems to have given up. He spends most of his time drinking beer in his trailer and is occasionally racked by ominous fits of coughing. Yet the two men have some affinities: both have done time, both were homophobic and therefore estranged from their sons, and both have a stubborn streak and a readiness to work outside of the law. Ike at first refuses Buddy Lee's proposal, but when Isiah and Derek's headstones are defaced with anti-gay slurs, he changes his mind. This odd couple begins a private investigation of their sons' deaths that quickly leads them into a world of violence and deceit.

Author S. A. Cosby seems to have steeped himself in the thriller and crime genres, and in this book and its acclaimed predecessor, *Blacktop Wasteland* (2020), he writes with a sure command of the form. Cosby has cited Elmore Leonard, Dennis Lehane, and Walter Mosley as some of his influences, and *Razorblade Tears* is reminiscent of their work. As in so many of those authors' novels, Cosby's heroes are not police officers or private detectives but rather people who have themselves been on the wrong side of the law. Ike and Buddy Lee draw on skills, knowledge, and connections from their former lives to access information and follow leads that escaped the police's attention. The novel has something of the dynamics of a buddy-cop movie, in that Ike and Buddy Lee have been thrown together by circumstances and have little choice but to work with each other. As they begin to investigate the life their sons had made for themselves, they must come to terms with each other and with the kinds of fathers they chose to be. In this regard, Cosby balances internal and external conflict deftly, creating a series of counterpoints between the two men's struggles to solve the murder, to deal with each other, and to reconcile their love for their sons with their own deep-seated prejudice.

As Ike and Buddy Lee investigate their sons' deaths, a series of compelling ironies develop. To solve the crime, the two men must finally learn about a relationship and a shared life of which each of them disapproved. Whether searching Isiah and Derek's apartment, asking questions at their workplaces, or gathering information from a gay bar the young couple frequented, the fathers must finally discover what kind of people their estranged sons really were. Isiah and Derek had told their friends that their fathers were unsupportive of their relationship, and so Ike and Buddy Lee are greeted with suspicion by those who might help. Then, when they tussle with two members of a motorcycle gang whom they find breaking into their sons' place, the fathers finally have a suspect for the murder. Yet the homophobic remarks of the bikers are uncomfortably similar to the kinds of sentiments that Ike and Buddy Lee themselves have expressed over the years. To avenge their sons' deaths, they will have to rethink their own bigoted attitudes toward gay people and their own sense of who deserves to be treated with dignity.

Cosby is equally at home writing action scenes and dialogue, and his careful plotting and pacing make this a gripping page-turner of a novel. In a typical sequence, Ike and Buddy Lee will discover a clue, engage in some banter as they drive across town to investigate it, and then find themselves drawn into a firefight, a brawl, or a chase. The drives in Ike or Buddy Lee's truck provide a running opportunity for character development and relationship building. The men share their regrets about how they treated their sons and also voice their confusion and discomfort with a world that has changed around them. Race further complicates their relationship. Ike is surprised, for example, at how light Buddy Lee's drug-related prison sentence was, and he implies that Black criminals draw heavier verdicts than White ones. For his part, Buddy Lee is not ready to accept the idea of White privilege: he points to Ike's thriving business, nice home, and new truck as evidence that many Black people are doing better than he himself is. These topical conversations can, at times, seem programmatic. Yet Cosby has a light touch, leavening serious conversations with colorful language and wickedly funny observations. Where Ike is dour and taciturn, Buddy Lee is irreverent and chatty, and the two are a tremendously entertaining pair of conversationalists and sparring partners. Of course, each one evolves over the course of the novel, gradually casting aside their old biases and coming to a fuller understanding of the world around them. By the same token, their relationship with each other also evolves, as they come to find a new respect for someone who had at first seemed very different. Cosby gives Ike and Buddy each their own story arc and provides smaller-scale arcs for the novel's supporting characters. As if to counterbalance a story that is, at its core, one of fathers and sons, he surrounds his protagonists with female characters. Mya, Arianna, and a mysterious woman named Tangerine—as well as even more tangential characters like Buddy Lee's next-door neighbor and Ike's office assistant—play important supporting roles.

Cosby's fight scenes are another of the book's strong suits, though the violence may be extreme for readers not used to crime fiction. Ike and Buddy Lee are street fighters, taking out their opponents with whatever comes to hand. Ike finds that any number of tools from his landscaping company can be used as a weapon, while Buddy Lee is quick to pull out the jackknife he carries in his back pocket. As their revenge campaign escalates, they acquire and deploy a small arsenal of guns and explosives. Visceral fight scenes are one of the pleasures of this genre, and Cosby uses them to animate and punctuate his story. Over the course of the novel, Cosby steadily raises the stakes for his two characters. For example, after they kidnap one of the bikers, they bring upon themselves the ire of the whole gang. There is no turning back from their bloody mission, as Ike's home, family, and business are now squarely in the bikers' sights. Buddy Lee and Ike find themselves running out of time as they struggle to locate Tangerine, who holds a secret that may have gotten their sons killed. As the action ramps up and the body count climbs, the two protagonists find themselves in an increasingly perilous situation.

By writing in the third person, Cosby gives the reader access not just to Ike and Buddy Lee's lives, but to scenes of the bikers and of other characters. This point of view allows him to release information strategically, such as showing the leader of the biker gang taking orders from an urbane gentleman over the phone, and therefore readers will likely see some of the novel's twists and revelations coming well before Buddy and Ike do. At times this means there are some elements of the plot that may be a little too predictable. Nevertheless, this is a genre in which readers assume that the protagonists will eventually solve the case, and getting there a few pages before the heroes do will not spoil this novel's appeal.

Razorblade Tears received strong reviews across many different kinds of publications. For *The New York Times*, Adam Sternbergh praised Cosby's prose and pacing, writing that "the book *moves*. It thrums. *Razorblade Tears* practically taunts you every time you try to put it down." He also applauded the fact that the noir-style crime novel is set "in the unexplored territory of poor rural Black Virginia," which opens many interesting social subtexts. If the novel has a flaw, Sternbergh argued, it is the thin characterization of Isiah and Derek, who "exist primarily to hover over the action like two saintly martyrs," a flatness that sticks out all the more because of "how successful Cosby is at breathing life into everyone else." Carol V. Bell echoed this criticism in her review for *NPR*: "It's a jarring juxtaposition—straight characters gain this growing awareness of and sensitivity to discrimination when the queer characters are marginalized in the narrative." Still, Bell also concluded that the book is "addictive, arresting entertainment" and that "Cosby's high-octane drama cements his ascension as a prince of the literary action thriller." *Razorblade Tears* received a starred review by *Kirkus* and numerous other positive notices, including an immediate clamor in Hollywood for the film rights.

Ultimately, this novel confirms S. A. Cosby as an exciting rising voice in the crime-fiction world. He can hit all the marks of the genre while also using it as a vehicle to explore deeper issues of race, class, and sexual identity, while representing diverse perspectives. *Razorblade Tears* is a powerful work that will leave readers eagerly anticipating Cosby's next book.

Author Biography
S. A. Cosby, a Virginia native, is known for his crime fiction that is often described as 'Southern noir.' His novel *Blacktop Wasteland* (2020) won the Los Angeles Times Book Prize and was a New York Times Notable Book, among other honors.

Matthew J. Bolton

Review Sources
Bell, Carol V. "Two Fathers Risk It All to Avenge Their Murdered Sons in This New Thriller." Review of *Razorblade Tears*, by S. A. Cosby. *NPR*, 23 July 2021, www.npr.org/2021/07/06/1012647702/two-fathers-risk-it-all-to-avenge-their-murdered-sons-in-this-new-thriller. Accessed 5 Oct. 2021.

Iglesias, Gabino. "Ghosts of Grief: On S. A. Cosby's 'Razorblade Tears.'" Review of *Razorblade Tears*, by S. A. Cosby. *Los Angeles Review of Books*, 24 Oct. 2021, www.lareviewofbooks.org/article/ghosts-of-grief-on-s-a-cosbys-razorblade-tears. Accessed 29 Oct. 2021.

Review of *Razorblade Tears*, by S. A. Cosby. *Kirkus*, 5 May 2021, www.kirkusreviews.com/book-reviews/s-cosby/razorblade-tears/. Accessed 29 Oct. 2021.

Sternbergh, Adam. "A Brawling, Go-for-Baroque Pulpfest." Review of *Razorblade Tears*, by S. A. Cosby. *The New York Times*, 3 July 2021, www.nytimes.com/2021/07/03/books/review/razorblade-tears-s-a-cosby.html. Accessed 5 Oct. 2021.

The Reading List

Author: Sara Nisha Adams
Publisher: William Morrow (New York). 384 pp.
Type of work: Novel
Time: 2017; 2019
Locale: The London, England, neighborhood of Wembley

In The Reading List, *an isolated widower meets a seventeen-year-old high school student who works as a librarian at his local library. When a chance occurrence takes place—the discovery of an anonymous reading list—the threads of their lives begin to tangle.*

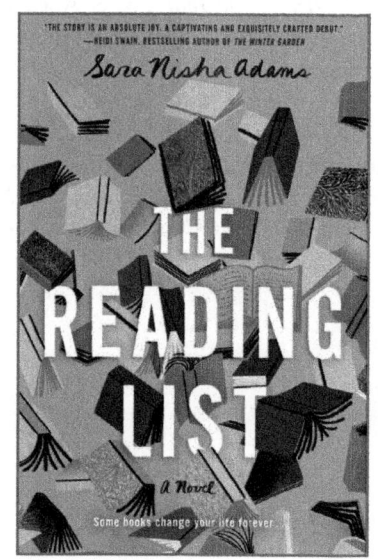

Principal characters
ALEISHA, a seventeen-year-old high school student and library assistant
AIDAN, her twenty-five-year-old brother
LEILAH, her mother, an artist and designer who struggles with mental illness
MUKESH, a recently widowed older man
NAINA, his wife who has passed away
DEEPALI, his acerbic daughter and the mother of twins
ROHINI, his industrious daughter
VRITTI, his kind and perceptive daughter
PRIYA, his granddaughter, Rohini's daughter

The Reading List (2021), the debut novel of Sara Nisha Adams, takes place in a suburban neighborhood of northwest London known as Wembley. The narrative moves primarily between the third-person perspectives of protagonists Aleisha and Mukesh, with the occasional addition of a chapter from the perspective of an auxiliary character. Aleisha is a teenager whose summer job as an assistant at the Harrow Road Library becomes a refuge and a place of solace as her home life begins to devolve. At seventeen and twenty-five respectively, she and her brother Aidan are caretakers for their mother, who suffers from debilitating episodes of mental illness that render her agoraphobic and volatile. This leaves Aleisha with little space to express herself and live a life not dictated by the needs and demands of others, while leaving Aidan with no option but to shelve his dreams of attending business school and opening a bike shop. Instead, he lives at home to care for his mother and works at a biscuit warehouse to support his family. Aleisha still has dreams of her own, the pursuit of a law degree,

Sara Nisha Adams

but she feels a deep and abiding guilt for the sacrifices her brother has had to make in order for her to follow them.

Mukesh is an older man seeking meaning and direction after the death of his wife, Naina. Entangled in the suffocatingly small, quaint world he has built for himself, he becomes increasingly anguished by his own socially avoidant habits. His discomfort with social interaction renders him reluctant to experience the outside world, but he resolves to venture out—if only to make Naina proud. His three grown daughters, Deepali, Rohini, and Vritti, are deeply concerned with his physical well-being, admonishing his cluttered house as unkempt and his propensity to eat meals that consist exclusively of mung beans and premixed chai as unbalanced. Mukesh reads these true concerns as perfunctory and mechanical; devoid of substantive emotional connection between father and daughters. His granddaughter Priya is consumed by the worlds she finds while reading books—worlds that Naina and Priya shared but from which Mukesh has been excluded by virtue of his own reluctance to read and his reticence toward connecting with his granddaughter. He feels that Naina always knew what to say to her, while he cannot quite find the words himself.

As Vritti, Rohini, and Deepali clear Naina's things from the house, Mukesh comes across a copy of *The Time Traveler's Wife* (2003) that Naina had checked out from the library before she died. He finds comfort in the pages—*The Time Traveler's Wife* was the last book she had read—but also wonders what she had been thinking as she read them. To find answers, he decides to make his way to the local library Naina had loved. Upon arrival, he finds Aleisha, her patience made thin by conflict at home. Flustered by her unfriendliness in response to him asking her for a book recommendation, he returns home empty-handed.

Meanwhile, Aleisha finds a mysterious scrap of paper that turns out to be a reading list that includes *To Kill a Mockingbird* (1960) among its titles. As a means of extending an olive branch to Mukesh after their contentious encounter, she resolves to read *To Kill a Mockingbird* and recommend it to him. Mukesh, to his delight, finds that he is enthralled and fascinated by the story line and characters of the novel, and what is more, so is Priya. They bond while discussing *To Kill a Mockingbird* and find an increasing commonality as they read the books on the reading list together. Aleisha and Mukesh, similarly, find a common ground of their own as they themselves make their way through the reading list. As Aleisha's home life intensifies and Mukesh faces the complicated task of navigating his familial relationships after his wife's death, they begin an odd friendship of sorts. And as they make their way through the list, they glean wisdom from the chapters that they bring to their lives and their interpersonal relationships.

Adams dedicates *The Reading List* to her grandparents and her parents, and states in the novel's "About the Author" section that she drew inspiration for the book from the bond she and her grandfather shared through their mutual love of reading. Like her characters, he lived in Wembley, and Adams writes about the neighborhood with the authority of an insider. With this authority comes a sense of familiarity that is extended to the reader as Adams relates Aleisha and Mukesh's story.

Adams lingers in the private, quotidian moments of Mukesh's life that demand a level of effort and hardship of him that he keeps hidden from public view. In doing so, she brings these moments to life. She spools out to the reader Mukesh's odyssey of a bus ride to reach the library for the first time; his apprehension at leaving the house and navigating the bus system alone and his chagrin at being unable to open the library's automatic door hold great weight to him. She also takes care to exhume his most inner feelings: his abiding love for his wife and his contention with the grief of losing her, as well as his struggle to connect emotionally with his family. Though predictable, Mukesh's perspective is refreshing.

At times, Adams's characterization of Aleisha fails to expand and grow in complexity to the same degree as her characterization of Mukesh, instead largely remaining in the well-trodden territory of teenage girls daydreaming about their love interests, or dodging vapid friends in a group chat. However, Adams hits her stride in detailing Aleisha's relationship with her mother, Leilah. Adams unfolds their complex and oft-changing dynamic, delving into their shared history, Leilah's varied experiences as a person with a mental illness, and Aleisha's insecurities in her perceived shortcomings in her role as her mother's caretaker and her ability to experience life as a teenage girl.

Adams has set *The Reading List* within the Indian community of Wembley in a way that highlights and celebrates the community. She has largely chosen to forgo prosaic language in favor of succinctness, language that drives plot and character motivation. Nonetheless, she has woven a cohesive and coherent narrative that moves between multiple points of view. Thematically, *The Reading List* explores the tension between isolation and community, ageism and the underreported obstacles and difficulties that older people face, the degenerative effect of mental illness and its far-reaching impact, the power of language and storytelling, the importance of family ties and the bonds of friendship, and the transformative experience of grief. Overall, *The Reading List*, though somewhat predictable in plot, is lucid and unflinching. Adams did not shy from uncomfortable moments and difficult conversations as she worked to highlight themes that are accessible to and suitable for a range of ages and discuss books that are widely known and read.

The Reading List enjoyed positive reviews from *Newsweek* and *Writer's Digest*. Deborah Dundas for the *Toronto* Star called the novel "a lovely story about how a love of reading can transport us to other worlds and also bring us together." *Publishers Weekly* praised Adams as having a gift for creating characters that are enthralling and make readers invested in them, while Stefanie Milligan for the *Christian Science Monitor* hailed *The Reading List* as being "an ode to the power of stories and the enchantment of reading." The reviewer for *Kirkus* praised *The Reading List* as showing "insightful empathy for difficulties faced at divergent life stages." Critics commented that the novel found strength in its pacing and its thematic agility, as well as Adams's ability to build characters who are likable, accessible, and relatable.

Author Biography
Writer Sara Nisha Adams works as an editorial director focused on commercial fiction. *The Reading List* is her first novel.

Annie Brown

Review Sources
Dundas, Deborah. "24 (Mostly Canadian) Books for a Summer's Worth of Reading." Review of *The Reading List*, by Sara Nisha Adams, et al. *The Toronto Star*, 4 June 2021, www.thestar.com/entertainment/books/opinion/2021/06/04/24-mostly-canadian-books-for-a-summers-worth-of-reading.html. Accessed 1 Nov. 2021.
Milligan, Stefanie. "Set among the Stacks: Four Enchanting Novels for Bibliophiles." Review of *The Reading List*, by Sara Nisha Adams, et al. *The Christian Science Monitor*, 13 Oct. 2021, www.csmonitor.com/Books/Book-Reviews/2021/1013/Set-among-the-stacks-Four-enchanting-novels-for-bibliophiles. Accessed 1 Nov. 2021.
Review of *The Reading List*, by Sara Nisha Adams. *Kirkus*, 16 June 2021, www.kirkusreviews.com/book-reviews/sara-nisha-adams/the-reading-list/. Accessed 1 Nov. 2021.
Review of *The Reading List*, by Sara Nisha Adams. *Publishers Weekly*, 3 Aug. 2021, www.publishersweekly.com/978-0-06-302528-8. Accessed 1 Nov. 2021.

Remote Control

Author: Nnedi Okorafor (b. 1974)
Publisher: Tordotcom (New York). 160 pp.
Type of work: Novel
Time: The near future
Locale: Ghana

In Remote Control, *a young girl with a frightening yet awe-inspiring power comes of age in near-future Ghana.*

Principal characters
SANKOFA, a.k.a. Fatima, the protagonist, a girl who discovers a "seed" that has fallen from the sky and subsequently gains a power capable of killing those around her
MOVENPICK, her fox companion
MRS. OKWAN, her mother
MR. OKWAN, her father
FENUKU, her older brother
PARLIAMENT MEMBER KUSI, a politician who purchases the seed from Fatima's family
THE ONE-EYED MAN, Kusi's bodyguard and later robber
ALHAJA UJALA, the owner of the RoboTown store Mr. Starlit Electronics
SISTER KUMI, a RoboTown resident and the wife of the local imam

The critically claimed author of the World Fantasy Award–winning novel *Who Fears Death* (2010) and the Hugo Award–winning novella *Binti* (2015), Nnedi Okorafor followed those works and others with the 2021 book *Remote Control*. The book is a short novel—sometimes described as a novella—set in a near-future incarnation of Ghana. It begins as a newcomer arrives in a suburb of the capital city of Accra: Sankofa, a petite fourteen-year-old who enters the town on foot and is accompanied only by her fox companion, who she has named Movenpick. Although Sankofa might seem an unimposing figure, her arrival frightens the town's residents, many of whom flee the streets and take refuge in their homes upon hearing of her arrival.

Undeterred by that reception, Sankofa approaches the house of a wealthy family and demands entrance, interrupting the family's Christmas Eve festivities. While the family is clearly frightened of her, they also treat her with respect, providing her with her preferred foods and drink—traditional Ghanaian dishes and room-temperature orange Fanta—and arranging for a seamstress to make her a new set of clothing in her preferred style. Sankofa builds a rapport with one of the family's children, a young boy who asks her to demonstrate the power for which she has become both known and feared. She agrees to do so and briefly emits an otherworldly green glow, the function of which is not yet revealed. When Sankofa leaves the house, however, the true potential of her power becomes apparent. The family's gateman confronts her and holds her at gunpoint, accusing her of having murdered his brother. Sankofa refutes that statement, explaining that she used her power to perform euthanasia on the terminally ill man in question, but the gateman is dissatisfied with that explanation and attempts to shoot her. In the face of that threat, Sankofa again emits the green glow, this time both stopping the bullet and killing the gateman, whose body burns until only a single bone remains.

This introduction aptly demonstrates both the extent to which Sankofa is known and feared and the reasons for her dual reputations as a murderer and a figure of mercy. Okorafor next moves the narrative backward in time by nearly a decade, to when the girl who will later become known as Sankofa is an ordinary five-year-old named Fatima. A sickly child who regularly suffers from malaria, Fatima lives with her family in the town of Wulugu, where her family operates a small shea tree farm. Interested in stargazing from a young age, Fatima entertains herself by writing what she calls sky words, designs she sees in the sky and reproduces in the dirt near her favorite shea tree. A turning point in her life comes during a meteor shower, when an extraterrestrial object that the young Fatima refers to as a "seed" lands on her family's property and sinks into the ground near the tree. When she investigates, the roots of the tree rise up and offer Fatima a wooden box with the seed inside, which becomes a prized possession. Some time later, her parents agree to sell the seed to a visiting politician who in turn hopes to sell it to LifeGen, a company that the politician's one-eyed bodyguard later describes as a "big American corporation that's probably going to eventually destroy the world." Shortly afterward, Fatima and her parents learn that the one-eyed man has betrayed his employer, stealing the seed from the politician and taking it to an unknown location.

Though no longer in her possession, the seed leaves Fatima with the strange ability to emit a green glow when she is in pain. She does not learn the extent of her power until she is seven years old, when she is struck by a car while going to the market with her brother. The pain and shock of the experience cause her power to flare, her light spreading throughout the entire town and felling its residents. While Fatima initially believes those around her to be sleeping, she quickly realizes that she has inadvertently killed every living being in Wulugu aside from herself and Movenpick, a fox that had escaped from a zoo and taken up residence in the shea tree near her home. Having lost her family and home and forgotten her own name, Fatima takes on the name of Sankofa and leaves Wulugu. She thus begins a lengthy journey throughout Ghana in search of the seed, which the one-eyed man is transporting from place to place. As she now

Nnedi Okorafor

causes all technological devices, including automobiles, to stop working when she touches them, Sankofa must make her journey on foot and encounters a host of dangers, both human and inhuman. Along the way, she learns to control her deadly power, which she finds can be used both for self-defense and to end the suffering of terminally ill patients without harming anyone else nearby. Although the one-eyed man and the seed long elude her, she at last catches up with him when he is dying of malaria.

As a writer best known for her contributions to the realm of speculative fiction, Okorafor is skilled at developing narratives that both fit within and expand the boundaries of that genre, and *Remote Control* is no exception. Existing in a potential near future, the world of *Remote Control* is at once futuristic and recognizable. Major automotive brands such as Mercedes and Tesla still exist in that world, for instance, but the vehicles are largely autonomous ones rather than traditional vehicles driven by humans. The residents of the communities Sankofa visits consume media content much like their early twenty-first-century counterparts; however, large "jelli tellis" capable of displaying three-dimensional content have replaced traditional televisions, and "personal windows" have joined mobile phones as must-have consumer technology. Even Sankofa's clothing, designed to reflect traditional Ghanian styles, is composed of a material known as BioSilk rather than a conventional textile.

The convergence between futuristic and recognizable is perhaps most apparent in the portion of *Remote Control* set in RoboTown. In this small town, residents at times line up outside establishments such as the Mr. Starlit Electronics store to purchase the latest gadgets, much as early twenty-first-century technology aficionados might line up to purchase the latest iPhone. The most striking feature of RoboTown is its robocop, also known as Steel Brother, a large robot that directs traffic at the town's most dangerous intersection and uses flying drones to monitor the goings-on in town. The robocop is continually surveilling the residents of RoboTown and collecting data, essentially representing an advanced form of the data-collection technologies already in widespread use at the time *Remote Control* was written. Sankofa draws inordinate attention from the robot and its drones, confounding them with her total lack of digital footprint and inability to use technology. Her existence confuses the robocop to such an extent that it malfunctions, making a fatal error in directing traffic that leads to the death of a young boy. Although Sankofa has lived in RoboTown for some time and has made a home for herself there, the people of RoboTown attack Sankofa after the incident. She quickly decides she must flee.

Sankofa's loss of both home and friends in RoboTown further emphasizes the loneliness of her existence, a state that is palpable throughout the work and is one of several hardships that shapes her character. Amid those hardships, she demonstrates a resilience and emotional complexity that make her an engaging and likable character capable of eliciting both sympathy and admiration from the reader. Her story is likewise a fascinating one, and its fast pacing and Okorafor's strong prose render *Remote Control* an engaging and enjoyable reading experience. The work is notably short in length, spanning a total of 160 pages in its original print edition. Some readers might be disappointed that Sankofa's story does not continue further and that certain aspects of the narrative remain ambiguous. Yet despite such ambiguity, the work succeeds in reaching a fitting conclusion: Sankofa's travels eventually lead her home to Wulugu, where she not only confronts her past but also takes decisive action to protect the future.

Remote Control received a largely positive critical response, with the anonymous reviewer for *Kirkus* describing the work's narrative as "gripping" and the world Okorafor presents as "captivating." In a review for *Locus*, Gabino Iglesias described *Remote Control* as "easy to read, emotionally gritty, and wildly imaginative" and called particular attention to the emotional complexity of the character of Sankofa as well as the strength of Okorafor's prose. Writing for the *New Scientist*, Layal Liverpool praised the ways in which Okorafor merges elements of science fiction and of West African language, culture, and folklore in the book. Liverpool further expressed the hope that Okorafor might one day return to the world of *Remote Control* and continue Sankofa's story in a later work. The relatively short length of the book did spark criticism from some reviewers, such as the *AV Club*'s Samantha Nelson, who wrote that the world presented in the book is "one with so much potential that it feels like it deserves more time." She expressed similar points about the narrative itself, arguing that the ending "feels rushed" and that the potential conflict with LifeGen "never manifests in any satisfying way." Nevertheless, Nelson appreciated many aspects of *Remote Control*, praising Okorafor's exploration of key themes such as grief.

Author Biography

Nnedi Okorafor is the author of numerous works of fiction for adults, including the acclaimed novel *Who Fears Death* (2010), as well as books for young adult and middle-grade readers.

Joy Crelin

Review Sources

Heller, Jason. "In 'Remote Control,' Drones Fly over the Yam Fields of a Near-Future Africa." Review of *Remote Control*, by Nnedi Okorafor. *National Public Radio*, 20 Jan. 2021, www.npr.org/2021/01/20/958499168/in-remote-control-drones-fly-over-the-yam-fields-of-a-near-future-africa. Accessed 6 Sept. 2021.

Iglesias, Gabino. "Gabino Iglesias Reviews *Remote Control* by Nnedi Okorafor." Review of *Remote Control*, by Nnedi Okorafor. *Locus*, 3 Apr. 2021, locusmag.com/2021/04/gabino-iglesias-reviews-remote-control-by-nnedi-okorafor/. Accessed 6 Sept. 2021.

Liverpool, Layal. "Remote Control Review: Fusing Ghanaian Stories with a Sci-Fi Thriller." Review of *Remote Control*, by Nnedi Okorafor. *New Scientist*, 20 Jan. 2021, www.newscientist.com/article/mg24933180-500-remote-control-review-fusing-ghanaian-stories-with-a-sci-fi-thriller. Accessed 6 Sept. 2021.

Nelson, Samantha. "A Young Girl Acquires Deadly Power in Nnedi Okorafor's Latest Sci-Fi Journey." Review of *Remote Control*, by Nnedi Okorafor. *AV Club*, 18 Jan. 2021, www.avclub.com/a-young-girl-acquires-deadly-power-in-nnedi-okorafor-s-1846035920. Accessed 6 Sept. 2021.

Review of *Remote Control*, by Nnedi Okorafor. *Kirkus*, 13 Jan. 2021, www.kirkus-reviews.com/book-reviews/nnedi-okorafor/remote-control-okorafor/. Accessed 6 Sept. 2021.

Review of *Remote Control*, by Nnedi Okorafor. *Publishers Weekly*, 9 Oct. 2020, www.publishersweekly.com/978-1-250-77280-0. Accessed 6 Sept. 2021.

The Removed

Author: Brandon Hobson (b. 1970)
Publisher: Ecco (New York). 288 pp.
Type of work: Novel
Time: Present day
Locales: Tahlequah, Oklahoma; Albuquerque, New Mexico

In Brandon Hobson's fourth novel, The Removed *(2021), a Cherokee family in Oklahoma celebrates its heritage as descendants of survivors from the brutal nineteenth-century Trail of Tears and commemorates the life of a family member lost to modern violence.*

Principal characters

Ernest Echota, the family patriarch in the early stages of Alzheimer's disease
Maria Echota, his wife, a retired social worker and mother of three
Sonja Echota, the eldest child, a library worker
Ray-Ray Echota, the middle child, a bright cheer person killed as a teenager by a police officer many years earlier
Edgar Echota, the youngest child, who struggles with drug addiction
Tsala, the spirit of an Echota ancestor killed for refusing to join the Trail of Tears
Wyatt, a charismatic young boy placed in temporary foster care at the Echota home

With the 2021 publication of *The Removed*, Cherokee novelist Brandon Hobson carries on his commitment to telling stories about contemporary Cherokee characters who grapple with trauma, displacement, and other heavy burdens yet maintain a measure of hope in spite of it all. In his previous novel, *Where the Dead Sit Talking* (2018), Hobson tells the story of a Cherokee boy in 1980s Oklahoma who ends up in foster care. *The Removed* retains the Oklahoma setting and touches on many of the same issues, including addiction, loss, and the fragmenting of American Indian families. However, with its deeper connection to Cherokee history and its complex narrative style, it also breaks exciting new ground.

The novel centers on the annual gathering of the Echota family to celebrate the Cherokee National Holiday, which marks the anniversary of the signing of the Constitution of the Cherokee Nation on September 6, 1839. This annual banquet and bonfire at the family home in Tahlequah, Oklahoma, in the heart of Cherokee Nation, not only honors Cherokee history, but also the life of the family's deceased son, Ray-Ray Echota. Years earlier, as a teenager, Ray-Ray got into an altercation with a White teenager, who fired a gun; despite Ray-Ray's innocence and the fact that he was only a teenager

Brandon Hobson

himself, a White police officer intervened and killed him. Afterward, the police department deemed the shooting justified and took no legal action against the officer.

While the trauma of Ray-Ray's violent death hangs over the gathering every year, preparations for this year's gathering are complicated even further by each family member's individual struggles. In an innovative approach, Hobson tells the story from each character's perspective in a constantly shifting first-person narration.

Family patriarch Ernest Echota is becoming frail and showing signs of mental deterioration from Alzheimer's disease. He is often confused, angry, and frustrated; at times his memory loss leaves him unable to perform basic tasks, such operating the television remote control. Maria, his wife and the family matriarch, struggles to care for him while dealing with her own demons. She has been in therapy to quell the rage she feels over her son's death. To control her depression, she keeps a journal and takes strong prescription medication. Writing about her late son, Maria notes, "I have always known grief is difficult and that forgiveness takes many years. I still haven't learned to completely forgive."

Their daughter, Sonja, who lives by herself down the road from her parents, has become obsessed with a younger White man, Vin Hoff, a musician and single father who lives across the street from the library where she works. As they grow closer, Sonja gradually discovers that Vin has a violent streak and is not the caring, sensitive person he seems on the surface. At the same time, Vin comes to realize that Sonja, beyond her sexual passion, has her own ulterior motive for dating him.

Least likely to make an appearance at Ray-Ray's commemoration is young Edgar Echota, who lives in Albuquerque, New Mexico. He is unemployed, still addicted to methamphetamine—despite an earlier family intervention—and has alienated his longtime girlfriend Desiree with his spiraling drug abuse.

Though prospects for a successful gathering seem dim, a new arrival brings a fresh breath of hope. Wyatt, a boy in the care of Indian Family Services and a virtual orphan with his father in jail and his mother no longer in Oklahoma, comes to live temporarily with the Echotas, as they are the only Cherokee family available to provide foster care. Wyatt stays in Ray-Ray's old bedroom and bears an uncanny resemblance to him, even performing the same impressions. Wise beyond his years, Wyatt's communication skills and apparent healing abilities allow him to offer the Echota family a glimmer of hope amid their suffering and trauma.

While the novel is set in the present day, the narrative weaves in Cherokee spirituality and history to draw parallels between the Echota family's present situation and the Cherokees' past. The Echotas celebrate the Cherokee National Holiday and other positive aspects of Cherokee culture but are also forced to reflect on darker moments in their people's history, particularly the forced removal of nearly sixteen thousand Cherokees from their traditional lands in the southeastern United States in 1838 and 1839. During this brutal displacement, known as the Trail of Tears, the United States military uprooted thousands of Cherokees from their homes east of the Mississippi River and forced them to march westward to their new territory in Oklahoma; during the march, thousands of Cherokees died from exposure, starvation, disease, and violence. Tsala, a deceased ancestor of the Echota family, provides the Echota family with a direct link to this historical trauma and serves as one of the "speakers of the dead, the drifters and messengers, the old and the young, lurking in the shadows . . . the removed." Tsala resisted the White soldiers' efforts to remove the Cherokees from their lands and was executed for his refusal to give in. From the spirit world, Tsala recounts events that happened in the past, tells stories about visionaries who saw the coming of the White men that brought suffering and death, and occasionally assists the living in subtle ways.

Cherokee religion and history filter into the narrative in other ways. *The Removed* focuses particularly on the symbolism of birds—red birds, owls, hawks, vultures—as messengers from beyond the human experience. These messengers are related to the ways individuals within a marginalized society are forced to confront grief and forgiveness. Hobson makes more explicit use of Cherokee spiritual belief through his depiction of the Darkening Land, a Purgatory–like place where Cherokee spirits await judgment. Edgar visits this place as his addiction worsens and his existence becomes increasingly hallucinatory; just like the spirits in the Darkening Land, Edgar is isolated and suffering, trapped in a surreal half-life from which he may not be able to escape.

While the narrative is steeped in the Cherokees' complicated past, it does not shy away from contemporary issues affecting the Cherokees and other Indigenous peoples. Ray-Ray's violent death at the hands of a police officer, and the lack of any subsequent justice or accountability, represents the tragic reality that Indigenous people are killed in disproportionate numbers by police officers in the US. The Echota family's present-day struggles, including mental illness and drug addiction, stem at least partially from Ray-Ray's death, and reflect the devastating impact of systemic racism on Indigenous families. However, Hobson injects this grim reality with a glimmer of hope through the character of Wyatt, who challenges stereotypes of children in foster care. Instead of being withdrawn, sad, or angry, Wyatt comes across as an outgoing and vibrant child, whose energy and insight may help provide the Echota family with the hope and healing they long for.

Critical reception of *The Removed* was widely enthusiastic and positive, with many reviewers considering the novel timely and powerful. John Domini, writing for the *Los Angeles Times*, declared, "What sets this novel apart, what stamps it as extraordinary, is the way it interweaves the grimly familiar with elements of fantasy, thereby illuminating both present and past." Though Domini noted minor issues with the *The Removed*'s "cultural blurring," including allusions such as the rebirth of the phoenix and a Rip Van Winkle–like story that are not typically associated with Indigenous lore, he extolled the work's "cosmic balance" and praises Hobson's novel as "his finest accomplishment." Marcela Davison Avilés agreed with this assessment, stressing to NPR that the story is "deeply resonant and profound," told with "exquisite lyricism." She said the novel invited a "reckoning as a society and civic culture with losses we created, injustices we allowed, and family separations we ignored." In the *New York Journal of Books*, Julie Cantrell echoed this praise for *The Removed*'s exploration of historical and contemporary traumas, calling the novel "a richly developed examination of the Cherokee people and the long-standing relationship they've had with injustice."

Other reviewers noted the novel's spirituality. K. L. Romo, writing for the *Washington Independent Review of Books*, felt it was "woven into the story like a soft thread of silk, binding the everyday lives of the characters with otherworldly warnings and messages of strength." While she referred to *The Removed* as a "gut-wrenching tale of broken hearts and shattered dreams," of "devastation caused by ongoing racism in our country," she felt it still struck an optimistic tone and offered a "ray of hope on the distant horizon."

One dissenting voice amid this widespread praise belonged to Emily West, who objected in *Main Street Nashville* that the novel had "too many stories in one," a reference to Hobson's blending of past and present and constant shifting among different narrators. She felt the "addition of Cherokee folklore in between switching characters" made the book "busy and hard to follow."

Hobson, as in his previous work, does not gloss over issues that are endemic to Indigenous peoples, including poverty, police brutality, unemployment, substance abuse, domestic fragmentation, and the hostility of the mainstream, dominant culture. The author adroitly blends the real, the surreal, and the supernatural through the constantly shifting narrative perspectives, a combination that may mirror how the Cherokees and other Indigenous peoples feel when trying to preserve their families and traditional culture amid the unnatural chaos of contemporary American society. While *The Removed* makes it clear how difficult this task can be, it also argues that it is not impossible.

Author Biography

An enrolled citizen of the Cherokee Nation, Dr. Brandon Hobson teaches creative writing at New Mexico State University. He has written multiple novels and short stories. His third novel, *Where the Dead Sit Talking* (2018) was shortlisted for the National Book Award, and his short fiction garnered the 2016 Pushcart Prize.

Jack Ewing

Review Sources

Avilés, Marcela Davison. "Powerful *Removed* Walks a Path between Memory and Mourning." Review of *The Removed*, by Brandon Hobson. *NPR*, 9 Feb. 2021, www.npr.org/2021/02/07/964593882/powerful-removed-walks-a-path-between-memory-and-mourning. Accessed 9 Dec. 2021.

Cantrell, Julie. Review of *The Removed*, by Brandon Hobson. *New York Journal of Books*, www.nyjournalofbooks.com/book-review/removed-novel. Accessed 9 Dec. 2021.

Domini, John. "In an Eerie Cherokee Novel, the Ghosts and the Grieving Have Their Say." Review of *The Removed*, by Brandon Hobson. *Los Angeles Times*, 3 Feb. 2021, www.latimes.com/entertainment-arts/books/story/2021-02-03/review-brandon-hobson-the-removed. Accessed 9 Dec. 2021.

Hokeah, Oscar. Review of *The Removed*, by Brandon Hobson. *World Literature Today*, vol. 95, no. 3, 2021, www.worldliteraturetoday.org/2021/summer/removed-brandon-hobson. Accessed 9 Dec. 2021.

Romo, K. L. Review of *The Removed*, by Brandon Hobson. *Washington Independent Revies of Books*, 22 Feb. 2021, www.washingtonindependentreviewofbooks.com/index.php/bookreview/the-removed-a-novel. Accessed 9 Dec. 2021.

West, Emily. "Review: *The Removed* Had Too Many Storylines." Review of *The Removed*, by Brandon Hobson. *Main Street Nashville*, 16 Sept. 2021, www.mainstreet-nashville.com/life/arts_culture/review-the-removed-had-too-many-storylines/article_3bbbf8f4-164e-11ec-b2c9-0fed9516a5ef.html. Accessed 9 Dec. 2021.

Rescuing the Planet
Protecting Half the Land to Heal the Earth

Author: Tony Hiss (b. 1941)
Publisher: Alfred A. Knopf (New York). Illustrated. 320 pp.
Type of work: Environment, nature, natural history, science, current affairs
Time: Prehistory through the present
Locale: Primarily North America

Tony Hiss's Rescuing the Planet: Protecting Half the Land to Heal the Earth *focuses on efforts underway across North America to conserve plant and animal habitats to slow climate change, reduce extinctions, preserve biodiversity, and protect 50 percent of US land and water by 2050.*

Principal personages

E. O. WILSON, a prominent American evolutionary biologist and sociobiologist who inspired the Half-Earth Project
STEVEN KALLICK, an environmental and human rights lawyer in the United States
STEPHEN KAKFWI, a Dene leader and politician who served as president of the Dene Nation (1983–87) and premier of Canada's Northwest Territories (2000–03)
VALÉRIE COURTOIS, an Inuk forester, the director of the Indigenous Leadership Initiative
HARVEY LOCKE, a Canadian conservationist and lawyer, a cofounder of Nature Needs Half movement
BENTON MACKAYE, the American forester who proposed constructing the Appalachian Trail
VLADIMIR IVANOVICH VERNADSKY, the Russian biogeochemist who coined the term "biosphere" in the twentieth century
CARL LINNAEUS, the Swedish scientist who developed the naming and counting system for plant and animal species used today
GEORGES CUVIER, a French zoologist considered the founder of paleontology

The existential question of the early twenty-first century has been whether civilization will survive beyond the twenty-second century. Researchers and experts in various scientific domains have proposed alarming scenarios—nuclear war, the impact of a planet-killing comet or asteroid, a global pandemic of some lethally contagious disease—as the potential exterminator of humankind. However, many have argued that a more likely cause for society's collapse and demise can be found in the mundane. An overwhelming majority of scientists agree that the side effects of modern human activities may well be the major agents of destruction. Such scientists note that aggressive industrialization since the eighteenth and early nineteenth century, and the consequent lifestyle shift from rural to urban, has resulted in global warming and climate change that is reaching a critical stage; by fouling the planet's air and water and by reducing plant and animal habitats, they emphasize, humans have upset the natural planetary order. This has set in motion cycles of extreme weather events (floods, fires, hurricanes, droughts, excessive temperature fluctuations) leading to increased species extinctions that may drastically disrupt quality of life and food security for all other species.

Acknowledging and effectively illustrating this reality, Tony Hiss also stresses in *Rescuing the Planet: Protecting Half the Land to Heal the Earth* (2021) that it is not too late to reverse the trend toward self-destruction. As evidence, the author highlights—with a profusion of photos, maps, and drawings, plus his own impressions from personal tours of the sites he writes about—numerous places across the North American continent where a diverse collection of dedicated individuals are doing their part to assist nature in staving off disaster. The goal, he explains, is to raise the level of protected land worldwide (currently at less than 15 percent in North America) to 50 percent by 2050, to achieve "50 by '50."

Hiss begins the discussion by explaining and expanding upon the concept of preserving half the earth, first advanced by evolutionary and sociological biologist E. O. Wilson, who wrote the introduction to Hiss's book. Hiss bluntly contends that this idea was reinforced by a 2019 global assessment totaling 1,500 pages to which 145 scientists from fifty countries contributed. Their conclusion, he writes, is that by their activities, humans as a species are "eroding the very foundations of our economies, livelihoods, food security, health and quality of life worldwide."

An intriguing starting point for saving the earth, Hiss presents, is the preservation of the North American Boreal Forest. This is one of three great forests, along with those of Siberia and the Amazon, that are being significantly deforested. He notes that at roughly 3,700 miles long and up to 1,000 miles thick, the Boreal, the world's biggest, most-intact wilderness at around 85 percent, is called "North America's bird nursery" and "the Fort Knox of carbon," for its ability to sequester (store) billions of tons of carbon in tree trunks and peat bogs that would, if released, speed up global warming beyond the point of no return. A key component in preserving the Boreal is the designation of Indigenous Protected Areas (IPAs), overseen by Indigenous Guardians, those who have lived in the areas and are descended of those who have stewarded the forest for millennia. Seven Indigenous nations are part of the Ungava Peninsula Caribou Aboriginal Round Table (UPCART), which inventories and monitors vast

Tony Hiss

Courtesy Michael Lionstar

herds on 370 million acres set aside to preserve herds of Boreal woodland caribou. Similar is the wilderness of the Mackenzie Valley in Canada, cradling the north-flowing, 2,600-mile-long Mackenzie River, the second-biggest river system on the continent. The region contains IPAs encompassing 28 million acres, with plans to protect millions more acres. Preserved within the Northwest Territories is the world's biggest zero light pollution preserve and Nahanni National Park Reserve, one of the Seven Wonders of Canada.

Informative, engaging, and persuasive, *Rescuing the Planet* ranges far and wide across the continent

as Hiss zeroes in on projects large and small that contribute to the goal of protecting 50 percent of the earth. Each section provides historical background, accessible pertinent facts about the area under discussion, and introductions of individuals or peoples associated with conservation efforts. To his credit, unlike certain prophets of doom, the author dwells less on the adverse effects of climate change and more on positive outcomes achieved in the past, in process during the present, and planned for the future. One such success story that Hiss highlights is the Appalachian Trail (AT), which Benton MacKaye proposed in the 1920s to lure humans to commune directly with nature. Completed in 1937, the over 2,000-mile-long walking path through some of the earth's oldest mountains, surrounded by wilderness and largely maintained by volunteers, extends from Maine to Georgia and attracts millions of hikers annually. The AT has inspired similar long-distance trails on other continents and was the model for additional popular North American wilderness exploratory areas. These include the Continental Divide Trail, the Pacific Crest Trail, the Bay Circuit in eastern Massachusetts, the City of Rocks in Idaho, and the nearly 5,000-mile-long Lewis and Clark Trail, among others.

Likewise, there are encouraging signs that governments around the world are waking up to the dangers of climate change. The fragility of the biosphere, the layer above and below the surface of earth where life can exist, is finally being recognized: Hiss details that more than seven hundred biospheres are now protected in 124 countries. He also points out entities like the Environmental Protection Agency and the United Nations Framework Convention on Climate Change have been created, and the United Nations has declared the 2020s the Decade on Ecosystem Restoration. Legislation such as the Endangered Species Act and the Convention on Biological Diversity has also been passed, while large-scale conservation projects tracking the movements of animals have resulted in such improvements as landscape bridges—wildlife highway overpasses and underpasses in migratory corridors that greatly reduce animal-vehicle collisions. In cities, builders are installing tinted or patterned nonreflective glass in skyscrapers to help cut down the millions of bird deaths caused by their impact with high-rise windows. More than one thousand holdfast zones, land recovered after exploitation by timber and mining concerns, are being identified across over 100 million acres to promote self-contained microclimates that provide survival options for organisms. Hiss demonstrates compellingly that these and other conservation programs, underway from Greenwich Village, New York, to Sonora, Mexico, from Alabama to Montana, from the Sierra to the Berkshires, will become more vital as the century advances. Scientists have predicted higher temperatures, widespread droughts, extensive flooding, and rising sea levels throughout the 2020s.

Critical reaction to *Rescuing the Planet* has been uniformly positive. The unnamed contributor for *Kirkus* called the book "a passionate argument for protecting the world's rapidly shrinking wilderness," calling attention to the "excellent natural history" as well as the tone, which was deemed "more optimistic than usual." John R. Wennersten, writing for the *Washington Independent Review of Books*, noted that Hiss "pays tribute to the outstanding work of women conservationists who have campaigned to save our forests and wildlife" and declared that the author has "crafted a valuable overview and inventory of land-use conservation." John Tierney, reviewing the book for the *Wall Street Journal*, agreed, calling Hiss "an indefatigable reporter and graceful writer, traversing the continent to observe the animals being saved and profile their saviors." Tierney cautioned that though the author "occasionally lapses into Soft Green doomsaying about endangered humanity and planetary catastrophe," he remains optimistic overall. Writing for the *New York Journal of Books*, Adrienne Ross Scanlan focused on the book's "stories of successful innovation and imagination" and stressed how it conveys "the importance of listening to often ignored voices," such as Indigenous leaders, and the stories that the animals themselves tell.

Rescuing the Planet is not a quick, easy read. It is full of authoritative numbers and facts—historical, geographical, biographical, and biological—that support the author's poignant argument that preservation of half the world's land and ocean resources is the absolute minimum needed to save the only planet in the universe known to sustain life. Hiss writes that despite the discovery in the last several decades of hundreds of potential earthlike worlds elsewhere in Earth's galaxy, most are too far away and too impractical to reach with current space technology. There is, as he notes, "no Planet B" to escape to.

The book presents myriad possible solutions to the problem of climate change. The greatest strength of *Rescuing the Planet* is the portraits of the remarkable and visionary individuals from all walks of life who are toiling, each in their own way, to improve a portion of Earth so that the 50 percent figure calculated as necessary for survival can be reached. The question that remains is whether their combined efforts will attract enough attention among the powerful and influential to inspire the timely action needed to preserve the natural world and, by so doing, to save the human species that has become an integral part of it.

Author Biography

Formerly a staff writer at the *New Yorker* for over three decades, Tony Hiss is a lecturer and the author of several books, such as 1990's *The Experience of Place*.

Jack Ewing

Review Sources

Review of *Rescuing the Planet: Protecting Half the Land to Heal the Earth*, by Tony Hiss. *Kirkus*, 15 Dec. 2020, www.kirkusreviews.com/book-reviews/tony-hiss/rescuing-the-planet/. Accessed 6 Nov. 2021.

Review of *Rescuing the Planet: Protecting Half the Land to Heal the Earth*, by Tony Hiss. *Publishers Weekly*, 11 Jan. 2021, www.publishersweekly.com/978-0-525-65481-0. Accessed 6 Nov. 2021.

Ross Scanlan, Adrienne. Review of *Rescuing the Planet: Protecting Half the Land to Heal the Earth*, by Tony Hiss. *New York Journal of Books*, www.nyjournalofbooks.com/book-review/rescuing-planet-protecting. Accessed 6 Nov. 2021.

Tierney, John. "'Rescuing the Planet' Review: Harder, Greener, Faster, Smarter." Review of *Rescuing the Planet: Protecting Half the Land to Heal the Earth*, by Tony Hiss. *The Wall Street Journal*, 31 Mar. 2021, www.wsj.com/articles/rescuing-the-planet-review-harder-greener-faster-smarter-11617229168. Accessed 6 Nov. 2021.

Wennersten, John R. Review of *Rescuing the Planet: Protecting Half the Land to Heal the Earth*, by Tony Hiss. *Washington Independent Review of Books*, 20 Apr. 2021, www.washingtonindependentreviewofbooks.com/index.php/bookreview/rescuing-the-planet-protecting-half-the-land-to-heal-the-earth. Accessed 6 Nov. 2021.

Revolution in Our Time
The Black Panther Party's Promise to the People

Author: Kekla Magoon (b. ca. 1980)
Publisher: Candlewick Press (Somerville, MA). Illustrated. 400 pp.
Type of work: History
Time: 1966–present
Locales: Oakland, California, and across the US

Kekla Magoon offers an exhilarating and deeply informative history of the radical Black Panther Party, countering their image as mainly a violent group with a thoughtful focus on their social work. She invites readers to think critically about the Panthers' legacy and see in themselves the capacity for political action and change.

Principal personages

HUEY NEWTON, a cofounder of the Black Panther Party
BOBBY SEALE, a cofounder of the Black Panther Party
ELDRIDGE CLEAVER, an early leader of the Black Panther Party who later split from the group
FRED HAMPTON, the leader of the Illinois chapter of the Black Panther Party and the Rainbow Coalition who was killed by law enforcement in 1969
ERICKA HUGGINS, a longtime member and leader of the Black Panther Party, a political activist and educator
ELAINE BROWN, a former chair of the Black Panther Party and a political candidate

"When people talk about the Black Panthers," author Kekla Magoon writes in her new award-winning history book for young people, "sometimes they speak in hushed tones, as if history itself could overhear. As if the Panthers are a secret no one should talk about." Magoon's *Revolution in Our Time: The Black Panther Party's Promise to the People* (2021) brings the conversation into the open, offering a thoughtful history of a movement that challenged, exhilarated, and terrified Americans in the late 1960s and 1970s. It is a deeply researched and thorough work, packed with detailed writing as well as illuminating photographs, but it remains accessible and very readable throughout. No matter their age, readers will likely find themselves engrossed in a fascinating and all-too-often ignored chapter of American history.

The book also makes clear that the Black Panthers, though long disbanded, still have the power to provoke. For example, pop superstar Beyoncé stirred controversy when she invoked the Panthers' image in her Super Bowl performance in 2016, appearing with her cadre of dancers dressed in black berets and black leather jackets adorned with hardware that looked like ammunition. But the overheated discourse surrounding that performance was hardly interested in who the Panthers actually were or what they really stood for, which is emblematic of the way the dominant White culture has always engaged with the Panthers: painting them as violent actors on the political fringe who sullied the legacy of Dr. Martin Luther King Jr. and his nonviolent resistance movement in the struggle for civil rights. That simplistic assessment is false, Magoon shows, and *Revolution in Our Time* offers a necessary corrective when it is most urgently needed. Young Black people are once again the vanguard of a new movement for social change and enduring its powerful and dangerous backlash. In a political moment when some perceive the words "Black Lives Matter" as a violent provocation, Magoon concedes that it may be hard to imagine the world of the Panthers, who lawfully observed police officers while visibly armed. But, as Magoon writes, the guns were just one aspect of the Panthers' rich history. *Revolution in Our Time* offers a reminder that we must not shrink our political imagination to fit the bounds of the world that exists, but rather expand it to conceive of the world that we want.

Kekla Magoon

Magoon is well known and critically acclaimed for her historical novels and nonfiction books for young readers, and here she continues to demonstrate her ability to write effectively for a young-adult audience. She also has much experience writing about the civil rights movement and related issues, including the turbulent 1960s–70s period specifically. Her award-winning 2010 novel *The Rock and the River* and its 2013 companion, *Fire in the Streets* (2013), are set in Chicago during the volatile summer of 1968. In *The Rock and the River*, a young boy must decide if he wants to follow the example of his father, a civil rights leader in the mold of King, or his older brother, a member of the Black Panther Party. Magoon also wrote a picture book about Thurgood Marshall, the NAACP lawyer and first Black Supreme Court Justice, and a biography of Ruby Bridges who, as a kindergartener in 1960, integrated the New Orleans school system. In 2015 Magoon partnered with Ilyasah Shabazz, the daughter of civil rights pioneer Malcolm X, to write *X: A Novel*, based on the activist icon's formative years.

While her familiarity with the subject matter made Magoon a prime candidate to write a history of the Black Panthers, she also felt a personal drive to communicate with younger audiences. As she explains in her author's note for *Revolution in Our Time*, she was frustrated as a child to be told that she was not old enough to understand something, as if she were not yet capable of forming opinions and taking action. "Adults found myriad ways to underscore the message that I was merely in training to someday become a person who mattered," she writes. Notably, the Black Panthers espoused a different view. Magoon quotes one of the party's founders, Huey Newton, who said that "revolution has always been in the hands of the young." Ericka Huggins, a prominent Panther and educator, emphasizes that the average age among the Panthers at their zenith was nineteen. As she lays out the history of the Black Panthers, Magoon also reminds readers of their own potential. "We don't have to wait," she notes. "We can change the world from the time we are very young, from the moment we realize there are injustices to correct."

For Huey Newton, that moment came as a student at Merritt College in Oakland, California. He met fellow student Bobby Seale, who was older because he had served in the air force before returning to school. The two studied political ideas, but they were eager to make political change in the community of Oakland. After talking with poor and struggling Black people in the community, they devised the Ten-Point Platform and Program that would serve as the Black Panther Party's foundational text. The platform outlined the new political party's goals, among them full employment for Black people, reparations for slavery, decent housing, and education about the "true history" of the United States and its exploitation of Black people. The platform also demanded an end to the police brutality that plagued Black communities. Addressing this violence became the Panthers' first order of business. The civil rights movement had focused changing laws, but as Newton and Seale talked to people in Oakland, they realized that monitoring how those laws were enforced was just as important.

For Newton and Seale, the rigorous nonviolent tactics of King had been effective, but they also demonstrated something rather chilling: White people were willing to commit terrible violence against Black people even when Black people refused to fight back. Ruby Bridges, a six-year-old child, required the armed protection of the National Guard to hold off the White mobs that wanted to hurt her for going to school. Newton and Seale organized to offer the same protection to the people of Oakland. As Magoon writes, "They wondered what would happen if Black people let would-be perpetrators of violence know that they were capable of fighting back, but would prefer not to fight at all." They put this idea in their name, calling themselves the Black Panther Party for Self-Defense, and set out on a program to "police the police." While King's movement was about civil disobedience, breaking laws to demonstrate that they were unjust, the Panthers sought to follow the law to the letter, demonstrating how it was applied very differently to Black people. If, say, a Black motorist were stopped by the police, the Panthers would appear to lawfully observe the interaction. They carried guns, and doing so was their legal right—they even read the laws out loud from a book to prove that their actions were legal. Magoon illustrates how this program ultimately made the Panthers an enemy of the police and how this adversarial relationship escalated and came to obscure, in the popular imagination, the rest of the Panthers' goals.

Magoon's book is invaluable for its willingness to engage with the Panthers in their totality. She captures their victories, their mistakes, and their uncertainty. She describes the legacy of their social programs to feed and educate people and considers the Panthers' views about gender and their relationship to the burgeoning women's liberation movement. She does not ignore their intentionally violent rhetoric ("off the pigs"), but rather explains why the Panthers chose to adopt this language and why it resonated with people. She even offers a glossary of the terms they used.

At every turn, Magoon invites the reader to think critically, offering thoughtful explanations of the Panthers' militant politics and placing them in an international political context. She urges readers to question accepted narratives about the Panthers and ask why they continue to endure.

Magoon also does a good job historically placing events that a reader might already have heard of in passing but may not entirely understand. One example is her explanation of the betrayal and 1969 killing of Fred Hampton, a Chicago-based Black Panther who had been tapped as the party's next leader and had significant success in reducing crime and working for social improvement with his multicultural Rainbow Coalition. Various other works have also covered who Hampton was and how an FBI program called COINTELPRO used an informant to engineer his murder. But Magoon's book shows these events as part of a larger history of the Panthers, clearly explaining developments such as the rise of various party chapters across the US and the incredible extent of COINTELPRO's blatantly illegal operations against the Panthers. Indeed, she even foregrounds the rise of the Black Panthers in other historical moments stretching back to the onset of the transatlantic slave trade. Just as importantly, she shows how the Black Panther Party has had a lasting impact well beyond its dissolution in 1982, with lingering influence in everything from free school breakfasts programs to social justice movements such as Black Lives Matter.

Critical reception to *Revolution in Our Time* was highly positive. It received starred reviews from *Kirkus*, *Publishers Weekly*, and *School Library Journal*, and was named a best book of the year by each of those outlets as well. The work went on to earn a Coretta Scott King Author Honor, was named a Michael L. Printz Honor Book, and was a finalist for the National Book Award for Young People's Literature. The *Kirkus* reviewer summed up the consensus, praising the "cinematic" narrative as a "not-to-be-missed story of America's history and current reality." Any student interested in the Black Panthers or the broader history of racial justice in the United States will find *Revolution in Our Time* to be a vital resource.

Author Biography

Kekla Magoon is an acclaimed author of both fiction and nonfiction for young people. Her honors include the Coretta Scott King/John Steptoe Award for New Talent, three Coretta Scott King Honor Books, the NAACP Image Award, the Boston Globe-Horn Book Award, and the American Library Association's Margaret A. Edwards Award.

Molly Hagan

Review Sources

Borgia, Amanda. Review of *Revolution in Our Time: The Black Panther Party's Promise to the People*, by Kekla Magoon. *School Library Journal*, 1 Oct. 2021, www.slj.com/?reviewDetail=revolution-in-our-time-the-black-panther-partys-promise-to-the-people. Accessed 20 Jan. 2022.

Njoku, Eboni. "Review of *Revolution in Our Time: The Black Panther Party's Promise to the People*." *The Horn Book*, 24 Nov. 2021, www.hbook.com/story/review-of-revolution-in-our-time-the-black-panther-partys-promise-to-the-people. Accessed 20 Jan. 2022.

Review of *Revolution in Our Time: The Black Panther Party's Promise to the People*, by Kekla Magoon. *Kirkus*, 8 July 2021, www.kirkusreviews.com/book-reviews/kekla-magoon/revolution-in-our-time/. Accessed 20 Jan. 2022.

Review of *Revolution in Our Time: The Black Panther Party's Promise to the People*, by Kekla Magoon. *Publishers Weekly*, 12 Aug. 2021, www.publishersweekly.com/978-1-5362-1418-5. Accessed 20 Jan. 2022.

Run: Book One

Authors: John Lewis (1940–2020) and Andrew Aydin (b. ca. 1983)
Illustrators: L. Fury and Nate Powell
Publisher: Abrams ComicArts (New York). Illustrated. 160 pp.
Type of work: Graphic nonfiction, memoir
Time: 1965–66
Locales: California; Georgia; Alabama; Washington, DC

Run: Book One *is the first book in a sequel to the congressman John Lewis's award-winning graphic trilogy,* March. *The* March *books told the story of Lewis's childhood as the son of Georgia sharecroppers and his rise as a prominent figure in the civil rights movement.* Run: Book One *lays the groundwork for Lewis's run for public office, as he grapples with national unrest following the passage of the Voting Rights Act of 1965.*

Principal personages

JOHN LEWIS, a civil rights activist, the head of SNCC (1963–66), and US congressman (1987–2020)
STOKELY CARMICHAEL, a civil rights activist, the head of SNCC (1966–67)
JULIAN BOND, the head of SNCC's communications department in 1966
DR. MARTIN LUTHER KING JR., a civil rights activist, the head of the Southern Christian Leadership Conference

Run: Book One (2021) tells another chapter in the fascinating life of the now-deceased activist and statesman John Lewis. Lewis died of pancreatic cancer on July 17, 2020, more than a year before *Run: Book One* was published, but as his coauthor, Andrew Aydin, notes in the book's foreword, Lewis had already approved most of its pages. Like Lewis's award-winning trilogy, March, published between 2013 and 2016, *Run* is written and illustrated in a graphic novel format and aimed at a young-adult audience. The March trilogy describes Lewis's childhood and early participation in the civil rights movement as the head of the Student Nonviolent Coordinating Committee, or SNCC. Picking up where March leaves off, *Run: Book One* describes the events that led to Lewis's decision to pursue electoral politics. Among these was his painful ouster from SNCC. The story follows Lewis between 1965 and 1966, shortly after playing an integral—if nearly fatal—role in pushing the passage of the Voting Rights Act of 1965, an historic act signed by Lyndon B. Johnson that aimed to end racial discrimination in voting.

Run: Book One / LEWIS AND AYDIN

John Lewis (Courtesy The 1Point8)

Run: Book One begins with images from the six-day uprising that took place in the Watts neighborhood of Los Angeles, California, in 1965, just after the passage of the act. In the dark of night, a White police officer stops a young Black motorist. A crowd gathers, and the young man's mother tries to intervene and stop his arrest. The officer aims his gun at her, and in the book's telling, a single rock flies through the air, landing on the hood of the police car with an evocative "KFFUD." The page is illustrated with minimal dark panels, which speak more to the violence that ensued than a literal depiction ever could. The Watts uprising highlights how the victories of the civil rights movement— in this case, the passage of the Voting Rights Act—often emphasized the myriad other ways in which Black people were oppressed, stoking righteous rage. White people, meanwhile, were ready to meet this rage with violence, as they saw the same victories as an infringement on their own power.

The Watts uprising—in which thirty-four people were killed and thousands more injured and arrested, almost all of them Black—began five days after the Voting Rights Act was signed into law. Activists like Lewis had risked their lives to meet this historic moment, and yet, as Watts clearly demonstrated, their work was far from finished. But just how that work would continue in the wake of the Voting Rights Act and its accompanying backlash was a matter of fierce debate that played out, in part, among the members of SNCC. In the March books, the young activists of SNCC organize sit-ins and marches. The upstart organization was not without their own internal struggles, but in *Run*, SNCC has become entwined with the larger political power structure. Lewis, now well known, has met with President Johnson and allied himself with the Kennedys, and not everyone in SNCC is happy about it. Throughout the book, Lewis and Aydin aptly introduce readers to the major players in SNCC at the time, including Julian Bond, one of Lewis's closest friends in the organization, and Stokely Carmichael, who would soon take over as head. (A lengthy section at the end of the book, titled "Biographies of the Movement," is also helpful.)

Lewis describes, with surprisingly fresh emotion, his shock at being ousted as the head of SNCC in 1966, replaced by Carmichael, who later became known as Kwame Ture. The ideological split between the two activists remains fresh, despite the passage of time; indeed, at Lewis's funeral, former president Bill Clinton took a shot at Carmichael (who died in 1998) in an effort to praise Lewis. (Even given their differences, it is difficult to believe that Lewis would have appreciated that.) For Lewis, Carmichael represented a revolt against Dr. Martin Luther King Jr.'s doctrine of nonviolence. As he writes in the March series, these principles were an extension of his religious faith; they were nonnegotiable. Carmichael, young and brash, urged Black people to defend themselves against what he saw as the violent backlash to the civil rights movement. It is important to remember that nonviolent activists were killed frequently during this period. When Lewis and others protested, they did so in full knowledge that they too might be killed. In *Run*, upon hearing of the murder of activist Jonathan Daniels, a White seminary student who was killed protecting a young Black woman named Ruby Sales in 1965, Lewis puts his head in his hands and thinks: "Even with the new protections of the Voting Rights Act, what could we do if they kept killing us?" In this anger and grief, Carmichael's views were forged.

As the new head of SNCC, Carmichael introduced "Black Power," an existing phrase first adopted by SNCC organizer Willie Ricks. Carmichael, as Lewis writes, "struck a nerve and captured a moment" when he said: "We want Black Power . . . We have begged the president. We've begged the federal government—that's all we've been doing, begging and begging. It's time we stand up and take over!" Carmichael was a separatist, who urged that SNCC, which had always had White members, be an entirely Black organization. Lewis took issue with this and also with what Lewis viewed as Carmichael's politically uncouth messaging. Lewis saw a path forward by allying himself with the Democratic Party; Carmichael wanted to break away and create his own political party, and partly out of that desire rose the Black Panther Party.

Andrew Aydin

One can tell that Lewis was still angry about his break with SNCC—he officially resigned in 1966, after a march in support of James Meredith, an activist best known as the first Black student to graduate from the University of Mississippi. Present-day activists might relate to Lewis's frustration here; while he was angry that Meredith had been shot and injured leading his own voting rights march, Lewis still expresses irritation with Meredith and his sloppy tactics, describing him as "a little all over the place" and "kinda strange, really." Even the seemingly untouchable figures of the civil rights movement could be embarrassed by one another. This very human aside relates to Lewis's resignation from SNCC. After the march in support of Meredith, Dr. King spoke, as did Carmichael and Floyd McKissick, the new head of the Congress of Racial Equality (CORE). McKissick criticized King, calling the doctrine of nonviolence "a dying philosophy." Carmichael was prepared to say much the same. It was not so much the views that irked Lewis, as the publicity of the argument. "All of the divisions in the movement were put on display for the world to see," he writes.

Run emphasizes that this moment in the movement did not exist in a vacuum. Questions about the military draft and the war in Vietnam—Lewis was vehemently against both—and apartheid in South Africa played an important role in people's thinking about the next chapter in the struggle for equal rights. Lewis had been focused on

Run: Book One / LEWIS AND AYDIN

Nate Powell

civil rights for Black Americans; these international crises made him consider the larger plight of the oppressed everywhere, and both issues are covered in detail in the book. This may seem a confusing stew of issues, but the authors and the illustrators, L. Fury and Nate Powell, do their best to tease out the complexities with cinematic panels rendered in grayscale. For instance, one does not need to understand the intricacies of Lewis's and Carmichael's conflict to see how Carmichael captured an international zeitgeist. A full-page spread of a crowd chanting, "Black Power!", coupled with an image of Lewis speaking forcefully for nonviolence to a dwindling crowd, says it all. Many reviewers likewise praised the book's artwork, most of which was created by L. Fury. (The illustrator of the March series, Nate Powell, completed the artwork that comes before this book's title page.) The anonymous *Kirkus* reviewer claimed that it "perfectly captures the tension and terror" of the times, and Eric Carpenter wrote in his *Horn Book* review that Fury "renders emotionally devastating, often violent events and quieter moments with equal finesse."

Run: Book One received starred reviews from *Publishers Weekly* and *Kirkus* and enthusiastic reviews from the *New York Times* and others as well. The *Kirkus* reviewer summed up many critics' sentiments by describing the book as "an intimate, powerfully revealing look at a crucial, complex time, though the eyes of a true American hero." *Run* is more convoluted than the March books, but necessarily so. It seeks to capture a profound shift in the movement and in American culture and, ironically, has been published during another such time. Several reviewers commented on *Run*'s timeliness, comparing the book's events to those of today. As the *Publishers Weekly* reviewer remarked, "the police brutality, voter suppression tactics, and segregationist politics of the 1960s are not so different" from those Lewis and others continued to fight against in the twenty-first century. As the activists in *Run* ask themselves what comes after the Voting Rights Act, the activists of today must ask what comes in its absence, as so many of the stipulations it put forth have been torn away. In the spirit of Carmichael, the present-day movement seeks to build its own power, but

L. Fury

remembering Lewis, it is also tasked with retrieving the civil rights that have been lost—a daunting multifaceted task requiring activists with various goals. Perhaps all can take strength from Lewis's plea to the living, published in the *New York Times* after his death. "Though I may not be here with you," he wrote, "I urge you to answer the highest calling of your heart and stand up for what you truly believe."

Author Biography

John Lewis (1940–2020) was a civil rights activist who was instrumental in the passage of the Voting Rights Act of 1965. He went on to serve in the US Congress from 1987 until his death in 2020.

Andrew Aydin served as Lewis's policy adviser before the publication of the March books, which he also cowrote. *March: Book Three* (2016) won multiple awards, including the Coretta Scott King Award, and became the first graphic novel to receive a National Book Award.

L. Fury is a Texas-based illustrator who has also worked as a concept artist and art director. *Run: Book One* is the first long-form comic she has illustrated.

Nate Powell, who also illustrated the March books, won an Ignatz Award and an Eisner Award for his 2008 graphic novel *Swallow Me Whole*.

Molly Hagan

Review Sources

Carpenter, Eric. Review of *Run: Book One*, by John Lewis and Andrew Aydin, illustrated by L. Fury and Nate Powell. *The Horn Book*, 6 Oct. 2021, www.hbook.com/story/review-of-run-book-one. Accessed 13 Jan. 2022.

Lacey, Marc. "John Lewis's Sequel to His Award-Winning Graphic Memoir, 'March.'" Review of *Run: Book One*, by John Lewis and Andrew Aydin, illustrated by L. Fury and Nate Powell. *The New York Times*, 10 Aug. 2021, www.nytimes.com/2021/08/10/books/review/john-lewis-run-book-one.html. Accessed 13 Jan. 2022.

Review of *Run: Book One*, by John Lewis and Andrew Aydin, illustrated by L. Fury and Nate Powell. *Kirkus Reviews*, 16 June 2021, www.kirkusreviews.com/book-reviews/john-lewis/run-lewis/. Accessed 13 Jan. 2022.

Review of *Run: Book One*, by John Lewis and Andrew Aydin, illustrated by L. Fury and Nate Powell. *Publishers Weekly*, 13 May 2021, www.publishersweekly.com/978-1-4197-3069-6. Accessed 13 Jan. 2022.

Vargas, Kiera. "Great Graphic Novels (#GGN2022) Featured Review of *Run: Book One* by John Lewis, Andrew Aydin, L. Fury, and Nate Powell." Review of *Run: Book One*, by John Lewis and Andrew Aydin, illustrated by L. Fury and Nate Powell. *Young Adult Library Services Association (YALSA)*, 2 Dec. 2021, www.yalsa.ala.org/thehub/2021/12/02/great-graphic-novels-ggn2022-featured-review-of-run-book-one-by-john-lewis-andrew-aydin-l-fury-and-nate-powell/. Accessed 13 Jan. 2022.

The Second
Race and Guns in a Fatally Unequal America

Author: Carol Anderson
Publisher: Bloomsbury (New York).
272 pp.
Type of work: Current affairs, history, law
Time: Largely eighteenth century to the present day
Locale: United States

Academic Carol Anderson's well-researched and meticulously sourced nonfiction work The Second: Race and Guns in a Fatally Unequal America *posits a compelling argument that the Second Amendment to the US Constitution was based on strong anti-Black bias that has continued to this day.*

Principal personages

GEORGE WASHINGTON, a Revolutionary War military leader, an enslaver, and the first American president
THOMAS JEFFERSON, a consultant for the US Constitution, an enslaver, and the third American president
JAMES MADISON, a contributor to the US Constitution, an enslaver, and the fourth American president
CHARLES DESLONDES, the Black leader of a revolt by a group of enslaved people in America
FREDERICK DOUGLASS, a Black former enslaved person who was an abolitionist and activist
DRED SCOTT, a Black enslaved person who legally battled to gain freedom as a US citizen
HUEY NEWTON, a founder of the Black Panther Party for Self-Defense
BOBBY SEALE, a founder of the Black Panther Party for Self-Defense
TRAYVON MARTIN, an unarmed Black teen who was shot and killed in 2012 by a White man who was part of a neighborhood watch
ALTON STERLING, a Black man who was carrying a gun in his pocket when he was shot and killed by police outside of a convenience store in 2016
PHILANDO CASTILE, a Black man who was pulled over in a traffic stop by a police officer in 2016 and was shot and killed after telling the officer that he had a firearm that was found to be legally permitted

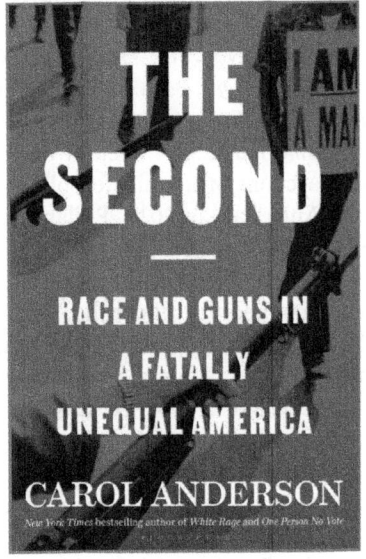

Longtime professor Carol Anderson is known for other prominent works of nonfiction revolving around both historical and current affairs, including the National Book Award long-list entry *One Person, No Vote: How Voter Suppression Is Destroying Our Democracy* (2018). Her book *The Second: Race and Guns in a Fatally Unequal America* (2021) opens with an affecting, direct account of a real-life police killing of a Black American. In 2016, Philando Castile was pulled over in a traffic stop by a police officer in Minnesota. In an attempt to prevent trouble, Castile notified the officer that he was carrying a firearm, which, Anderson stresses, he had a permit to carry. After hearing this information, the officer shot and killed Castile. Similar incidents are later laid out involving names that many readers will recognize from headlines: Alton Sterling, Trayvon Martin, Tamir Rice, Breonna Taylor. Throughout the book, Anderson presents such cases in an effort to illustrate the sentiment that she sums up by quoting *The Atlantic*'s David A. Graham: "'The Second Amendment does not apply to black Americans the same way it does to white Americans.'"

Carol Anderson
Courtesy Stephen Nowland-Emory

Anderson poignantly backs up this point with evidence from the designing of the Second Amendment in the eighteenth century to the present day. Along the way, she argues that "the societal fear of Black people" and "anti-Blackness" play a dominant role in police violence against Black people, a longstanding phenomenon that began to draw heightened public scrutiny in the 2010s. To Anderson, police shootings such as the killing of Castile highlight a racially disparate response to the exercising of rights such as bearing arms, standing one's ground, protecting one's property, or defending oneself. The bulk of *The Second*, bookended by a brief introduction and epilogue, is a passionate, well-reasoned study divided into four succinct, fact-packed, heavily referenced chapters. In the end, Anderson tells an appalling story of a checkered history and uneven application of the Second Amendment that will likely jar many readers.

Chapter 1 concentrates on the origin of the problem. Anderson examines the background of the Second Amendment between the earliest days of the nation and the immediate aftereffects of the Revolutionary War (1775–83). The successful colonial uprising resulted in the wresting of American independence from Great Britain. Victory inspired the development of the US Constitution (created in 1787 and ratified June 21, 1788), the document that more than two centuries later still provides the legal framework for American society. The exclusively White, male, mostly slaveholding landowners representing the original thirteen colonies who wrangled over the language of the Constitution—and the first ten amendments, called the Bill of Rights—were, according to Anderson, operating in part from a position of fear. The men who made the rules that Americans would afterward live by were terrified of what a growing population of enslaved Black people might do to seek retribution or threaten their dominance.

As Anderson details, from the beginnings of the transatlantic slave trade in the seventeenth century onward enslaved Black people had fought for the right to defend themselves, to save their own lives, to exist. Enslaved people desiring freedom, attempting to prove they were human beings with certain rights and not merely property, had frequently rebelled against their enslavers. Major uprisings occurred or were planned in 1687, 1709, 1722, 1723, 1730, and 1739, especially in the Southern colonies. All were brutally suppressed, mainly because enslaved people often had to fight for their rights with inadequate implements against White foes armed with guns. White legislators in the various colonies passed laws (such as the Negro Acts of 1722 and 1740) to ensure Black people remained disarmed and vulnerable. Militias, which came to be seen as an effective support for patrols of enslaved people and suppressing rebellions, also confiscated weapons so that enslaved people would stay subjugated. Though such militias occasionally participated in the Revolutionary War, Anderson notes that General George Washington considered them unreliable: they were poorly trained, often did not show up, or ran away during battles.

Despite their inconsistent performance, militias would be forever linked to gun ownership by the Second Amendment. Anderson argues the idea behind the amendment was in effect a bribe to Southern states, guaranteeing White enslavers would always have the upper hand in confrontations—without which those states might have refused to ratify the Constitution, thus disrupting the fledgling nation-building. The bargain was sweetened with other constitutional concessions to the Southern bloc and their insistence upon preserving the institution of chattel slavery: they could continue the transatlantic slave trade for another twenty years; a "fugitive slave clause" provided for the return of escaped enslaved people, wherever they fled; and another clause counted each enslaved person as three-fifths of a person—enough to give enslaving states a numerical political advantage without granting enslaved people the rights of citizenship. Additional impetus for passage of the Second Amendment (ratified in December 1791) was provided by the successful Haitian Revolution, which erupted in August 1791.

Subsequent chapters of *The Second* compellingly show how the original intent of the Second Amendment to deny Black people—from enslavement and beyond—the right to bear arms, serve in a well-regulated militia, or defend themselves has been reinforced. Chapter 2 covers the postcolonial era up to the US Civil War. During this time, the Naturalization Act (1790) defined "who could become a US citizen" and therefore have access to specified rights. By terms of the act, driven, Anderson contends, by persistent "white fear, white suspicion, white contempt, and white rage," people of African descent in America qualified for neither. As the author points out, race would not be eliminated as a basis for naturalization until 1952. To further enhance the divide between Black and White people in America, Black people were in most jurisdictions denied the right to vote, to sit on juries, or to testify in court against a White person. Following planned or successful uprisings by enslaved people in 1800 and 1811, more restrictive gun laws were passed to keep weapons out of the hands of both enslaved and free Black people. Despite such laws, a trained, professional militia composed of free Black people in Louisiana helped Andrew Jackson defeat the British at the Battle of New Orleans during the War of 1812. After the battle, however, the Black militia was disarmed and dismissed. In the wake of other slave revolts and aborted uprisings, many states (Virginia, Florida, Georgia, Tennessee, Arkansas, Florida, Texas, Mississippi) passed laws banning Black people from owning and/or using weapons. An important US Supreme Court decision, *Dred Scott v. Sandford* (1857), ruled that Black people were not US citizens, and thus had no rights "'that a white man is bound to respect.'"

The third chapter, titled "The Right to Kill Negroes," deals with the Civil War and Reconstruction, and carries the narrative into the mid-twentieth century. A number of laws were passed that seemingly intended to improve the lot of Black Americans: the 1862 Militia Act, the Thirteenth Amendment abolishing slavery (1865), the Freedmen's Bureau Bill (1866), and the Fifteenth Amendment (1870) establishing the right to vote. However, Anderson provides examples showing that, as with the Second Amendment, these laws were applied unequally, keeping Black Americans defenseless. She relates with striking detail how private groups of White people, such as the Ku Klux Klan, slaughtered Black people attempting to protect election results in Colfax, Louisiana, in 1873 and massacred others in South Carolina in 1876. State-sanctioned lynchings became common between 1890 and 1920. In the early twentieth century, White people went on murderous rampages against Black communities in Atlanta, Georgia; Elaine, Arkansas; Washington, DC; and elsewhere.

The final chapter focuses on efforts to "overcome the anti-Blackness embedded in the Second Amendment." Highlights include the foundation of the Black Panther movement, the race riots of the mid-1960s, the establishment of Second Amendment refinements—"stand your ground," open carry, etc.—and the increasing but racially inconsistent influence of the National Rifle Association (NRA). The narrative carries right into the contemporary state of affairs, particularly the continued disparity between the way laws across the legal system are applied to Black and White Americans.

Critical reception to *The Second* was largely positive. Philip V. McHarris, writing for the *Washington Post*, declared the book important as it offers "an opportunity to rethink our attachment to the Constitution and our entire body of laws." The reviewer for *Kirkus* agreed, stating, "Writing evenhandedly and with abundant examples, Anderson makes a thoroughly convincing case," and concluding that *The Second* is "an urgent, novel interpretation of a foundational freedom that, the author makes clear, is a freedom only for some." Jeff Calder, in a review for the *Atlanta Journal-Constitution*, noted Anderson's "gift for elegant summary," adding, "Her writing has clarity of style and a cool zeal."

Among those offering critiques was *New York Times* reviewer Randall Kennedy. While praising certain elements of the book, Kennedy found fault with aspects of the narration. He took issue with what he perceived as Anderson's main contention "that the aim to protect slavery was the predominant motive behind the Second Amendment." He also asserted that the book "provides little useful guidance regarding contemporary approaches to the matter of 'race and guns.'" While this may be true,

Anderson's role in writing *The Second* was from the perspective of a historian and chronicler rather than a policymaker, and she carries this out effectively.

In the end, besides the main text, the book contains several pages of notes referencing dozens of authoritative resources. Collectively, they present a large and persuasive body of circumstantial evidence that supports the author's main premise: that centuries after the ratification of the Second Amendment, its "inherent anti-Blackness" persists, to the continuing detriment of Black Americans. Whether readers ultimately agree or not, *The Second* is a timely, thought-provoking book about a significant issue that is well worth reading.

Author Biography

A 2018 recipient of a Guggenheim Fellowship, Carol Anderson is the chair of African American Studies at Emory University. The author of several books, her third, *White Rage: The Unspoken Truth of Our Racial Divide* (2016), won the National Book Critics Circle Award for criticism.

Jack Ewing

Review Sources

Calder, Jeff. "*The Second* Eyes Racial Implications of the Right to Bear Arms." Review of *The Second: Race and Guns in a Fatally Unequal America*, by Carol Anderson. *The Atlanta Journal-Constitution*, 14 June 2021, www.ajc.com/life/arts-culture/the-second-eyes-racial-implications-of-the-right-to-bear-arms/6XOPOKUMI5GQVJZN3W2KNKRAZA/. Accessed 5 Nov. 2021.

Kati, Rebekah. Review of *The Second: Race and Guns in a Fatally Unequal America*, by Carol Anderson. *Library Journal*, 1 May 2021, www.libraryjournal.com/?reviewDetail=the-second-race-and-guns-in-a-fatally-unequal-america-2116346. Accessed 7 Oct. 2021.

Kennedy, Randall. "Was the Constitutional Right to Bear Arms Designed to Protect Slavery?" Review of *The Second: Race and Guns in a Fatally Unequal America*, by Carol Anderson. *The New York Times*, 28 May 2021, www.nytimes.com/2021/05/28/books/review/the-second-carol-anderson.html. Accessed 7 Oct. 2021.

McHarris, Philip V. "The Long Tension Between the Second Amendment and Black Gun Ownership." Review of *The Second: Race and Guns in a Fatally Unequal America*, by Carol Anderson. *The Washington Post*, 25 June 2021, www.washingtonpost.com/outlook/the-long-tension-between-the-second-amendment-and-black-gun-ownership/2021/06/23/e48626c4-c2f9-11eb-93f5-ee9558eecf4b_story.html/. Accessed 7 Oct. 2021.

Review of *The Second: Race and Guns in a Fatally Unequal America*, by Carol Anderson. *Kirkus*, 17 Mar. 2021, www.kirkusreviews.com/book-reviews/carol-anderson/the-second/. Accessed 7 Oct. 2021.

Second Place

Author: Rachel Cusk (b. 1967)
Publisher: Farrar, Straus and Giroux (New York). 192 pp.
Type of work: Fiction
Time: Unknown
Locale: Ambiguous marsh location

Second Place *is a novel written in the form of a long letter from a woman known as "M" to her correspondent "Jeffers." The novel centers around the relationship between M and a painter, "L"—or, rather, how M's relationship with L's paintings fatefully intertwined the lives of M and L over the months with which the novel is concerned.*

Principal characters
M, the narrator
TONY, her second husband
JUSTINE, her daughter
KURT, Justine's boyfriend
L, a renowned painter
BRETT, a socialite and sometime companion of L
JEFFERS, the recipient to whom the text is addressed

Rachel Cusk's eleventh novel and her first publication following the conclusion of her well-received, nonlinear *Outline* trilogy, the highly anticipated *Second Place* (2021) is an epistolary story in which the author returns to a clear plot. The novel is a letter written by M, a lonely woman longing for something to excite her idyllic but isolated life, to her friend, a writer named Jeffers. As M begins her letter, she explains her past as a woman trapped in a marriage she did not enjoy, how she was inspired to leave and start anew after seeing a painting by the artist L, and her life fifteen years later, living with her second husband in a remote location near the sea on a tidal marsh. The title of the book references the name that M and her second husband, Tony, give to a second house that they have built on their remote property. Their property is far removed from the nearest town and M, who is an author of some repute, conceives of the "Second Place" as a visiting artist's/author's retreat that will bring some element of companionship and culture to their isolated corner. She tells Jeffers that she wrote to L and invited him to visit the Second Place, and the rest of her letter dictates her experiences with the artist when he finally takes her up on her offer.

The location of their home is never fixed for the reader. M might be French—she makes periodic references to a younger life in France and to a fateful trip to Paris as

Rachel Cusk

a young woman. Tony, by contrast is "the only dark-skinned person for miles around," brought to the marsh as a child adopted by a "marsh family." Although his biological heritage is unknown, the narrator comments "I have seen photographs of Native Americans, and more than anything he looks like one of them, though how that could be I don't know." Her offhand comment about Tony resonates as racist—a possibility that is emphasized elsewhere in the manner through which her text associates Tony with the land, romanticizes his limited education but extensive natural knowledge, and characterizes him in opposition to the high-strung and cosmopolitan artist L. Similarly, L, who describes his only home as his studio in New York City, has no specific geographic mooring, as he was reared in an unnamed "desolate part of the world" and has spent the decades since his early success as a painter traveling the world at will.

Although the reader never learns what state, country, or continent the story takes place in, the marsh and the characteristics of its landscape shape the mood of the book. Critics have noted that certain aspects of the plot—the fact that there has been a significant and global economic "crash" of the art and stock markets, and the fact that the outside world has been "shut down" for unstated reasons—tie the novel to the secluded and entrapped life experienced by most of the world's population after the start of the coronavirus disease 2019 (COVID-19) pandemic in spring 2020. Yet, critics have also noted that the text seems to come from a different historical moment, in which gender roles are more traditional and the artist-identity is more clearly linked to heroic masculinity. In its characterizations of both place and time, the book plays alternatively with the tension between the local and the global, alongside movement among past, present, and future. This fluidity contributes to what Randy Rosenthal, in a review of the novel for the *Washington Post*, identified as the novel's central concern—the ability of "true art" to transcend observation of the world and, instead, to pursue the "unreal."

Art is certainly at the heart of this novel. The text itself offers a meta-commentary on writing and the worlds it creates. At the conclusion of the book, Cusk offers a dedication that acknowledges the correlation of *Second Place* to the 1932 memoir *Lorenzo in Taos*, written by Mabel Dodge Luhan, concerning her relationship with the writer D. H. Lawrence. Cusk describes her text as a "tribute to [Luhan's] spirit," but Rosenthal more pointedly characterizes this as an "appropriation" of Luhan's text. Indeed, the characters' names (M, L, Jeffers, and Tony) are drawn directly from *Lorenzo in Taos* and the Indigenous characterization of Tony in Cusk's novel is modeled on Luhan's American Indian spouse. While the interweaving of *Second Place* with *Lorenzo in Taos* is central to the novel, readers are given no tools within the text to dig into this relationship between the two texts, and critics have only engaged with this relationship in a limited fashion.

By contrast, *Second Place* is more open about its reflections on the relationship between visual art and the art of writing. M is a writer, L is a painter. M is drawn to, and even understands her life to have been profoundly altered by, L's paintings. By contrast, L is dismissive of M and even expresses an interest in "destroying" her. Both have reached an age where youth is behind them and they face mortality. Similarly, both struggle with their worth as artists, though in different terms and for different reasons. Comparisons abound throughout the novel of visual art and text. Perhaps the most relevant of such references is one that compares these mediums with respect to the passage of time. Cusk writes, "Language is the only thing capable of stopping the flow of time, because it exists in time, is made of time, yet is eternal—or can be. . . . An image is also eternal, but it has no dealings with time—it disowns it." In *Second Place*, the two artists struggle with the increasing realization of their own mortality and of the powers wielded by their "eternal" art forms.

The relationship between creator, subject, and work is also central to the struggles of L and M with one another. Although M is drawn specifically to L's landscapes, when she learns that L is currently painting portraits, she asks him to paint her. Instead, he wishes to paint Justine and Tony, refusing to paint M because he says he cannot see her. Similarly, though M feels a close affinity to L's paintings, she struggles to see the man himself with any clarity, instead relentlessly pursuing the image of the artist she has long cultivated in her mind. If art is eternal, the artist clearly is not. The discussion of the artist's invisibility here is tied not just to fear of death, but also to the individual's ability to control (or not) the narrative of how their work and their selves are perceived by others.

Another theme that is worked throughout the book is gender and, specifically, the ways that power and gender are associated. When M first encounters L's paintings, she sees in them "a freedom elementally and unrepentingly male down to the last brushstroke." A young mother in an unhappy marriage, M is drawn to this male freedom even if, as a woman, she feels it must be "translated" into something that she can recognize and connect with. Putting on the "borrowed finery" of L's paintings, M finds the spark she needs to divorce her husband and forge a new direction for her life.

Yet, while M routinely mentions the gendered imbalance of power that has defined her personal life, the men around her renounce these claims of powerlessness. At stake, among other things, is her motherhood, which, at some level, forces her into a position of power and authority. As she reflects, "parenthood is the closest most people get to an opportunity for tyranny." Perhaps for this reason, Tony tells M that she does not know her own power. L, meanwhile, seems to chafe against M's maternal nature as somehow oppressive and overbearing of his artistic freedom. By denying her a portrait but later including her in a shocking mural he paints in Second Place, L undercuts the power of M's female aura and represents her in a way that he knows she will find abhorrent.

Within these gender-based characterizations, Tony occupies a significant space. He eschews M's existing understanding of the woman as the highly critiqued underdog in heterosexual relationships. His difference from the other men in M's life, the novel suggests, has to do with his minority status. After Justine and her boyfriend separate, her mother encourages her to pursue some of her own dreams, reassuring Justine that "she would always be able to find a white man to be obliterated by, if that was what she decided she wanted." As other reviewers noted, M's honesty and dedication in her relationship with Tony are questionable. While the novel foregrounds assertions of race and feminine disempowerment, the intersection of race and gender within the novel deserves further exploration.

Second Place was long-listed for the 2021 Booker Prize. Overall, critics gave *Second Place* positive reviews, with *Publishers Weekly* claiming that the novel's "brilliant prose and piercing insights convey a dark but compelling view of human nature." In addition, as Judith Shulevitz noted in a review of the novel for the *New York Times*, *Second Place* is a slippery text, which presses the boundaries of the novel genre while also taking on the moralizing tone of a fable. In the opening scenes of the book, M recalls meeting the devil on a train leaving Paris. When the incident occurs, she has just encountered L's paintings for the first time, which some suggest is foreshadowing. Elsewhere in the novel, religion appears in symbolic ways, but what seems more at stake, ultimately, is the concept of truth or reality versus fiction or the unreal.

In the end, if this is a fable, then M's final words on this topic are, perhaps, the most significant. She writes, "It seemed to me there was nothing stable, no actual truth in all the universe, save the immutable one, that nothing exists except what one creates for oneself."

Author Biography

Rachel Cusk is a prolific and celebrated author who has published eleven novels and four nonfiction books. She is the recipient of numerous awards, including a Guggenheim Fellowship.

Julia A. Sienkewicz, PhD

Review Sources

Cummins, Anthony. "*Second Place* by Rachel Cusk Review—Psychodrama in the Shape of Social Comedy." *The Guardian*, 2 May 2021, www.theguardian.com/books/2021/may/02/second-place-by-rachel-cusk-review-psychodrama-in-the-shape-of-a-social-comedy. Accessed 8 Jan. 2022.

Dederer, Claire. "Women Refusing to Be Like Other Women: New Novels by Rachel Cusk and Jhumpa Lahiri Explore the Liberating Power of Isolation." Review of *Second Place*, by Rachel Cusk, and *Whereabouts*, by Jhumpa Lahiri. *The Atlantic*, June 2021, www.theatlantic.com/magazine/archive/2021/06/rachel-cusk-second-place-jhumpa-lahiri-whereabouts/618706/. Accessed 8 Jan. 2022.

Rosenthal, Randy. "Rachel Cusk's *Second Place* Goes to Some Profoundly Insightful Places." Review of *Second Place*, by Rachel Cusk. *The Washington Post*, 4 May 2021, www.washingtonpost.com/entertainment/books/rachel-cusk-second-place-book-review/2021/05/04/bd609c66-acdb-11eb-b476-c3b287e52a01_story.html. Accessed 8 Jan. 2022.

Review of *Second Place*, by Rachel Cusk. *Publishers Weekly*, 1 Feb. 2021, www.publishersweekly.com/978-0-374-90778-5. Accessed 24 Jan. 2022.

Shulevitz, Judith. "A Rachel Cusk Novel in a Mystical and Enigmatic Key." Review of *Second Place*, by Rachel Cusk. *The New York Times*, 4 May 2021, www.nytimes.com/2021/05/04/books/review/second-place-rachel-cusk.html. Accessed 8 Jan. 2022.

Seek You
A Journey through American Loneliness

Author: Kristen Radtke (b. 1987)
Publisher: Pantheon Books (New York). 352 pp.
Type of work: Graphic nonfiction

Graphic artist and writer Kristen Radtke's second book, Seek You: A Journey through American Loneliness, *dissects America's growing epidemic of loneliness and social isolation. Radtke first conceived of the book in 2016, four years before a global pandemic made such suffering painfully acute, and it casts a wide net among disparate concepts while also drawing on experiences and observations from Radtke's own life with the hope that in shared affliction people might reach out to one another to save themselves.*

Principal personages

KRISTEN RADTKE, the author, who serves as the book's narrative voice
MY DAD, her father, who, as a child, sought communication via ham radio
HARRY HARLOW, a twentieth-century psychologist who conducted experiments on rhesus monkeys to learn more about love and development through the exploration of the mother-infant relationship

Seek You: A Journey through American Loneliness (2021) is the second graphic book of nonfiction from Kristen Radtke, the former art director of *The Believer*. The book's title is a reference to CQ, a code amateur radio operators use to establish contact with one another. As Radtke explains, the French pronunciation of the letters "CQ" is similar to the first two syllables of the word *sécurité*, which can be intended to mean "pay attention." In a poetic twist, English speakers mistook the acronym for the words "seek you." Radtke's book—part memoir, part social history—is about loneliness, and with it, the universal desire for connection. Noting that people were suffering from loneliness long before the widespread forced isolation of the coronavirus disease 2019 (COVID-19) pandemic, she illustrates, both through her artwork and accompanying words, that as it turns out, being lonely is a startlingly serious health concern in itself. In a September 2021 report, Dr. Vivek Murthy, whom Radtke refers to in her book, described loneliness as one of his most pressing concerns as US Surgeon General. Simply, people who describe themselves as lonely often do not live as long as those who describe themselves as socially fulfilled. People who feel lonely, Radtke notes, are more prone to engage in risky behaviors in terms of health like eating poorly, drinking too much, or smoking cigarettes. But this does not begin to address the number of deaths in which loneliness has played a part. As Radtke emphasizes, loneliness and aloneness are two distinct modes of being. Lonely people are everywhere; alone, certainly, but also surrounded by people. Loneliness is an intangible sense of disconnection, and it is killing people. Radtke writes that loneliness will officially be considered an epidemic by the year 2030.

In an effort to understand loneliness, Radtke casts a wide net, arguably too wide, but nonetheless compelling. She explores loneliness in her own life and in the lives of her friends. She also writes about the increase in suburban populations and the invention of the television laugh track, as well as the myth of the American cowboy and the tendency to describe mass shooters as "loners." At a later point in *Seek You*, she brings the reader's attention to Harry Harlow, a psychologist who conducted studies on love and social relationships' effect on development through experimentation of maternal deprivation using rhesus monkeys in the 1950s. While Radtke's various threads never quite come together, *Seek You* offers an absorbing, multifaceted—and as several reviewers noted, communal—view of a common affliction many people share but know so little about.

Kristen Radtke

Radtke published her first book, *Imagine Wanting Only This*, in 2017. Like *Seek You*, it is a difficult book to classify. In it, she contemplates desire, impermanence, and the makings of a meaningful life. The book established her distinctive personal style, a mixture of minimalist graphic images and poetic, philosophical prose. Heller McAlpin, who reviewed *Seek You* for the *Los Angeles Times*, wrote that Radtke's books are "part of a growing trend" in graphic literature, with "narratives that hybridize memoir with social history rendered both verbally and visually." McAlpin cites Nora Krug's 2018 book *Belonging*, in which the author reckons with her family ties to Nazi Germany, and Alison Bechdel's book about exercise, *The Secret to Superhuman Strength* (2021). But Radtke's style makes her work unique. Though she writes in the first person, actively interpreting the information she shares, she only rarely appears as a drawn character. Her art tends toward the interpretative, leading McAlpin to observe, "The word 'graphic' is a far more appropriate descriptor of her work than 'comic.'"

Seek You begins with an explanation of the CQ code and Radtke's discovery that, as a child, her strict, emotionally reserved father rigged an antenna on his family's roof and would often stay up through the night looking for other amateur radio operators to talk to. The information shocked her. She writes that she never saw her father as a person who might desire anything but order. In her illustrations, Radtke imagines him as an abstracted figure floating through space, carried by a string of beeps—the CQ call in Morse code. It is just one example of how Radtke successfully conveys what it feels like to be lonely on the page. On a panel several pages later, a woman's legs dangle in murky grey ink. "Loneliness feels to me like being underwater, fumbling against a muted world in which the sound of your own body is loud against the quiet of everything else," she writes. Juxtaposed with her father's experience growing up in rural Wisconsin, Radtke describes her own early adult years in which she went away from rural Wisconsin to New York City, a place curiously lonely, not for its lack of people but for its incredible abundance of them. Radtke writes about being lonely during this time, and how she projected similar feelings onto the people she saw on the subway or passed on the street. She is filled with tenderness for these strangers and wonders if this tenderness is its own kind of CQ call.

Unsurprisingly, loneliness is exacerbated by the structures of modern American life. People are physically isolated in suburbs or city apartments and are more likely than their ancestors to live alone. Radtke also points to the pervasive myth of the American cowboy, a self-reliant figure who thrives by making his way in the world alone. This kind of loneliness is presented as an enviable trait, but as human beings with a real, biological need for meaningful connection, the promise of fulfillment through rugged independence can never be fulfilled. The thread connecting the ethos of the American cowboy to Radtke's next point of discussion is a bit convoluted, but suffice it to say that, citing political theorist Hannah Arendt, she considers how feelings of loneliness and isolation, like the familiar childhood anguish of being left out of a group, can lead people to become more withdrawn and fearful of those outside of one's familiar sphere. In other words, isolation, real and perceived, is a fertile breeding ground for violence. When Radtke turns her attention to gun violence and mass shooters, Taylor Griggs, for the *Chicago Review of Books*, wrote that the book "loses its way." Griggs's criticism can be applied to the book as a whole. Despite "rich analysis," Griggs wrote, "Radtke does not reach a sensical conclusion about her thoughts on gun violence and its place in our culture. This is completely understandable—it's a big issue!—but it becomes a bit tiring to read such meandering thoughts, even if they are written beautifully and accompanied by engaging illustrations."

Radtke moves on to consider the lure and alienation of social media, and then, the unusual ways people use technology—phones, a robotic toy—to fill a void of human intimacy. Touch, Radtke writes, is such a serious biological need that psychologists call it "skin hunger." This evocative phrase leads to one of the more compelling, if also more disturbing, sections of the book: her discussions of Harlow and his research. Providing context, she explains how Harlow noticed that rhesus monkeys his lab bred themselves behaved differently than the monkeys that were sent from their natural habitats. He saw that the monkeys he raised in the lab were fearful and nervous, and he wondered what that might mean for human children. At the time, doctors cautioned parents not to coddle their babies. Too much contact, it was believed, made a child psychologically weak—a "sissy" as Radtke writes—and, thanks to a host of dreadful diseases, possibly very sick. Successfully challenging this notion, he proved just how strongly living beings need contact and love to survive. But she also shows that his conclusions came at a great cost, as he subjected the monkeys in his lab to experiments of profound physical deprivation and psychological torment. Driven, Radtke suggests, by his own feelings of profound isolation, he devised progressively sadistic experiments, culminating in one he called "the pit of despair." Baby monkeys were placed at the bottom of an enclosure that looked like an upside-down triangle with a window at the top. Monkeys would climb up to the window to attempt escape, only to slide back down into the pit, over and over again. One of his colleagues described the experiment as a "personal metaphor" for Harlow's troubled personal life. Through this exploration, Radtke shows that while Harlow's discoveries were important, projecting his own loneliness onto his test subjects caused great harm. Radtke, who tells readers that loneliness can be contagious, thought-provokingly wonders what that means for everyone else. How do people use their own feelings of isolation to hurt others?

Radtke writes that her mission, however scattered in its presentation, is to find a "solution" for loneliness; "a way for each of us to swim toward a once-invisible ledge and reach for it." Indeed, *Seek You* is a comforting beacon for seekers. As a reviewer for *Publishers Weekly* wrote in a starred review, "For a treatise about the perils of being alone, it creates a wonderful sense of being drawn into conversation." Similarly, Gabino Iglesias wrote for NPR, "The beauty of *Seek You* is that it feels like a communal experience." Perhaps to that point, it also serves as a reminder that personal pain can serve as the basis for communion. As Iglesias wrote, "This book is loneliness dissected, and the dissection involves all of us in a personal way that's impossible to not care about."

Author Biography

Kristen Radtke is a graphic artist and writer. Formerly the art director at *The Believer*, she became the art director at *The Verge* in 2021. She published her first book, *Imagine Wanting Only This*, in 2017.

Molly Hagan

Review Sources

Griggs, Taylor. "A Simple Thesis in 'Seek You.'" Review of *Seek You: A Journey through American Loneliness*, by Kristen Radtke. *Chicago Review of Books*, 14 July 2021, chireviewofbooks.com/2021/07/14/seek-you/. Accessed 20 Oct. 2021.

Iglesias, Gabino. "Loneliness Is a Communal Experience in 'Seek You.'" Review of *Seek You: A Journey through American Loneliness*, by Kristen Radtke. *NPR*, 13 July 2021, www.npr.org/2021/07/13/1015618618/loneliness-is-a-communal-experience-in-seek-you. Accessed 20 Oct. 2021.

McAlpin, Heller. "Review: Feeling Lonely? Join the Club with an Intense New Graphic Memoir." Review of *Seek You: A Journey through American Loneliness*, by Kristen Radtke. *Los Angeles Times*,13 July 2021, www.latimes.com/entertainment-arts/books/story/2021-07-13/feeling-lonely-join-the-club-with-an-intense-new-graphic-memoir-suggests. Accessed 20 Oct. 2021.

Review of *Seek You: A Journey through American Loneliness*, by Kristen Radtke. *Kirkus*, 10 Mar. 2021, www.kirkusreviews.com/book-reviews/kristen-radtke/seek-you/. Accessed 20 Oct. 2021.

Review of *Seek You: A Journey through American Loneliness*, by Kristen Radtke. *Publishers Weekly*, 30 Apr. 2021, www.publishersweekly.com/978-1-524-74806-7. Accessed 20 Oct. 2021.

The Sentence

Author: Louise Erdrich (b. 1954)
Publisher: Harper (New York). 400 pp.
Type of work: Novel
Time: Early 2000s–2020
Locale: Minneapolis, Minnesota

In The Sentence, *Louise Erdrich's eighteenth novel, the employees of a Native American–owned bookstore in Minneapolis try to survive a pandemic, police brutality, and unfriendly visits from the ghost of a former customer.*

Principal characters
TOOKIE, the narrator; a middle-aged bookstore employee with Ojibwe (Anishinaabe) roots
POLLUX, her husband, a former tribal policeman
HETTA, Tookie's niece and housemate during the pandemic
JARVIS, Hetta's baby
LAURENT, the father of Hetta's baby, an aspiring writer
JACKIE, Tookie's childhood teacher, mentor, and coworker
LOUISE, the owner of a bookstore featuring Native American books and crafts
FLORA, the ghost of a deceased White woman who haunts the bookstore

Ghosts and hauntings have been major features in stories about bookstores at least since Christopher Morley's *The Haunted Bookshop* (1919), in which the ghosts are those "of all great literature;" that is, of books that have lived on long after their authors passed away. Hauntings and ghosts, including both good and bad spirits, are also found frequently in Indigenous cultures all over the world, particularly those that still preserve strong oral traditions. In her 2021 novel *The Sentence*, author Louise Erdrich combines these traditions, sometimes with cutting irony and always with an eye on pressing contemporary issues.

The Sentence is Erdrich's eighteenth novel, and not her first to combine history, folklore, and social commentary. For example, two of her earlier novels, *Plague of Doves* (2008) and *The Night Watchman* (2020), both used shifting narrative perspectives to tell stories about Native American characters, particularly those of Ojibwe descent; Erdrich, who herself is of partial Ojibwe descent, draws heavily on the folklore and history of her own family and ethnic background to inform these narratives. *The Sentence* strikes a similar tone to Erdrich's earlier works and uses a familiar structure but tackles contemporary issues in a particularly explicit manner.

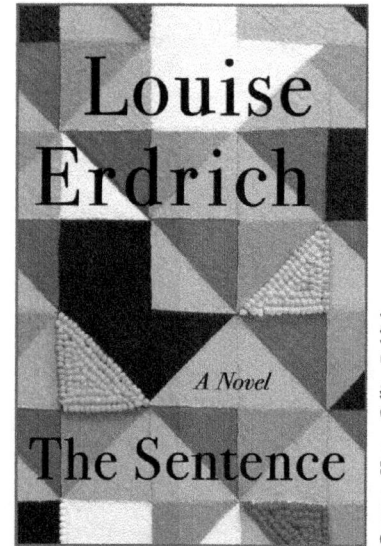

Louise Erdrich

Tookie, the middle aged, first-person narrator, seems to have built a stable life out of a dysfunctional past. She considers herself "an ugly woman" on both the outside and the inside. When she was younger, Tookie battled addiction and spent time in prison. Now she is "rehabilitated" and works at a bookstore in Minneapolis, Minnesota, that mainly sells Native American books and crafts. Tookie's attempts to deal with the consequences of her earlier lifestyle take up the first two parts of this much longer story, though details from those years still haunt her memories and inspire her to try and be a better person in the present day.

A Native American woman who works with Tookie at the bookstore often complains about White people who want to read or tell stories of homesteads haunted by Native Americans; Tookie's coworker finds this ironic and maintains that the Indigenous people of the United States are haunted by White colonists and their descendants. Tookie thinks that the history of Minnesota haunts everything from race relations to politics but tells her fellow employees that they must not think like victims. Their main priority is to sell books and keep the store in business in the new digital economy.

This "haunting" becomes quite literal when a regular customer dies on November 2, 2019, on the holiday of All Souls' Day. As Tookie notes, this holiday represents the moment when the line is thinnest between heaven and earth and between the living and the dead. The customer, named Flora, was a White woman who irritated Tookie and the other employees with her dubious but persistent claims of American Indian ancestry. To Tookie's distress, Flora's ghost keeps reappearing at the store, especially when Tookie is working alone, and retraces Flora's old steps around the store's various sections. Worse still, Flora's daughter Kateri delivers a handwritten book that her late mother was reading just before she died. Tookie begins to come mentally undone as she tries to make sense of the book and the ghost's appearances. She tries talking to the store's owner, Louise, about the disturbances at the store and in her life but struggles to understand what is happening.

About halfway through the novel, while the characters are still dealing with Flora's ghost and their own personal challenges, the novel takes a sudden turn and pulls in plot elements directly from contemporary headlines. There is news of a "novel virus," soon identified as SARS-CoV-2, the virus responsible for the deadly coronavirus disease (COVID-19) pandemic that began in 2020. For Tookie and the other characters, everything begins to change. People begin hoarding more than everyday necessities and families shelter together, despite interpersonal conflicts; for Tookie, this means sharing her home with her estranged niece, Hetta, and Hetta's infant son, Jarvis.

As Tookie and the other characters adjust to life during the pandemic, another tragedy rocks Minneapolis. When a White police officer murders George Floyd, a Black man, widespread protests grip the city and eventually the rest of the country. Hetta is determined to join the protests; she feels a strong connection to the Black Lives Matter movement's fight for an end to racist policing practices and sees parallels between the police's treatment of Black Americans and the centuries of racism against Indigenous people in the US. She says that the Minneapolis police have killed American Indians since the city was founded, and she feels obligated to fight for social change. However, Tookie remains preoccupied dealing with Flora's ghost.

As the protests heat up, Tookie's first-person narration yields to a third-person omniscient narration that gives readers insight into the feelings of other characters, including Tookie's husband Pollux, a former policeman, who tries to feed protestors without meeting the police himself. Earlier breaks from Tookie's narrative appear under section titles introducing details about a particular character's nightmares or personal habits.

Amid the chaos and trauma of the pandemic, Floyd's death, and the subsequent protests, Erdrich depicts scenes of hopeful organizing and community building, particularly through healing dances. On one occasion, the dancers are mothers of all races who have lost sons to fatal police beatings and shootings. Bookstore employees have a powwow, a type of religious gathering held by many Native American communities, as they try to make sense of the chaotic events around them, including Flora's death. They decide to hold a ritual that will help Flora leave the bookstore and move on.

The Sentence gets its title from the definition of the word "sentence" in a dictionary that Tookie receives as a gift from Jackie, her tribal teacher as a child and her lifelong mentor. As stated in the dictionary, a sentence can be a grammatical unit of words, or it can be a judgment passed on a lawbreaker. In a flashback set prior to Tookie's rehabilitation, while she is serving a prison sentence, she feels that she is "on the wrong side of language," since the English language of the European settlers who occupied Native American lands does not square with the experiences captured in the languages of the Indigenous people these settlers killed or displaced. However, Tookie loves the dictionary's brief examples of sentences, such as "The door is open" and "Go!" When she finds herself in solitary confinement, she uses this opportunity to educate herself, relishing words and reading with "murderous intensity." As Tookie transforms into an educated woman, she impresses Louise, her future employer at the bookstore in Minneapolis, where her lifelong mentor Jackie has already found work. As Tookie learns more about the books sold there, she begins to think that a sentence in a book can kill a person or set a person free, and this realization eventually helps her come up with a plan to confront Flora's ghost.

Befitting the major role books play in Tookie's life, the text of the novel is followed by a long and "totally biased" list of Tookie's favorite books, arranged in categories that include "ghost managing," "pandemic reading," and "sublime books," as well as books of poetry, fiction, and nonfiction about the Native American experience. At the end of this list, Erdrich repeats Tookie's opening comment from her introduction in the novel's first section: "Books contain everything worth knowing except what ultimately matters." This statement makes it clear that while books can be powerful and transformative, they are often not enough to solve the types of problems—racism, disease, and police brutality, to name a few—endemic to modern society.

The Sentence's supernatural themes are enhanced by Erdrich's inclusion of Native American, particularly Ojibwe, folklore. Many of the novel's characters mention the Rougarou, the Ojibwe culture's interpretation of the werewolf. It is related to the European werewolf, specifically the *loup-garou* myth that French explorers brought to North America, which also has parallels to later monsters in American folklore, such as Bigfoot and the Bogeyman. While the Rougarou does not typically feed on humans, it lives a long life, and can turn humans into other Rougarou.

Three characters in the novel talk about the Rougarou. The bookstore's owner Louise, who serves as a stand-in for the novel's author, introduces the story of the Rougarou when Tookie wants to know how the deceased Flora can still seem quite alive, knocking over books and moving things around the store. Later, Pollux, who leads spirit dances, tells Tookie what he learned from his grandmother about this mythic figure. This myth comes even more to the forefront when Laurent, a Métis writer and the father of Hetta's child, identifies himself as the descendant of a French *loup-garou* who came to North America and fathered children with a Native American woman.

Reviews of *The Sentence* were generally quite favorable. Ron Charles of the *Washington Post* predicted that it may prove the best of the many pandemic-themed novels that are bound to follow it, partly for the versatility of its writing style but also for incorporating elements of magical realism. Additionally, he praised the characters, particularly the "gruff charm" of Tookie. Writing for the *New York Times*, Malcolm Jones complimented Erdrich's ability to work details about events of 2020 into an engaging work of fiction. While he conceded that the novel occasionally felt "baggy" due to the presence of so many elements and plotlines, Jones considered this complaint insignificant compared to Erdrich's ability to depict deep characters, tackle heavy themes, and write "passages that stop you cold."

On a more critical note, Jennifer Wilson, writing for *Vulture*, recognized the novel as a genuine and appropriate continuation of Erdrich's literary corpus; however, Wilson complained that Erdrich wrote with a "false optimism" regarding social conditions in the US at the end of 2020. Jo Livingstone in *The New Republic* also took issue with Erdrich's hopeful tone, remarking that her novels have been "uniquely generous" to their characters, and that *The Sentence* continues this trend. Despite this critique, Livingstone praised Erdrich's ability to create an unusual type of horror narrative loaded with social commentary. Livingstone singled out Erdrich's inversion of the traditional "Native American burial ground" trope as a particularly successful twist; instead of having Native American ghosts haunt White protagonists, Erdrich depicts a White ghost haunting her Native American protagonists. For Livingstone, these supernatural elements did not feel out of place; after all, in Erdrich's imaginative world, the living are "ghosts-in-waiting," seeking ways to communicate with those who lived before them, who live among them, and will live on after them.

Author Biography
Louise Erdrich has won many awards for books of fiction and poetry that feature Native American characters, settings, and themes. Her novel *The Round House* (2012) won the National Book Award for Fiction, and her 2020 novel *The Night Watchman* won the Pulitzer Prize for Fiction.

Thomas Willard

Review Sources
Charles, Ron. "*The Sentence* Is Among Louse Erdrich's Most Magical Novels." *The Washington Post*, 9 Nov. 2001, www.washingtonpost.com/entertainment/books/louise-erdrich-sentence-book-review/2021/11/08/0a18fd34-40af-11ec-a88e-2aa4632af69b_story.html. Accessed 17 Nov. 2017.
Jones, Malcolm. "A New Novel by Louise Erdrich Haunted by Covid and George Floyd's Death." Review of *The Sentence*, by Louise Erdrich. *The New York Times*, 9 Nov. 2021, www.nytimes.com/2021/11/09/books/review/the-sentence-louise-erdrich.html. Accessed 17 Nov. 2017.
Livingstone, Jo. "The Haunting of Louise Erdrich." Review of *The Sentence*, by Louise Erdrich. *The New Republic*, 29 Oct. 2021, newrepublic.com/article/164199/haunting-louise-erdrich-sentence-book-review. Accessed 22 Nov. 2021.
Wilson, Jennifer. "*The Sentence* Shows the Downside of Urgency." *Vulture*, 10 Nov. 2021, www.vulture.com/article/the-sentence-louise-erdrich-book-review.html. Accessed 17 Nov. 2017.

She Who Became the Sun

Author: Shelley Parker-Chan
Publisher: MacMillan (New York). 416 pp.
Type of work: Novel
Time: 1345–56
Locale: China

She Who Became the Sun is the debut novel of Australian Shelley Parker-Chan, a former diplomat in Southeast Asia. This fantasy novel centers on a girl who assumes her brother's identity to fulfill her destiny in Mongol-ruled fourteenth century China, as it ponders the nature of fate, queer identity, and desire.

Principal characters

ZHU CHONGBA, a peasant girl who assumes the identity of her dead brother
MA XIUYING, her future wife
XU DA, her friend; a former monk
GENERAL OUYANG, eunuch and former slave to Mongolian prince Esen
ESEN-TEMUR, Mongolian prince

She Who Became the Sun (2021) is the first in an announced pair of fantasy novels that feature a reimagining of the early life of the fourteenth century monk who became emperor of China, Zhu Yuanzhang, the founder of the Ming dynasty. In Parker-Chan's reimagining, however, *She Who Became the Sun* is not the story of a boy who rose through skill and strength from humble beginnings to the highest position in the empire. Instead, it is about a girl who assumes a male identity to fulfill that destiny. Promoted as "*Mulan* meets *The Song of Achilles*," and "a bold, queer, and lyrical reimagining," *She Who Became the Sun* explores the internal conflict that attends the two main characters, Zhu Chongba (Parker-Chan's rendition of Zhu Yuanzhang) and her eventual rival General Ouyang, both of whom live outside the acceptable gender norms of their time.

Zhu Chongba is introduced as an unnamed girl whose fate is to be nothing. She is certainly treated as nothing by her family, whose fortunes are pinned on her brother, Zhu Chongba, foretold to be destined for greatness. Such greatness seems far away as the novel opens, however. A multiyear drought and starvation have reduced her family, once consisting of her father's parents, her own parents, and six siblings, to three survivors: her, one of her brothers, and her father, who still considers her to be completely expendable. He offers her as a bribe to the bandits who raid their home before they murder him. After the attack, she watches her brother die of despair and realizes that she has something he lacks—the will to live at any cost. Taking her brother's name and identity, Zhu Chongba believes that as long as she is him, she can share his foretold greatness. This grim determination earns her a place at a monastery, which saves her life. It is there that she meets Xu Da, an older pupil who knows her secret but is a faithful and reliable friend. It is at the monastery where she meets a person whose fate is inexorably intertwined with her own.

General Ouyang is also an outsider. The leader of the monastery where Zhu Chongba lives will not allow him to enter, forcing him to wait outside while his former master and friend, the Yuan prince Esen, is brought inside. Ouyang is a eunuch who was enslaved and mutilated by Esen's father after he murdered the rest of Ouyang's family. Esen's father only spared Ouyang's life because he—like Zhu Chongba—was willing to do anything to survive. Ouyang also lives between genders, physically feminine in some ways, but so resentful of the mutilation that caused these similarities that he despises women. He is deeply attracted to Esen, and the feeling seems to be mutual, though he also knows that it falls to him to avenge the murder of his family. The conflict between who he really is and who he must appear to be is at the heart of his story, and connects him with Zhu Chongba as well.

Shelley Parker-Chan

After the monastery is destroyed, Zhu Chongba, passes as a male monk and joins rebels known as Red Turbans, a hotbed of power plays and manipulation. They are fighting against the Mongol-led Yuan Dynasty, whose army is led by Esen and Ouyang. And so, the primary conflict is established between two people who are not what they seem to be, but who share the intense desire to fulfill their destiny.

Parker-Chan is not shy about delving into the complicated, often contradictory identities of the two queer protagonists at the heart of this story. Both feel betrayed by their bodies and both are unable to reconcile their thoughts and desires with their biological selves. Their identities are able to shift and change as well, as Zhu Chongba moves through periods of time when she feels male, but is forced to engage with her female body, if only to disguise it, and feels ungendered.

Parker-Chan also offers cisgender, straight characters as reference points for Zhu Chongba and Ouyang. Xu Da is a cisgender, straight man, who exemplifies traditionally male attributes. He is sexually active with a variety of women and feels comfortable in his own skin, able to enjoy such mundane pleasures as going shirtless on a hot summer day and a hot communal bath. His friendship with Zhu Chongba is based on a shared male-ness, a brotherhood, even though he knows the truth about her gender identity. The prince Esen, clearly attracted to Ouyang, also wears his masculinity easily. Ma Xiuying is a young woman who is treated like a servant by her betrothed and then marries Zhu Chongba after he dies. She is feminine, nurturing, kind, maternal, and attracted to Zhu Chongba even after her identity is revealed. The two fall deeply in love, though Zhu Chongba continues to be detached from her physical body and does not solicit pleasure, though she offers it freely.

Aside from the complications of fraught gender identities and complex sexual desires, there is the larger perilous world of power and struggle in a multiethnic empire where warring factions are constantly jostling for power. Parker-Chan offers language cues to explore how ethnic identity can lead to conflicting loyalties and assumed familiarities. She also astutely examines ambition and ethics, noting the ways that murder, betrayal, and manipulation are justified by those who consider their actions necessary to reach a greater good. Zhu Chongba's pursuit of her destined greatness and General Ouyang's desire for revenge propel these characters to take drastic, ugly steps to get what they want.

After an epic ascent to power, complete with sweeping battles, ghostly visitations, and treachery, *She Who Became the Sun* culminates in a pair of brutal assassinations that may make the reader question whether either Zhu Chongba or General Ouyang is a hero in any sense. The result is certainly accurate—there are few leaders who rose from slavery and peasantry to power without a certain amount of disconcerting bloodshed—but it feels cynical. The only loyal, ethical person in the story seems to be Zhu Chongba's childhood friend Xu Da. Even Ma Xiuying must put her misgivings aside to support Zhu Chongba in her relentless pursuit of power, which she believes to be her destiny.

In the end, it is the two characters who are outsiders, unable and unwilling to conform to the rigid expectations of gender identity that are constantly reinforced around them, who change the course of the empire. They are bound together by their shared otherness and their drive, despite their physical limitations, to fulfill their destinies. They are able to understand each other in a way that no other character can.

Many reviewers praised the frank and nuanced exploration of gender and sexuality that sets *She Who Became the Sun* apart from its peers. In their review on *Tor.com*, Lee Mandelo praised the "intense, grasping, often amoral desires of two queer protagonists," pointing out that the book allows the characters' "deeply complicated relationships to gender and their bodies" to be at the heart of the book. In the *Chicago Review of Books*, Greer Macallister praised the book as "original" and noted the ways that it examines "gender and identity, prejudice and violence, history and humanity." In her review in *Locus Magazine*, Liz Bourke found that there is a great deal to unpack in the book's "use and interpretation of gender and sexuality," worthy of an entire separate study. In *USA Today*, Eliot Schrefer called *She Who Became the Sun* an "important entry in the LGBTQ fantasy canon."

The complex and nuanced examination of ethics and power dynamics in pursuit of power was also noted by several reviewers. Schrefer noted that the world Parker-Chan creates is "structured by ambition above all else," and the characters within manipulate, murder, and connive to get ahead in a hardscrabble world. In her review on the *Geek Girl Authority* website, Alex Faccibene summed up the moral ambiguity of the book as a test of the reader's enjoyment of "studies of power or stories of revenge and ambition."

Though reviews were positive overall, Alex Brown commented in a review for *Locus* that the fantasy elements were "thin." Aside from being able to see ghosts, who seemed passive and ancillary, and the summoning of colored fire, there was not much in the way of complex fantasy in this work. In addition, Macallister found the romantic relationship between Zhu Chongba and Ma Xiuying "surprisingly underdeveloped," while Schrefer commented on the book's "restricted emotional range" and found the plot dragged at times.

Overall, critics agreed that *She Who Became the Sun* is an important work of fantasy fiction with original and compelling main characters. The book is praised widely for its handling of gender identity and sexuality, demonstrating a nuanced and complex understanding of how the characters express and embody themselves. *She Who Became the Sun* speaks to complex issues of morality, power, and identity that will resonate with most readers.

Author Biography

Shelley Parker-Chan is an Asian Australian former diplomat and advisor who worked in human rights and gender equality in Southeast Asia. She was awarded the 2017 Otherwise (Tiptree) Fellowship for work expanding our understanding of gender. *She Who Became the Sun* is her debut novel.

Bethany Groff Dorau

Review Sources

Bourke, Liz, and Alex Brown. "Liz Bourke and Alex Brown Review *She Who Became the Sun* by Shelley Parker-Chan." Review of *She Who Became the Sun*, by Shelley Parker-Chan. *Locus Magazine*, 30 July 2021, locusmag.com/2021/07/liz-bourke-reviews-she-who-became-the-sun-by-shelley-parker-chan/. Accessed 1 Nov. 2021.

Faccibene, Alex. Review of *She Who Became the Sun*, by Shelley Parker-Chan. *Geek Girl Authority*, 12 Aug. 2021, www.geekgirlauthority.com/she-who-became-the-sun-review/. Accessed 1 Nov. 2021.

Macallister, Greer. "Gender and Greatness in '*She Who Became the Sun*.'" Review of *She Who Became the Sun*, by Shelley Parker-Chan. *Chicago Review of Books*, 28 July 2021, chireviewofbooks.com/2021/07/28/she-who-became-the-sun/. Accessed 1 Nov. 2021.

Mandelo, Lee. Review of *She Who Became the Sun* by Shelley Parker-Chan. *Tor.com*, 28 July 2021, www.tor.com/2021/07/28/book-reviews-she-who-became-the-sun-by-shelley-parker-chan/. Accessed 1 Nov. 2021.

Schrefer, Eliot. "Review: '*She Who Became the Sun*' Is an Important Entry in the LGBTQ Fantasy Canon." Review of *She Who Became the Sun* by Shelley Parker-Chan. *USA Today*, 21 July 2021, www.usatoday.com/story/entertainment/books/2021/07/20/she-who-became-sun-important-entry-lgbtq-fantasy-canon/7973314002/. Accessed 1 Nov. 2021.

A Sitting in St. James

Author: Rita Williams-Garcia (b. 1957)
Publisher: Quill Tree Books (New York).
  480 pp.
Type of work: Novel
Time: 1860
Locale: St. James, Louisiana

A Sitting in St. James is a sweeping work of historical fiction by young adult author Rita Williams-Garcia. Set on a sugar plantation in St. James Parish, Louisiana, the novel is an unflinching portrait of slavery in the pre–Civil War South that focuses on the members of a White enslaving family.

Principal characters

MADAME SYLVIE BERNARDIN DE MARET DACIER GUILBERT, the French-born, royalist head of Le Petit Cottage
THISBE, her personal attendant, a sixteen-year-old enslaved woman
LUCIEN GUILBERT, her son, the abusive, alcoholic manager of Le Petit Cottage
BYRON GUILBERT, her grandson, a West Point cadet
JANE CHATHAM, a teenage girl, the Guilberts' eccentric neighbor
ROSALIE, Lucien's daughter, conceived by the rape of an enslaved woman named Camille

A Sitting in St. James (2021), a stunning novel by award-winning young adult author Rita Williams-Garcia, begins with a modest apology. "Gentle reader," the omniscient narrator writes, "It gives me no pleasure to disturb you with this story, for who wants to read about slavery?" Indeed, Williams-Garcia herself, as she explains in the book's afterword, once vowed that she would never write a book about slavery or the civil rights era. Like many Black authors, she was frustrated by the lack of fiction about contemporary Black characters living outside the bounds of chattel slavery or Jim Crow. Williams-Garcia first broke her vow with *One Crazy Summer* (2010), a middle-grade novel set in Oakland during the early days of the Black Panther movement; it was a Newbery Medal Honor Book and a finalist for the National Book Award for Young People's Literature.

Williams-Garcia breaks her vow again with *A Sitting in St. James*, and does so, once again, with purpose. The novel, about a White family in pre–Civil War Louisiana and the people whom they enslave, is written for an audience of older teens and adults, and readers should be warned that it contains scenes of brutal sexual violence; though it can be difficult to read, it is ultimately deeply rewarding in its complexity of plot and character. Williams-Garcia's well-researched novel seeks to expose the roots of American racism, illustrating how White supremacy is entwined with each characters' conception of self. At a panel on police brutality, a young Black boy once asked the author "Why do they hate us?"; she laments that she did not have an adequate response to explain the depth of disregard for Black life. This book, she writes in the afterword, is an attempt to answer that young boy, illustrating how deeply identity is formed (and perpetuated) by social conditions, and begging questions about what someone from the future might think of contemporary society viewed through the same unblinking eye.

Though the bulk of the novel is set in Louisiana in 1860, the story begins with a prologue set in revolutionary France. A young girl named Sylvie, friend to the fallen royal court, is orphaned and hidden away in a convent. Her only escape is through marriage to a stranger, a wealthy, French-born planter named Bayard Guilbert—an uncouth man who was once in love with her mother. Guilbert whisks her away from her beloved country. They settle in Haiti but are driven from their plantation, or forced labor camp, by another revolution, engineered by the country's enslaved population. Husband and wife flee to the Louisiana bayou, a primitive wilderness to young Sylvie's eyes, and build a sugar plantation in St. James Parish. Madame Sylvie, now an elderly, widowed matriarch, has "retired" from her role as plantation head, appointing her only living son, Lucien, as its manager. Lucien, like so much else in Madame Sylvie's life, has revealed himself to be a disappointment, an incompetent alcoholic known for his violent abuse of enslaved women.

Madame Sylvie, an avid card player, often speaks of the necessity of playing the hand one is dealt—an extreme irony to the ears of the enslaved women in her presence. While she has made the best of her lot, she is perpetually aggrieved. True, she has endured real tragedy—namely the unexpected death of her only daughter—but she has also engineered it. Of course, Madame Sylvie would never see it that way. In her eyes, she is a long-suffering victim and, as such, must seek her own reward. She decides to take a personal servant. A teenage girl, plucked from her family at the age of six, attends to Madame Sylvie's every physical need, eyes downcast, lips unspeaking. She fetches the playing cards for Madame Sylvie but also bathes and dresses her, and wipes her after she relieves herself. She endures punishment, having her hands beaten with the back of a hairbrush, for the smallest infraction or suggestion of smile. Madame Sylvie will only call her servant Thisbe, the name of Queen Marie Antoinette's beloved dog.

The omniscient narrator begs patience as the threads of the tale come together. The lives and bloodlines of the characters are so tangled that to explain the circumstances of one requires telling the story of another, like Jesse, the murdered young son of Lily,

Rita Williams-Garcia

Courtesy HarperCollins Publishers

the cook. Their stories must be told in order to understand Byron Guilbert, Lucien's son. Unlike his father, Byron is a moderate drinker and refuses, to Lucien's disdain, to harass and assault the enslaved women of Le Petit Cottage. Byron is studying at West Point and is engaged to the niece of a countess—but he has a dangerous secret. He is in love with a man named Pearce, one of his fellow West Point cadets. Pearce, a charming Northerner, comes to visit his beau, but his irreverent ways clash, often in serious ways, with the iron-clad social mores of the South. Some critics questioned the author's portrayal of Pearce and Byron. For instance, a reviewer for *Publishers Weekly* suggested that aspects of their story fetishize queer pain—a fruitful point for discussion. But Williams-Garcia offers a mostly nuanced portrait of what a queer romance might have looked like at the place and time. (She cites Michael Bronski's 2011 book *A Queer History of the United States* as a reference.) Most interesting, however, is how Byron, a born Southerner, navigates his identity. As a gay man who is not out, he is empathetic to White women who are also bound by archaic social rules, but this empathy does not extend to enslaved people. He chafes against only those rules of the Old South that apply to him specifically and vows to protect the same "way of life" he seeks to escape at war.

The principal cast also includes a young woman named Jane Chatham, who was raised on a neighboring plantation. Her refusal to live according to the complicated strictures of White womanhood has driven her mother to desperation. Jane is sent to live with the Guilberts, with Madame Sylvie serving as her social instructor. The invitation is not entirely benevolent. Lucien is happy to use the money for Jane's room and board to pay some of the plantation's mounting debts, while Madame Sylvie embraces the arrangement out of a complicated sense of spite. Jane offers a refreshing twist on a familiar archetype. She is not a pretty, clever tomboy, but a rough eccentric who rejects social niceties simply because she does not comprehend them. Another character of interest is Rosalie, Lucien's teenage daughter. Rosalie, a talented seamstress, was conceived through the violent rape of her mother, Camille. The child is, thus, a "quadroon," meaning that she is "one-quarter" Black according to her lineage. Rosalie, who has returned from the convent where she had been attending school, must navigate the precarious, liminal space among her roles as daughter, sister, and enslaved person. She is an outsider in every circle. Save for her mother and brothers, she is ostracized by other enslaved people, her relative privilege magnified by Lucien's decision to have her live in the overseer's cottage. Meanwhile, her mother's husband, pained by the memory of Camille's rape, rejects her, as does Madame Sylvie, who refuses to acknowledge any mixed-race Guilbert. Lucien could be said to care for her, but his love is tempered by the ever-present knowledge that she is his property and, as such, can be used for profit.

The book's title—*A Sitting in St. James*—refers to its central event. Madame Sylvie makes plans to sit for a portrait. An old-fashioned practice even in 1860, the portrait will be painted by a descendant of a woman who once painted Marie Antoinette. The story of the painting, and the lengths Madame Sylvie will go to have it, illustrates one of the novel's central themes, best described by a reviewer for *Publishers Weekly*, who claimed the novel "offers an unvarnished look at a slowly toppling power structure obsessed with artifice and tradition, hinting . . . that new generations may, slowly and not without suffering, move away from antiquated ideology." Madame Sylvie, eighty years old but ever loyal to her long-dead monarch, is an absurd figure to the younger people in her life. Her understanding of the world is shaped by ideas that no longer have any power or meaning, yet she is unable to understand the world or her place in it without them. So, too, are Lucien and Byron shaped by the institution of chattel slavery. In the book's afterword, Williams-Garcia references an interview with the late Nobel Prize–winning novelist Toni Morrison. Asked about racism, Morrison poses a question to White people: "What are you without racism?" Lucien and Byron, so different in character yet the same in their understanding of the world, are threatened by the impending war and what it might mean for their way of life. But Williams-Garcia ensures the reader looks closer. If Lucien's identity is built on his wealth, his sense of worth is wholly dependent on the brutal subjugation of Black people, be they a stranger to him, like Lily, or his own daughter. Williams-Garcia illustrates how a person like Lucien is able to normalize rape, torture, and murder within the context of his own self-interest. To dismiss people who enslaved other people as merely bad lets them off the hook. How were racism and exploitation so thoroughly absorbed into the fabric of American life? Only when people ask the question can they begin to remove the stain.

Author Biography
Rita Williams-Garcia published her first novel, *Blue Tights*, in 1987. Her 2009 young adult novel *Jumped* was a finalist for the National Book Award for Young People's Literature, as were *One Crazy Summer* (2010), and *Clayton Byrd Goes Underground* (2017). She has also won the Coretta Scott King Award and the Newbery Honor Book award.

Molly Hagan

Review Sources
Bracy, Pauletta Brown. Review of *A Sitting in St. James*, by Rita Williams-Garcia. *Horn Book*, 15 June 2021, www.hbook.com/?detailStory=review-of-a-sitting-in-st-james. Accessed 23 Sept. 2021.

Peebles, Donald. Review of *A Sitting in St. James*, by Rita Williams-Garcia. *School Library Journal*, 1 May 2021, www.slj.com/?reviewDetail=a-sitting-in-st-james. Accessed 23 Sept. 2021.

Review of *A Sitting in St. James*, by Rita Williams-Garcia. *Kirkus*, 3 Mar. 2021, www.kirkusreviews.com/book-reviews/rita-williams-garcia/a-sitting-in-st-james/. Accessed 23 Sept. 2021.

Review of *A Sitting in St. James*, by Rita Williams-Garcia. *Publishers Weekly*, 1 Apr. 2021, www.publishersweekly.com/978-0-06236729-7. Accessed 23 Sept. 2021.

Skinship

Author: Yoon Choi
Publisher: Alfred A. Knopf (New York). 304 pp.
Type of work: Short fiction
Time: 1980s–present
Locales: United States; South Korea; London, England

Yoon Choi's debut fiction collection, Skinship, *features eight stories about the varied experiences of Koreans, Korean immigrants, and Korean Americans.*

Principal characters

HAN SOO-AH, formerly known as Park Soo-ah; a Korean immigrant who runs a bodega with her husband
HAN JAE-WOO, her husband
HONG KI-TAE, her English tutor in Korea; a famous pastor
ALBERT UHM, a classical pianist
SAE-RI AHN, also known as Kim Sae-ri; a woman who got pregnant as a teen in Korea
KIM MIN-SOO, also known as Matthew; Sae-ri's son
JAMES AHN, also known as Ahn Jun-ho; Sae-ri's Korean American husband
MINYOUNG HWANG, also known as Song Minyoung; a wealthy stay-at-home mom
CHARIS HWANG, Minyoung's teenage daughter
SONG MINJI, Minyoung's younger sister who lives in London
LIM SO-HYUN, a teenage girl who moves to the US with her mother and brother to escape their abusive father
JI-WON LI, a young girl attending a diverse elementary school in Queens, New York
ANJALI ANAND, Ji-won's first real friend; an Indian American girl

In "On Romanizing Korean Names and Writing Immigrant Stories in an Acquired Language," an August 2021 essay for *Literary Hub*, Yoon Choi notes that when she first started writing fiction she did not intend to write about Korean characters or anything Korean. While she was a creative writing graduate student at Johns Hopkins University, she aspired to write stories like those by her literary heroes, Vladimir Nabokov and John Cheever, and subsequently spent a lot of time researching European-sounding names for her characters. Although she did not realize it at the time, she was grappling with the belief that many people from immigrant families internalize: that their heritage is something to "transcend" in order to become great in America. It was not until years later when she had started a family and given up her literary dreams that Choi sat

Yoon Choi

Courtesy Aaron Jay Young

down one day, suddenly inspired to write a few lines about Han Mo-Sae, a Korean grandfather. The character evolved into a story, which in turn led to the 2021 short-story collection *Skinship*.

Choi's collection is a spectacular debut that comprises eight stories, each of which focuses on a different set of characters. "The Church of Abundant Life," for example, follows a frustrated fifty-something woman named Soo who runs a corner store with her husband and wonders what her life would have been like if she never married him. "Solo Works for Piano" is about a brilliant pianist named Albert who exhibits neurodiverse behavior and refers to himself as "a person who retreats." In "Song and Song," a stay-at-home mom comes to appreciate her artistic, rebel sister after their mother dies. Other stories follow children learning to navigate their place in the world, grandparents struggling with dementia, immigrants born in Korea, and second-generation Korean Americans. There is a queer character in one story and an adopted character in another. Ultimately, by ensuring the collection comprises a diverse spectrum of people and experiences, Choi establishes that Koreans and Korean Americans are not monolithic. Indeed, all of the characters who populate the pages of *Skinship* are beautifully wrought, three-dimensional beings with their own unique fears, hopes, and challenges.

Choi is the kind of gifted writer who knows how to transport her readers directly into her characters' minds and lives. Many of her stories opt for small, everyday moments rather than complex, dramatic plots. To demonstrate why these moments are significant to her characters, Choi often provides readers with context in the form of memories or flashbacks. "The Church of Abundant Life," for example, begins when protagonist Soo sees a newspaper advertisement for an upcoming sermon by a man named Hong Ki-tae, a famous pastor who had a crush on her when he was her English tutor in Korea. She remembers that it was Hong Ki-tae who first introduced her to her husband, Jae-woo, whom she found attractive because he had endured much hardship in his life but always managed to persevere. After they married, Jae-woo brought Soo to New York City so that they could run a corner store in a rough neighborhood, and she began to resent him. It becomes clear then that for Soo, Hong Ki-tae represents the "road not traveled"—she could have been the wife of a respected pastor. Her assessment of her life changes after she interacts with a member of his congregation. Soo's story, as Choi tells it, is relatable and poignant.

Women who are struggling with feelings of inadequacy is a reoccurring theme among several of *Skinship*'s stories. "First Language," for example, follows a woman named Sae-ri who is traveling to Pennsylvania with her husband, James, to pick up her son, Min-soo (also known as Matthew), from a religious camp for troubled boys.

The couple were originally set up by a matchmaker back in South Korea who did not tell James that Sae-ri had Min-soo when she was a teenager. James does not learn this truth until five years into their marriage, after they have twin girls together, when Sae-ri's mother can no longer take care of Min-soo in Korea. As Min-soo gets older, he makes their lives increasingly difficult, which forces Sae-ri to confront her own shortcomings.

Another woman in the collection who is in the midst of questioning herself and her life decisions is Minyoung from the story "Song and Song." A Columbia University graduate who is married to a doctor and lives an affluent life, Minyoung becomes overwhelmed with feelings of inadequacy when her teenage daughter, Charis, gives a class presentation about how she did not respect her mother for being a stay-at-home mom until she realized that feminism had given her that choice. Minyoung's insecurities come to the forefront when she and Charis go to London to visit her younger sister Minji, a struggling writer who has chosen an impoverished life but seems fulfilled. Minyoung's story illustrates how much pressure there is on women of Korean heritage to fulfill the cultural expectations of being a good mother and wife. An even more resonant example of this arguably sexist phenomenon can be found in the title story, "Skinship." In it, narrator So-hyun, her brother, and their mother leave Korea to escape her alcoholic father and end up living with her maternal aunt and uncle in the United States. So-hyun's mother is so ashamed that she cannot provide a better life for her children that she becomes a self-loathing ghost of her former self who is constantly humiliated by her sister and brother-in-law.

One of the aspects that makes *Skinship* such an enjoyable read is Choi's beautiful prose, namely her careful use of sensory details. Often these details are so well-crafted that it is easy to assume that she has plucked them from her own life. Choi's family immigrated from South Korea to New York when she was three years old. Similarly, many of her characters live in New York City and she captures the sounds, people, and overall atmospheres of their distinct neighborhoods with expertise. She also paints a vivid picture of Korean American homes through what her characters eat and drink, writing engagingly about purple yams, steamed glutinous corn, vodka in butterfly mugs, and dried squid that sticks to the back of one's teeth.

Another talent of Choi's that shines in *Skinship* is her ability to relay the subtext behind characters' relationships through their body language, carefully chosen words, and silences. In the story "Skinship," so much of the power structure of So-hyun's aunt's house is conveyed by who makes dinner, who cleans, and where everyone sits at the table. In "A Map of the Simplified World," it becomes clear that elementary school student Ji-won's relationship with her best friend Anjali is beginning to fray when the two girls have a tense conversation about whether guinea pigs are cute or just rodents. Again and again, Choi is able to capture how characters' feel about themselves and one another through small yet significant details. In turn, she adds a richness and universality to the stories is extremely engaging.

It is difficult to find flaws in *Skinship*. Some readers might not like the fact that its eight narratives are almost twice the length of the average short story. However, others will appreciate the opportunity to spend time with Choi's characters. This has been the consensus among literary critics, the overwhelming majority of whom had nothing but praise for *Skinship*, which was a finalist for the 2022 PEN/Robert W. Bingham Prize for Debut Short Story Collection. The reviewer for *Kirkus* stated that Choi's book is "the rare story collection that draws you in so completely that the pages turn themselves." Similarly, Hamilton Cain wrote in his review for the *Star Tribune*, "Choi's collection of short stories is an inventive, dazzling work that probes the Korean-American experience from myriad angles and perspectives, wielding the double-edged sword of the hyphen to superb effect. Each piece is a banger." Most readers will be hard pressed to find a piece within the collection that they do not enjoy or find meaning in. There is no filler in *Skinship*—each beautifully written, poignant story stands on its own.

Another common point of praise for *Skinship* has been the way in which it tells immigrant stories in a completely new way. In her review for NPR, Maureen Corrigan wrote, "I know: immigration is hardly a fresh subject and it's especially popular in memoirs and fiction these days. But, it's Choi's approach, the way her stories unexpectedly splinter out from a single life to touch upon decades of family history shaped by immigration that make them something special." Ashley Duong had a similar comment in her Associated Press review for ABC News, writing, "Her collection is a fresh take on the experience of newcomers to America—stories of love, disappointment and sacrifice." Indeed, *Skinship* focuses on experiences that go beyond the familiar immigrant tropes of reaching for the American dream, experiencing racism and xenophobia, and navigating the challenges of cultural assimilation. Choi's decision to have most of her characters' conflicts be with their friends, family members, classmates, and themselves demonstrates that there is much more to these characters' lives and identities beyond being an immigrant. In interviews, Choi has stated that she set out to write the kind of book she wished that she had in her bookshelf growing up. It is safe to say that with *Skinship* she succeeded.

Author Biography
Yoon Choi has a MA from John Hopkins and was a recipient of the 2017 Wallace Stegner Fellowship in Fiction Writing from Stanford University. Her stories have been published in the *New England Review, Michigan Quarterly Review, The Best American Short Stories 2018*, and elsewhere.

Emily E. Turner

Review Sources
Cain, Hamilton. Review of *Skinship*, by Yoon Choi. *The Star Tribune*, 13 Aug. 2021, www.startribune.com/review-skinship-by-yoon-choi/600087529. Accessed 13 Jan. 2021.

Corrigan, Maureen. "Think You Know Where the Stories in *Skinship* Are Going? Think Again." Review of *Skinship*, by Yoon Choi. *NPR*, 25 Aug. 2021, www.npr.org/2021/08/25/1030611449/skinship-review-yoon-choi-short-story-collection. Accessed 13 Jan. 2021.

Duong, Ashley. "Examining Korean American Duality in *Skinship*." Review of *Skinship*, by Yoon Choi. *ABC News*, 23 Aug. 2021, abcnews.go.com/Entertainment/wireStory/review-examining-korean-american-duality-skinship-79601745. Accessed 13 Jan. 2021.

Review of *Skinship*, by Yoon Choi. *Kirkus*, 16 June 2021, www.kirkusreviews.com/book-reviews/yoon-choi/skinship. Accessed 13 Jan. 2021.

Smile
The Story of a Face

Author: Sarah Ruhl (b. 1974)
Publisher: Simon and Schuster (New York). 256 pp.
Type of work: Memoir, medicine
Time: 1974–2020
Locales: New York, Rhode Island, Connecticut, Illinois

In this memoir recounting a decade living with a serious case of Bell's palsy, a condition that causes facial paralysis, noted playwright Sarah Ruhl meditates on many different topics relevant to her sudden inability to smile.

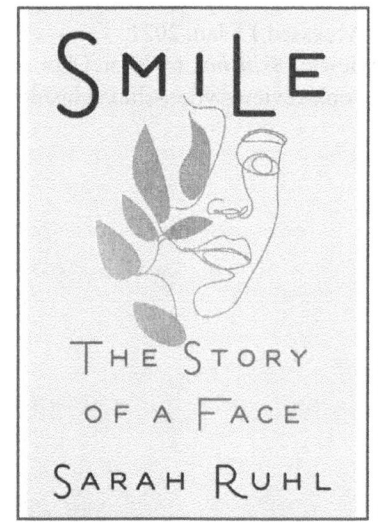

Principal personages
SARAH RUHL, an acclaimed playwright who develops a serious case of Bell's palsy after giving birth
TONY CHARUVASTRA, her husband, a child psychiatrist
ANNA, her eldest daughter
HOPE, her daughter, twin of William
WILLIAM, her son, twin of Hope

In this wise, witty, and ultimately inspiring book, the respected playwright Sarah Ruhl describes her effort to manage, for over a decade, a severe case of Bell's palsy, which descended on her shortly after she gave birth to fraternal twins in 2010. *Smile* (2021) is intriguingly structured so that several important details of Ruhl's life and medical condition are saved for close to the very end of the volume. In the pages in between the book's opening and conclusion, Ruhl offers an engaging, multigeneric narrative that is part memoir, part medical case history, with a healthy dose of humor thrown in for good measure. The book is likely to intrigue almost anyone who enjoys good writing and a compelling story, but it will, of course, be especially interesting to those who have lived with Bell's palsy, a condition in which nerve damage causes facial paralysis, as well as to parents trying to raise small children while attempting to meet the demands of professional obligations. Ruhl includes many revealing photographs from throughout her life in the book, including her life with Bell's palsy. Many of these she did not wish to be taken at the time, but they serve to help readers better understand precisely the challenges she faced not only as a person trying to live with Bell's palsy but also as a fairly prominent person trying to do so in the public eye. Altogether, *Smile* is a thoughtful and winning book that reminds readers of the common struggles people face from the often unexpected challenges of life.

Simply as a compendium of scientific information and of medical facts and theories, the book is hard to put down. One learns, for instance, many facts about pregnancy, including that "twins run on the mother's side, skipping a generation," that bed rest frequently results in depression both before and after delivery, and that pregnant women are generally denied full knowledge of the potentially negative outcomes of their pregnancies. Ruhl's many experiences with members of the medical profession also shed light on that field—namely, that while most medical professionals are compassionate heroes, a few can be appallingly insensitive. Along the way, Ruhl also peppers her narrative with many tidbits of trivia. Readers learn, for example, that it is actually harder to frown than to smile. Additionally, Ruhl shares the various advantages men have over women in living with Bell's—men can grow beards, for instance, and, besides, they are not, according to social gender norms, *expected* to smile as often as women are.

Sarah Ruhl

One also, of course, learns plenty about the condition of Bell's palsy, a mysterious disease that while known to the ancient Greeks, the causes of which remain mostly unknown and very difficult (and sometimes impossible) to cure. The condition can come and go quickly or linger for years, as is the outcome in Ruhl's case. While almost all people living with Bell's improve after a year, Ruhl herself is one of the 5 percent of people whose palsy lasts especially long (and never, in fact, entirely disappears). Ruhl explains ways of treating the condition, such as acupuncture and other "non-Western" approaches to medicine, and she details her visits with many members of the medical field, from chiropractors to neurologists. The distortion that Bell's palsy can cause to a person's face also reveals a great deal about cultural and social biases that most people rarely stop to think about. Ruhl, by being *forced* to think about them, reveals much about how people interact with one another in a society that prizes smiles, especially in women. Ruhl reports that most of humans' emotions are shown on the left sides of their faces (the very side damaged by Ruhl's case of the palsy) and that beauty is—and always has been—associated with symmetry. She shares with readers how Americans smile more than people in many other countries, in part because the United States consists of such a heterogenous population; people smile more to connect with other cultures that may not speak the same language. Further, Americans tend to value broad smiles that show many teeth, whereas such smiling in other cultures is often considered in bad taste. Ruhl discusses the fact that smiling in painted portraits was and remains unusual; the *Mona Lisa*, for example, is intriguing partly for that reason. Moreover, Ruhl explores how having Bell's palsy impacts other people's reactions to her—how they can be sometimes crude and sometimes compassionate when coming into contact with her.

But Ruhl, as it turns out, had not only Bell's palsy to deal with. Well into her attempt to manage the condition, she was also diagnosed with celiac disease, an autoimmune condition in which the body attacks itself when gluten is ingested. It turns out that this condition may have helped prevent Ruhl from recovering from Bell's, and it may also have played a major part in her father's premature death from cancer—an event to which Ruhl alludes throughout the book. (She does not fully recount his death until the book is moving toward its conclusion, at which point she includes a powerful description of this period in her life.) Ruhl was often sick as a child, probably because of undetected celiac disease, and the disease may also have had an impact on the complicated pregnancy that preceded her development of the palsy. Moreover, people contending with celiac disease have a higher chance than most of suffering from depression—another problem afflicting Ruhl (for lots of understandable reasons) in the aftermath of her diagnosis with Bell's.

And yet this is not, remarkably, a very depressing book. Ruhl is lucky enough to have an exceptionally loving husband, spirited and often funny children, a wide circle of compassionate friends and family, and an innate sense of good humor that lends a lightness to the memoir. Indeed, as the book develops, one is more and more impressed by Ruhl's ability to find humor in the challenges life has thrown in her path. By the end, the work seems life-affirming rather than one long account of a series of unfortunate events. One is reminded of how precious life is, and how especially precious good health is, and of how, ultimately, people have little choice but to try to make the best of the suffering and disappointments to which almost no one is immune. Ruhl's palsy led her to worry that she was unintentionally conveying irritation or anger in her facial expression, which is why her condition was often so hard for her to accept. Ruhl is a person who *wanted* to smile, especially when she could no longer easily do so, and reading her narrative will often bring real smiles to the faces of her readers.

Ruhl acknowledges that in many ways she has led an unusually privileged life. Raised by talented, White, upper-middle-class parents (her mother was a teacher and a noted amateur actor), educated at Brown University, married to a gifted doctor, and successful in her career as a playwright, Ruhl has had remarkable advantages (including a healthy income and a nanny) in coping with her various conditions. Yet the author rarely, if ever, comes across as conceited or self-important; in fact, just the opposite, especially when she pays generous tributes to the friends, colleagues, family members, and medical professionals who have helped her not only survive (she briefly contemplated "erasing" herself) but even thrive, despite the various ways in which her body became a kind of enemy. She seems an especially affectionate wife and a deeply appreciative mother who can find humor in the trials of parenthood. (An account of various kinds of vomiting by her children, on one occasion all taking place at once, is especially funny.) Her accounts of her relationships with numerous other people are often heartwarming, and her husband emerges as a particularly kind partner. In short, there is much in this book that balances the darkness it undeniably explores, so that by the end one values the work not only for the medical information it imparts but for the real-life wisdom it often conveys.

A one-time agnostic who eventually reconnected, on her own terms, with her childhood Catholic faith, Ruhl also draws on teachings by people from other religions, especially Buddhism, and other intellectual orientations. She explores her condition from almost every conceivable psychological, historical, sociological, cultural, and intellectual angle, while maintaining a writing style that is winningly simple, clear, understated, and often clever. One can easily comprehend why Ruhl is a successful dramatist because she manages to bring many people (especially herself) alive on the page, particularly when recounting her sometimes quirky thoughts and comments. The book was accused by at least one reviewer, with some justice, of being overlong, and others noted its digressive nature, a common element in Ruhl's work. As Helen Epstein wrote for the *Arts Fuse*, "If you are looking for a medical memoir about learning to live with Bell's palsy, you will be frustrated with this book and find it rambling." However, many reviewers had positive comments. Kristen Martin praised Ruhl in her review for NPR for her "engaging and insightful" writing, especially when writing about the trials of parenting. Martin also enjoyed Ruhl's physical description of her condition, explaining that "these insights allow for the reader to empathize, a crucial function of any illness narrative." Likewise, the anonymous reviewer for *Kirkus* called the book a "captivating, insightful memoir." By the time *Smile* winds to its conclusion, Ruhl's condition has greatly improved. Ultimately, one feels that one has not only followed her through a very difficult journey but has also met, on the page, someone it would be a pleasure to meet in person.

Author Biography
Sarah Ruhl is an accomplished playwright who was the recipient of a MacArthur Fellowship in 2006. Her play *In the Next Room, or the vibrator play* (2009) was nominated for both a Tony Award and the Pulitzer Prize for Best Drama in 2010. She is also the author of four books of nonfiction.

Robert C. Evans, PhD

Review Sources
Epstein, Helen. "Book Review: Sarah Ruhl's 'Smile: The Story of a Face.'" *The Arts Fuse*, 16 Oct. 2021, artsfuse.org/238882/book-review-sarah-ruhls-smile-the-story-of-a-face. Accessed 14 Jan. 2022.
Feng, Rhoda. "Emotions Take Flight in 'Smile: The Story of a Face.'" Review of *Smile: The Story of a Face*, by Sarah Ruhl. *Chicago Review of Books*, 15 Oct. 2021, chireviewofbooks.com/2021/10/15/smile-the-story-of-a-face. Accessed 14 Jan. 2022.
Martin, Kristen. "Writer with Bell's Palsy Ponders How to Experience Joy When Expression Is Limited." Review of *Smile: The Story of a Face*, by Sarah Ruhl. *NPR*, 6 Oct. 2021, www.npr.org/2021/10/06/1043641296/sarah-ruhls-smile-records-her-experience-with-bells-palsy. Accessed 14 Jan. 2022.
Review of *Smile: The Story of a Face*, by Sarah Ruhl. *Kirkus*, 7 July 2021, www.kirkusreviews.com/book-reviews/sarah-ruhl/smile-ruhl. Accessed 14 Jan. 2022.

A Snake Falls to Earth

Author: Darcie Little Badger (b. 1987)
Publisher: Levine Querido (Hoboken, New Jersey). 384 pp.
Type of work: Novel
Time: Near future
Locales: Texas; the Reflecting World

A Snake Falls to Earth is an Indigenous Futurist young adult novel based in Apache tradition, telling the intersecting coming-of-age stories of a young human girl and a snake boy from the spirit world.

Principal characters

NINA, a Lipan Apache girl
OLI, a cottonmouth snake boy from the Reflecting World who visits Earth
AMI, a toad person in the Reflecting World, Oli's friend
RISK AND REIGN, coyote sisters from the Reflecting World, Oli's friends
BRIGHTEST, a hawk person from the Reflecting World, Oli's friend
GRANDMA, Nina's grandmother, who has some mysterious connections to the spirit world
ROSITA, Nina's great-great grandmother; the keeper of the family's stories, who lives to be 150 years old

In 2020, Darcie Little Badger burst onto the literary scene with her superb debut novel *Elatsoe*. A young adult work that seamlessly blends the fantasy and mystery genres, *Elatsoe* quickly earned several prestigious awards and was even named one of the hundred best fantasy books ever written by *Time* magazine. The novel received acclaim for Little Badger's exceptional writing, but also gained attention for having a Lipan Apache protagonist. While prominent and richly drawn American Indian characters in general have historically been few and far between, there had never been a Lipan Apache character in mainstream literature before. In her follow-up novel, *A Snake Falls to Earth* (2021), Little Badger continues to bring her people and their culture to readers as she tells the story of two teenagers from very different worlds who are willing to sacrifice everything to save the people they love.

While *A Snake Falls to Earth* is set in the near future, it has an epic, timeless quality to it. The book alternates between two story lines, the first of which is presented in third-person narration and follows a Lipan girl named Nina living in Texas. When she was nine years old, Nina recorded her great-great grandmother Rosita telling a story while on her deathbed that seemed to contain a clue about how she lived to be 150 years old. Nina could not understand the story, however, because Rosita told it to her in a mixture of Spanish and Lipan—a language that had been mostly lost over the years as a result of the genocide of the Lipan people. Over the next few years Nina works on deciphering the story, which she believes is about her family's connection to a magical world that separated from Earth thousands of years ago but still remains tethered to it. When her grandmother's life is put in danger because she cannot leave her home as severe weather approaches, Nina must try to save her by finding a way to use the information that Rosita left her.

The second story line is told in the first person by Oli, a teenage cottonmouth snake person who lives in that magical realm, known as the Reflecting World. Oli's story harmonizes perfectly with Nina's despite the fact that the two are quite different in both their plots and narrative style. When it comes to introducing Oli's environment, Little Badger conducts flawless worldbuilding, drawing on Apache traditions to show how spirits, monsters, and animal people all live in the Reflecting World. Like all animal people, Oli can alternate between his "true form" as a snake and his "false form" as a human. When the book begins, Oli leaves his mother's nest for the first time and must struggle to make it in the wild on his own. After settling on the banks of a bottomless lake, he befriends a toad named Ami and two fearless coyote sisters named Risk and Reign. When a mysterious illness puts Ami on the brink of death, Oli, the coyotes, and a hawk named Brightest must travel to Earth to try and stop the forces that are killing his species.

Darcie Little Badger

A large part of what makes *A Snake Falls to Earth* so enjoyable is its storytelling style. While *Elatsoe* was a brilliant debut, Little Badger's voice feels more fully formed and shines even brighter in *A Snake Falls to Earth*. In interviews, the author stated that while writing the novel she decided to use elements of the Lipan storytelling tradition that she learned from her mother. It is thanks to this decision that *A Snake Falls to Earth* stands out from so many other works of young adult fiction. Not only does it move at a different pace, but it also presents the world, humans, and animals from a perspective outside of the typical White Western lens. Little Badger enriches the story further by blending the Lipan stories she heard growing up about animal people with her own imagination to create the mythology of the Reflecting World.

Both longtime fans of the genre and newcomers will find *A Snake Falls to Earth* to be an exciting work of Indigenous Futurism—a growing artistic movement in which Little Badger has been recognized as a leading member. Where the mainstream media often depicts American Indian people as only figures of the past, Indigenous Futurists use their art to demonstrate that not only have their people survived centuries of genocide and cultural erasure to exist today but will continue to exist in the future. Like many other works that are classified as part of this movement, *A Snake Falls to Earth* includes elements of fantasy and science fiction. But Little Badger also harnesses the futurist lens by focusing on realistic issues that will impact the world in the years to come. This is evident in the novel's two biggest threats: the imminent hurricane and the extinction of Ami's species on Earth. Both of these events are related to the broader climate change crisis—something that many young people are anxious about. To demonstrate that there is hope for the future, Little Badger showcases characters who use optimism, grit, kindness, and teamwork to find solutions to their problems. Their actions also parallel the generations of Lipan and other Native American people who faced extinction from external forces for centuries but ultimately did not give up.

One of the key themes of *A Snake Falls to Earth* is the importance of one's cultural heritage, family, and identity. Rosita's story, for example, holds the key to Nina understanding how to find the magic that could save her grandmother's life, but she initially cannot access it because she does not speak Lipan. Nina's struggle here borrows from the real world where there are no longer fluent Lipan speakers. By making this conflict a central part of the plot, Little Badger demonstrates how much has been lost as a result of the forced assimilation of American Indians and other Indigenous cultures. Not only do many young Indigenous people today no longer know their ancestral languages, but they have been denied access to a wealth of knowledge and culture that is their birthright. Nina's determination to learn the Lipan language and more about her family's connection to the magic of the Reflecting World feels like an inspirational call-to-arms. Notably, Little Badger has Nina use a fictional app called St0ryte11er as a platform to tell the world about her heritage, indicating how technology can still be put to good use. Ultimately, the novel showcases just how important it is for younger generations to connect with their elders so they can keep their ancestors' wealth of knowledge alive while also having a better understanding of themselves.

Another interesting element of *A Snake Falls to Earth* that Little Badger has continued from *Elatsoe* is the Lipan matrilineal tradition. In both novels, the protagonists look for guidance, wisdom, or inspiration from their female family members, who are presented as the keepers of ancestral knowledge and magic. It is through Rosita that Nina learns about the animal people, spirits, and monsters that live in the Reflecting World. Her grandmother, who has healing powers, can be interpreted as a guardian figure in the way that she is tied to the family's ancestral land. Nina's father is also a source of wisdom and help; his bookshop turns out to be a place where animal people have been coming for years for books to bring back to the Reflecting World. Ultimately, however, it is Nina's mother, a linguist, who helps her crack Rosita's story in Lipan, further underlining the intergenerational power of women.

Any flaws of *A Snake Falls to Earth* are few and far between. It could be argued that the narrative's third act feels slightly overwhelming because the protagonists must face many different antagonistic forces instead of focusing on a few. However, this is a minor quibble, and many readers will likely find all of these conflicts to make for an engaging narrative rather than an overstuffed one. Tellingly, reception of *A Snake Falls to Earth* was overwhelmingly positive, with most critics quick to heap praise on Little Badger's writing and creativity. The book was longlisted for the National Book Award for Young People's Literature and was named the best young adult novel of 2021 by

Publishers Weekly, for which a reviewer stated: "Fun, imaginative, and deeply immersive, this story will be long in the minds of readers." *Kirkus Reviews* was similarly enthusiastic in its review, calling it "A coming-of-age story that beautifully combines tradition and technology for modern audiences" and "evokes the timeless feeling of listening to traditional oral storytelling."

Many critics emphasized how important *A Snake Falls to Earth* feels thanks to its presentation of diversity and major real-life social issues. In a review for *Tor.com*, Mahvesh Murad noted that "There is no pretension in the writing, no forced attempts at being on trend, and yet it is completely relevant—whether it is that certain characters are asexual, or use the pronoun they, or the power of the internet, or whether it is the frightening, timely talk of rapid climate change." Indeed, Little Badger's writing never feels didactic nor heavy handed; instead, she just seems to be relaying the world as she and her readers' see it. This is particularly evident in the way she presents her characters' gender and sexual identities. "Little Badger's casual inclusion of they/them pronouns and same-sex couples feels refreshingly natural, so much so that I had not noticed that a character was non-binary until I was two-thirds through the novel," Chandler Treon wrote for the *Porter House Review*. "Such inclusion is important for normalizing underrepresented identities and contextualizing them for young adult readers."

Ultimately, *A Snake Falls to Earth* is a highly engaging book thanks to Little Badger's vivid imagination and deft ability to write charismatic characters and compelling plot. A fresh addition to the crowded field of young adult literature, it is a novel that is likely to delight readers of all ages and backgrounds.

Author Biography
A trained Earth scientist, Darcie Little Badger has written short stories as well as the YA novel *Elatsoe* (2020). She received the 2021 Locus First Novel Award and a Golden Kite Award for Young Adult Fiction.

Emily E. Turner

Review Sources

Gall, Elisa. Review of *A Snake Falls to Earth*, by Darcie Little Badger. *The Horn Book Inc.*, 16 Nov. 2021, www.hbook.com/story/review-of-a-snake-falls-to-earth. Accessed 13 Jan. 2021.

Murad, Mahvesh. "Remember Our History: *A Snake Falls to Earth* by Darcie Little Badger." *Tor.com*, 23 Nov. 2021, www.tor.com/2021/11/23/book-reviews-a-snake-falls-to-earth-by-darcie-little-badger. Accessed 10 Jan. 2022.

Review of *A Snake Falls to Earth*, by Darcie Little Badger. *Kirkus Reviews*, 13 July 2021, www.kirkusreviews.com/book-reviews/darcie-little-badger/a-snake-falls-to-earth. Accessed 10 Jan. 2022.

Review of *A Snake Falls to Earth*, by Darcie Little Badger. *Publishers Weekly*, 18 Aug. 2021, www.publishersweekly.com/978-1-64614-092-3. Accessed 10 Jan. 2022.

Treon, Chandler. "Modernized Folklore: Blending the Natural, Spiritual, and Technological in *A Snake Falls to Earth*." Review of *A Snake Falls to Earth*, by Darcie Little Badger. *Porter House Review*, 3 Jan. 2022, porterhousereview.org/articles/modernized-folklore-blending-the-natural-spiritual-and-technological-in-a-snake-falls-to-earth/. Accessed 10 Jan. 2022.

Somebody's Daughter

Author: Ashley C. Ford (b. 1987)
Publisher: Flatiron Books (New York). 224 pp.
Type of work: Memoir
Time: Late 1980s to the present
Locales: Fort Wayne, Indiana; Brooklyn, New York

In this riveting memoir, writer Ashley C. Ford recalls growing up with an incarcerated father and a volatile, temperamental mother. The book reveals how these relationships permeated every aspect of Ford's early life, from the challenges of poverty to her very sense of identity.

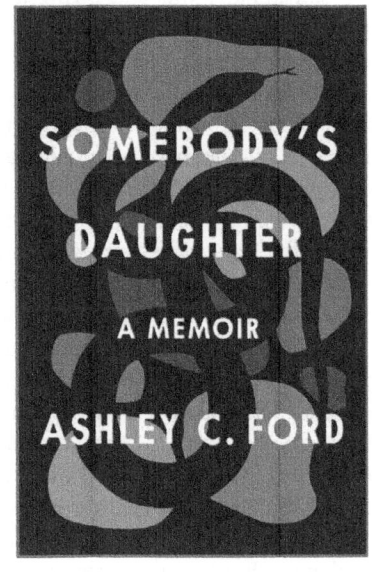

Principal personages

ASHLEY, the author and narrator
ASHLEY'S MOTHER, with whom she has a tense relationship
ASHLEY'S FATHER, who is incarcerated for reasons initially unclear to Ashley
BILLIE, Ashley's beloved grandmother

Ashley C. Ford's writing has been published by outlets including *New York*, *BuzzFeed*, the *Guardian*, and *Slate*. She also hosted several successful podcasts, and in 2017 she was named one of *Forbes* magazine's "30 Under 30 in Media." Yet it is with her debut book, *Somebody's Daughter* (2021), that she truly breaks out as a vivid literary voice. This wrenching, heartfelt memoir is in some ways a classic account of coming of age in the face of adversity. But it also provides insight into experiences that are rarely afforded mainstream attention, particularly that of Black American families and the unique pain of growing up with an incarcerated parent.

The great power of *Somebody's Daughter* lies in Ford's ability to consider people—and specifically her own family members—in their full complexity, even when doing so means challenging prevailing notions of right and wrong. The book is framed above all by her father's lengthy incarceration. It begins with the adult Ford receiving news that the parent whom she has only ever known behind bars is being released. The narrative then jumps back to relate Ford's life leading up to that point, so her father is mostly physically absent from the story, but his presence looms large nevertheless. Ford grapples to reconcile her deep love for her father with her limited actual connection to him, especially after she finally learns of the crime for which he was imprisoned. Eventually, she is able to hold these conflicting realities at once, and this complexity forms the heart of *Somebody's Daughter*. "To the world, he was a bad man," she writes. "To me, he was my dad who did a bad thing. I was still trying to figure out what it means to love someone who had done such a bad thing, but I did love him."

Ford employs the same empathy when she writes about her mother, the other towering personality in the book. Remaining unnamed throughout, her mother is fiercely loving but also frighteningly abusive, both physically and emotionally. Ford writes honestly about fearing her mother's fury while simultaneously recognizing the tremendous pressures her mother faced as a young, single parent of four children, dependent for a number of years on an abusive boyfriend. There are even plenty of happy times between mother and daughter, presented without apology alongside the unhappy ones. Ultimately, the key theme is again the great complexity of familial love, especially amid adverse social conditions. In a telling exchange in the first chapter, Ford, in response to her mother's invitation that she can "always come home," thinks, "Mama, I love you, but I'll work myself past the white meat, down to the bone, and fistfight every stranger I run across on the street before we live under the same roof again." Ford never explicitly forgives either of her parents for the harm they caused, but her writing exhibits a tenderness that makes the book a remarkable portrayal of humanity.

Ashley C. Ford

For Ford, the impact of her family situation is an aching need for a more ideal parent throughout her early life. While her father offers unwavering love and support in his letters to her (and on the rare occasions when she visits him in prison), his physical absence compels her to seek comfort elsewhere. Most often she finds it in her beloved grandmother, Billie. Like everyone else, Billie is flawed. She is judgmental and prickly, but offers Ford the most consistent safe harbor from the volatile forces that shape her world. Billie even briefly takes Ford, then five or six years old, to live with her own parents on a farm in Missouri. Ford recalls this as a peaceful time, in which she was offered the quiet solitude to think about her place in the world.

The time at the farm provides one of the book's most arresting symbolic images. After an unsuccessful visit from Ford' mother, Billie walks Ford to the edge of the property, where the grass grows wild. She digs a hole, and when Ford leans over the edge to look, the dirt is writhing with snakes. They seem to move together as one. When Ford asks what the snakes are doing, Billie replies, "They're loving each other, baby," before promptly dousing the hole with lighter fluid and dropping in a lit match. Instead of trying to escape, the snakes cling to one another tighter. Watching them shrivel and die, Ford is horrified and begins to cry. But Billie has a point to make about families and love. "We don't give up on our people. We don't stop loving them," she says. "Not even when we're burning alive." The image serves as a poignant symbol of Ford's broader experience, a heart-rending mix of trauma and unshakeable bonds.

The main arc of *Somebody's Daughter* describes Ford's journey as she learns to love on her own terms. She gives her love generously, but she learns to guard it generously too. Young Ford is vulnerable to her mother's rages but also to untrustworthy adult men and boys. An important thread of the book explores Ford's sexual coming of age. She describes her discomfort with her changing body and how it made her a target of suspicion. In one passage, for example, a catcaller reprimands Ford when he learns she is a child, as if she had provoked his harassment by willfully masquerading as a young woman. Later, when Ford, who fears being home alone after school, hangs around a male teacher's classroom asking questions, he accuses her of trying to seduce him. Like many Black girls, Ford is seen, with shocking combativeness, as an adult long before she actually is one. This pattern comes to a head when she is sexually assaulted as a young teenager, a deep trauma that greatly impacts her sense of self for years to come.

Ford does offer hope that love is still possible after suffering. She writes frankly about how she eventually embraces sex and desire after the violence of rape. Even when she learns the terrible truth that it was rape for which her father was incarcerated, she remains capable of love. Indeed, learning the truth in a way helps her process the realities of life. While her identity as a Black girl undeniably creates difficulties in society, it proves to be a foundational strength as she tells her story, one born of authentic experience and emotion. Ford might not subscribe to the same self-immolating kind of love as her grandmother, but the underlying sentiment is the same: she never gives up on loving her family, even when she must forge her own path to do it.

Forging that path ultimately means establishing her independence and healthy boundaries. Ford becomes the rare member of her family to attend college, and she embraces the freedom this affords her. Notably, however, the book does not end when she escapes her volatile home; as Billie knows, family ties extend beyond physical space. The first time Ford returns to visit her mother's home, she relishes the knowledge that she can leave whenever she wants. But as she gets older, she mourns the growing distance between herself and other members of her family. How can she remain close to them without getting burned? There is no single satisfying answer, but in her desire to nurture and maintain relationships, Ford resolves to visit her father for the first time since she was a preteen. The myriad complications of visiting a loved one in prison—from the paperwork to the seemingly arbitrary list of items banned from the visitation room to the strict rules policing physical touch—are described in detail, showcasing an all-too-real experience for many Americans. Yet it is the emotional reality of Ford's encounter with her father that illuminates the bigger theme: how incarceration divides families, punishing not only the incarcerated but also their loved ones. While Ford by no means downplays her father's crime, she shows that love and forgiveness, including of oneself, are vital to positive change, both on the individual and societal levels.

Somebody's Daughter was met with great critical acclaim, debuting on the New York Times Best Sellers list and earning recognition as one of the best books of the year by numerous publications. It received a starred review from *Publishers Weekly*, which called it a "blistering yet tender account" that "astounds." *Kirkus* also gave a starred recommendation, with the reviewer comparing the book to Tara Westover's 2018 hit memoir *Educated* in its depiction of breaking away from a damaging home life, as well as to Tayari Jones's 2018 novel *An American Marriage* in its exploration of the profound effects of incarceration on family. In a review for the *Washington Post*, professor and author Allyson Hobbs noted how, with some 1.8 million incarcerated people in the United States, *Somebody's Daughter* touches on a subject that is of widespread importance in American society yet receives little attention: "The disruption of family life that mass incarceration leaves in its wake." As Hobbs wrote, Ford "painfully and poignantly shows us that life goes on, even when a parent is not there."

Author Biography
Ashley C. Ford has written for numerous publications and also hosted programs such as the fiction podcast *The Chronicles of Now* and several web series. She was named one of *Forbes* magazine's "30 Under 30 in Media" in 2017. *Somebody's Daughter* is her first book.

Molly Hagan

Review Sources
Davis, Bridgett M. "Ashley C. Ford's Memoir Recalls Life with a Single Mom and Jailed Dad." Review of *Somebody's Daughter*, by Ashley C. Ford. *The New York Times*, 30 May 2021, www.nytimes.com/2021/05/30/books/review/ashley-c-ford-somebodys-daughter.html. Accessed 1 Dec. 2021.
Hobbs, Allyson. "What Happens to a Family When a Father Goes to Prison." Review of *Somebody's Daughter*, by Ashley C. Ford. *The Washington Post*, 25 June 2021, www.washingtonpost.com/outlook/what-happens-to-a-family-when-a-father-goes-to-prison/2021/06/23/57736b1c-d2ac-11eb-a53a-3b5450fdca7a_story.html. Accessed 1 Dec. 2021.
Onwuamaegbu, Natachi. "*Somebody's Daughter* Will Leave Readers Gasping for Air." Review of *Somebody's Daughter*, by Ashley C. Ford. *The Boston Globe*, 20 May 2021, www.bostonglobe.com/2021/05/20/arts/somebodys-daughter-will-leave-readers-gasping-air/. Accessed 1 Dec. 2021.
Review of *Somebody's Daughter*, by Ashley C. Ford. *Kirkus*, 23 Mar. 2021, www.kirkusreviews.com/book-reviews/ashley-c-ford/somebodys-daughter-ford/. Accessed 1 Dec. 2021.
Review of *Somebody's Daughter*, by Ashley C. Ford. *Publishers Weekly*, 8 Apr. 2021, www.publishersweekly.com/978-1-250-30597-8. Accessed 1 Dec. 2021.

The Souvenir Museum

Author: Elizabeth McCracken (b. 1966)
Publisher: Ecco (New York). 256 pp.
Type of work: Short stories
Time: Present day
Locales: The United States, the United Kingdom, Ireland

The Souvenir Museum is a collection of tragicomic short stories about oddball characters dealing with love, grief, fear, and heartbreak as they explore the many variations of family relationships.

Principal characters
SADIE, a young American woman
JACK, her boyfriend, born in the United States to a British family
LOUIS LEVINE, an elderly man who has recently lost his wife
DAVID LEVINE, Louis's son
LOTTIE STANLEY, a ventriloquist
MISTRESS MICKLE, an American actor who plays a villain on a British television show
LEONORA, a mother who has lost her children
BRUNO, a gay man with a four-year-old son
ERNEST, Bruno's partner
THEA, a woman awaiting the birth of her first grandchild
JOANNA, a woman on a trip to Denmark

Elizabeth McCracken has written several novels and a memoir but is perhaps best known for her short stories, which combine humor and pathos. *The Souvenir Museum* (2021), which collects pieces first published in venues such as *Zoetrope All-Story*, *Harper's*, and the *Atlantic* is generally lighter than her previous collection, *Thunderstruck* (2014), but there is still a great deal of heartbreak to be had in its pages.

Five of the stories—"The Irish Wedding," "A Splinter," "The Get-Go," "Two Sad Clowns," and "Nothing, Darling, Only Darling, Darling"—revolve around the characters Jack and Sadie, providing a through-line for the collection as a whole. Jack (whose real name is Leonard) is the American-born child of a British family, always a bit out of place among his relatives. Sadie, his girlfriend and eventual fiancée, is American, raised by a widowed Jewish mother. They are introduced in "The Irish Wedding" on their way to Jack's sister's destination wedding, where Sadie meets, and is overwhelmed by, Jack's family. ("I've had anxiety dreams more relaxing," she tells him.) The competing tensions and strengths that emerge in any relationship become

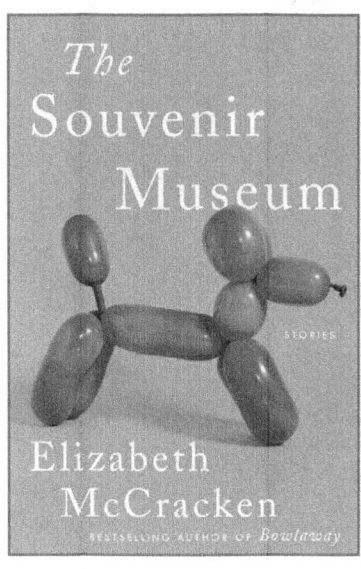

Elizabeth McCracken

a key theme, not only in the stories about Sadie and Jack but throughout the collection.

"A Splinter" elaborates on a somewhat absurd episode mentioned in "The Irish Wedding," in which a teenaged Jack runs away with an older ventriloquist, Lottie. The relationship falls apart, but Jack remains a puppet enthusiast for the rest of his life. In "The Get-Go," Jack meets Sadie's mother and finds out more about her father's death. "Two Sad Clowns" depicts Jack and Sadie's first meeting in a bar in Boston and foreshadows a bleak future that the stories in the collection never quite reach: "Even Punch and Judy loved each other once," it begins. "These people too, Jack and Sadie." Later on, the story enumerates the many differences between Jack and Sadie that the two are unaware of at this first meeting, concluding, "They never should have married, probably." But they do marry, in the collection's final story, "Nothing, Darling, Only Darling, Darling." Their wedding in England and subsequent honeymoon in Amsterdam are, however, overshadowed by the recent suicide of Jack's nephew Thomas.

The other seven stories in the collection are unrelated to the Jack and Sadie stories, and to one another. Their content varies widely, though again relationships are typically central themes. "Proof" is about a bird-watching enthusiast, Louis, who is taken by his son, David, on an expedition to see puffins on a rocky island off the coast of Scotland. The seemingly innocuous excursion is fraught with emotion for the pair, as David's mother, Louis's wife, has only recently died. David also must grapple with Louis's incipient mental decline: in the story's climactic moment, Louis briefly forgets David's name.

In "It's Not You," an unnamed first-person narrator recounts her trip to the Narcissus Hotel in the "long-ago days of 1993." Nursing a recent heartbreak, she encounters a married radio host with a "beef bourguignon voice" who has been stood up by a woman—a regular caller to his show—with whom he has been having a long-distance affair. The protagonist of "Mistress Mickle All at Sea" is an American woman with an Irish passport living in Surrey, England, where she plays the villain on a children's TV program. Though her real name is Jenny Early, the story refers to her throughout by the name of her character. She is returning from a New Year's visit to Rotterdam, where her brother lives. "Expatriation was the family disease, hereditary," she reflects.

"Birdsong from the Radio" follows Leonora, whose love for her three children manifests as a desire to nibble on them. As small children, they enjoy this ("Children long to be eaten. Everyone knows that."), but as they grow older they are less amenable to it, and Leonora only grows hungrier. When all three children are killed in a car accident—the fault of a drunk-driving babysitter—Leonora attempts to fill the empty space inside herself with loaves of bread instead. "Robinson Crusoe at the Waterpark" deals with similar themes of parents' fears for their children and desire to somehow insulate them against all harm. In the story, Bruno and Ernest take their four-year-old son, Cody, on his first trip to a water park. The more laid-back Ernest is enjoying the trip, but Bruno is unable to stop thinking of all the disasters that could occur: "Survivors of the Whaleship *Essex* at the Waterpark. The *Lusitania* at the Waterpark. *The Poseidon Adventure* at the Waterpark."

Thea, the protagonist of "A Walk-Through Human Heart," has a daughter, Georgia, who is expecting a first child of her own. Thea goes from store to store looking for a gift for her unborn grandchild: a specific baby doll, "Baby Alive," that Georgia longed for when she was eight, but that Thea was unwilling to buy her. "Georgia would find it touching, or she'd be hurt," McCracken writes. "Thea wasn't sure which reaction she hoped for." The title story, "The Souvenir Museum," follows a woman, Joanna, whose father has recently died. As a last request, he wanted Joanna to take his watch to her ex, Aksel, who always admired it. Aksel, however, now lives and works in a recreation Viking village in Denmark—"off the grid," as Joanna says, to which Aksel replies, "You just don't know my coordinates." The setting gives the encounter a surreal flavor, as if it is taking place outside of time.

When stripped down to the bare facts of their plots, the stories seem melancholic, but they are in fact frequently leavened by humor, from sharp observations to little bits of absurdity to, perhaps unexpectedly, scatological humor. ("The Irish Wedding" has an extended bit in the latter vein and also features a dog named "S——head.") "Proof," for example, has Louis, who is Jewish, reflecting on his wedding to his Scottish wife, Arlene; he wanted a Scottish wedding, but she refused, expressing a particular hatred for kilts and bagpipes. "What could be sadder in a marriage than incompatible feelings about bagpipes?" McCracken asks. "Ought they still to marry?" In "Robinson Crusoe at the Waterpark," Ernest and Bruno argue about open-plan houses, which Bruno is strongly against: "Do you know who else likes to see everything from the kitchen? The Devil. Hell is entirely without doors."

The characters in the stories are often geographically or culturally displaced. Many of the stories find their protagonists away from home, but it goes deeper than that. Jack is an odd man out in both the United States and the United Kingdom; Mistress Mickle is an American living in Britain visiting a brother who lives in the Netherlands; Bruno is British, raised by a German adoptive mother, and now living in the United States, while his partner, Ernest, is Cuban American. The characters' multicultural backgrounds contribute to their loneliness and complicate their relationships with their families.

Family, of course, is central to the majority of the stories in *The Souvenir Museum*, with "It's Not You" as the only exception. Parent-child relationships are a frequent focus, from parents with young children dealing with the fact that they cannot fully insulate their children from the world's dangers to adults with elderly parents dealing with their parents' decline or death. Sibling relationships are also foregrounded in several of the stories, particularly the strange dynamic that comes from two (or more) people growing up together but then having their lives diverge so completely that in some ways they are strangers to one another. This is exacerbated by geographical displacement; both "Mistress Mickle All at Sea" and "The Irish Wedding" make a point of noting that the siblings central to the story have different accents, an audible sign of their separation.

The Souvenir Museum was widely praised by critics. Many noted McCracken's evocative turns of phrase and unexpected visual descriptions. Jackie Thomas-Kennedy, writing for the *Harvard Review Online* noted that the "prose is so plush that it may be read happily for the language alone, though there is much more at work here." An anonymous reviewer for *Publishers Weekly* wrote that "McCracken has a gift for surprising similes . . . that ignite the reader's imagination, making great fun out of ordinary settings and scenery." Critics also praised the endearingly quirky characters that populate the stories, whom Heller McAlpin, for NPR, referred to as "appealing oddballs" and "wonderfully eccentric." In a review for the *Boston Globe*, Joseph Peschel called them "a goluptious coterie of eccentric and fascinating, if not entirely likable, characters." The author's keen observation of human behavior was another strength that many critics noted. An anonymous reviewer for *Kirkus* described the stories as "searingly realistic." Writing for the UK publication *TLS*, Desirée Baptiste commented that "English social foibles are sharply observed," while in a review for the *Guardian* John Self noted that McCracken "has a gift for spotting the comic potential in situations many of us have endured" and that the stories are "stippled with just-so observations."

Taken as a whole, *The Souvenir Museum* is a tightly constructed set of narratives in which powerful depictions of love and loss intertwine with wry humor and striking prose. While each story can stand on its own, exploring the same themes from different angles enhances the impact of the stories and allows them to add up into a unique and memorable reading experience.

Author Biography

Elizabeth McCracken is the author of two other collections of short stories, *Here's Your Hat What's Your Hurry?* (1993) and *Thunderstruck and Other Stories* (2014), winner of the 2015 Story Prize. She has also written three novels and a memoir. Her novel *The Giant's House* (1996) was a finalist for the National Book Award.

Emma Joyce

Review Sources

Baptiste, Desirée. "Bread, Cake, Doughnuts: Life and Death Recollected, in Various Voices." Review of *The Souvenir Museum*, by Elizabeth McCracken. *TLS*, 4 June 2021, www.the-tls.co.uk/articles/the-souvenir-museum-elizabeth-mccracken-review-desiree-baptiste/. Accessed 20 Feb. 2022.

McAlpin, Heller. "*The Souvenir Museum* Is an Exhibit to Savor." Review of *The Souvenir Museum*, by Elizabeth McCracken. *NPR*, 13 Apr. 2021, www.npr.org/2021/04/13/985537989/the-souvenir-museum-is-an-exhibit-to-savor. Accessed 20 Feb. 2022.

Peschel, Joseph. "This Thing Called Life in Elizabeth McCracken's *The Souvenir Museum*." *Boston Globe*, 15 Apr. 2021, www.bostonglobe.com/2021/04/15/arts/this-thing-called-life-elizabeth-mccrackens-souvenir-museum. Accessed 20 Feb. 2022.

Self, John. "*The Souvenir Museum* by Elizabeth McCracken Review—Delightful Domestic Stories." *The Guardian*, 8 June 2021, www.theguardian.com/books/2021/jun/08/the-souvenir-museum-by-elizabeth-mccracken-review-delightful-domestic-stories. Accessed 20 Feb. 2022.

Review of *The Souvenir Museum*, by Elizabeth McCracken. *Kirkus*, 26 Dec. 2020, www.kirkusreviews.com/book-reviews/elizabeth-mccracken/the-souvenir-museum. Accessed 20 Feb. 2022.

Review of *The Souvenir Museum*, by Elizabeth McCracken. *Publishers Weekly*, 22 Oct. 2020, www.publishersweekly.com/978-0-06-297128-9. Accessed 20 Feb. 2022.

Thomas-Kennedy, Jackie. Review of *The Souvenir Museum*, by Elizabeth McCracken. *Harvard Review Online*, 9 July 2021, harvardreview.org/book-review/the-souvenir-museum. Accessed 20 Feb. 2022.

Squirrel Hill
The Tree of Life Synagogue Shooting and the Soul of a Neighborhood

Author: Mark Oppenheimer (b. 1974)
Publisher: Alfred A. Knopf (New York). 320 pp.
Type of work: Current affairs, religion
Time: October 2018–March 2020
Locale: Pittsburgh, Pennsylvania

Squirrel Hill is the account of how a Jewish community in Pittsburgh fared after an anti-Semitic attack took the lives of eleven worshippers at the Tree of Life synagogue in the deadliest attack on Jewish people in American history.

Principal personages
JEFFREY MYERS, the rabbi of Tree of Life
JONATHAN PERLMAN, the rabbi of New Light
TAMMY HEPPS, a prominent Jewish resident of Squirrel Hill
GREG ZANIS, a retired carpenter and founder of Crosses for Losses
ROBERT BOWERS, the White nationalist accused of killing eleven parishioners at the Tree of Life synagogue
SHAY KHATIRI, an Iranian student who started a GoFundMe for Tree of Life
DONALD TRUMP, the former president of the United States, who caused controversy by visiting Squirrel Hill after the shooting

In the prologue to *Squirrel Hill: The Tree of Life Synagogue Shooting and the Soul of a Neighborhood* (2021), Mark Oppenheimer takes the reader back to the fatal morning of October 27, 2018, when White nationalist Robert Bowers opened fire on Jewish worshippers at the Tree of Life synagogue located in Squirrel Hill, a Jewish neighborhood in Pittsburgh, Pennsylvania. He explains that his book is about how "people behaved in the aftermath of the Tree of Life shooting." Oppenheimer's own ancestral roots date back to the 1840s in Squirrel Hill, and his father grew up in the close-knit neighborhood, giving him a unique insider/outsider perspective. He navigates the terrain with the sensibilities of a participant and an observer in an ethnographic inquiry. Through interviews, half of which took place a week after the shooting, with community members, survivors, witnesses, emergency personnel, business owners, rabbis, and many others from outside of the neighborhood, Oppenheimer provides a complex and nuanced narrative of how events evolved during and after the shooting. His inquiry reveals a much more diverse community than appears on the surface. Oppenheimer explains that "Squirrel Hill has never been all Jewish or even mostly

Jewish... In fact, it is one of the most diverse places in very white western Pennsylvania." This diversity is depicted in multiple ways in the book—through the political perspectives of traditional and modern Orthodox Jews; the customs of non-Orthodox Jews and the affiliations of progressive Jews; and the experiences of people who are not Jewish. These voices are all a part of the mosaic of life in the Squirrel Hill community. Through intricate storytelling, Oppenheimer describes everything from the differences in the feelings and responses of mourners, to the overwhelming community support, to how the anniversary of the tragedy was planned and carried out a year later.

Mark Oppenheimer

The assortment and quality of support Squirrel Hill residents received in the immediate aftermath of the shooting ranged from professional crisis responders who were experts at their jobs to less-knowledgeable amateurs, according to the stories told to Oppenheimer. Thankfully, not all support required people to be physically present, as some mourners preferred that onlookers stay away to give them the space to bury their loved ones and grieve. One of the first narratives Oppenheimer retells between a mourner and an ally who is not Jewish and did come to Squirrel Hill is that of the Crosses for Losses founder Greg Zanis and Squirrel Hill resident Tammy Hepps. Zanis drove five hundred miles from Aurora, Illinois, to deliver crosses as a memorial to Squirrel Hill victims, as he had done for countless other tragedies over the past several years. Zanis is initially regarded with hostility when Hepps, a member of Beth Shalom synagogue, spots the crosses in the back of his truck. When she realizes that he has Stars of David sitting in the passenger seat that he plans to add to the crosses, Hepps is more receptive. Ultimately, Hepps even helps Zanis by sharing the names of the victims with him. However, as Oppenheimer clarifies, "Zanis had demonstrated admirable cultural sensitivity in affixing Stars of David to the crosses, but crosses are still crosses... [and] a cross of white wood planted on the synagogue grounds, with a victim's name on it, seemed discordant."

Another heartwarming yet dissonant experience is conveyed by Oppenheimer in the story of Shay Khatiri, an Iranian expatriate who started a GoFundMe campaign page that raised over $1 million for Tree of Life specifically—but failed to include the other two congregations that shared the building, Dor Hadash and New Light. Oppenheimer explains that the imbalance in funding support was quickly recognized by the congregants, and they started their own GoFundMe pages. (Tree of Life eventually shared the money it received with the other two congregations.) Not all encounters between the Jewish community and people outside of the community turned out as cooperative, however. Oppenheimer devotes a whole chapter, titled "The Visitors," to the many people who came to help but who ended up requiring assistance themselves, such as help finding hotel rooms or other services. These often-unwelcome visitors, sometimes referred to as "trauma tourists," included Catholic parishioners, dog therapy handlers, and college students. Oppenheimer pointedly raises the question of "whether such well-meaning visitors were right to accept the community's hospitality, in the same week that Squirrel Hill was burying eleven men and women."

In his discussions with high school students in a chapter titled "The High School," Oppenheimer observes conflicting feelings among students on how the community and the world responded to the mass shooting of eleven Jews, in contrast to the ongoing murders of Black people on an everyday basis. The students seem to suggest that the difference is racial. Oppenheimer, on the other hand, frames the contrast as the difference in the number of people who die at one point in time. He explains that mass shootings seem to go national only when they exceed more than five or six victims, and that, by contrast, one or two homicides at a time does not tend to make national news. One cannot help to be inclined to believe that national attention is likely related to both racism *and* the number killed at one point in time. Like the historical impact of anti-Semitism in Jewish communities, racism has been deadly in its impact on Black communities for centuries.

A prominent feature of *Squirrel Hill* is the way in which Oppenheimer weaves the intimate details of people's lives into a larger historical and contemporary commentary on the intersections of the politics of anti-Semitism and White supremacy. This is most notable in the chapter titled "The Trump Visit," regarding President Donald Trump's visit to Squirrel Hill. The geopolitical landscape of the area is complicated and is illustrated by how divided the Jewish residents of Squirrel Hill were in their reception of the presidential visit. Jewish activists planned a march protesting the visit, while traditional Jews prioritized the need to provide Trump with a hospitable reception. Still other Jewish residents felt Trump was grandstanding and that his visit would interfere with the week of funerals and mourning. Another, more penetrating consideration that Oppenheimer advances is the community's differing viewpoints on anti-Semitism. Many were concerned with Trump's controversial history, including his refusal to condemn the White nationalists who gathered at the Unite the Right rally in Charlottesville, Virginia, in 2017. Furthermore, many shared their fear that the shooter had been emboldened by the racist and anti-Semitic ideology for which the president had become known. When Trump arrived in Squirrel Hill days after the shooting, he was greeted by protestors and supporters, as well as by the Tree of Life synagogue's rabbi, which pleases some congregants and angers others. These conflicting political positions and opinions surface a year later among the Squirrel Hill residents in the planning of the first anniversary of the shooting as residents continue to struggle with the ongoing threats of White supremacy and gun violence.

Media critics responded favorably to *Squirrel Hill*. It received a starred review from *Kirkus*, which described it as "a stunning book that offers an eloquent portrait of an antisemitic attack and its effect on a neighborhood." Oppenheimer received praise from the anonymous *Kirkus* reviewer for taking an "approach rarely seen in books about mass shootings," with his efforts to focus on those affected by the tragedy beyond the killer or the victims. Similarly, Oppenheimer was applauded by reviewer

Jared Cohon, writing for the *Wall Street Journal*, for his "expertise and knowledge" and choice to "focus on the community" instead of the killer and the victims. Cohon also appreciated Oppenheimer's "keen long-term [observations] of Judaism, Jews and their experiences in America" as an author, columnist, and journalist with roots in Squirrel Hill. Cohon further credited Oppenheimer with raising the issue of racial tensions through the high school students with whom he met, especially "in the midst of the Black Lives Matter movement and the beginning of the nation's racial reckoning."

However, Cohon, who lives in Squirrel Hill himself and knew both a victim and a survivor of the shooting, took issue with some of Oppenheimer's portrayal of events. For example, Cohon stated that the community gathering three days after the attack was not an anti-Trump rally but instead "much more a coming together of neighbors in a show of solidarity." He also criticized the author's constant mentioning of declining synagogue membership as if it "were the only or dominant way to engage Jewishly." He pointed to the community's response to the shooting as evidence that Jewish life thrives beyond low synagogue attendance. Moreover, Cohon explicitly contradicted Oppenheimer's claim that the Jewish Federation is less relevant and "solicited donations after the shootings." Cohon, as a member of the committee that helped distribute donations, wrote, "I can state that this is simply not true." Despite these three criticisms, Cohon ended his review on a positive note, praising the book for providing "a window into a complex and still unfolding story . . . and lessons to be learned."

Irina Reyn, reviewer for the *New York Times*, also lives in Squirrel Hill. In her review, Reyn noted how Oppenheimer's personal and professional roots in religion, Jewish culture, and Squirrel Hill, particularly, gave him a kind of familiarity and sympathetic approach to the treatment of the story. Diane Cole, reviewer for the *Washington Post* and survivor of the 1977 anti-Semitic attack in Washington's B'nai Brith Building, described *Squirrel Hill* as "an emotionally draining terrain, flecked with occasional, unexpected pockets of consolation," as well as a "powerful meditation on the changing meaning of community and belonging in an age of disconnection and isolation." One of her criticisms with the book was that she "wanted Oppenheimer to dig deeper into the psychological impact and the enduring ache that trauma leaves behind." Cole also stated that more than a history lesson about global anti-Semitism, she would have preferred that Oppenheimer explore the intersection of White supremacy and anti-Semitism in modern times and its implications in fueling acts of violence toward anyone considered "other." Additionally, Cole felt that Oppenheimer could have explored why people seem to forget anti-Semitic attacks so quickly after the media coverage ends. As Reyn, who drives by the Tree of Life synagogue daily, observed, "it still stands cordoned off by a wire fence" and brightened by the many pieces of student art that reflect the sentiments of the community, with posters reading slogans like "Stronger Together" and "You Are Not Alone."

Author Biography

Mark Oppenheimer is an author and director of the Yale Journalism Initiative. He has written five books and numerous articles on religious subjects for publications such as the *New York Times* and *Mother Jones*.

Valandra, MBA, MSW, PhD

Review Sources

Cohon, Jared. "'Squirrel Hill' Review: A Synagogue Endures Hate." Review of *Squirrel Hill: The Tree of Life Synagogue Shooting and the Soul of a Neighborhood*, by Mark Oppenheimer. *The Wall Street Journal*, 3 Dec. 2021, www.wsj.com/articles/squirrel-hill-book-review-tree-of-life-synagogue-pittsburgh-endures-hate-11638544546. Accessed 29 Jan. 2022.

Cole, Diane. "A Diverse Community, an Antisemitic Attack and What Came Next." Review of *Squirrel Hill: The Tree of Life Synagogue Shooting and the Soul of a Neighborhood*, by Mark Oppenheimer. *The Washington Post*, 15 Oct. 2021, www.washingtonpost.com/outlook/a-diverse-community-an-antisemitic-attack-and-what-came-next/2021/10/13/4211b260-1190-11ec-882f-2dd15a067dc4_story.html. Accessed 29 Jan. 2022.

Reyn, Irina. "What Happened After the Most Deadly Antisemitic Attack in American History?" Review of *Squirrel Hill: The Tree of Life Synagogue Shooting and the Soul of a Neighborhood*, by Mark Oppenheimer. *The New York Times*, 27 Oct. 2021, www.nytimes.com/2021/10/27/books/review/mark-oppenheimer-squirrel-hill.html. Accessed 29 Jan. 2022.

Review of *Squirrel Hill: The Tree of Life Synagogue Shooting and the Soul of a Neighborhood*, by Mark Oppenheimer. *Kirkus*, 14 July 2021, www.kirkusreviews.com/book-reviews/mark-oppenheimer/squirrel-hill/. Accessed 29 Jan. 2022.

The Storyteller
Tales of Life and Music

Author: Dave Grohl (b. 1969)
Publisher: Dey Street Books (New York). Illustrated. 384 pp.
Type of work: Memoir
Time: 1970s to the present
Locales: Springfield, Virginia; Seattle; Los Angeles; various performance venues around the world

The Storyteller is a memoir by one of the most prominent American rock musicians of the late twentieth and early twenty-first centuries, Dave Grohl, the onetime drummer for Nirvana and the founder and lead vocalist of the Foo Fighters.

Principal personages

DAVE GROHL, author and narrator, a successful rock musician
VIRGINIA GROHL, his mother, whom he credits for her unwavering support
JORDYN BLUM, his wife
VIOLET, his daughter
HARPER, his daughter
OPHELIA, his daughter
TRACEY, a friend whom he considered a cousin, and credits for introducing him to punk music
KURT COBAIN, lead vocalist of the band Nirvana, which Grohl joined
PAUL MCCARTNEY, a former member of the Beatles and a friend of Grohl's family
JIMMY SWANSON, Grohl's best friend from childhood; later a roadie
TAYLOR HAWKINS, a member of Grohl's band Foo Fighters

Dave Grohl is among the most noted musicians of contemporary times and is considered by some to be one of the greatest drummers in the history of rock music. He joined the iconic grunge band Nirvana at the height of their fame in the early 1990s, and after that band's demise founded the Foo Fighters, a group that became highly successful and influential in its own right. After the March 2020 declaration of the coronavirus disease 2019 (COVID-19) pandemic disrupted everything, Grohl decided to write a memoir. He admits in his acknowledgments that he knew nothing about writing a book, but claims he followed the mantra that has shaped his entire career: "Fake it till you make it." Such an approach could lead to disaster for the untalented, but it seems to have worked for Grohl in writing just as it has in music. He has produced a lively, honest memoir, 2021's *The Storyteller: Tales of Life and Music*, that is well and engagingly written with numerous flashes of insight and humor.

Although he had little formal musical education, Grohl knew from an early age that music was going to be a big part of his life. In his introduction he notes that he has always measured his life "in musical increments rather than months or years." The music he has listened to or played at the time has defined his life in any period. He notes that he does not collect "stuff" but rather collects "moments" in his memory, and given his career, it is no surprise that these moments are "full of music." There was a point when music was simply "sounds" to him, he explains, until the day when the songs he heard and played "became the air I breathed."

Dave Grohl

In telling his life story, Grohl generally follows a chronological order, but not entirely. Still, while some events are mentioned out of sequence because they relate to another story he is telling at that point, the pieces of his life and their meaning in shaping his identity remain clear and compelling. Exploring his introduction to punk rock, for example, he details how it came from Tracey, a teenage girl whom he considered a cousin because their mothers were such close longtime friends. He and his mother and sister often visited Tracey and her family at their home in Evanston, Illinois. On one trip, when he was thirteen, she showed him her collection of punk rock records and took him to a concert, his first. Punk rockers at that time were often producing their own records, printing the covers on photocopiers and basically doing everything themselves. Tracey's record collection was "a virtual treasure trove of underground, independent punk rock, something I had never known existed up until that point," he writes. Throughout the book, lines of text set in a typeface that resembles handwriting occur occasionally; these usually denote and emphasize a summary or mark a transition in the narrative with great, even more personal effect. After learning first-hand about punk rock, he writes in one such section, "This was the first day of the rest of my life."

Grohl taught himself how to play drums, often banging on pillows while listening to the music of Scream, a local punk rock group in the Washington, DC, area. Then, when he was seventeen, he had the chance to become part of Scream. Since the band toured extensively, this meant he would have to drop out of school. As his mother was a schoolteacher, he thought she would be reluctant to approve. But she simply told him, "You'd better be good." His mother would continue to be constant supporter throughout his career, and even wrote her own book about the mothers of rock stars.

As one might expect, Grohl had to "pay his dues" in the early stages of his career. Scream was not wildly successful at that point but was known well enough to tour across the country and occasionally in Europe. When touring in the United States, the band often slept in their van, on a plywood platform built over a space for storing their gear, or stayed with friends or relatives. In the period just after he joined Nirvana, he lived off convenience store corn dogs, bought three for a dollar, to stretch his per diem living payout. Even later, when he and Nirvana started making some significant money, there was little immediate change to his lifestyle because with touring and recording sessions, there was little time to go out and spend the money.

Grohl's leap to become part of Nirvana began in 1990, when a friend told him that the grunge band was looking for a new drummer. Following an audition, he was invited to join and accepted, despite some reservations about leaving his first musical "family," and he began playing drums with Nirvana in September of that year. This transition ultimately took some adjustment, as Nirvana was really beginning to become wildly popular around that time. They drew large crowds of rambunctious fans, and Grohl began to realize there was some danger in these environments. The band's music expressed rage and contempt for authority, and the band members often wrecked equipment as a kind of crazed conclusion to their concerts. So, it was not surprising that they attracted fans that rushed the stage or surged so close that everyone's safety could be at risk. In January 1992 the band's album *Nevermind* reached number one on the Billboard album charts, and that same week they performed for the first time on *Saturday Night Live*. As if to prove they were now in the big time, that night Weird Al Jankovic called to ask permission to do a parody of their hit mainstream song "Smells Like Teen Spirit." Another sign that Grohl had "arrived" personally came about this same time—his first credit card.

Given Grohl's strong musical fit with Nirvana, no one could have envisioned that his time with the band would be quite brief. After being with the group only a few months, he learned that frontman Kurt Cobain was using heroin. While Grohl admits to copious use of marijuana and alcohol, he claims to have generally stayed away from hard drugs himself. Cobain soon checked into a rehab facility in Los Angeles, which his friends took as a hopeful sign. But he continued to struggle with drugs, coming near death after an overdose in March 1994 before killing himself the following month. As Grohl reflects, "Those three and a half years that I knew Kurt, a relatively small window of time in the chronology of my life, shaped and in some ways still define who I am today. I will always be 'that guy from Nirvana,' and I am proud of it."

Grohl felt "lost" after Cobain's death, and for the first time in his life music brought him no peace. After several months of depression and mourning, however, he started writing songs and recording them himself. Eventually, he scheduled some time in a professional studio. Although he had no idea of starting a new band at this point, he released these largely solo songs on a 1995 album under the name Foo Fighters. The project continued, and by the time of 1997's *The Colour and the Shape* he had recruited other musicians, making Foo Fighters a group with Grohl as the lead vocalist.

The latter part of the book deals more with Grohl's family and some stories of him individually performing in various venues, such as at the Kennedy Center Honors in a tribute to the Who, and later playing a tribute to Paul McCartney, during which the former Beatle sat next to President Barack Obama. Grohl does not delve deeply into the history of the Foo Fighters, even though in the early days of the band, most of the members lived at Grohl's house and they recorded their music in his basement studio. He does describe how the music of the Foo Fighters differed from much of the rock mainstream at that time: "Popular rock music at the time had turned its focus to a new genre, nu metal, which I appreciated but wanted to be the antithesis of, so I intentionally moved in the opposite direction. There was a glaring absence of melody in most nu metal songs, and it was my love of melody (inspired by the Beatles from an early age) that led me to write from a much gentler place." After the Foo Fighters won a Grammy Award for the Best Rock Album in 2001, Grohl realized they had reached a level of success and financial reward that meant they did not have to go on working, but in one of the text's "handwritten" sections, he describes the conclusion they came to: "We didn't have to do this anymore. We wanted to do this forever."

Part of the fascination of this book is that Grohl is in some ways a typical rock star, but in other ways not at all. He has worked the long hours and has gone on the worldwide tours, and there were parties, drugs, and alcohol at times. He is devoted to his music with a passion that is clearly evident. However, he is also a devoted husband and father, who rearranged a concert and flew home from Australia to take his daughter to her first father-daughter dance. He loves his hometown and still considers his mother a best friend and confidant. Though he seems to know everyone who is anyone in the music world, he does not drop names simply to impress the reader. Rather, he expresses a genuine awe of some of the older artists who inspired him, and remains grateful to have met some of the legends of rock music after he had become a legend himself.

Readers with little background in modern pop music may be confused by the various subgenres of music Grohl describes, such as punk rock, grunge, alternative, and heavy metal. But familiarity with this vocabulary is not really needed to enjoy the book. While music is rightly at the center of the work, Grohl never gets technical in his treatment. Though he has been associated primarily with some of the edgier genres of modern pop music, he has a deep appreciation of many styles, dating back to singing along with his mother to the tunes on the car radio and the jazz played in the clubs she took him to visit as a young man.

Reviewers generally treated *The Storyteller* kindly, with *Publishers Weekly* giving it a starred review. Grohl's reputation within the music world as a "nice guy" is reflected by many critics. The title alone of Allison Stewart's review for the *Washington Post* reveals much about both the book and its author: "Dave Grohl's 'The Storyteller' Is Just as Upbeat as You'd Expect." As Stewart wrote, there is no "score-settling or dirt-dishing" in this book. In fact, Grohl rarely makes any critical comment about any musician. At times this can be almost off-putting: Kitty Empire, writing for the *Observer*, noted that Grohl "pulls his punches" and suggested that "the book feels like an intentionally PG take on what could be a much rowdier, more hair-raising tale." Yet the story that emerges from this book and its many engrossing anecdotes is indeed upbeat—a story of pursuing and achieving a lifelong dream, and of making rock music stardom coexist with a strong family life.

Author Biography
Musician Dave Grohl has continued to record and release music with the Foo Fighters, including 2021's *Medicine at Midnight*.

Mark S. Joy, PhD

Review Sources
Empire, Kitty. "*The Storyteller* by Dave Grohl—a Foo Fighter Pulls His Punches." *The Observer*, Guardian News and Media, 17 Oct. 2021, www.theguardian.com/books/2021/oct/17/the-storyteller-by-dave-grohl-a-foo-fighter-pulls-his-punches. Accessed 14 Jan. 2022.

Stewart, Allison. "Dave Grohl's 'The Storyteller' Is Just as Upbeat as You'd Expect." *The Washington Post*, 6 Oct. 2021, www.washingtonpost.com/entertainment/books/dave-grohl-memoir-storyteller/2021/10/06/91d95d72-2610-11ec-8831-a31e7b3de188_story.html. Accessed 14 Jan. 2022.

Review of *The Storyteller: Tales of Life and Music*, by Dave Grohl. *Kirkus*, 17 Aug. 2021, www.kirkusreviews.com/book-reviews/dave-grohl/the-storyteller-grohl/. Accessed 21 Jan. 2022.

Review of *The Storyteller: Tales of Life and Music*, by Dave Grohl. *Publishers Weekly*, 20 Aug. 2021, www.publishersweekly.com/978-0-06-307609-9. Accessed 21 Jan. 2022.

The Sum of Us
What Racism Costs Everyone and How We Can Prosper Together

Author: Heather McGhee (b. 1980)
Publisher: One World (New York). 448 pp.
Type of work: Current affairs, history, sociology
Time: The present day, with references to various points in American history
Locales: Various locations in the United States

Focusing on the intersection of economics, politics, and race, Heather McGhee argues that America has a long history of enacting policies that are designed to target people of color, but that also have a profoundly damaging impact on White people.

Principal personages
DONALD TRUMP, president of the United States between 2017 and 2021
CHARLES KOCH, billionaire business executive who has funded various libertarian causes
DAVID KOCH, Charles's late brother, a billionaire businessperson who, along with him, funded various libertarian causes
JANICE TOMLIN, a schoolteacher who won a class-action suit on behalf of subprime loan borrowers
SANCHIONI BUTLER, a union organizer for a Mississippi automobile factory
CHIP WELLS, an automobile factory worker who switched from pro-union to anti-union
ANGELA KING, a reformed White supremacist who devotes herself to antiracist work

The Sum of Us: What Racism Costs Everyone and How We Can Prosper Together (2021) is a powerful study of the far-reaching effects of racist political, social, and economic policies and practices on American life and culture. An economist and social policy advocate who, after working for the organization for several years, headed the public policy think tank Demos between 2014 and 2018, author Heather McGhee focuses on the intersection of economics, politics, and race. Her central, less commonly explored contention in this sweeping book is that racist polices targeting people of color have also had a profoundly damaging effect on White communities.

Why would White Americans enact policies that are ultimately to their own detriment? In the course of her work and research, McGhee realized that many Americans view the success of various racial groups as a zero-sum equation: if one group is

Heather McGhee

thriving, it must be at the expense of the other. McGhee argues that "the narrative that white people should see the well-being of people of color as a threat to their own is one of the most powerful subterranean stories in America." This zero-sum thinking, according to McGhee, leads White Americans to hollow out public goods that they themselves would benefit from. In each chapter of her wide-ranging study, McGhee focuses on a different area of American economic and social life, including housing, schools, wages, voting rights, and the environment. She compellingly and engagingly illustrates how racist ideology and policy and the zero-sum myth have exacted a cost on the lives of all Americans and have kept them from developing the social networks, economic protections, voting rights, and public goods that most other prosperous democracies take for granted. Despite all of this, McGhee is, at her core, an optimist, and her book is animated by a vision of how Americans of all backgrounds could reject the zero-sum proposition and instead work together to create a nation in which everyone thrives.

McGhee asks a commonsense question in her introduction: "Why can't we have nice things?" The United States is a political and economic powerhouse that has boasted, for most of its history, the largest economy in the world. Yet Americans do not have some of the basic public goods that so many other nations do: a public health-care system, a social safety net, reasonably priced colleges, secure prospects for retirement, high voting rates, and a political system that is not unduly influenced by lobbyists and special interests. Working on Capitol Hill as a researcher and policy advocate, McGhee began to realize that there is not a purely economic or political explanation for these profound gaps in America's social infrastructure. Rather, they are the deliberate, constructed products of a long legacy of racism and White supremacy. White Americans believed in public amenities, investments in infrastructure, and social dividends when their recipients would be primarily or exclusively White.

It was only in the wake of the civil rights movement, when Black Americans and other people of color would benefit from these systems, that White Americans reversed their beliefs and lost their faith. To illustrate her point, McGhee uses the example of public swimming pools. In the first half of the century, American towns across the country boasted pools that were a point of civic pride and an integral part of their communities. They were also overwhelmingly segregated, not just in the Jim Crow South but also in many northern towns. In the 1950s, the Supreme Court struck down the doctrine of separate but equal, ordering the integration of public facilities such as schools, libraries, and swimming pools. Faced with this mandate, many towns made an appalling choice: rather than integrate their pools, they drained them, filled them in with concrete, or sold them to private owners. The drained pool becomes a powerful metaphor for less-visible ways in which White Americans have sacrificed their own prosperity to keep others from sharing in it. For example, America once boasted an affordable public university system that educated generations of students. Yet, as the number of Black students and other students of color rose, states began disinvesting from their universities. At the same time, the federal government shifted its form of student aid from scholarships and grants (which did not need to be repaid) to loans. The result of what McGhee calls this "stealth privatization" of the public university system is that students—and a disproportionate number of students of color—must take on crippling levels of debt to earn a degree. As with the swimming pool, the university was drained of its resources as soon as it became clear that people of color might benefit from using it.

In each chapter of her book, McGhee focuses on a different aspect of American life, tracing the ways in which racism has informed the country's public policy choices. She begins by presenting a brief history of America, one that focuses on the way racial differences have been constructed and invoked to justify the slaughter and displacement of American Indians, the enslavement of Black people, and a century of Jim Crow. The very concept of "Whiteness," she notes, is an American one, a new category and privilege that European colonists and immigrants bestowed on themselves to escape the caste system of their home countries and to distinguish themselves from enslaved and Indigenous people. The new social capital of "Whiteness" went together with a new capitalist system founded on ostensibly "free" land, taken from American Indians, and ostensibly "free" labor, exacted from enslaved people. The economic underpinnings that would allow the United States to become a world power were grounded in the displacement and enslavement of people of color. This concept of "freedom built on slavery" is the original example of the zero-sum equation; after all, an enslaver's wealth is directly threatened by enslaved peoples' freedom or autonomy.

McGhee goes on to contend that this zero-sum logic continued to prevail well after the Civil War and the end of slavery. Fearing the potential political and economic power of emancipated Black people, White landowners used both the law and mob violence to keep them from exercising their right to vote, hold office, attain an education, own businesses or receive loans, and share in public goods and spaces. They also worked to drive racially charged wedges between Black people and poor White people; it was critical that the latter group identify with White holders of power, rather than with Black people who shared their socioeconomic status. In other words, race needed to trump class. Whiteness itself was so powerful an identifier that generations of poor White people have rejected policies that would be to their own benefit, out of a resentment that it would also benefit Black people, whom they deemed as undeserving. McGhee's book is therefore a powerful counterargument to the classical economic theory that people make their financial choices out of enlightened self-interest. As she explores the gutting of the American public university system or the decline of the unions, McGhee shows that White people have made many choices that are not at all in their own self-interest. Understanding the White supremacist nature of early

American social, political, and economic life helps one to understand the many policy choices and cultural biases that have continued to shape America's present.

McGhee's chapter on the subprime loan crisis offers a powerful example of how White people suffer from policies that originally targeted people of color. Banks first developed predatory lending schemes, in which they convince homeowners to refinance their mortgages through risky subprime packages, by targeting homeowners of color, particularly Black people. Most of the individuals trapped in these new loans had already been making regular payments on traditional thirty-year mortgages. Lenders used all manner of tricks to talk them into switching into complicated and unnecessarily expensive subprime loans, even though most of them qualified for better rates. As the banks hiked the rates on these variable loans or levied exorbitant fees, many of the recipients lost their homes. McGhee powerfully stresses that as early as 1992, state legislators and community activists knew about this practice, and there were many attempts to get the federal government to act. Yet, because the targets of the predatory practices were Black, the issue was largely ignored. Rather than seeing the banks and lenders as being at fault, White lawmakers and regulators were quick to see this phenomenon as fitting into the traditional stereotype of Black people, viewed as financial liabilities, being unable to manage their money. Having honed their practices on Black targets, the predatory lenders went on to grant subprime loans in White communities, a widespread practice that would lead to the subprime stock market collapse of 2008 and the Great Recession.

McGhee animates her book by including the stories of many individual people whose lives intersect with contemporary social and economic realities. Her interviews with and portraits of these individuals help to put a human face on broader social issues, and she deftly combines historical perspectives, economic data, and personal narratives. Janice Tomlin's story, for example, shows the damage that subprime loans caused for Black homeowners and communities. An unassuming schoolteacher, Tomlin successfully brought a class-action suit against Chase bank for targeting her and others in her community with predatory loans. McGhee's chapter on unions is also full of fascinating people, like Sanchioni Butler, a labor organizer attempting to unionize a Nissan automobile plant in Mississippi. In this racially stratified factory, the better jobs seem to go to White workers, and for a union to succeed the White employees would need to identify more with their Black coworkers than with their White managers. Chip Wells, a White maintenance worker, started out supporting the unionization efforts. However, after increasing pressure and veiled threats from his White coworkers, he switched sides. At the same time, in his final interview with McGhee, he spoke longingly of the sense of purpose and community he felt when he was part of a cross-racial movement. Some of McGhee's most revealing interviews are with White people who have been on both sides of the fight. Angela King grew up under prejudiced parents and gravitated toward drugs, crime, and a White supremacist gang. Yet in prison, she found herself befriended by a group of Black women, and she gradually began to rethink her earlier belief system. Once released, King helped found an organization dedicated to challenging White supremacy. McGhee's portrayals of these and many other individuals help to show the cost of zero-sum thinking and the potential for people to recognize the "Solidarity Dividend" that would come from thriving together.

The Sum of Us received overwhelmingly positive reviews. In the *New York Times*, Jennifer Szalai wrote, "There is a striking clarity to this book; there is also a depth of kindness in it that all but the most churlish readers will find moving." The *Washington Post* reviewer likewise found it a "stunning, sobering, oddly hopeful" book. John Warner, writing for the *Chicago Tribune*, said that *The Sum of Us* is "perfectly timed to the moment and has the potential to radically shift our cultural conversation." He concludes his review by pondering what would happen if the book "busts out of the liberal demographic to impact others who are not already on board." This book will fill readers both with dismay at the racist underpinnings of America's past and with hope for its future.

Author Biography
Heather McGhee, whose work focuses on addressing American inequality, was president of the advocacy and research organization Demos from 2014 to 2018 before going on to chair racial justice group Color of Change's board of directors beginning in 2019.

Matthew J. Bolton, PhD

Review Sources
Szalai, Jennifer. "*The Sum of Us* Tallies the Cost of Racism for Everyone." Review of *The Sum of Us: What Racism Costs Everyone and How We Can Prosper Together*, by Heather McGhee. *The New York Times*, 23 Feb. 2021, www.nytimes.com/2021/02/23/books/review-sum-of-us-heather-mcghee.html. Accessed 25 Aug. 2021.

Taylor, Paul C. "Racism Targets Some but Works against Everybody." Review of *The Sum of Us: What Racism Costs Everyone and How We Can Prosper Together*, by Heather McGhee. *The Washington Post*, 12 Mar. 2021, www.washingtonpost.com/outlook/racism-targets-some-but-works-against-everybody/2021/03/11/47abc28c-7484-11eb-948d-19472e683521_story.html. Accessed 25 Aug. 2021.

Warner, John. "Heather McGhee's *The Sum of Us*: Required Reading to Move the Country Forward—Together, Writes John Warner." *The Chicago Tribune*, 23 Feb. 2021, www.chicagotribune.com/entertainment/books/ct-books-biblioracle-0228-20210223-absfuzxupjd53h4w5k3e7hrn5y-story.html. Accessed 25 Aug. 2021.

The Sunflower Cast a Spell to Save Us from the Void

Author: Jackie Wang
Illustrator: Kalan Sherrard
Publisher: Nightboat Books (New York). Illustrated. 120 pp.
Type of work: Poetry

In her debut full-length poetry collection, The Sunflower Cast a Spell to Save Us from the Void, *Jackie Wang uses dream-like imagery and language to touch on a variety of topics, from identity and interpersonal connection to memory and loss.*

Poet and scholar Jackie Wang is an assistant professor of American studies and ethnicity at the University of Southern California. In her 2018 essay collection, *Carceral Capitalism*, she provides a deep reflection on the inequities of America's capitalist system and the ways that mass incarceration, racism, and debt combine to reinforce existing patterns of inequity and to create populations vulnerable to commodification and economic exploitation. At the end of *Carceral Capitalism*, she utilizes poetic prose in a series of "conversations," with poems presented alongside quotes from important figures in the literature of revolutionary politics. In the discussion that follows, she posits that dreams are an important dimension of "abolitionist thinking," allowing a person to envision a world separated from the constraints of the world as it is. In exploring the connection between dreams and revolutionary vision, Wang says that the "job" of the poet is to dream, a job she takes on in her poetry collections.

The Sunflower Cast a Spell to Save Us from the Void (2021) is Wang's third collection of "dream poetry" and her first full-length collection. Wang published the first of these collections, *Tiny Spelunker of the Oneiro-Womb: Dream Selections* (2016), was published as part of a chapbook series, *Say Bye to Reason and Hi to Everything*, by the New York–based arts foundation Capricious. In the chapbook, Wang attempts to transform the illogical qualia of the dream world so that the feelings and impulses of her dreams can be shared. She started sharing her dreams in poetic form, typically using the monostich format, which helps to translate the sometimes-dizzying shifts that occur in the mind when one is dreaming. Wang's second chapbook, *The Twitter Hive Mind Is Dreaming* (2018) continued this theme, with a selection of poems plucked from Wang's active Twitter account and curated by Tamryn Spruill. In the 2010s, while working towards her graduate degrees, Wang took to using Twitter to replay her dreams, sharing a new dream every morning for months. Many of these became part of the *Tiny Spelunker of the Oneiro-Womb*, while others became part of Spruill's

Jackie Wang

curated collection from Wang's Twitter account. Though her poems touched on profound subject matter, such as incarceration, social justice, and trauma, she kept them short and concise, often operating within Twitter's 140-character limit.

While *Tiny Spelunker of the Oneiro-Womb* and *The Twitter Hive Mind Is Dreaming* are chapbooks, short collections of poetry typically containing ten to thirty individual pieces, *The Sunflower Cast a Spell to Save Us From the Void*, is a far longer and more diverse approach to the dream-poem theme. Here, she delves into dreams in many different ways. Some poems convey the fractured spatial and temporal logic of the dream state. Some reflect on the way that dreams spill over into waking life with echoes of emotion and by shifting one's perceptions. Others draw on Wang's other interests and foci, blending her poetry with her academic explorations.

One of the recurring themes in Wang's poetry collection is the idea of "fellow travelers," the individuals who share the dream spaces with Wang. She mentions these individuals frequently throughout the book. In one passage, she writes,

> All I remember is the coppiced terrain I crossed to find a house to rest in. Who is the woman lurking in the woods? A fellow traveler. I'm not used to seeing others. She is lost and I am lost but the difference is she is a novice at being lost, whereas I have always been without country. Without planet.

In her dreams, Wang encounters strangers, people she knows, people she has read about, political figures drawn from her studies of history, fellow students, old friends, and members of her family. She reflects on dreams as meditations on connection and distance, longing, and desire. Dreams serve as the setting for encounters, but also symbolize the emotional connections and disconnections between individuals. In "The Future Is between Us," in which the dreamer meets an old friend within a dollhouse, Wang writes, "Because the body of our book has been incinerated by the judgement I have to transmit consciousness diagonally, through the coiled spine of the immaterial nexus," reflecting on the immateriality, uncertainty, and ephemerality of the digital domain, while the same poem also reflects one of Wang's repeated points of interest, the process of sharing dreams.

> Before the technological catastrophe of separation I felt excited that there was at least one person with whom I could share the urgency of THINGS MUST BE DIFFERENT.

As in: after such an experience, things can never be the same.

The notion that "things must be different" is not only at the heart of Wang's poetry, but also imbues her academic analysis of race, politics, and economics. In her writings, both poetic and otherwise, Wang has been developing an interesting thesis about the political importance of dreams. Dreams, according to Wang, do some of the work needed to achieve a revolution, on the political or personal level, creating what she called, in *Carceral Capitalism*, "openings where there were previously none."

That dreams provide a space for a person to work out various emotional, social, and personal issues is certainly not new, but Wang's contribution to this discussion is that it is in the sharing and extrapolation of dreams that real changes to the world are made. Tweeting her dreams to her network of familiar and unfamiliar virtual connections and taking this further by using the communication of dreams to anchor her collections of poetry is not only personal but social, and potentially political. For Wang, writing out her dreams is akin to asking others to share in her visions, but also to share the experience of anxiety, fear, and shame that are common themes in dreams, as dreamers reflect on the important emotional twists that occur in their waking lives, through the fractured and confusing logic of the dream state.

The poems in Wang's collection are all primarily constructed in lyrical prose, and all are united by the dreaming or dreamscape theme, though some more explicitly than others. At times, Wang's poems seem more or less realistic in theme until some surreal detail reminds readers that they are inhabiting a fragmented reflection of a dream. Another theme that Wang uses to bind the collection together is the image and symbolism of the sunflower. Interspersed with her poetry, Wang includes quotes about sunflowers from a number of different historic, scholarly, and artistic figures and the flower appears in the equally dreamlike illustrations that appear in the book, created by avant-garde New York performance artist Kalan Sherrard. In using this familiar botanical archetype of sun worship, idyllic pastoralism, and potent political symbolism, Wang suggests a connection to these larger reflections.

The title poem of Wang's collection evokes the sunflower in its many symbolic roles:

> You were never no locomotive, Sunflower, you were a sunflower! You were never yourself. You were octopus, you were the face of a book we won at the arcade. You were sutra, or a social movement in Taiwan.

In this poem, Wang references Allen Ginsburg's "Sunflower Sutra," the 2014 Sunflower Movement in Taiwan, and even the use of sunflower tissue to make a healing poultice, reflecting the many ways that various cultures have embraced the sunflower as a symbol of hope, especially for those who feel trapped in a world that feels oppressive and unkind. To dream of a sunflower, in Wang's poetry, is to dream of future possibilities, of as yet unimagined utopian versions of oneself and one's world. The shared and yet intimately personal symbolism of the sunflower is a reflection of Wang's attitude towards dreams, which are both a person's internal reorganization of the mind and are also opportunities for social connectivity, and visions of potential futures, whether personal or political.

The Sunflower Cast a Spell was well received by critics. Elisa Gabbert, poetry columnist for the *New York Times Book Review*, listed it among her seven favorite poetry collections of 2021 and wrote, "Here dreams are spaces of radical possibility, and as in the real world, the possibilities are sometimes magical . . . and sometimes nightmarish . . . and sometimes both, like dress rehearsals for the apocalypse." Reviewer Amanda Auerbach, writing in *The Brooklyn Rail*, also invoked the magical and the real, "The spell of this book preserves the multiple-layers, multiple-petaled nature of life. Wang's collection professes the potency of dream and sunflower; it professes the persistence of powers that save." Wang's collection was included in many notable books lists for the year, and was a finalist for a National Book Award as well. For many reviewers, one of the things that made Wang's poetry so gripping was the promise and hopefulness of her vision, that the process of sharing our visions, nightmares, fantasies—our dreams—might be more than a simple exercise in self-expression, but might actually be the key to creating shared strategies for meeting the potentially apocalyptic futures facing the human collective.

Author Biography

Award-winning poet, scholar, and harpist Jackie Wang is an assistant professor of American studies and ethnicity at the University of Southern California. *The Sunflower Cast a Spell to Save Us from the Void* was a poetry finalist for the 2021 National Book Awards. Her collection of political essays, *Carceral Capitalism*, was published in 2018.

Kalan Sherrard is an experimental anarchist puppeteer.

Micah Issitt

Review Sources

Auerbach, Amanda. "Jackie Wang's *The Sunflower Cast a Spell to Save Us From the Void*." *The Brooklyn Rail*, Mar. 2021, brooklynrail.org/2021/03/books/Jackie-Wangs-The-Sunflower-Cast-a-Spell-to-Save-Us-From-the-Void. Accessed 16 Feb. 2022.

Ballard, Thea. "Jackie Wang's Dream Poetics." Review of *The Sunflower Cast a Spell to Save Us from the Void*, by Jackie Wang. *The Nation*, 26 Aug. 2021, www.thenation.com/article/culture/jackie-wang-sunflower-poetry-review/. Accessed 16 Feb. 2022.

Carroll, Rachel. "The Luminous World Should Be Shared: On Jackie Wang's *The Sunflower Cast a Spell to Save Us from the Void*." *Los Angeles Review of Books*, 26 Mar. 2021, lareviewofbooks.org/article/the-luminous-world-should-be-shared-on-jackie-wangs-the-sunflower-cast-a-spell-to-save-us-from-the-void/. Accessed 16 Feb. 2022.

Gabbert, Elisa. "The Best Poetry of 2021." *The New York Times*, 10 Dec. 2021, https://www.nytimes.com/2021/12/10/books/review/best-poetry-books-2021.html. Accessed 21 Feb. 2022.

The Sweetness of Water

Author: Nathan Harris (b. ca. 1992)
Publisher: Little, Brown (New York). 368 pp.
Type of work: Novel
Time: Just after the American Civil War
Locale: Old Ox, Georgia

The Sweetness of Water presents a look at life in rural Georgia in the confusing weeks and months following the American Civil War. White landowner George Walker, his wife Isabelle, their veteran son Caleb, and the formerly enslaved brothers Prentiss and Landry all find their lives intertwined in unexpected ways.

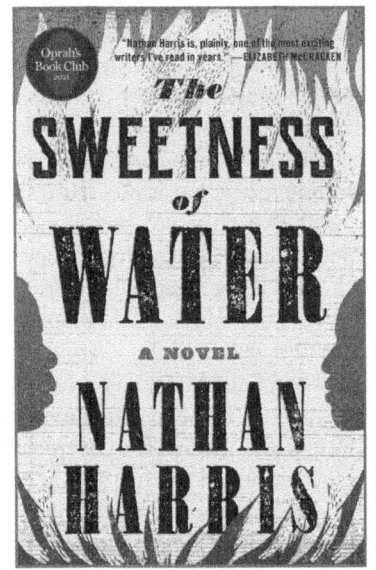

Principal characters

GEORGE WALKER, a middle-aged White landowner, seeking a mysterious, mystical beast
ISABELLE WALKER, his wife, from whom he is emotionally disconnected
PRENTISS, a young Black man recently freed from slavery
LANDRY, Prentiss's largely silent older brother, also recently freed
CALEB WALKER, George and Isabelle's son, a Confederate veteran
AUGUST WEBLER, a former Confederate soldier from a wealthy family, Caleb's lover

The Sweetness of Water (2021), the debut novel from writer Nathan Harris, is set in the fictional small town of Old Ox, Georgia, just after the end of the American Civil War. The Union victory has officially freed those who were enslaved, but in many ways this has done little to change the status quo. In Old Ox, some freed people gather in makeshift tent communities, foraging for food. Others continue to work the plantations, clinging to some semblance of stability in a time of profound upheaval. The two freedmen at the heart of Harris's novel, Prentiss and his nearly mute brother, Landry, have chosen a path somewhere between these two poles of existence. Having left the plantation on which they were born and raised, the men find themselves shut out of the larger, tightknit groups of freed people in Old Ox but incapable of leaving the town altogether. Landry, the older of the two, resists leaving the only place he has ever known. Prentiss, who wants to head north in search of their mother, loves and relies on his brother, but he is also aware that Landry, a gentle giant with traumatic brain injuries and a disfigured face from years of brutal beatings, might struggle to survive on his own. The two men vow to stick together and make a crude home for themselves in the woods.

When the book opens, George Walker, an aging White landowner, limps through the trees, tracking a strange, mythical beast he has sought since childhood. George knows how ridiculous that might sound, but he swears he has seen the animal long ago, and now it haunts his sleep. "I often wake to its image, as if it's trying to alert me to its presence nearby. . . It travels through my head like an echo, bounding through my dreams," George says in the opening pages, which hints at the deep metaphoric significance of the creature. Having lost his sense of direction in the fading light, George comes upon Prentiss and Landry, who have left the neighboring plantation. The two Black men are cautious and respectful, aware that the rules that govern the racial caste system are still in place despite their recent freedom. But George is too obtuse, too eccentric to obey any social norm—and he is also consumed by grief, having just learned that his only son, Caleb, has died in the war. This grief makes him lonely, and it is out of loneliness that he reaches out to the two wayward brothers. He invites them to stay on his property and offers to pay them to help him clear his land for a peanut farm—a totally foreign venture for George. The brothers, hoping to save enough to be able to travel north, ultimately agree to the deal.

Nathan Harris

As George, Prentiss, and Landry work the fields together, a bond is formed. The unlikely (and at times frustrating) friendship among these men forms the novel's emotional core. The circumstances of the newly freed brothers are particularly interesting and complex, as they must navigate a world that is at once totally new and yet much the same as ever. Prentiss is hyper-aware of the bounds of his and Landry's freedom. He understands, implicitly, that their freedom is not the same as George's freedom as a wealthy White man, or even the freedom of George's wife, Isabelle, a White woman. Freedom means that Prentiss and Landry will no longer be forced to work the fields without compensation—but if they do choose to work, does it mean they will be fairly paid? Does freedom mean that they can sit at a dinner table with a White woman, or accuse a White man of murder? Such questions trouble Prentiss's plans, narrowing their scope, and create a spiritual rift between him and his beloved brother. Emancipation has allowed them to finally embrace their true natures—Prentiss, chatty but also practical and cautious; Landry, the silent dreamer. But in a hostile world, these differences make it harder for Prentiss to keep them safe. Prentiss calls it the "burden of freedom," though it is clear that these new challenges are still far better than enslavement.

While Prentiss and Landry are perhaps the book's most intriguing characters, the plot centers on George, Isabelle, and Caleb, who, it would not be revealing too much to say, turns out to be alive. Caleb is cowardly and painfully reserved, even with his parents. He guards a secret, given more weight in light of his presumed death. Caleb is involved in a romantic relationship with August Webler, his longtime friend and fellow Confederate soldier. August is the most eligible bachelor in Old Ox, the arrogant son of a wealthy planter. Harris challenges readers to consider queerness in a historical context, though the relationship between Caleb and August is not exactly a loving one. Like his enslaver father, August can be brutal, and Caleb, doggedly devoted, is ever willing to stand his abuse.

Harris provides another twist on the societal norms of the 1860s with the character of Isabelle, who contemplates her own kind of independence. The initial news of Caleb's death drives a wedge between her and her husband, forcing her to consider a future where she might be on her own. Like George, Isabelle strains against social expectation. Attending a rare luncheon, she is unable to finish her meal without challenging the host, not entirely out of true conviction for what she is saying, but in principled rebellion against the politesse that society demands of her. Harris's vivid prose makes her discomfort palpable. "She closed her eyes, ignored the whine of a caged hog, the ring of hammer meeting anvil," he writes in a passage when Isabelle is forced to make the trip to town. "Sounds of excess, vice not of the religious order but of the human order, the noises of society fending off despair with routine."

In short: George and his family are not like other White people in Old Ox. They are outsiders, resistant to the calcified social mores of the antebellum South. George holds no overtly offensive opinions about race or sex. He respects his wife, and when he seeks the company of a young mixed-race woman at a brothel, he pays her just to talk. He does not, and has never, enslaved human beings; he lives off of his family's wealth, selling off small pieces of land instead of farming it. (The peanut farm complicates this arrangement.) Isabelle, and even Caleb, too, are shown to be kindhearted and empathetic. As August's efforts to preserve the secret of his relationship with Caleb lead to an outburst of racism and violence, the Walkers continually display human decency.

These unusual traits are admirable but can also be somewhat difficult to believe when considering the book in the context of its historical setting. In a review for the *New York Times*, novelist Martha Southgate pointed this out as a major flaw in an otherwise strong and ambitious debut novel. She noted that the Walkers are not merely out of step with the people of Old Ox, but sharply at odds with the attitudes of most White Southerners—indeed, most White Americans—of the time, to the point that she questioned the historical accuracy of the narrative. Indeed, at times Harris seems to go out of his way to create a White character wholly set apart from violent mechanisms of chattel slavery, a system that suffused every aspect of Southern economic and social life. There is no clear reason given for why George's views are so progressive, or why Prentiss and Landry are relatively quick to trust George and Isabelle. "The novel doesn't do the world-building work that would make the civil, supportive relationships among the four characters convincing," Southgate argued.

The Sweetness of Water may fall short of its grand ambition to challenge assumptions about the post–Civil War era in service of understanding contemporary social issues. But there are nevertheless many things to admire about it. Indeed, most reviewers offered enthusiastic praise. The book received a starred review from *Publishers*

Weekly, which called it a "deeply moving" character study, and was recommended by *Kirkus* as "an impressive debut by a storyteller with bountiful insight and assurance." In a review for *Texas Monthly*, Daniel Peña effused that "this novel is simply the best I have read in years." Peña saw in the book echoes of the 2020 killing of George Floyd that sparked racial justice protests throughout the United States, and the mob violence of the January 6, 2021, insurrection at the US Capitol. Harris's novel "asks us to consider white-supremacist ideology not as a uniquely Southern phenomenon, but as an uncomfortable truth and feature of the entire American endeavor," Peña wrote. "Old Ox is in Georgia, but it is also everywhere today."

Many critics specifically applauded the sharpness of Harris's prose. For example, the book's title refers to a recurring image that offers hope for a more humane future. As a young boy, Landry is hypnotized by the beauty of a gawdy water fountain on display at the plantation. Once, in the middle of the night, he escapes his cabin to swim in it—an illicit act for which he could have been killed. Once free, Landry seeks similarly simple pleasures, roaming the woods to sit in fields of dandelion flowers and swim in pristine creeks. He finds joy in these excursions, and with joy comes hope. "All danger carried the faint trace of comfort, all wrongs the hint of what may be right," Harris writes in Landry's voice. "How else to explain a world of cruelty that had also carried in it the great joy of watching his mother at the mercy of Little James's fiddle on a Sunday afternoon, the miracle of a fresh tick mattress, the sweetness of water after a day spent picking in the fields?"

The Sweetness of Water has proven to be a hit with general readers as well as critics. It was selected for Oprah's Book Club, among many other high-profile recommendations, and made the New York Times Best Sellers list. It also found success on the literary awards circuit, earning spots on the longlists for both the Booker Prize and the Carnegie Medal for Excellence.

Author Biography

Nathan Harris made his mainstream literary debut with *The Sweetness of Water*. He won the Kidd Prize from the University of Oregon and was named a finalist for the Tennessee Williams Fiction Prize.

Molly Hagan

Review Sources

Charles, Ron. "Oprah's Latest Book Club Pick, 'The Sweetness of Water,' Is a Miraculous Debut." Review of *The Sweetness of Water*, by Nathan Harris. *The Washington Post*, 15 June 2021, www.washingtonpost.com/entertainment/books/sweetness-of-water-nathan-harris-book-review/2021/06/15/286d9178-ce04-11eb-a7f1-52b8870bef7c_story.html. Accessed 14 Oct. 2021.

Peña, Daniel. "Set after Civil War, 'The Sweetness of Water' Is Eerily Relevant." Review of *The Sweetness of Water*, by Nathan Harris. *Texas Monthly*, 15 June 2021, www.texasmonthly.com/arts-entertainment/sweetness-of-water-novel-review/. Accessed 14 Oct. 2021.

Southgate, Martha. "A Civil War Novel Imagines More Racial Kinship Than Horror." Review of *The Sweetness of Water*, by Nathan Harris. *The New York Times*, 15 June 2021, www.nytimes.com/2021/06/15/books/review/the-sweetness-of-water-nathan-harris.html. Accessed 14 Oct. 2021.

Review of *The Sweetness of Water*, by Nathan Harris. *Kirkus*, 19 May 2021, www.kirkusreviews.com/book-reviews/nathan-harris/the-sweetness-of-water/. Accessed 14 Oct. 2021.

Review of *The Sweetness of Water*, by Nathan Harris. *Publishers Weekly*, 3 May 2021, www.publishersweekly.com/978-0-316-46127-6. Accessed 14 Oct. 2021.

A Swim in a Pond in the Rain
In Which Four Russians Give a Master Class on Writing, Reading, and Life

Author: George Saunders (b. 1958)
Publisher: Random House (New York).
    432 pp.
Type of work: Essays
Time: Nineteenth century

In A Swim in a Pond in the Rain: In Which Four Russians Give a Master Class on Writing, Reading, and Life, *author and professor George Saunders gathers seven Russian short stories that he has used in his creative writing classes, commenting on what each one can teach the aspiring writer about the craft of fiction.*

Principal characters
MARYA VASILYEVNA, a middle-aged schoolteacher who is the protagonist of "In the Cart"
YASHKA THE TURK, a young factory hand who wins a singing contest in "The Singers"
OLENKA PLEMYANNIKOVA, a woman who transfers her affections among a series of husbands and lovers in "The Darling"
VASILI ANDREEVICH BREKHUNOV, an arrogant landowner in "Master and Man"
NIKITA, one of Vasili's laborers in "Master and Man"
COLLEGIATE ASSESSOR KOVALYOV, a middle-ranked bureaucrat who loses his nose in "The Nose"
IVAN IVANYCH, a veterinarian who goes for a walk in the country in "Gooseberries"
BURKIN, a friend who accompanies Ivan Ivanych in "Gooseberries"
ALYOHIN, a gentleman farmer who hosts the two friends in "Gooseberries"
ALYOSHA, an obedient peasant in "Alyosha the Pot"

In *A Swim in a Pond in the Rain* (2021), author and longtime Syracuse University professor George Saunders reprints the text of seven Russian short stories and discusses how each of them can teach one to become a better reader and writer. Having used and analyzed these stories in his creative writing classes over the years, Saunders has a deep understanding of how they work and can help the reader plumb their hidden depths. Reading this book is, therefore, reminiscent of attending a high-caliber creative writing workshop. Saunders is not a literary critic, per se, nor does he read Russian. Rather, his interest in these stories is that of a craftsperson who admires

George Saunders (photo, Courtesy Penguin Random House)

how each piece is put together and who muses on what lessons each can offer aspiring writers. His book's subtitle, *In Which Four Russians Give a Master Class on Writing, Reading, and Life*, aptly sums up his intentions in this remarkable and generous book. Saunders is an insightful and genial guide through the rich world of Russian fiction, and his volume will appeal to readers and writers alike.

Saunders has gathered a compelling collection of seven stories that underscore just how varied the field of nineteenth-century Russian literature really is. The book includes three stories by Anton Chekhov ("In the Cart," The Darling," and "Gooseberries"), two by Leo Tolstoy ("Master and Man" and "Alyosha the Pot"), Ivan Turgenev's "The Singers," and Nikolai Gogol's "The Nose." Manuals on creative writing often involve the author summarizing stories, relying on excerpts, or assuming that author and reader are familiar with the same works. By including the text of all of the stories he wishes to study, Saunders ensures that his reader knows the works at hand and can follow a detailed and intimate discussion of them. Saunders takes a particularly detailed approach to the first of these stories, "In the Cart," by presenting it a page at a time. After each page of Chekhov's work, Saunders comments on how the story is developing and readers react. This method will be familiar to readers who have taken literature classes or creative writing workshops. It also goes to the heart of one of Saunders's core beliefs about fiction, expressed in the brief explanatory introduction to his approach for "In the Cart": "A story (any story, every story) makes its meaning at speed, a small structural pulse at a time." Saunders argues throughout this book that good fiction must hold the reader's interest from line to line or beat to beat, setting up a series of expectations that the reader wishes to see resolved. A great story is "a continual system of escalation" that stokes the reader's fascination in its protagonist and their situation.

Chekhov was largely responsible for creating the modern short-story form, and "In the Cart" offers a series of lessons on how a writer can hold the reader's interest. Like so many Chekhov stories, this one is a subtle study in character. As Marya Vasilyevna, a rural schoolteacher, rides in a cart, she thinks wistfully about her happy childhood and her deceased parents. The story culminates with a case of mistaken identity. Marya mistakes a woman she glimpses on the train platform for her long-dead mother, a slip that reveals just how deeply the protagonist longs for her old life. In discussing this story, Saunders argues that "the short story form is ruthlessly efficient." He demonstrates how each part of the piece builds on what came before and is essential to the whole. Any aspiring short-story writer should read Chekhov, and Saunders's commentary on "In the Cart" effectively underscores how relevant and contemporary his work still is.

In each subsequent section of the book, Saunders first presents the text of an entire story and then discusses it. Saunders often puts his finger on a pattern or technique that holds the key to understanding any number of other works of fiction. In analyzing Chekhov's "The Darling," for example, he notes that the story is structured around a repeating pattern. The protagonist, Olenka Plemyannikova, takes on the opinions and habits of her husband, a regional theater manager. When her husband dies, Olenka is grief-stricken but eventually remarries. She soon adopts the opinions and worldview of her new husband. As this pattern continues, the reader is primed both for repetition and for variations on the theme. For Saunders, this pattern underscores an essential truth of storytelling: that the reader stays with a story to see how the expectations that it raises will be fulfilled. The third Chekhov story, "Gooseberries," contains the scene that Saunders's title refers to: three friends take a swim in a pond in the rain. Saunders analyzes this story late in the collection and applies all of the concepts he has explored earlier in the book to its narrative structure. The story raises question about the nature of happiness but refuses to offer a fixed or simplistic answer. Saunders admires "how free of agenda" Chekhov is, and the way the author is "interested in everything but not wedded to any fixed system of belief." He sees this as an important corrective for young writers, who often believe that a story is "a delivery system for their ideas."

There is a real range to the stories in this collection: while the three Chekhov stories are realistic, Gogol's "The Nose" is absurdist. In this story, a bureaucrat wakes to find that his nose is missing. He later spots it—ambulatory, human-sized, and wearing dress clothes—as it makes the rounds of town. Saunders sees Gogol's work as animated by joy, even as it targets the banality and hypocrisy of everyday life. He argues that "The Nose" reminds the reader that words and sentences are not reality, but a simulacrum of it. A story like Gogol's challenges the reader's understanding of language and reality itself, jostling them out of their everyday perception of the world to focus solely on meaning regardless of the real or fictional world in which events take place. While Turgenev's "The Singers" has a realistic setting, the author's narrative approach can likewise unsettle a reader. Saunders reports that Turgenev's narratorial asides annoy his students, who want the narrator to get out of the way of the story that they are telling. For Saunders, though, this discursiveness and occasional clumsiness were essential to Turgenev and to every story he told. He argues that "The Singers" significantly suggests "how little choice we have about what kind of writer we'll turn out to be." Turgenev's style may not please every reader, but it was his way of expressing something true and beautiful.

Two stories by Tolstoy demonstrate the range that can exist within a single author's oeuvre. "Master and Man" is a suspenseful tale that culminates in a moving spiritual conversion. The arrogant landowner Vasili Andreevich Brekhunov, intent on concluding a business deal, takes his sleigh out in the middle of a snowstorm. He is accompanied by the peasant Nikita. Again and again, the pair loses sight of the snow-covered road and instead passes through a little town that could offer them refuge. Having already explored the pattern story in "The Darling," Saunders notes how Tolstoy exploits this device in "Master and Man." Saunders catalogues the subtle changes to the town each time the men encounter it and points out the ways in which Tolstoy continually raises the stakes of his story. Thinking only of his financial dealings, Vasili eventually strands himself and his servant in the snowstorm. With death imminent, Vasili must reconsider how he has lived his life and what he has prioritized. As powerful as this tale is, Saunders is never reverential, and his impulse is still to take the story apart to see how it works. In the spirit of a creative writing workshop, he also has a suggestion for revision: Tolstoy's depiction of Nikita, he contends, is too idealized. Nikita lacks the depth that Vasili possesses, perhaps because Tolstoy saw more of himself in the landowning "master" than in the simple "man." Saunders challenges his reader to rewrite the last few pages of the story to present Nikita in less romanticized terms. Contrasting "Master and Man" with Tolstoy's earlier, more compressed "Alyosha the Pot" reveals something of the author's evolution in style.

Saunders's book includes a series of "Afterthoughts," short chapters that range far beyond the stories at hand. These thoughtful and lively digressions help to expand the scope of the book and to offer new ways for readers and writers to think about the craft of fiction. In "Afterthought #5," for example, Saunders explains how an awkwardly written paper that a student submitted for one of his classes inspired him to write a new story. The clumsy, earnest voice of the academic paper became that of a teenage protagonist, and a story developed around them organically. Saunders encourages writers to "follow the voice" and to try other novel ways of generating new stories.

A Swim in a Pond in the Rain was generally well received by critics and readers. Writing for *The New York Times*, Parul Sehgal described Saunders's commentary on Russian fiction as "one of the most accurate and beautiful depictions of what it is like to be inside the mind of the writer that I've ever read." Sehgal was wary, however, of Saunders's sweeping claims for the transformative power of fiction, seeing them as "naïve" and "solipsistic." Gary Saul Morson, in his review for the *Wall Street Journal*, had a different objection to Saunders's analyses: he seems too ready to project onto nineteenth-century authors a twenty-first-century progressive view. Morson argued that Saunders is most comfortable with Chekhov but fails to understand what drives Tolstoy and Gogol's fiction. Nevertheless, Morson acknowledged the "enticing brilliance of his careful analyses." Writing for the *Washington Post*, Lisa Zeidner praised Saunders's "idiosyncratic, high-spirited way of approaching fiction." Robert Allen Papinchak, reviewing the book for the *Los Angeles Review of Books*, called *A Swim in a Pond in the Rain* "an overwhelmingly constructive book" that is meant for "anyone who reads and admires short stories or might aspire to writing one—or better ones."

Readers of Saunders's fiction and essays know how inventive and creative a writer he is. He brings a distinctive voice and point of view to whatever topic he is exploring. In *A Swim in a Pond in the Rain*, he finds an innovative way of discussing creative writing. This engaging rather than technical book, enhanced further by his personalized anecdotes, effectively recreates the experience of attending a college literature course or a creative writing workshop, and it will prove interesting to a variety of both readers and writers.

Author Biography
George Saunders is a short-story writer, novelist, and educator. He was a finalist for the National Book Award for his short-story collection *Tenth of December* (2013) and won the Man Booker Prize for his novel *Lincoln in the Bardo* (2017).

Matthew J. Bolton

Review Sources
Morson, Gary Saul. "*A Swim in a Pond in the Rain* Review: From Russia with Love." Review of *A Swim in a Pond in the Rain: In Which Four Russians Give a Master Class on Writing, Reading, and Life*, by George Saunders. *The Wall Street Journal*, 5 Feb. 2021, www.wsj.com/articles/a-swim-in-a-pond-in-the-rain-review-from-russia-with-love-11612540987. Accessed 15 Aug. 2021.

Papinchak, Robert Allen. "How to Read an Artichoke: On George Saunders's *A Swim in a Pond in the Rain*." *The Los Angeles Review of Books*, 14 Jan. 2021, lareviewofbooks.org/article/how-to-read-an-artichoke-on-george-saunderss-a-swim-in-a-pond-in-the-rain/. Accessed 15 Aug. 2021.

Sehgal, Parul. "George Saunders Conducts a Cheery Class on Fiction's Possibilities." Review of *A Swim in a Pond in the Rain: In Which Four Russians Give a Master Class on Writing, Reading, and Life*, by George Saunders. *The New York Times*, 19 Jan. 2021, www.nytimes.com/2021/01/12/books/review-swim-pond-rain-george-saunders.html. Accessed 15 Aug. 2021.

Zeidner, Lisa. "Thrilling Little Machines: George Saunders Analyzes Russian Short Fiction." Review of *A Swim in a Pond in the Rain: In Which Four Russians Give a Master Class on Writing, Reading, and Life*, by George Saunders. *The Washington Post*, 21 Jan. 2021, www.washingtonpost.com/outlook/thrilling-little-machines-george-saunders-analyzes-russian-short-fiction/2021/01/21/c41146ba-4876-11eb-a9d9-1e3ec4a928b9_story.html. Accessed 15 Aug. 2021.

The Tangleroot Palace

Author: Marjorie Liu (b. 1979)
Publisher: Tachyon (San Francisco). 256 pp.
Type of work: Short fiction
Time: Unknown
Locales: Various

The Tangleroot Palace collects seven of Marjorie Liu's previously published stories exploring powerful magic, hostile landscapes, and complex women.

Though primarily known for her longform work, including the novels in the Dirk & Steele and Hunter Kiss series, and for the creator-owned comics series *Monstress*, author and comic book writer Marjorie Liu wrote and published a variety of short stories over the first decades of her career. Her shorter works are collected in a single volume for the first time with the publication of *The Tangleroot Palace* (2021), which collects seven stories mostly written during the first decades of the twenty-first century. The stories span a variety of genres and subgenres, from fairy tales to steampunk to postapocalyptic horror, showcasing Liu's range as a writer and command of language and storytelling. In some cases, the stories presented differ somewhat from the versions originally published in earlier anthologies. The title of the piece "The Light and the Fury" was changed, for example, and Liu notes in her introduction to the collection that others have been edited to varying extents. Still, as Liu explains, the stories collected were written during a specific era in her career, and in many ways reflect her interests and preoccupations from that period. This grants readers unfamiliar with Liu's work a retrospective view of her development as an artist.

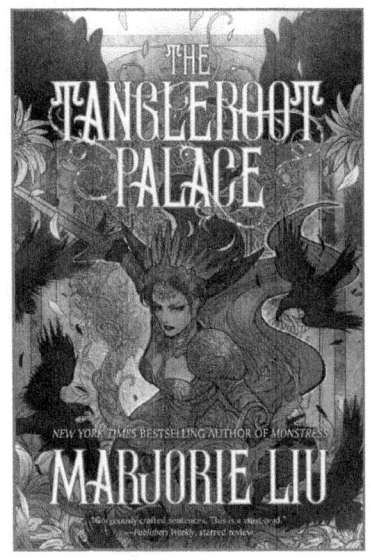

The first story in *The Tangleroot Palace*, "Sympathy for the Bones," follows the character Clora, a young woman who has been taken in and raised by an elderly woman named Ruth. Ruth is a hoodoo woman capable of creating poppets, sewn with bone needles and filled with sympathetic magic, that can be used to harm or even kill the people they are created to resemble—including Clora herself. Hoping to escape Ruth's control, Clora plots against her powerful mentor. Liu follows "Sympathy for the Bones" with a brief note in which she provides some context for the writing of the story, as well as information about the anthology in which it was originally published, a practice she continues for each story in the book.

Next, the collection presents the story "The Briar and the Rose," a reimagined take on the Sleeping Beauty fairy tale. The story focuses on Briar, often referred to as the

Duelist, a skilled warrior employed as a guard by a beautiful courtesan known as Carmela. Carmela, however, is in fact a body-stealing witch, and when she falls into a heavy sleep one day each week, the woman whose body she has stolen, a princess named Rose, awakens. Having fallen in love with Rose, the Duelist works to free her from the witch's control, delving into ancient history to find the witch's true name.

The next story in the collection, "The Light and the Fury," is reminiscent of the steampunk subgenre of speculative fiction, which incorporates futuristic technology inspired by nineteenth-century settings and machinery. This story is in an alternate history universe in which China colonized portions of western North America prior to the arrival of the British on the continent and subsequently sided with the rebelling colonists during the American Revolutionary War (1775–83). Technological development accelerated rapidly in that world following the discovery of mysterious crystal skulls, which facilitate the growing of crystals capable of powering machines such as airships and submersibles. The strange power the skulls possess has also accidentally granted superhuman abilities to protagonist Xīng MacNamara, also known as the ex-Lady Marshal, a widely known and feared fighter—a superhero of sorts—who has come out of retirement amid a war between Great Britain and China. Facing the threat of human fighters who have allowed themselves to be purposely transformed into superpowered monstrosities, Xīng must also confront her past in the form of Maude, a former friend and lover who once betrayed Xīng and her cause.

The concepts of superheroes, supervillains, and dangerous technology are also explored in "The Last Dignity of Man," in which technology executive Alexander Lutheran styles himself after the comic book villain Lex Luthor, Superman's archnemesis, because of his own fascination with the fictional hero Superman. Alexander believes that for someone like Superman to exist, he must himself play the role of the hero's villainous counterpart. Alexander's perspective begins to change, however, after he meets and hires Richard, an older man who has fallen on hard times but has valuable lessons for Alexander. "The Last Dignity of Man" in some ways feels out of place in *The Tangleroot Palace*, in part because of its male protagonist, but more significantly because of its setting. Unlike the other stories in the volume, which are set in fantastical pasts, postapocalyptic landscapes, or entirely fictional worlds, "The Last Dignity of Man" takes place in a world that is very similar to our own and references pop culture figures, such as Superman, with which the reader will likely be familiar. The comic book references in the story are particularly appropriate in light of Liu's own extensive work in comics.

While most of the stories in *The Tangleroot Palace* are unrelated to Liu's longform work, two of the stories have ties to Liu's Dirk & Steele series, a series of detective novels that incorporates fantasy themes. "Where the Heart Lives," a prequel to that series, begins when a young woman named Lucy Steele leaves home to take a position as a domestic servant for a woman named Miss Lindsay. While traveling to Miss Lindsay's home, she passes through a frightening forest, where she encounters a woman who is trapped and seeking help. The trapped woman, Mary, is the long-lost wife of Henry Lindsay, Miss Lindsay's brother, who was abducted many years before by a mysterious being living in the forest. After confronting this forest entity and freeing Mary, Lucy marries fellow employee Barnabus, setting in motion events that will later result in the formation of the Dirk & Steele Detective Agency. "After the Blood," on the other hand, represents what Liu describes as a "possible future" for the Dirk & Steele series, and is set in a postapocalyptic world in which much of the population has died from a disease known as the Big Death. The story's narrator, Amanda, survived the Big Death; since then, she has lived on her family's property in a rural area with a significant Amish population. Now, however, grotesque monsters that were once men lurk in the forest and emerge to hunt both Amanda and her neighbor Henry, who became a vampire years before amid the same traumatic event that gave Amanda's blood a strange power. Circumstances come to a head after Henry's secret is revealed, and Amanda and her friends face greater danger than ever before.

Forests feature prominently in several of Liu's stories, as Liu herself observes in one of her notes, and the stories aptly demonstrate the ability of forests to conceal, confound, and terrify those traveling through, trapped within, or conspicuously avoiding them. The forest in "After the Blood" is dangerous, not only because of the monsters within, but also because it is a place of personal trauma for Amanda. In "Where the Heart Lives," the forest has a distinctly otherworldly feel, as it is home to a queen who is loath to give up anyone she traps within the forest's borders.

The final and longest story in the collection, "Tangleroot Palace," follows a similar vein; in that case, however, the evil force within the forest is herself trapped there and longs to be freed. This story focuses on a princess named Sally, who learns that her father intends to marry her off to a foreign warlord with a terrifying reputation. Hoping to find a different path, she seeks out the cursed Tangleroot Forest and soon experiences the forest's strange and disorienting power. Sally escapes the forest's thrall with the help of a group of travelling performers, led by a man calling himself Mickel Thorn, but ultimately leaves the group to return to the forest, where she confronts the evil there with some unexpected assistance. As Sally discovers, relationships with friends and family can be key to overcoming daunting evil.

Indeed, the importance of friendship and family is clear in many of Liu's stories in this collection. For example, Lucy's dedication to her newfound family gives her strength in "Where the Heart Lives;" Amanda, Henry, and Steven's teamwork ensures their survival in in "After the Blood;" and Alexander and Richard's friendship in "The Last Dignity of Man" reshapes much of Alexander's worldview. The pain that arises when such a relationship is betrayed is also evident in "The Light and the Fury," during which Xīng, still processing Maude's betrayal, is willing to come out of retirement only after rumors about Maude's whereabouts arise. Aided by Liu's beautiful prose and strong plotting, the stories ultimately combine to form an intriguing collection that is entertaining as well as thought provoking, with haunting imagery and complex characters that linger long after the book's conclusion.

The Tangleroot Palace received largely positive reviews upon its release from both general review publications and periodicals dedicated to speculative fiction. Critics widely praised Liu's strong prose and fascinating narratives. The anonymous reviewer for *Kirkus* described the collection as "a masterclass in the art of storytelling," while the critic for *Publishers Weekly* wrote that Liu's "ear for language carries each story forward on gorgeously crafted sentences," describing the collection as "a must-read." Writing for *Strange Horizons*, a speculative fiction magazine, Stephen Case likewise described Liu's prose as "gorgeous" and praised her "tight plotting and richly imaginative storytelling." He cited "The Light and the Fury" as a particular highlight of the collection, and was impressed by the wide range of genres overall. Case added that, since this marks the first time Liu's short fiction has been published in a single volume, *The Tangleroot Palace* offers a valuable opportunity to enjoy a strong selection of her work in one collection. In a review for *Locus*, a publication dedicated to reviewing horror, science fiction, and fantasy writing, critic Maya C. James was somewhat more critical of the collection. She described the characterization and plotting of some stories, most notably "The Last Dignity of Man," as less developed than others. However, she expressed particular appreciation for "The Briar and the Rose," which she described as "swoon worthy and well-paced," and praised Liu's ability to balance "evocative, romantic writing" with "gritty, electric scenes of violent revenge."

Author Biography

Marjorie Liu is the author of many novels, including the works in the Dirk & Steele series, and is the writer and cocreator of the comics series *Monstress*. *The Tangleroot Palace* is her first collection of previously published short stories.

Joy Crelin

Review Sources

Case, Stephen. Review of *The Tangleroot Palace: Stories*, by Marjorie Liu. *Strange Horizons*, 24 Jan. 2022, strangehorizons.com/non-fiction/the-tangleroot-palace-stories-by-marjorie-liu/. Accessed 14 Feb. 2022.

James, Maya C. "Maya C. James Reviews *The Tangleroot Palace* by Marjorie Liu." *Locus*, 22 Aug. 2021, locusmag.com/2021/08/maya-c-james-reviews-the-tangleroot-palace-by-marjorie-liu/. Accessed 14 Feb. 2022.

Review of *The Tangleroot Palace: Stories*, by Marjorie Liu. *Kirkus*, 10 Feb. 2021, www.kirkusreviews.com/book-reviews/marjorie-liu/the-tangleroot-palace/. Accessed 14 Feb. 2022.

Review of *The Tangleroot Palace: Stories*, by Marjorie Liu. *Publishers Weekly*, 18 Dec. 2020, www.publishersweekly.com/978-1-61696-352-1. Accessed 14 Feb. 2022.

Tastes Like War

Author: Grace M. Cho (b. 1971)
Publisher: Feminist Press (New York). 296 pp.
Type of work: Memoir
Time: 1961–2008
Locales: Chehalis, Washington; Providence, Rhode Island; New York City

In her memoir Tastes Like War, *Grace M. Cho looks back on her relationship with her mother, a Korean immigrant who struggled with schizophrenia.*

Principal personages

GRACE, the author and narrator, a sociology professor and aspiring pastry chef
KOONJA, her mother, a survivor of the Korean War who is later diagnosed with schizophrenia
JAMES, her father, a White merchant marine who was much older than his wife and often away from the family
HER HALF BROTHER, six years older, who later houses their mother in an in-law apartment
JENNY, her only friend while living in the xenophobic town of Chehalis, Washington
CESAR, her longtime partner, a musician

While there is no standard format for memoirs, it is easy to associate the genre with thick-spined books written by politicians, celebrities, business gurus, and war heroes. Often these authors are at the end of their careers and seeking to solidify their legacy or provide some insight on an event that came to define them. Typically, their memoirs move chronologically through time, recounting the most important moments of their lives while also offering advice for readers who might have similar aspirations. In *Tastes Like War* (2021), however, Grace M. Cho shatters this restricted idea of what a memoir can be. At its core a meditation on her mother's struggles with schizophrenia, the book also incorporates elements of history, sociology, and even food writing, blending transcendent prose and emotionally wrought memories with sharp journalistic insights. Although it is a deeply personal story that focuses primarily on Cho's experiences, the book also has qualities that are comparable to a detective novel. It revolves around the propulsive mystery of how her mother's life was shaped by the Korean War and especially how the hardships she endured may have intersected with her mental illness. Through meticulous research and small clues that

Grace M. Cho

her mother unwillingly revealed over time, Cho tries to put the fragmented pieces of her mother back together and honor her legacy.

One of the most enjoyable aspects of *Tastes Like War* is the highly unconventional literary style that Cho employs. Early in the prologue, she states that she experienced three versions of her mother throughout her life: the beautiful, dynamic mother of her childhood; the mother whose schizophrenia spiraled frighteningly out of control for fifteen years; and the mother who began to show vestiges of her former self in the years before she died, bonding with Cho over Korean food. The book's four sections are organized in a somewhat linear way, but within each Cho jumps back and forth between memories of the three different versions of her mother as she tries to contextualize information. This stylistic decision to provide the story with a loosely chronological structure while also seamlessly moving around in time infuses the prose with a fluid, dreamy feeling that is easy to get drawn into. It also makes all of the memories that Cho shares seem interconnected, blended together in their shared relevancy. In this way, the book often reads as though it is a portal into Cho's rawest, most intimate thoughts.

Another remarkable aspect of *Tastes Like War* is how much important information Cho conveys about world history and the delicacy of mental health in general, all filtered through a personal lens. In the earliest years of her life, Koonja lived in a Korea under the colonial rule of imperial Japan. After World War II Korea was divided into Soviet-backed North Korea and US-backed South Korea, and the Korean War that broke out in 1950 became a key proxy conflict in the so-called Cold War between the global superpowers. Many members of Koonja's immediate family were among the estimated two to three million civilians who were killed or disappeared during the three years of active fighting in the Korean War. While Cho's mother very rarely mentioned this time in her life, Cho deduces from research that her mother likely experienced horrific violence and malnutrition. For example, Cho connects other historical and eyewitness accounts of this mass suffering with a memory of her mother making an offhand comment about eating insects, rodents, and small birds. Similar poignant intersections continue to emerge throughout the book, providing deeper insight into both general history and Koonja's individual experience. One of these is reflected in the title: Koonja states that she does not want to drink powdered milk because it "tastes like war," which jolts Cho into recalling her discovery that one of the few things American soldiers brought for starving Koreans in the 1950s was cases of powdered milk—which many could not drink because they were lactose intolerant.

Tastes Like War is about many different things, but at its heart it is the story of Koonja. Cho's love for her mother thrums on the pages as she demonstrates that the woman who was devalued first by Korean society for having a biracial child and later by American society for being an immigrant was not only a human being but someone incredible. In postwar South Korea there were no jobs or real infrastructure, and the US military stations were the only source of a better life. It was there that the tenacious Koonja met Cho's father, whom she eventually married and followed to the rural town of Chehalis, Washington. Cho is open and honest as she grapples with the realization that her mother was likely part of the Korean government's initiative to provide "comfort women" to American soldiers, a reality rife with sexual and racial politics that resonate into the present day. As Cho establishes a vivid portrait of her mother's humanity throughout the book, it becomes clear how necessary it is to destigmatize sex workers and provide them with emotional and psychological support.

Throughout the narrative of *Tastes Like War*, it becomes clear that Cho has an incredible ability to capture the humanity of people. And while she is not afraid to depict their flaws, she never sets her readers up for judgment—just empathy. This talent becomes especially clear in the way in which she presents both of her parents. Cho's father, James, was working in Korea in the early 1970s when he met Koonja, who was twenty years younger than him and already had a child with an unknown father. The two had a tumultuous relationship that vacillated between passion and disdain for one another. At one point, Cho recalls witnessing her father hitting her mother and her mother breaking a chair over him. Cho's father was also deeply conservative and at times racist; he once voted for KKK leader David Duke to be nominated as the Republican Party's presidential candidate. Yet though she admits that she and her father did not have a friendly relationship in his later years because of these problematic aspects of his personality, Cho still shares moments where he was loving, kind, and a good father. She also offers insights rather than excuses into why he acted that way, speculating that it could be related to the hardships he experienced while growing up during the Great Depression. In turn, he comes across as very human rather than a one-dimensional antagonist.

Cho's depiction of her mother is tender and encourages readers to reexamine their understanding of people who live with schizophrenia and other mental illnesses. In the book's early sections, she focuses on the incredible, loving woman that her mother was—someone who woke Cho up every morning by rubbing her legs and made her "birthday" meals consisting of her favorite foods so she would not be afraid to go to school. Cho also topples the perception that her mother was an uneducated immigrant or a "war bride," as many racist people in their small Washington town believed her to be, instead showing her to be an extremely intelligent, resourceful survivor. She reveals that Koonja taught herself English word by word from the dictionary back in Korea. To ensure that Cho and her brother were treated well by their teachers, she hosted a lavish dinner party every year for the school's faculty. At one point she began foraging wild blackberries and gourmet mushrooms in the woods and selling them, making a tidy profit in addition to her graveyard shift job at a juvenile correction center. It is Cho's depiction of the strong, vivacious woman Koonja was that makes the eventual onset of her psychosis feel even more tragic. As Cho watches her mother become a recluse who believes she is being followed and refuses to eat because voices named "Oakie" will not let her, readers will feel their hearts break and wonder if there is anything that might bring back Koonja.

Critical reception of *Tastes Like War* was very positive, with numerous reviewers citing it as one of the best books of the year. A New York Times Best Seller, it was also named a finalist for the 2021 National Book Award. Many critics highlighted how well written, insightful, and ultimately powerful the memoir is. "Cho hauntingly captures the fragility of life in its most painful and beautiful moments," the reviewer for *Publishers Weekly* wrote, for example. "This heartfelt and nuanced tribute is remarkable." It is true that most people who read *Tastes Like War* will by moved by Cho's unfiltered presentation of her emotions and her exploration of the deep suffering that her mother endured.

However, some critics did note that the narrative is ultimately rather open ended, which could perhaps frustrate some readers. As the *Kirkus* reviewer wrote, "Cho refuses to settle on a specific explanation for her mother's illness, which creates some sense of an unresolved narrative." It is important to note here that throughout the memoir Cho uses her skills as a sociologist to speculate about how her mother's early life might have contributed to her schizophrenia. She includes facts from various studies that suggest that schizophrenia is not just a genetic condition but something that can possibly be triggered by extreme emotional duress during one's childhood, a drop in estrogen during menopause for women, or even being the only minority in an all-White neighborhood—all factors that align to Koonja's own experiences. Although it is impossible for Cho to decisively state what contributed to her mother's illness, she presents enough information that readers will likely start looking at the long-term mental health consequences of trauma in a new light.

Other critics focused their reviews on the way in which Cho made food such an enjoyable cornerstone of the memoir. Sonja Flancher wrote for the *Rumpus*, "*Tastes Like War* reminds readers of the extremes of the human condition. There is trauma and hate and bigotry and ignorance, but there is also hope and light and the importance of small pleasures—like finding the perfect cabbage for a batch of kimchi, or ripe blackberries in the brambles of the Washington forest." Indeed, food is one of the most prevalent thematic threads that ties all four sections of the memoir together as Cho explores fond memories of her mother's cooking growing up, the tastes that had cultural meaning to them as Koreans, and how she began to connect with her mother later in life by cooking her food. There are lush descriptions of dishes like japchae, bulgogi, sogogi soup, and miyeok-guk, which will no doubt resonate with readers familiar with Korean cuisine and intrigue those who are not.

Ultimately, *Tastes Like War* is a beautiful, haunting examination of the mysteries of who one's parents really are and how family history shapes one's own life. It is a literary success spiritually akin to Alison Bechdel's graphic novel *Fun Home* (2006) and other unique, gripping, family-oriented memoirs. It is a book that readers of all backgrounds will get something from—whether they have family members of their own with mental illness, want to know more about the personal toll of the Korean War, or are simply looking to be engrossed in superb writing.

Author Biography
A sociologist and academic at the College of State Island, Grace M Cho has published numerous journal articles as well as creative writing. Her book *Haunting the Korean Diaspora: Shame, Secrecy, and the Forgotten War* (2008) earned an American Sociological Association award.

Emily E. Turner

Review Sources
Flancher, Sonja. "The Trauma of Surviving." Review of *Tastes Like War,* by Grace M. Cho. *The Rumpus*, 20 Oct. 2021, therumpus.net/2021/10/20/tastes-like-war-by-grace-m-cho. Accessed 17 Feb. 2022.
Review of *Tastes Like War*, by Grace M. Cho. *Kirkus*, 3 Mar. 2021, www.kirkusreviews.com/book-reviews/grace-m-cho/tastes-like-war/. Accessed 17 Feb. 2022.
Review of *Tastes Like War*, by Grace M. Cho. *Publishers Weekly*, 2 Nov. 2021, www.publishersweekly.com/978-1-952177-94-1. Accessed 17 Feb. 2022.

These Precious Days

Author: Ann Patchett (b. 1963)
Publisher: HarperCollins (New York). 320 pp.
Type of work: Essays
Time: 1960s to the present day
Locales: Nashville, Tennessee; California; New York

This collection of essays by acclaimed novelist Ann Patchett explores varied subjects such as friendship, death, memory, and the life of a writer and bookstore owner.

Principal personages

ANN PATCHETT, the author, who co-owns the Parnassus bookstore in Nashville
KARL, her husband, a doctor in Nashville
TAVIA CATHCART, her longtime friend from childhood
SOOKI RAPHAEL, her friend and houseguest during the COVID-19 pandemic, who works as an assistant to actor Tom Hanks
FRANK PATCHETT, her father

These Precious Days (2021), a collection of twenty-two essays (along with an introduction and epilogue that feel very much like additional chapters) spans decades and topics and people. At the same time, its title indicates how the book is very much in the zeitgeist of the coronavirus disease 2019 (COVID-19) pandemic, embracing a feeling that it is time to slow down, remember, ponder life and death, and pay attention to each moment. The title essay itself, first published in *Harper's* early in 2021, tells the story of actor Tom Hanks's assistant, Sooki Raphael, who came to Nashville with pancreatic cancer to be part of a clinical trial and then was forced into an isolated intimacy with her hosts—Patchett and her husband, Karl—during the pandemic. Of course, the pandemic was doing the forcing, as it did for so many others, requiring configurations of people and living situations unfathomable before lockdown. The Patchetts and Raphael formed a family during this time, and the piece becomes a reminder that real life is unpredictable, capricious, surprising, and beautiful. Patchett asks the reader to pay attention to what is happening right now, outside of their desire to know how the story ends. She surrenders to not knowing Raphael, not being able to see the arc of her story or know its ending, just as, at the time of the book's publication in late 2021, people still did not know exactly how the pandemic would end or what it would mean to them.

If there is a theme to this collection, it is a confrontation with death, or at least with loss. It provides a clear-eyed view into the life of a woman who knows herself and, now in her late fifties, is unapologetic about her talent, her privilege, and her good luck. Because Patchett is who she is—a best-selling author, wealthy bookstore owner, and celebrity—she can view her life without bitterness or illusion. The result is a generosity that borders on eulogy at times. Still, she manages to avoid coming off as too self-satisfied or revisionist by telling some truths that might be wielded as weapons in the hands of a more insecure writer.

In her opening essay, "Three Fathers," Patchett recounts her gifts from all, but primarily the first two, of her fathers. Her biological father, a Los Angeles police officer who wanted her to take up a practical career so she could have a steady income and stability, gave her the gift of self-possession. Rather than assuring his talented daughter that she should be a writer, he thought perhaps she should be a dental hygienist. Patchett writes, "Having someone who believed in my failure more than my success kept me alert." She would have to be a writer with or without his support, as she notes, "My father taught me at a very early age to give up on the idea of approval." She describes her second father, her stepfather Mike, with whom she lived for fifty-one weeks of the year after her mother took up with him and they moved to Nashville, as a dynamic, complicated figure, who "broke plates and put his fist through hollow doors and thought I was the second coming of Christ." He wanted to be a writer like his stepdaughter. Patchett can see that both the criticism and the praise, and later editing requests, were acts of love from these men who were very different parents to her. Her third father, Darrell, arrived later in her life and gave her an unexpected gift. "He let me be just one more person around a crowded table, a valued addition," she writes. For a woman whose problem had always been too much attention, too much identification with her beautiful mother, this was, indeed, a gift.

"Three Fathers" also accepts openly and with good humor one of the secrets of those who live intimately with a writer: at any moment, particularly an important one, they are likely thinking about what they will write about it. This is also explicitly stated in "These Precious Days," as Patchett told her friend Sooki that she would write about her but understood that she could not shape the story. In fact, there is not a piece in this collection where Patchett does not address her role in the story not just as a person, but as a writer. The voice in this collection is that of a mature, self-confident woman who has been moving through her whole life as a writer, putting all her eggs in that basket (as she puts it) since she was very young. Because of her success, and her father's lesson to ignore what other people think, she is able to be astute about both her faults and her triumphs, acknowledging her talent, her many awards, her celebrity status, and her privilege while also understanding that much of life is capricious. "We

Ann Patchett

Courtesy Heidi Ross

don't deserve anything," she says, "not the suffering and not the golden light. It just comes."

In her essay "A Talk to the Association of Graduate School Deans in the Humanities," a lively, humorous piece, Patchett recounts her education, which culminated with an MFA program at the Iowa Writers' Workshop. Her stories in this piece, some horrifying, some hilarious, are tied together with the unifying lesson of how important it was for her to find other people who were dedicated to the life of the writer, just as opening her bookstore in Nashville helped her create such a community of readers. The bookstore, Parnassus, is clearly one of the great passions of Patchett's life, a place where she is able to be herself most clearly and others are welcome to do the same. This is another recurrent theme: the moments in people's lives when they can be their "best and most complete selves," with dear friends, in a beloved bookstore, or with a nun at a bar. This awareness of joy and beauty and comfort often comes, as it seems to have for Patchett, in middle age, and after a whole lot of life experience and loss.

Of course, loss is always looming, when people are brave enough to look past the bulwarks, a theme Patchett takes up directly in multiple essays In "How to Practice." In the latter, she describes how cleaning out the condo of her friend's father led her to confront her own accumulated possessions, suggesting to Karl that in order to downsize they could pretend they were going to move, without ever actually doing so. She muses, "I could have said, 'I wonder if we could just pretend to die,'" but of course that was a bridge too far. Similarly, in "My Year of No Shopping" she does just that, giving up shopping for a year. In both these essays, Patchett explores how possessions are both part of people's journey—a beloved typewriter features prominently—and distract people from the inevitability of loss, busying them with unnecessary things. Not shopping, she discovered, was a wonderful timesaver.

One of the strongest essays in the collection, "Flight Plan," is an insight into a mature, secure marriage in which there are nevertheless still moments of selfishness, doubt, and fear. Karl has had a lifelong obsession with planes and flying—Patchett catalogues his airplanes with the kind of detail that a collector will appreciate. Meanwhile, she worries about this inherently dangerous hobby, her expression of concern serving to cool his enthusiasm only temporarily. In the end, she finds the kind of peace expressed throughout this collection. When a mistake was made that could have had deadly consequences, it was her error, not his, and so she decided to let go of her wish to control their fate, realizing that life offers no guarantees. Life and death are capricious and unpredictable, she muses, and Karl will probably not die in a way she has predicted: "It will be life and time, the things that come for us all."

Another intriguing aspect of the book is that Patchett proves unafraid of taking on a topic that other writers may avoid: the fact that she did not want to have children. In "There Are No Children Here," she catalogues the interactions she has had with other people who cannot and will not accept this as truth. One famous writer told her that she would not know what it meant to love, and therefore could not write about real love, until she had children. A radio talk-show host, she further candidly details, asked her a stream of intrusive questions about her choices. She does not shy away from the complexity of her feelings, confessing to a broken heart the one time she wanted to adopt a child. There is no pat answer here, no secret trauma or obvious repulsion, just the knowledge that she wanted to devote herself to writing and did not feel like there was enough energy in her to also raise children. In a question posed to the talk-show host, Patchett also broaches the gendered nuances of the topic—male writers are not often asked how they juggle parenthood and their craft, and they are hardly ever critiqued when they are childless. At another point, she also considers what a dark and lonely journey childhood can be, not for any particular reason but just because life is hard; she does not want to place another human in the center of it.

Reviews of *These Precious Days* were generally effusive, finding Patchett's clarity around death, loss, beauty, and friendship especially praiseworthy. Michele Filgate, reviewing the book for the *Washington Post*, praised Patchett's "discipline as a writer and her deep understanding of herself," noting that after reading the title essay in a single sitting, she wept and sent it to a friend. Filgate quoted Patchett's introduction, as she evaluated her essays and found that "again and again, I was asking what mattered most in this precarious and precious life." In her *New York Times* review, Alex Witchel lauded "Patchett's heart, smarts and 40 years of craft," noting that she writes without extraneous detail but with great tenderness and "plenty of love to spread around." In a review for the *Chicago Review of Books*, Meredith Boe called the collection "sharp and honest," asserting that Patchett writes about the people she loves "with endless gratitude." Reviewer Abhrajyoti Chakraborty, writing for the *Guardian*, was one of the few to strike a more critical note, approaching the book as a "collection of warm and affectionate eulogies" and finding some pieces redundant. Though acknowledging that repetition can be inevitable in pieces that were originally written for individual publication, Chakraborty wondered if the selection could have been made with more care. Similarly, in her NPR review, Annalisa Quinn found that some of Patchett's essays seem like "excuses to brag about her friends." Still, the essential message of this collection resonates, and Patchett's desire to remain open-hearted and appreciate the gifts she has been given shines through in the end.

Author Biography

Ann Patchett is an award-winning writer and a co-owner of Parnassus Books in Nashville, Tennessee. She is best known for her novels, including *The Patron Saint of Liars* (1992), *State of Wonder* (2011), *Commonwealth* (2016), and *The Dutch House* (2019). She has also written children's books and numerous essays.

Bethany Groff Dorau

Review Sources

Boe, Meredith. "Endless Gratitude in *These Precious Days*." Review of *These Precious Days*, by Ann Patchett. *Chicago Review of Books*, 21 Dec. 2021, chireviewofbooks.com/2021/12/21/these-precious-days/. Accessed 2 Feb. 2022.

Chakraborty, Abhrajyoti. "*These Precious Days* by Ann Patchett Review—a Reckoning with Loss." *The Guardian*, 18 Nov. 2021, www.theguardian.com/books/2021/nov/18/these-precious-days-by-ann-patchett-review-a-reckoning-with-loss. Accessed 2 Feb. 2022.

Filgate, Michele. "Ann Patchett's *These Precious Days* Is a Beautiful Reminder of What's Important." *The Washington Post*, 26 Nov. 2021, www.washingtonpost.com/entertainment/books/ann-patchett-these-precious-days/2021/11/26/1870d420-4d29-11ec-b0b0-766bbbe79347_story.html. Accessed 2 Feb. 2022.

Quinn, Annalisa. "Ann Patchett Reflects on Love and Relationships in New Essay Collection." Review of *These Precious Days*, by Ann Patchett. *NPR*, 23 Nov. 2021, www.npr.org/2021/11/23/1058263105/ann-patchett-on-love-and-relationships-in-these-precious-days. Accessed 2 Feb. 2022.

Witchel, Alex. "Ann Patchett Has Thoughts on a Bunch of Subjects." Review of *These Precious Days*, by Ann Patchett. *The New York Times*, 19 Nov. 2021, www.nytimes.com/2021/11/19/books/review/these-precious-days-ann-patchett.html. Accessed 2 Feb. 2022.

Three Girls from Bronzeville
A Uniquely American Memoir of Race, Fate, and Sisterhood

Author: Dawn Turner (b. 1965)
Publisher: Simon & Schuster (New York). 336 pp.
Type of work: Memoir
Time: 1960s–present
Locales: Bronzeville neighborhood of Chicago, Illinois; Champagne, Illinois; Indianapolis, Indiana

In this memoir, novelist Dawn Turner shares her lived experiences from childhood to the present day shaped by community, love, loss, and self-reflection. From Chicago's South Side to college a few hours away to putting down roots in a rural community, Turner shows the impacts of urban planning, inequitable education, and how a couple of poor decisions can have lifelong implications at the intersection of race and gender.

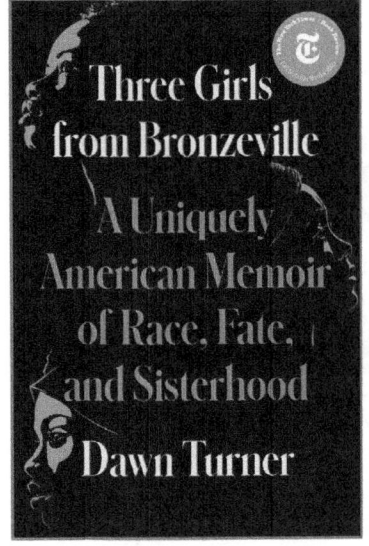

Principal personages
DAWN TURNER, the author
BARB TURNER, a.k.a. Mom, her mother
KIM TURNER, her younger sister
MR. TURNER, a.k.a. Dad, her father
GRANNY, her maternal grandmother
AUNT DORIS, her maternal aunt
DEBRA TRICE, her best friend and neighbor
ANDREW MCDONALD, her stepfather

In *Three Girls from Bronzeville* (2021), her third book and first nonfiction title, Dawn Turner "seeks to understand how three Black girls with very similar aspirations ended up with wildly divergent fates," as Linda Villarosa put it in her review for the *New York Times*. Turner was one of the titular three girls who grew up together in Chicago's South Side neighborhood of Bronzeville; the other two were her younger sister, Kim Turner, and her best friend, Debra Trice. Turner went on to graduate college, marry, move into a house, and enjoy success as an award-winning novelist and journalist; Kim developed a dependence on alcohol and died of a heart attack in her twenties; and Debra was convicted of murdering a fellow crack smoker in 2000 and served twenty-one years of a fifty-year sentence. *Bronzeville* started as a series about Debra that Turner had written as a columnist for the *Chicago Tribune* during the 2000s.

Bronzeville begins by chronicling how Turner and her family became inhabitants of Bronzeville. While the complex history of how three generations of women on her maternal side came to live in the Bronzeville community is rich in detail, it is also lengthy and delays the story's heart, Turner's coming of age. Bronzeville is a character more than just a location where characters exist. Turner writes about how the community grew during the Great Migration as Black people fled from the Jim Crow South seeking out better opportunities and how it became a testament to the generational resilience that she benefited from time and again. She also takes great pride and joy in acknowledging prior residents of Bronzeville, such as Ida B. Wells, Gwendolyn Brooks, Louis Armstrong, Richard Wright, and Sam Cook. Turner does an outstanding job describing her world, transporting the reader back to 1970s and '80s Chicago to experience the heyday of a proud, protective, and appreciative community of Black people.

Turner was a toddler living in an apartment in the Lawless Gardens complex with her parents when her sister was born in July 1968. Members of her extended maternal family, such as Granny and Aunt Doris, lived nearby. Built by Black developers in the late 1960s for middle-class people displaced by urban development, the Lawless Gardens apartment complex was not a housing project, nor was it where most middle-class families chose to live. The community primarily consisted of working-class families, and it was well kept, safe, and comfortable through the early 1980s.

Growing up, Turner lived a typical life of school, church, and family. Her mother was strict and had high expectations of her daughters. Mrs. Turner often reminded her daughters that they were to remain virgins until marriage and postpone marriage until they had lived independently and explored the world at least a little bit. Mr. Turner, a dispatcher at a local cab company, lacked financial management skills, which caused constant conflict with his wife.

Early in the memoir, Mrs. Turner was preparing to separate from her husband when she discovered she was expecting their second child. She believed the baby would be male and decided she would leave her son with his father to raise while she and Dawn moved on with their lives. To her surprise and disappointment, Mrs. Turner bore Kim and decided to stay with her husband. Mr. Turner was not an active participant in either of his daughters' lives, but he was closer to Kim. One night Turner was woken from her sleep by sounds of screaming and items breaking in her parents' bedroom. What she walked in on not only resulted in her parents divorcing, but further alienated her from her dad. This moment was the catalyst for changes that she and Kim would respond to in markedly different ways. After their parents' divorce, Mrs. Turner and the children moved from a third-floor apartment to one on the twelfth floor for a new start.

As an introvert with no friends, Turner spent a great deal of her time eavesdropping on the conversations between her mother, Granny, and Aunt Doris. Turner's life began to change once again when she entered third grade. Her teacher, Mrs. Love, had an unorthodox style of classroom management that exposed Turner to self-control and emotional regulation—aspects of health and wellness that were new to her. In Mrs. Love's class, she also met Debra, whom she had seen before but with whom she had never conversed. As it turned out, Debra lived on the thirteenth floor of Turner's building, and her bedroom was above Turner's. Almost immediately, the two became best friends. Debra was more extroverted and outspoken, and they balanced one another out over the next few years. Kim was also indirectly a part of their friendship because she often tagged along behind her older sister, plus she and Turner shared a room, so when Debra visited, it was with both girls. The school they and other kids who reside in Lawless attended was good enough but not great. A couple of years into their friendship, Debra transferred to a school with better academic outcomes. Turner and Debra maintained their relationship while attending different schools by leaving notes for one another under their welcome mats and their typical adventures throughout their neighborhood. While the friends managed to weather this storm, there was a more significant change on the horizon. Debra was heartbroken when she informed Dawn that her family was relocating to Indianapolis. The close friends promised to maintain their bond through letters and phone calls.

Turner transferred to a preparatory academy for high school while consuming several literary works by Black authors. She gained access to these texts through her stepfather, Andrew McDonald, who worked at the city library. Unfortunately, due to drinking, Andrew became her mother's second ex-husband. In high school Turner sought out additional academic enrichment opportunities and prepared herself for college. On the other hand, Kim cut class, missed assignments, and was overall dismissive of school, as she had been since age ten. Neither Turner nor her parents could get Kim to straighten up her act, so Turner decided to focus on her own future. Kim agreed with that approach and reminded her older sister not to act as her third parent.

Turner was accepted to college and prepared for her first move away from home. While she was away at school, Kim's behavior worsened. At the same time, Debra seemed to have minimal direction or focus as she not only decided not to attend college but struggled to maintain employment or any type of stability.

Following a difficult start at college, Turner refocused and graduated with an undergraduate degree in communications in four years and returned to Bronzeville, where she accepted a job at the *Chicago Tribune*. Although she noticed that Lawless Gardens and Bronzeville had declined over the years, her childhood neighborhood was nearly unrecognizable when she returned after college. The once clean and cared-for apartment complex had become a neglected, gang-controlled community that city officials did not prioritize. It was evident that Chicago was no longer interested in the well-being of the South Side, and Turner believed this was due to the city's anti-Black racism and classism toward the community's residents. She began to hope that her mother would consider relocating as their other family members had.

Things were going well for Turner, both personally and professionally, as a young adult. She maintained a healthy relationship with her high school sweetheart, whom she eventually married. Conversely, by the age of nineteen, Kim had dropped out of high school and experienced a devastating loss that she coped with by drinking. Turner wanted to be there for her younger sister but did not know how best to support her. Kim promised Turner that she would turn her life around, secure employment, complete her GED, and stop drinking. Meanwhile, Debra also lived on the edge, experimenting with drugs and working as a stripper. Turner found herself constantly wondering why her best friend and sister were on such different trajectories from hers and how best to help them get back on track. She continued to manage these relationship dynamics while excelling professionally. *Bronzeville* is an excellent example of others' decisions shaping individuals' experiences and the struggles to manage one's responses to these decisions. The three friends had very different reactions to the cards life dealt them, and their lives went in three very different directions resulting in various successes, second chances, and a great deal of pain.

Bronzeville received starred reviews before and upon its publication. Villarosa keenly observed that the memoir's "episodic chapters . . . read like self-contained short stories woven together into a whole." Indeed, nearly every chapter could evolve into a standalone book. One of the strengths of this text is the self-reflection it may ignite in its readers. Terri Schlichenmeyer, in her review of *Bronzeville* for the *Washington Informer*, asked, "Have you ever wondered what life might've been like if you'd made different choices, picked a different spouse, or another job? Yep, then 'Three Girls from Bronzeville' is for you." Schlichenmeyer goes on to add, "And yet, this book isn't entirely about choices; it's also about taking what life seems to hand you and molding it to fit." One of the most challenging elements of this memoir is how Turner is influenced and impacted by others' decisions. Despite, or perhaps because of, such challenges, reviewers have found Turner's memoir, and the three women at its heart, so compelling. As Tina McElroy Ansa wrote for the *Washington Post*, "It makes one hope that Turner might return to this memoir in 10 or 20 years for a second volume. I'm hooked on these women."

Author Biography
Dawn Turner's previous novels include *Only Twice I've Wished for Heaven* (1996) and *An Eighth of August* (2000). A former columnist and reporter for the *Chicago Tribune* and contributor to NPR's *Morning Edition*, Turner was a 2014–15 Harvard University Nieman Journalism Fellow and a 2018 fellow and journalist in residence at the University of Chicago's Institute of Politics.

LaShawnda Fields

Review Sources

Ansa, Tina McElroy. "*Three Girls from Bronzeville* Is a Story about Growing Up on Chicago's South Side—and So Much More." Review of *Three Girls from Bronzeville: A Uniquely American Memoir of Race, Fate, and Sisterhood*, by Dawn Turner. *The Washington Post*, 8 Sept. 2021, www.washingtonpost.com/entertainment/books/three-girls-from-bronzeville-book-review/2021/09/08/408d431c-0cd8-11ec-aea1-42a8138f132a_story.html. Accessed 9 Dec. 2021.

Schlichenmeyer, Terri. "Book Review: *Three Girls from Bronzeville*: *A Uniquely American Memoir of Race, Fate and Sisterhood* by Dawn Turner." *The Washington Informer*, 15 Sept. 2021, www.washingtoninformer.com/book-review-three-girls-from-bronzeville-a-uniquely-american-memoir-of-race-fate-and-sisterhood-by-dawn-turner/. Accessed 9 Dec. 2021.

Villarose, Linda. "Dawn Turner Looks Back on Her '70s Girlhood, and Those Who Got Left Behind." Review of *Three Girls from Bronzeville: A Uniquely American Memoir of Race, Fate, and Sisterhood*, by Dawn Turner. *The New York Times*, 6 Sept. 2021, www.nytimes.com/2021/09/06/books/review/dawn-turner-three-girls-from-bronzeville.html. Accessed 9 Dec. 2021.

The Twilight Zone

Author: Nona Fernández (b. 1971)
First published: *La dimensión desconocida*, 2016, in Chile
Translated from the Spanish by Natasha Wimmer
Publisher: Graywolf Press (Minneapolis). 232 pp.
Type of work: Novel
Time: 1970s–present
Locales: Santiago, Chile, and environs

The second novel of Nona Fernández to be translated from Spanish to English, The Twilight Zone *continues the author's unique blend of fact and fiction in its examination of the violence of the Pinochet dictatorship in Chile.*

Principal characters
ANDRÉS ANTONIO VALENZUELA MORALES, a Chilean soldier and intelligence agent during the Pinochet regime
FERNÁNDEZ, the female narrator, a television documentary writer
GENERAL AUGUSTO PINOCHET, coup leader and later military dictator of Chile
M, the father of Fernández's teenage son

By 2021, two of Chilean author Nona Fernández's novels had been translated into English: *Space Invaders* (2019) and *The Twilight Zone* (2021). Both are similar in subject matter, style, structure, and concept. These works are imagined semi-autobiographies, blending fact and fiction, and focus on personalized aspects of the trauma generated throughout Chile by the dictatorship of General Augusto Pinochet. During the Pinochet's rule, which lasted from 1973 to 1990, thousands of Chileans fled the nation out of fear of government brutality or persecution for their political beliefs. Tens of thousands of individuals, including many dissidents and democratic activists opposed to Pinochet's regime, were tortured or executed by the government. Thousands of others simply disappeared, often executed and buried in secret.

Fernández grew up in Chile during Pinochet's regime and became more aware of the horrific events of this era as a teenager; like many other Chilean authors of her generation, including Alejandro Zambra and Lina Meruane, she has drawn on this violent history and its complex aftermath to inform her work. The narratives of both *Space Invaders* and *The Twilight Zone* consist of excerpts from various media, including clippings, recordings, and letters, plus conversations, dreams, memories, and imaginations, which the author weaves together to try and make sense of the crimes of

Pinochet's regime and analyze how those years are, and ought to be, remembered.

Both of Fernández's novels are divided into four parts that each reference the metaphorical device contained in the novel's title. *Space Invaders* takes its title from the pioneering arcade game created in 1978, and its four parts are entitled "First Life," "Second Life," "Third Life" and "Game Over," likening the novel's events to a vicious high-stakes game. *The Twilight Zone* takes a similar form; Fernández named the novel after the famous science fiction series that ran from 1959 to 1964, and the titles of its four parts—"Entry Zone," "Contact Zone," "Ghost Zone," and "Escape Zone"—all harken back to the television series' title.

Nona Fernández

Courtesy Sergio López Isla

The novel's connection to the *Twilight Zone* television series goes beyond the title. To reinforce the surreal nature surrounding what was happening in Chile during the dictatorship—sudden abductions, extended torture, public and private murders, mysterious disappearances—Fernández makes frequent references to particularly memorable or appropriate episodes of the television series, which is noted for its use of surreal science fiction plotlines to comment on social issues. It is somewhat interesting that Fernández uses an American television show to illustrate the excesses of a South American regime, given the considerable support Pinochet received from the United States during his 1973 overthrow of his socialist predecessor, Salvador Allende.

The narrative of *The Twilight Zone* centers on a real-life controversial figure who first came to the attention of the public in 1984, in the midst of Pinochet's dictatorship. Andrés Antonio Valenzuela Morales, "a man with a bushy mustache," appears on the very first page of the novel. He enters the offices of a leftist magazine, *Cauce*, and asks to speak with a reporter. He then confesses to the journalist to being a willing participant in the torture, murder, and disappearance of various Chilean citizens. Valenzuela, himself tortured by what he has seen and done, feels he must unburden himself because his professional life is adversely affecting his personal life. He cannot eat or sleep. His relationships with his wife and son and friends have suffered. He is full of guilt and "trapped in a reality he didn't know how to escape." After baring his soul, his photo appears on the cover of the magazine under the headline "I Torture People."

This real event and many others are woven into *The Twilight Zone*, and the narrator Fernández, a writer and documentary filmmaker, is based on the author herself. As a child, Fernández sees the magazine cover with Valenzuela's photo, and forever remembers him as "the man who tortured people." The story picks up speed when, decades later, the narrator encounters Valenzuela again. As part of her research for a documentary television series about Pinochet's dictatorship, Fernández views and listens to taped interviews with victims of the dictatorship. One recording contains an interview with Valenzuela, who was smuggled out of Chile after giving his original confession the magazine and returned thirty years later to give testimony in court. Hearing the plain voice and apparent remorse of the man who tortured and killed people with live rats, electricity, and other brutal methods inspires Fernández to try and speak with Valenzuela and hear him explain how he came to feel remorseful. She writes, but never sends, a letter to him, asking multiple questions about what he did and how he felt. She imagines various scenarios involving the torturer and his involvement in the disappearance of specific people. As the narrator continues to work on her documentary, she retells the story of Valenzuela's attempts to uncover and make amends for his own crimes and those of his ex-colleagues, risking his life in the process.

While Fernández's narration frames the novel, Valenzuela is undoubtedly its complex moral center. Although his confessed involvement in the worst of the Pinochet regime's crimes seems to set Valenzuela up as a clear villain, he instead emerges as a vaguely sympathetic figure. The author achieves this in a few different ways, particularly through the inclusion of Valenzuela's own voice in the form of courtroom testimonies and other confessions. One particular excerpt replicates Valenzuela's blunt language and offers insight into his troubled state of mind:

> They ordered me to bind El Pelao's hands and feet. They ordered me to tie stones to him. They ordered me to push him off the cliff. I remembered the last time we had lunch together. It hadn't been so long ago. We'd talked about soccer. We'd told jokes.

In this matter-of-fact description, the author contrasts the brutality of the execution with the tenderness of Valenzuela's final lunch with the victim, emphasizing Valenzuela's continued sensitivity and humanity despite his evil actions. The narrator also sympathetically compares him to a character from a *Twilight Zone* episode, an astronaut who crashes on a strange planet who will never be able to return home. Much like the astronaut's journey into space, Valenzuela's confession has taken him into dangerous uncharted territory, stranding him all alone far from the comforts of his old life. In his isolation, Valenzuela is resigned to the reality that someone will find him, "and one of them will be willing to stain their pants with my blood." This is a reference to the constant danger Valenzuela faces from other former agents of the Pinochet regime eager to keep their crimes covered up; this constant danger not only heightens the narrative tension and helps the novel read more like a thriller, but also emphasizes Valenzuela's selflessness in making such a confession. However, despite these admirable traits in Valenzuela, Fernández resists the temptation of fully redeeming him, and retains a strong sense of moral ambiguity.

Critical reception of *The Twilight Zone* was largely positive. The novel was a finalist for the National Book Award for Translated Literature and was longlisted for the Andrew Carnegie Medal for Excellence in Fiction. Ariel Dorfman of the *New York Times*, a former Chilean exile who lost friends to Pinochet's oppressive government, called Fernández's novel "wildly innovative, a major contribution to literature, in Chile and beyond, that deals with trauma and its aftermath." Dorfman especially praised the author's incorporation of multiple genres into her fiction, including autobiography, journalism, and poetry, considering it a groundbreaking approach to storytelling.

Anjanette Delgado, of the *New York Journal of Books*, credited the unsent letter the novel's narrator composes to Valenzuela as "a key moment" that addresses important philosophical issues. She felt that the questions in the letter addressed "human susceptibility to corruption by force, violence, and fear for oneself or others . . . and ultimately speak to the issue of collective responsibility." Delgado also praised the novel's "tight plot, with suspense born of the prose, so precise it often reads like a mystery caper."

Other reviews were more mixed. J. D. Debris of the *Harvard Review Online* agreed in part with Dorfman's assessment of the narrative's success, and stressed how "Fernández's conversational, essayistic narration guides the reader surefootedly through a minefield of political absurdity." The reviewer also praised how the author "excels in chronicling the proximity of the banal and the brutal," perhaps a reference to Valenzuela's dry recollections of the torture and executions he carried out, but noted that Fernández is "less successful when mapping pop culture exactly onto history," in part a critique of the novel's repeated references to the *Twilight Zone* television series.

Reviewer Lucas Iberico Lozada of *The Nation* had an even more negative view of *The Twilight Zone*. While recognizing the author's "experiments with form in order to examine the malleability of memory," Lozada criticized the ambiguous role of the narrator in the novel, calling out Fernández's "inability, or her unwillingness, to involve herself." He concedes that the narrator's distance from the events of Valenzuela's life helps her tell the story more effectively, but added, "It has the unfortunate effect of turning the reader into a helpless spectator staring into a screen." Lozado went on to criticize the narrator's involvement as "unsatisfying" and "glancing," which he felt undermined the story's mystery, tension, and other strengths.

It is possible that neither the narrator of *The Twilight Zone* nor its author were directly affected by the events described in the novel. For example, there is no mention of any specific family member abused during the dictatorship. However, it must be remembered that both the character and author Fernández, as human beings and Chilean citizens, could not remain untouched by the incidents that unfolded during the Pinochet era. *The Twilight Zone* is a rich, imaginative, thought-provoking interpretation of childhood first impressions that matured into complex adult considerations of timeless issues—right versus wrong, accountability and responsibility, the strengths and weaknesses of human nature—that are applicable in any age or place, particularly whenever and wherever totalitarianism rears its ugly head.

Author Biography

A novelist, playwright, and actor, Nona Fernández has published six novels, including her first to be translated into English, *Space Invaders*. The *Twilight Zone* won the Sor Juana Inés de la Cruz Prize for a book written in Spanish by a woman upon its original publication in 2016 and was considered for other prestigious literary awards.

Natasha Wimmer has translated nine of Chilean author Roberto Bolaño's works from Spanish to English, as well as both of Nona Fernández novels thus far translated into English.

Jack Ewing

Review Sources

Debris, J. D. Review of *The Twilight Zone*, by Nona Fernández, translated by Natasha Wimmer. *Harvard Review Online*, Harvard University, 17 May 2021, harvardreview.org/book-review/the-twilight-zone/. Accessed 18 Nov. 2021.

Delgado, Anjanette. Review of *The Twilight Zone*, by Nona Fernández, translated by Natasha Wimmer. *New York Journal of Books*, www.nyjournalofbooks.com/book-review/twilight-zone-novel. Accessed 18 Nov. 2021.

Dorfman, Ariel. "When a Nation's Torturous Past Resembles *The Twilight Zone*." Review of *The Twilight Zone*, by Nona Fernández, translated by Natasha Wimmer. *The New York Times*, 15 Mar. 2021, www.nytimes.com/2021/03/16/books/review/nona-fernandez-twilight-zone.html. Accessed 18 Nov. 2021.

Lozada, Lucas Iberico. "The Distortions of Pinochet: Nona Fernández's Novels Reckon with the Chilean Dictatorship through Surreality and Memory." Review of *The Twilight Zone*, by Nona Fernández, translated by Natasha Wimmer. *The Nation*, 19 Aug. 2021, www.thenation.com/article/culture/twilight-zone-nona-fernandez-review/. Accessed 18 Nov. 2021.

Rayapati, Nitya. "'Your Imagination Is Clearer than My Memory': The Gray of Complicity in *The Twilight Zone*." Review of *The Twilight Zone*, by Nona Fernández, translated by Natasha Wimmer. *Chicago Review of Books*, 22 Mar. 2021, chireviewofbooks.com/2021/03/22/your-imagination-is-clearer-than-my-memory-the-gray-of-complicity-in-the-twilight-zone/. Accessed 18 Nov. 2021.

Tepper, Anderson. Review of *The Twilight Zone*, by Nona Fernández, translated by Natasha Wimmer. *Bomb Magazine*, no. 155, 10 Mar. 2021, bombmagazine.org/articles/nona-fern%C3%A1ndezs-the-twilight-zone/. Accessed 18 Nov. 2021.

Unbound
My Story of Liberation and the Birth of the Me Too Movement

Author: Tarana Burke (b. 1973)
Publisher: Flatiron Books (New York). 320 pp.
Type of work: Memoir
Time: 1970s–Present day
Locales: New York City; Philadelphia; Selma, Alabama

Unbound *is a memoir by activist Tarana Burke covering major events in her life, from the sexual assault she endured in childhood to her founding of the "Me Too" movement, one of the most influential social movements in contemporary American history.*

Principal personages
TARANA BURKE, the author and narrator
MR. WES, her stepfather
KAIA, her daughter
JAMES BEVEL, a reverend and civil rights leader, who was also a known child molester
MRS. SANDERS, a lawyer and cofounder of the organization 21st Century Youth Leadership Movement
HEAVEN, a young Black girl who attends a youth camp led by Burke and a sexual abuse survivor

An instant *New York Times* best seller, *Unbound: My Story of Liberation and the Birth of the Me Too Movement* (2021), the debut memoir of activist and Me Too founder Tarana Burke, is a powerful testimony of survival written with brutal honesty, style, humor, and grace. Burke leaves no stone unturned as she narrates the life that led her to become an organizer, activist, and advocate for survivors of sexual violence, particularly for Black girls and youth not so different from herself. Her journey from silence, shame, and self-blame to empowerment, healing, and liberation offers inspiration to survivors of sexual violence everywhere. She shines a light of accountability on adults in positions of power within families, communities, churches, and society who fail in their responsibility to protect children. Burke takes the reader through the many twists and turns, and betrayals and loyalties, she experiences in her long road to recovery and healing. In doing so, she exposes the cruelty of the world but also emphasizes how she endured such challenges, describing the alienation, condemnation, and embrace she experienced from various family and friends in her community. Her tenacity, devotion, and perseverance reflect a remarkable resilience of spirit. Moreover, through

Tarana Burke
Courtesy Dougal MacArthur

her journey, Burke succeeds in creating a space for young Black girls to get in touch with themselves and their feelings while maintaining what agency they have.

Reading *Unbound* is almost like watching a movie with rich, vivid cinematography. Burke's prose is powerful in its emotion and its clarity, allowing readers to derive a visceral sense of her surroundings and the magnitude and impact of the traumas she endures. Whether she is on the bus verbally sparring with rude boys, in the kitchen washing dishes, in a classroom correcting a teacher about Black history, getting her own Black history lesson from her grandfather, or running down a stairwell trying to flee from a neighborhood predator, the environments are an integral part of her truth-telling. Her dialogue further pulls the reader into the story like a witness to the experience as it is happening. It can be jarring at times, as well as emotionally invigorating and challenging all at once. Notably, survivors of sexual trauma should be warned that they may be triggered.

Sexual violence is not the only trauma Burke survives, however. The book provides ample examples of how race, class, and gender oppression are intricately connected and impact Burke's life and her ability to help other Black survivors. This is most visible when she realizes just how inaccessible and essentially nonexistent resources are in her community. The patriarchal behaviors and poverty-related roadblocks she constantly navigates can be frustrating and exhausting, but they are so grounded in the reality of her lived experiences that they press the reader to stay present. As Burke's passion and skills in advocacy grow, she comes to grips with the realization that her own coping strategies are becoming less effective and undermining her ability to support young girls who disclose sexual abuse. Burke explains clearly in the last chapter of the book, entitled "for colored girls," how her own healing and recovery are intimately intertwined with her activism and advocacy. She writes: "No matter how hard the work, no matter how meager the resources, no matter how tired or frustrated or burned out I was, I always returned to it, not just because I loved my kids and I loved supporting survivors but because I needed to make the things I endured mean something. I was trying to make more space in the movement for Black women to find validity, accountability, community, and value. Even after all the work I had done to get myself where I was, I still needed that support too."

Burke skillfully discusses how racism and sexism impact the ways sexual violence is often addressed within Black communities. As she explains, the historical legacy "of false accusations of sexual violence against Black men" resulted in racial terror lynchings at the hands of White mobs. This history, in combination with Black communities' turbulent relationship with law enforcement, has historically complicated efforts to hold Black men accountable for sexual violence within Black families and communities. Burke also recognizes how addressing structural racism and poverty can make sexual violence seem almost minor, especially in a culture in which people tend to place blame on Black girls for their own abuse. She offers readers a multifaceted and complex context for understanding why "when it comes to sexual violence in the Black community, the culture of secrecy and silence is more complex than just wanting to protect the perpetrator." This context might also be helpful to understanding, in part, why Burke chose not to confront her own abuser when she saw him many years later at an annual community function. She explains that at that time, her priority and responsibility was self-care and survival, not confrontation. Her decision challenges one of the oldest formulaic notions in the field of sexual trauma recovery—that confrontation is critical to healing from sexual abuse.

Overall, though, Burke is not conflict-avoidant and does not hesitate to use confrontation to hold sexual abuse perpetrators and those complicit in their violence accountable. There are several instances in the book of her confronting revered community members, pastors, senators, and lesser-known individuals to disclose sexual abuse that has already occurred. She draws on all of the resources and networks available to her and puts herself in situations to build her skills and knowledge along the way. Burke also does an excellent job in her book of identifying structural barriers *within* the helping profession, such as the protocols for reporting abuse in schools by teachers and administration, and other policies and procedures that were clearly not developed with Black girls living in poverty in mind. Burke's descriptions of these encounters with so-called helping professionals are delivered with humor and sarcasm in some instances, perhaps to demonstrate the ludicrousness and irony of those situations, relative to their real helpfulness in achieving her goal in getting support for the children with whom she works.

Over the course of *Unbound*, Burke reveals the seeds of the Me Too movement that later came into existence. As a community organizer, she spent decades before the movement went mainstream doing advocacy work on behalf of Black girls, many of whom were survivors of sexual abuse. She details her work leading organizations in Selma, Alabama, such as the Black Belt Arts and Cultural Center and Just Be, Inc., that aimed to instill confidence in Black girls. After moving from Selma to Philadelphia, Burke begins running workshops where she encourages women to share stories of sexual abuse and assault, often by simply writing the words "me too" on a piece of paper. When the social media hashtag #metoo goes viral in 2017, Burke initially has no involvement in the movement's sudden trajectory, and she finds the co-opting of the term by mostly White women in Hollywood "jarring." Burke shares her worries at the time that social media would dampen her life's work, but eventually comes to appreciate and embrace her role as the movement's founder.

Critics responded positively to *Unbound*. It received starred reviews from *BookPage*, *Kirkus*, and *Publishers Weekly*, for example. For *BookPage*, Amy Scribner wrote that "Burke writes with humor and gratitude about her experiences" in an "unflinching, open-hearted, beautifully told account of becoming one of the most consequential activists in America." Scribner further described *Unbound* as "not just a thoroughly engrossing read . . . [but] also an important book that helps us understand the woman who has been so influential as our country struggles to acknowledge women's trauma." Similarly, the anonymous reviewer for *Kirkus* described *Unbound* as "a soul-baring memoir" and "an unforgettable page-turner of a life story rendered with endless grace and grit." Moreover, Burke's story is defined in the *Kirkus* review as "raw and sobering but also a source of healing and hope for other survivors." The unnamed reviewer for *Publishers Weekly* agreed, characterizing the book as "intensely moving and unapologetically frank."

Shannon Melero of *Jezebel* made a point of recognizing that, as the M Too movement's founder, Burke "has the first and final say on what it truly means to live and say 'me too.'" Melero described *Unbound* as "an unwavering, unapologetic claim of ownership of two small yet powerful words that played a crucial role in Burke's life and, ultimately, in the lives of the women and girls she guided." Unlike some other critics, Melero did not avoid the race, gender, and class implications of White Hollywood women actors taking over the movement in many ways, noting the power of "Burke's claim on #MeToo, especially in the current cultural environment where creators of color frequently have their ideas repurposed and repackaged for a profit they never see." As Melero put it, "reading the first-hand account of a Black woman refusing to step aside for women with more clout is a much-needed reminder for organizers and creators of color who face a similar landscape." With equal conviction, Melero addressed the potentially difficult impact of the subject matter, warning readers that "getting through Burke's stories of sexual and emotional abuse requires a degree of mental fortitude" with which the reviewer herself struggled. She recommended that unlike "some books that you can't put down because they're so appealing; with *Unbound*, you must put it down frequently to remind yourself to breathe."

Speaking to those who have survived against the odds, and especially the young Black women too often left out of other movements, Burke ends *Unbound* with a powerful and definitive declaration. She writes: "I am the woman who organized and fought and taught, the woman who despite all odds and in the face of trauma, kept traveling until she found her healing and her worth. I am her. She is me. And we are free."

Author Biography

Tarana Burke is an activist and founder of the Me Too movement. The recognitions bestowed upon her for her work have included the 2017 *Time* magazine Person of the Year and the 2019 Sydney Peace Prize, among many others.

Valandra, MBA, MSW, PhD

Review Sources

Melero, Shannon. "'And We Are Free': The Power of Tarana Burke's Memoir." Review of *Unbound: My Story of Liberation and the Birth of the Me Too Movement*, by Tarana Burke. *Jezebel*, 23 Sept. 2021, jezebel.com/and-we-are-free-the-power-of-tarana-burkes-memoir-1847689454. Accessed 30 Dec. 2021.

Scribner, Amy. Review of *Unbound: My Story of Liberation and the Birth of the Me Too Movement*, by Tarana Burke. *BookPage*, Sept. 2021, www.bookpage.com/reviews/26604-tarana-burke-unbound-nonfiction/. Accessed 30 Dec. 2021.

Review of *Unbound: My Story of Liberation and the Birth of the Me Too Movement*, by Tarana Burke. *Kirkus*, 16 June 2021, www.kirkusreviews.com/book-reviews/tarana-burke/unbound-my-story-liberation/. Accessed 30 Dec. 2021.

Review of *Unbound: My Story of Liberation and the Birth of the Me Too Movement*, by Tarana Burke. *Publishers Weekly*, 8 June 2021, www.publishersweekly.com/9781250621733. Accessed 5 Feb. 2022.

Under a White Sky
The Nature of the Future

Author: Elizabeth Kolbert (b. 1961)
Publisher: Crown (New York). 256 pp.
Type of work: Natural history, nature, environment, science
Time: Largely the early twenty-first century
Locales: United States, Australia, Iceland, Greenland, and Switzerland

Under a White Sky: The Nature of the Future *is the follow-up to Elizabeth Kolbert's Pulitzer Prize–winning book* The Sixth Extinction, *in which she wrote that human beings are living through a mass extinction event. In* Under a White Sky, *she assesses the damage humans have wrought and offers a grim prescription.*

Principal personages
RUTH GATES, a marine biologist and a foremost coral expert, the director of the Hawai'i Institute of Marine Biology
MADELEINE VAN OPPEN, an ecological geneticist breeding hardier coral
MARK TIZARD, a biochemist who hopes to reduce invasive species through genetic editing
KLAUS LACKNER, the physicist often credited with pioneering "negative carbon emissions"
FRANK KEUTSCH, a lead scientist for Harvard University's Solar Geoengineering Research Program
DAVID KEITH, an applied physics professor at Harvard who spearheaded the development of its Solar Geoengineering Research Program

Elizabeth Kolbert's book *Under a White Sky: The Nature of the Future* (2021) further explores ideas introduced in her 2014 book *The Sixth Extinction*, which won the Pulitzer Prize in 2015. In that book, Kolbert writes that human beings are living through a period of mass extinction; in *Under a White Sky*, she assesses how humans are grappling with it. Some chapters of the book were first published in the *New Yorker*, where she is a member of the magazine's staff. Like her colleague John McPhee, a veteran author and 1999 Pulitzer Prize winner, Kolbert writes about science and nature in clear, evocative prose any reader can understand—a blessing given the urgency of what she is saying. In *Under a White Sky*, she offers a simple thesis to illustrate a frustratingly complex concern. When humans set out to solve an ecological problem, she writes, they all too frequently end up creating new ones.

By way of example, Kolbert cites the conundrum of the Asian carp. In the 1960s, scientists brought the fish to the United States, theorizing that it would eat the aquatic weeds clogging American waterways. It seemed like a good idea at the time and, in fact, was inspired by the idea of using biological controls proposed by Rachel Carson, a pioneering environmentalist and the author of the groundbreaking 1962 book *Silent Spring*. The fish were seen as a biological solution, as Carson termed it, as opposed to a polluting, chemical one. However, the introduction of the carp turned out to be its own disaster—made worse by the fact that, decades earlier, engineers had reversed the flow of Chicago's wastewater. As predicted, the carp ate the weeds, but they also ate everything else, upending the fragile balance of the various environments into which they were introduced. By the early 2000s, the carp problem had become so dire that the Army Corps of Engineers was forced to address it on a massive scale, erecting electrified underwater barriers that would keep the carp from continuing to spread. Kolbert quotes Carson, whom, she notes, almost titled *Silent Spring* "The Control of Nature." Carson wrote that "control of nature" was "a phrase conceived in arrogance" and born of the philosophy "that nature exists for the convenience of man." Carson saw chemicals and pesticides as humans' most perverse instrument of control, but Kolbert shows that even "biological solutions," like Asian carp, can have catastrophic consequences. Kolbert also argues, powerfully, that humans have no other choice but to keep seeking them out: "If there is to be an answer to the problem of control," she writes, "it's going to be more control."

Elizabeth Kolbert

The book provides an audacious assessment presented in plain terms. Kolbert's "narrative voice is steady and restrained—the better, it sometimes seems, to allow an unadorned reality to show through, its contours unimpeded by frantic alarmism or baroque turns of phrase," Jennifer Szalai wrote in her review of *Under a White Sky* for the *New York Times*. Kolbert offers a sobering picture of humans' plight through stories about Asian carp, cane toads, and the Devils Hole pupfish. In the case of the Devils Hole pupfish, one of the rarest fish species in the world, Kolbert chronicles the elaborate measures scientists are taking to encourage them to breed. "I was struck, and not for the first time," she writes, "by how much easier it is to ruin an ecosystem than to run one." Humans know so little about ecosystems, even one as small as Devils Hole, but again, Kolbert argues, humans must assume the risk of meddling in them. Kolbert writes about Ruth Gates, a famous coral scientist who died in 2018. Gates was a proponent of breeding coral to be more resistant to changing temperatures and other stresses; she called it "assisted evolution." "A lot of people want to go back to something," Gates told Kolbert when they met. "They think, if we just stop doing things, maybe the reef will come back to what it was." But this is simply not the case. Gates argued that people need to get used to the idea of a future "where nature is no longer fully natural" in the rosy sense that most people understand it.

While Gates, and ecological geneticist Madeleine van Oppen, hoped to help species survive, Mark Tizard, a biochemist, wants to help reduce some species' numbers. Tizard is working to alter bits of an invasive species' DNA—in this case, cane toads—to reduce the population to a manageable size. Cane toads are toxic, and unlike carp, they are far more deadly as prey. Tizard is overseeing attempts to tinker with the production of the enzyme that increases the toxin's potency. He understands that the idea might make people queasy. Tizard does not see himself as "playing God," as some people suggest; he says he uses available tools to "benefit a system that is in trauma." But as Kolbert writes, genetic editing invites all kinds of unforeseen consequences. The line from the 1993 film *Jurassic Park*—"Life finds a way"—comes to mind, but Kolbert chooses a different reference. She instead discusses the comparison of gene editing to ice-nine, the fictional deadly substance engineered by scientists in Kurt Vonnegut's 1963 novel *Cat's Cradle*; the tiniest sliver of ice-nine could freeze every drop of water worldwide. Comparisons to science fiction are apt. Echoing Gates, Kolbert writes that people must not think of returning to an ideal nature, but of creating a new, livable one—but what this future might look like raises its own troubling questions. Among them, do people have a right to decide which species will live and which will die? Kolbert argues that given the cumulative effects of humanmade climate change, refusing to answer this question provides its own answer. She quotes Stewart Brand, editor of the serial publication *Whole Earth Catalog*, who wrote in 1968, "We are as gods and might as well get good at it," while noting that he has become more pointed, saying, "We are as gods and *have to* get good at it."

Few of the ideas presented in the book evoke the power of gods more viscerally than changing the color of the sky. The title of Kolbert's book comes from a possible consequence of solar geoengineering, a concept she explores in the last quarter of the book. Reducing carbon emissions alone, Kolbert writes, will not save Earth from climate catastrophe; thus, it is necessary for people to explore "negative carbon emissions," pioneered by physicist Klaus Lackner. Some new companies, like Climeworks, whose main plant is in Iceland, are exploring ways to suck carbon out of the air and bury it underground where it is turned to stone. Others espouse ideas that would impress Vonnegut in their intriguing absurdity. Inspired by volcanoes, which blast sulfur dioxide that then becomes sulfuric acid, into the stratosphere, other scientists are exploring a concept called "solar geoengineering." This concept could entail shooting reflective particles into the sky in the interest of reducing the amount of energy that reaches Earth and, theoretically, the heat it captures. One leading researcher in that field is Frank Keutsch. The best possible material for such an endeavor, Keutsch told Kolbert, is diamond. The idea of shooting billions of tiny diamonds into the sky, Kolbert writes, "struck me as magical, like sprinkling the world with pixie dust." The observation captures the futility the gesture implies. As Kolbert notes, solar geoengineering treats one symptom of climate change, not its cause, and runs the risk of making people dependent on a stopgap measure. She details that it has been compared to treating a heroin addiction with methadone: "two addictions in place of one." Of course, as with everything else, solar geoengineering also offers a Pandora's box of consequences. One small but unsettling outcome is that the particles would likely turn the sky white.

Reviewers have praised Kolbert's book, even as they have lamented its contents. In a starred review for *Publishers Weekly*, one reviewer called *Under a White Sky* "brilliantly executed and urgently necessary." Carlos Lozada, writing for the *Washington Post*, described Kolbert as "a writer confident enough to acknowledge ambiguity," a wise observation, but one that does not quite capture the profound ambiguity of the unknown future humans have created for themselves. In her *Times* review, Szalai notes that Kolbert is a rare science writer who communicates the breadth of the climate crisis in terms both concrete and existential. In a review for the *Guardian*, Ben Ehrenreich observed that Kolbert mostly ignores the world power structure's explicit interest in keeping things as they are, even at their own expense, and lamented that in response to so profound a crisis, Kolbert "can imagine only additional technological fixes. The possibility of social change has been excluded from the start."

Author Biography

Elizabeth Kolbert is the author of *Field Notes from a Catastrophe: Man, Nature, and Climate Change* (2006) and the Pulitzer Prize–winning *The Sixth Extinction* (2014). She became a staff writer at the *New Yorker* in 2009.

Molly Hagan

Review Sources

Ehrenreich, Ben. "*Under a White Sky* by Elizabeth Kolbert Review—the Path to Catastrophe." *The Guardian*, 26 Mar. 2021, www.theguardian.com/books/2021/mar/26/under-a-white-sky-by-elizabeth-kolbert-review-the-path-to-catastrophe. Accessed 13 Nov. 2021.

Lozada, Carlos. "Why Humanity Can't Be Trusted to Repair Its Own Environmental Damage." Review of *Under a White Sky: The Nature of the Future*, by Elizabeth Kolbert. *The Washington Post*, 11 Feb. 2021, www.washingtonpost.com/outlook/2021/02/11/kolbert-white-sky/. Accessed 13 Nov. 2021.

Szalai, Jennifer. "Electrified Rivers and Other Attempts to Save the Environment." Review of *Under a White Sky: The Nature of the Future*, by Elizabeth Kolbert. *The New York Times*, 10 Feb. 2021, www.nytimes.com/2021/02/10/books/review-under-white-sky-elizabeth-kolbert.html. Accessed 13 Nov. 2021.

Review of *Under a White Sky: The Nature of the Future*, by Elizabeth Kolbert. *Kirkus*, 22 Dec. 2020, www.kirkusreviews.com/book-reviews/elizabeth-kolbert/under-a-white-sky/. Accessed 13 Nov. 2021.

Review of *Under a White Sky: The Nature of the Future*, by Elizabeth Kolbert. *Publishers Weekly*, 30 Nov. 2020, www.publishersweekly.com/978-0-593-13627-0. Accessed 13 Nov. 2021.

Velvet Was the Night

Author: Silvia Moreno-Garcia (b. 1981)
Publisher: Del Rey (New York). 304 pp.
Type of work: Novel
Time: 1970s
Locale: Mexico City, Mexico

Velvet Was the Night, a tense neo-noir set in 1970s Mexico City during a period of violent political turbulence, follows an unhappy secretary and a low-level government enforcer as they stumble across dangerous secrets while searching for a missing woman.

Principal characters

MAITE JARAMILLO, a lonely legal secretary
LEONORA TREJO, her neighbor, an art student and leftist activist
RUBÉN, her neighbor's ex-boyfriend, a member of her underground artist collective
ELVIS, a member of a right-wing paramilitary group
EL MAGO, the leader of the paramilitary group to which Elvis belongs

Silvia Moreno-Garcia is a Mexican Canadian author best known for her fantasy and supernatural horror fiction. After the success of *Mexican Gothic* (2020), a surreal gothic melodrama about a Mexican socialite who visits the mansion of a mysterious family, audiences largely expected her follow-up novel to be in a similar vein of gothic horror. However, with *Velvet Was the Night* (2021), Moreno-Garcia demonstrates her versatility by writing a historical noir thriller with no fantasy elements.

Yet despite this genre shift, *Velvet Was the Night* is a fitting successor to the author's previous best seller, as both novels take genres with their roots in Europe and the United States and put a distinctly Mexican spin on them, seamlessly integrating the history and culture of that setting into genres not typically associated with Mexican literature. Because *Velvet Was the Night* is a work of noir, Moreno-Garcia incorporates some of the genre's standard tropes—morally ambiguous characters, dark settings, and political corruption—with some unique twists. Moreno-Garcia also redefines the role of women in noir; instead of relying on the genre's traditionally limited and often sexist roles for female characters, the author places fully developed female characters at the heart of her narrative.

The novel takes place in Mexico City in the 1970s, at a time of political turmoil in Mexico known as the Dirty War. An outgrowth of the Cold War, the decades-long standoff between the United States and the Soviet Union, the Dirty War saw the Mexican government capturing, torturing, and killing leftist activists, many of whom were university students. The government also shut down venues where these activists gathered, particularly "singing cafes" where pop and rock music were performed; ironically, the government regarded popular music with the same suspicion harbored by the Communist governments they opposed. The United States helped to fund the Mexican government's actions, hoping to prevent communism from gaining a foothold in the country. The Soviet Union intervened as well, attempting to advance their own pro-Communist agenda but not always benefitting the protesters and activists they claimed to support.

The novel begins on June 10, 1971, the day of the Corpus Christi massacre, a real-life event in which the Mexican government retaliated violently against a mass student protest in Mexico City, killing almost one hundred-twenty protesters. The massacre is also known as *El Halconazo*, the Hawk strike, due to the involvement of a government-backed paramilitary group known as *Los Halcones*, or the Hawks. Elvis, the first of the book's protagonists to be introduced, is a young member of this group. His responsibilities include infiltrating student groups and beating up journalists. He hates violence and would much prefer to explore the worlds of music and film and teach himself a new word every day out of an illustrated dictionary. Elvis resents his assignments; he considers them pointless and does not view other people's political loyalties as a "big deal." However, despite his lack of political commitment, Elvis struggles to find a way out of this life. After growing up in poverty and then failing out of high school due to an undiagnosed learning disorder, Elvis doubts he has any options outside of working for the Hawks.

Meanwhile, Maite, a thirty-year-old legal secretary, keeps her head down and tries to avoid any involvement in the unrest boiling all around her. She prefers to focus on her pet parakeet, her extensive record collection, and her favorite comic book, *Secret Romance*. She lives for "love, frail as gossamer, stitched together from a thousand songs and a thousand comic books." Like Elvis, Maite is dissatisfied with her life, though her complaints are far more ordinary—an underpaid job, a nagging mother, a lack of romantic success. She has only one friend: her coworker Diana, to whom she lies about her weekend activities, inventing imaginary dates.

When Maite's next-door neighbor, the glamorous art student Leonora, asks her to watch her cat, Maite agrees without a second thought. She frequently takes on cat sitting and other menial jobs for her neighbors, since she is always home and believes that she knows what to expect: a few days of easy work and a little extra money to supplement her lackluster income. But Leonora's scheduled return date comes and goes, and Leonora does not appear to retrieve her pet.

Silvia Moreno-Garcia

More out of annoyance at being stiffed on her pet-sitting fee than concern for her neighbor, Maite begins trying to find out where Leonora has gone. She soon enlists the help of the missing woman's charming ex-boyfriend, Rubén, and begins to uncover hidden parts of Leonora's life. As it turns out, Leonora has been involved with the student activists, and Maite finds herself drawn into Mexico's political underground as her search for Leonora widens. Maite finds this search for Leonora adds some much-needed excitement to her life—suddenly she finds herself the heroine of the kind of darkly romantic story that she could previously experience only through her comics. However, just as Maite begins to experience real excitement, she also comes closer to very real danger.

Elvis's boss, the charismatic El Mago—the leader of the Hawks, whom Elvis describes as "a dark god"—also seeks Leonora. He believes she has some incriminating photographs and is willing to go to extremes to prevent these photos from falling into the wrong hands. El Mago assigns Elvis to the task, and the novel alternates between Elvis and Maite's points of view as they circle each other, catching glimpses but not quite meeting, in their respective searches for Leonora. The pursuit brings them into contact with a varied cast of characters, from secret police and Soviet agents to dissident artists and student activists, who all have a part to play in Mexico's sprawling political drama.

The plot is complex and winding without ever becoming confusing, despite the large number of moving pieces—a government conspiracy, the involvement of Russian and American spies in Mexico's domestic affairs, the interpersonal dramas of Leonora's group of artist-activists, and more. While the novel begins at a slower pace, once the plot takes off, the simmering tension never lets up. Moreno-Garcia also manages to weave in exposition about a turbulent period of Mexican history without resorting to a dry, textbook-like recitation of facts or disrupting the narrative flow.

While the plot is deftly constructed, the true strength of the novel is the characterization of Elvis and Maite, both flawed people living unhappy lives and searching for escape through art. Maite's pettiness and refusal to engage with the political situation, which she considers "terribly dull," makes her, at times, an unsympathetic character. Maite can also be quite selfish and unempathetic, evident from her treatment of Leonora's dangerous situation as merely an exciting adventure for herself. Elvis's willingness to commit violence against innocent people for a cause in which he does not even believe also gives him antiheroic qualities. But despite these considerable negative traits, Elvis and Maite become sympathetic through their palpable loneliness and yearning to break out of their narrow existences and find deeper meaning and happiness. As both navigate around the mystery of Leonora's disappearance, their affinity for each other becomes clear and propels them toward an actual meeting. The anticipation of this long-awaited meeting complements the mysteries of the plot, adds tension, and helps bring everything to a stunning conclusion.

Music plays a noticeable role in *Velvet Was the Night*, whose title comes from the 1950 pop ballad "Blue Velvet". The singing cafes frequented by Leonora and her fellow students serve as hotbeds of activism; the government recognizes the political and cultural influences of these cafes and moves to shut them down, highlighting the important role music can play in inspiring revolutionary change. Maite and Elvis, both devout music fans, use it as a form of escape from the dreariness and violence that surrounds them. In the end notes, the author even provides a Spotify playlist of songs mentioned in the novel.

Upon its publication in 2021, critics gave *Velvet Was the Night* near-universal praise. A reviewer for *Kirkus* described it as a "noir masterpiece," with "memorable characters, taut pacing, an intricate plot, and antiheroes you can't help but root for." In a starred review for *Publishers Weekly*, a reviewer agreed with this praise for the novel's "distinctive characters." While the reviewer noted Moreno-Garcia's use of "seductive" neo-noir elements, the reviewer also complimented the novel's "pleasing touch of romance."

Much of the critical praise focused on Moreno-Garcia's ability to cultivate emotional investment in her characters, despite their antiheroic qualities. Writing for *Slate*, Laura Miller called the characters "fascinating creations, bristling with contradictory but convincing traits," She also praised the plot's noir elements, praising their ability to "satisfy familiar cravings without resorting to mere pastiche." In a review for National Public Radio, Gabino Iglesias called Maite and Elvis "unique, flawed, and sad in a way that burrows into your heart." He also lauded Moreno-Garcia's ability to create "a complicated plot that's easy to read" and noted that even readers completely unfamiliar with the Mexican historical context would "be able to keep up."

Iglesias joined many other reviewers in expressing appreciation for Moreno-Garcia's versatility and ability to bring fresh elements to familiar genres. He compared Moreno-Garcia's writing to "a wild pendulum that swings from horror to fantasy to noir" and felt her work succeeded despite its range of genres. Elizabeth Hand wrote in the *Washington Post*, "Moreno-Garcia always leaves her own indelible stamp on any seemingly familiar genre."

Velvet Was the Night succeeds as a thrilling, page-turning work of noir full of twists and turns. However, it also adds a level of complexity through its reckoning with a dark period in Mexico's history, refusing to shy away from exploring how powerful countries on both sides of the Cold War meddled in Mexico's domestic conflict for their own gain. At the heart of the story are two complex, profoundly human characters who are endearing despite their flaws. For all these reasons and more, *Velvet Was the Night* is a noteworthy modern entry into the noir canon.

Author Biography

Silvia Moreno-Garcia is the best-selling author of *Mexican Gothic* (2020), *Gods of Jade and Shadow* (2020), and many other works. She also served as editor of the World Fantasy Award–winning horror anthology *She Walks in Shadows* (2015).

Emma Joyce

Review Sources

Hand, Elizabeth. "Silvia Moreno-Garcia's *Velvet Was the Night* Is a Noir-Thriller as Captivating as Its Title." *The Washington Post*, 17 Aug. 2021, www.washingtonpost.com/entertainment/books/silvia-moreno-garcias-velvet-was-the-night-is-a-noir-thriller-as-captivating-as-its-title/2021/08/14/e5280e10-fa46-11eb-943a-c5cf30d50e6a_story.html. Accessed 7 Dec. 2021.

Iglesias, Gabino. "This Noir Adventure Shows Silvia Moreno-Garcia Can Do It All, with Style to Spare." Review of *Velvet Was the Night*, by Silvia Moreno-Garcia. *National Public Radio*, 20 Aug. 2021, www.npr.org/2021/08/20/1029522252/this-noir-adventure-shows-silvia-moreno-garcia-can-do-it-all-with-style-to-spare. Accessed 7 Dec. 2021.

Miller, Laura. "Mexican Noir." Review of *Velvet Was the Night*, by Silvia Moreno-Garcia. *Slate*, 17 Aug. 2021, slate.com/culture/2021/08/velvet-was-the-night-review-silvia-moreno-garcia.html. Accessed 7 Dec. 2021.

Review of *Velvet Was the Night*, by Silvia Moreno-Garcia. *Kirkus Reviews*, 16 June 2021, www.kirkusreviews.com/book-reviews/silvia-moreno-garcia/velvet-was-the-night. Accessed 7 Dec. 2021.

Review of *Velvet Was the Night*, by Silvia Moreno-Garcia. *Publishers Weekly*, 1 June 2021, www.publishersweekly.com/978-0-593-35682-1. Accessed 7 Dec. 2021.

Wake
The Hidden History of Women-Led Slave Revolts

Author: Rebecca Hall (b. 1963)
Illustrator: Hugo Martínez
Publisher: Simon & Schuster (New York). 208 pp.
Type of work: Graphic nonfiction
Time: 1999–2002; 1712; 1708; 1769–70
Locales: New York City; Santa Cruz, California; England; West Africa; Atlantic Ocean

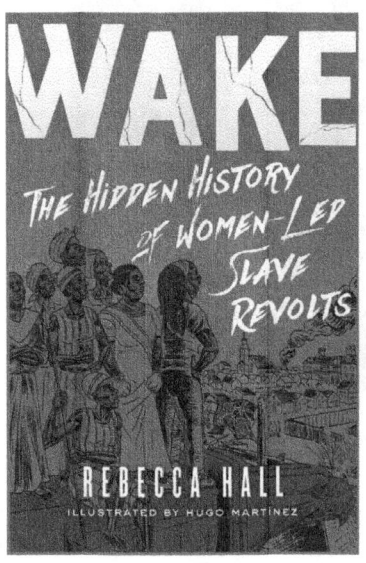

Wake: The Hidden History of Women-Led Slave Revolts gives life to historian Rebecca Hall's extensive, thorough research about resistance in the era of chattel slavery, exploring the experiences of enslaved women in eighteenth-century New York and African women who revolted on transatlantic slaving ships. Unusually, Wake also depicts Hall's efforts to uncover these stories, digging, often fruitlessly, through archives in New York City, London, and Liverpool.

Principal personages

REBECCA HALL, the author, a lawyer and historian
BEA, her partner and co-parent
SARAH OR ABIGAIL, one of her research subjects, a pregnant woman involved in a 1712 slave revolt in New York City
THE NEGRO FIEND, another of her research subjects, an unnamed enslaved woman who led a 1708 revolt in Newtown, New York

Rebecca Hall began her career as a tenant's rights lawyer, but after eight years, she had grown frustrated by the legal system, shaped as it is by centuries of racism and sexism. She quit her practice, hoping to gain a deeper understanding of the law through academic study. In the late 1990s, Hall returned to school, earning a PhD in history, with a focus on the emergence of chattel slavery in the British North American colonies. The dominant history has long preferred to remember this period as both inevitable and isolated: enslaved people submitted to the plantation system until it was ended by an act of law. Through painstaking research, Hall unearths a different story—set not merely in the South but in the cities of the North and Europe and shaped by countless uprisings and other acts of resistance—that continues to the present day. Her book *Wake: The Hidden History of Women-Led Slave Revolts* (2021), a work of graphic nonfiction illustrated by Hugo Martínez, tells this multifaceted, multigenerational tale

Rebecca Hall
Courtesy Cat Palmer

with true grace. It compellingly captures Hall's quest to uncover the stories of enslaved women who resisted bondage, driven by her own experiences with racism, the separation from her partner and son that her research requires, and memories of her paternal grandparents, who were both enslaved.

Etelka Lehoczky, who reviewed *Wake* for National Public Radio (NPR), notes that the book is unique for its depiction of the act of historical research. Clean historical narratives, she wrote, are easy to draw. "What's hard is illustrating the historical process: squinting one's way through sheaves of correspondence, scanning documents for any mention of a key name, and simply thinking a lot," she wrote. Illustrator Martínez finds countless ways to depict both the excitement of discovery and the anguish of being thwarted by a dead end. As Hall writes, her work is all the more difficult because it requires her to read "against the grain," meaning that she must scour crumbling documents for omissions, cobbling together stories from those details that have been omitted from the historical record. "This is one way history erases us," Hall writes. "You think you are reading an accurate chronicle written at the time, but if who we are and what we care about are deemed irrelevant, it won't be in there." Martínez captures the intangible practice of reading against the grain as well, drawing Hall amid a sea of other researchers as a negative space. Martínez's black-and-white drawings lend urgency to the voices of the past, manifesting an observation Hall makes at the beginning of the book. "Sometimes when you think you're hunting down the past," she writes, "the past is hunting you." The people Hall is trying to reach are constantly lurking in Martínez's haunting illustrations. The puddles on a New York City street, beneath buildings constructed by the hands of the enslaved, and skyscrapers built by the wealth amassed through their labor, offer a window to another city, where men walk in chains and women fetch water from the neighborhood well for their enslavers. Through these drawings, Hall's frustration is made clear: the stories she seeks are everywhere and nowhere.

Early in her research, Hall uncovers the story of a slave revolt in New York City in 1712. Historians often portray enslaved women as submissive and incapable of acting on their own, but tantalizing clues from the 1712 uprising challenge this narrative. Among the twenty-seven people tried for the revolt, at least four were women. Two were acquitted, while the others were found guilty. Either Sarah or Abigail was pregnant, and because her child was considered the property of her enslaver—and in a larger sense, the property of the state—she was not executed immediately but incarcerated. As Hall explains, this was very unusual at the time. In the early eighteenth century, jails held prisoners for a few days before they received their punishment; Sarah or Abigail might well have been among the first people, if only due to oversight, to endure years-long imprisonment as a punishment in and of itself.

Drawing on information gleaned from other historical accounts, Hall imagines how these women might have come together to plan and execute a revolt. Her tale is a radical act of invention intended to counteract the erasure of these women's stories, and though the details may not reflect the reality of those particular women, it reveals the essential truth of their humanity: they once lived in slavery and resisted it.

In an effort to uncover the story behind an earlier eighteenth-century revolt—planned and carried out by a woman referred to in official documents as the "Negro fiend"—Hall journeys to London, England, where she stumbles on a larger story. Archives in London and Liverpool offer a wealth of information about uprisings on slave ships ferrying captives from West Africa to North America. In the 1990s, Hall explains, historians pooled their data about the Middle Passage, and made several surprising discoveries. Analyzing over thirty-six thousand crossings, researchers found that one out of every ten ships experienced a slave revolt and most notably, "the more women onboard a slave ship, the more likely a revolt," Hall notes. Hall offers a few explanations for why this was so. While men were held in chains below deck, women and children were commonly unchained among the crew upon reaching open water. This arrangement made them vulnerable to sexual abuse, but it also provided opportunities to access the ship's weapons, which were also commonly kept above deck. Still, some historians questioned the results of the study, arguing that women rarely appeared in historical narratives of revolts. Hall finds this reasoning circular. Enslaved women were not included in the historical record because they were believed to lack the agency to revolt, she argues, and now historians argue that enslaved women lacked agency because they do not appear in the historical record.

In an effort to explore what a women-led revolt on a slave ship might have looked like, Hall—and the impressively versatile Martínez—take the reader back to two precolonial kingdoms of West Africa. Hall uses information about one particular voyage, aboard a ship called the *Unity* in 1770, and imagines, with compelling evidence, that some of the women aboard are Ahogi, elite female soldiers of the West African kingdom of Dahomey. Her imagined reconstruction about a couple of ill-fated Ahogi warriors evokes a rich lore about African captives who chose to die in the Atlantic, rather than face the horrors of slavery. "Sound waves travel so slowly in water and the ocean is so vast, the sound can last centuries underwater," she writes of the voices of the Ahogi. "Maybe, if we listen carefully, we can hear them."

In telling the story of the Ahogi, Hall also illuminates the complexities of African participation in the transatlantic slave trade. African kingdoms, like many societies, enslaved captives of war. Europeans, trading guns for humans, exploited this practice to erect a massive international system of chattel slavery. Chattel slavery, distinct from slavery as it had been practiced before, was inherited and based entirely on race. It was also, Hall emphasizes, enormously lucrative, building fortunes and companies that continue to thrive.

Hall visits Lloyd's of London, an insurance company that made its wealth insuring slave ships, in hopes of seeing the company's archives. She meets with resistance when it becomes clear she hopes to understand the company's role in the slave trade. It is one of a few scenes in the book in which Hall's research provokes anger. In other scenes, Hall herself is met with racist suspicion. A security guard trails her through the Victoria Tower in London. "Wow, here too?" her avatar mutters. These moments are integral to Hall's larger point about power. Like Sarah or Abigail, power—personified in many of Hall's historical documents as Dom Regina, an all-encompassing term for the state—is both everywhere and nowhere. Hall references Michel-Rolph Trouillot, a Haitian anthropologist and historian who wrote the book *Silencing the Past: Power and the Production of History* (1995). Trouillot was a pioneer of the theories Hall explores in her book: who gets to be a part of history, and who is erased. Flying home to California from New York after having met another dead end, Hall quotes Trouillot: "The ultimate mark of power may be its invisibility; the ultimate challenge, the exposition of its roots."

Wake received starred reviews from major publications including *Publishers Weekly*, *Library Journal*, and *Kirkus*. The *Kirkus* reviewer used the word "excavation" to describe Hall's purpose, but Hall employs a different word, connoting an inward action instead of an outward one. In an early scene in the book, Hall imagines enslaved people gathering to mourn the death of a friend. Several women take turns remembering her before lowering her coffin into the earth. The very title of the book echoes this ritual remembrance before a burial, and Hall returns to this image in the book's last pages, in an effort to explain what she calls "the final stage of healing from trauma." At a wake, people speak about the dead so that they might better remember them. Likewise, Hall writes: "The past is not a ghost we want to banish or exorcise. It is something we want to internalize."

Author Biography

A former lawyer, Rebecca Hall is an educator, activist, and historian. She was a 2020–21 scholar in residence at the New York Public Library's Schomburg Center for Research in Black Culture. *Wake*, her first book, is based on her dissertation, "Not Killing Me Softly: African American Women, Slave Revolts, and Historical Constructions of Racialized Gender."

Hugo Martínez is an illustrator and graphic designer. *Wake* is his first graphic book.

Molly Hagan

Review Sources

Cornog, Martha. Review of *Wake: The Hidden History of Women-Led Slave Revolts*, by Rebecca Hall and Hugo Martínez. *Library Journal*, 21 May 2021, www.libraryjournal.com/?reviewDetail=wake-the-hidden-history-of-womenled-slave-revolts-1782855. Accessed 1 Oct. 2021.

Lehoczky, Etelka. "A Stunning Graphic Novel Uncovers the History of Enslaved Women Who Fought Back." Review of *Wake: The Hidden History of Women-Led Slave Revolts*, by Rebecca Hall and Hugo Martínez. *NPR*, 30 May 2021, www.npr.org/2021/05/30/1001430516/a-stunning-graphic-novel-uncovers-the-history-of-enslaved-women-who-fought-back. Accessed 16 Sept. 2021.

McNatt, Rosemary Bray. "*Wake* Review—a Must-Read Graphic History of Women-Led Slave Revolts." *The Guardian*, 31 July 2021, www.theguardian.com/books/2021/jul/31/wake-review-hidden-history-of-women-led-slave-revolts-rebecca-hall-hugo-martinez. Accessed 16 Sept. 2021.

McShane, Julianne. "New Graphic Novel Reveals Black Women's Hidden Role in Slave Revolts." Review of *Wake: The Hidden History of Women-Led Slave Revolts*, by Rebecca Hall and Hugo Martínez. *NBCBLK*, NBC Universal, 3 Aug. 2021, www.nbcnews.com/news/nbcblk/new-graphic-novel-reveals-black-womens-hidden-role-slave-revolts-rcna1573. Accessed 16 Sept. 2021.

Review of *Wake: The Hidden History of Women-Led Slave Revolts*, by Rebecca Hall and Hugo Martínez. *Kirkus Reviews*, vol. 89, no. 9, May 2021. *Literary Reference Center Plus*, search.ebscohost.com/login.aspx?direct=true&db=lkh&AN=150019975&site=lrc-plus. Accessed 16 Sept. 2021.

Review of *Wake: The Hidden History of Women-Led Slave Revolts*, by Rebecca Hall and Hugo Martínez. *Publishers Weekly*, vol. 268, no. 19, May 2021, pp. 54–55. *Literary Reference Center Plus*, search.ebscohost.com/login.aspx?direct=true&db=lkh&AN=150199394&site=lrc-plus. Accessed 16 Sept. 2021.

We Begin at the End

Author: Chris Whitaker
Publisher: Henry Holt (New York). 384 pp.
Type of work: Novel
Time: 1975; 2005
Locales: Cape Haven, California; Montana

We Begin at the End *takes place in a small town devastated by the tragic death of seven-year-old Sissy Radley. Thirty years later, the boy held responsible for her death is released from prison, setting off a new chain of violent events.*

Principal characters

DUCHESS DAY RADLEY, a thirteen-year-old girl who considers herself an "outlaw"
CHIEF "WALK" WALKER, the local police chief
STAR RADLEY, Duchess's mother
VINCENT KING, Star's former lover, a convicted criminal
MARTHA MAY, Walk's former girlfriend, a lawyer
ROBIN, Duchess's six-year-old brother
RICHARD "DICKIE" DARKE, a local businessman

We Begin at the End (2021) is British writer Chris Whitaker's third adult crime novel. Beginning with his first novel, *Tall Oaks* (2016), which won the Crime Writers' Association John Creasey New Blood Dagger Award, Whitaker established a reputation as an important new voice in crime fiction. In *We Begin at the End*, Whitaker crafts another dark, suspense-laden mystery set in the United States, but expands his range to incorporate a moving coming-of-age story into the narrative.

This novel begins with a brief prologue taking place in the small town of Cape Haven, California, thirty years before the main story. The prologue depicts the childhoods of eventual police chief Walker, known as Walk, and his three best friends, and also provides background information on the death of seven-year-old Sissy Radley, for which Walk's friend Vincent King is blamed and sent to prison. The next ten chapters are organized into "Part One: The Outlaw," and jump ahead in time. Walk is now chief of police, Vincent is about to be released from prison, and Sissy Radley's older sister Star is struggling with drug abuse and alcoholism. Star loves her two children, thirteen-year-old Duchess and five-year-old Robin, but is incapable of properly caring for them. As a result, Duchess has become the adult in the family, taking on the care of not only her younger brother but also her mother.

Further tragedy strikes the family when Star is murdered, forcing Duchess and Robin to move to Montana to live with their grandfather. The sixteen chapters focusing on this event, organized into "Part Two: Big Sky," are tragic, yet still offer a sense of hope for the children, as well as for Walk himself. They also highlight the separate lines of investigation Walk and Duchess follow to try and solve Star's murder.

In "Part Three: Restitution," which contains another sixteen chapters, Walk continues to search for Star's killer. He also defends Vincent, who punishes himself for his youthful transgressions that led to his imprisonment but is trying to prove his innocence in Star's death. Meanwhile, in the wake of her mother's death, Duchess struggles to understand her place in life. She is too old to settle into foster care, and her rebellious behavior complicates things as a social worker tries to find a new home where she and Robin can stay together. The novel ends with "Part Four: Heartbreaker." In this four-chapter portion, Walk's and Duchess's lives completely diverge as they learn to hold on to the parts of their past that keep them sane while letting go of those pieces that tear them apart, all while closing in on the truth behind the mystery of Star's death.

Chris Whitaker

The title of the novel indicates one of the most striking thematic elements, and touches on the theme of reinventing one's self and starting over. Hal Radley, Star's father and Duchess's grandfather, tells Walk about a sermon he heard about the idea of starting over when one thing ends. The pastor's message hints of an eternity in heaven, but Hal had a hard time grasping this after the death of his child, Stella, and the subsequent suicide of his wife. Later, Hal repeats this mantra to Duchess, who struggles to understand the reality of a grandfather who had abandoned his living daughter, Star, due to his all-consuming sadness of losing his other daughter. Duchess only begins to comprehend Hal's responses later in the novel, when she learns secrets from his past that explain his need for a fresh start. For Vincent, the end of his prison sentence offers him a chance at a new life, but in an ironic twist, he is thrown back into jail, once again leaving him searching for freedom. Vincent, like the novel's other characters, spends the novel trying to move beyond the sins and trauma of his past, and in a new direction of hope and healing.

Friendship, and the selflessness it often requires, is another significant theme in the novel. Walk's childhood friendship with Vincent has been a motivating factor for most of his life. The teenage friend group of Walk, Vincent, Star, and Martha May, who was in a romantic relationship with Walk, provided a base for all four young people. This leads Walk to frequently act in ways he thinks are best for his friends, even when it requires him to sacrifice what he wants. As a teen, he let Martha May leave shortly after her father forced her to have an abortion. As an adult, he continues to demonstrate this selfless streak; he takes care of Star and her children and puts his career on the line to fight for Vincent's freedom. As the plot unfolds, Vincent tries to repay Walk for his loyalty, and Martha May becomes a central part of his life again.

Star's children also struggle to navigate their friendships and other relationships. Five-year-old Robin is lovable, but the parents of his friends do not trust their children in Star's care, so his social life is limited while in Cape Haven. Too busy taking care of her mother and her brother, the prickly and defensive Duchess also has no friends until she moves to Montana to live with her grandfather. While there, a local boy, Thomas Noble, pursues a friendship with her, the first time a peer has ever reached out to her. Though Duchess tries to hold onto the cold exterior she has always shown to the world, Thomas manages to connect with her, and Duchess learns that not all people her age are the same.

The theme of family, particularly the "families" people choose for themselves, is an important aspect of the novel. Walk's friendship with Vincent is more like a brotherhood, and he also becomes a surrogate father to Star's children. Star loves her children, but the past has traumatized her to a point where she is unable to be an effective parent. This requires Duchess to be her family's caretaker, despite the fact that she is too young to carry that responsibility. Meanwhile, Robin is torn between the love he has for his mother, the security he has with his sister, and the desire to be part of a more stable and conventional family. When Star is killed and Duchess and Robin are sent to live with Hal, Robin settles in easily, eager for the love his grandfather is willing to share, but Duchess struggles to accept the man she sees as central to Star's downfall. As she is forced to reckon with her own choices alongside the choices of others, Duchess learns that family comes not only from blood, but also from those she chooses to love.

Whitaker intertwines a variety of side issues to add to the story's impact. For instance, the pitfalls of the foster care system are examined through the lives of Duchess and Robin, who endure abusive and selfish foster families during their time in the system. They also encounter a lack of sympathy from employees of the foster care system, who find Duchess difficult to deal with due to her understandably rebellious attitude. While Duchess and Robin suffer bullying from their foster siblings, this is hardly the only time the novel touches on this theme. The children have been the victims of bullying their entire lives because of their poverty and their mother's behaviors. Due to a birth defect affecting his arm, Thomas also endures bullying from the other children. As an "outlaw," Duchess takes it on herself to protect Thomas, transforming herself from a victim into a resilient survivor. In another example of how the novel deals with the complexities of social perceptions, Duchess and many of the townspeople believe Walk is an alcoholic, but he is actually dealing with the effects of Parkinson's Disease. Society's lack of understanding or compassion for people with chronic illnesses and disabilities is a unique aspect of the book and heightens the struggles many characters must face.

Though the novel is largely character-driven, with the emotional bildungsroman of Duchess and Walk's reckoning with his past placed at the center of the story, the mystery element is essential for carrying the plot and building suspense. The primary question is who killed Star Radley, and Walk spends most of the story searching for answers that will both solve that mystery and vindicate Vincent. In his search, Walk confronts Dickie Darke, a local businessman with a mysterious past and a strong desire to acquire Vincent's property. Dickie also has a vendetta against Duchess, who earns his ire after she makes a misguided attempt at vengeance for her mother. Other suspects include the local butcher, whose interest in Star suggested a more problematic obsession, and a neighbor who still longs for his glory days as a popular high school jock. Walk's investigation reopens old wounds and creates new tensions among the townspeople, resulting in a pleasingly messy conflict that will keep readers entranced.

Upon its publication in 2021, *We Begin at the End* was met with popular and critical acclaim. It won the Gold Dagger for Best Crime Novel from the Crime Writers' Association (UK) and the award for Best International Crime Fiction from the Australian Crime Writers' Association. In addition, it became an immediate New York Times Best Seller. Many reviews praised the novel's character development; writing for *School Library Journal*, Samantha Hull called the characters "raw, real, and relatable," while the critic for *Publishers Weekly* noted that the novel is "powered by extraordinarily deep character development." However, not all feedback was universally positive. In Liz Moore's review for the *New York Times* she argued that Whitaker's descriptions of both setting and characters lack substance. She took particular issue with what she felt were contrived character names and dialogue that lacked the "rhythm of human speech," and also felt the author's violation of grammar conventions made his writing, at times, hard to follow.

Despite her reservations about some aspects of the novel, Moore praised the plot, calling it "moving" and "propulsive." Other reviewers echoed this praise; the review in *Publishers Weekly* lauded the plot as "impressively intricate." Another reviewer, writing for *Kirkus*, said, "Whitaker crafts an absorbing plot around crimes in the present and secrets long buried, springing surprises to the very end." Reviewers also had varying opinions on the genre of the novel, who noted that it functions as a bildungsroman, a mystery, and a thriller, but also incorporates elements of romance and literary fiction. Ultimately, *We Begin at the End* will likely interest a wide variety of readers, especially those looking for a different twist on crime fiction.

Author Biography
Chris Whitaker is the acclaimed crime writer of novels for adults and young adults. His fiction debut, *Tall Oaks*, was published in 2016.

Theresa L. Stowell, PhD

Review Sources
Gillette, Sam, et al. Review of *We Begin at the End*, by Chris Whitaker. *People*, vol. 95, no. 12, Mar. 2021, p. 31. *EBSCOhost*, search.ebscohost.com/login.aspx?direct =true&db=asn&AN=149211085. Accessed 5 Jan. 2022.

Hoffert, Barbara. Review of *We Begin at the End*, by Chris Whitaker. *Library Journal*, vol. 145, no. 10, Oct. 2020, p. 51. *EBSCOhost*, search.ebscohost.com/login.aspx?direct=true&db=asn&AN=145926940. Accessed 5 Jan. 2022.

Hull, Samantha. Review of *We Begin at the End*, by Chris Whitaker. *School Library Journal*, vol. 67, no. 5, May 2021, p. 92, www.slj.com/?reviewDetail=we-begin-at-the-end. Accessed 5 Jan. 2022.

Moore, Liz. "Go West: This Novel Begins with One Ending - and Then Another." Review of *We Begin at the End*, by Chris Whitaker. *The New York Times*, Mar. 2021, p. 19, www.nytimes.com/2021/03/09/books/review/we-begin-at-the-end-chris-whitaker.html. Accessed 5 Jan. 2022.

Review of *We Begin at the End*, by Chris Whitaker. *Kirkus*, 25 Dec. 2020, www.kirkusreviews.com/book-reviews/chris-whitaker/we-begin-at-the-end/. Accessed 5 Jan. 2022.

Review of *We Begin at the End*, by Chris Whitaker. *Publishers Weekly*, 18 Dec. 2020, www.publishersweekly.com/978-1-250-75966-5. Accessed 5 Jan. 2022.

When the Stars Go Dark

Author: Paula McLain (b. 1965)
Publisher: Ballantine Books (New York). 384 pp.
Type of work: Novel
Time: 1993
Locale: California

When the Stars Go Dark is a thriller by bestselling author Paula McLain that follows the kidnapping of three different girls through the eyes of a detective who is grappling with her own traumatic past.

Principal characters

ANNA HART, a homicide detective based in San Francisco
WILL FLOOD, a local sheriff and her childhood friend from Mendocino
CAMERON CURTIS, the fifteen-year-old adopted daughter of a famous actor who has gone missing
POLLY KLAAS, a twelve-year-old girl who was kidnapped from her house
SHANNAN RUSSO, a seventeen-year-old girl from a poor family whose whereabouts are unknown
JENNY LEDFORD, Anna and Will's friend who was murdered when they were teenagers

Paula McLain is not an easy writer to categorize. After launching her literary career as a poet, she wrote a memoir about her childhood experiences in foster care titled *Like Family: Growing Up in Other People's Houses* (2003). McLain then transitioned to writing novels and established her literary niche with *The Paris Wife* (2011), a fictionalized account of Hadley Richardson, Ernest Hemingway's first wife while the couple lived in 1920s Paris. The book quickly became a New York Times Best Seller and made McLain a rising star in the literary world. She followed its success with two more works of historical fiction about forgotten female figures: *Circling the Sun* (2015), focused on Beryl Markham, the first woman to fly an airplane across the Atlantic, and *Love and Ruin* (2018), the story of Ernest Hemingway's third wife, Martha Gellhorn—one of the most important war correspondents of her generation.

Although it contains themes and stylistic elements of her previous works, McLain's latest novel is in many ways unlike anything she has written before. *When the Stars Go Dark* (2021) follows the story of a San Francisco homicide detective named Anna Hart who has just returned to her hometown of Mendocino, California, after being sent away by her husband for reasons that are initially unclear. While in Mendocino, Anna

Paula McLain

Courtesy Penguin Random House

tries to distract herself from her own emotional turmoil by joining a former childhood friend, local sheriff Will Flood, in solving the case of a missing fifteen-year-old girl named Cameron Curtis. As Anna works Cameron's case, she notices that it has similarities to two other nearby disappearances involving a twelve-year-old girl named Polly Klaas and a seventeen-year-old girl named Shannan Russo. The experience of investigating the tragic disappearances of these young women forces Anna to reflect on her own childhood trauma.

What makes *When the Stars Go Dark* somewhat unique within the context of McLain's oeuvre is that it is her first thriller. Additionally, it is helmed by a fictional character rather than a historical figure. This has not stopped McLain from blending some historical facts into her fiction, however, as Polly Klaas is a girl who was kidnapped in real life in 1993; her case gained national attention and led to significant changes in California's legal system. Another interesting way in which *When the Stars Go Dark* differs from McLain's previous novels is that it reflects her own personal story. Like the protagonist, Anna, McLain also lost her parents at a young age and subsequently lived with foster families, where she suffered sexual abuse. While McLain never became a homicide detective who specialized in missing children's cases, it is easy to assume that Anna functions as a stand-in for her in other ways—specifically how the traumas of her past inform her worldview as an adult.

The central narrative of *When the Stars Go Dark* feels fresh simply because it is driven by multiple mysteries. In its first few pages, the book grabs readers with the mystery of what tragedy Anna is running from in San Francisco that caused her to return to Mendocino. Anna herself comments on what a bizarre story her life has become in a gripping passage from the first chapter when she states, "I can't imagine any stranger correctly guessing at the plot. I'm having a hard time understanding it myself, and I'm the main character; I'm writing it." While Anna's dark, nebulous story line sets the novel's tone, it quickly takes a backseat to the mystery of what happened to Cameron, Polly, and Shannan. The girls' disappearances ultimately function as the primary plot engine of the novel. However, the book consists of so many other strange events that at times it borders on magical realism. For example, there are the mysteries of Anna's foster father's disappearance and her childhood friend Jenny's unsolved murder that continue to haunt Mendocino. At one point, Anna befriends a psychic and later a stray dog—both of whom seem to have preternatural abilities.

Beyond its skillfully subtle use of mysticism, *When the Stars Go Dark* differs from traditional thriller novels in its literary style. McLain's MFA degree in poetry is on full display throughout her dreamy, intimate prose, which she crafts in the first-person, present tense to provide readers with unfiltered insights into Anna's damaged psyche. Additionally, McLain avoids the well-worn homicide detective trope of investigating the disappearance of pretty teenage girls for salacious purposes. Instead, she uses the disappearances of Cameron, Polly, and Shannan to shine a light on how vulnerable young women are in the world. Through the book's chapters, it becomes clear how all three of these girls were failed by societal systems that were supposed to keep them safe. Even the systems designed to find them and bring them home prove to be flawed. While Polly's disappearance gets media attention because of her personality and family background, Shannan's does not because she came from a lower-class home and had a reputation for being sexually precocious. Ultimately, McLain demonstrates how society and absent parents sometimes enable young women to become the victims of predators.

If there is one system that *When the Stars Go Dark* examines the most it is that of foster care. As Anna investigates Cameron's disappearance, she discovers that, like her, Cameron lost her parents at a young age, was separated from her siblings through foster care, and was sexually abused by someone who was supposed to be a guardian. McLain leverages these similarities into Anna's superpower; specifically, that Anna is able to identify how Cameron was feeling and what trouble she might have gotten herself into because she shares similar psychic wounds. McLain also uses the characters of Anna and Cameron to illustrate the complex emotions that former foster children often suffer from. This is most evident in Anna, who still struggles with feelings of guilt and self-loathing after years of blaming herself for her mother's death, her father's disappearance, and her half siblings' separation. It is through Anna's journey that McLain provides readers with a much-needed look at the mental toll that the foster care system takes on former wards of the state well into their adulthood.

Like McLain's previous novels, *When the Stars Go Dark* was well received by readers and became a New York Times Best Seller. Critics had a similarly positive response, with many being quick to deem the novel an excellent addition to the genre. For example, Maureen Corrigan wrote in her review for the *Washington Post* that it was "an atmospheric and intricately plotted suspense novel." Similarly, the reviewer for *Kirkus* called it "a muted yet thrilling multilayered mystery." It is true that despite the fact that McLain's novel is much more emotionally and socially complex than the average thriller, fans of detective novels will still find it highly engaging. McLain may use *When the Stars Go Dark* as an opportunity to depict the vulnerability of young women within the context of flawed societal systems; however, it also succeeds in maintaining the traditional story beats of its genre by making readers feel as though they are alongside Anna as she investigates crimes. As Claire Fullerton wrote for the *New York Journal of Books*, the novel "is an enthralling foray into the step-by-step mechanics behind the hunt for a child abductor that grows with surprising linkages into the search for a serial killer hiding in plain sight."

Another common point of praise for *When the Stars Go Dark* was directed at McLain's writing. In addition to highlighting her beautiful writing style, many critics commended her ability to create sympathetic characters despite the novel's dark, twisted subject matter. *Publishers Weekly* stated in its review that "McLain matches poetic prose with deep characterizations as she shines a light on the kindness in her characters' souls." Similarly, Chandler Baker wrote in her review for the *New York Times* that she appreciated how Anna differed from the gruff, hardboiled detective stereotype that helms most thrillers. To this point, Baker wrote that Anna's "outspoken empathy feels downright refreshing in a fictional detective, and entirely believable because of the trauma in her own story." Indeed, one of McLain's many talents as a writer is her ability to create characters who are deeply flawed but relatable. Will Flood, for example, is a messy, vulnerable character who at one point tries to kiss Anna in an act that is more about depression and reaching out for human connection than lust. Perhaps the most blatant display of McLain's skill at writing characters is how she depicts Cameron as a complex, multidimensional human with a rich interior life. This differs from most thrillers, which often present their female victims as innocent ingenues.

When the Stars Go Dark is not a perfect novel. At times, it can feel overstuffed with all the mysteries that it is juggling. "A glut of names, places and time periods occasionally had me mentally scurrying to play catch-up," wrote Baker in her review, while also acknowledging that these mental gymnastics were worthwhile in the end. Additionally, certain mysteries are easier to solve and in turn deflate some of the narrative's suspense. Despite these minor flaws, however, it is a difficult book to put down. McLain is an excellent storyteller who wields suspense in an expert manner. Her enchanting literary style, compelling characters, and intimate insights into the type of people who become the victims of predators will draw readers in and provide them with a new and necessary worldview. *When the Stars Go Dark* may be McLain's first foray into the thriller genre, but it is unlikely to be her last.

Author Biography
Paula McLain is a *New York Times* best-selling author and the recipient of fellowships from the Ohio Arts Council and the National Endowment for the Arts.

Emily E. Turner

Review Sources
Baker, Chandler. "Missing Girls and a Bit of Mysticism, in Paula McLain's Debut Thriller." Review of *When the Stars Go Dark*, by Paula McLain. *The New York Times*, 13 Apr. 2021, www.nytimes.com/2021/04/13/books/review/when-the-stars-go-dark-paula-mclain.html. Accessed 29 Nov. 2021.

Corrigan, Maureen. "In Her Novel 'When the Stars Go Dark,' Paula McLain Draws on Abuse Cases, Including Her Own." *The Washington Post*, 23 Apr. 2021, www.washingtonpost.com/entertainment/books/in-her-novel-when-the-stars-go-dark-paula-mclain-draws-on-abuse-cases-including-her-own/2021/04/22/211e29c4-a14e-11eb-85fc-06664ff4489d_story.html. Accessed 29 Nov. 2021.

Fullerton, Claire. Review of *When the Stars Go Dark*, by Paula McLain. *New York Journal of Books*, 13 Apr. 2021, www.nyjournalofbooks.com/book-review/when-stars-go-dark-novel. Accessed 29 Nov. 2021.

Review of *When the Stars Go Dark*, by Paula McLain. *Kirkus*, 3 Mar. 2021, www.kirkusreviews.com/book-reviews/paula-mclain/when-the-stars-go-dark/. Accessed 29 Nov. 2021.

Review of *When the Stars Go Dark*, by Paula McLain. *Publishers Weekly*, 13 Jan. 2021, www.publishersweekly.com/978-0-593-23789-2. Accessed 29 Nov. 2021.

When We Cease to Understand the World

Author: Benjamín Labatut (b. 1980)
First published: *Un verdor terrible*, 2020, in Spain
Translated from the Spanish by Adrian Nathan West
Publisher: New York Review of Books (New York). 192 pp.
Type of work: Short fiction, novel, history
Time: Twentieth century
Locale: Europe

Benjamín Labatut's When We Cease to Understand the World *is a series of increasingly fictional accounts of major scientific breakthroughs of the twentieth century, the modes of destruction each one offers, and the price of progress.*

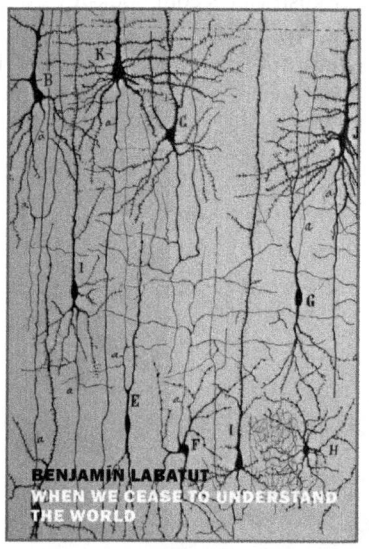

Principal characters

HERMANN GÖRING, Nazi war criminal; based on the historical figure of the same name

FRITZ HABER, German chemist who developed the Haber-Bosch process; based on the historical figure of the same name

CLARA IMMERWAHR, German chemist; Haber's wife; based on the historical figure of the same name

KARL SCHWARZSCHILD, German physicist and astronomer whose calculations predicted black holes; based on the historical figure of the same name

WERNER HEISENBERG, German quantum physicist who proposed the uncertainty principle; based on the historical figure of the same name

NIELS BOHR, Heisenberg's mentor; the physicist who modeled the atom; based on the historical figure of the same name

ALEXANDER GROTHENDIECK, German French mathematician; based on the historical figure of the same name

SHINICHI MOCHIZUKI, Japanese mathematician; based on the historical figure of the same name

ERWIN SCHRÖDINGER, German physicist who proposed the wave mechanics formulation of quantum mechanics; based on the historical figure of the same name

When We Cease to Understand the World, Adrian Nathan West's 2021 translation of Chilean writer Benjamín Labatut's *Un verdor terrible* (2020), was short-listed for both the International Booker Prize and the National Book Award for Translated Literature. Labatut describes *When We Cease* in his acknowledgments as a "work of fiction based on real events," namely, the major scientific breakthroughs of the twentieth century. As the book progresses, he relies more and more on fiction, imagining the inner lives of the scientists who engineered these breakthroughs as they ponder the consequences of their discoveries. Labatut has an eye for the surreal. He offers off-kilter, real-life details that dovetail—beautifully, grotesquely—with his imagined ones. Without the aid of the internet, it is sometimes hard to separate the two.

The book's first chapter, titled "Prussian Blue," begins with the Nazi war criminal Hermann Göring killing himself before he can be hanged by crushing a cyanide capsule between his teeth. Cyanide, the fast-working, deadly poison, is a byproduct of the first synthetic pigment, a color dubbed Prussian Blue by Johann Jacob Diesbach, the Swiss pigmenter and dyer who discovered it. Diesbach's discovery was an accident, Labatut writes, arrived at by crushing the bodies of millions of parasitic insects in search of the color red. Diesbach was enchanted by his discovery, believing that he had found the revered shade of blue rumored to have been used by the ancient Egyptians. This holy hue, Labatut notes, stained the gas chambers of Nazi concentration camps, as cyanide was a component of Zyklon B, the gas the regime used to kill millions of Jews during the Holocaust. In Labatut's hands, this convoluted chain of images and events—all true—hypnotize with the force of poetry. The chapter demonstrates Labatut's query without explicitly stating it: Is the price of all knowledge destruction?

Labatut, who published a collection of short stories in 2009 and a novel in 2016, writes in the tradition of the celebrated twentieth-century German author W. G. Sebald, whose work combined history, memoir, and fiction in similarly oblique ways. *When We Cease to Understand the World* also appears to draw inspiration from nineteenth-century writer Mary Shelley, who pondered similar questions about the bounds of scientific thought. Labatut mentions her in the book's first chapter, writing that in her classic novel *Frankenstein* (1818), "she warned of the risk of the blind advancement of science, to her the most dangerous of all human arts." To this point, Labatut tells the story of Fritz Haber, a German chemist who developed the chlorine gas used in World War I. Labatut describes the scene of the first gas attack in Ypres, Belgium, in 1915, and how the slow-moving, "greenish" cloud moved across no-man's land, killing every living thing in its path. "The leaves withered on the trees as it passed, birds fell dead from the sky," he writes. Men convulsed, choking on their own mucus, their skin turning blue from lack of oxygen. Labatut suggests the gas stunned even those who released it. He quotes one soldier, Willi Siebert, who later wrote, "It was a beautiful day, the sun was shining. . . . We should have been going on a picnic, not doing what

Benjamin Labatut

Courtesy Juana Gomez

we were doing." But at least one man present that day was pleased. Haber was proud of his work, and later blindsided, upon his return to Berlin, by the reaction of his wife, Clara Immerwahr. A celebrated chemist in her own right, Immerwahr was so horrified by her husband's creation that she killed herself. Haber, who was Jewish, went on to develop the pesticidal fumigant that would be used to create Zyklon B, the chemical weapon that would kill several members of his own family during the Holocaust.

Haber, Labatut writes, was a true genius. He was the father of the Haber-Bosch process, which the author describes as "the most important chemical discovery of the twentieth century." Because the process creates artificial nitrogen for fertilizing crops, the press called him "the man who pulled bread from air." Millions would have died from famine had Haber not invented this process. The duality of help and harm is demonstrated quite profoundly in Haber's chapter; other figures in the book work in more theoretical realms. The existential dread of their discoveries—which suggest as-yet-unfathomable real-world applications—is demonstrated in the story of Karl Schwarzschild, a German physicist and astronomer who first predicted the existence of black holes. Schwarzschild made the discovery, which he called the singularity, while serving in World War I. In Labatut's imagination, the physicist is haunted by the specter of a void in which time and space have no meaning, and it appears to him in the senseless destruction of the war. Schwarzschild was not so much concerned with how his discovery could be used but what it meant in terms of people's understanding of the world. On his death bed—in Labatut's telling—he names his fear to a mathematician. "The true horror, he said, was that the singularity was a blind spot, fundamentally unknowable."

Other figures in the book, some sliding into madness and wild hallucinations, are similarly unmoored by their discoveries. Werner Heisenberg and Erwin Schrödinger grapple with the implications of quantum physics, a realm that does not obey the laws of physical reality as people perceive them. Labatut has said that the amount of fiction in the book grows as it progresses, and by the time he arrives to these characters, he is spinning stories out of air. Schrödinger, who really did suffer from tuberculosis, the illness from which he eventually died in 1961, formulated his wave theory of quantum mechanics while he was being treated at a sanatorium. In Labatut's telling, Schrödinger develops a romance with the daughter of the sanatorium's owner, who is also ill. Labatut's writing, with no small thanks to translator West, is as hypnotic as always, but the story rankles. Both tender and lurid, it depicts Schrödinger's obsession with a frail young girl. It is a consensual relationship, but it reads as a romanticization of the real Schrödinger, a serial abuser who groomed young girls for sex. Labatut seems to offer no reason for romanticizing this aspect of Schrödinger's life other than that he can. He similarly seems to celebrate the trope of the mad genius. In his telling, thinkers who might have had mental illnesses rage and hallucinate, writing their equations in a fervor. It makes for very beautiful reading but lacks a clear purpose. As Labatut's story takes over, the book grows less critical of the relationship between scientific discovery and destruction; in fact, it seems to revel in it.

Despite its faults, *When We Cease to Understand the World* makes for thought-provoking reading, even for those who may not be well versed in chemistry or physics.

Labatut's explanations of scientific and mathematical theories are clear and evocative. They are so effective that readers will want to continue to monitor the saga of Shinichi Mochizuki, a hermetic, brilliant mathematician who, in a six-hundred-page proof, claimed to have solved the "unsolvable" $a + b = c$ conjecture of number theory in August 2012.

When We Cease to Understand the World received an enthusiastic review in the *Guardian* from the novelist John Banville, who described the book as a "nonfiction novel" that was "ingenious, intricate and deeply disturbing." He further praised the book's "intricate web of associations," relating to character, image, and event, that echo what becomes the scientists' obsession: seeking to understand not the thing itself, but how all things are connected. In writing about Heisenberg's mentor, Niels Bohr, Labatut writes that Bohr was as much a philosopher as he was a physicist; to Heisenberg's frustration, Bohr embraced both Heisenberg's theory of how subatomic particles behave and also Schrödinger's opposing theory. In Bohr's view, Labatut writes, "the attributes of elementary particles were only valid in a given context and arose from a relationship. No single frame of reference could encompass them."

Author Biography

Benjamín Labatut is the author of the 2009 short-story collection *La Antártica empieza aquí* (Antarctica starts here) and *Después de la luz* (2016; After the light). His first book to be translated into English, *Un verdor terrible* (2020; *When We Cease to Understand the World*), was short-listed for the 2021 International Booker Prize and was a finalist for the 2021 National Book Award for Translated Literature.

Adrian Nathan West is the author of *The Aesthetics of Degradation* (2016) and *My Father's Diet* (2022). In addition to his honors for translating *When We Cease to Understand the World*, West is an award-winning translator of about thirty books, most from German and Spanish.

Molly Hagan

Review Sources

Banville, John. "*When We Cease to Understand the World* by Benjamín Labatut Review—the Dark Side of Science." *The Guardian*, 10 Sept. 2020, www.theguardian.com/books/2020/sep/10/when-we-cease-to-understand-the-world-by-benjamin-labatut-review-the-dark-side-of-science. Accessed 14 Jan. 2022.

Fonseca-Wollheim, Corinna. "The Ecstasy of Scientific Discovery, and Its Agonizing Price." Review of *When We Cease to Understand the World*, by Benjamín Labatut, translated by Adrian Nathan West. *The New York Times*, 24 Sept. 2021, www.nytimes.com/2021/09/24/books/review/benjamin-labatut-cease-understand-world.html. Accessed 14 Jan. 2022.

Franklin, Ruth. "A Cautionary Tale about Science Raises Uncomfortable Questions about Fiction." Review of *When We Cease to Understand the World*, by Benjamín Labatut, translated by Adrian Nathan West. *The New Yorker*, 6 Sept. 2021, www.newyorker.com/magazine/2021/09/13/a-cautionary-tale-about-science-raises-uncomfortable-questions-about-fiction. Accessed 14 Jan. 2022.

Review of *When We Cease to Understand the World*, by Benjamín Labatut, translated by Adrian Nathan West. *Kirkus*, 16 June 2021, www.kirkusreviews.com/book-reviews/benjamin-labatut/when-we-cease-to-understand-the-world/. Accessed 14 Jan. 2022.

Review of *When We Cease to Understand the World*, by Benjamín Labatut, translated by Adrian Nathan West. *Publishers Weekly*, 22 June 2021, www.publishersweekly.com/978-1-68137-566-3. Accessed 14 Jan. 2022.

Whereabouts

Author: Jhumpa Lahiri (b. 1967)
First published: *Dove mi trovo*, 2018, in Italy
Translated from the Italian by Jhumpa Lahiri
Publisher: Alfred A. Knopf (New York). 176 pp.
Type of work: Novel
Time: Present day
Locale: An unnamed city in Italy

Whereabouts, Jhumpa Lahiri's fourth book of fiction and her first novel originally written in Italian, explores a woman's solitary life in spare and haunting prose.

Principal characters

THE NARRATOR, an author and professor living in the unnamed Italian city of her birth
HER MOTHER, a widow with whom she has a strained relationship
A FRIEND'S HUSBAND, with whom the narrator finds herself flirting
A FORMER LOVER, with whom the narrator continues to socialize

Whereabouts (2021) is a spare and elegiac novel narrated by a woman who has constructed a rigidly solitary life for herself. The narrator writes in her apartment, visits the university where she teaches, frequents local cafes and shops, and interacts with a group of friends and lovers whom she keeps at emotional arms-length. She is likewise distanced from her own past and her inner motivations. She knows that she has been shaped by her difficult parents—a combative mother and a passive father—but she seems unwilling to confront or move beyond the traumas of her childhood. The novel unfolds in a series of vignettes, each designated by its setting: "On the Sidewalk," "At the Trattoria," and so on. By eschewing proper nouns, and hence never naming the Italian city she lives in or any of her friends and acquaintances, the narrator further expresses her sense of isolation and anonymity. Over the course of the short chapters a plotline gradually develops, and by novel's end the narrator seems poised to break at last from her self-imposed solitude and to make a change for the better.

Acclaimed author Jhumpa Lahiri wrote *Whereabouts*, her fourth work of fiction, in Italian rather than the English of her breakthrough works. Her previous book, *In Other Words*, her first written in Italian, described her decision to move to Italy to immerse herself in a study of the language. With *Whereabouts* (or *Dove mi trovo*, in the original Italian), Lahiri further commits herself to Italian by writing fiction in the language.

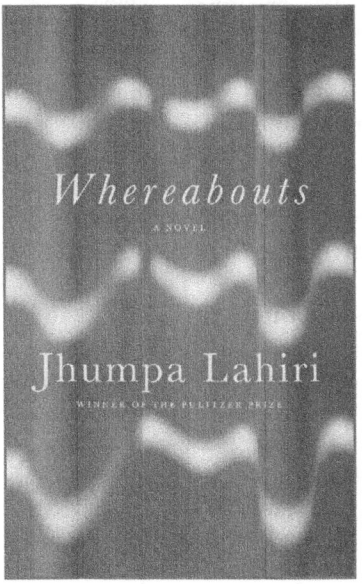

Lahiri is not the first English-language writer to cross languages. Samuel Beckett, for example, composed most of his work in French and then translated it into English. Vladimir Nabokov switched from writing novels in Russian to writing them in English, while Ha Jin switched from Chinese to English. Nevertheless, it is still a striking and unusual decision for a contemporary American author to make. It is one that perhaps only an author as well-established as Lahiri could pull off. A Pulitzer Prize winner and a finalist for the National Book Award, Lahiri is a literary icon, and it is fascinating to watch her reinvent herself in a new language and culture.

One of the most interesting aspects of Lahiri's narrator is the fact that she is a native-born Italian, rather than an immigrant or a visitor. Raised in the unnamed Italian city in which she still resides, with a widowed mother living a train ride away, she is firmly rooted in a single culture, language, and location. Nor is there any indication that either of her parents were immigrants. This narrator therefore stands in sharp contrast to the protagonists of Lahiri's other books and to the author herself. It is a bold choice on Lahiri's part, because it strips *Whereabouts* of much of the material and many of the themes that fueled her earlier two novels. *The Lowland* (2013) is a story of immigration and of creating a new life in America, while *The Namesake* (2003) focuses on a first-generation protagonist who finds himself navigating the cultures of his immigrant parents and of the America in which he was raised. In *Whereabouts*, the narrator's relationship to culture is far simpler—this city and culture are the only life she has ever known. This helps to explain the austerity of her narration and of her world; from the coffee she drinks to the notebooks she uses, everything the narrator encounters bears a familiar name and provenance. Some readers may find in this austerity a sense of loss, as the rich cultural cross-currents that animate Lahiri's earlier works are largely absent from this one. By the same token, the narrator's circumscribed life may seem at times more like that of an expatriate, someone who is a visitor and observer in a country and culture rather than a product of it.

Yet the brevity of this novel and the austerity of its narrator's lifestyle produce their own form of power and momentum. Though she has lived in the same city her whole life, the narrator is profoundly alienated from others. Simple interactions and incidents therefore carry more weight than they might with someone who was living a fuller and more interconnected life. As the novel progresses, incidents of disorientation, menace, or conflict seem to multiply. At a dinner party, the narrator finds herself exasperated with an opinionated tablemate, and makes a rude comment that she is later ashamed of. The aggressive husband of a visiting friend tries to borrow a book from the narrator, and the reader feels along with her what a violation it would be to let this man walk off with anything from her library. While housesitting for a friend in the countryside, the narrator's momentary sense of tranquility is shattered when she finds a dead mouse with its head neatly severed. A change is coming to narrator, whether she likes it or not, as the careful world that she has constructed for herself begins to come undone. So effective is Lahiri's evocation of this character that the reader feels the magnitude of ostensibly minor incidents. For example, when the narrator's favorite stationery store suddenly closes and is replaced by a shop selling luggage to tourists, we feel it as a genuine loss. While the novel's individual chapters play out as partially self-contained vignettes, there is an overarching story concerning the narrator's growing realization that she will have to rethink aspects of her life.

It would perhaps be easy for an American expatriate in Italy to enthuse about aspects of life in that country, and to dwell only on the most beautiful, historic, or appealing aspects of Italian culture. If anything, Lahiri does the opposite. Her unnamed city is described as "godforsaken" and "run-down." The narrator and her circle of friends are not living *la bella vita*, or the beautiful life. Rather, they seem tired and disaffected, and even their extramarital affairs and secret liaisons seem passionless. It is hard to write in Italian without invoking Dante Alighieri, whose *La divina commedia* (*The Divine Comedy*) stands at the center of the Italian canon. *Whereabouts* seems, in many respects, to draw on *Inferno* and *Purgatorio*, the first two parts of the *Commedia*. In fact, Lahiri's Italian title, *Dove mi trovo,* or "Where I find myself," uses the same verb that governs the famous first two lines of the *Inferno*: "*Nel mezzo del cammin di nostra vita, / Mi ritrovai per una selva oscura*" ("Midway on our life's journey, / I found myself in a dark wood"). The circuit of cafes, shops, office, and home that Lahiri's narrator makes seem to echo the descending rings of Dante's Hell or the spiraling path up the mountain of Purgatory. For the souls in Hell, such circling is endless, whereas those in Purgatory have the consolation of eventually being released from their torment. If the unnamed city of *Whereabouts* is a modern version of Dante's cosmos, the question for the narrator is whether she can, like the purgatorial souls, eventually deliver herself from her current miseries and ascend to a better life. As the Italian title suggest, this novel is not about exploring one's surroundings, per se, but about finding oneself. The narrator's walks, train rides, trips to the countryside, and eventual decision about whether to go abroad or stay home are all manifestations of an inner journey of self-discovery.

Yet at times, the narrator's disaffection can feel self-indulgent. At an academic conference, she describes herself as full of "dread," while the other participants are "mostly men dressed in gray, herds of them, all of them laughing too loudly, too often." Surely, at any conference for writers or academics, Lahiri's narrator would not be alone in seeing herself as uniquely sensitive, self-aware, and set apart from the other less-enlightened participants. An element of solipsism starts to creep into this and other scenes in which the narrator ascribes to herself a higher degree of consciousness than the people around her. In a similar vein, at a party after a friend's child has been baptized, the narrator feels compelled to leave the event to watch the sea instead. There is something sophomoric and performative about this act. In truth, how could a luncheon not be excruciatingly boring in a narrative world stripped of all proper nouns? The narrator's choice to avoid all specificity regarding people and places goes hand in hand with her contempt for most of the individuals she encounters. Sometimes, her narrative teeters on the edge of parody. She says of attending the baptism: "She told me it meant a lot to her, so I said yes, even though to be honest I was tempted to decline the invitation. Another colleague of ours gave me a ride. He's irritating, but unfortunately, I don't have a car." Is the narrator a sensitive existentialist, or a peevish misanthrope? One begins to wonder whether the people who invite the narrator to events and shuttle her around are really so blind to her faults, or whether they have their own opinions about her. Ultimately it is not clear to what extent Lahiri herself sympathizes with or judges her narrator's degree of humorless self-importance.

Perhaps reflecting this ambiguity, *Whereabouts* received mixed reviews, with some readers finding its austerity off-putting. Writing for the *New York Times*, Madeleine Thein noted that the novel's chapters "sometimes sing and sometimes perplex," and opined that Lahiri's "polished words sometimes seem to lose contact with living existence, providing a skillful description of a two-dimensional world—a picture of a picture." Ron Charles was harsher in a review for the *Washington Post*, seeing the book as an entry in the subgenre of "slim, grim novels [that] offer a flatlined vision of life reduced to its terrifying aimlessness." He recognized the innate difficulty of writing about something as intensely inward as depression but felt that Lahiri's "descriptions of chilled despair have been so aggressively honed that there's little for us to hang on to but the sighs." Yet others gave a more positive assessment of the book. "As always, Lahiri writes with subtlety and delicacy," Heller McAlpin wrote for *NPR*. "*Whereabouts* is the literary equivalent of slow cooking; it demands patience." In a glowing review for the *Guardian*, Tanjil Rashid argued that "Where her English thrived on the particular, Lahiri's Italian reaches for the universal." Rashid speculated that "perhaps, in Italian, Lahiri saw the possibility of writing the everywoman English denied her."

An austere and demanding novel, *Whereabouts* marks a dramatic departure for Lahiri. Even readers who find aspects of the book frustrating should admire the boldness of the author's commitment to a new language and wonder how her work will continue to evolve in the future.

Author Biography
Acclaimed author Jhumpa Lahiri is known for her work focusing on the experience of immigrants. She won the Pulitzer Prize and the PEN/Hemingway Award for her short-story collection *Interpreter of Maladies* (1999), and received the National Humanities Medal in 2014.

Matthew J. Bolton

Review Sources

Charles, Ron. "Jhumpa Lahiri's Novel *Whereabouts* Is a Delicate Exploration of Despair." Review of *Whereabouts*, by Jhumpa Lahiri. *The Washington Post*, 20 Apr. 2021, www.washingtonpost.com/entertainment/books/jhumpa-lahiris-novel-whereabouts-is-a-delicate-exploration-of-despair/2021/04/20/8c1fce0c-a1cc-11eb-a7ee-949c574a09ac_story.html. Accessed 25 Nov. 2021.

McAlpin, Heller. "Jhumpa Lahiri's New *Whereabouts* Is about Places Both Geographic and Emotional." Review of *Whereabouts*, by Jhumpa Lahiri. *NPR*, 29 Apr. 2021, www.npr.org/2021/04/29/991671844/jhumpa-lahiris-new-whereabouts-is-about-places-both-geographical-and-emotional. Accessed 25 Nov. 2021.

Rashid, Tanjil. "*Whereabouts* by Jhumpa Lahiri Review—A Fascinating Shift." Review of *Whereabouts*, by Jhumpa Lahiri. *The Guardian*, 6 May 2021, www.theguardian.com/books/2021/may/06/whereabouts-by-jhumpa-lahiri-review-a-fascinating-shift. Accessed 25 Nov. 2021.

Thien, Maeleine. "Jhumpa Lahiri's New Novel Pares a Shrinking Life Down to Its Essence." Review of *Whereabouts*, by Jhumpa Lahiri. *The New York Times*, 27 Apr. 2021, www.nytimes.com/2021/04/27/books/review/whereabouts-jhumpa-lahiri.html. Accessed 25 Nov. 2021.

Review of *Whereabouts*, by Jhumpa Lahiri. *Kirkus*, 27 Jan. 2021, www.kirkusreviews.com/book-reviews/jhumpa-lahiri/whereabouts-lahiri/. Accessed 13 Dec. 2021.

Review of *Whereabouts*, by Jhumpa Lahiri. *Publishers Weekly*, 29 Dec. 2020, https://www.publishersweekly.com/978-0-593-31831-7. Accessed 13 Dec. 2021.

White Smoke

Author: Tiffany D. Jackson
Publisher: Katherine Tegen Books (New York). 384 pp.
Type of work: Novel
Time: Present day
Locale: A small town called Cedarville

New York Times *best-selling young adult author Tiffany D. Jackson's novel* White Smoke *is a gothic horror set in a small Midwestern town where Mari's mother has won a three-year writing residency that offers a rent-free home. Struggling with profound anxiety, a very particular phobia, and addiction, Mari is unmoored when strange things start happening around the family's newly renovated old house.*

Principal characters
MARIGOLD, a.k.a. Mari, a teenage girl desperate to escape her past mistakes
SAMMY, her little brother
PIPER, her ten-year-old stepsister
RAQUEL, her mother
ALEC, her stepfather
YUSEF, her new friend in Cedarville

New York Times best-selling young adult author Tiffany D. Jackson's novel *White Smoke* (2021) is a horror novel, aptly marketed as a cross between Shirley Jackson's 1959 gothic *The Haunting of Hill House* and *Get Out* (2017), the blockbuster horror film with pointed racial commentary. In the tradition of the prolific young adult horror novelist R. L. Stine—who lends an enthusiastic blurb to Jackson's book—*White Smoke* collides the experience of being young with the unsettling tropes of horror. Marigold, Jackson's teenage protagonist, is haunted by her past. Now, as her family moves from the sunny beaches of California to a chilly Midwestern town, she finds herself being haunted for real. Jackson makes this classic setup her own, turning it into a commentary on gentrification and the politics of power without losing the plot or dulling the thrills. Jackson has written thrillers before—among them *Allegedly* (2017) and *Monday's Not Coming* (2018)—but *White Smoke* is her first foray into horror. Alex Brown, who reviewed the book for the science-fiction magazine *Locus*, wrote that *White Smoke* is "horrifying enough to keep me on the edge of my seat" and "bristles with tension from the first page to the last."

Tiffany D. Jackson

Mari is moving to Cedarville because of her mother—or, at least, that is what people think. Mari's mother, Raquel, is a writer and has won a three-year residency to live rent-free in a newly renovated home on Maple Street. Tagging along are Mari and her beloved younger brother, Sammy, as well as Raquel's new husband, Alec, and his ten-year-old daughter, Piper. Relations among the newly mixed family are fragile. Piper is jealous of the attention her father lavishes on Raquel as well as the friendship between Mari and Sammy. Another flash point is food. Owing to Sammy's severe allergies, Mari, Raquel, and Sammy are vegan; Alec and Piper are not. Yet another, though mostly unspoken, distinction is race. Mari, her mother, and her brother are Black, while Alec and Piper are White. Differences aside, the family is collectively surprised upon their arrival in Cedarville, a small Midwestern town struggling to turn the page on its sordid history. Driving down Maple Street, Mari cannot help but notice that every other home is abandoned or blackened by fire. The shifty behavior of the residence's hosts does not soothe the family's trepidation. In a tour of their new and cavernous home they are warned, without explanation, that they must never enter their own basement.

But Mari has only two things on her mind. The first is her consuming phobia of bed bugs, borne of experience. Mari's obsession with the bugs is a manifestation of her profound anxiety. Brown praised Jackson's handling of Mari's anxiety as "nuanced and evocative." They further noted, "Good anxiety representation means not shying away from the messiness of it all and how it can override your common sense and logic until it's all-consuming." Mari's fear of bed bugs exhausts her. The warning about the basement is drowned out by her anxieties about the house's wood paneling. Creepy noises and unsettling smells are just a backdrop to her furious inspection and cleaning.

The other thing on Mari's mind is weed, or rather, her lack of it. She is desperate for a fix to quell her racing thoughts. There are thousands of miles between Mari and her usual hookups, but she faces a much larger obstacle. Fresh out of rehab after an overdose, Mari knows that she cannot simply ask a new friend for help. She must be more cautious lest she be sent back to rehab or worse. She hatches an outrageous plan to grow her own marijuana in one of the abandoned houses on Maple Street and pursues it with zeal. She joins the local gardening club, where she befriends Yusef, a handsome teen and one of the few boys at her new school. Yusef has no clue about Mari's "secret garden," as she calls it. He is adamantly against the drug, and for good reason. Half of his family is in prison for possession, as are, Mari is horrified to discover, most of the Black men in Cedarville.

Some critics took issue with the amount of time Jackson devotes to Mari's fixation on weed. A reviewer for *Publishers Weekly* wrote that "Mari's addiction-induced tunnel-vision takes center stage to the detriment of other components" of the story; Breanna Henry, writing for the *New Orleans Review*, offered a similar critique. Other critics, however, argue that Mari's "tunnel-vision" feels like a believable representation of addiction, even as she pursues her quest to extreme ends. Jackson also offers thoughtful commentary balancing addiction issues with the racism of the War on Drugs. "Jackson digs into the reasons a person might self-medicate and what happens in the aftermath of drugs taking over a community," Brown wrote. It is to Jackson's credit that she explores the relationship between addiction and punishment instead of moralizing about Mari's behavior. (Yusef offers this perspective, but authentically and with heart.)

Even more impressive, Jackson weaves Mari's guilt about her addiction into the plot. Mari oscillates between excitement for her impending harvest and shame. She feels personally responsible for uprooting her family, noting that her mother spent their savings to help her get clean. Mari wants to start fresh, but in her mind, a new start means punishing herself for her past. A star athlete, she refuses to join the track team at her new school, telling herself that she does not deserve the good things she had before. Thus, when truly strange things start happening around the house, Mari is afraid to speak up about them. She does not want to make her mother think she is smoking again or ruin the work she has done to regain the personal freedom she lost after the accident. Her mother knows about her bed bug phobia—a disorder called delusional parasitosis—and Mari believes that, should she give the impression that she is really losing it, she might never be allowed to leave the house again.

As if Mari did not have enough problems, there is also Piper, a smirking tattletale who, in Mari's mind, exists only to make her life miserable. But as frustrating as Piper can be, any reader can see that the child is lonely. In her loneliness, Piper reaches out to an imaginary friend named Ms. Suga. When household items inexplicably vanish or frightening notes appear beneath Mari's door, Piper blames Ms. Suga; Mari, not without cause, blames Piper. In addition to this ghostly figure is the Hag, an urban legend about a demon woman who inhabits human bodies to steal their skin. The Hag is said to reside in Mari's new house, which might explain why most of her new classmates keep her at arm's length. There is so much Mari does not know about her new town, including why the other homes on her block are entirely abandoned. Exploration of those homes yields more questions: why did the inhabitants leave all of their belongings behind? These mysteries lead Mari to the town's most powerful force, the Sterling Foundation, the same foundation that hosts Mari's mother's residency, which is aimed at attracting new residents to displace the old. Learning about the various wealthy, White patrons of the foundation, Mari uncovers the structures of inequity that shape the town.

White Smoke received a starred review from *Kirkus*, which wrote that it "begs to be finished in one sitting"—another reviewer, for the blog *Nerds & Beyond*, used the same words—and presents "a masterful juxtaposition of searing social commentary and genuinely creepy haunts." The disembodied footsteps in the hall are just as unsettling as the massive prison complex that casts a literal shadow over the town; the apparition with burning skin frightens as does the sickly-sweet politeness of the foundation's top executive. Critics were divided regarding the book's ending, but Brown found much to admire, calling it one of the novel's "best parts." "Given the topics Jackson is dealing with, a pat ending would do a disservice to the characters and the readers," they wrote. Clearly, Jackson is working on a larger canvas; her characters are a part of a historical drama written through centuries of racism and oppression. Their individual resolutions are necessarily small compared to the questions the book raises. As Brown wrote, "The ending may not be what every reader wants, but it's the best ending the book could have." There are several final twists, sensitively deployed, that will surprise readers and hopefully encourage them to question who the story's villain really is.

Author Biography
Tiffany D. Jackson got her start working in television and film, and in 2009, wrote and directed a short horror film called *The Field Trip*. She published her first young adult novel, *Allegedly*, in 2017, followed by *Monday's Not Coming* in 2018. Her first *New York Times* best seller was *Grown* (2020).

Molly Hagan

Review Sources
Brown, Alex. Review of *White Smoke*, by Tiffany D. Jackson. *Locus*, 25 Nov. 2021, locusmag.com/2021/11/alex-brown-reviews-white-smoke-by-tiffany-d-jackson/. Accessed 12 Jan. 2022.
Henry, Breanna. Review of *White Smoke*, by Tiffany D. Jackson. *New Orleans Review*, 2021, www.neworleansreview.org/white-smoke/. Accessed 12 Jan. 2022.
Review of *White Smoke*, by Tiffany D. Jackson. *Kirkus*, 29 June, 2021, www.kirkusreviews.com/book-reviews/tiffany-d-jackson/white-smoke-jackson/. Accessed 12 Jan. 2022.
Review of *White Smoke*, by Tiffany D. Jackson. *Publishers Weekly*, 8 July 2021, www.publishersweekly.com/978-0-06-302909-5. Accessed 12 Jan. 2022.
"*White Smoke* Review: A Terrifyingly Good Story from Tiffany D. Jackson." Review of *White Smoke*, by Tiffany D. Jackson. *Nerds & Beyond*, 7 Sept. 2021, www.nerdsandbeyond.com/2021/09/07/white-smoke-review-a-terrifyingly-good-story-from-tiffany-d-jackson/. Accessed 12 Jan. 2022.

The Wild Fox of Yemen

Author: Threa Almontaser
Publisher: Graywolf Press (Minneapolis, MN). 112 pp.
Type of work: Poetry
Locales: United States, Yemen

The Wild Fox of Yemen, *the debut poetry volume of Yemeni American writer Threa Almontaser, is a powerful collection of poems that explore themes of identity, history, and survival.*

In many ways, *The Wild Fox of Yemen* (2021) feels like an unprecedented book of poetry. This is due to its author, Threa Almontaser, whose talent for crafting vibrant verse about what it means to be an Arab American woman is largely unmatched. Born and raised in New York to a Yemeni family, Almontaser has a bifurcated worldview that toggles back and forth between its two parts when expressed on the page. This stylistic trait is perhaps most evident in the way that Almontaser writes in both English and Arabic throughout the book. In interviews she has explained that her use of language reflects how her mind works in everyday life as she interacts with young children in her family and during her day job teaching English as a Second Language to immigrants and refugees. Almontaser is not the first poet of Middle Eastern descent to use Arabic in her work; however, the way in which she integrates the language is transformative. While most of the poems are written primarily in English, Arabic words, phrases, and verses are included throughout many of them. Some of these words are spelled phonetically with the English alphabet while others appear in Arabic script. Almontaser also enhances the book's sense of bilingual codeswitching by including verses that are written in English but must be read from the right side of the page to the left like Arabic. In these instances, it is easy to deduce that certain words in Arabic capture her thoughts and feelings more accurately than their English equivalents ever could. It also seems to be an act of cultural preservation as her poem "Recognized Language" suggests when she writes: "Where did my old words go, my first words? Sometimes I dream / in Arabic without understanding. . . I try calling Arabic back / like calling wild horses."

One of the most interesting effects of Almontaser's decision to not provide translations of any Arabic that appears in the book is that it facilitates a role reversal between her and her English readers. As Almontaser points out in several poems, she is often treated as a foreigner in the United States, despite being born in the country, simply because she wears a hijab, a traditional Muslim head covering. By ensuring that her poems reflect the world as she experiences it as a Yemeni American Muslim woman,

English-speaking readers suddenly become the outsiders or foreigners who exist on the edges of her world. This may initially seem alienating to some, but it amplifies the collection's overall atmosphere of intimacy. In the end, readers are given a look at the way that the poet's mind really works.

Indeed, *The Wild Fox of Yemen* is a raw and deeply personal collection of poems that gets much of its resonance from the unfiltered way that Almontaser shares her thoughts and feelings. As a writer, she is not one to hold back—a quality that becomes particularly clear whenever she explores painful subjects like the different types of racism that she has experienced in post–September 11 America. For example, in the poem "Hunting Girliness" she writes:

Threa Almontaser

> I say, Truth is,
>
> > I quit being cautious in third grade
> > when the towers fell &, later, wore
>
> the city's hatred as hijab.

In a later poem, "Hidden Bombs in My Coochie," Almontaser discusses how in the US she is treated like a terrorist, or the wife of one. She also demonstrates how racism does not always manifest as blatantly anti-Muslim behavior but sometimes instead as people fetishizing or "othering" her. In the poem "Muslim Girl with White Guys, Ending at the Edge of a Ridge," for example, she recounts incidents where White men asked her to write their names in Arabic so that they can get her language, which they do not understand or have a connection to, tattooed on their bodies later. Again and again, Almontaser proves that she is not afraid to make her readers uncomfortable by telling the truth—even when it means criticizing a culture that they likely participate in on some level.

Another recurring theme that Almontaser explores throughout *The Wild Fox of Yemen* is the tension that exists around the intersection of her identity's two nationalities. While the aforementioned racism is perhaps the most obvious example of the inherent conflict that comes from being a Yemeni Muslim in the US, Almontaser also uses several of her poems to discuss how being an American negatively impacts her experiences as a Yemeni Muslim. In the poem "Portraits of This Country," for example, she reflects on how her mother and other family members often view the US as a dangerous, corruptive, and sinful force. As a result, they blame every bad thing that happens on the country that "ruined" her. In other poems, she writes about how growing up in

America has made her feel less connected to her mother tongue, heritage, and who she really is as a person. By the end of the collection, it becomes clear that Almontaser feels torn between two cultures but not fully accepted by either—she is American when she goes back to Yemen and Yemeni when she is in America.

Arguably, the book's most powerful subject is the current socioeconomic state of Yemen, one of the world's poorest countries. Since the mid-2010s, the nation has been embroiled in a multilateral civil war that has devastated its infrastructure and led to the extreme poverty and hunger of roughly 20 million Yemeni people. Almontaser draws attention to this crisis in her family's homeland through a series of five poems that are grouped together. Each provides readers with another glimpse of how dire the situation is in Yemen and the myriad factors that contributed to its calamitous state. For example, in "Coffee Arabica as a Maelstrom of Endless Aftershocks," Almontaser describes being approached by a young child in Yemen who is offering her body in exchange for money. In "Guide to Gardening Your Roots," she explains how British colonizers divided Yemen into competing halves. In "Yemen Rising as Poorest Country in the World," she writes about the myriad challenges her people face:

> The water here is weaponized. The water here
> is full of parasites and pirates. If you swim too long,
>
> either one can steal you. The politicians that dug themselves
> into our gospeled fields were bad seeds.

Many Western readers will find these poems to be both enlightening and heartbreaking. As *The Wild Fox of Yemen* demonstrates, Almontaser is a highly descriptive writer with a talent for crafting potent imagery. In "Etymology of Hair," she describes the aftermath of a haircut as strands that stick to everyone "like pollen." In a poem called "Stained Skin," she talks about the magical combination of henna and her aunts who are "birthed from the bottom of their mother's / tea cup" with "skin simmering darker, darker." Just as she excels at depicting the beauty of life, Almontaser has a way of capturing its mundane moments and ugliness, too. She is an exceptional worldbuilder who excels at transporting her readers to different memories. Reading *The Wild Fox of Yemen*, it is easy to imagine what it is like to be a Yemeni American girl in New York in the late 1990s and early 2000s, who uses henna to paint images from the popular Dragon Ball cartoon on her hands and who listens to both Britney Spears and her parents' fears of their family being attacked for being Muslim after the September 11 terrorist attacks.

A playful yet defiant tone to *The Wild Fox of Yemen* that many readers may find intoxicating becomes most evident in the book's recurring motif of womanhood. Through sporadic snapshots of Almontaser's life that are peppered throughout different poems, she creates a coming-of-age narrative about how she forged her own definition of what it means to be a woman in the world of the twenty-first century. For example, in the book's opening poem, "Hunting Girliness," she writes about how her femininity is not soft, sweet, nor demure, but more comparable to Cerberus—the monster in Greek mythology that guards the gates of hell. Her signature cheeky wordplay that scaffolds the book's defiance reappears in "When White Boys Ask to See My Hair," a poem that begins with the humorous line, "My hair isn't taking any visitors right now." Even the creative use of space that Almontaser employs when crafting her poems reveals how she as an artist is not willing to conform. In this way, her work feels comparable to other boundary-pushing poets of her generation, such as the Black nonbinary poet Danez Smith.

Reception of *The Wild Fox of Yemen* has been overwhelmingly positive. In 2020, its manuscript won the Walt Whitman Award—a coveted prize that led to its publication by Graywolf Press, as well as $5,000 and a residency in Umbria, Italy. According to the judges who selected it, *The Wild Fox of Yemen* won because it had the Whitman-like qualities of being "vibrant," "rebellious," and "linguistically diverse," while acknowledging the self's myriad identities. After *The Wild Fox of Yemen* was published, critics continued to sing its praises. In her review for the *Guardian*, Kate Kellaway wrote that Almontaser's debut collection was "a dazzling exploration of a life caught between different cultures."

Not all critics called the book flawless, however. Zoha Khan wrote in her otherwise positive review for the *Michigan Daily* that, "At times, the language and the structure seemed to intentionally confuse the reader, though that might've been Almontaser's purpose." Indeed, at first glance many of the poems that populate *The Wild Fox of Yemen* feel impenetrable because of their unconventionality. For some readers, it may take time to adjust to reading Almontaser's unique style. Others may not be up for the challenge or may find it to be too much work. It would be their loss, however, as Almontaser's poetry only becomes richer and easier to comprehend the more one engages with it.

For many critics, Almontaser's original voice and poetic style were not hurdles to overcome but triumphs to celebrate. For example, Rachel Hadas wrote for *TLS Magazine*: "Almontaser's verbal richness doesn't stall or cloy; rather, her bold poems convey the spaciousness afforded by freedom and truth-telling. They keep moving, and we try to keep pace." It is true that there is a provocativeness and rhythm to Almontaser's verses that at times can feel comparable to rap music. This feeling is amplified by the fact that she occasionally namechecks the hip-hop artists she listened to growing up, such as Lil Wayne and the Fugees.

Ultimately, *The Wild Fox of Yemen* is a collection of poetry that should not be missed. It will sate anyone who has been looking for representation of the contemporary American Muslim woman's experience. Similarly, its depiction of Yemeni culture and the humanitarian crisis in Yemen are especially critical for Western readers to understand. More than that, however, Almontaser's exploration of raw, personal subject matters blended with her incredible poetic style make for an intrepid piece of art. It is likely to inspire many others to push the boundaries of their own work.

Author Biography
Threa Almontaser is a Yemeni American writer, educator, translator, and multimedia artist. A Fulbright scholar, she is the winner of the Unsilenced Grant for Muslim American Women Writers and the Brett Elizabeth Jenkins Poetry Prize, among other honors.

Emily E. Turner

Review Sources
Boe, Meredith. "The Body of History and the Memory of Home in 'The Wild Fox of Yemen.'" Review of *The Wild Fox of Yemen*, by Threa Almontaser. *Chicago Review of Books*, 12 Apr. 2021, chireviewofbooks.com/2021/04/12/the-body-of-history-and-the-memory-of-home-in-the-wild-fox-of-yemen/. Accessed 17 Feb. 2022.

Hadas, Rachel. "Cats and Cerberus." Review of *The Wild Fox of Yemen*, by Threa Almontaser. *TLS Magazine,* 25 July 2021, www.the-tls.co.uk/articles/the-wild-fox-of-yemen-threa-almontaser-review-rachel-hadas. Accessed 11 Feb. 2022.

Kellaway, Kate. "Darting between Two Worlds." Review of *The Wild Fox of Yemen*, by Threa Almontaser. *The Guardian*, 3 Aug. 2021, www.theguardian.com/books/2021/aug/03/the-wild-fox-of-yemen-by-threa-almontaser-review-darting-between-two-worlds. Accessed 11 Feb. 2022.

Khan, Zoha. "'The Wild Fox of Yemen' and Finding the Little Wild Fox Inside All of Us." Review of *The Wild Fox of Yemen*, by Threa Almontaser. *The Michigan Daily*, 19 Sept. 2021, www.michigandaily.com/arts/the-wild-fox-of-yemen-and-finding-the-little-wild-fox-inside-all-of-us/. Accessed 11 Feb. 2022.

Winter in Sokcho

Author: Elisa Shua Dusapin (b. 1992)
First published: *Hiver à Sokcho*, 2016, in Switzerland
Translated from the French by Aneesa Abbas Higgins
Publisher: Open Letter (Rochester, New York). 160 pp.
Type of work: Novel
Time: Present day
Locales: Sokcho, South Korea, and environs

Elisa Shua Dusapin's debut novel, Winter in Sokcho, *originally published in French in 2016 and translated into English in 2021, tells the tells the story of a young biracial woman grappling with her identity and relationships in a desolate Korean resort town.*

Principal characters

NARRATOR, a young French Korean receptionist
MOTHER, her Korean mother, a fishmonger
YAN KERRAND, a middle-aged French graphic novelist visiting South Korea
JUN-OH, the narrator's boyfriend, an aspiring model
OLD PARK, the owner of a disreputable guest house in Sokcho

The South Korean city in the title of Elisa Shua Dusapin's first novel, *Winter in Sokcho* (2021), originally published in French in 2016, is a popular seasonal destination for locals and tourists. A port situated on the Pacific coast in northeastern South Korea, Sokcho is a two-hour drive from the capital, Seoul. The resort is also about forty miles from the border of North Korea; between Sokcho and this border lies the Demilitarized Zone (DMZ), a heavily guarded neutral area that stretches across the Korean Peninsula and has separated North and South Korea since the 1953 ceasefire in the Korean War. During the summer, visitors to Sokcho can enjoy sandy beaches, hot springs, boating, fishing, and other outdoor activities, and the city boasts distinctive cuisine, cultural events, natural scenery, and other features typical of many resort towns. However, Sokcho is a vastly different place during the winter months. When the weather turns cold and bleak, residents retreat indoors, and visitors mostly stay away.

Winter is when the novel's protagonist and first-person narrator, an unnamed twenty-four-year-old French Korean woman (the same ethnicity as the author, and the same age she was at the time of publication) returns to Sokcho, her hometown. Her Korean mother, a fishmonger, works at the market during the day and shares a bed

Elisa Shua Dusapin
Courtesy Romain Guélat

with her daughter at night. The narrator, having completed her French and Korean literature studies at the University of Seoul, is trying to decide what to do with the rest of her life. She is in a holding pattern and has been working part-time for a month as a receptionist, cook, and maid at a second-rate guest house run by a man known as Old Park. The decrepit facility, featuring "orange and green corridors, lit by blueish light bulbs," consists of a main structure with a kitchen, lounge and guest rooms, and a separate addition, a traditional house on stilts with paper walls dividing rooms. Old Park's, which is not listed in any guidebook, is where people "washed up . . . by chance, when they'd had too much to drink or missed the last bus." When temperatures sink below zero in winter, water pipes and sewage lines tend to freeze, detracting from the already bleak ambiance.

The only visitors in town as the novel opens are a Japanese mountain climber and a bandage-swaddled young woman recovering from extensive facial plastic surgery; the thick gauze wrapped around her head makes her "look like a panda." The second tenant helps introduce one of the novel's main themes, the concept of self-image and the possibility of change. Plastic surgery has become a major industry in South Korea, thanks to the many specialists and the comparatively inexpensive cost for a wide variety of cosmetic procedures, ranging from nose jobs and hair transplants to complete facial reconstruction and breast augmentation. The narrator's self-centered boyfriend, Jun-oh, who shuttles back and forth between Seoul and Sokcho, is himself contemplating elective surgery to enhance his chances of becoming a successful model. The narrator's hypercritical mother, eager for her daughter to be married, feels that her daughter, who wears glasses and suffers weight fluctuations from bingeing and purging due to an eating disorder like bulimia, might also benefit from reconstructive work.

The main narrative begins with the arrival of a new guest, a French national from the Normandy region. He looks at the narrator while she checks him in without apparently seeing her—though she desperately wants to be seen through the eyes of someone she can respect. The man is Yan Kerrand, a graphic novelist and cartoonist "with a Western face," old enough to be the narrator's father but mysterious enough to become an object of secret desire. His presence sets off a complicated psychological reaction in the narrator. Her own father, who she never knew, was French; he disappeared, never to be seen again, soon after her mother became pregnant. Casually, Kerrand and the narrator—both outcasts because of their looks amidst a tight-knit and homogeneous society—begin a loose relationship that hinges on mutual dependence. Kerrand needs the narrator as a guide while he searches for landscapes to inspire dynamic backdrops for his drawings; he is working on the final installment in a successful comic book series about an Indiana Jones-type archaeologist who has previously experienced adventures in Egypt, Peru, Italy, and elsewhere. The narrator needs Kerrand to add variety and spice to what, even at her young age, has become a stagnant, perhaps even purposeless, existence.

Their tenuous association begins by accident and builds slowly but tensely toward an uncertain climax through a succession of small, unimportant acts that apparently bear more significance to the narrator than to Kerrand. For example, the narrator is distracted by Kerrand's unexpected appearance in the guesthouse kitchen, and she cuts her hand while chopping ingredients for a guest dinner. He sops up her blood with his handkerchief, and while he seems indifferent to the incident, his touch electrifies the narrator.

Since he renders his black-and-white drawings in ink on paper, Kerrand enlists the narrator's aid in finding appropriate materials for his art. At a supermarket, he rips open packages of paper to feel and taste the different textures of the products, and she becomes complicit in his misdemeanors by hiding the packages he damaged. Her fascination with Kerrand leads her to sneak into his room when he is absent. She also spies on him at night, watching silently at his half-opened door or listening through the paper wall separating their rooms to the scratching of his pen on paper as he creates his artwork. Kerrand wants to draw the "perfect woman," but is unsure how to proceed, so his drawings become overworked: "He daubed ink slowly and purposefully over the paper until the woman was nothing more than a black, misshapen blob." Though Kerrand is a professional artist, there is something infantile about him. He carelessly drips ink on his bedding and the moth-eaten rug covering the floor of his tiny room, and chews scraps of paper while he works.

The artist's oral fixation touches on another thematic undercurrent, the topic of food preparation and consumption. The narrator's mother is an expert chef licensed to prepare fugu, a dish made from blowfish flesh, which is potentially lethal if toxic organs are not properly removed. The mother has taught her daughter how to make sashimi, stuffed squid, baby octopus with sticky rice, and other delicacies for the guests. However, the narrator is unable to persuade Kerrand to eat these meals. The artist, who dislikes spicy dishes, usually dines in his room on fast food from Dunkin' Donuts and instant noodles from a nearby convenience store.

As time passes, the narrator begins to accompany Kerrand to nearby beaches, mountains, and waterfalls on her days off. Their relationship deepens in moments of fleeting touches and fleeting conversation; Kerrand grabs the narrator to save her from a falling icicle, and he warms her chilly fingers in his pocket. They discuss a few interests they have in common, such as a fondness for the stories of French author Guy de Maupassant and the art of French painter Claude Monet. Though the narrator speaks passable French, she insists on conversing in English. The pair visit an observation point in the DMZ, where they view the heavily fortified towers and barbed wire fences that separate the two Koreas. While there, Kerrand and the narrator notice similarities between Kerrand's home in Normandy, France—the site of the Allied invasion of Nazi-occupied Europe that helped lead to the defeat of Nazi Germany in World War II—and the DMZ, an area that serves as a stark reminder of the ongoing hostility between

North and South Korea. The narrator relates an incident when someone was killed by trigger-happy guards, and Kerrand mentions that waves on Normandy beaches still uncover the bones of dead soldiers buried in the sand.

Winter in Sokcho was widely praised by critics. It won several prestigious European literary awards upon its publication in French in 2016 and won the National Book Award for Translated Literature when it was published in English in 2021. Anandi Mishra of the *Harvard Review* noted the "subtle language and atmospheric setting," calling the novel "one of the best literary noirs in recent memory . . . [it] delivers an unassuming but potent story that lingers." Catherine Taylor of the *Guardian* agreed, especially about the language used, pointing out that "Dusapin's terse sentences are at times staggeringly beautiful, their immediacy sharply and precisely rendered from French by Aneesa Abbas Higgins." Taylor concluded, "*Winter in Sokcho* is a noirish cold sweat of a book."

Writing for the *Asian Review of Books*, Peter Gordon likewise focused on the author's skillful wordplay, praising the novel's "well-observed, sometimes wry detail," the "economic language," the "quick cuts in scene," and "abridged dialogue" that recall Kerrand's comic-book style. In a review for *Litro Magazine*, Jess Gulliver also freely acknowledged the author's and translator's linguistic skills, and focused particular praise on *Winter in Sokcho*'s depictions of relationships. Gulliver considered the thin wall between the narrator's bedroom and Kerrand's, dividing their individual worlds, as something symbolic of the border between North and South Korea. Gulliver also dwelled upon the numerous references to food, particularly fish, which are manipulated into various shapes. She compared this process to South Korea's plastic surgery industry, by which individuals undergo processes to meet regional beauty standards, including paler skin, larger eyes, thinner lips, less prominent cheekbones, and narrower face.

Winter in Sokcho offers something for everyone: romance, intrigue, suspense, character studies, cultural insights, culinary advice, and even a travelogue, all in well-composed verbal snapshots. Dusapin's distinctive, oblique style adds an air of mystery to even the most superficial encounters and maintains suspense right up until the final pages.

Author Biography
Elisa Shua Dusapin is the author of several novels in French, including *Les Billes du Pachinko* (2018) and *Vladivostok Circus* (2020).

Aneesa Abbas Higgins is a translator who specializes in translating works from French into English. Her translations have won two PEN Translates Awards, as well as a National Book Award.

Jack Ewing

Review Sources

Cheesman, Tara. Review of *Winter in Sokcho*, by Elisa Shua Dusapin. *Barrelhouse Magazine*, 13 May 2021, www.barrelhousemag.com/onlinelit/2021/05/winter-sokcho-dusapin. Accessed 4 Feb. 2022.

Gordon, Peter. Review of *Winter in Sokcho*, by Elisa Shua Dusapin. *Asian Review of Books*, 23 Jan. 2020, asianreviewofbooks.com/content/winter-in-sokcho-by-elisa-shua-dusapin/. Accessed 4 Feb. 2022.

Gulliver, Jess. Review of *Winter in Sokcho*, by Elisa Shua Dusapin. *Litro Magazine*, 10 Feb. 2020, www.litromagazine.com/literature/book-review-winter-in-sokcho-by-elisa-shua-dusapin/. Accessed 4 Feb. 2022.

Mishra, Anandi. Review of *Winter in Sokcho*, by Elisa Shuan Dusapin, translated by Aneesa Abbas Higgins. *Harvard Review*, 20 July 2021, harvardreview.org/book-review/winter-in-sokcho/. Accessed 4 Feb. 2022.

Pierson-Hagger. "Elisa Shua Dusapin's *Winter in Sokcho*: A Masterful Short Novel." *The New Statesman*, 27 July 2021, www.newstatesman.com/culture/2020/05/winter-in-sokcho-elisa-shua-dusapin-review. Accessed 4 Feb. 2022.

Taylor, Catherine. "*Winter in Sokcho* Review—Broodingly Atmospheric." *The Guardian*, 28 Feb. 2020, www.theguardian.com/books/2020/feb/28/winter-in-sokcho-review-elisa-shua-dusapin-first-novel-south-korea. Accessed 4 Feb. 2021.

Winter Recipes from the Collective

Author: Louise Glück (b. 1943)
Publisher: Farrar, Straus and Giroux (New York). 64 pp.
Type of work: Poetry

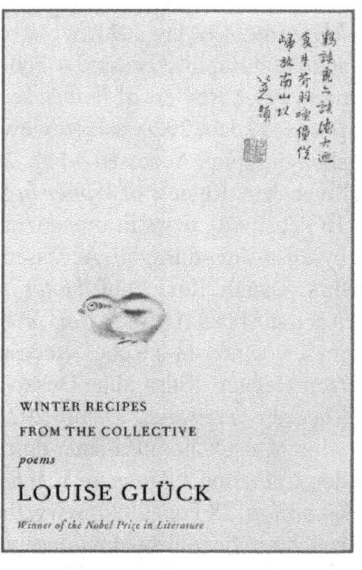

Winter Recipes from the Collective is a haunting collection of poems that meditate on the nature of life, death, and memory.

Winter Recipes from the Collective (2021) is Louise Glück's first collection of poetry since she won the 2020 Nobel Prize in Literature. This volume finds Glück mining a rich vein of thought and feeling as she explores a theme that has long preoccupied her: the transitory nature of life and the need to come to terms with one's inescapable death. These poems are full of moments of striking beauty and stark honesty. As the title poem implies, the voices in this collection are often collective in nature. Like the chorus of a Greek play, Glück's speakers seem to represent not just themselves, but a whole society. The knowledge that they pass on and the fears and delights that they voice are not just their own, but those of a people or an era. One of the great pleasures in reading Glück's newest collection of poetry lies in her ability to shift from the deeply personal and individual to the universal and collective. It is a bravura performance, the work of a poet who has mastered her craft and who uses it to speak to the essential nature of being human.

The collection's title poem is a prime example of Glück's multivalent voice. "Winter Recipes from the Collective" unfolds in an unspecified village, presumably somewhere in Asia, where men gather moss that their wives transform into a bitter but sustaining meal. During the snowy months, villagers pass the time crafting bonsai trees. There is a tension between the bleak, snow-covered world outside and the artificial light and heat that sustains the miniature trees. When the narrator holds the bowl of a bonsai tree in their hands, they see "a pine blowing in high wind / like man in the universe." The tree's life in miniature parallels the life of each of us: a small existence sheltered for a while from the void beyond. As the narrator dwells on the beauty of the trees and the sadness that is felt when one of them dies, the reader suspects they are also talking about humanity. After all, death is the great leveler: "The trees were miniature, as I have said, / but there is no such thing as death in miniature." The poem features a first-person speaker who is reflexively self-effacing. They speak in terms of "we" and "us" as often as they speak of "I" and "my," as if their existence were inextricable from that of the village collective. The speaker's own particular lived experiences—for example, walking to the arboretum while thinking of an absent friend—seem to flow ineluctably into the thoughts and words of their grandmother, instructor, or fellow villagers. Their voice is therefore not so much individual as representative, an expression of the collective experience and wisdom of generations.

In the hands of a lesser poet, this tendency toward universalizing might prove disastrous. After all, readers are generally taught that specificity gives life to a poem. Yet Glück modulates brilliantly between the poles of the universal and the particular, such that the two binaries often collapse into each other. The speaker in "Winter Recipes" is both a specific individual and the voice of a whole culture—as, in many respects, we all are. This ability to contain many voices in one is a great strength of Glück's collection, and one revered by many. Reviewing *Winter Recipes from the Collective* for the *Washington Post*, Troy Jollimore commented, "It is an end-of-life book, where the life in question could be anyone's: the poet's, the reader's, the planet's." Though the reader's own life may unfold in very different circumstances from that of the villager in the title poem, the reader nevertheless identifies with them. When they hold up the sheltered bonsai tree, one sees both a specific miniature tree and one's own fragile lives and planet.

Louise Glück

While poems in the collection are more narrative in nature, these, too, have the quality of an allegory or a fable. In "The Denial of Death," for example, a narrator loses their passport and is rejected by their companion, who simply continues the journey without them. Stranded outside of a hotel that will not admit them, the narrator is befriended by a concierge who allows them to live in an adjacent orange grove and who serves as a mentor figure. The concierge eventually conveys his perspective on their situation: "You have begun your own journey, / not into the world, like your friend's, but into yourself and your memories." On the far side of this journey, the narrator may realize that "everything returns, but what returns is not / what went away." A poem that began in a narrative mode shifts subtly into a different register, as the concierge and the traveler engage in a philosophical discussion about the nature of life, loss, and the creative impulse.

"The Denial of Death," like several of the other works in this collection, is a poem that acknowledges its own artifice. In a remarkable moment at the poem's end, the concierge and the reader collapse into a single, undifferentiated audience:

> *Concierge*, I said. *Concierge* is what I called you.
> And before that, *you*, which is, I believe,
> a convention in fiction.

Having served his purpose and spoken his truth, the concierge is revealed to be a fictional construct—as is, of course, every aspect of every poem ever written. This sort of metanarrative turn occurs several times in the collection, as Glück's speakers give a nod to the fictional nature of their narratives and the artifice of an implied relationship between a poem and its reader. It is as if there are moments in which the poem itself must fall away if Glück is to be cosmic in her scope and all-encompassing in her gaze.

"A Children's Story" is another of Gluck's poems that seems to function on an allegorical level. The brief poem's opening lines establish an uneasy tension between the mythic and the real:

> Tired of rural life, the king and queen
> return to the city, all the little princesses
> rattling in the back of the car, singing the song of being:

It is unclear whether this is a story of everyday children who see themselves as princesses, or of royalty living in a decidedly plebian fashion. As the journey to the city progresses, the poem takes on darker overtones, as the speaker reveals the truth that is known to the parents, that "all hope is lost." The "princesses" may be sheltered from this harsh reality for a while longer, but it is a burden that they will eventually inherit. Glück's poems, even ones as short as this, are puzzle boxes that call on the reader to continually reexamine them, looking for an elusive meaning. While this poem purports to be a story, it is so elliptical that no reader can piece its whole narrative together. And while its title would suggest that it is meant for an audience of children, its bleak view of the world is one that only a timeworn adult could hold. The poem has elements of an allegory, yet Glück has hidden the key that would unlock its meaning. Part of the haunting power of this and other poems in the collection are the ways in which they resist an easy explanation or a single interpretation. They abide in the reader's mind precisely because they are unresolved and unresolvable.

Readers may also find themselves studying the many connections and resonances across the various poems in this collection. For example, the children in the allegorical "A Children's Story" may echo the ones in "Winter Journey." These children, too, were ferried about in their mother's car as young girls; as adults, they reminisce in the common room of a hospital or clinic. An adult sister will also show up in "Autumn," to be joined by the speaker and their sentimental mother in "Second Wind." The teacher in "The Setting Sun" refers to "those misshapen trees the Chinese grow. / *Pun-sai*, they're called." The reference might prompt one to think not only of the bonsai trees in "Winter Recipes from the Collective," but of the great number of references to Chinese culture that course through this slim book. Another teacher, Leo Cruz, appears in "Song," the final poem of the collection. As with the concierge from "The Denial of Death," Cruz seems to recede, in the poem's final lines, into a dreamlike, imaginary figure. There is an overstory to *Winter Recipes from the Collective*, with each of the poems somehow contributing to the larger meaning of the collection itself.

Winter Recipes from the Collective has been praised as a challenging but rewarding collection that distills the themes and elements that have long animated Glück's work.

In his *Washington Post* review, Jollimore wrote that "reading Glück's new poems is a joyful experience, as reading great poetry always is. It is a grim joy, yes, but one that feels true to its moment, one that we need, and one that readers of this bleakly elegant collection will find themselves savoring." The reviewer for *Publishers Weekly* likewise called the collection "magnificent," remarking on the "reflective poems that are deeply engaged with the idea of being alone with oneself." Poet Elisa Gabbert, writing in the *New York Times*, saw the collection as giving "an impression of exhaustion, as though language and material have been nearly depleted." This is a form of praise because Gabbert concludes that "Glück's preoccupations are what poetry is for . . . poems are confrontations with the void." In the *Chicago Review of Books*, Mandana Chaffa called *Winter Recipes* "an exquisitely small collection—the way an atom that contains the world is small—that further solidifies Glück's place as one of the eminent poets of our time."

The audience for serious poetry has shrunk dramatically over the past century, though it did experience a notable resurgence during the coronavirus pandemic. The form simply does not approach the popularity of the novel, to say nothing of newer media such as film, television, and the internet. Yet while the readership for a new collection of poetry is narrower than it would have been generations ago, it is nevertheless ardent. Louise Glück's new collection will reward the attention and patience of readers willing to grapple with the essentially transitory nature of human existence. Glück is not afraid to look into the abyss and to consider the inevitability that, because of our inherently mortal natures, we will each lose all that is dear to us. Spending time with Glück's work may prepare the reader to look squarely at this reality, and to find joy despite—or even because of—the fleeting nature of our existence.

Author Biography

The author of thirteen collections of poetry and two books of essays, Louise Glück has received many prizes and awards, including the Nobel Prize, the Pulitzer Prize, the National Book Award, and a National Humanities Medal.

Matthew J. Bolton

Review Sources

Chaffa, Mandana. "The Transformative Simplicity of Louise Glück's 'Winter Recipes from the Collective'." Review of *Winter Recipes from the Collective*, by Louise Glück. *Chicago Review of Books*, 28 Oct. 2021, chireviewofbooks.com/2021/10/28/winter-recipes-from-the-collective/. Accessed 30 Dec. 2021.

Gabbert, Elisa. "Louise Glück's Stark New Book Affirms Her Icy Precision." Review of *Winter Recipes from the Collective*, by Louise Glück. *The New York Times*, 26 Oct. 2021, www.nytimes.com/2021/10/26/books/review/louise-gluck-winter-recipes-from-the-collective.html. Accessed 30 Dec. 2021.

Jollimore, Troy. "Louise Glück's First Collection since her Nobel Gracefully Captures Our Fragility." Review of *Winter Recipes from the Collective*, by Louise Glück. *The Washington Post*, 4 Nov. 2021. www.washingtonpost.com/entertainment/books/louise-glucks-first-collection-since-her-nobel-gracefully-captures-our-fragility/2021/11/03/2047ae94-2d3f-11ec-baf4-d7a4e075eb90_story.html. Accessed 30 Dec. 2021.

Review of *Winter Recipes from the Collective*, by Louise Glück. *Publishers Weekly*, 17 Oct. 2021, www.publishersweekly.com/978-0-374-60410-3. Accessed 9 Feb. 2022.

The Woman They Could Not Silence
One Woman, Her Incredible Fight for Freedom, and the Men Who Tried to Make Her Disappear

Author: Kate Moore
Publisher: Sourcebooks (Naperville, IL). 560 pp.
Type of work: Biography, history
Time: 1860–97
Locales: Manteno, Illinois; Jacksonville, Illinois; Granville, Illinois; Chicago, Illinois

The Woman They Could Not Silence follows the story of Elizabeth Packard, a woman who was involuntarily admitted without trial in the nineteenth century to an institution for people with mental illness by her husband. Packard's intelligence and will are explored through her journey to legally prove her sanity as well as inspire change for women and people with mental illness.

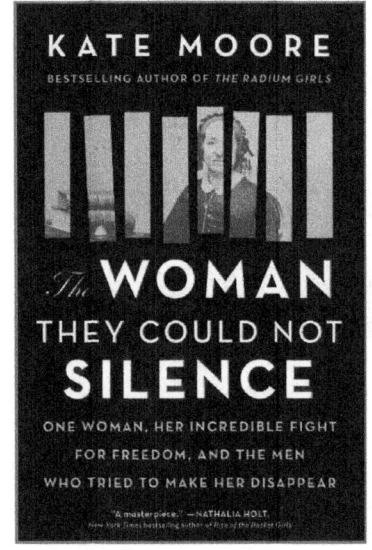

Principal personages

ELIZABETH PACKARD, an activist for the rights of women and people with mental illness
THEOPHILUS PACKARD, her husband, a pastor
DR. ANDREW MCFARLAND, a doctor interested in the field of psychiatry and superintendent of Illinois State Hospital for the Insane
SARAH MINARD, another woman held at the Illinois State Hospital whom Packard became close to
GENERAL ALLEN C. FULLER, Illinois politician hired to lead the team investigating McFarland

June 18, 1860, was Elizabeth Packard's final day at her family home in Manteno, Illinois, for what would prove to be over three years. On that day, her husband, Theophilus, a pastor, had made arrangements to have her admitted against her will to the Illinois State Hospital for the Insane in Jacksonville, Illinois. Even though she was an intelligent and articulate forty-three-year-old woman who had become a fervent believer in women's rights, Packard had no recourse to fight her husband's decision to send her away. In fact, veteran writer Kate Moore argues in her 2021 book *The Woman They Could Not Silence: One Woman, Her Incredible Fight for Freedom, and the Men Who Tried to Make Her Disappear* that it was Packard's very ability to express her mind, especially publicly, on multiple subjects, and her disagreements

Kate Moore

with her husband's religious philosophy, that led Theophilus to have her held involuntarily at the institution.

Throughout the work, Moore effectively and engagingly illustrates, via a mixture of accessible historical context and storytelling, how this moment began a new era in Packard's life. While she had largely been, according to the traditional gender roles she had been brought up on, an obedient wife and loving mother to six children for over twenty years, her forced removal fundamentally changed the relationship she had with her family. Among other issues, her youngest children would not be as familiar with her when they saw her next, they would be taught by her husband not to respect her, and her only daughter, a ten-year-old child, was traumatically burdened with taking over her mother's duties despite her young age. Even though Packard viewed her children as her whole world, Moore poignantly relates that "Elizabeth was lost to all her children now." During her time in Jacksonville, she had to learn to adapt if she wanted freedom, and that meant, in part, that she had to emotionally close off the grieving mother.

Moore uses this first part of Packard's biography to stress the lack of women's rights, particularly for married women during the 1860s, rights that would have allowed her to fight being sent to the institution and to remain with her children. One of the strengths of *The Woman They Could Not Silence* is Moore's ability to intertwine the humanized biography of Packard with a treatise on historical attitudes toward women. Built into the story of Packard's life experiences, readers find evidence of Moore's own dedicated research as the author sources various primary documents, including, most affectingly, Packard's own writings, to illustrate the historical facts. Two examples appear in the third chapter, where Moore relays that married women "could be received at an asylum simply 'by the request of the husband,'" because they were legally viewed as "civilly dead." In these examples, Moore quotes the 1863 publication *Reports of the Illinois State Hospital for the Insane, 1847–1862* as well as the Seneca Falls Convention's 1848 Declaration of Sentiments. This reliance on primary sources establishes the veracity of the authentic history behind Packard's experiences. Moore also sprinkles helpful tidbits throughout the text to help contemporary readers understand the differences between the twenty-first century and the nineteenth. For instance, when monetary amounts are mentioned, such as Theophilus's debt, Moore shares what the present-day cost would be. Another aspect of the time period Moore discusses in conjunction with Packard's state of affairs is the Civil War. Moore introduces the issues of slavery, abolition, oppression, and freedom as they connected to the war happening in Elizabeth's own home and the larger scale civil unrest.

While women's issues are a significant concern in the book, Packard's years in the state facility, as captivatingly presented by Moore, showcase the misogyny of the criteria used for institutionalizing women, the often-horrible conditions of Jacksonville and other asylums, and Packard's own indomitable spirit. It is important to acknowledge, as Moore notes, that 1860 was not the first time Packard had been placed into such a facility. At nineteen years old, she had already started to demonstrate her vast intelligence while serving as Randolph College's principal in Massachusetts. Her father placed her at the State Lunatic Hospital, citing "insanity" brought on by "'mental labor.'" With a piercing bluntness characteristic of the book, Moore points out that "doctors were policing women who stepped outside society's strictly defined gender spheres—work and intellect for men, home and children for women—in what could be described as a 'medicalization of female behavior.'" In 1860, her forced admittance to the state institution, an act that was in accordance with state law regarding married women, was a result of her husband's desire to take away her freedom for having the nerve to disagree with him publicly. The doctors Theophilus consulted to back his claims against his wife certified her as "insane" on the grounds of "'incessant talking'" along with "'unusual zealousness'" and "'strong will.'"

Packard's three years in the state institution in Jacksonville were somewhat contradictory. Upon admittance to the facility, she was treated like a respected guest. She was given her own room in a ward where other women had also been admitted by husbands seen as controlling. The women enjoyed companionship, decent accommodations, and gentle care, and she became a favorite. Dr. Andrew McFarland, the superintendent of the institution, seemingly treated her as his equal. However, as she grew confident in his perception of her, she studiously observed and noted inequities and unkindness in, or general lack of, real treatment, and began to freely express her opinions as well as her hatred of her husband. McFarland responded poorly to Packard's opinions and observations and became convinced that she was mentally ill. In an act of vengeance against her written self-defense and reproof demanding better conditions for all people held in the institution, he removed her from the fellowship of the women with whom she had become friends, placing her in a ward where "the smell hit her in a noxious wave," and "ahead of her, she heard noise: 'screaming, fighting, running, hallooing.' Women with 'rough, tangled, flying and streaming hair' ran riot around the ward, their skin pitch-black with dirt." This description, powerfully supported by Packard's own firsthand language, is just one of many that Moore employs to illustrate the true conditions of the institution. Packard became frightened by the abuse carried out by other patients, the attendants, and even McFarland himself. Additionally, Moore takes this opportunity to expand on the horrors some women experienced in other institutions due to such unscientifically based theories as a female genital mutilation "cure." Packard routinely heard the screams of patients whose heads were held under cold water by cruel attendants.

Contrary to McFarland's expectation that he could break Packard, in actuality his actions toward her gave her a new venue for rebellion. Rather than falling apart, she confronted the problems of the wards head-on, treating the other patients as humans and recording the abuses she observed as well as others' stories. Though McFarland ordered that she not be allowed paper or pen, she found ways to write. She recorded both surface problems in the hospital, such as McFarland refusing to keep bearable temperatures in the winter season and serving inedible food, alongside deeper concerns like physical abuse. Her careful recordings would eventually become the basis for permanent change at a legislative level.

After three years, Packard was released from the Jacksonville institution against her husband's wishes, partially because McFarland no longer wanted to deal with her. Once she regained her freedom, she attempted to return to her family. Theophilus had turned her younger children against her, and when it looked like they might be considering her as a mother again, he fled to Massachusetts with the children. Packard had no recourse because the law was in favor of her husband; not even divorce, which she initially rejected as an option, would give her any rights to her children. Moore continues to highlight Packard's unconquerable spirit over the next few years, when she took charge of not only her own life but grabbed legal reins to make a change not only for the friends she had left behind at the Illinois State Hospital but for women everywhere.

The rest of the book shares the battles Packard fought for herself, for other women, and for people with mental illness. Moore traces her efforts to prove her sanity, clear her name through an official trial, and self-publish her account of Jacksonville along with several other writings, including a treatise against McFarland. Moore demonstrates Packard's perseverance in being able to support herself financially through creative means such as crowdsourcing and going door-to-door sharing her story to pay for the publication costs. She also tracks Packard's quest for change and success in adjusting the legal system's view of women and people with mental illness. Her adamance in speaking out led to a reconsideration of the ways people could be admitted to institutions and a new state law that prevented women from being institutionalized against their will without a trial. She continued to campaign for the causes of women and people with mental illness for the remainder of her life, ensuring the passage of further legislation in a number of states, instituting reforms such as independent inspection bodies for facilities designed to treat people with mental illness.

Many critics have praised *The Woman They Could Not Silence* as a significant and worthwhile read overall. While Annalisa Quinn, in a review for National Public Radio (NPR), critiqued the biography for not fully exploring the complexity of Packard's character, other reviewers noted that its effective highlighting of an integral but lesser-known activist is timely given the prominent calls for social justice made by several groups by the 2020s. Michelle Ross, reviewing the work for *Booklist*, called it a "veritable tour de force," and an anonymous reviewer for *Publishers Weekly* lauded Moore's blending of storytelling with "historical fidelity," noting that she also "paints Elizabeth's fierce intelligence and unflagging ambition with vibrant brushstrokes."

Author Biography
Kate Moore has worked as an editor and is an acclaimed writer of nonfiction works. Her 2017 book *The Radium Girls: The Dark Story of America's Shining Women* was a *New York Times* Best Seller.

Theresa L. Stowell, PhD

Review Sources
Quinn, Annalisa. "A Woman Is Committed to an Asylum for Thinking in 'The Woman They Could Not Silence.'" *NPR*, 23 June 2021, www.npr.org/2021/06/23/1009355765/the-woman-they-could-not-silence-book-review. Accessed 26 Oct. 2021.

Ross, Michelle. Review of *The Woman They Could Not Silence: One Woman, Her Incredible Fight for Freedom, and the Men Who Tried to Make Her Disappear*, by Kate Moore. *Booklist*, vol. 117, no. 15, Apr. 2021, p. 10. *Literary Reference Center Plus*, search.ebscohost.com/login.aspx?direct=true&db=lkh&AN=149629874&site=lrc-plus. Accessed 18 Oct. 2021.

Spydell, Anna. Review of *The Woman They Could Not Silence: One Woman, Her Incredible Fight for Freedom, and the Men Who Tried to Make Her Disappear*, by Kate Moore. *BookPage*, July 2021, www.bookpage.com/reviews/26423-kate-moore-woman-they-could-not-silence-history/. Accessed 18 Oct. 2021.

Statler, Chad E. Review of *The Woman They Could Not Silence: One Woman, Her Incredible Fight for Freedom, and the Men Who Tried to Make Her Disappear*, by Kate Moore. *Library Journal*, 1 June 2021, www.libraryjournal.com/?reviewDetail=the-woman-they-could-not-silence-one-woman-her-incredible-fight-for-freedom-and-the-men-who-tried-to-make-her-disappear-2114775. Accessed 26 Oct. 2021.

Review of *The Woman They Could Not Silence: One Woman, Her Incredible Fight for Freedom, and the Men Who Tried to Make Her Disappear*, by Kate Moore. *Publishers Weekly*, 10 May 2021, www.publishersweekly.com/978-1-4926-9672-8. Accessed 26 Oct. 2021.

A World on the Wing
The Global Odyssey of Migratory Birds

Author: Scott Weidensaul (b. 1959)
Publisher: W. W. Norton (New York).
 Illustrated. 400 pp.
Type of work: Nature
Time: Mostly the early twenty-first century
Locales: The United States, Canada, China, India, Cyprus, the Bahamas

In A World on the Wing: The Global Odyssey of Migratory Birds, *nature writer and birder Scott Weidensaul explores the lengthy and often-dangerous migrations undertaken by numerous bird species and the efforts to track, study, and ultimately protect migratory birds and their habitats.*

A nature writer, avid birder, and wildlife researcher, Scott Weidensaul made an influential contribution to the public understanding of migratory birds in 1999 with *Living on the Wind: Across the Hemisphere with Migratory Birds*, a volume that delves into the impressive migrations carried out by millions of birds each year. He returns to that topic with the 2021 publication *A World on the Wing: The Global Odyssey of Migratory Birds*. This follow-up of sorts highlights relevant updates to the scientific understanding of migration, covers new ground, and offers further insights and perspective into the area of study that has so fascinated both Weidensaul himself and the many dedicated researchers and volunteer birders he encounters.

A World on the Wing begins with a prologue that offers readers a preview of the sort of work the book will be. Opening in medias res, the prologue finds Weidensaul on the tundra of Alaska's Denali National Park and Preserve, where he and a small group of researchers have traveled to capture and place geolocators on local birds. The group is hoping to place such devices on gray-cheeked thrushes to track their migrations, which take the birds from Alaska and northern Canada all the way to South America and back, and determine where, specifically, in South America the birds go. The process of catching the thrushes is tricky work on its own, and the researchers' location in the Alaskan wilderness leads to further, and far more dangerous, complications. While waiting to trap thrushes in a patch of nearby willows, they accidentally cross paths with a grizzly bear and her cub and narrowly escape death or severe injury when the charging adult bear abruptly decides to flee rather than attack. In addition to providing an exciting opening for *A World on the Wing*, this anecdote aptly demonstrates the lengths to which scientists studying migratory birds are willing to go to gather the data they need—and the uncomfortable and even dangerous situations in which Weidensaul is willing to put himself for the sake of his book. That willingness persists throughout the work, which sees Weidensaul and his companions navigate washed-out roads while searching for Amur falcons in northeastern India, pursue illegal songbird trappers in Cyprus, and spend hours counting birds in China's coastal wetlands.

The dangers and discomforts faced by Weidensaul and his fellow researchers, however, are often trivial in comparison to the trials of the migratory bird populations they work to track. While the basic concept of bird migration will be familiar to most readers, for whom flocks of birds traveling with the seasons is likely a common sight, the extent of the migrations taking place and the physically strenuous work required to make such journeys may be far less obvious. While Weidensaul's firsthand experiences in the field make up a portion of the book, much of *A World on the Wing* is dedicated to exploring migratory patterns and the science underlying them. Perhaps one of the most stunning topics of discussion is the sheer distance birds are capable of traveling while navigating between their summer and winter habitats. A whimbrel wearing a tracking device, Weidensaul notes, was found to have migrated 18,000 miles over the course of a year. Other birds travel even farther: Arctic terns, for instance, have been documented to fly as many as 57,000 miles in the timespan of a year, migrating between sites as far flung as the Netherlands and Australia. These long journeys can be dangerous, for a multitude of reasons. In addition to facing predation from other birds as well as human and nonhuman animals, migratory birds must at times travel through dangerous weather, including hurricanes, and risk arriving at their final destination only to discover that a once-forested area has been lost to logging or construction.

The long distances and strenuous activity required of many migratory birds have led to intriguing physical adaptations in those species. In some cases, Weidensaul notes, birds' internal organs—such as those belonging to their digestive system—atrophy over the course of the journey, ensuring that the birds expend energy only on the processes and organs most essential to migration. After the birds arrive at their destinations, the organs resume normal function until the birds must embark on their next migration. Some birds may likewise be able to endure long, sustained flights through the process of unihemispheric sleep, in which one side of the brain sleeps while the other remains awake. Weidensaul further notes that some birds undergo periods of extensive feeding and weight gain as the time of migration approaches, which ultimately grants species such as black-tailed godwits the fat reserves needed to fly for more than a week without a break while migrating between destinations such as Alaska and New Zealand. While the phenomenon of stockpiling body fat in preparation for a period of sustained exercise and little food is a relatively easy process for a lay reader to understand, the means by which birds actually navigate between their summer and winter habitats and return to the same places year after year are far more complex. Weidensaul notes that birds' navigational abilities have long fascinated researchers, who, over the decades, have proposed a host of explanations for those abilities. Among the most intriguing—and mindboggling—of those theories involves the phenomenon of quantum entanglement, which may contribute to birds' apparent abilities to sense and navigate based on Earth's magnetic field.

The environmental threats posed by climate change and human activities such as land-clearing are common concerns in many books dealing with the natural world, and *A World on the Wing* is no exception. Indeed, Weidensaul discusses efforts both to protect bird populations, some of which declined significantly during the twentieth and twenty-first centuries, and to conserve the habitats on which they rely for survival. Such efforts are, much like the technology used to track migrating birds, continually evolving in conjunction with advancements in the understanding of birds' behaviors and preferred habitats. Weidensaul makes the important point that while conservationists long worked to protect the forests of South and Central America, which serve as vital wintering habitats for many North American species, less attention was historically paid to those birds' North American habitats, which were subject to deforestation, forest fragmentation, and the elimination of the transitional spaces known as early successional habitats. In addition, he calls attention to the importance of areas known as stopover sites, places where some birds on long migratory journeys land to rest and feed. Even if a bird population's place of origin and eventual destination are protected, the loss of that population's typical stopover sites could prove devastating. Stopover sites can be particularly vulnerable to human development because their importance to birds has not always been documented. Nevertheless, Weidensaul points out that hope remains—as of the writing of the book, crucial stopover sites in coastal China had recently gained protected status from the Chinese government, which researchers hoped would help protect the sandpipers and other birds prone to stopping there.

An experienced nature writer, Weidensaul is skilled at explaining complex scientific concepts in an engaging and comprehensible manner. This skill is evident in his explanations of birds' often-bizarre biology and of the array of technologies used to track them. Among the most prominent tracking technologies are devices placed directly on the birds, enabling researchers to document those specific birds' journeys for later analysis. Advances in miniaturization and tracker technology have benefited the migration-research community enormously. As Weidensaul explains, earlier tracking devices were suitable for certain large birds but were much too heavy and cumbersome for small birds. Small geolocators and even smaller nanotags, on the other hand, are suitable for use on much smaller birds and, in the case of nanotags, can offer more geographically precise data. However, Weidensaul notes, such technological advances have not completely superseded earlier methods of tracking migrations and enumerating the birds passing through a given area. Radar, for instance, is capable of detecting large flocks of birds and can be used to assess migrations that take place at night and are largely invisible to the general population. Methods that integrate low-tech forms of recordkeeping and internet technology likewise remain useful: the online initiative eBird, for instance, enables birders from around the world to upload digital records of the birds spotted in their regions, creating a substantial dataset that researchers can use to analyze the movement of migratory birds as well as to support conservation initiatives. An informative and engaging work, *A World on the Wing* may very well prompt more people to join the ranks of birders contributing to initiatives such as eBird, as Weidensaul conveys both the appeal of birding as a pastime and the success of collaborations between researchers and hobbyists over the previous decades.

A World on the Wing received several positive reviews, with the anonymous critic for *Publishers Weekly* describing Weidensaul's work as "remarkable" and the *Kirkus* critic stating that the book "belongs in every birder's library." In a review for the *New York Times*, Christian Cooper identified *A World on the Wing* as a strong follow-up to Weidensaul's early book *Living on the Wind* and noted that "the difference this go-round is time and skin in the game," calling attention to the author's passion for bird migration, which has only deepened over time, as well as his access to a wide range of experts in the field. Cooper further praised Weidensaul's prose itself, commenting positively on his "knack for evocative passages and immersive scenes." Critics also noted that *A World on the Wing* is particularly successful in demonstrating the appeal of birding, the fascinating and essential roles birds play in the wider ecosystem, and the daunting threats they face. In a review for the *Guardian*, for instance, Ashish Ghadiali noted, "I'm not a birder, but Weidensaul persuades me that I could be." Ghadiali further wrote that while the book warns of the dangers phenomena such as deforestation pose to birds, the work is not solely negative and, in fact, serves as "an emphatic statement of confidence in nature's resilience." Tellingly, *A World on the Wing* was well received by critics and publications dedicated to birding and wildlife. In a birding column for the Portland, Maine, *Press Herald*, ornithologist Herb Wilson commented positively on the author's broad geographic focus as well as his emphasis on conservation and developing technologies. Writing for the *Habitat Herald*, a publication of Virginia's Loudon Wildlife Conservatory, Steve Allen also praised Weidensaul's work, ultimately deeming it "required reading for everyone who loves birds."

Author Biography

Scott Weidensaul is the author of several books, such as *Living on the Wind: Across the Hemisphere with Migratory Birds* (1999) and *Of a Feather: A Brief History of American Birding* (2007). He is an American Ornithological Society fellow.

Joy Crelin

Review Sources

Allen, Steve. Review of *A World on the Wing: The Global Odyssey of Migratory Birds*, by Scott Weidensaul. *Habitat Herald*, vol. 26, no. 4, 2021. *Loudon Wildlife Conservancy*, loudounwildlife.org/2021/11/book-review-a-world-on-the-wing/. Accessed 14 Dec. 2021.

Cooper, Christian. "Christian Cooper on a New Book That Asks: Why Are Migratory Birds Vanishing?" Review of *A World on the Wing: The Global Odyssey of Migratory Birds*, by Scott Weidensaul. *The New York Times*, 30 Mar. 2021, www.nytimes.com/2021/03/30/books/review/a-world-on-the-wing-scott-weidensaul.html. Accessed 14 Dec. 2021.

Ghadiali, Ashish. "*A World on the Wing* by Scott Weidensaul Review—Incredible Journeys Taken by Migratory Species." *The Guardian*, 30 Mar. 2021, www.theguardian.com/books/2021/mar/30/a-world-on-the-wing-by-scott-weidensaul-review-incredible-journeys-taken-by-migratory-species. Accessed 14 Dec. 2021.

Wilson, Herb. "Birding: *A World on the Wing* Shares Amazing Stories of Migration." *Portland Press Herald*, 26 Sept. 2021, www.pressherald.com/2021/09/26/birding-a-world-on-the-wing-shares-amazing-stories-of-migration/. Accessed 14 Dec. 2021.

Review of *A World on the Wing: The Global Odyssey of Migratory Birds*, by Scott Weidensaul. *Kirkus*, 31 Dec. 2020, www.kirkusreviews.com/book-reviews/scott-weidensaul/a-world-on-the-wing/. Accessed 14 Dec. 2021.

Review of *A World on the Wing: The Global Odyssey of Migratory Birds*, by Scott Weidensaul. *Publishers Weekly*, 31 Dec. 2020, www.publishersweekly.com/978-0-393-60890-8. Accessed 14 Dec. 2021.

The Wrong End of the Telescope

Author: Rabih Alameddine (b. ca. 1959)
Publisher: Grove Press (New York). 368 pp.
Type of work: Novel
Time: Present day
Locale: Lesbos, Greece

Mina Simpson, a doctor who emigrated from Lebanon to the United States, agrees to volunteer at a refugee camp in Greece at the request of a friend. As the novel unfolds, she shares the stories of the refugees she meets, reflects on her own life, and criticizes the author telling her story.

Principal characters

MINA SIMPSON, a Lebanese American doctor
MAZEN, her brother
EMMA, her friend, who oversees a refugee camp in Greece
AN UNNAMED WRITER, her friend, who is struggling to write a novel about refugees
SUMAIYA, a Syrian refugee who has cancer

Rabih Alameddine, a writer born to Lebanese parents who spent his younger years in Kuwait and Lebanon before settling in California and pursuing his higher education, published his first novel, *Koolaids*, in 1998. A nonlinear narrative, *Koolaids* explores both the AIDS crisis in San Francisco's gay community and the Lebanese civil war. This set the tone for the rest of his career; his novels largely revolve around characters who are LGBTQ, Arab American, or both, and have complex, fragmented narrative structures.

The Wrong End of the Telescope (2021) is no exception. It follows Mina Simpson, a transgender woman married to another woman, who emigrated from Lebanon to Massachusetts and then Chicago and has spent decades avoiding any contact with her family or the part of the world in which she grew up. It is with conflicted feelings that she agrees to the plea of a friend, Emma, to volunteer her services as a doctor at a refugee camp on the Greek island of Lesbos ("As close as I'd been to Lebanon in decades," as she says), run by the NGO that Emma works for. But Mina does want to help, if she can—though both she and the novel as a whole are compellingly ambivalent on the question of whether it is possible for her to do so in any meaningful way.

Meeting her in Lesbos is her brother, Mazen, "the only family member who crossed my picket line after years of silence." This reunion prompts her to reflect on her life, with her history dealt out piecemeal, interspersed with stories of the refugee camp. She discusses growing up with an emotionally and sometimes physically abusive mother,

her discovery of her gender identity, her journey to America to attend Harvard University, how she reinvented herself once there, and her over-thirty-year relationship with her wife, Francine, among other things. Refreshingly, while being transgender is certainly significant in Mina's life, it is not the sole focus of her part of the narrative, as it often is in stories with transgender characters. Her identity is multifaceted and her status as a transgender woman does not define her particularly more than her status as a doctor, immigrant, sister, or wife, among other things.

The third strand of the novel concerns a friend of Mina's, an unnamed gay Lebanese American writer (addressed as "you"), who volunteered at the same camp several years ago but eventually fell into despair regarding his inability to help—unlike Mina, he has no practical skills to contribute. This character closely resembles Alameddine himself, who in real life has volunteered at a refugee camp on Lesbos. In a metafictional twist, Mina frequently excoriates this writer for his relative privilege, his inability to write directly about his experience at the camp, and his belief in the power of fiction to bring about any kind of change or improvement in the world, or even to help the writer himself to make sense of things. "When has writing explained anything to you?" she asks. "Writing does not force coherence onto a discordant narrative." Though the writer is her friend and she clearly has affection for him, she is unsparingly harsh when it comes to the shortcomings that have caused him to struggle to write this particular story.

Rabih Alameddine

Courtesy Benito Ordonez; Grove Atlantic website

Mina's criticism apparently gives expression to the author's self-doubt about whether he is the right person to tell this story, and the tension between his desire to serve as a witness for the refugees' stories and his skepticism regarding whether this will accomplish anything. Looking into the wrong end of a telescope makes things that are close up seem farther away; the title may refer to the distance with which Westerners view refugees from the Arab world, even when those refugees are on their doorsteps, but equally it may refer to the narrative convolutions that allow the author to put some distance between himself and his experiences at the refugee camp, which seem to have shaken the foundations of his worldview. "Lesbos not only broke your wall," Mina tells him, referring to the metaphorical wall that insulates the privileged from the suffering of others, "it broke you."

At the camp, Mina meets a woman named Sumaiya, a Syrian refugee with late-stage liver cancer who is trying to conceal her condition from her husband and three children. The family has enough troubles as it is, Sumaiya feels, without having to worry about her as well. She has no control over the larger situation and very little ability to alleviate her family's distress; this is the one thing she can do for them. Mina is the only person she takes into her confidence. The camp is woefully unequipped to treat Sumaiya's illness, but Mina does her best to provide comfort. In doing so, she becomes close to Sumaiya and her family. She begins working to get them permission to go to Athens and beyond, where Sumaiya will have better access to medical care.

The majority of the refugee camp thread of the narrative is focused on Sumaiya, but there are also one-chapter vignettes revolving around other refugees. Some are lighthearted—in one, a refugee woman in Lebanon brightens up her surroundings by bedazzling the inside of her tent with sequins ("with results Liberace would have envied"). In another, a man tells a probably untrue (or at least exaggerated) story about fleeing Lebanon, after having fled from Syria, to avoid being forced to rob a jewelry store. Others are bleaker—a would-be music student drowns in the Aegean, clutching his violin; a gay couple are refused entry into the European Union because they do not seem stereotypically "gay" enough. Mina also discusses run-ins with volunteers, mostly college students, who treat the experience as a kind of tourism, taking selfies with the refugee boats, and with cynical journalists who sift through the refugee stories for the ones that best fit the existing Western narrative of the crisis.

There are many grim aspects to the refugee camp, Mina's own life, and even the writer's life (despite his self-recrimination regarding his relative comfort, he too has experienced violence and discrimination). Despite the heaviness of much of the subject matter, however, Mina maintains a sense of humor throughout. Her breezy wit is expressed in chapter titles such as "Avoid Getting Liver Cancer If You Can" and "When You Don't Know What to Say, Have a Cookie." Sometimes this becomes a sort of gallows humor; talking about the writer's experience of being suspected of terrorism, for instance, Mina says that of course he would never build an improvised explosive device—it "would ruin your manicure."

The Wrong End of the Telescope was long-listed for the 2022 PEN/Faulkner Award for Fiction and received significant critical acclaim. Reviewers appreciated its blunt honesty about the issues with even well-meaning Western interventions into the problems of the Arab world. "This is the first novel I've read that gives ample room to the ugliness of certain camp volunteers . . . and the many humiliations some inflict on the displaced," Dina Nayeri wrote for the *New York Times*, also calling Mina "refreshingly honest" and noting that she "is able to observe what European volunteers can't." Casey Plett, reviewing the novel for the *Guardian*, called it "plain, unflinching and deeply observed, without being sentimental or cloying."

The novel's sense of humor also received particular praise. Nayeri described *The Wrong End of the Telescope* as "irreverent" and "full of wit, returning always to human absurdity," while an anonymous critic for *Publishers Weekly* noted in a starred review that the novel "can still locate humor in the pit of hell." Mark Athitakis, writing for the *Los Angeles Times*, lauded the novel for being "unafraid of humor while addressing a humanitarian crisis." Another aspect of the novel much commented on by reviewers was the metafictional element. Critics largely felt that the inclusion of the unnamed author's grappling with how and why to tell the story enriched the book. "Telling this story in a linear way, with well-worn gestures of compassion, would not suffice," Athitakis concluded. Nayeri found the writer's struggle "deeply poignant," and noted that it resonated with concerns that Arab American writers—"the ones who carry our people's narratives westward, who shape how they're seen (and used) by those in power"—often face.

The Wrong End of the Telescope is ultimately an ambitious and kaleidoscopic novel that is not only an exploration of the refugee crisis but a meditation on how to write about such a crisis. In Mina, it creates a strong character with a memorable narrative voice who provides a clear-eyed look at the shortcomings of refugee camps. All of these elements come together to make it a memorable experience and a standout among similar novels.

Author Biography

Rabih Alameddine is the award-winning author of six novels, including *Koolaids* (1998), *The Hakawati* (2008), *An Unnecessary Woman* (2014), and *The Angel of History* (2016), as well as one collection of short stories. In 2019 he won the John Dos Passos Prize for Literature for his overall body of work.

Emma Joyce

Review Sources

Athitakis, Mark. "This Refugee Novel Knows It Can't Change the World." Review of *The Wrong End of the Telescope*, by Rabih Alameddine. *Los Angeles Times*, 13 Sept. 2021, www.latimes.com/entertainment-arts/books/story/2021-09-15/this-refugee-novel-knows-it-cant-change-the-world. Accessed 4 Feb. 2022.

Nayeri, Dina. "An Irreverent Novel Trains Its Gaze on Refugees and Their Rescuers." Review of *The Wrong End of the Telescope*, by Rabih Alameddine. *The New York Times*, 21 Sept. 2021, www.nytimes.com/2021/09/21/books/review/the-wrong-end-of-the-telescope-rabih-alameddine.html. Accessed 4 Feb. 2022.

Plett, Casey. "*The Wrong End of the Telescope* by Rabih Alameddine Review—Beyond Empathy." *The Guardian*, 9 Oct. 2021, www.theguardian.com/books/2021/oct/09/the-wrong-end-of-the-telescope-by-rabih-alameddine-review-beyond-empathy. Accessed 4 Feb. 2022.

Rungren, Lawrence. Review of *The Wrong End of the Telescope*, by Rabih Alameddine. *Library Journal*, 1 Sept. 2021, www.libraryjournal.com/review/the-wrong-end-of-the-telescope-1784283. Accessed 4 Feb. 2022.

Silman, Roberta. "Book Review: *The Wrong End of the Telescope*—A Stunning Achievement." Review of *The Wrong End of the Telescope*, by Rabih Alameddine. *The Arts Fuse*, 8 Nov. 2021, artsfuse.org/240518/book-review-the-wrong-end-of-the-telescope-a-stunning-achievement. Accessed 4 Feb. 2022.

Review of *The Wrong End of the Telescope*, by Rabih Alameddine. *Publishers Weekly*, 16 June 2021, www.publishersweekly.com/978-0-8021-5780-5. Accessed 4 Feb. 2022.

You Don't Have to Be Everything
Poems for Girls Becoming Themselves

Editor: Diana Whitney
Illustrators: Cristina González, Kate Mockford, and Stephanie Singleton
Publisher: Workman (New York). Illustrated. 176 pp.
Type of work: Poetry

In You Don't Have to Be Everything, *Diana Whitney has compiled an empowering anthology of poems that foster self-understanding and explore the complexity of adolescent girls and their wide range of emotions, from longing to rage and everything in between.*

In her introduction to *You Don't Have to Be Everything: Poems for Girls Becoming Themselves* (2021), editor Diana Whitney elaborates on the purpose of the poetry anthology she has compiled. Notably, she quotes the first line of the poem "Wild Geese" by Mary Oliver—"You do not have to be good"—as a key inspiration. Whitney explains how she noted to her own daughter that the somewhat startling statement is not necessarily an invitation to be bad, but rather a reminder that "you're more than just good or bad. You're strong and complicated and worthy of love. You don't need to apologize for yourself. You don't have to be everything." As the book's title suggests, this empowering message ultimately underlies every aspect of what proves to be a remarkable collection of poems.

To help young women understand that they "do not have to be good," Whitney includes a wide range of poetic voices. She also divides the anthology into eight sections, each based on an emotion. They are titled, in order of appearance, "Seeking," "Loneliness," "Attitude," "Rage," "Longing," "Shame," "Sadness," and "Belonging." Within each section, each poem offers a unique connection to its corresponding emotion. This diversity helps encourage self-reflection in multiple ways, across multiple facets of every individual personality, but the poems are also linked at a broader level in that they are chosen for their relevance to adolescent girls in particular. Taken as a whole, the poems validate the message "you are enough." It is a powerful message, and *You Don't Have to Be Everything* is successful in communicating it in various ways.

Although not a defining factor in most books, the physicality of this volume stands out and appears carefully chosen for ease of use and maximum readability. Anthologies are often known for their heft, but this book is a small paperback—it fits easily in backpacks and is both small and light enough to carry in a handbag, making it portable for any teen's active lifestyle. It is also a book that encourages engagement. Most anthologies publish every poem in portrait orientation rather than landscape orientation, regardless of the fact that line length can vary widely across works. Here, however, Whitney and her design team change the page orientation depending on the poem; a half dozen in the collection are in landscape orientation. Readers, then, must turn the book to the right or left to read certain poems, making the entire experience more interactive while also adhering to the poet's intent of how the poem should look on the page. Most poets choose their line breaks carefully, and both line lengths and line breaks contribute to the meaning of poems. A good example in the anthology is Tarfia Faizullah's "Self Portrait as Mango," which repeats the word "mango" at the end of numerous long lines, emphasizing the injustice of stereotyping as misinterpretation and symbolizing the speaker's anger at these injustices. Had the poem's long lines been shortened to fit on a page in portrait orientation, or even the font size reduced, the poem would have lost some of its power. The book's interesting layout, then, offers authenticity as well as engagement.

Diana Whitney (editor)

The numerous illustrations in the anthology also foster engagement with the text and offer realistic and positive images of strong young women. Colorful art by one of the three illustrators—Cristina González, Kate Mockford and Stephanie Singleton—are included on most pages. Some illustrations focus on repeating patterns, such as the crescent moons, clouds, sunflowers, and butterflies opposite Maya Angelou's poem "Phenomenal Woman." Others offer engaging portraits of young women of many diverse backgrounds, sizes, and shapes, such as the young woman of color opposite the title page for the "Attitude" section titled. The woman is in a red halter top and jeans. She has a small but evident scar on her stomach, but not one she is trying to hide; she is also not ashamed or uncomfortable exposing her underarm hair. She has her hands on her hips and looks directly at the reader with curiosity and strength. The pleasantly wide range of representation in the illustrations should allow most young women to see some element of themselves on one or more pages.

Similarly, another strength of the anthology is its diverse mix of poets. There are plenty of long-established and easily recognizable artists, including Maya Angelou, Joy Harjo, and Mary Oliver, but also many lesser-known writers and up-and-coming figures, such as Evie Shockley, Elizabeth Acevedo, and Amanda Gorman. While some of the poets are literary icons whose work has already been included in many other anthologies, others have developed their followings in the age of social media. The roster is diverse not only in terms of race and ethnicity, but also sexual orientation and gender identity, with prominent representation from the LGBTQ community. As with the illustrations, this level of diversity ensures that most young adult readers will identify with one or more of the poets and their experiences.

The attention to a diversity of voices also has the added benefits of providing established poets with a new audience and newer poets with a larger platform. Sharon Olds is an example of the former, having won the Pulitzer Prize and many other honors across her distinguished career known for confessional poetry about her own life. She is represented here by the poem "I Go Back to May 1937," which discusses her parents, suggesting that their marriage is a mistake yet recognizing that if they had not married, Olds herself would not exist. She cannot change or reverse that mistake, but she can, as she states, "tell about it." This poem was published in Olds's book *The Cell* (1987) and has been reprinted many times, but it finds a new audience in this anthology with contemporary young women, who will likely also have incidents from their past they might wish to change. Reflecting the book's overall empowering message, Olds shows readers they have the power to write, to create, to bear witness.

While it is always empowering, the anthology makes clear that there is room for difficult subjects and negative feelings. For example, Andrea Gibson's poem "No Filter," in the "Sadness section" of the book includes the lines:

> I am hardly every stable.
> Last week I busted my knuckle
> on the steering wheel
> because I believed for a moment
> I'd made a wrong turn
> when I became who I am.
> I'd go into detail but it will hurt too much.

More of an emerging voice compared to Olds, Gibson is a queer poet who uses they/them pronouns and often focuses on issues of identity. The narrator of "No Filter" fixes themselves in the internet era, noting the "unspoken promise we all make / to be in real life whoever we are on instagram." The piece expresses a common complaint about social media, such as Instagram and Facebook: that contributors only post about the positive aspects of their lives—the awards, the successes, the parties, the new house or car, the new love—reinforcing the perception that their life is always wonderful. Gibson instead acknowledges the hurt and trauma that people can face under the surface and expresses both fear and hope. Serious, unsentimental poems like this help *You Don't Have to Be Everything* validate even the more challenging experiences readers may go through. And the inclusion of contemporary poets like Gibson ensures that the anthology cannot be dismissed as out of touch with current realities, while also often giving voice to experiences that have received little attention in the past.

Whitney has also been careful in choosing poems that have a degree of clarity and transparency, rather than works that have many allusions or are opaque in their meaning. The included poems still lend themselves to multiple interpretations and depth of meaning, but they are not the kinds of pieces that include footnotes or make numerous references to obscure historical events. They are mainly poems grounded in the realities of life and personal experience that make their intentions clear. And of course, because the anthology is organized around the emotions of adolescent girls, Whitney has chosen poems that this audience is especially likely to relate to. In Dominique Christina's "The Period Poem," for example, the speaker is blunt in chastising a male poster on Twitter who claimed to have dumped his girlfriend because she got her period while they were having sex. The piece loudly declares itself as "an anatomy lesson infused with feminist politics," but this bluntness does not detract from the poetry:

> You're the reason my daughter cried funeral tears
> When she started her period.
> The sudden grief all young girls feel
> After the matriculation from childhood and
> The induction into a reality that they'll have to negotiate
> People like you and your disdain
> For what a woman's body can do.

Christina goes on to identify the ways women are strong and blessed, and by the end of the poem she addresses her daughter directly, exhorting women to "Spill your impossible scripture / All over the good furniture." She ends the poem on the word "period," where it does double duty as both a reference to the menstrual cycle and a pointed end to an unpleasant conversation. It is an excellent example of a spoken word poem, focusing on natural speech and clever word play. It and many others show how Whitney's selection of accessible works for the anthology still demonstrates masterful command of classic poetic elements.

You Don't Have to Be Everything earned a positive critical reception, with many reviewers citing it as a valuable resource for young women. For example, *Publishers Weekly* noted that "this empowering assemblage of poems by an inclusive group of women writers offers insight and community to readers navigating adolescence," while *Kirkus Reviews* called the anthology "An engrossing, comforting collection" and "A helpful companion." Equally complimentary was Shanta Lee Gander, who in a review for *Literary Mama* wrote, "Today's adolescent girls, their mothers, and mother-figures, now have a guide to help ease the rocky road to adolescence." Gander further suggested that while the anthology speaks first and foremost to adolescent girls, but it will also likely resonate with adult women who are "invited to revisit their younger selves." Ultimately, the diverse poets and illustrators of *You Don't Have to Be Everything*, convincingly arranged by Whitney's editorial eye, do a great job communicating the empowering message of the title, opening the conversation being yourself is enough.

Editor Biography
Feminist activist and author Diana Whitney has published poetry, essays, reviews, and literary criticism in various outlets. Her debut poetry collection, *Wanting It* (2014), won the Rubery Book Award, and she earned a Vermont Arts Council Creation Grant in 2021.

Cristina González is an artist and designer based in Ecuador whose colorful style celebrates diversity and creativity.

Kate Mockford is a UK-based freelance illustrator. She is also a teacher of art and photography.

Stephanie Singleton is a Toronto-based illustrator. Much of her work combines decorative and surreal styles.

Marybeth Rua-Larsen

Review Sources

Gander, Shanta Lee. Review of *You Don't Have to Be Everything: Poems for Girls Becoming Themselves*, edited by Diana Whitney. *Literary Mama*, 2021, literarymama.com/articles/departments/2021/05/a-review-of-you-dont-have-to-be-everything-poems-for-girls-becoming-themselves. Accessed 21 Dec. 2021.

Pino, Kristina. Review of *You Don't Have to Be Everything: Poems for Girls Becoming Themselves*, edited by Diana Whitney. *Booklist*, vol. 117, no. 13, 1 Mar. 2021, p. 40.

Speer, Elizabeth. Review of *You Don't Have to Be Everything: Poems for Girls Becoming Themselves*, edited by Diana Whitney. *School Library Journal*, 1 June 2021, www.slj.com/?reviewDetail=you-dont-have-to-be-everything-poems-for-girls-becoming-themselves. Accessed 21 Dec. 2021.

Review of *You Don't Have to Be Everything*, edited by Diana Whitney. *Kirkus Reviews*, 10 Dec. 2020, www.kirkusreviews.com/book-reviews/diana-whitney/you-dont-have-to-be-everything/. Accessed 21 Dec. 2021.

Review of *You Don't Have to Be Everything: Poems for Girls Becoming Themselves*, edited by Diana Whitney. *Publishers Weekly*, 14 Jan. 2021, www.publishersweekly.com/978-1-5235-1099-3. Accessed 21 Dec. 2021.

Category Index

Autobiography
All In (Billie Jean King with Johnette Howard and Maryanne Vollers), 11

Biography
All That She Carried (Tiya Miles), 16
American Baby (Gabrielle Glaser), 21
The Code Breaker (Walter Isaacson), 129
The Doctors Blackwell (Janice P. Nimura), 162
Empire of Pain (Patrick Radden Keefe), 167
Four Hundred Souls (Ibram X. Kendi and Keisha N. Blain), 212
Garbo (Robert Gottlieb), 232
King of the Blues (Daniel de Visé), 301
The Outlier (Kai Bird), 459
The Woman They Could Not Silence (Kate Moore), 707

Current Affairs
Empire of Pain (Patrick Radden Keefe), 167
From a Whisper to a Rallying Cry (Paula Yoo), 222
The Hospital (Brian Alexander), 276
Invisible Child (Andrea Elliott), 291
Rescuing the Planet (Tony Hiss), 530
The Second (Carol Anderson), 545
Squirrel Hill (Mark Oppenheimer), 596
The Sum of Us (Heather McGhee), 606

Environment
Islands of Abandonment (Cal Flyn), 296
Rescuing the Planet (Tony Hiss), 530
Under a White Sky (Elizabeth Kolbert), 654

Essays
The Anthropocene Reviewed (John Green), 41
Broken (Jenny Lawson), 104
Girlhood (Melissa Febos), 237
On Juneteenth (Annette Gordon-Reed), 439
A Swim in a Pond in the Rain (George Saunders), 620
These Precious Days (Ann Patchett), 634

Ethics
American Baby (Gabrielle Glaser), 21

Fiction
Second Place (Rachel Cusk), 550

Graphic Nonfiction
And Now I Spill the Family Secrets (Margaret Kimball), 36
Run: Book One (John Lewis and Andrew Aydin), 540
Seek You (Kristen Radtke), 555
Wake (Rebecca Hall), 663

History
All That She Carried (Tiya Miles), 16
American Baby (Gabrielle Glaser), 21
American Republics (Alan Taylor), 31
Black Birds in the Sky (Brandy Colbert), 84
The Black Church (Henry Louis Gates Jr.), 89
The Doctors Blackwell (Janice P. Nimura), 162
Empire of Pain (Patrick Radden Keefe), 167
The Failed Promise (Robert S. Levine), 177

Four Hundred Souls (Ibram X. Kendi and Keisha N. Blain), 212
The Free World (Louis Menand), 217
From a Whisper to a Rallying Cry (Paula Yoo), 222
The Ground Breaking (Scott Ellsworth), 247
How the Word Is Passed (Clint Smith), 281
A Little Devil in America (Hanif Abdurraqib), 338
Major Labels (Kelefa Sanneh), 354
The Outlier (Kai Bird), 459
Revolution in Our Time (Kekla Magoon), 535
The Second (Carol Anderson), 545
The Sum of Us (Heather McGhee), 606
When We Cease to Understand the World (Benjamín Labatut), 678
The Woman They Could Not Silence (Kate Moore), 707

Law
Fuzz (Mary Roach), 227
The Second (Carol Anderson), 545

Letters
The Letters of Shirley Jackson (Shirley Jackson), 315

Medicine
The Doctors Blackwell (Janice P. Nimura), 162
Empire of Pain (Patrick Radden Keefe), 167
The Hospital (Brian Alexander), 276
Smile (Sarah Ruhl), 578

Memoir
1000 Years of Joys and Sorrows (Ai Weiwei), 1
Beautiful Country (Qian Julie Wang), 59

Between Two Kingdoms (Suleika Jaouad), 69
Broken (Jenny Lawson), 104
Crying in H Mart (Michelle Zauner), 148
Finding the Mother Tree (Suzanne Simard), 188
Four Hundred Souls (Ibram X. Kendi and Keisha N. Blain), 212
Girlhood (Melissa Febos), 237
Halfway Home (Reuben Jonathan Miller), 252
How the Word Is Passed (Clint Smith), 281
A Little Devil in America (Hanif Abdurraqib), 338
My Broken Language (Quiara Alegría Hudes), 401
Poet Warrior (Joy Harjo), 478
Punch Me Up to the Gods (Brian Broome), 502
Run: Book One (John Lewis and Andrew Aydin), 540
Smile (Sarah Ruhl), 578
Somebody's Daughter (Ashley C. Ford), 587
The Storyteller (Dave Grohl), 601
Tastes Like War (Grace M. Cho), 629
Three Girls from Bronzeville (Dawn Turner), 639
Unbound (Tarana Burke), 649

Music
Major Labels (Kelefa Sanneh), 354

Natural History
A Most Remarkable Creature (Jonathan Meiburg), 396
Rescuing the Planet (Tony Hiss), 530
Under a White Sky (Elizabeth Kolbert), 654

CATEGORY INDEX

Nature
Fuzz (Mary Roach), 227
Islands of Abandonment (Cal Flyn), 296
A Most Remarkable Creature (Jonathan Meiburg), 396
Rescuing the Planet (Tony Hiss), 530
Under a White Sky (Elizabeth Kolbert), 654
A World on the Wing (Scott Weidensaul), 712

Novel
Aristotle and Dante Dive into the Waters of the World (Benjamin Alire Sáenz), 46
Arsenic and Adobo (Mia P. Manansala), 50
Beasts of a Little Land (Juhea Kim), 54
Beautiful World, Where Are You (Sally Rooney), 64
Bewilderment (Richard Powers), 74
Billy Summers (Stephen King), 79
The Book of Form and Emptiness (Ruth Ozeki), 100
The Chosen and the Beautiful (Nghi Vo), 119
Cloud Cuckoo Land (Anthony Doerr), 124
The Committed (Viet Thanh Nguyen), 134
Concrete Rose (Angie Thomas), 139
Crossroads (Jonathan Franzen), 143
Damnation Spring (Ash Davidson), 153
Falling (T. J. Newman), 183
Firekeeper's Daughter (Angeline Boulley), 193
The Five Wounds (Kirstin Valdez Quade), 203
Great Circle (Maggie Shipstead), 242
Harlem Shuffle (Colson Whitehead), 257
Heaven (Mieko Kawakami), 262
Hell of a Book (Jason Mott), 267
Intimacies (Katie Kitamura), 286
Klara and the Sun (Kazuo Ishiguro), 306

Last Night at the Telegraph Club (Malinda Lo), 311
Libertie (Kaitlyn Greenidge), 320
The Life I'm In (Sharon G. Flake), 324
Light Perpetual (Francis Spufford), 328
The Lincoln Highway (Amor Towles), 333
The Love Songs of W. E. B. Du Bois (Honorée Fanonne Jeffers), 343
The Madness of Crowds (Louise Penny), 349
Malibu Rising (Taylor Jenkins Reid), 358
A Marvellous Light (Freya Marske), 363
Mary Jane (Jessica Anya Blau), 367
Matrix (Lauren Groff), 372
The Memoirs of Stockholm Sven (Nathaniel Ian Miller), 381
The Mirror Season (Anna-Marie McLemore), 391
My Heart Is a Chainsaw (Stephen Graham Jones), 406
The Night Always Comes (Willy Vlautin), 416
No Gods, No Monsters (Cadwell Turnbull), 421
No One Is Talking about This (Patricia Lockwood), 426
Noor (Nnedi Okorafor), 431
Oh William! (Elizabeth Strout), 435
Once There Were Wolves (Charlotte McConaghy), 444
The Other Black Girl (Zakiya Dalila Harris), 449
A Passage North (Anuk Arudpragasam), 464
People We Meet on Vacation (Emily Henry), 469
Project Hail Mary (Andy Weir), 482
The Promise (Damon Galgut), 487
The Prophets (Robert Jones Jr.), 492
The Queen of the Cicadas (V. Castro), 507
Razorblade Tears (S. A. Cosby), 511

The Reading List (Sara Nisha Adams), 516
Remote Control (Nnedi Okorafor), 520
The Removed (Brandon Hobson), 525
The Sentence (Louise Erdrich), 560
She Who Became the Sun (Shelley Parker-Chan), 565
A Sitting in St. James (Rita Williams-Garcia), 569
A Snake Falls to Earth (Darcie Little Badger), 582
The Sweetness of Water (Nathan Harris), 615
The Twilight Zone (Nona Fernández), 644
Velvet Was the Night (Silvia Moreno-Garcia), 658
We Begin at the End (Chris Whitaker), 668
When the Stars Go Dark (Paula McLain), 673
When We Cease to Understand the World (Benjamín Labatut), 678
Whereabouts (Jhumpa Lahiri), 683
White Smoke (Tiffany D. Jackson), 688
Winter in Sokcho (Elisa Shua Dusapin), 697
The Wrong End of the Telescope (Rabih Alameddine), 717

Novella
My Monticello (Jocelyn Nicole Johnson), 411
A Psalm for the Wild-Built (Becky Chambers), 497

Philosophy
Everybody (Olivia Laing), 172

Poetry
American Melancholy (Joyce Carol Oates), 26
Call Us What We Carry (Amanda Gorman), 109

Floaters (Martín Espada), 208
Four Hundred Souls (Ibram X. Kendi and Keisha N. Blain), 212
Playlist for the Apocalypse (Rita Dove), 474
Poet Warrior (Joy Harjo), 478
The Sunflower Cast a Spell to Save Us from the Void (Jackie Wang), 611
You Don't Have to Be Everything (Diana Whitney), 721
The Wild Fox of Yemen (Threa Almontaser), 692
Winter Recipes from the Collective (Louise Glück), 702

Psychology
Chatter (Ethan Kross), 114
Everybody (Olivia Laing), 172

Religion
The Black Church (Henry Louis Gates Jr.), 89
Squirrel Hill (Mark Oppenheimer), 596

Science
The Code Breaker (Walter Isaacson), 129
Finding the Mother Tree (Suzanne Simard), 188
Islands of Abandonment (Cal Flyn), 296
Rescuing the Planet (Tony Hiss), 530
Under a White Sky (Elizabeth Kolbert), 654

Short Fiction
Afterparties (Anthony Veasna So), 6
Blackout (Dhonielle Clayton, Tiffany D. Jackson, Nic Stone, Angie Thomas, Ashley Woodfolk, and Nicola Yoon), 94
The Dangers of Smoking in Bed (Mariana Enríquez), 157
First Person Singular (Haruki Murakami), 198

CATEGORY INDEX

Milk Blood Heat (Dantiel W. Moniz), 386
My Monticello (Jocelyn Nicole Johnson), 411
The (Other) *You* (Joyce Carol Oates), 454
Skinship (Yoon Choi), 573
The Tangleroot Palace (Marjorie Liu), 625
When We Cease to Understand the World (Benjamín Labatut), 678

Short Stories
The Souvenir Museum (Elizabeth McCracken), 591

Sociology
Everybody (Olivia Laing), 172
From a Whisper to a Rallying Cry (Paula Yoo), 222

Halfway Home (Reuben Jonathan Miller), 252
Invisible Child (Andrea Elliott), 291
A Little Devil in America (Hanif Abdurraqib), 338
The Sum of Us (Heather McGhee), 606

Travel
A Most Remarkable Creature (Jonathan Meiburg), 396

Verse Novel
Home Is Not a Country (Safia Elhillo), 272
Me (Moth) (Amber McBride), 377

Title Index

1000 Years of Joys and Sorrows (Ai Weiwei), 1

Afterparties (Anthony Veasna So), 6
All In (Billie Jean King with Johnette Howard and Maryanne Vollers), 11
All That She Carried (Tiya Miles), 16
American Baby (Gabrielle Glaser), 21
American Melancholy (Joyce Carol Oates), 26
American Republics (Alan Taylor), 31
And Now I Spill the Family Secrets (Margaret Kimball), 36
The Anthropocene Reviewed (John Green), 41
Aristotle and Dante Dive into the Waters of the World (Benjamin Alire Sáenz), 46
Arsenic and Adobo (Mia P. Manansala), 50

Beasts of a Little Land (Juhea Kim), 54
Beautiful Country (Qian Julie Wang), 59
Beautiful World, Where Are You (Sally Rooney), 64
Between Two Kingdoms (Suleika Jaouad), 69
Bewilderment (Richard Powers), 74
Billy Summers (Stephen King), 79
Black Birds in the Sky (Brandy Colbert), 84
The Black Church (Henry Louis Gates Jr.), 89
Blackout (Dhonielle Clayton, Tiffany D. Jackson, Nic Stone, Angie Thomas, Ashley Woodfolk, and Nicola Yoon), 94

The Book of Form and Emptiness (Ruth Ozeki), 100
Broken (Jenny Lawson), 104

Call Us What We Carry (Amanda Gorman), 109
Chatter (Ethan Kross), 114
The Chosen and the Beautiful (Nghi Vo), 119
Cloud Cuckoo Land (Anthony Doerr), 124
The Code Breaker (Walter Isaacson), 129
The Committed (Viet Thanh Nguyen), 134
Concrete Rose (Angie Thomas), 139
Crossroads (Jonathan Franzen), 143
Crying in H Mart (Michelle Zauner), 148

Damnation Spring (Ash Davidson), 153
The Dangers of Smoking in Bed (Mariana Enríquez), 157
The Doctors Blackwell (Janice P. Nimura), 162

Empire of Pain (Patrick Radden Keefe), 167
Everybody (Olivia Laing), 172

The Failed Promise (Robert S. Levine), 177
Falling (T. J. Newman), 183
Finding the Mother Tree (Suzanne Simard), 188
Firekeeper's Daughter (Angeline Boulley), 193

First Person Singular (Haruki Murakami), 198
The Five Wounds (Kirstin Valdez Quade), 203
Floaters (Martín Espada), 208
Four Hundred Souls (Ibram X. Kendi and Keisha N. Blain), 212
The Free World (Louis Menand), 217
From a Whisper to a Rallying Cry (Paula Yoo), 222
Fuzz (Mary Roach), 227

Garbo (Robert Gottlieb), 232
Girlhood (Melissa Febos), 237
Great Circle (Maggie Shipstead), 242
The Ground Breaking (Scott Ellsworth), 247

Halfway Home (Reuben Jonathan Miller), 252
Harlem Shuffle (Colson Whitehead), 257
Heaven (Mieko Kawakami), 262
Hell of a Book (Jason Mott), 267
Home Is Not a Country (Safia Elhillo), 272
The Hospital (Brian Alexander), 276
How the Word Is Passed (Clint Smith), 281

Intimacies (Katie Kitamura), 286
Invisible Child (Andrea Elliott), 291
Islands of Abandonment (Cal Flyn), 296

King of the Blues (Daniel de Visé), 301
Klara and the Sun (Kazuo Ishiguro), 306

Last Night at the Telegraph Club (Malinda Lo), 311
The Letters of Shirley Jackson (Shirley Jackson), 315
Libertie (Kaitlyn Greenidge), 320

The Life I'm In (Sharon G. Flake), 324
Light Perpetual (Francis Spufford), 328
The Lincoln Highway (Amor Towles), 333
A Little Devil in America (Hanif Abdurraqib), 338
The Love Songs of W. E. B. Du Bois (Honorée Fanonne Jeffers), 343

The Madness of Crowds (Louise Penny), 349
Major Labels (Kelefa Sanneh), 354
Malibu Rising (Taylor Jenkins Reid), 358
A Marvellous Light (Freya Marske), 363
Mary Jane (Jessica Anya Blau), 367
Matrix (Lauren Groff), 372
Me (Moth) (Amber McBride), 377
The Memoirs of Stockholm Sven (Nathaniel Ian Miller), 381
Milk Blood Heat (Dantiel W. Moniz), 386
The Mirror Season (Anna-Marie McLemore), 391
A Most Remarkable Creature (Jonathan Meiburg), 396
My Broken Language (Quiara Alegría Hudes), 401
My Heart Is a Chainsaw (Stephen Graham Jones), 406
My Monticello (Jocelyn Nicole Johnson), 411

The Night Always Comes (Willy Vlautin), 416
No Gods, No Monsters (Cadwell Turnbull), 421
No One Is Talking about This (Patricia Lockwood), 426
Noor (Nnedi Okorafor), 431

TITLE INDEX

Oh William! (Elizabeth Strout), 435
On Juneteenth (Annette Gordon-Reed), 439
Once There Were Wolves (Charlotte McConaghy), 444
The Other Black Girl (Zakiya Dalila Harris), 449
The (Other) You (Joyce Carol Oates), 454
The Outlier (Kai Bird), 459

A Passage North (Anuk Arudpragasam), 464
People We Meet on Vacation (Emily Henry), 469
Playlist for the Apocalypse (Rita Dove), 474
Poet Warrior (Joy Harjo), 478
Project Hail Mary (Andy Weir), 482
The Promise (Damon Galgut), 487
The Prophets (Robert Jones Jr.), 492
A Psalm for the Wild-Built (Becky Chambers), 497
Punch Me Up to the Gods (Brian Broome), 502

The Queen of the Cicadas (V. Castro), 507

Razorblade Tears (S. A. Cosby), 511
The Reading List (Sara Nisha Adams), 516
Remote Control (Nnedi Okorafor), 520
The Removed (Brandon Hobson), 525
Rescuing the Planet (Tony Hiss), 530
Revolution in Our Time (Kekla Magoon), 535
Run: Book One (John Lewis and Andrew Aydin), 540

The Second (Carol Anderson), 545
Second Place (Rachel Cusk), 550
Seek You (Kristen Radtke), 555
The Sentence (Louise Erdrich), 560

She Who Became the Sun (Shelley Parker-Chan), 565
A Sitting in St. James (Rita Williams-Garcia), 569
Skinship (Yoon Choi), 573
Smile (Sarah Ruhl), 578
A Snake Falls to Earth (Darcie Little Badger), 582
Somebody's Daughter (Ashley C. Ford), 587
The Souvenir Museum (Elizabeth McCracken), 591
Squirrel Hill (Mark Oppenheimer), 596
The Storyteller (Dave Grohl), 601
The Sum of Us (Heather McGhee), 606
The Sunflower Cast a Spell to Save Us from the Void (Jackie Wang), 611
The Sweetness of Water (Nathan Harris), 615
A Swim in a Pond in the Rain (George Saunders), 620

The Tangleroot Palace (Marjorie Liu), 625
Tastes Like War (Grace M. Cho), 629
These Precious Days (Ann Patchett), 634
Three Girls from Bronzeville (Dawn Turner), 639
The Twilight Zone (Nona Fernández), 644

Unbound (Tarana Burke), 649
Under a White Sky (Elizabeth Kolbert), 654

Velvet Was the Night (Silvia Moreno-Garcia), 658

Wake (Rebecca Hall), 663
We Begin at the End (Chris Whitaker), 668
When the Stars Go Dark (Paula McLain), 673

When We Cease to Understand the World (Benjamín Labatut), 678
Whereabouts (Jhumpa Lahiri), 683
White Smoke (Tiffany D. Jackson), 688
The Wild Fox of Yemen (Threa Almontaser), 692
Winter in Sokcho (Elisa Shua Dusapin), 697
Winter Recipes from the Collective (Louise Glück), 702

The Woman They Could Not Silence (Kate Moore), 707
A World on the Wing (Scott Weidensaul), 712
The Wrong End of the Telescope (Rabih Alameddine), 717

You Don't Have to Be Everything (Diana Whitney), 721